HISTORICAL DICTIONARIES OF
DISCOVERY AND EXPLORATION
Series Editor: Jon Woronoff

1. *Australia,* by Alan Day, 2003.
2. *Pacific Islands,* by Max Quanchi and John Robson, 2005.
3. *Northwest Passage,* by Alan Day, 2006.
4. *Northwest Coast of America,* by Robin Inglis, 2008.

Historical Dictionary of the Discovery and Exploration of the Northwest Coast of America

Robin Inglis

Historical Dictionaries of Discovery and Exploration, No. 4

The Scarecrow Press, Inc.
Lanham, Maryland • Toronto • Plymouth, UK
2008

SCARECROW PRESS, INC.

Published in the United States of America
by Scarecrow Press, Inc.
A wholly owned subsidiary of
The Rowman & Littlefield Publishing Group, Inc.
4501 Forbes Boulevard, Suite 200, Lanham, Maryland 20706
www.scarecrowpress.com

Estover Road
Plymouth PL6 7PY
United Kingdom

British Library Cataloguing in Publication Information Available

Library of Congress Cataloging-in-Publication Data

Inglis, Robin, 1942–
 Historical dictionary of the discovery and exploration of the Northwest Coast of
America / Robin Inglis.
  p. cm. — (Historical dictionaries of discovery and exploration ; no. 4)
 Includes bibliographical references.
 ISBN-13: 978-0-8108-5551-9 (hardcover : alk. paper)
 ISBN-10: 0-8108-5551-8 (hardcover : alk. paper)
 1. Northwest Coast of North America—Discovery and exploration—
Dictionaries. 2. Northwest, Pacific—Discovery and exploration—Dictionaries.
3. Northwest Passage—Discovery and exploration—Dictionaries. 4. Explorers—
Northwest Coast of North America—Biography—Dictionaries. 5. Pioneers—
Northwest Coast of North America—Biography—Dictionaries. 6. Fur traders—
Northwest Coast of North America—Biography—Dictionaries. 7. Frontier and
pioneer life—Northwest Coast of North America—Dictionaries. 8. Indians of
North America—Northwest, Pacific—History—Dictionaries. 9. Northwest Coast
of North America—Description and travel—Dictionaries. 10. Northwest Coast of
North America—Biography—Dictionaries. I. Title.

F851.5.I48 2008
979.5003—dc22   2007043069

For Bev

Contents

Editor's Foreword

Although discovery and exploration might seem somewhat abstract concepts related more to adventure than real life, in practice they had extremely important consequences for world history. For their motives were very real, very practical, and often very commercial. This has rarely been clearer than in early activities along the Northwest Coast of America, which were undertaken largely by the leading imperial powers of the day—Britain, France, Spain, and Russia—and by the upstart United States. While no doubt interested in finding and exploring new places, the expeditions were busy staking claim to huge chunks of territory (with no particular concern for those living there), collecting items that might advance one country or the other, while private companies and individuals were busy trading whatever they could find of value, the fur traders being the most active. Thus, there ensued not only an extremely active period of discovery and exploration primarily from the mid-18th to the early 19th century but also a "scramble" for territory not very different from the more celebrated one in Africa.

This was, indeed, a scramble and not a very organized process, with different expeditions flying different flags covering the same very approximate geographical area—namely from California north to Alaska—and discovering, and then gradually exploring, discontinuous areas. It would be quite impossible to keep track of all of them without something like this extremely useful *Historical Dictionary of the Discovery and Exploration of the Northwest Coast of America*. Since the time element is so important in many cases, and just who came first is more than a mere talking point, the history of this extraordinary effort is first traced in the chronology. It is then seen more broadly, and logically, in the introduction. The countless details, who did what, and when, and how, and just what was discovered, and what other advances (cartographic, navigational, scientific, and other) were made, and—not to be forgotten—how those who happened to be there already reacted, can be found in greater detail in the dictionary itself. Obviously, this book can say only so much on the subject, and therefore readers interested in learning more are encouraged to find other routes to information through the bibliography.

This volume has been written by Robin Inglis who, as a former director of the Vancouver Maritime Museum and the North Vancouver Museum and Archives, lives in the middle of the subject region. As such, he was the curator of exhibitions dealing with the visits of La Pérouse and Malaspina to the Northwest Coast of America. He has also written articles and lectured on these and related topics; edited a collection of essays entitled *Spain and the North Pacific Coast*; and served as regional editor of the Hakluyt Society's edition of the Malaspina journal. To this can be added his role as president of the Instituto de Historia del Pacífico Español in Vancouver. These latter points are mentioned not just to show the breadth of his interests but because, in this particular field, and even centuries after the events, there is a tendency toward scholarly patriotism—or just laziness. Thus the greatest merit of the author is to have placed equal and fair emphasis on all of the actors, including the Spanish, French, and Russian, who all too often and unfairly come in a very distant second to the British and Americans. Thanks to such balance, this book is a particularly valuable addition to the series of Historical Dictionaries of Discovery and Exploration.

Jon Woronoff
Series Editor

Preface

"One day the Mowachaht discovered Captain Cook in their bay."

Exhibition label:
Royal British Columbia Museum

On the Northwest Coast of America at the present time the concept of discovery is not held in particularly high regard. It is too easily linked with the history of colonialism, a legacy that makes many uneasy and sensitive to the feelings of those descendants of the first Americans to whom the historical period has been, and remains, particularly painful. For the native peoples themselves, whose ancestors lived in the region for at least 10,000 years before the arrival of the explorers, and who had before that contact developed a sustainable lifestyle and successful societal organization, with a rich and complex cultural component, the notion is frankly incomprehensible. As elsewhere in the world, discovery and exploration involved encounter. There was little comprehension of "the other" as both sides sought to turn the experience to their advantage. Initially, change for the peoples of the Northwest Coast was more subtle than obvious, and the meetings became more significant in retrospect as the decades unfolded. Certainly the long-term results were not so subtle as the implications of disease, violence, appropriation of land, and ultimately marginalization manifested themselves.

For the Europeans and Euroamericans who have come to the region in the wake of the encounter, the story of discovery and exploration is the start of their own story, of occupying and "improving" the land and of building nations. Such men as Vitus Bering and James Cook are heroes and loom large as precursors of the North America we know and the civilization we enjoy. For those who were here before, and who have lived through the depopulation and loss of power over their own lives, the encounter is viewed very differently. Thus the same event, as symbol, has the ability to make some celebrate and others weep; emotions are conflicted.

Nevertheless the stories of Juan Francisco de la Bodega y Quadra, Grigorii Shelikhov, Aleksandr Baranov, George Vancouver, and Dionisio Alcalá Galiano are each in their own way heroic, worthy of the telling and deserving of respect. Although obviously men of their time with a commitment to a certain view of progress and the creation of empires, both political and commercial, most of the explorers and many of the traders and others who followed them were men who tried to meet "the other" as fellow human beings. They may not have found them attractive or "civilized" but on the whole they meant them no harm or ill will. And there was at least one legacy that has been beneficial to Native Americans. The written descriptions of native life, the annotated maps of their lands, and the drawings of people and places that resulted from the voyages and expeditions are of immense value and complement the rich oral traditions that have been passed down from generation to generation. Perhaps fair reflection and assessment of the historical record is preferable to celebration or despair.

In this light it is hoped that this work of reference will be useful. My interpretation of discovery and exploration is a wide one; it is not just about surveying and maps, but also about the work of scientists and artists who explored the natural history and people and landscapes of the Northwest Coast, and about the material culture of the civilization they found. Thus we find here not only sailors and trailblazers and mapmakers, but also men who brought other talents to draw and paint, to collect and to write about their impressions.

My first debt of gratitude is to editor Jon Woronoff for trusting me to undertake the task, and for acting on the suggestion of my friend and colleague John Robson that I be given the opportunity to do so. John has been a source of interest and great support throughout. I thank him particularly for the help that he and Max Quanchi provided in drawing and producing the maps. Over the years I have benefited greatly from sharing my enthusiasm for this period with many people. They are really too numerous to mention but I would be remiss without listing a few: Donald Cutter, Iris Engstrand, John Kendrick, Christon Archer, Freeman Tovell, the late Kaye Lamb, Andrew David, Barry Gough, Robert King, John Gascoigne, Glyndwr Williams, the late Lydia Black,

Richard Inglis, Derek Hayes, Nick Doe, Mercedes Palau, Eric Beerman, and Pilar San Pio. Sadly I now miss a constant debating of the issues with the late John Crosse. Needless to say, the conventional disclaimer applies; any errors in fact or interpretation are mine, and I am acutely aware that a book like this is only as good as its first mistake.

My bases of operation have been the library at the University of British Columbia and the Vancouver Public Library, and I am grateful to their staffs, particularly in the Special Collections Divisions. I have found myself working in public and university libraries from San Diego and Seattle to Anchorage, Montreal, Ottawa, New York, London, and Madrid. I have found each in their own way to have been welcoming and their staffs most helpful. In this journey of exploration, I myself have discovered much that was new and of interest: I thank my colleagues at the North Vancouver Museum and Archives and particularly my family for bearing with my regular need and desire to retreat into the 18th century.

Acronyms and Abbreviations

EIC	East India Company
HBC	Hudson's Bay Company
PWS	Prince William Sound
RAC	Russian–American Company

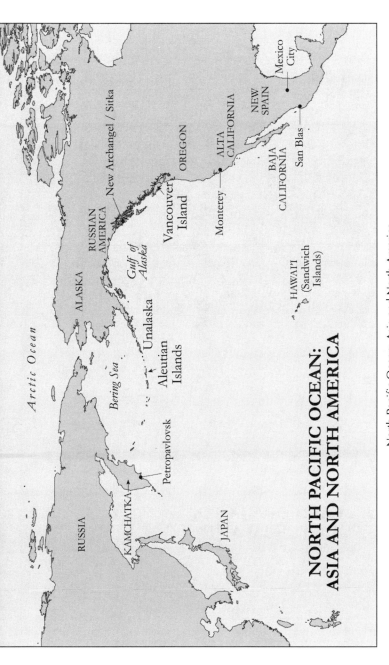

NORTH PACIFIC OCEAN: ASIA AND NORTH AMERICA

North Pacific Ocean: Asia and North America

Maps drawn for this publication by John Robson and produced by Max Quanchi.

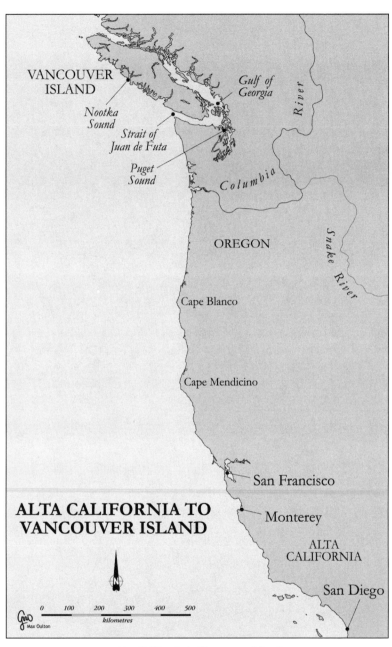

Alta California to Vancouver Island

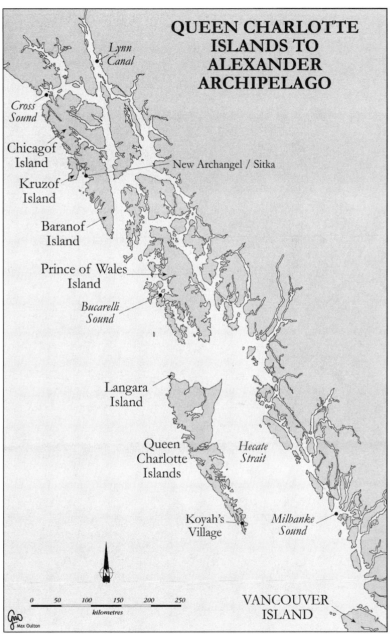

QUEEN CHARLOTTE
ISLANDS TO
ALEXANDER
ARCHIPELAGO

Lynn
Canal

Cross
Sound

Chicagof
Island

New Archangel / Sitka

Kruzof
Island

Baranof
Island

Prince of Wales
Island

Bucarelli
Sound

Langara
Island

Queen
Charlotte
Islands

Hecate
Strait

Koyah's
Village

Milbanke
Sound

VANCOUVER
ISLAND

N

0   50   100   150   200   250
kilometres

Max Oulton

Queen Charlotte Islands to Alexander Archipelago

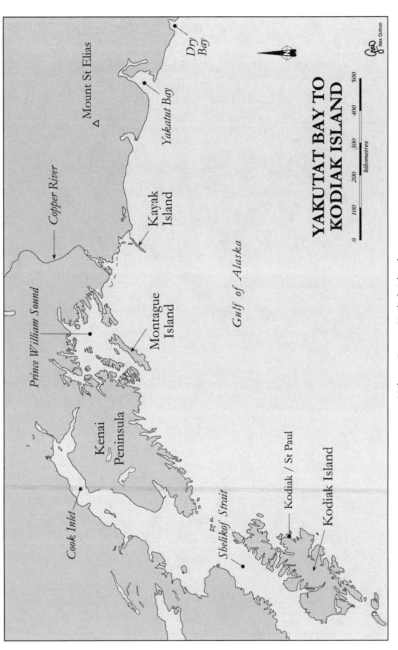

Yakutat Bay to Kodiak Island

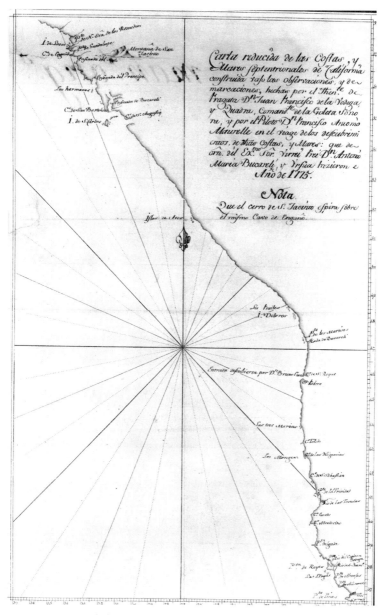

Juan Francisco de la Bodega y Quadra/Francisco Mourelle: Carta reducia
de las Costas y Mares Septentrionales de California, 1775. *Archivo
del Museo Naval, Madrid.*

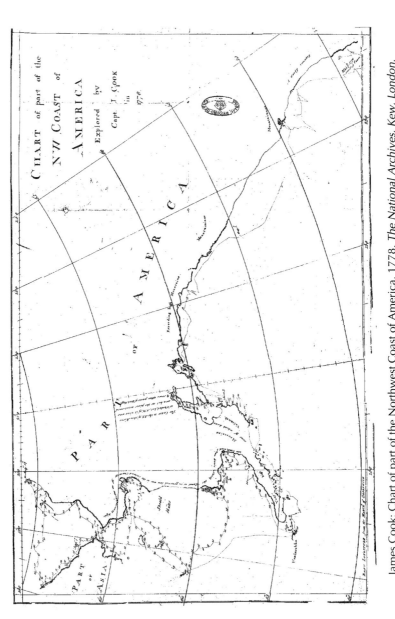

James Cook: Chart of part of the Northwest Coast of America, 1778. *The National Archives, Kew, London.*

Francisco de Eliza: Carta que comprehende los interiores y veril de la costa desde los 48° de Latidud N hasta los 50°, 1791.
Archivo del Museo Naval, Madrid.

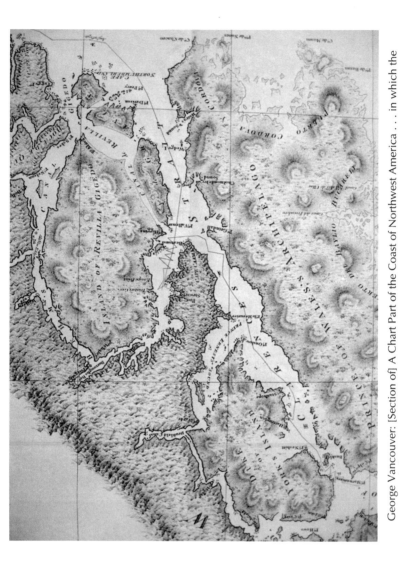

George Vancouver. [Section of] A Chart Part of the Coast of Northwest America . . . in which the Continental Shore has been correctly traced and determined from latitude 51°45′ longitude 232°08′ east to latitude 57°30′ N and longitude 226°44′ E [1793]. Atlas to A Voyage of Discovery to the North Pacific Ocean, 1798. Vancouver Public Library.

John Webber: A View in Ship Cove, Nootka Sound, 1778. *The British Library, London.*

John Meares: The Country of New Albion (1788). *Voyages Made in the Years 1788 and 1789 from China to the North West Coast of America,* 1790. Image from Collection des Cartes Geographiques . . . relative aux voyages du Capitaine J. Meares. *University of British Columbia Library, Rare Books and Special Collections.*

José Cardero: Pira y Sepulcros de la Familia del Actual Ankau en el Puerto de Mulgrave, 1791. *Archivo del Museo Naval, Madrid.*

Friedrich Heinrich von Kittlitz: Inhabitants of Ounalachka with their canoes, 1827. Atlas to Frederic von Litke, *Voyage autour du monde . . . sur la corvette Le Séniavine dans les années 1826, 1827, 1828, et 1829* (1835). *University of Washington Libraries, Special Collections.*

Chronology

The Northwest Coast of America was discovered and explored by Asian peoples crossing the land bridge of Beringia in the Pleistocene age, perhaps as early as 25,000 BC and as late as 10,000 BC. In the era of prehistory and the historical period there is also clear evidence that boats carrying people from Japan and China were swept across the North Pacific by the prevailing winds and currents to land upon the shores of America. The general chronology that follows, however, highlights only those known events and achievements of specific people that are substantiated by the historical record. The geographical range of the list covers the North Pacific from California to Eastern Siberia, allowing the reader to appreciate a few of the earliest approaches to the Northwest Coast that preceded and made possible its discovery and exploration during the 18th century.

1494   Treaty of Tordesillas between Spain and Portugal divides the world between them with papal blessing. This becomes the basis for Spanish claims of sovereignty over the Northwest Coast of America.

1513   Vasco Nuñez de Balboa crosses the Isthmus of Darien and sights the Pacific. He claims the "South Sea" for Spain.

1522   Explorers sent out by conquistador Hernán Cortés from Mexico City reach the Pacific Ocean coast of New Spain.

1533   Baja California is discovered by Fortún Jiménez on a voyage sponsored by Cortés.

1535   Cortés travels to Baja California and establishes the short-lived settlement of Santa Cruz in the Bay of La Paz. It is abandoned the next year.

1539 Francisco de Ulloa explores the east coast of Baja California and the continental coast of the Gulf of California. He proves that "California" is not an island.

1540 Ulloa continues his explorations by rounding the tip of the California peninsula and sailing up the west coast, perhaps as high as 30°N. Hernando de Alarcón also explores the Gulf of California and confirms Ulloa's discovery that "California" is not an island.

1542 Juan Rodríguez Cabrillo, sailing from the Mexican port of Navidad, explores the coast of what is later known as Alta California. He discovers San Diego Bay, which he names Bahia de San Miguel, and Monterey Bay, naming it Bahia de los Pinos.

1543 Bartolomé Ferrer continues the coastal explorations of Cabrillo and likely sails beyond Cape Mendocino towards the modern California–Oregon border at 42°N.

1564 Abraham Ortelius presents his influential map "Orbis Terrarum." It codifies the idea of a Strait of Anian leading into a Northwest Passage across the top of America. The concept was to endure for over 200 years.

1565 Andrés de Urdaneta proves his theory that a west–east crossing of the Pacific to New Spain from the Philippines is possible. Within a few years (1571) the Spanish begin to exploit the famous Manila galleon trade route. It ends in 1815.

1579 Francis Drake on his voyage around the world looks for the Northwest Passage and spends the early summer on the lower Northwest Coast off Oregon and California. Landing somewhere north of San Francisco, he names the country New Albion and takes possession in the name of Elizabeth I.

1584 Francisco Gali commanding an east-bound Manila galleon sails as high as Vancouver Island. His report of a "strong current" sparks renewed interest in New Spain in the Strait of Anian, and concern that the English may have found it.

1587 Thomas Cavendish captures the great *Santa Ana*, a treasure-laden Manila galleon, off Cabo San Lucas.

1588   The year of the supposed, but fictional voyage of Spanish cosmographer Lorenzo Ferrer Maldonado through the Northwest Passage, entering the Pacific at 60°N.

1592   The year in which Greek pilot Apostolos Valerianos, or Juan de Fuca, maintains that he sailed north from New Spain and discovered the Strait of Anian at 49°N. His tale is not told in print until 1625 and, although the "Strait of Juan de Fuca" later proves to be a substantial opening in the coast, it is not the entrance to any passage to the Atlantic.

1595   Sebastián Cermaño sailing to Acapulco on a Manila galleon explores the California coast looking for safe harbors. His ship is wrecked in Drake's Bay north of San Francisco.

1602–1603   Sebastián Vizcaíno in the *San Diego* leads an expedition to explore the California coast. He identifies Monterey Bay and reaches Cape Mendocino. Another of his ships, the *Tres Reyes*, under Martín de Aguilar, finds a "voluminous river" close to the California–Oregon border.

1620   Influential cosmographer Antonio de la Ascensión maintains that "California" is an island, and that the "gulf" leads directly into the Strait of Anian. This opinion affects the cartography of California for a century.

1625   Samuel Purchas publishes *Hakluytus Postumus; or, Purchas his Pilgrimes*. It introduces the world to the fable of Juan de Fuca's voyage across America.

1639   Russian Cossack and explorer Ivan Moskvitin reaches the Sea of Okhotsk. An *ostrog* (small fort) is built close to the future site of Okhotsk. A settlement is continuously enlarged on the present site from 1665 onwards, and becomes a formal naval and shipbuilding base early in the 18th century.

1640   The year of the supposed, but apocryphal, "voyage" of Bartholomew de Fonte through a passage across America. The publication of his "adventures" in 1708 inspires widespread belief in such a waterway for much of the 18th century.

1648   Semen Dezhnev, a Cossack leader and arctic navigator, makes a successful voyage from the Kolyma River around the northern tip of

Eastern Siberia, through the Bering Strait to the Anadyr River. He thus proves that Asia and America are not joined.

1662 The Royal Society of London for the Improvement of Natural Knowledge is granted its charter. In the 18th century it becomes influential in promoting discoveries and exploration in the Pacific Ocean, especially after Sir Joseph Banks becomes president in 1778.

1670 The Hudson's Bay Company receives its charter to trade into Hudson Bay from a huge territory that encompasses most of the far northern part of the then-known continent of North America.

1702 Jesuit missionary Eusebio Francisco Kino descends the Colorado River and the east coast of California. He proves that it is not an island as had been thought for 75 years.

1708 Publication in London of *Monthly Miscellany or Memoirs for the Curious*. It introduces the false tale of Bartholomew de Fonte's voyage in a passage across America and becomes the prime source for speculation about the geography of the Northwest Coast that lasts for much of the 18th century.

1719 Peter the Great dispatches Ivan Evreinov to explore the coast and waters to the south and east of Kamchatka. The aim is to establish its relationship to Japan and America. The work takes place in the summer of 1721.

1724 A dying Peter the Great instructs Vitus Bering to establish the relationship of the Asian coast of his empire to America.

1726 Jonathan Swift places Brobdingnag, the mythical land of giants visited by Lemuel Gulliver, on the "unknown" Northwest Coast.

1728 Vitus Bering, sailing north from Kamchatka, discovers St. Lawrence Island, negotiates Bering Strait, and reaches 67°18' N, but does not find America.

1730 The idea of a "River of the West" promising a route from the center of the continent to the Pacific is born through a map constructed by Pierre de la Vérendrye. It is redrawn and published by Philippe Buache in 1754.

1732 Mikhail Gvozdev and Ivan Fedorov, sailing from the Gulf of Anadyr on the coast of Siberia, are the first Russians to see the "Great

Land" of America. They were off Cape Prince of Wales, named 16 years later by James Cook. The Russian government launches the Great Northern Expedition under Vitus Bering. It will include his second Kamchatka Expedition that discovers the Northwest Coast in 1741.

1741 Vitus Bering and Aleksei Chirikov sail from Kamchatka to the Northwest Coast. After searching for the mythical Gamaland they become separated from each other. Bering lands on Kayak Island near Mount St. Elias, and Georg Wilhelm Steller conducts the first scientific investigations on the coast. The Shumagin Islands are discovered and some of the Aleutian Islands sighted. Bering dies on Bering Island in December. Chirikov reaches the Alexander Archipelago and sights Mount Edgecumbe, which he calls Mount St. Lazaria. Rounding the Gulf of Alaska heading home, he sights the islands off the Alaska Peninsula, and later touches the Aleutian Islands.

1743 Emel'ian Basov becomes the first of the pioneer fur-trading navigators to take advantage of the discovery of islands and furs to the east of Kamchatka by the Vitus Bering and Aleksei Chirikov Expedition of 1741–1742. Over the next 56 years, prior to the establishment of the Russian–American Company, nearly 100 hunting and trading expeditions sail from Okhotsk and Kamchatka. They progressively discover and explore the chain of Aleutian Islands and the inlets of the continental coast round the Gulf of Alaska.

1744 Arthur Dobbs publishes his influential *Account of the Countries adjoining Hudson's Bay*. It continues a belief in some quarters about a navigable Northwest Passage, despite earlier explorations to the contrary on the west coast of that bay.

1752 Joseph Nicolas de l'Isle and Philippe Buache produce highly influential maps that impose details of Bartholomew de Fonte's completely fictitious voyage, through a passage across America, upon the geography revealed by the Russians in the north and Spaniards in the south. They bolster the claims of a de l'Isle memoir of 1750 and feed a belief in the mythical geography of the coast for another 30 years. One element of this mythology is a great "Sea of the West" in the interior of western America.

1758 Stepan Glotov reaches Unmak and Unalaska to become the discoverer of the Fox Islands, the nearest Aleutian Islands group to the

Alaska Peninsula. On the expedition's return to Kamchatka in 1762, Petr Shishkin presents the first map of the region to Russian authorities, complementing Glotov's report on their discoveries and the native peoples.

1761 Gavriil Pushkarev reaches the Alaska Peninsula and thus becomes the first Russian trader to visit mainland America, although at the time he considers it to be another of the Aleutian Islands. Gerhart Friedrich Müller's *Voyages from Asia to America,* with a famous map reflecting both fact and speculation, appears in English. (It was published in Russian in 1758.) It shows the relationship between the landings of Bering and Chirikov (1741), that of Gvozdev (1732), and the discoveries of the fur traders in the Aleutians.

1762 Catherine the Great ends state monopoly on trade with China, which encourages larger consortia to enter the Aleutian fur trade, thus expanding exploration.

1763 Stepan Glotov lands on Kodiak Island, discovering Three Saints Bay. Unknown to the Russian hunters, Bering and Chirikov had previously sighted the "island" separately in 1741. Nikolai Daurkin travels by kayak from the Chukotskii Peninsula to St. Lawrence Island, the Diomede Islands, and to the Seward Peninsula in Alaska, his travels resulting in an important early map of the region.

1763–1764 Natives in the Eastern Aleutian Islands launch a counterattack against invading Russian *promyshlenniki* in what becomes known as the Aleut–Russian War.

1765 José de Gálvez becomes *Visitador-General* (royal inspector) to New Spain. His interest in defense of the northern frontier leads to the founding of Alta California and voyages to the Northwest Coast.

1766 Ivan Sindt discovers St. Matthew Island in the Bering Sea and explores the coast of western Alaska.

1768 The expedition of Petr Krenitsyn and Mikhail Levashov, which had been commissioned by Catherine the Great as early as 1764, finally explores the eastern Aleutian Islands. The first official maps are produced along with reports on the Aleuts. The Naval Department of San Blas is founded on the northwestern coast of New Spain. It will become the base of operations for expeditions to supply Alta California, to explore the Northwest Coast of America, and to supply the Spanish settlement at Nootka.

1769 The Sacred Expedition under Gaspar de Portolá, which includes Franciscan Father Junípero Serra, begins the exploration and settlement of Alta California. San Diego is founded. A detachment of the expedition moves beyond Monterey and sights San Francisco Bay.

1770 Spanish explorers found a settlement at Monterey. A presidio and a mission, dedicated to San Carlos Borremeo, are established. From Monterey, Pedro Fages makes an overland trek to San Francisco, explores the eastern part of the bay and is the first to see the Golden Gate. Junípero Serra moves the San Carlos mission from Monterey to the nearby Carmel River valley. Visits to it are later recorded by Bodega y Quadra (1779), La Pérouse (1786), Malaspina (1791), and George Vancouver (1792).

1771 Samuel Hearne reaches the mouth of the Coppermine River proving that there is no low-latitude Northwest Passage exiting Hudson Bay or anything resembling it east of 115°W or south of 65°N.

1774 Juan Pérez undertakes the first Spanish voyage north of Alta California and, accompanied by Esteban José Martínez, reaches Langara Island at the northern end of the Queen Charlotte Islands. He later anchors off Nootka Sound.

1775 A second Spanish expedition leaves San Blas for the Northwest Coast. Its ships become separated. Juan Francisco de la Bodega y Quadra and Francisco Mourelle reach the Alexander Archipelago and discover Bucareli Bay. The commander, Bruno de Hezeta, explores the coast farther south and discovers the presence of a great river. The "Entrada de Hezeta" is later confirmed in 1792 as the mouth of the Columbia River. Juan Manuel de Ayala makes the first maritime entrance into San Francisco Bay. It is surveyed by pilot José Cañizares, who constructs the first chart of the port.

1778 James Cook's Third Voyage to the Pacific in the ships *Resolution* and *Discovery* runs the Northwest Coast from Oregon and Nootka Sound to Prince William Sound and Cook Inlet. Entering the Bering Sea off Unalaska Island, Cook negotiates and names Bering Strait, crosses the Arctic Circle and reaches 70°41′ N in search of the Northwest

Passage. On his return south, he meets the Russian fur trader Gerasim Izmailov on Unalaska Island and receives information including maps about Russian discoveries. The influential Sir Joseph Banks becomes president of the Royal Society.

1779   Without Cook, who has been murdered in Hawaii in February, the English expedition, at first under Charles Clerke and later under John Gore, makes two visits to Petropavlovsk in Kamchatka before and after further probing of the icepack in the Arctic Ocean. The third Spanish expedition to the northern coasts is launched. Led by Ignacio de Arteaga and including Bodega and Mourelle, it visits Bucareli Bay, Prince William Sound, and Port Chatham—Ensenada de Nuestra Señora de la Regla—on the southwest tip of the Kenai Peninsula.

1780   The first of four editions of William Coxe's *Account of the Russian Discoveries between Asia and America* is published and brings Russian activity in the North Pacific to the attention of the English-speaking world.

1781   Daines Barrington publishes his *Miscellanies* with Francisco Mourelle's account of the 1775 Spanish voyage to Alaska. John Rickman, an officer on the *Discovery*, publishes the first unauthorized account of Cook's Third Voyage and confirms the widespread rumors of the high prices received in China for furs collected at Nootka.

1783   Russian hunters begin to establish a presence in Prince William Sound. More than 300 are involved including Potap Zaikov, Filipp Mukhoplev, and Evstrat Delarov. They reach Kayak Island after Leontii Nagaev discovers the Copper River. The American John Ledyard publishes an account of Cook's visit to the Northwest Coast.

1784   The official account, with atlas, of James Cook's Third Voyage, *A Voyage to the Pacific Ocean in the years 1776, 1777, 1778, 1779 and 1780*, completed by James King, is published. It precipitates the maritime fur trade.

1785   The first of the maritime fur traders, James Hanna, arrives on the Northwest Coast. He successfully collects furs in Nootka Sound, the site of Cook's unexpected success.

1786   A French naval expedition under Jean François de La Pérouse visits Alaska, anchoring in Lituya Bay (Port des Français), and charting the outside coast south beyond Vancouver Island to Monterey. Gavriil Pribylov discovers the first of the Pribilof Islands, St. George; the next year he explores St. Paul. Fur traders arrive on the coast in earnest. James Strange and James Hanna (on his second visit) come to Nootka Sound. They both explore the northwest coast of Vancouver Island and enter Queen Charlotte Sound. Strange then continues north to Prince William Sound; Hanna sails south to Clayoquot Sound. Traders Nathaniel Portlock and George Dixon spend the first of two seasons on the coast, exploring Cook Inlet where they encounter Russians establishing trading posts. John Meares also arrives in Alaska; he explores Shelikhov Strait and trades in Prince William Sound, where he winters over and loses many men.

1787 Portlock and Dixon spend a second season on the coast. After exploring around Hinchinbrook Island at the entrance to Prince William Sound, where they encounter John Meares, the former sails south to Chichagof Island. Dixon visits Yakutat Bay, Baranof Island and discovers, explores, and names the Queen Charlotte Islands. Fur trader Charles Barkley visits Nootka Sound. He then discovers and names Barkley Sound before becoming the first European to discover the entrance to the Strait of Juan de Fuca. James Colnett makes his first visit to the Northwest Coast, trading for furs and exploring from Prince William Sound to the Queen Charlotte Islands and making charts.

1788 Spanish navigators Esteban José Martínez and Gonzalo López de Haro visit Prince William Sound and Unalaska. Their voyage results in a decision to establish a post in Nootka Sound the following year to forestall an expected move by the Russians. Pioneer American fur trader Robert Gray arrives at Nootka with John Kendrick. He explores the west coast of Vancouver Island, entering the Strait of Juan de Fuca in the south and penetrating Queen Charlotte Sound in the north. He also sights Prince of Wales Island. He becomes the first American to circumnavigate the world on his return to Boston in 1790. English trader John Meares makes his second visit to the coast. He later maintains that Chief Maquinna sold him land for a trading post in Nootka Sound, and this claim becomes a central issue in the Nootka Crisis. He explores the coast south as far as Tillamook Bay. After a second season on the Northwest Coast, James Colnett meets John Meares in Canton at the end of the year and enters into a fateful contract to establish a trading settlement in Nootka Sound in 1789. Fur trader Charles Duncan explores and maps the islands of the continental coast of central British Columbia. He also draws a chart and coastal profile of the entrance to the Strait of Juan de Fuca. Russian fur traders Gerasim Izmailov and Dimitrii Bocharov explore the coast south from Prince William Sound and leave specially created possession plaques at prominent sites.

1789 Esteban José Martínez sets up a temporary Spanish post at the entrance to Nootka Sound on Vancouver Island. This action is prompted by fear of a Russian advance from the north. The site in Friendly Cove becomes the scene of the Nootka Sound Incident in which English fur traders are arrested and their ships impounded. James Colnett and his men are sent to San Blas. This precipitates the Nootka Crisis. Alexander Dalrymple publishes his *Plan for Promoting the Fur Trade,* a reflection of the intensity of discussions in London as to how Britain should control the emerging fur trade on the Northwest Coast. Alexander Mackenzie voyages down the Mackenzie River to the Frozen Sea. The Count of Revillagigedo arrives in New Spain; as viceroy he oversees a period of intense Spanish exploration on the Northwest Coast, 1790–1792.

1790 Francisco de Eliza and Pedro de Alberni establish a permanent Spanish military establishment at Yuquot (Friendly Cove) in Nootka Sound. It is the first nonnative settlement between San Francisco and Prince William Sound. Manuel Quimper explores the north and south shores of the Strait of Juan de Fuca as far as its eastern end. Salvador Fidalgo leads another Spanish expedition to the far north, concentrating on Prince William Sound and Cook Inlet. He also visits the Russians in Three Saints Bay on Kodiak Island. Joseph Billings's expedition visits Unalaska, Kodiak Island, Prince William Sound, and down the Northwest Coast to Kayak Island and Yakutat Bay. Influential French geographer Jean-Nicolas Buache de Neuville announces in Paris that he believes in the apocryphal voyage of Ferrer Maldonado in 1588, and thus in the existence of a navigable Northwest Passage. England and Spain avert war by agreeing to the first Nootka Convention. It effectively breaches the Spanish claim to exclusive sovereignty over the Northwest Coast.

1791 Aleksandr Baranov arrives on Kodiak Island to assume management of the fur trading interests of Grigorii Shelikhov. He remains in Russian America until 1818. A major Spanish naval expedition under

Alejandro Malaspina explores and charts the coast, visiting Yakutat Bay and Nootka Sound. Francisco de Eliza leads a Spanish expedition into the Strait of Juan de Fuca. José María Narváez explores beyond the San Juan Islands into the Strait of Georgia as far north as Texada Island. French navigator Etienne Marchand trades and explores in the Alexander Archipelago and at the northern end of the Queen Charlotte Islands.

1792 After wintering over in Clayoquot Sound, Robert Gray discovers Gray's Harbor and then, in May, crosses the bar of Hezeta's "entrada" to discover the Columbia River. Dionisio Alcalá Galiano and Cayetano Valdés, and George Vancouver and William Broughton explore the waters behind Vancouver Island. The English explorers discover Puget Sound and are the first Europeans to prove conclusively that Vancouver Island is an island, although strictly speaking the Spaniards, coming and going from Nootka in the same year, are the first to actually complete a circumnavigation. Jacinto Caamaño explores the waters off the continental coast, the Queen Charlotte Islands, and southern Alaska to effectively dispose of the fiction of the voyage of Bartholomew de Fonte. Bodega, at Nootka on the Limits Expedition, and George Vancouver fail to negotiate a satisfactory turnover of the Spanish settlement to the British under the terms of the Nootka Convention of 1790. Salvador Fidalgo sets up the Spanish establishment of Nuñez Gaona at Neah Bay. It is the first European settlement in Washington State, but is abandoned at the end of one summer when the authorities decide to maintain their site at Nootka. Aleksandr Baranov moves his headquarters on Kodiak Island from Three Saints Bay to St. Paul's Harbor at the northeastern end of the island. He initiates the practice of sending an annual fleet of kayaks with Aleut hunters south, down the continental coast from Prince William Sound.

1793 George Vancouver spends his second season surveying the continental coast and numerous islands north of Vancouver Island to the southern part of the Alexander Archipelago. Alexander Mackenzie becomes the first European to cross the continent "from Canada by land" reaching the Pacific Ocean at Dean Channel, British Columbia. English shipbuilder James Shields, working for Aleksandr Baranov, establishes a shipyard in Resurrection Bay on the Kenai Peninsula; it makes possible a more sustained Russian advance down the Northwest Coast.

1794   George Vancouver's expedition spends its third and final summer on the Northwest Coast; it starts its meticulous survey in Cook Inlet and, coming south, completes the task in the Alexander Archipelago. The first mission of the Russian Orthodox Church arrives on Kodiak Island.

1795   Baranov establishes the Russian trading post of Novorossiik at George Dixon's Port Mulgrave in Yakutat Buy. Spain formally abandons its establishment in Friendly Cove, Nootka Sound.

1796–1797   Dimitrii Tarkhanov explores the coast between Yakutat Bay and the Copper River, and surveys the central and upper reaches of the river itself.

1798   The publication of George Vancouver's *A Voyage of Discovery to the North Pacific Ocean and round the World,* with atlas, finally establishes the basic geography of the Northwest Coast.

1799   The Russian–American Company (RAC) is formally established by a *ukase* of Czar Paul I. Aleksandr Baranov has established enough of a Russian presence in the Alexander Archipelago to found the settlement of New Archangel with a fort dedicated to St. Michael. Successful American fur trader and entrepreneur William Sturgis makes the first of four commercial voyages to the Northwest Coast.

1802   New Archangel, the first Russian settlement significantly south of Prince William Sound, on the west coast of Baranof Island in the Alexander Archipelago, is destroyed by the Tlingit.

1804   Meriwether Lewis and William Clark and the U.S. Corps of Discovery reach the mouth of the Columbia River, thus making the first transcontinental crossing south of the 49° parallel. Russians successfully recapture New Archangel thanks to the timely arrival of Iurii Lisianskii in the *Neva.* He is in the North Pacific as part of Russia's first round-the-world expedition commanded by Ivan Kruzenshtern. The settlement and fort are rebuilt on a new site close by (present-day Sitka), which becomes the headquarters of the Russian–American Company and the capital of Russian America.

1808   Nor'wester Simon Fraser navigates down the Fraser River from central British Columbia, following the course of a great river but finding out that it is not the Columbia.

1810 Influential naval officer Vasilii Golovnin visits New Archangel and is critical of the administration of the Russian colony in America. He later recommends the appointment of governors who are naval officers, but this does not happen until Baranov leaves in 1818.

1811 Representatives of John Jacob Astor's Pacific Fur Company establish Fort Astoria at the mouth of the Columbia River. After exploring in the Rocky Mountains for a number of years, David Thompson descends the Columbia River and produces a survey of its entire length.

1812 Fort Ross is established by the Russians north of San Francisco.

1813 The North West Company takes over Fort Astoria at the mouth of the Columbia River and renames it Fort George.

1815–1816 Georg Schaeffer's attempt to establish an effective Russian presence in Hawaii ends in miserable failure.

1816 Otto von Kotzebue's expedition explores the coast of Alaska, north and south of Bering Strait, and enters and names Kotzebue Sound.

1819 The Transcontinental Treaty negotiated by John Quincy Adams and Luís de Onís signals Spain's formal retreat on the Northwest Coast to the 42° parallel. Fur trader and explorer Petr Korakovski establishes the Alexander Redoubt in Bristol Bay. It expands the reach of the Russian–American Company.

1820 Gabriel Franchère publishes his memoir of life at the mouth of the Columbia River in the period 1811–1813.

1821 The British government forces a merger between the Hudson's Bay Company and the North West Company. As the Hudson's Bay Company, it comes to dominate commercial and exploration activity on the central and lower Northwest Coast.

1821–1822 Adolf Etholen and Vasilii Khromchenko undertake an important two-season survey of the Bering Sea coast of Alaska between Bristol Bay and Norton Sound.

1824 Father Ioann Veniaminov begins his ministry to the Aleuts on Unalaska Island.

1824–1825   Treaties between Russia and the United States and Russia and Britain essentially determine the southern and eastern boundaries of Russian America.

1825   The Hudson's Bay Company founds Fort Vancouver on the Columbia River. Fort Vancouver becomes headquarters of the Hudson's Bay Company sprawling Columbia Department.

1826   The first Russian atlas to reflect the results of a century of Russian exploration in the North Pacific is published by the noted hydrographer and explorer Gavriil Sarychev. Frederick Beechey explores Kotzebue Sound and the Alaskan coast north beyond Icy Cape.

1827   The scientifically important expedition of Fedor Litke visits Russian America.

1828   Russian navigator Mikhail Staniukovich undertakes a precise survey of the entire Bering Sea coast of the Alaska Peninsula.

1833   The Russian–American Company establishes St. Michael's Redoubt in Norton Sound. The Hudson's Bay Company establishes Fort Nisqually in Puget Sound. Working for the Russian–American Company, Andrei Glazunov begins four years of exploration in the valleys of the Yukon and Kuskokwim Rivers.

1836   Edward Belcher visits Russian America, Nootka Sound, and California. His explorations are supported by Henry Kellett.

1839   George Simpson (Hudson's Bay Company) and Ferdinand Wrangell (Russian–American Company) negotiate an agreement between their respective companies that gives the former access to the coast in the north, and the latter vital supplies for New Archangel. Edward Belcher makes a second visit for surveying on the Northwest Coast; he comes to the Columbia River before heading north to Russian America and the Aleutian Islands.

1840   The Russian scholar Il'ia Voznesenskii begins to amass his great collection of natural history specimens and ethnographic artifacts from Russian America.

1841   A major round-the-world American expedition commanded by Charles Wilkes visits the coasts of California and the Oregon country.

1842–1844 Lavrentil Zagoskin explores and surveys the Yukon and Kuskokwim River systems in west-central Alaska, bringing the natives of the interior formally into the trading orbit of the Russian–American Company.

1843 Fort Victoria is founded at the southern end of Vancouver Island as a Hudson's Bay Company trading post. In the wake of the Oregon Boundary settlement (1846) it becomes the capital of the Crown Colony of Vancouver Island in 1849.

1846 The Oregon Treaty divides the old Oregon Country between the United States and Britain at the 49° parallel. Vancouver Island is retained by Britain and Henry Kellet surveys its southern coastline.

1852 Mikhail Teben'kov, governor of Russian America in the 1840s, publishes his *Atlas of the Northwest Coast of America from Bering Strait to Cape Corrientes and the Aleutian Islands.*

1857 British hydrographer George Henry Richards arrives to survey the coasts of Vancouver Island, initially in the southeast and the adjacent continental shoreline.

1859 The "Pig War" demonstrates that the United States–Canada boundary in the San Juan Islands remains unresolved despite the Oregon Treaty of 1846. The issue is not settled for another 13 years when an arbitration panel headed by German Emperor Wilhelm I decides in favor of the United States and fixes the boundary in Haro Strait.

1867 Russian America is sold to the United States. Sitka (New Archangel) becomes the capital of the new territorial administration of Alaska.

Introduction

THE LAST COAST

The concept of a "Northwest Coast" of America emerged in the final decades of the 18th century as explorers searching for a Northwest Passage, and traders pursuing a maritime fur trade, roamed the North Pacific from New Spain to Kamchatka. When Joseph Nicolas de l'Isle published his famous map in 1752 he gave the region a shape, but in combining known facts with fantasy he created an image more confused than accurate. His was, however, a speculative attempt to fill what had been for two hundred years a cartographic blank between California and the Strait of Anian, generally understood to separate America from Asia. This unknown coast from Cape Mendocino to the Gulf of Alaska was the last temperate zone to guard its secrets from a Eurocentric world. Once "discovered" and initially explored—remarkably rapidly between 1774 and 1794—however, it was placed on the world map against a backdrop of imperial maneuvering and fierce competition for commercial advantage.

The reasons for the coast remaining a mystery are not hard to understand. It is a very long way from Europe to the Pacific, and once ships arrived they tended to be kept in the south by the prevailing winds and currents. To properly explore the north and to extend commercial enterprise into it required new approaches to shipbuilding and the health of men at sea, as well as a revolution in navigation. Until new solutions to age-old problems like scurvy or determining longitude emerged in the second half of the 18th century there were no compelling reasons, imperial or commercial, to undertake the expense and risks of lengthy voyages into the unknown. The ebb and flow of European interest in the Pacific as a whole reflected this uncertainty, which was reinforced by the existence of colonial settlements and trading opportunities in more easily accessible regions, such as eastern North America, the Caribbean, Africa, and even India.

The English search for a Northwest Passage had stalled early in the 17th century. By that time Spain, which claimed sovereignty, had declined to show any interest in the region, preferring to consolidate its empire in central and South America and to rely on the stable and lucrative transoceanic trade represented by the Manila galleon. Russia had expanded across Siberia with great energy during the 17th century, but still had much to keep it occupied in Europe and Asia without considering a comparable leap into the Pacific. In China, the Ch'ing dynasty concentrated on maintaining internal stability and economic prosperity and exerting its influence in Mongolia, Tibet, and central Asia. And Japan under the Tokugawa shogunate became, from the 1630s, increasingly self-absorbed and isolationist. Finally the Spaniards, French, and British, who might have uncovered—overland—the mysteries of the Pacific coast of North America, were slow to break out of their colonial settlements in the east and south. The populations were small, the distances large, and the topography increasingly difficult. Again, without compelling reasons for exploration, the expense and risks involved were daunting.

NATIVE PEOPLES AND ANCIENT VISITORS

In northern California, Oregon, and Washington the coast assumes a low profile with forests coming to the shore. Great waves break upon dramatic headlands that separate long stretches of lowland and beach, across which rivers flow to sea. North of the Strait of Juan de Fuca, however, the western edge of the continent undergoes remarkable change. Increasingly high, forested mountains rise above deep, sheltered fjords, and the coasts of British Columbia and southeast Alaska are labyrinths of thousands of islands, narrow waterways, hidden coves, and deep inlets. By the time Cross Sound is reached, snowcapped peaks and glaciers falling into the ocean signal the presence of the highest mountains on the continent. Rounding the Gulf of Alaska the volcanic peaks of the Alaska Peninsula stand guard over the Bering Sea, leading the way down to the islands of the Aleutian chain and the route to Kamchatka.

Occupying this narrow strip of coast were Native Americans whose aboriginal culture was unlike any other on the continent. Owing nothing to the influences that spread onto the Great Plains from Mexico, it was Asian in origin and resulted from migration across a land bridge and the Aleutian Islands as long as 25,000 years ago. While anthropologists, linguists, and archaeologists speculate about the "when" of this arrival, the native people themselves prefer to speak of "time immemorial" and to explore in their mythology the "how" of becoming fully human and learning to live with their environment, the animal world and their fellow human beings.

Although Alutiiq and Aleut peoples living to the west of Prince William Sound endured a harsh, cold maritime environment, which defined a life of bleak subsistence, natives exhibiting the classic Northwest Coast culture from Yakutat Bay to northern California inherited a region of plenty. It gave them rich salmon streams and the bounties of the sea, as well as the rain forest in which they found plants and animals and wood, especially cedar, from which they made house planks, cordage, clothing, basketry, and canoes. The village and tribal societies that developed were highly complex. Authority resided in a chiefly class, and privilege based on wealth created from a surplus of resources came to be emphasized. Ceremonial activity, which celebrated significant events or seasonal observances through dance or the potlatch, sought to acknowledge the spirit world that provided the gifts of abundance, to redistribute the wealth, and to reinforce the principles of cooperation and community.

Had they foreseen their future after sustained contact with visitors to their coast, these native peoples could only have expressed satisfaction that their lands were, for so long, a blank on European maps of the world. The fact that Jonathan Swift could safely place Gulliver's Brobdingnag on the far west coast of North America signified their remoteness. But their isolation was never absolute for, over the millennia, thousands of ships were driven across the North Pacific by the winds and current. No doubt the many Asians who survived these accidental crossings were enslaved and absorbed into the culture. But more important than the people were the ships as a principal source of iron. This prized metal increased the ability of Native Americans to work the wood that was so central to their existence. Less clear is the number of planned voyages from China or Japan. The Chinese certainly possessed the ability to visit America, and knowledge of "eastern shores" appears in both writing and art. In the 16th century there were sightings of strange ships off California. Historians tend to be uncomfortable with such circumstantial evidence and are loath to admit the validity of much ancient, non-European activity in the Pacific. But this does not negate its reality; legend has its own truth, and the memory of man recorded in text and map is not the only memory written in the sea. Nevertheless, the arduous voyages involved in establishing practical commercial links with America could not have appeared worthwhile, and the Asians contented themselves with maritime activity in local waters. What is clear is that those who arrived on the Northwest Coast before the 18th century created no dramatic change to the evolution of native culture, its cycle of seasonal activities and its ceremonies.

SPANISH APPROACHES, 1533–1603

In 1528 Hernán Cortés, conqueror of the Aztec Empire, was granted a monopoly over exploration in the South Sea, as the Pacific Ocean was then known, with rights to occupy any lands discovered. His maritime endeavors never brought him wealth or glory, but they did lead to the discovery of Baja California, accidentally found by Fortún Jiménez off the coast of New Spain in late 1533. It was an inhospitable place—isolated, arid, and containing hostile natives—but reports of pearls brought Cortés himself in 1535 to take possession in the Bay of La Paz. Exploration round Cabo St. Lucas and some way up the Pacific coast followed, but when Cortés left in 1537, his settlement collapsed. In 1539 Francisco de Ulloa explored the Gulf of California, proved that Baja California was a peninsula, and sailed up its outer coast as far as the Isla de Cedros at 28° N.

In 1542 Viceroy Antonio Mendoza launched a coastal expedition in search of rich cities believed to exist beyond the northern horizon. Commanded by Juan Rodríguez Cabrillo it was responsible for discovering the bays of San Diego and Monterey. After Cabrillo's accidental death, Bartolomé Ferrer was believed to have reached as high as the California–Oregon border at 42° N in early 1543. As a result, the voyage is considered the true beginning of the discovery and exploration of the Northwest Coast of America. At the time, however, it marked the end of the first phase of Spanish exploration. Various land and sea expeditions had found neither advanced civilizations nor exploitable minerals, and the coast and its inhabitants were generally unappealing.

The coast north of "California" next became of interest to authorities with the establishment of the Manila galleon trade route in the 1570s, and the unexpected arrival of Francis Drake and Thomas Cavendish to cause havoc off the Pacific coast of New Spain. Their appearance and, more ominously, their disappearance at a time when the English were known to be searching diligently for the Northwest Passage, suggested that it had been found and that they had used it to return home. If this were the case then Spain's long-held claim of sovereignty over the "Spanish Lake" and the safety of her China ships would be in jeopardy. Consequently it was decided to use the galleons to search for a safe harbor on the coast where Cabrillo and Ferrer had sailed. The success of Pedro de Unamuno in 1587, however, was limited and the experience of Sebastián Rodríguez Cermeño in 1595 was downright disastrous. Exploration using cumbersome and heavily laden galleons was clearly inadvisable, and demand increased for a purpose-specific expedition with low draft ships for work in shallow, rocky waters. In one of his last acts in September 1598, Philip II issued a royal order for such an initiative, and an experienced, well-connected merchant Sebastián Vizcaíno was chosen to lead the voyage.

Three ships were outfitted, an experienced Manila galleon pilot Francisco Bolaños was found, and the cosmographer Antonio de Ascensión was made responsible for assembling existing charts and preparing others during the expedition. The *San Diego*, *Santo Tomás*, and *Tres Reyes* left Acapulco in May 1602 with orders to survey the coast up to Cape Mendocino. As they made their way north, Vizcaíno replaced most of Cabrillo's toponyms. After charting San Diego Bay, the expedition reached Monterey, later described in glowing terms, but with a number of men sick the *Santo Tomás* was sent home, also carrying reports of the expedition's progress. In January 1603 the ships were separated in a storm off Point Reyes. After being driven north of Cape Mendocino by another storm, Vizcaíno identified Cape Blanco close to 43° N in southern Oregon. The *Tres Reyes* also sailed beyond Cape Mendocino where the Spaniards found "a very large bay" into which emptied a "heavily flowing river." Initially thought to be the entrance to the Strait of Anian this later became, as the Rio de Martín Aguilar, an important feature of the mythical geography of the Northwest Coast in the 18th century.

Although the expedition was considered a success due to the ports of San Diego and Monterey being considered acceptable for the Manila galleons, and because of the production of remarkably accurate charts, events transpired to effectively stop the idea of either settlement (except on the inside coast of Baja California) or further exploration of the Pacific Coast for another 165 years. Primary among these was the belief that with improved construction and provisioning and armament, the galleons did not need a port of refuge so close to Acapulco after all, and that any attempt by foreign powers at settlement on the coast would fail because of the problems of isolation and supply already experienced by the Spanish themselves. There remained some ongoing anxiety about the Strait of Anian but the strait itself and any threat now seemed quite remote from Mexico City, and the expense of doing anything about it beyond the practical resources of the Crown. In the end the authorities gambled on its nondiscovery despite the "rumored evidence" to the contrary, believing that exploration and the production of definitive charts would only highlight its existence and damage Spanish interests. Although settlers and missionaries moved into Baja California, successive viceroys refused to use money from the royal coffers to finance nautical enterprises. Voyages to California became purely private initiatives aimed at exploiting the pearl beds.

THE STRAIT OF ANIAN AND ISLAND OF CALIFORNIA

The abstract vision of the world inherited from classical and medieval times by European mariners in the 16th century held that the polar regions were surrounded by water. The high latitude voyages of Vasco de Gama and Ferdinand Magellan in the southern hemisphere only served to reinforce belief that navigable waters would also be found across the top of Europe and America. After the discovery of America and the Pacific Ocean, mapmakers were troubled by the need to show a relationship between Asia and America. For a short time it was believed they were joined, but in the 1560s maps appeared to show them separated by a strait, which led to open water reaching east to the Atlantic. From this time on, the Strait of Anian was a cartographical given, underlined by stories like that of Juan de Fuca, which was widely disseminated in the 1590s (and formally published in 1625) and in which the old Greek mariner told of sailing through it in 1592. This account probably inspired another that surfaced in Madrid in 1609, in which the cosmographer Lorenzo Ferrer Maldonado claimed that he had entered the Northwest Passage in 1588 and sailed through it to Anian and the Pacific. A year earlier, in 1608, the influential Antonio de la Ascensión, who had sailed with Vizcaíno, sent a memorandum to the Spanish Crown in which he not only reiterated belief in the strait, but also proceeded to alter the geography of California by stating that the gulf explored by Ulloa was in fact a strait between the "Island of California" and the continent. At the northern end of the island, where it opened into the Pacific, the entrance to the Strait of Anian began. So credible was the opinion of Antonio de la Ascensión that Baja California was shown as an island on maps throughout the 17th century until it was finally disproved by the explorations of the Jesuit missionary Father Eusebio Kino. Because it was cartographically necessary to the identity of North America, the Strait of Anian was never disproved because it actually did exist in the form of the Bering Strait. Although Alejandro Malaspina went looking for it in 1791 at the 60° N reported by Ferrer Maldonado, it had already been found by Bering in 1728 and rediscovered by James Cook in 1778. While the two explorers did indeed discover the fabled strait, they also shattered the two-centuries-old belief that it was the Pacific entrance to a great navigable passage. The icepack of the Northwest Passage proved that to be a cruel illusion.

RUSSIAN APPROACHES, 1724–1784

By the time Spanish authorities had firmly withdrawn from any idea of sponsorship of further exploration or settlement on the Pacific coast of California, Russian traders and hunters were nearing the end of their advance across Siberia to the Pacific. Combining exploration of Russia's northern coastline in the ultimately forlorn hope of finding a Northeast passage, they penetrated the interior by moving up and portaging between the numerous rivers that flow into the Arctic Ocean. By the 1640s they had reached the Kolmya River and the polar shores of the Chukotskii Peninsula, and the mouths of the Amur and Anadyr Rivers, which flow into the Okhotsk and Bering seas. In 1648 Semen Dezhnev left the mouth of the Kolyma with a group of *promyshlenniki* (free-spirited fur hunters and traders) to follow the coast east and south in an attempt to reach the Anadyr region reputed to be rich in sable. Most of the *koches* (small two-masted boats with a rounded hull design for operation in icy seas) did not survive the voyage, but two managed to round the peninsula and negotiate the Bering Strait, thus unwittingly proving that Asia and America were indeed separated. In the end, Dezhnev and his immediate companions were the only survivors, and history has credited the voyage to his name. A number of other expeditions probably followed the same route in subsequent years, and its navigation and the vague existence of a "great land" across the "eastern sea" from the land of the Chukchi became a part of local folklore.

Although massively distracted by his efforts to reform Russian government and society and to secure a place in the political and economic life of Europe, Peter the Great (1682–1725) maintained an ongoing interest in the possibility of a Northeast Passage, gaining a greater understanding of the Pacific Coast of his empire, and opening trade with China and Japan. In 1716 a sea route was pioneered from Okhotsk to Kamchatka, and the formal exploration of the peninsula and attempts to subjugate its natives began. In 1719 the czar authorized the first topographical survey of the region under Ivan Evreinov and Fedor Luzhin. They were ordered "to travel to Kamchatka and beyond" to chart new lands, to determine "whether Asia and America are joined by land," and to examine the coastal areas "not only south, but east and west, and to place everything onto a map." Because official news of Dezhnev's voyage did not reach St. Petersburg until the 1730s, there were lingering doubts about the relationship of Asia to America although, from his visit to Holland in 1697 and knowledge of the maps available to him, Peter would have had the opinion that they were not joined. When the Great Northern War with Sweden ended in 1721 the czar not only had the opportunity to satisfy his curiosity but also to discover if finding America might lead to exploitation of its natural resources and the opening of trade with Spanish America. He clearly understood the gains to be made by advancing not just south to Japan and the Philippines but also on to America, and there was a direct connection between this appreciation of the potential of America and the commissioning of Vitus Bering to undertake the first Kamchatka Expedition in 1724.

There are many interpretations of what Peter had in mind, but the most appealing is that he expected Bering to sail east along the southern coast of the "unknown land" depicted on the map of Johann Homann (1722). This would make sense if he hoped that Bering might ascertain the location of any European (i.e. Spanish) settlements. As it was, Bering sailed north in the summer of 1728 and only made a short trip east in 1729. Finding no "great" or "unnamed" land he proved that the Russians had underestimated the distance to America across what is now the Bering Sea from Kamchatka. Farther to the north, America comes close to Asia across the Bering Strait, but fog had prevented the Danish-born navigator from seeing the continent to the east. That first sighting took place in July 1732 when Mikhail Gvozdev and Ivan Federov, continuing the exploration of the Kamchatkan and Chukchi coasts, stood off Cape Prince of Wales and made the first Russian contact with a native American.

Despite the disappointment of his voyage, Bering was put in charge of what was the greatest exploratory initiative ever undertaken—the Great Northern Expedition of 1733–1742. It sought to survey the vast extent of Siberia to the north and east, and to culminate with voyages to Japan and America. The logistical challenges of the task meant that Bering and Aleksei Chirikov were unable to set off for America until June 1741. Parted by a storm, Bering in the *St. Peter* and Chirikov in the *St. Paul* finally discovered, separately, the Northwest Coast of America in late July. When Chirikov lost two longboats off the Alexander Archipelago he decided to return to Kamchatka by following the coast north and west, which took him past Kodiak Island, the Shumagin Islands and a number of the Aleutian Islands before his scurvy-ridden ship limped into Petropavlovsk in October. Bering was less fortunate; although he landed on Kayak Island and also visited the Shumagins, where Aleuts were encountered, the *St. Peter* was beset by storms and had to stop over on Bering Island where the captain-commander and others died during the winter. The survivors finally reached Kamchatka in the summer of 1742. Although America had been found, the results were disappointing. The distances were huge, the cartographic record meager, and the contacts with natives cursory and uneventful. No settlements with which to trade had been located, and the loss of life was significant. The real success—the remarkable scientific achievements of Georg Wilhelm Steller—was unplanned and would only be appreciated later; the immediate result—a rich and frenzied fur rush across the Aleutian Island chain to the Alaska Peninsula—was unintended. Not until there was a need to follow up the rough cartography of the fur traders and to respond to the alarming "encroachment" of James Cook would the Russian navy again launch formal expeditions into the North Pacific.

Beginning in 1743, the advance of the *promyshlenniki* to America was rapid. Drawn by the proximity of Bering Island and reports of abundant sea otters and seals, they essentially continued their march across Siberia onto the ocean, island-hopping to Kodiak and the Alaska Peninsula within 20 years. The shipbuilders, navigators, and hunters were descendants of families who were already familiar with gathering furs in Okhotsk and Kamchatkan waters and the Kurile Islands. Tough and resourceful, they endured great hardships; many died, but others like Stepan Glotov undertook numerous voyages, most lasting several years at a time. Key entrepreneurs such as Nikifor Trapeznikov received government encouragement, loans, and access to supplies in return for reports and maps of what they found. Fedor Soimonov was one of several officials who supported the traders and provided an important link with the authorities in St. Petersburg. In the 1760s the government again sponsored voyages of exploration. Although Ivan Sindt's voyage across the Bering Sea to survey the American coast enjoyed limited success and produced suspect maps, the expedition of Petr Krenitsyn and Mikhail Levashov to the eastern Aleutians, 1767–1768, was much more important, completing a comprehensive geographical survey and providing valuable information about the Aleuts, whose resistance to the invaders and their firearms had collapsed only a few years earlier.

The ascent of Catherine II to the throne in 1762 brought change to the fur trade. The gradual exhaustion of hunting sites coincided with her early abolition of the state's monopoly on the sale of furs into China. With the need for longer voyages and better ships came more competition, and the nature of the trade began to change. Then, in 1774, the empress rescinded the obligatory tax rate of 10 percent on the catch of furs, which immediately made the trade more attractive to new investors. Larger companies were formed and for the balance of the century they competed mercilessly to control the profitable business. Principal among these were a succession of companies developed by Grigorii Shelikhov and Pavel Lebedev-Lastochkin, which sponsored the beginning of Russian settlements in Alaskan waters. The idea was to establish fortified villages on the coast and islands so as to save the time and money required to mount numerous voyages, and to improve the efficiency of hunting conditions. A key feature of the trade was the Russian enslavement of the Aleuts: unlike later traders on the Northwest Coast from Britain and New England, who trafficked with local natives, the Russians enserfed the Aleut and Koniags, forcing them to hunt from their kayaks in return for meager rations and other goods.

Although the village of Iliuliuk had been developed on Unalaska Island in the mid-1770s, it was the decision of Shelikhov to found a major base in Three Saints Bay on Kodiak Island (1784), and his dreams of building an empire on the Northwest Coast of America that marked the beginning of a new permanence in Russia's presence, and the start of a period of intensive Russian exploration around the Gulf of Alaska. Profitable commerce was not Shelikhov's only concern. He also dreamed of a land in which settlers would build cities and be economically self-sufficient, producing their own food, building ships, developing industry, and trading with the world.

As the Russians moved inexorably towards colonization of a huge segment of the American coast, word of their activities gradually filtered into western Europe. Despite the fact that the results of naval and commercial voyages took some time to be organized for publication within the country, and Russia's political and cultural estrangement from the rest of Europe fed a certain xenophobia that encouraged secrecy in the hopes of discouraging curiosity, visitors came home with information, materials were stolen and smuggled out, and published works were translated. Thus Gerhardt Friedrich Müller's *Voyages from Asia to America* (1761) and Steller's *Beschreibung von dem Lande Kamtschatka* (1774) became available, and were joined in 1780 by William Coxe's important *Account of the Russian Discoveries between Asia and America.* For the Spanish, in particular, information about the Russians was of major concern, as activity in the North Pacific was considered an encroachment on their sovereignty and a potential threat to New Spain. As early as 1750 Spaniards were present when Joseph Nicolas de l'Isle gave a talk on the subject in Paris, and in 1757 the Jesuit Andrés Marcos Burriel published a new edition of Miguel Vengas's *Noticia de la California* in which he discussed the nature of Russian expansion. A year later, in 1758, the Franciscan José Torrubia produced *I Moscoviti nella California, o sia dimostrazione della verity del passo all' America Settentrionale* in which he warned that it was entirely possible for the Russians to expand south to California.

SPANISH RESPONSE TO THE RUSSIANS, 1774–1779

Spain was slow to respond to this perceived threat as well as another one that also emerged in the 1750s. This was the presence on the maps of de l'Isle and Philippe Buache of the long-rumored passage between the Pacific and Atlantic, an idea that had been resurrected during the 18th century through the publication (1708) and promotion in the 1740s of the story of a voyage through it by the entirely fictional Bartholomew de Fonte. However, the appointment of José de Galvez as *visitador general* (royal inspector) to New Spain, and the ascension of the reform-minded Carlos III to the throne signaled a new interest in the viceroyalty. The security of the northern frontier became a prime concern and in a very short period of time resulted in the establishment of the Naval Department of San Blas, and the Sacred Expedition that founded Alta California with its presidios and missions in San Diego, Monterey, and San Francisco. When, in the early 1770s, the Spanish ambassador to St. Petersburg relayed to Madrid more specific information about the naval and commercial activities of the Russians, the government felt obliged to respond to what appeared to be a sustained attempt to challenge its perceived hegemony on the as-yet-unknown coast north of California.

The result was a strengthening of San Blas with officers trained for exploration in the use of new navigational instruments, and the launching of a series of voyages to find the Russians and to assess the nature of the threat. The first voyage of Juan Peréz in the *Santiago* in 1774 proved inconclusive. Instructed to sail as high as 60° N he only reached the northern end of the Queen Charlotte Islands, made no landings, and therefore did not perform any Acts of Possession; he did bring back interesting information about the natives he encountered off Langara Island and later off Nootka Sound, but there was no sign of any Russians. A second voyage involving some of the recently-arrived young officers was therefore prepared for 1775. Commanded by Bruno de Hezeta in the *Santiago*, it launched the career of Juan Francisco de la Bodega y Quadra in the *Sonora*. A number of landings were made and possession ceremonies performed. Separated from Bodega off the Strait of Juan de Fuca (which had not yet been discovered) Hezeta sailed up the coast of Vancouver Island before identifying the mouth of the Columbia River, which he actually thought might be the legendary strait. The more adventurous Bodega, accompanied by Francisco Mourelle, "pressed on taking fresh hardship for granted" and reached 58° N, sighting Mount Edgecumbe, and taking possession of Sea Lion Cove on Kruzof Island and Bucareli Sound off Prince of Wales Island. It was a triumphant advance, which provided a good, general indication of the trend of the coast—west instead of the expected east—but again no Russians had been found.

This might have been the last voyage for a time had not Madrid received news in May 1776 of the imminent departure of James Cook for the North Pacific to search for the western entrance to the Northwest Passage. A desire to intercept the celebrated English navigator and to search themselves for the passage prompted Spanish plans for a third voyage, but it did not sail until 1779, long after Cook had left the Northwest Coast. With Ignacio de Arteaga in the *Princesa* and Bodega in the *Favorita*, Bucareli Bay was reached and the Spaniards explored Prince William Sound and the coast of the Kenai Peninsula before, with the appearance of scurvy, they turned for home. They probably should have done better, found Cook Inlet and, like Cook, sailed down to the Aleutian Islands and into the Bering Sea.

Nevertheless, the voyage was considered successful, particularly as possession had been taken above 60° N and once again there was no sign of any Russians. Dominion over the coastline appeared secure by virtue of prior discovery and the all-important Acts of Possession; Russian establishments, if they actually existed, seemed sufficiently distant to pose no problem. This, however, was not true. Madrid had been lulled into a false sense of security and by the time its ships again ventured north, in 1788, 1790, and 1791, any hope of control in the far north had been lost. Unaware of the achievements, let alone the consequences, of Cook's voyage as they became embroiled in the American Revolutionary War, the Spanish would ultimately find out that official voyages by Russia, England, and France, and the presence of numerous fur traders roaming at will over the entire region, meant that defense of their sovereignty would have to be focused much lower on the coast.

THE APPEARANCE OF JAMES COOK, 1778

Between the end of the Seven Years' War in 1763 and the outbreak of the French Revolution in 1789, England and France played out a good deal of their imperial rivalry in the Pacific. The search for imperial advantage motivated the voyages of Philip Carteret and Louis Antoine de Bougainville, but they also introduced a new element—the enlightened expedition. The Age of Enlightenment demanded that inherent in voyages to find and chart new lands, and to pursue new trading opportunities, was an obligation to investigate their wider geography, the flora, fauna, and minerals, and naturally any native people encountered. The voyages of James Cook in the 1760s and 1770s became models of the exploratory voyage, and influenced all subsequent major naval initiatives including those of Jean François de La Pérouse, Joseph Billings, Alejandro Malaspina, George Vancouver, and Ivan Kruzenshtern. As a result, scientists and artists were added to the corps of officers well trained in navigation and surveying.

In 1760 there still remained two overwhelming mysteries in world cartography. Was there a great southern continent? And was there a navigable passage across the top of the world, either a Northeast Passage or a Northwest Passage, or both? Cook's first two Pacific voyages destroyed the concept of *Terra Australis*; his third was directed at finding the supposed waterway above North America. Leaving England in 1776, the expedition took place shortly after news of Samuel Hearne's trek to the Coppermine River had reached London and suggested that any navigable passage would only be found far to the north. Cook's instructions therefore advised him to move rapidly from his landfall at 45° N, in Francis Drake's New Albion, to 65° N where he was expected "very carefully to search for, and to explore such Rivers or inlets as may appear to be of considerable extent" and which might offer the promise of a link to Hudson Bay or Baffin Bay.

These instructions to concentrate his efforts in more northerly latitudes combined with adverse late winter weather to mean that Cook's usual meticulous surveying did not really start until he came close to 60° N in the Gulf of Alaska. After visiting Prince William Sound and Cook Inlet he ran down the Alaska Peninsula to seek a way into the Bering Sea. Finally finding open water to the north, he sailed as far as the ice pack at 70° N. It would appear inconceivable that had he undertaken on the lower coast the kind of surveys accomplished in New Zealand on his first two voyages, he would not have found the Strait of Juan de Fuca and explored in the Alexander Archipelago to disprove the "Pretended Strait of Admiral de Fonte." As it was the *Resolution* and the *Discovery* hurried past Fuca in the fog and off the Queen Charlotte Islands and Alaska Panhandle were forced by the weather to sail away from the coast. His sojourn in Nootka Sound, however, did allow for some useful repairs to the ships, some survey work to determine their precise location, and extensive contact with a group of natives that proved very different from those encountered in the South Seas. In addition John Webber and a number of the officers began to compile their significant artistic record of places and people. The Nootka stopover also allowed the sailors to trade for furs, which they acquired to combat the dampness and cold they were experiencing and expected to get worse.

Despite an intense frustration with the inaccuracies of the early Russian charts, the disappointments of "Sandwich Sound" and "Cook's River," and the barrier to progress encountered at Icy Cape, Cook's achievement in defining the trend of the coast and charting, first the entire Gulf of Alaska and then the far north where America approaches Asia, was substantial. In particular, the expedition's work in 1778 in this latter region and again in 1779, after Cook's death, resulted in the most important charts of the entire voyage. With added information received from the Russians his work soon became the reference point, not only for the navigators who followed him, but also for the Russians themselves. As the first transmittal of information to England came back from Unalaska and Kamchatka via St. Petersburg, officials there and indeed the empress herself were keen to benefit from what Cook had discovered about the remote and unexplored parts of the empire.

During their visit to Petropavlovsk in the fall of 1779 the men sold their best sea otter skins to the Russians. They were delighted with the profits achieved and later became ecstatic when they reached Canton and realized that the furs from Nootka were worth nearly twice as much there as in Kamchatka. Immediately a number of officers began to harbor dreams of returning to the Northwest Coast to engage in trade and make their fortunes. Word of their commercial success began to emerge even before the ships reached London in October 1780, and four unauthorized accounts of the voyage were published before the official one appeared with a full atlas of charts and drawings in 1784. In this official account James King provided a blueprint of what was necessary to establish a profitable fur trade between America and Asia.

There were two key results of Cook's voyage for the Northwest Coast: first the launching of an intense maritime fur trade; and secondly an equally intense maneuvering for imperial advantage. Both ensured that by the turn of the century feverish maritime activities would result in publications that essentially removed forever any lingering mysteries of the geography of the Pacific coast of North America.

FUR TRADE EXPLORATION, 1784–1804

Long before the publication of Cook's journal in 1784, rumor and the unauthorized accounts had made it clear that a lucrative fur trade was possible between the Northwest Coast and China. In the early 1780s such entrepreneurs as Richard Cadman Etches, John Cox, and William Bolts dreamed of entering the trade and found Cook's former officers keen to enter the discussion. When the journal was finally published the result was immediate.

The first trader, James Hanna, in the appropriately named *Sea Otter*, arrived on the coast in 1785. He returned again in 1786. That year also saw the arrival of Nathaniel Portlock and George Dixon, working for Etches's King George's Sound Company, for a visit to Cook Inlet, and the voyage of James Strange to Vancouver Island and Prince William Sound. Both Hanna's and Strange's exploits led to some pioneering exploration along the central and northern coast of Vancouver Island and in Queen Charlotte Sound. In Prince William Sound in the fall of 1786, Strange encountered William Tipping, attached to an expedition that had also set out from India under John Meares. Early on, the ships had lost contact with each other. They proceeded to America separately, and Tipping had left Prince William Sound by the time Meares arrived and spent a disastrous winter (1786–1787) before limping back to Macao.

The next year, 1787, proved to be a particularly important one; Portlock and Dixon returned from Hawaii to Alaska and from Prince William Sound proceeded to trade and explore down the coast for the entire summer. Dixon entered Yakutat Bay, stopped on Baranof Island in the Alexander Archipelago and discovered and named the Queen Charlotte Islands. Portlock also came south to Chichagof Island. Also connected with Etches, James Colnett arrived to trade and explore, making rough charts of the coast from Prince William Sound to the Queen Charlotte Islands. Farther south his colleague Charles Duncan spent time in Nootka Sound and explored the west coast of Vancouver Island. As well, Charles Barkley arrived at Nootka, traded successfully and then proceeded down the west coast of Vancouver Island to the sound that bears his name before, to his immense surprise because the great Cook himself had declared its nonexistence, he discovered the entrance to the Strait of Juan de Fuca.

Through various machinations in China, Meares acquired Barkley's charts and immediately laid plans to sail to Nootka Sound and enter into an agreement with the local chief, Maquinna, that would allow him to set up a trading post and forestall any similar move by the Etches company. Undeterred by the fact that he was again trading illegally without permission from the East India Company, which owned the rights to the coast under British law, he arrived at Nootka in 1788. There he was able to establish a shore station and, while he was away exploring, his men constructed the first ship built on the coast, the schooner *Northwest America*. His grand idea, imagined also by a number of other traders and their sponsors, was to create a permanent base served by coastal vessels from which a transoceanic link with China could be maintained. After overseeing the creation of his post at Nootka, Meares sailed south. He visited the Makah Indians at the entrance to Fuca, but he did not explore the strait, preferring to press on to see if he could find the great River of the West. However he failed to identify the entrance to the Columbia River and had to content himself with discovering Tillamook Bay.

The field was by no means limited to English traders for, by 1787, the Boston merchant Joseph Barrell was prepared to sponsor a voyage. This was due at least in part to the ceaseless promotion of John Ledyard, who had been with Cook and had published one of the unauthorized accounts of his voyage in 1783. But economic conditions did not favor the financing of a voyage until a few years later, which meant that John Kendrick and Robert Gray did not arrive at Nootka until late in 1788. The energetic Gray spent 1789 on the west coast of Vancouver Island and sailed some way into the Strait of Juan de Fuca before heading north to Queen Charlotte Sound and Hecate Strait. Crossing Dixon Entrance he sighted Prince of Wales Island. He initiated American trade with the Haida, and thus pioneered exploration and commerce in a region of the coast that the "Boston Men" would soon come to dominate. Gray completed the first American circumnavigation before setting out again from New England in 1790. His years on the coast, 1791 and 1792, took him from Oregon to southern Alaska and in May 1792, exploring south from Vancouver Island, he made arguably the most important discovery of all by crossing the bar of the Columbia and thereby finding the greatest river system of the Pacific Northwest. Other Americans such as Joseph Ingraham, John Boit, and later William Sturgis contributed greatly to an understanding of the geography and native peoples of the Northwest Coast as far north as the Alexander Archipelago, but none matched Gray in importance. Americans loomed large as the 1790s progressed into the 19th century. They developed a successful system of commerce that relied more and more on goods produced on the coast itself, such as leather, whale oil, and abalone shells, in addition to goods from Hawaii and China. Taking advantage of the turmoil in Europe they came to dominate the trade, and their journals, maps, art, and shared experiences all helped to advance the exploration of the Northwest Coast of America.

Although confined to the far north in the early period, it was not long before Russian traders also continued their advance with exploration east and south along the continental coast. From Shelikhov's base on Kodiak and Lebedev-Lastochkin's strength on the Alaska Peninsula, they consolidated their presence in Cook Inlet and Prince William Sound in the 1780s. The arrival of Aleksandr Baranov in 1791 and the establishment of St. Paul's Harbor on Kodiak coincided with the start of a rapid decline in sea otters around the Gulf of Alaska, which resulted in his assault in earnest on the northern Alexander Archipelago in the 1790s and early 1800s. A shipyard was constructed on the Kenai Peninsula and a permanent post on Hinchinbrook Island in 1793. In 1795 a post was created at Yakutat and by this time the Copper River and its delta had been explored, great hunting fleets of Aleut kayaks were being sent out annually from Kodiak, and James Shields had undertaken a general survey of the coast north from the Queen Charlotte Islands.

The Russians explored Lituya Bay and Cross Sound and began to investigate the numerous bays and islands off the continent, an activity that was driven by their insatiable appetite for furs. Once the Russian–American Company had received its charter and Baranov had begun construction of New Archangel in 1799 (permanently established in 1804) the Russians continued to improve upon the charts they inherited from George Vancouver's surveys in 1793–1794, and which had been published in 1798. The final details of the northern coast revealed themselves as a result of the sustained presence of ships of the imperial navy, which began to arrive regularly in the colony beginning with the voyage of Iurii Lisianskii in the *Neva*, 1804–1805, and from communication between American and Russian traders as the 19th century got underway. Although they continued to travel south to Vancouver Island, Oregon, California, and Hawaii and founded Fort Ross in 1812, the Russians did not contribute anything particularly substantial to the geographical knowledge of the southern coast.

IMPERIAL MANEUVERING AND THE NOOTKA CRISIS

The end of the American Revolutionary War and publication of Cook's journal made it almost inevitable that the Northwest Coast would become the scene of imperial rivalries.

The first navy into the field was that of France, which was keen to build on its success in the war and presence in the South Pacific to launch a voyage to match that of Cook, to increase national prestige, and to contribute to the advancement of knowledge. The result was the voyage of Jean François de La Pérouse that followed an ambitious plan to roam the Pacific to complete some of the work left undone by the English navigator. Louis XVI and his ministers were also keen to have the potential of the fur trade on the Northwest Coast investigated and to see if any evidence of a navigable passage across the top of America might exist after all. La Pérouse spent the best part of the summer of 1786 on the coast, where he discovered Lituya Bay in Alaska and visited the Spanish settlement at Monterey. A boat tragedy delayed his departure from Alaska so he did little more than run the outside of the coast, and fog prevented any visit to Nootka Sound or investigation of the still-unknown Strait of Juan de Fuca. Nevertheless, the navigational, cartographic, written and artistic record, and reports on the fur trade meant that Paris was as knowledgeable about the coast as London or Madrid or St. Petersburg at that time. The loss of the expedition after leaving Australia in 1788, and the turmoil of the French Revolution and its Napoleonic aftermath, ensured that the voyage would not be followed up by any national initiative, and the only other French presence was provided five years later by the privately financed fur trader Etienne Marchand.

La Pérouse's appearance did, however, renew Spain's concern about its assumed sovereignty over the coast, already heightened by the prospect of other nations capitalizing on a fur trade with Asia. This was particularly the case when he seemed to bring information, first to Concepción in Chile and later to Monterey, that suggested the Russians were on the move and intended to establish a post at Cook's anchorage in Nootka Sound as a preemptive strike against traders from other nations. It was time for another Spanish investigation. As a result Esteban José Martínez and Gonzalo López de Haro were sent to the far north in 1788. They performed Acts of Possession at various locations, including Prince William Sound and Unalaska, and met Russian fur traders on Kodiak and Unalaska Islands. They also confirmed what they took as a serious threat, the imminent arrival of a naval expedition to establish a Russian presence at Nootka and other places and to challenge the fur traders who were already operating at will in a region that St. Petersburg considered, as strongly as did Madrid and Mexico City, to be in its sphere of hegemony. As it was, the planned expedition of Grigorii Mulovskii was reluctantly cancelled by Catherine the Great when war broke out in Europe, and the Russians, forestalled at Nootka by Spain and England, never successfully (except in the unique case of Fort Ross) advanced farther south than the Alexander Archipelago. When a naval expedition did arrive under Joseph Billings, it came late, in 1790, and never proceeded farther than Yakutat Bay. It was left to Aleksandr Baranov and the Russian–American Company to consolidate, through commercial activity, whatever sovereignty Imperial Russia was able to establish.

The threat of serious Russian activity goaded Viceroy Manuel Flórez into responding, in 1789, with another Spanish voyage. This brought Spain to Nootka Sound, where Esteban José Martínez set about establishing a post, performed an Act of Possession and encountered both English and American traders. To Martínez the English presence, flying Portuguese colors, was much the more sinister. These traders belonged to the syndicate organized by John Meares. They were following up his visit in 1788 and his apparent agreement with Chief Maquinna for land upon which to set up a trading post. When James Colnett, sent by Meares, arrived with Chinese laborers and materials to establish the post, he was not about to agree with Martínez that the English had no rights in the region, that Spain had sovereignty, and that he must leave immediately and not engage in any trade. The clash that soon ensued resulted in the arrest of Colnett, his men, and the ships, and their transport as prisoners to San Blas. Not considering the Spanish presence at Nootka in 1789 to be permanent, the viceroy had sent word to Martínez during the summer that he was to leave in the fall. Given what had transpired he did so reluctantly, returning to New Spain to tell his version of what was later referred to in England as an "insult to the British flag."

When word of what had happened to his plans for Nootka reached Meares in China, he immediately set off to London to persuade the government of William Pitt to demand redress for his grievances and compensation for his losses from Madrid. He arrived in April 1790. The government, which had already been formulating a policy of "freedom of the seas" and "freedom to trade" by which it maintained the right of English ships to sail the oceans at will and to trade and establish posts and supply centers on coasts and islands unoccupied by other Europeans, was only too keen to challenge what it considered to be Spain's outdated pretensions of sovereignty over such places in both the Atlantic and the Pacific. Pitt was already under pressure from commercial interests in London for a similar "preposterous" Spanish action on the coast of Patagonia, and he immediately regarded the Nootka Sound Incident as even more serious, taking place as it did in the very location where the English had rights due to James Cook's "first discovery." Over the next few months, as negotiations proved unsatisfactory, both England and Spain prepared for war. By the fall, however, Spain was obliged to back down primarily because the French Revolution had, at a crucial juncture, robbed it of the support of its natural ally. The Nootka Convention of October 1790 provided for restitution of "English territory" at Nootka, compensation for Meares, and agreement that British ships would be free to trade on the "unoccupied" Northwest Coast of America.

The true implications of the Spanish "defeat" and British "victory" were, however, not immediately apparent and are clearer in retrospect than they were at the time. The Spanish moved decisively to set up a permanent military establishment in Nootka Sound in the spring of 1790, and laid plans to continue exploration to remove the lingering doubts about the veracity of the tales of Juan de Fuca and Bartholomew de Fonte. In England meanwhile, voices from within and without the government had been calling for action to capitalize on the exploration and commercial success of the fur traders. Returning from the coast in 1788, George Dixon had advocated with Sir Joseph Banks and others to support settlements and establish sovereignty through trade. In 1789 Alexander Dalrymple published *A Plan for Promoting the Fur-Trade, and Securing it to this Country* in which he argued for a united effort by the East India Company and the Hudson's Bay Company to control the coast and the interior of Northwest America. In doing so they would also control the Northwest Passage that he remained convinced still awaited discovery and exploration. In response the government, which had been planning a voyage to be led by Henry Roberts, a veteran of Cook's last two voyages, to locate secure harbors for whalers in the South Atlantic, expanded the scope of the expedition to find as well a spot for a settlement near King George's Sound (Nootka). The mobilization of the navy in preparation for war with Spain in 1790 delayed these plans, but when they were revived, with George Vancouver in command, the focus had shifted to the Pacific and the Northwest Coast. Vancouver was to undertake an accurate survey of a region that had now fallen so fortuitously into the sphere of British interest, and to accept restoration of the buildings and lands of which the Nootka Convention had presumed John Meares had been dispossessed.

THE SPANIARDS AND GEORGE VANCOUVER: THE COAST REVEALED, 1790–1794

In late 1789 a new energetic viceroy, the Count of Revillagigedo, had arrived in Mexico with a group of well-trained naval officers, led by the experienced Juan Francisco de la Bodega y Quadra, to bolster the situation at San Blas in support of the supply of California and the defense of Spanish interests on the Northwest Coast. The immediate outcome was the reoccupation of Nootka in 1790 and the construction of a fort to guard a military establishment set up in Friendly Cove. The commandant, Francisco de Eliza, sent Manuel Quimper to make the first serious reconnaissance of the Strait of Juan de Fuca and, when he returned to New Spain and reported to the viceroy that channels proceeded to the north, orders went out that further investigations should take place in 1791.

The summer of 1790 also saw another Spanish voyage to the far north. After coming to Nootka with Eliza, Salvador Fidalgo set out for Prince William Sound, Cook Inlet, and Kodiak Island. He met Russian traders, and performed Acts of Possession and improved Spanish cartographical understanding of the coast, but he made no new discoveries and essentially explored areas already well known.

The Quimper voyage into Fuca, however, led directly to another by Eliza himself in 1791 and the discovery and exploration of the Strait of Georgia behind Vancouver Island by José María Narváez in the *Santa Saturnina.* Meanwhile, an assertion in Paris in November 1790 by geographer royal, Jean-Nicolas Buache de Neuville, that the 16th-century voyage of Lorenzo Ferrer Maldonado through a Northwest Passage was believable, led to the great expedition of Alejandro Malaspina, already in the Pacific to survey the coasts and report on the prospects of Spanish territories, being diverted to the Northwest Coast. In the summer of 1791 the *Descubierta* and *Atrevida*, with their highly trained officers using the best navigational and survey instruments available, along with the scientist Tadeo Haenke and the artists Tomás de Suria and José Cardero, concentrated their efforts on Yakutat Bay and Nootka Sound. The result of their efforts was a mass of documentation—cartographic, scientific, ethnographic, and artistic—but in terms of new discoveries and exploration it was quite limited. More important in that context was the work in 1792 of Malaspina's officers Dionisio Alcalá Galiano and Cayetano Valdés, who were detached from the main expedition and, in concert with George Vancouver, completed the work of Quimper, Eliza, and Narváez by continuing the exploration of the Strait of Georgia. This led directly to the circumnavigation of Vancouver Island by the English ships *Discovery* and *Chatham* and the Spanish schooners *Sutil* and *Mexicana.*

Vancouver had been instructed to make a detailed survey of the coast from 30° to 60° N. Like Cook before him, he made landfall off Drake's New Albion in April 1792. Instead of proceeding to Nootka Sound, where Bodega was waiting for him as Spain's commissioner to hand over the establishment under the terms of the Nootka Convention, he ran up the coast as far as the entrance to the Strait of Juan de Fuca reported by various fur traders. Unaware of Spanish activities in 1790–1791, and later "mortified" to find that he was following others into the Strait of Georgia, he was determined to pursue the traders' leads as the initial part of his grand survey. His most important accomplishments that summer were the discovery of Puget Sound and proving the insularity of Vancouver Island. Also, by deciding that to undertake a proper survey much of the work would have to be done by small boats, he began what would become one of the major cartographic achievements of any age—a remarkably detailed survey that followed the ins and outs of the coast and its islands for over 10,000 miles.

Before breaking off his survey for the year and sailing to Nootka, where his negotiations with Bodega were largely cordial but inconclusive, and then on to a winter in Hawaii (his consort William Broughton explored the Columbia River and then took the expedition's papers and charts back to England from New Spain), Vancouver had edged his way up the continental coast north of Vancouver Island. Before departing Nootka in the fall of 1792 he had the benefit of meeting with Jacinto Caamaño, who shared with him his charts and experiences of a summer in the waters of the Queen Charlotte Islands and southern Alaska and the adjacent continental coast. Caamaño's exploration of the inlets and islands had essentially disproved the fiction of Fonte, and his information set Vancouver up for his next survey season in full knowledge that the whole tale was an absurdity.

Vancouver began his work in 1793 where he had left off in the vicinity of Rivers Inlet and Fitzhugh Sound. The innumerable channels and islands of the northern British Columbia coast proved to be, in his own words, an "intricate inhospitable labyrinth." The "tedious, arduous and hazardous" work fell largely to James Johnstone and Joseph Whidbey, who directed the small boat excursions that sometimes took them over 100 miles from the ships. This was microexploration, a "slow and irksome process . . . on account of the divided state of this extraordinary inhospitable region." One boat excursion barely advanced the latitude of the survey yet covered nearly 800 miles in the Behm Canal surrounding Revillagigedo Island. By September they had had enough and stopped at Cape Decision at the southern end of Kuiu Island after exploring Sumner Strait in the middle of the Alexander Archipelago. The third and final season started with a voyage from Hawaii to "Cook's River" which was soon found to be an inlet. In Prince William Sound, Vancouver confirmed what others had already discovered—that its various arms were, too, all dead ends. Focused on the priority of completing his survey, he did not seek out Aleksandr Baranov on Kodiak Island nor tarry long before sailing south to Cross Sound. He had already been off this continental shore with Cook, and it was clear from the Russians encountered at Yakutat that there was little new to learn. He was well aware also of the tedious work that lay ahead to reach the endpoint of the previous summer. That moment was finally achieved in mid-August after the boat excursions had successfully explored Lynn Canal, Stephens Passage, Chatham Strait, and Frederick Sound. As a result of his extraordinary achievement that allowed his maps to be used by traders and navigators well into the second half of the 19th century, the possibility of a transcontinental passage was finally put to rest. With pride and certainty Vancouver could safely write: "I trust the precision with which the survey of the coast . . . has been carried into effect, will remove every doubt, and set aside every opinion of a northwest passage, or any other communication navigable for shipping between the North Pacific, and the interior of the American continent."

THE OVERLANDERS

Exploration across northern and northwestern North America was driven by two imperatives: the search for an easy passage through the continent, and the nature of the fur trade, which required continual expansion. English explorers operating out of Hudson Bay and French explorers traveling west from the St. Lawrence Valley never found the passage, but they did create the fur trade. Some 20 years after the fall of New France in 1763, two rival enterprises had emerged as active instruments of British imperial ambition. In carrying the fur trade to the Arctic and Pacific, the Hudson's Bay Company and the North West Company were almost exclusively responsible for the exploration of western Canada and, by limiting the Russians and effectively challenging the Americans, for securing most of the northern part of the continent for the British Empire. In the 1750s Anthony Henday and others approached the Great Plains from the north; in the early 1770s Samuel Hearne journeyed to the mouth of the Coppermine River; and by the early 1780s Peter Pond had become familiar with the Athabasca country from where he pressed on to Great Slave Lake.

Discovering a land of lakes and rivers, Pond became convinced that they would lead him to the western sea, and in James Cook's report of "Cook's River" in 1784 he seemed to find proof for his optimism. Each of his four surviving maps speculated that the lakes gave birth to rivers that flowed north and west as the Mackenzie and Peace indeed do; but in fashioning the image of "Cook's River" leading directly to the Pacific from "Slave Lake" he conveniently ignored the Rocky Mountains and wildly underestimated the distances involved. In his writings, however, he correctly promoted the concept of a chain of trading posts as the best way to hold the region in the face of the imperial interests of others. Pond's mantle as explorer-trader fell upon Alexander Mackenzie and it was he who set out in 1789 to follow Cook's River to the sea. Instead he found that the river exiting Great Slave Lake, and which now bears his name, turned north; thus instead of tracing it to the Pacific he arrived at the Arctic Ocean. In 1792 he set out again, this time ascending the Peace River from Lake Athabaska. Guided by native information he crossed the Continental Divide and found himself on the upper reaches of what today is the Fraser River, which he descended for about 250 miles. Again, guided by natives he left what he was sure was the Columbia River to strike due west in search of the Pacific Coast. Carrying Cook's chart and following a well-established native trade route he arrived "from Canada by land" in July 1793 in Dean Channel, some six weeks after a boat from George Vancouver's *Discovery* had surveyed the same area. Mackenzie had finally achieved the British dream of linking its settlements in eastern America with the Pacific, but the complexity of the journey through the mountains, although it promised a future rich in the supply of furs, had proven anything but easy. His was no practical trade route to the coast, and Simon Fraser's descent of the Fraser River in 1808 would also disappoint, when his river proved not to be the Columbia explored by William Broughton in 1792. Indeed the Hudson's Bay Company, as it sent its trader-explorers into the mountains of what was to become central and northern British Columbia, the Yukon, and Alaska in the first half of the 19th century, never did find that elusive river route to the coast to equal the Columbia system in the south. When in mid-century John Bell and Robert Campbell finally brought together the last pieces of the complex puzzle of mountain geography, they discovered that the great river of the north, the Yukon, was too far north to be useful; and, as it flowed into Russian America, its navigation to the ocean was closed to the Company.

The remarkable transcontinental journey of Lewis and Clark, 1804–1806; the founding of Astoria and appearance of David Thompson at the mouth of the Columbia in 1811; and the arrival of Wilson Price Hunt in 1812 all ensured that the great river of the west and the surrounding Oregon Country would become the focus of exploration and commercial activity as the 19th century got underway. One of the key players in the unfolding history of this part of the Northwest Coast was Thomas Jefferson, who had long been interested in the west as fertile soil for the development of republican values and insurance for future prosperity. He was also fearful that a continued Spanish and British presence in the west would become increasingly hostile and confining for the new republic. His launch of Lewis and Clark's Corps of Discovery was in direct response to the publication of Mackenzie's journal and its accompanying map. By the time the Americans left St. Louis in May 1804, Jefferson's government had negotiated the Louisiana Purchase, which made the whole project even more important as it would now proceed on American soil to the foot of the Rockies.

With the triumphant return of the expedition from its winter sojourn on the Pacific, 1804–1805, Jefferson hoped that the next stage of American exploration would come from a commercial initiative, which did indeed happen when the prosperous New York fur merchant John Jacob Astor founded the Pacific Fur Company and targeted the mouth of the Columbia River for establishment of a trading post by land and by sea. With his ambitious plan for Fort Astoria as a base to control the Columbia, Astor sought to replicate for the United States what was occurring farther north, the de facto seizure of the west for Britain by creation of an integrated fur-trading system. But before the voyage of the *Tonquin* and the second American crossing of the continent by Wilson Price Hunt, 1811–1812, could realize Astor's dream, David Thompson had extended the reach of the North West Company from his explorations in the Kootenay region of the upper Columbia, by canoeing downriver to oppose it. The inherent strength of the North West Company and the vulnerability of Fort Astoria during the War of 1812 soon led to a British takeover, and British control over the Columbia, initially in the hands of the Nor'westers and after 1821 the Hudson's Bay Company, was to last for a generation.

RUSSIANS IN WESTERN ALASKA

For a number of years after the establishment of Kodiak (1792) and New Archangel (1804), Aleksandr Baranov concentrated on pursuing the interests of the Shelikhov Company and the Russian–American Company in the coastal areas bordering the Gulf of Alaska. Efficient Aleut hunting and competition from American traders and the Hudson's Bay Company, however, gradually depleted the supply of furs, causing

the Russians to shift their sights to the north, across the Alaska Peninsula to the coast of the Bering Sea and into the arctic, where Otto von
Kotzebue had gone looking for the Northwest Passage in 1816. The
initial goal in exploring the beaver-rich region was to gain an intimate
knowledge of the coast and then to penetrate the interior by using the
great river systems of the Nushagak, Kuskokwim, and Yukon. By
establishing an effective working relationship with the native people,
the Russians sought, successfully, to divert for their own benefit the
well-established trading relationship that was in place from the Alaskan
interior across the Bering Strait to the Chukchi of eastern Siberia.

In 1818 Petr Korakovsky and Fedor Kolmakov crossed the Alaska
Peninsula into Bristol Bay exploring the coast in detail for the first time
and pushing north round Cape Newnham into Kuskokwim Bay. A year
later Kolmakov established the Novo Aleksandrovskii Redoubt at the
mouth of the Nushagak River, and it became his base in the south for
exploration of the interior and the organization of a lucrative fur trade
during the 1820s and 1830s. Another important figure in developing the
trade was Ivan I. Vasil'ev in the years 1829–1830. During 1821–1822
Adolf Etholen and Vasilii Khromchenko surveyed the coast from
Bristol Bay to Norton Sound where, in 1833, a second trading post,
the Mikhailovskii Redoubt, was founded to control and support access
to the Yukon. In the early 1830s Aleksandr Kashevarov continued the
coastal survey with a detailed examination of the mouth of the Yukon
River and in 1838 explored the arctic shore well beyond Kotzebue
Sound almost as far as Point Barrow. The Russians had been mindful
of the earlier presence of Frederick Beechey (1826) and the continuing
English interest in the Northwest Passage and were keen to make their
own reconnaissance and presence felt. Meanwhile the most important
interior explorations, based primarily on the Yukon and Kuskokwim
Rivers, were undertaken by Andrei Glazunov in 1835 and Lavrentii
Zagoskin who, in the period 1842–1844, completed an ambitious expedition far into the Alaskan interior.

THE OREGON TERRITORY AND THE "END OF EXPLORATION"

In spite of the swift demise of John Jacob Astor's Astoria project,
the American claim for a window onto the Pacific in Oregon always

remained strongly in play thanks to his initiative and the previous achievements of Robert Gray and Lewis and Clark. When an unexpected outcome of the Treaty of Ghent (1814), which ended the War of 1812, was discussion of a boundary in the far west, the Americans argued persuasively that they had indisputable rights to the Oregon Country based on prior discovery, exploration, and settlement. Other pressing matters determined that this was not a question that either could or had to be solved immediately, with the result that in 1818 the vast region west of the Rocky Mountains was declared "free and open" without prejudice to either nation's claims. The British had wanted the Columbia River as the boundary but the Americans adamantly refused any agreement that would bring Britain south of the 49° parallel. The "Oregon Territory" was, however, further defined in the south by the Transcontinental Treaty of 1819 that confirmed the retreat of Spain to the 42° parallel, and in the north by British and American treaties with Russia in 1824–1825 that fixed the southern boundary of Russian America at 54°40'.

The activities of David Thompson in the Kootenays paved the way for the Northwest Company (merged with its rival Hudson's Bay Company after 1821) to move south with the result that the western interior of Oregon and Idaho were explored and hunted by two of the greatest explorer-traders of the period, David Mackenzie and Peter Skene Ogden. In Oregon, the famous "Snake River Brigades" also realized the plan of Hudson's Bay Company governor George Simpson to strip bare, or hunt out, the country most likely to appeal to rival American traders. In 1829–1830 Ogden journeyed south from the Columbia River through the intermountain west as far as the Gulf of California. His travels on this trek and earlier in the Snake Country added much new information to the Aaron Arrowsmith maps being produced in London.

In 1825 Fort Vancouver, some 100 miles upriver, became the headquarters of the Hudson's Bay Company's flourishing Columbia Department under the direction of chief factor John McLoughlin. As such it was also the nerve center for ongoing exploration activity not only in the interior but also up and down the coast from California to Russian America. Governor Simpson's plan to confront American maritime fur traders by building a series of trading forts such as Fort Simpson (1831) serviced by coastal vessels like the *Vancouver*, *Cadboro*, *Broughton*, and *Beaver* meant that further exploration of the more hidden areas of the coast was undertaken, and the details of general maps improved.

As the Columbia region of Oregon, along with Puget Sound, the Strait of Georgia, and the lower Fraser River became more developed by ongoing Hudson's Bay Company activity, the Northwest Coast shrank in size, with more attention being paid to the west coast of Vancouver Island, the Queen Charlotte Islands, and what is today the coast of northern British Columbia. In 1821 the Hudson's Bay Company knew little about the coast; some 20 years later its coasting trade had revealed the region anew.

With the development of national consciousness in the United States came a bold initiative in 1836 to send an Exploring Expedition around the world. In its concept and scope the Wilkes Expedition harkened back to the great scientific voyages of Cook, La Pérouse, Malaspina, and Kruzenshtern. It lasted from 1838 to 1842, explored the coast of Antarctica and visited hundreds of Pacific islands. More importantly, in support of Washington's long-term view of "natural dominion" over much of the Pacific seaboard of North America, it was instructed to visit the coasts of California and the Oregon Country. As a result, the expedition undertook important hydrographic work in the Strait of Juan de Fuca and Puget Sound, at the mouth of the Columbia River, and at San Francisco. It was the precursor to the work of such British hydrographers as Henry Kellet and George Richards in the wake of the Oregon Treaty of 1846. The subtle shift from exploration to hydrographic surveying, and the kind of reporting on natural resources and the future of agriculture and industry found in the reports of such observers as Eugène Duflot de Mofras, mark the real end of discovery and exploration and the beginning of a new phase of historical development highlighted by surveying, settlement, and exploitation.

In 1846, not without acrimony and threats of war, Britain and the United States finally settled the Oregon question. With the boundary fixed at the 49° parallel after all, the Americans retained the Columbia and Puget Sound on which to build the future states of Washington and Oregon, but left the Hudson's Bay Company in control of Vancouver Island and the coast north of Fuca to Russian America. These were subsequently managed by the Hudson's Bay Company through a period of colonial transition towards responsible government and the entry of British Columbia into the Canadian confederation in 1871.

After 1846 there remained three final acts in the drama of dividing up the Northwest Coast. The absorption of Alta California into the United

States in 1848 as a result of the Mexican War, an arbitrated settlement of the San Juan Islands dispute in 1872, and the purchase of Alaska by the Americans in 1867, with its subsequent controversial agreement on an Alaska–Canada Boundary in 1903. Of the three, the San Juan question was perhaps the most interesting for, in deciding the international boundary between the Strait of Georgia and the Strait of Juan de Fuca, German Emperor Wilhelm I invoked the ghosts of the Spanish explorers who in 1791–1792 had preceded George Vancouver into the area. The Americans argued that in 1819 they had inherited the rights to the Spanish discoveries and explorations of José María Narváez and Dionisio Alcalá Galiano; the emperor agreed and the boundary line was drawn in Haro Strait. In this way, with its reference to a heroic past, the San Juan arbitration brought to an end the period of discovery and exploration.

THE DICTIONARY

– A –

ABORIGINAL MIGRATION. The first people to discover and explore Northwest America migrated from Asia across a land bridge known as **Beringia**. The most recent bridge seems to have existed from as long as 25,000 years ago to as recently as 10,000 years ago. On the American side, dry land provided a route through the region north of the Yukon River, which offered abundant wildlife, and gradually opened up into a corridor east of the Rocky Mountains through which, as climatic change dictated, people were able to move south and east, eventually spreading out onto the Great Plains.

Between 12,000 and 7,000 years ago, the coast north of the **Strait of Juan de Fuca** was discovered, explored, and occupied by people moving south. Initially they moved from one ice-free refuge to another. By boat or advancing along sections of now submerged coastal plain, they brought with them arctic fishing and hunting technology and lived on a variety of sea mammals, fish, shellfish, plants, and berries. They moved up the river valleys in response to the availability of salmon, use of which was crucial as it underpinned development of a cultural system and social organization based on catching, preserving, and storing the fish.

A third route of movement followed the trench of central **British Columbia** between the Rockies and Coastal Mountains; it began to open up about 8,000 years ago, and was the way the migrants reached the lower coast and arrived in **Washington** and **Oregon**. Again, the use of salmon encouraged settlement and the largest populations ultimately developed on the resource-rich lower sections of the **Fraser River** and the **Columbia River**. *See also* NATIVE AMERICANS OF THE NORTHWEST COAST.

1

ACT OF POSSESSION. An act of possession ceremony was performed by naval representatives of the leading imperial powers of Europe, usually upon the discovery of lands they believed other Europeans had not already visited. This was done in an intellectual context that considered the world empty unless "discovered" from Europe. Settlement by native peoples—"savages"—did not count. In 1786 on Maui, **Jean François de La Pérouse** wrote that the practice was "too utterly ridiculous" in its disregard of native rights, but this did not prevent him later from taking possession of an island in **Lituya Bay**, Alaska with the usual formalities; it was, after all, a place safely positioned between the Russians and the Spaniards that potentially held commercial riches for France.

The formalities involved a number of variations which might include: the raising of the national flag, some kind of verbal declaration (ideally in front of the natives so that they could be seen to accede to the surrender of their lands), the carving of the king's name on a tree, the planting of a cross, and the burying of coins and a written declaration in a bottle under a cairn of stones. From **Francis Drake** in **California** in 1579, to **Juan Francisco de la Bodega y Quadra** in **Bucareli Bay** in 1775, **James Cook** in **Cook Inlet** in 1778, **Gerasim Izmailov** placing metal possession plates and imperial crests in strategic locations along the coast south of **Prince William Sound** in 1788, and **Manuel Quimper** presiding over a solemn ceremony in the **Strait of Juan de Fuca** in 1790, acts of possession were performed up and down the Northwest Coast in the discovery and exploration period.

Such acts proved meaningless. While Cook and **George Vancouver** performed their share of acts, it was English refusal in the **Nootka Crisis** to accept sovereignty without settlement or negotiated agreement that determined final control. Thus, although sovereignty became generally accepted as a result of early Spanish and Russian settlement in California and Alaska respectively, for the rest of the coast, boundaries had to be negotiated, and sovereignty finally decided, by treaty between the United States, Spain, Russia, and Britain.

ADAMS-ONÍS TREATY. *See* TRANSCONTINENTAL TREATY, 1819.

ADMIRALTY CHARTS, BRITISH. During the second half of the 18th century British naval captains on voyages of exploration were directed to undertake surveys and prepare charts. At the end of the journey these were collected, along with any journals, and forwarded to the Admiralty. In 1795 the first hydrographer to the Admiralty, **Alexander Dalrymple**, was appointed to manage the collection and to compile and disseminate navigational information for the benefit of captains of naval vessels sailing to the four corners of the globe, a task in which he had already been unofficially engaged.

When chart publication was initiated at the beginning of the 19th century the Navy's Hydrographic Office had inherited work on the Northwest Coast from **James Cook, George Vancouver**, and such fur traders as **George Dixon, Nathaniel Portlock**, and **John Meares**. Between 1792 and 1794 Vancouver had incorporated into his charts a good deal of information produced by his Spanish and fur-trading contemporaries. For close to 50 years after the publication of his charts in 1798 there was little British survey work done on the Pacific Coast of North America although **Henry Kellett** and **Edward Belcher** worked in **Russian America, Nootka Sound**, and at the mouth of the **Columbia River** in 1837.

With the establishment of the Canadian west coast boundary under the terms of the **Oregon Treaty**, 1846, the Admiralty undertook the first formal surveys of the coast since Vancouver. Operating out of **Fort Victoria**, Kellett in the *Herald* and James Wood in *Pandora* did the initial work at the southern end of **Vancouver Island** and along the **Strait of Juan de Fuca**. The most intensive period of surveying was undertaken by **George Henry Richards** in the *Plumper* and *Hecate* between 1857 and 1862. Initially drawn to the area of the San Juan Islands, where the boundary had been left in dispute by the treaty, Richards completed an entire survey of Vancouver Island and its adjacent continental coast. His work was carried on by Daniel Pender in the **Hudson's Bay Company**'s steamship *Beaver*. His focus of activity was principally the coastline from the northern end of Vancouver Island to Alaska. By complementing Richards's work farther south, Pender ensured that by 1870 charts and sailing directions existed to make the coastline of British Columbia relatively safe for **navigation**—certainly as safe as its often adverse climate of wind, rain, and fog would allow.

AGUILAR, MARTÍN DE. *See* Rio de Martín de Aguilar.

ALARCÓN, HERNANDO DE (fl. 1540–1541). An explorer of the **Gulf of California**, Hernando de Alarcón accompanied **Francisco de Ulloa** in 1539, and was sent north again in 1540 to support the overland expedition of Francisco Vazquez de Coronado, exploring beyond the Sonoran desert for the fabled Seven Cities of Cíbola. Although he ascended the Colorado River in August 1540, he found no sign of Coronado, but his chart of the gulf improved upon Ulloa's and confirmed **Baja California** as a peninsula. Despite these early voyages and the explorations of **Eusebio Francisco Kino** at the turn of the 18th century, this information never became widely disseminated and was ignored by many mapmakers for another 200 years because of the influence of cosmographer **Antonio de la Ascensión**, who maintained that California was an island.

ALASKA. Alaska is the largest state in the United States of America. Prior to its purchase from Russia in 1867, the upper northwestern edge of North America was known as **Russian America**. The name Alaska is thought to have come from an **Aleut** term meaning "great land" used by the natives to differentiate their islands from the **Alaska Peninsula**. The name for the new state, variously attributed to Secretary of State William Seward, Massachusetts Senator Charles Sumner, or General William Halleck, Commander of the Military Division of the Pacific, was likely a simple application of the name for the peninsula to the larger area.

ALASKA PENINSULA. Extending over 500 miles southwest from Iliamna Lake, between **Bristol Bay** and **Cook Inlet**, the Alaska Peninsula's nature was not fully appreciated until charted by the **Petr Krenitsyn** and **Mikhail Levashov** Expedition in 1768. It had been reached by *promyshlenniki* (fur hunters) as early as 1761 when **Gavriil Pushkarev** spent the winter of 1761–1762 near the **Shumagin Islands**. **Stepan Glotov** sailed along the peninsula to discover **Kodiak** Island in 1762, after which other hunters ventured into the region. Skirting Kodiak in June 1778, **James Cook** approached "Alaschka" and ran southwest off the coast to **Unimak** Island. In July he traced its northern coast into Bristol Bay. From his survey and information received from the Russians, Cook's charts, published in 1784, accurately defined the peninsula (except in the area of Kodiak Island) and confirmed that it was an extension of the American continent. In the 1780s fur traders were active in Shelikhov Strait. In 1787 **Evstrat Delarov** established outposts from **Three Saints Bay** (Kodiak Island) at Karluk (on the north side of the island) and Katmai, the site of a native trading fair (on the peninsula), and men working for **Pavel Lebedev-Lastochkin** moved into the interior of the upper peninsula, pioneering cross-country routes between Cook Inlet and Bristol Bay to lakes Iliamna, Naknek, and Becharov [*sic*]. The latter was named after **Dmitrii Bocharov**, who charted the northern coast and portaged across the peninsula in 1791.

ALBERNI, PEDRO DE (1745–1802). An army officer who joined the Free Company of Volunteers of Catalonia, Pedro de Alberni came to **New Spain** in 1767. In 1790 he arrived on the Northwest Coast with **Francisco de Eliza**, bringing 80 soldiers to develop a military establishment at **Friendly Cove** in **Nootka Sound**. Alberni supervised the building of a fort at the entrance to the cove, the erection of other buildings, the digging of wells, the keeping of livestock, and the planting of gardens. He also kept meteorological records. Above all he developed a good working relationship with the local **natives**, notably Chief **Maquinna**, and compiled a 633-word Spanish–Nootkan dictionary. **José Mariano Moziño** later used this work in *Noticias de Nootka*, his account of Nootka Sound.

ALCALÁ GALIANO, DIONISIO (1760–1805). An interest in science and astronomy brought Dionisio Alcalá Galiano to the attention of the influential Vicente Tofiño, who was engaged in a hydrographic survey of Spain that resulted in the *Atlas Marítimo de España* (1789). This experience formed the basis of his considerable expertise as an astronomer, surveyor, and cartographer. In 1788 he proposed an expedition to update the charts of the coasts of Argentina and Chile, and his ideas became folded into the larger expedition of **Alejandro Malaspina**, which he joined, to visit all the Spanish possessions in the Pacific.

Malaspina recruited Alcalá Galiano as his principal astronomer and Alcalá Galiano made a major contribution to the expedition as it rounded South America, 1790–1791. After its arrival in Acapulco, and while Malaspina and **José Bustamante** were away for the summer of 1791 on the Northwest Coast, Alcalá Galiano remained in **New Spain** to finish the charts made so far, to gather documents of potential value to the voyage, and to undertake astronomical observations. In the fall of 1791, when the viceroy, the **Count of Revillagigedo**, and Malaspina received news of the **Francisco de Eliza** Expedition's explorations in the **Strait of Juan de Fuca**, they agreed that another expedition was necessary. Alcalá Galiano was chosen to lead this reconnaissance accompanied by **Cayetano Valdés**.

The expedition left Acapulco in two ships, the *Sutil* and *Mexicana*, on 8 March 1792, arrived at **Nootka Sound** on 13 May and entered the strait to visit **Nuñez Gaona** on 6 June. The ships then proceeded through the San Juan Islands. No attempt was made to explore the opening seen by **José María Narváez** the previous year that would have led into **Puget Sound**; rather they hastened north, hugging the continental shore until they reached Punta de Cepeda (Point Roberts). The ships then crossed Eliza's Gran Canal (the **Strait of Georgia**) and ran up the outside of the islands off **Vancouver Island** before anchoring at the northern tip of Gabriola Island and visiting what is today the harbour of Nanaimo. Recrossing the strait Alcalá Galiano encountered **George Vancouver** off Punta de Lángara (Point Grey) on 21 June. The two commanders agreed to work together as they proceeded north, but not before Spanish launches had explored Burrard Inlet.

The expedition sailed northwest through the maze of islands that separated the continent from Vancouver Island. Like the English, the Spaniards took to their small boats to explore what are today the long fjords of Toba, Bute, Loughborough, and Knight Inlets. In Toba Inlet they found a curious wooden tablet covered with hieroglyphics (now thought to be a native tide chart), which was drawn by **José Cardero**, whose sketches of people and places greatly enhanced the narrative of the voyage. Exiting the Canal de Descubierta (Johnstone Strait) the Spaniards visited a large village, Majoa, the subject of a fine panorama drawing by Cardero, in the vicinity of Port McNeill. They then sailed along the north coast of **Vancouver Island**, out into the Pacific through the Salida de las Goletas (Goletas Channel), and south to Nootka.

Alcalá Galiano wrote that while the voyage might have served to satisfy the curiosity of those armchair geographers who still held out hope of a passage across America, it was "in no way of use to navigators." But the expedition gave important information to **Juan Francisco de la Bodega y Quadra** for his negotiations with Vancouver, and disproving falsities is almost as vital an aspect of exploration as making new discoveries. The Alcalá Galiano and Valdés Expedition was, therefore, one of many that undertook the surveys necessary to solve the northern mystery of a passage to the Atlantic. Galiano's journal was published in embellished form as *Relación del Viaje hecho por las Goletas Sutil y Mexicana en el año 1792 para reconocer el Estrecho de Juan de Fuca* in 1802. It was Spain's response to the **Jean François de La Pérouse** and Vancouver publications after the fall of Malaspina, in 1795, had caused abandonment of the publication of the Spanish commander's comprehensive account of the entire expedition. Alcalá Galiano's name, therefore, became synonymous with Spanish exploration on the Northwest Coast. With its long introduction covering the whole sweep of Spanish activities on the coast since the 1770s, the *Relación* finally dispensed with Spain's penchant for secrecy and added immeasurably to European knowledge of the North Pacific, its geography, and its native peoples.

Alcalá Galiano died commanding a ship-of-the-line at the Battle of Trafalgar on 21 October 1805. His glorious death, coupled with a distinguished career, placed him in the Pantheon of Spanish Naval Heroes and makes him one of the more famous of the explorers who sailed the waters of the Northwest Coast at the end of the 18th century.

ALEUT/ALUTIIQ. The coast stretching west from **Prince William Sound** (PWS), down the **Alaska Peninsula**, and out along the volcanic islands of the Aleutian chain is the home of a southern Eskimo people whose marine environment has shaped a culture at least 8,000 years old. The Alutiiq live in PWS, the **Kenai Peninsula**, and on **Kodiak** Island and much of the Alaska Peninsula; the Aleuts, who called themselves "Unangan" at the time of contact, lived in the archipelago. The sea was their highway and the source of their subsistence. Long ago the rich resources of the sea enabled them to develop complex societies with hereditary classes. They were expert fishermen and hunters, building villages on bays where they could be protected yet near the ocean. The explorers marveled at their skilled use of the *baidarka* in which they traveled hundreds of miles between islands and hunted whales and other mammals with poison-tipped harpoons.

The advance of Russian *promyshlenniki* (fur hunters) quickly compromised the Aleut way of life. Warfare, **disease**, slavery, and forced relocation inflicted swift and terrible damage. Early resistance, though fierce and painful for the invaders, was ultimately overcome and the Aleut–Russian War in the eastern islands in 1763–1764 marked the end of Aleut independence. Thereafter their lives became intertwined with those of the Russian traders and settlers, an influence still existing in both cultures today primarily through the **Russian Orthodox Church**. The early trading companies and ultimately the **Russian–American Company** quickly recognized the natives' skill as hunters, and pressed them into service, first locally and then farther afield; by the end of the 18th century flotillas of hundreds of kayaks moved southeast down the Alaskan coast to exploit the waters of the **Alexander Archipelago**. Later, operating from **Fort Ross**, the Aleuts hunted in San Francisco Bay. This enslavement of native men, however, cost many their lives and undermined the culture of the island villages they left behind. *See also* NATIVE AMERICANS OF THE NORTHWEST COAST.

ALEUTIAN ISLANDS. The Aleutian Islands extend over 1,200 miles west from the **Alaska Peninsula** towards **Kamchatka**. They facilitated Russian exploration and occupation of the Northwest Coast of America. When the survivors of **Vitus Bering**'s voyage to America reached Kamchatka in 1742 with reports that islands to the east were rich in fur-bearing animals, *promyshlenniki* (fur hunters) immediately recognized the opportunity to expand their hunting grounds and within a year had landed on **Bering Island**. By 1745 one ship had wintered over on Attu, the most westerly of the Aleutians in the Near Islands. Thereafter, the advance was swift through the remaining island groups—Rat, Andreanof, and Fox. *See also* ALEUT/ALUTIIQ.

ALEXANDER ARCHIPELAGO. A group of over 10,000 islands between **Cross Sound** and **Dixon Entrance**, the Alexander Archipelago was not definitively surveyed until after the sale of **Russian America** to the United States in 1867. Named by the Americans in honor of Alexander II, czar of the Russian Empire at the time of the sale, the archipelago is dominated by seven large islands—Chichagof, Admiralty, and Baranov in the north, and Prince of Wales, Revillagigedo, Kiui, and Kupreanoff in the south.

The first of the 18th century explorers in the region, **Aleksei Chirikov**, was off Noyes and Baker Islands, west of Prince of Wales Island on 15 July 1741; he believed himself close to Spanish America, but he was actually some 18 degrees north of **San Francisco** and also not in sight of the continent proper. **Juan Francisco de la Bodega y Quadra** and **Francisco Mourelle,** the next visitors to the outer islands, anchored on Kruzof Island on the western edge of Baranov Island on 18–21 August 1775 before discovering **Bucareli Bay**, inside Baker Island, on 24 August. Bodega, Mourelle, and **Ignacio de Arteaga** returned to this bay in 1779. Neither they nor the great exploring expeditions of **James Cook, Jean François de La Pérouse,** and **Alejandro Malaspina,** which ran the outside of the coast—in 1778, 1786, and 1791 respectively—had any comprehension of the labyrinthine archipelago that separated them from the continent. The first full appreciation of this reality fell to **George Vancouver** and his companions in 1793 and 1794, although fur traders had begun to probe the numerous bays and channels in the late 1780s.

By the mid-1790s the first giant flotillas of hunting kayaks, directed from **Kodiak** Island into the area by **Aleksandr Baranov,** moved beyond **Yakutat Bay** and Cross Sound to reach the archipelago. This was the beginning of a sustained Russian presence, which, despite persistent **Tlingit** opposition, led to the establishment of a settlement in **Sitka Sound** in 1799. Although the fort and trading post of **New Archangel** was destroyed in a native attack in 1802, it was reestablished in 1804 and became the capital of Russian America. As it grew into an international port and center of the maritime **fur trade**, all of the waterways of the archipelago were revealed.

ALTA CALIFORNIA. Early voyages from **New Spain**—such as those of **Juan Rodríguez Cabrillo** and **Sebastián Vizcaíno,** and **Manila galleons** commanded by **Sebastián Rodríguez Cermeño** and **Pedro de Unamuno**—had discovered and explored, in a cursory way, the coast of southern California in the period 1542–1603. The bays of **San Diego** and **Monterey** had been identified.

Neuva (New) or Alta California, so named to distinguish it from the peninsula of Antigua (Old) or **Baja California**, was not explored in any serious way until the second half of the 18th century. The push into the region from New Spain was a defensive measure designed by **José de Gálvez** to prevent the Russians from extending their northern activities to the edge of the Spanish Empire. This action effectively reaffirmed Spain's claim to the coast between San Diego and **San Francisco**—Alta California—and beyond. In 1769 two maritime and two land expeditions known as the **Sacred Expedition** were dispatched to accomplish the twin goals of securing San Diego and locating Monterey Bay. Exploring beyond Monterey without recognizing it, a scouting party reached San Francisco Bay. In June 1770, the Spanish flag was raised at Monterey, which became the capital of the new province. That same year, **Pedro Fages** pioneered an overland route to San Francisco via the Santa Clara Valley and the eastern shores of San Francisco Bay, from which he saw its entrance, later named the Golden Gate by John C. Frémont in 1846. The first nautical survey of the bay was undertaken in 1775 by **Juan Manuel de Ayala** and **José Cañizares**.

The instruments of Spanish control were the missions, presidios, and pueblos. The 21 missions were designed to absorb the scattered native populations into a series of religious centers; the four presidios at San Diego, Santa Barbara, Monterey, and San Francisco introduced the military dimension; and the three pueblos (before 1800) were government-sponsored civilian settlements.

Initially, Spanish exploration was confined almost exclusively to the coastal areas. But in 1772 Fages discovered and crossed the southwest corner of the great central valley and, in 1774, **Juan Bautista de Anza** traveled overland from Sonora to Monterey.

ANIAN. *See* STRAIT OF ANIAN.

ANZA, JUAN BAUTISTA DE (1735–1788). Born and raised in Sonora, Juan Bautista de Anza became an experienced soldier defending the northern frontier of **New Spain**. In the early 1770s he opened a land route between Sonora and **Alta California**, which was crucial in establishing a viable Spanish presence on the coast. In 1774 he reached the Pacific at the mission of San Gabriel Arcángel (1771) near present-day Los Angeles, and then proceeded north to **Monterey**. His success prompted Viceroy **Antonio María de Bucareli** to draw up plans to strengthen the new province by sending more soldiers, settlers, and livestock. In the autumn of 1775 a party of 240 soldiers and 60 other men, women, and children, with a thousand head of cattle, set out from Tubac with the goal of establishing a presidio and mission at **San Francisco**. When he reached San Gabriel in January 1776, however, Anza was obliged to detour to **San Diego** to help put down an Indian uprising against the mission. He reached Monterey in March and proceeded north with a small party to explore the San Francisco peninsula and select sites for the presidio and mission, thus complementing the maritime explorations of **Juan Manuel de Ayala** in 1775.

ARKHIMANDRITOV, ILLARION (ca. 1820–1872). The Creole navigator Illarion Arkhimandritov sailed in the service of the **Russian–American Company** for nearly 30 years commanding numerous vessels, principally in the **Aleutian Islands**, to the **Pribilof Islands** and to western **Alaska**. He assisted **Il'ia Voznesenskii**, the natural scientist and ethnographer, in building his important collections in the 1840s, and in 1843 undertook an important hydrographic assignment for **Mikhail Teben'kov**, completing a precise survey of the eastern coast of **Cook Inlet**, **Montague Island**, adjacent areas in **Prince William Sound**, and the entire coastline of **Kodiak** Island. The results of his work were reflected in Teben'kov's *Atlas of the Northwest Coast of America* (1852). Another specific contribution to Northwest Coast exploration was his production of nine charts of the region made for the Kodiak office of the Russian–American Company and delivered in 1861. He continued his hydrographic work in the waters of **Unalaska**, the **Pribilof Islands**, and **Norton Sound** in the years leading up to the 1867 sale of **Russian America** to the United States.

ARROWSMITH, AARON (1750–1823). English cartographer and map publisher, Aaron Arrowsmith established his reputation with an 11-sheet world map in 1790. He owed much to an association with **Alexander Dalrymple**, whom he assisted in his work as hydrographer to the Admiralty. Arrowsmith became known for the accuracy and trademark functional simplicity of his maps, which he himself engraved.

In 1795 he published his great map of Canada based on information received from individual explorers and traders, the **Hudson's Bay Company**, and the Royal Navy. That same year **Samuel Hearne**'s trek to the Coppermine River (1771) was not generally appreciated until his journal was published with an Arrowsmith map. His "Map of America . . . exhibiting Mackenzie's Track . . . 1801" accurately reflects not only the discoveries of that explorer, but also the work of the Pacific coast explorers and traders including **George Vancouver** as far north as the beginning of the **Alaska Peninsula**. In the preface to his *Voyages from Montreal . . . through the Continent of America to the Frozen and Pacific Oceans . . .* (1801) **Alexander Mackenzie** praised the professional abilities of his cartographer. This earlier map formed the basis of Arrowsmith's famous "Map Exhibiting all the New Discoveries in the Interior Parts of North America" (1802), which better than any other showed the results of late-18th-century exploration across the continent and on the west coast, from **Baja California** to **James Cook**'s **Icy Cape**, and from the Great Lakes to Hearne and Mackenzie's "frozen sea." It was this map that influenced **Thomas Jefferson**'s launch of the **Lewis and Clark Expedition**.

ARTEAGA Y BAZAN, IGNACIO DE (1731–1783). Appointed commandant of the Naval Department of **San Blas** in 1774, Ignacio de Arteaga was chosen by Viceroy **Antonio María de Bucareli** in 1777 to command a third Spanish voyage from Mexico to the Northwest Coast. But there were not enough ships to meet the needs of both **California** supply and exploration. This meant that **Juan Francisco de la Bodega y Quadra** had to go to Peru to purchase the *Favorita*, while Arteaga was obliged to complete construction of his own ship, the *Princesa*, which was not launched until the summer of 1778. The final plans for the voyage took shape over the winter of 1778–1779: Ferdinand Quirós, the pilots **José Camacho** and **Juan Pantoja y Arriaga**, and the priest **Juan Antonio García Riobo** would sail with Arteaga; and **Francisco Mourelle**, the pilots **José Cañizares** and Juan Bautista Aguirre, and the priest Cristóbal Díaz would sail with Bodega. The latter gathered together all available information about the coast, secured adequate supplies, determined sailing routes, and constructed a composite chart, using Russian sources.

The expedition left San Blas on 12 February 1779. One of its goals was to intercept and arrest **James Cook**, whom the Spaniards expected on the coast at the same time in violation of the Laws of the Indies. Unbeknownst to them he had already come and gone. The other goal was to reach 70° N, only possible if the Spaniards were prepared to sail far into waters explored by the Russians. From the available information, based largely on the erroneous chart of **Jacob von Stählin**, they thought like Cook that a passage existed to take them into the northern sea.

The two frigates were separated in a storm off northern California but proceeded to their planned rendezvous at **Bucareli Bay**, where they met again on 2 May. The expedition's stopover is noteworthy for two main reasons: Mourelle's extensive survey of the waterways of that part of the **Alexander Archipelago**, and the sustained contact between the Spaniards and the **Tlingit** and **Haida** of the area. The first took place between 18 May and 12 June; the second principally at the anchorage site in Port Santa Cruz on the west side of Suemez Island. At Santa Cruz, Arteaga performed the **act of possession**, raising a cross in the same location that Bodega had planted his four years earlier. The Spaniards remained at Bucareli Bay for two months, and natives came from the surrounding area, setting up temporary encampments on the beaches to be near the ships. The journals of Arteaga, Bodega, Pantoja, and Riobo are replete with valuable information about all aspects of the encounter. The Spanish captains were able to identify and deal with men who were obviously chiefs, and there were much trade and native visitation to the ships. There were moments of tension, including hostage taking, but overall efforts to eliminate **violence** and to treat "the other" with respect prevailed.

The ships finally got away from the bay on 1 July. This did not augur well for their attempt to reach the intended high latitudes and check on the Russians; the summer season was already far advanced, and Cook, in 1778, had passed the same location two months earlier in the year. Nevertheless, three good weeks of sailing brought them to **Prince William Sound** and a fine anchorage at Puerto de Santiago (**Port Etches** on Cook's **Hinchinbrook Island**, which they named Santa María Magdalena). On 22 July Arteaga again took possession at 61°17′ N. This became the basis for Spain's continued claim to sovereignty in the North Pacific under the **Treaty of Tordesillas**.

Cañizares and Pantoja explored along the coast of the island, and from their report of a wall of mountains to the east and north (the Chugach Range), Arteaga quickly surmised that the sound offered no entrance to any **Northwest Passage**. At a junta (meeting of officers) Arteaga expressed serious concern about the appearance of scurvy, but it was decided to continue sailing west in search of any other openings to the north.

The ships left Santiago on 29 July. After battling stormy seas, strong winds, and incessant rain they eventually found safe haven in today's Port Chatham, inside Elizabeth Island at the end of the **Kenai Peninsula**. Another act of possession was performed on 2 August and the place was called Ensenda de Nuestra Señora de la Regla after the patron saint of monastic orders. Pantoja made a survey of the bay upon which several charts were constructed. Although native dwellings were found, they were unoccupied. Canoes approached the frigates but there was no formal contact. On 3 August the weather was clear enough for the Spaniards to see the active volcano of Mount Iliamna, but the return of heavy rains and fog meant that when they left their anchorage on 8 August they failed to appreciate either the entrances to Shelikhof Strait or **Cook Inlet**, which would certainly have merited the same attention paid to it by James Cook the previous year.

It appears that Arteaga, even before leaving Regla, had convinced himself that the Russian passage to the north did not exist. Furthermore the trend of the island-strewn coast was to the southwest and the scurvy showed no sign of abating: seven sailors had already died and ten more were affected. Poor weather and the lateness of the season suggested an immediate return to San Blas. They were off Afognak Island when Arteaga informed Bodega and Mourelle of his decision; both were fiercely critical of their commander. **San Francisco** was reached on 14 September and the expedition stayed for 45 days. With fresh fruit and vegetables the sick sailors soon recovered. Fortunately, a fire in the hut in which the pilots were working on the charts of the expedition did not engulf their work. The ships finally arrived in San Blas towards the end of November.

At the time the expedition was deemed a success: it had reached 61° N, found no Russians, and performed crucial Acts of Possession. In hindsight it appears less so: too long had been spent at Bucareli Bay when the goal was 70° N, and Arteaga's decision to turn back, while understandable, proved him to be a less than determined explorer.

ARTIFACTS. The collection of native artifacts was incidental to exploration and the **fur trade** except in the case of the **Alejandro Malaspina** and **George Vancouver** expeditions (and later the **Lewis and Clark** and **Charles Wilkes** expeditions), which were instructed to gather such items. The practice of trading for souvenirs and curiosities as reminders of their adventures became an everyday occurrence in the lives of the earliest visitors to the coast. **Georg Wilhelm Steller**, with **Vitus Bering** in 1741, collected some hunting and fishing items (and smoked salmon) on **Kayak Island** for which the Russians left in payment some cloth, tobacco, knives, and beads. Later the first items from **Aleuts** were collected in the **Shumagin Islands**. **Mikhail Levashov** began collecting in the **Aleutian Islands** in the late 1760s and started the practice, carried forward by **John Webber** and **Tomás de Suría**, of making accompanying drawings to establish context. Collecting artifacts started on the central coast off the **Queen Charlotte Islands** with **Juan Pérez** in 1774 and was lively in **Nootka Sound** when **James Cook**'s expedition arrived there in 1778. The Englishmen collected fishing hooks and spoons and masks, and the first examples of the famous chief's hat with the whale hunt motif. Arms and ceremonial items, such as masks depicting the human face, were more costly. During the period of their establishment at Nootka, the Spanish collected many items of which a few still exist. One of the most interesting transactions was the purchase of a mask from Chief **Maquinna** by **Alexander Walker**, who was at Nootka with **James Strange** in 1786; it was only completed after protracted negotiation held in secret, no doubt because the item had special ceremonial meaning. In 1791 at **Yakutat Bay**, where **Tadeo Haenke** made a unique personal collection of toys, or models for larger carvings, Malaspina noted that items such as spoons and baskets were quickly being made specifically for trading purposes, and this manufacture to satisfy demand became more common as British, American, and Russian fur traders descended on the region.

The curio collections made in the early exploration and fur trade period were often widely scattered or lost at a time when natural history specimens were deemed more interesting and important.

Items collected by Cook's men and **George Dixon** and **Archibald Menzies** made their way into the British Museum, in part given by Sir **Joseph Banks**. Others went to hometowns; for example **James King** gave items to Trinity College Dublin. Many items in England went to Sir Ashton Lever's private museum and were dispersed, when it closed in 1806, to British and European museums from Cambridge to Vienna and Florence. The official nature of the many Spanish and Russian voyages led to the retention of important collections now preserved at the Museo de América in Madrid and the Museum of Anthropology and Ethnography of the Academy of Sciences in St. Petersburg. American domination of the fur trade for a number of decades resulted in a significant number of artifacts returning to New England, where 241 in museum collections, primarily in the Peabody Essex Museum in Salem, Massachusetts, were documented by Mary Malloy in the 1990s. Her research and that of John King, Adrienne Kaeppler, and Paz Cabello Carro has admirably built upon the pioneering work of Erna Gunther to develop whatever provenance might still be established for the items that have survived. The collections made by officials of the **Russian–American Company**, and notably by **Il'ia Voznesenskii** in the 1840s, enriched immeasurably the holdings in St. Petersburg, and the Wilkes materials ultimately became one of the founding collections of the Smithsonian Institution.

These early collections now take pride of place in museums alongside the large European and American collections created in the late 19th century as part of the development of the disciplines of anthropology and ethnology. These later collections were gathered to represent a Northwest Coast culture that was expected to disappear in the face of the onslaught of the modern world, and most of the items were created to feed that collecting frenzy. In the context of the modern renaissance of Northwest Coast culture and art, the oldest artifacts are especially valuable for their purity; like the drawings and the journals of the visitors they are not just cultural items, but vital documents of contact. *See also* NATIVE AMERICANS OF THE NORTHWEST COAST.

ARTISTS. One of the most enduring legacies of the discovery and exploration period on the Northwest Coast are the drawings and paintings of views, events, and **native** peoples that have survived to complement the extensive written record set out in log books, journals, and reports.

In reality only a handful of professional artists, such as **John Webber**, **Gaspard Duché de Vancy**, **Tomás de Suría**, and **Louis Choris**, served on the formal voyages of exploration sent out under the auspices of the British, French, Spanish, and Russian navies. Their contribution was vital, but just as important for the historical record were the efforts of many talented amateurs, such as the **scientists Georg Heinrich von Langsdorff** and **Friedrich Heinrich von Kittlitz**; surgeon's mate **William Ellis**; and the erstwhile housepainter with a talent for drawing **George Davidson** (1768–1801); and a significant number of officers, who had some training in drawing sea views and coastal profiles, and who used their natural ability and interest in what they were seeing to make sketches. The earliest examples are the Russians **Sven Waxell** and **Mikhail Levashov;** later ones include **Henry Roberts**, **Joseph Baker**, Lieutenant **Blondela**, **Felipe Bauza**, **Iurii Lisianskii**, **Frederick Beechey**, and **William Smyth**.

Perhaps the most remarkable story is that of **José Cardero**, who within three years with the **Alejandro Malaspina** expedition had risen from cabin boy and willing natural history illustrator to official artist with a major Northwest Coast contribution to his name.

The valuable experience of **James Cook** with formally trained artists Sydney Parkinson and William Hodges on his first two voyages, and his success in adding John Webber to his Northwest Coast expedition, gave the naval planners for other major initiatives (i.e. the **La Pérouse** and Malaspina expeditions which included de Vancy and Suría respectively) examples of the tangible benefits that could result. Thus **Luka Voronin** went with **Joseph Billings**, Choris went with **Otto von Kotzebue**, **Mikhail Tikhanov** with **Vasilii Golovnin**, and **Pavel Mikhailov** with **Mikhail Staniukovich**. The most surprising exception was **George Vancouver**'s voyage. Fortunately, officers **Joseph Baker** and **Zachary Mudge** and midshipmen **Thomas Heddington**, **Henry Humphrys**, and **John Sykes** filled the gap admirably.

Few of the early fur-trading voyages produced much artwork, but because former naval officers were often involved, there were some contributions. Examples include the work of **George Dixon**, **John Meares**, **Robert Haswell**, and **Joseph Ingraham**.

Two other very important contributors were **Atanásio Echeverría**, the natural history artist who also did important views and native portraits when at **Nootka Sound** in 1792, and surgeon **Sigismund Bacstrom**, who was on the coast in fur-trading vessels in the early 1790s. *See also* BANKS, JOSEPH.

ASCENSIÓN, ANTONIO DE LA (fl. 1569–1632). Carmelite Father Antonio de la Ascensión studied at the pilot academy at Seville. He sailed with the **Sebastián Vizcaíno** Expedition and later wrote an account of the voyage. Increasingly influential as a cosmographer he produced, between 1608 and 1632, a series of exaggerated memoria extolling the benefits of colonization of **Baja California** and the bounties of its surrounding seas. Most importantly he stated that it was an island and his views were crucial in promoting that fiction. A map drawn by him was copied by the Englishman Henry Briggs and published with his treatise about the **Northwest Passage** in Samuel Purchas's *His Pilgrimes* in 1625. Remarkably, less than 100 years after the explorations of **Francisco de Ulloa** and **Hernando de Alarcón**, the **Gulf of California** had become a completely apocryphal inland passage linking the coast of Mexico to the **Strait of Anian**. It remained that way on many maps until well into the 18th century.

ASIAN VOYAGES. Whether by design or accident, it is clear that thousands of ships arrived on the Northwest Coast from China or Japan prior to the historical period, which dates from the 1740s. This assumption is based on the fact that during the 18th and 19th centuries numerous disabled fishing vessels were driven by the prevailing winds and currents across the North Pacific, landing along the coast from the **Aleutian Islands** to **Oregon**. Evidence is particularly strong that prior to the arrival of Europeans such vessels were an important source of iron for **Native Americans** in the region, and that many Asians survived the crossing. The Clatsop at the mouth of the **Columbia River** even had a term for their visitors: *Tlon-hon-nipts*—"those who drift ashore."

What is less obvious is the number of voyages specifically aimed at America. The Chinese, particularly those living on the coast of Kwantung province near Canton, certainly possessed the seamanship, knowledge of astronomy, and shipbuilding skill to allow them to range at will far from home, sailing among the Pacific Islands and visiting America. Knowledge of the "eastern shores" of the American continent is referred to in both writing and art, and in 1540 and 1573 there were Spanish sightings of ships at the mouth of the Colorado River and off Jalisco that, at the time, were considered to be Chinese. *See also* FUSANG.

ASTORIA. During the 1780s the American entrepreneur John Jacob Astor became interested in entering the **fur trade** and established links with the **North West Company** in Montreal. Expanding his operations into the interior of the continent, particularly after the Louisiana Purchase (1803), Astor shipped large quantities of fur to the Orient. In 1808 he organized the American Fur Trade Company. Two years later, dreaming of pushing his activities to the Pacific Ocean, he established the Pacific Fur Company. In 1811 his representatives, arriving by sea in the *Tonquin*, established Fort Astoria at the mouth of the **Columbia River**. During the War of 1812, however, this isolated post was sold (under duress) to the North West Company and renamed Fort George. Despite this failure, Astor was successful in consolidating his activities on the Great Plains and moving into the Rockies and this brief presence on the coast was later used to bolster the United States' claim to **Oregon**.

AYALA, JUAN MANUEL DE (1745–?). Juan Manuel de Ayala is credited with making the first discovery of **San Francisco** Bay from the sea in August 1775. Almost immediately after his 1774 arrival in **New Spain**, he was assigned to command the *Sonora*, as consort to **Bruno de Hezeta**'s *Santiago*, on a northern voyage planned for 1775. After the commander of a third ship, the *San Carlos*, became delusional shortly after leaving **San Blas** in March 1775, Ayala took over that vessel, sent his fellow officer back to San Blas in the ship's launch and headed to **Monterey** to deliver supplies. Viceroy **Antonio María de Bucareli** had issued instructions that the *San Carlos* was to explore and chart the bay north of the **California** capital first seen in 1769 by members of the **Sacred Expedition**. This was to complement the overland expedition of **Juan Bautista de Anza** from Sonora.

The *San Carlos* left Monterey on 27 July and arrived off San Francisco Bay on 5 August. The actual entry is credited to pilot

José Cañizares, who undertook an initial reconnaissance in the longboat; and it was he who undertook the survey that resulted in the Plano del Puerto de San Francisco now in the Archivo General de Indias in Seville, although it bears Ayala's name. Most of the names given to the harbor's landmarks have been changed (Punta del Angel de la Guarda is now Point Lobos) but Angel Island retains its name from Isla de Santa María de los Angeles, and the infamous prison of Alcatraz (now closed) on Yerba Buena Island took its name from Ayala's Isla de Alcatraces because he found so many pelicans there. The chaplain on the *San Carlos*, **Vicente Santa María**, was less interested in navigational matters, and his journal discusses friendly encounters with the **natives**. Ayala stayed in San Francisco Bay for over a month, leaving on 18 September. He never did meet up with Anza, who only managed to reach the area some seven months later.

– B –

BACSTROM, SIGISMUND (fl. 1763–1801). After Dutch naval service, physician and artist Sigismund Bacstrom was employed by Sir **Joseph Banks** to travel on **James Cook**'s Second Voyage to the Pacific. Instead Bacstrom accompanied Banks on a scientific voyage to Iceland, after which he served on a variety of merchant vessels. In 1791 he sailed to the Northwest Coast on the *Butterworth*, transferring a year later to another fur-trading vessel in **Nootka Sound** and then visiting **Hawaii**. Back at Nootka in 1793, he spent the trading season on an American brig in the **Queen Charlotte Islands** and along the adjacent continental coast. All the while Bacstrom made sketches, some of which he turned into watercolors. Twenty-nine coastal works have survived, all characterized by an attention to detail reminiscent of the Spanish artist **José Cardero**. Bacstrom's drawings of the Spanish establishment in **Friendly Cove** are particularly noteworthy, as is his striking portrait of the daughter of **Haida** chief, Cunneah. He also painted two **native** village sites at the entrance to Fitzhugh Sound.

BAIDARA. See BAIDARKA.

BAIDARKA. The word *baidarka* derives from the Russian *baidara*, and refers to a native boat found in the **Aleutian Islands** and Gulf of Alaska. With the use of *baidarka* to refer to a kayak or small, distinctly hatched, deck-covered boat, *baidara* came to identify a larger, open, skin-covered fishing and group travel boat, which had a much larger carrying capacity. *Baidara*s were akin to the large ocean-going **Tlingit** canoes encountered by the early explorers that held up to 20 people. The **Aleut** kayak, made of sea mammal skins stretched over a light frame of carved driftwood, was a remarkable piece of engineering; long and narrow, it was built for speed and buoyancy. Every able-bodied man in the Aleutian Islands at the time of contact had his own *baidarka*, and the Russians and other European visitors marveled at the natives' skill in building and handling these craft in even the stormiest seas. The operator got into an open hatch, which was made watertight with a drip skirt tied tightly around his waist; he then tied his tunic over the opening to make himself one with his craft. The Aleuts used double-bladed paddles, took on board sealskin floats for added buoyancy in case of emergency, and invented an ingenious mouth-operated pump, in which water was sucked into a hollow tube and emptied over the side. The classic kayak of the eastern Aleutians was a single-hatch boat with a distinctive bifid bow and a three-piece keelson. The early explorers noted regional differences in types and style of kayak; in **Prince William Sound** they were less narrow and had two hatches, a feature also found in the far west.

In their early island exploration, the Russians made simple maps by utilizing *baidarka*s and native orientation and navigational methods. The first illustration of a kayak was a crude drawing by **Sven Waxell** in 1741. Much more important was the work of **John Webber** in 1778. **Friedrich Heinrich von Kittlitz** also executed a fine and detailed drawing of two **Unalaska** hunters in 1827.

BAJA CALIFORNIA. Mariners in the service of **Hernán Cortés** were the first to discover and explore the outlines of **California** as it was first known. It only became Baja (Lower) California with the colonization of **Alta** (Upper) **California** in the 1770s, and the administrative division of the two provinces did not actually take place until 1804. A short-lived settlement was set up on the bay of La Paz in the southeast in 1535–1536, but the dry, barren land was unable to sustain agriculture, and the natives were hostile. Despite the fact that the expeditions of **Francisco de Ulloa** (1539–1540), **Hernando de Alarcón** (1540) and **Sebastián Vizcaíno** (1602–1603) established the general nature of its east and west coasts, the idea that Baja California was an island rather than a peninsula persisted well into the 18th century. Neither these early voyages, nor the pearl hunting ventures that followed contributed to any real understanding of the place, or to its early colonization. Far from the centers of power and population in **New Spain**, and seemingly inaccessible except by a perilous sea journey, its desert conditions ensured that an estimated 20,000 natives remained beyond direct Spanish influence for 150 years. The pioneering efforts of the Jesuits, notably Fathers **Eusebio Francisco Kino** (1683–1685 at La Paz) and Juan de Salvatierra (1697 at Loreto) began the establishment of a series of missions at the end of the 17th century. There were 17 of these in existence in 1767, when the Jesuits were expelled from the Spanish Empire and the settlements passed into the hands of the Franciscans under **Junípero Serra**. A few years later they were handed over to the Dominicans, when the Franciscans concentrated on the more fertile environment, both human and natural, that had presented itself in Alta California. Ultimately there were 26 missions in Baja California, but in 1800 the population of the province was estimated at only 5,500 Spaniards and 7,000 natives, a 60 percent decline of the original aboriginal population.

It was from the most northerly of the missions, Santa María, that the **Sacred Expedition** set out to colonize Alta California on 11 May 1769. In 1776 the capital of the two Californias was moved from Loreto to **Monterey**.

BAKER, JOSEPH (1768–1817). The naming of the majestic mountain on the border of **British Columbia** and **Washington** in his honor, in 1792, demonstrates the high esteem in which British naval officer and cartographer Joseph Baker was held by **George Vancouver**. He became first lieutenant on *Discovery* when **Peter Puget** took over command of the *Chatham* from **William Broughton** in January 1793.

In the published atlas of the Vancouver Expedition, the large folio charts of the Northwest Coast—eight in all—were each "prepared under [Vancouver's] immediate inspection by Lieut. Joseph Baker." Baker was a central figure in the cartographic achievement of the expedition, and his own log, in which he recorded observations of many of the places visited, was the most extensive of all of the officers' personal records.

Once Vancouver entered the **Strait of Juan de Fuca** and realized his survey could only be done effectively by small boat excursions, Baker was employed to reduce the field notes, sketches, and calculations into preliminary and then finished charts. No matter how organized the process of gathering the raw information was, the task of creating a coherent whole from the collection of damp triangulation data sheets; finger-stained sketches of waterways; distances, some measured, others estimated; and notes hastily scribbled, was tedious, exacting, and frustrating. Supervised by Vancouver and aided by **Joseph Whidbey** and **James Johnstone**, under whom almost all of the boat surveys were carried out in 1792–1794, Baker executed this crucial assignment so well that he was Vancouver's obvious choice, after the voyage, to prepare the final charts for the engravers to produce the atlas volume that appeared with the journal in 1798.

BANKS, JOSEPH (1743–1820). After inheriting his father's fortune in 1764, English baronet Joseph Banks devoted himself to study and collecting, patronage and advocacy. From 1773 he was active in the development of the Royal Botanic Gardens at Kew. After 1776 his home became a cabinet of natural history and ethnology, an institute of research open to scholars of all nationalities, and a social gathering place for the most influential figures in British science and politics. From this base Banks entered into a voluminous correspondence with politicians, **scientists**, and explorers all over the European world; his advice was ceaselessly sought—by such explorers as **Jean François de La Pérouse** and **Alejandro Malaspina**—and generously dispensed.

Elected a fellow of the **Royal Society** in 1766 and president in 1778, Banks developed its reputation as an advisor to the government and the Admiralty, the latter through his membership on the boards of the Royal Observatory and Longitude. By this time he had participated in three voyages including the first of **James Cook** to the South Pacific. His experiences introduced him to men who would play a key role in Cook's Third Voyage, and provided him with an enduring belief in the value of naval and commercial voyages to advance scientific enquiry. As well, using an understanding of **navigation** and enthusiasm for exploration learned from Cook, he became custodian of the model of the "exploratory voyage." His influence is clear not only in the voyages of La Pérouse and Malaspina, but also of **Nathaniel Portlock** and **George Dixon, James Strange, William Bligh**, Arthur Philip, George Macartney, **George Vancouver**, Matthew Flinders, and the Russian circumnavigations of the first half of the 19th century.

One of the keys to Banks's influence was his placement of appointees on a number of voyages, for example the botanist-surgeon **Archibald Menzies** on the voyages to the Northwest Coast by **James Colnett** and Vancouver. During the **Nootka Crisis** he provided the government with information on Spanish voyages and claims in the North Pacific. He helped draft Vancouver's instructions for the Northwest Coast survey, and advised on navigational instruments, the charts and journals to be scrutinized and carried on board, articles to be used in trade with the **natives**, and the care of plants at sea.

Banks's influence broadened the perspective of his own and other governments, beyond their obvious interest in discovery towards a wider view of exploration for the advancement of knowledge. He believed that discovery was only the beginning: the real importance lay in knowledge and the analysis of new lands, and in their potential for trade and resource development. Through voyages like those of Dixon and Vancouver, Banks helped to ensure that science would be put at the service of empire.

BARANOV, ALEKSANDR (1746–1819). A towering figure in the early history of **Alaska**, Aleksandr Baranov's administration of the interests of the Shelikhov-Golikhov Company in the 1790s, followed by 20 years as manager of the **Russian–American Company** (1799–1818), firmly established Russia's presence on the Northwest Coast of America.

Baranov was first employed by **Grigorii Shelikhov** to manage his company's affairs on **Kodiak** Island. He was given wide latitude to pursue its best interests in the struggle with its rivals (notably the **Pavel Lebedev-Lastochkin** Company), to control all trade and relationships with foreigners, to found new settlements, and to extend Russian control over newly explored territories. Baranov sailed for Alaska in the summer of 1790 and wintered over on **Unalaska** Island before arriving in **Three Saints Bay** in June 1791. He soon decided to move his headquarters to St. Paul's Harbor, where he founded the present-day settlement of Kodiak. English fur traders had already been active in **Cook Inlet** and **Prince William Sound** (PWS), but with the ability to press local natives into his service Baranov was much better situated to maintain a sustained presence in the region and to establish settlements. He reinforced an earlier Shelikhov trading post at English Bay in Cook Inlet, and himself visited **Montague Island** and **Hinchinbrook Island** in PWS. As early as 1792 he began to send out large fleets of **Aleut** hunters along the coasts of the Alaska and **Kenai Peninsula**s, preferring to have his own people hunt directly than relying on trade with the local natives. In 1793 a fleet of 170 *baidarka*s reached **Yakutat Bay**, the prelude to a swift advance southeast down the coast in the years that followed. Because of **Tlingit** hostility, the Russians came to rely on the Aleuts as both hunters and warriors.

Between 1792 and 1794 Baranov spent much of his time on the mainland and, as a key to future developments, in 1793 established a settlement and shipbuilding facility under **James Shields** in Resurrection Bay on the site of the present-day town of Seward. By 1795 an outpost had been established at Yakutat (Novorossiik) and that same year Shields made a voyage of exploration as far as the **Queen Charlotte Islands** in response to the presence on the coast of **George Vancouver**. Also in 1795, and in subsequent years, Baranov himself voyaged beyond **Cross Sound**. Surveys of the **Alexander Archipelago** by Shields and Gavriil Talin in the years 1797 and 1798, as well as his own explorations and the need to provide more permanent support for his Aleut hunting parties, finally persuaded Baranov to found a major new settlement in the area. He had also become convinced that the presence of heavily armed British and American merchantmen, and their trading success with the local Tlingit, posed a major threat to Russian sovereignty and his company's interests.

Establishment of the new post was accomplished in July 1799 when Baranov bought a tract of land from a local Tlingit chief and founded **New Archangel**, a few miles north of present-day Sitka. He wintered over and, after a ceremony involving the formal presentation to Chief Mikhail (his baptized Russian name) of a possession plate, and written certificate stating that the surrounding territory had been freely ceded to the Russians for appropriate payment, Baranov left for Kodiak. But the situation in the archipelago was less than stable, despite the success of a major long-range hunting party out of Kodiak under **Ivan Kuskov** in 1801. Proceeding south again in 1802, Kuskov met unexpected hostility from the Tlingit, and picked up information about an imminent attack on New Archangel. This duly took place, aided and abetted by British and American fur traders, in June 1802. The Russian outpost was burned to the ground and most of its inhabitants were killed. Baranov, recognizing that future success in the **fur trade** lay in control of the Alexander Archipelago, determined to recapture the site. Gathering four ships and a fleet of Aleut *baidarka*s, he proceeded to the region in 1804, where he was fortunate to find the navy frigate *Neva*, under **Iurii Lisianskii**, ready to assist him. The Russian victory was swift and decisive and the ensuing peace treaty heralded an end to formal hostilities between the Tlingit and the Russians although periodic outbreaks, such as an attack on the Yakutat settlement the following year, made it clear that tension was never far from the surface. The **natives** continued to exercise political independence and accepted no Russian interference in their internal affairs. Mutual tolerance and the benefits of trade prevailed. New Archangel was rebuilt on the site of Sitka and was rapidly developed by Baranov into a shipbuilding center and international port.

In 1802 Baranov learned that Shelikhov's heirs had been granted a monopoly over commercial activities in Alaska and had confirmed his status as chief manager of the new Russian–American Company (RAC). Once control at New Archangel was restored it quickly became his new capital and center of administrative and commercial operations in the colony. Looking to extend his company's influence and gain access to the all-important agricultural products that could help sustain the infant colony, Baranov sent ships south along the coast of **Vancouver Island** and **Oregon** as far as **California**. As early as 1803, recognizing the importance and success of Yankee traders in southern Alaska, he entered into a number of commercial agreements by which, in exchange for much needed supplies, he provided Aleuts and kayaks to hunt as far south as California in return for a share of the profits from sales in Canton. It was an interest in the southern coast that culminated in the establishment of **Fort Ross** in 1812. Baranov was likewise interested in forging links with

Hawaii, but the attempt to establish a foothold on the island of Kauai, 1815–1817, was short-lived.

Although the publication of George Vancouver's journal and atlas in 1798 eclipsed the efforts of his contemporary explorers on the Northwest Coast, the persistent fur-hunting, trading, and surveying efforts of Baranov and his employees in the decade 1792–1802 meant that Russian activity was equally important in creating knowledge of the coast, especially the intricacies of the straits, bays, and inlets of the Alexander Archipelago. And Russian appreciation and understanding of the different native peoples and their cultures clearly surpassed that of any other visitors to the coast in the period 1775–1825. Baranov was instrumental in the consolidation of Russian power around the Gulf of Alaska, and in extending that power south to the natural boundary of **Dixon Entrance**. He successfully met the initial competition of rival companies, reorganized the **sea otter** hunt by forcing Aleuts into his service, neutralized Tlingit opposition, came to an accommodation with American traders for the benefit of his fledgling colony, and battled churchmen and naval officers who tried to limit his authority.

In January 1818 an increasingly irascible Baranov, who regularly quarreled with naval officers sent to report on the colony, was replaced as general manager by **Ludwig von Hagemeister**. Thereafter, governorship of the RAC's affairs in New Archangel was given to navy men. In the fall he left for St. Petersburg to give an account of his 28-year stewardship, but he died as his ship negotiated the islands of Indonesia.

BARKLEY, CHARLES WILLIAM (1759–1832). Charles William Barkley sailed in the service of the **East India Company** (EIC) before resigning in 1786 to make a trading voyage (sponsored surreptitiously by a number of Company directors) to the Northwest Coast in the English-built *Imperial Eagle*. The ship left Ostend in November, flying the Austrian flag to avoid the monopoly regulations of the EIC in the North Pacific. At 400 tons with 20 guns, she was the largest vessel to visit the coast up to that time. A month earlier Barkley had married a young wife, Frances, the first European woman known to visit **British Columbia**, and whose reminiscences (first published in 1978) provide an intriguing insight into life and activities aboard an 18th-century trading vessel.

The *Imperial Eagle* reached **Nootka Sound** in June 1787. Here Barkley met **John Mackay**, a ship's surgeon who had been left there the previous summer by another trader, **James Strange**. Mackay offered valuable information about local trading activities and the geography of the coast, which suggested that Nootka was on an island, not the American continent. As a result Barkley sailed his ship south and traded successfully in **Clayoquot Sound** and another large indentation in the coast, which he named Barkley Sound after himself. Proceeding farther south he was astonished to find, at the end of July, that he was off the entrance to a great strait, which he promptly named after the legendary navigator **Juan de Fuca**, who was said to have discovered a strait in the same latitude on the American west coast in 1592. He was particularly surprised because the strait's existence had been discounted by **James Cook** a mere nine years earlier in 1778. Tragedy then befell the voyage when, near Destruction Island and the mouth of the Hoh River in **Washington**, six men landed a small boat but were promptly killed by local natives. It was an event eerily reminiscent of the nearby murder of Spanish sailors voyaging with **Juan Francisco de la Bodega y Quadra** in 1775. Barkley sailed immediately for Canton to sell his cargo of furs. There he found not only an already saturated market but also, more ominously, that the EIC had discovered the threat to its monopoly. As he planned a second voyage his partners disassociated themselves from the venture to save their positions; their agents sold the *Imperial Eagle*, and Barkley's charts, journals, and stores were acquired by **John Meares**. Meares used the information in the account of his own voyages to the Northwest Coast, published in 1790, in which contrary to popular understanding he credited Barkley with the discovery of the **Strait of Juan de Fuca**.

After a few years trading in the Indian Ocean, Barkley and his wife made a second voyage to the Northwest Coast in the brig *Halcyon*. He traded in the **Alexander Archipelago**, the **Queen Charlotte Islands**, and on northern **Vancouver Island**.

BARRINGTON, DAINES (1727–1800). English jurist, antiquarian, amateur naturalist, and member of the council of the **Royal Society**, Daines Barrington's importance lies in his pursuit of the idea of a **Northwest Passage**, and his 1781 publication of **Francisco**

Mourelle's journal of his 1775 voyage from **New Spain** to **Alaska** with **Juan Francisco de la Bodega y Quadra**.

His Royal Society connections and friendship with First Lord of the Admiralty, the Earl of Sandwich, gave Barrington an audience within the scientific community and government for his promotion of a route to the East Indies via the polar sea. In June 1773 this resulted in the arctic voyage to 80° N (near Spitzbergen) of John Phipps (later Baron Mulgrave). Undaunted by Phipps's failure, due to a "bad year" of ice, Barrington transferred his attention to the idea of searching for the Pacific entrance to the Northwest Passage, recalling the instructions (never carried out) to John Byron, who voyaged to the Pacific in 1764, to seek his way home across the top of America. In 1774 Barrington succeeded in persuading the Royal Society to petition the Admiralty to sponsor another voyage; it was delayed for some years but was the genesis for **James Cook**'s third expedition in 1778.

In 1781 Barrington published some of his articles in an eclectic collection titled *Miscellanies*. Today it is best remembered for Mourelle's journal, accompanied by a map of the coast from **San Blas** north to Puerto de los Remedios (on Kruzov Island) which, in advance of the appearance of Cook's atlas (1784), noted "Cook's Harbour 1778" (**Nootka Sound**) and identified **New Albion**. In his introduction, Barrington wrote that Spain jealously guarded its sovereignty over the Northwest Coast, but had more to fear from the Russians than the English.

BASHMAKOV, PETR (fl. 1753–1763). One of the early navigators in the Aleutian **fur trade**, Petr Bashmakov made four voyages along the western and central **Aleutian Islands** during the years 1753–1763. These were voyages of exploration as much as hunting and trade. In 1753–1754 he reported sighting eight unknown islands before his ship was wrecked on one of the Near Islands. Building another vessel from the remains, he wintered over before returning to **Kamchatka**. Setting out again in 1756, he ventured farther east and claimed to have discovered 13 new islands. The Rat Islands were initially called the "Bashmakov Islands," although by then some islands to the east, in the Andreanoff Group—Kanaga, Adak, and Atka—were already well known. Bashmakov made two more voyages to the Near Islands in 1759–1761 and 1762–1763, and evidence (on a map later produced by **Potap Zaikov**) suggests that he died in a shipwreck on Tanaga Island.

BASOV, EMEL'IAN (fl. 1733–1756). After **Vitus Bering**'s men returned to **Kamchatka** in 1742, Emel'ian Basov organized the first hunting voyage to the "Eastern Sea." The Russian thus pioneered the maritime **fur trade** and the discovery of the **Aleutian Islands**. A small ship, the *St. Peter*, was built during the winter of 1742–1743 and in 1743 Basov set out with Petr Verkhoturov, a veteran of Bering's voyage, to show him the way. A year later, after voyaging beyond **Bering Island** far enough to see the Near Islands, they returned to Kamchatka with a rich catch of sea otter and fox pelts, having also sighted Mednoi Island.

Other expeditions followed, with Basov in partnership with the Irkutsk merchant **Nikifor Trapeznikov**. In 1747 Mednoi Island was visited and named for the discovery of its copper deposits. From then onwards, while others entered the scramble for furs and quickly pushed the hunt east into the Near Islands and beyond, Basov invested in a fruitless attempt to finance an expedition to exploit the copper. It ruined him and his contribution to the earliest voyages towards America was largely forgotten.

BAUZA Y CAÑAS, FELIPE (1764–1834). Aboard the *Descubierta*, Felipe Bauza was one of the most productive members of the **Alejandro Malaspina** Expedition, which he joined as director of charts and plans. He took responsibility for a key priority of the voyage to the Pacific—the creation of up-to-date charts of the coasts of the Spanish Empire in the Americas and Philippines, and the other places visited. The high quality and extensive cartographic documentation from the voyage is a testament to his energy, skill, and administrative abilities, and Malaspina was fulsome in his praise of Bauza's contribution.

On the Northwest Coast, Bauza was responsible for over 20 manuscript charts and plans including details of the ports of **Mulgrave**, **Nootka**, **Monterey** and Acapulco; also no less than 15 coastal profiles from **Alaska** to **California**. Bauza was on Malaspina's exploration by launch to the head of **Yakutat Bay**, 2–4 July 1791. He drew a plan showing the track of the expedition through the ice field to the Hubbard Glacier, and it was probably his sketch (now lost) of the scene in Disenchantment Bay that was later worked up into a finished painting by Juan Ravenet. This was one of a few drawings Bauza completed to add to the artistic output of the expedition. There is a sketch of natives in a kayak off **Prince William Sound**, and full-length studies of native men at Mulgrave and Nootka.

Following the expedition Bauza spent time drafting the **cartography** based on the expedition's surveys and astronomical observations. He then served at sea before beginning an extended career in the Hydrographic Office of the Navy, initially serving with **José Espinosa**. As a liberal member of the Spanish parliament, he was forced into exile by the restoration of the reactionary Ferdinand VII in 1823. Carrying with him a collection of sketches, charts, and plans, many of them related to his work during the Malaspina Expedition, he escaped to London. There he became involved with the **Royal Society** and British Hydrographic Office. He shared both his overall knowledge and skill as a draughtsman, as well as a number of charts and plans from his collection, with his British counterparts. He also presented a copy of Espinosa's two-volume *Memorial concerning astronomical observations undertaken by Spanish navigators in different parts of the globe* to the Office. In London he worked on a third volume and provided the Office with lists of geographical positions, some of which related to the Northwest Coast of America as far north as **Mount St. Elias**. Thus, despite the disgrace and fall of Malaspina and the consequent Spanish failure to publish a full journal and atlas of his voyage, valuable information gathered during the expedition did filter out in a variety of forms to the great benefit of mariners in the 19th century. In this context, the influence of Bauza's work in Spain and his years in Britain cannot be overestimated.

BAYLY, WILLIAM (1738–1810). When plans were developed for **James Cook**'s Third Voyage, William Bayly, having served on the Second Voyage, was appointed astronomer on *Discovery*. With Cook and **James King** on the *Resolution*, he was responsible for observations to obtain latitude and longitude both at sea and on land. At sea he also had to keep records of the speed of the ship and meteorological and oceanographical data. On shore he worked in the portable observatories so well depicted by **John Webber** and **William Ellis** in their drawings of Ship Cove, **Nootka Sound**. He used a variety of instruments, including K3, Larcum Kendall's chronometer; sextants by Jesse Ramsden and Peter Dolland; and compasses and telescopes. Prior to the voyage he had been responsible for designing more effective tripod suspension stands for the large but delicate astronomical (pendulum) clocks used in the observatories.

Bayly executed a fine chart of the North Pacific tracing the voyage's progress. He also produced rough charts showing details of the east coast of **Kodiak** Island, the **Alaska Peninsula**, the **Shumagin Islands**, and Cape Newnham in the **Bering Sea**.

On Cook's death, King transferred with **John Gore** to the *Discovery*, and Bayly moved with **Charles Clerke** to the *Resolution*. On his return to England in 1780, he was immediately commissioned by the Board of Longitude to prepare the observations of Cook, King, and himself for publication. They appeared in 1782.

BEECHEY, FREDERICK (1796–1856). After action in the War of 1812 and service on numerous ships, British naval officer Frederick Beechey became associated with John Franklin and attempts to traverse the **Northwest Passage**. He made two arctic voyages in 1818 and 1819–1820 before being given command of the *Blossom* in 1825 and ordered to proceed through the **Bering Strait** and wait in **Kotzebue Sound** for a rendezvous with Franklin, who was coming west overland from the mouth of the **Mackenzie** River. After a stopover at Petropavlovsk in June 1826, Beechey reached Kotzebue Sound in July. There was no sign of Franklin and no meeting ever took place, but Beechey proceeded to survey the sound and explore the coast beyond **Icy Cape** in hopes of finding the Northwest Passage that had eluded Cook and other explorers. One of the expedition's small boats reached Point Barrow at 71°23′. Beechey was a competent artist and two of his sketches were published in his *Narrative of a Voyage to the Pacific and Beerings* [*sic*] *Strait*.

BEHM, MAGNUS (1727–1806). Magnus Behm was governor of **Kamchatka** when the ships of **James Cook**'s Expedition, minus Cook and with an ailing **Charles Clerke** in command, arrived in Petropavlovsk in April 1779. **James King**, **John Gore**, and **John Webber** traveled across the peninsula to Bol'sheretsk to meet with Behm, who proved to be a charming and generous host, loading them up with provisions and tobacco for the men of the *Resolution* and *Discovery*. Webber painted his portrait. When Behm returned to the ships with the officers, he was received with full honors as a representative of Empress **Catherine II**. The importance of the contact was that he was about to leave for St. Petersburg, and Clerke was impressed enough to entrust him with a letter to the Admiralty, and with Cook's journal about their discovery of the Sandwich Islands **(Hawaii)** and exploration of the Northwest Coast that included a chart of their discoveries. These duly reached London on 10 January 1780, nearly nine months before the return of the expedition. Praise and admiration for the achievements of the voyage were combined with dismay and acute sorrow at the news of Cook's death.

BELCHER, EDWARD (1799–1877). Naval surveyor and explorer Edward Belcher served on the *Blossom* under **Frederick Beechey** and visited the **Bering Sea** and Arctic Ocean in 1826 and 1827. In 1837 he took command of the *Sulphur* from an ailing Beechey to undertake an extensive survey of the Pacific coasts of North and South America. With **Henry Kellett** in the *Starling* he worked in **Prince William Sound**, established the location and height of **Mount St. Elias**, and visited the **Alexander Archipelago** in the neighborhood of **New Archangel** before sailing south to **Nootka Sound** and **San Francisco** Bay. Following work in Central and South America, Belcher returned to the North Pacific in 1839. He re-engaged with **Russian America** and surveyed the Stikine River in the wake of the dispute between the **Hudson's Bay Company** and the **Russian–American Company**. Coming south to the **Columbia River**, he surveyed its bar and inner anchorages.

BELL, JOHN (1799–1868). In the 1830s and 1840s when the **Hudson's Bay Company** was interested in exploiting the vast region west of the **Mackenzie** River, fur trader and explorer John Bell was active on the Peel River, 1839–1840, where he established Fort McPherson. In 1842 he crossed the Richardson Mountains and descended the Rat River to the Porcupine, a significant tributary of the Yukon River. When, in 1845, he followed the Porcupine to its confluence with the Yukon he had, without fully appreciating it, established a vital link between the Mackenzie and Yukon River systems. Two years later

Alexander Murray established Fort Yukon at this location. Bell's achievement, and the exploits of **Robert Campbell**, finally solved the puzzle of the relationship between the interior river systems of the far northwest and the Arctic and Pacific oceans.

BERING, VITUS (1681–1741). In 1704 after whaling experience in the North Atlantic and voyages to America, the West Indies, and East Indies, the Danish-born Vitus Bering was recruited to help modernize and strengthen the Russian navy. In wars against Turkey and Sweden he rose to the rank of captain by 1720 but, disappointed by lack of advancement, resigned in early 1724. He was soon back in service, however, and by the end of the year had been appointed to lead an expedition that **Peter the Great** was keen to get underway to further his interest in the eastern seas of the empire.

This expedition aimed to complete the **Kamchatka** coastal survey of **Ivan Evreinov** and Fedor Luzhin, which the czar had hoped would determine more precisely the relationship between Asia and America. Assisted by **Martin Spanberg** and **Aleksei Chirikov**, Bering left St. Petersburg in February 1725 with the goal of exploring the seas north and east of Kamchatka and finding America. He was to "endeavor to discover . . . whether the country towards the North, of which at present we have no Knowledge, is Part of America or not." If it was joined to America, he was to follow the coast "if possible to reach some Colony belonging to a European Power. . . ." If ships were encountered, he was to "diligently enquire the Name of the Coasts" and learn anything else that would allow him to write reports upon which a map could be created.

The administrative and physical challenges of crossing Siberia were enormous, and it took two years to reach Okhotsk. Men were then ferried to Kamchatka but only when the *St. Gabriel* had been built could Bering launch his first **Kamchatka Expedition**. On 13 July 1728 he sailed north to the Gulf of Anadyr. The expedition discovered **St. Lawrence Island**, negotiated the **Bering Strait** without being aware of **Cape Prince of Wales**, and sailed as far as latitude 67°24′ N. At that point, on 16 August, Bering became fearful of getting caught in the ice and fog. Confirming that there was no northern land bridge between the continents and no obvious sign of an island or peninsula that could signify America, he turned for home.

Returning south and sighting the **Diomede Islands**, the explorers were prevented by fog from actually seeing America as they sailed through the Bering Strait. They encountered Chukchi natives on 20 August but Bering did not have interpreters who could communicate effectively, and so was unable to understand anything substantial about any lands to the north or east. Nevertheless, wintering over in Kamchatka, he became more aware of the strong rumors about islands to the east and decided on a second reconnaissance, in June 1729, before his return to Okhotsk. However, frustrated by fog, he failed to discover any lands. The Russians had no knowledge of the substantial distance between Kamchatka and America between latitudes 50° and 60° N and, misled by Chukchi talk of a "great land" close to their homeland, believed that, farther south, America was also not too far away.

Bering reached St. Petersburg in March 1730. His failure to find America or any islands leading to it caused disappointment. Nonetheless his skill, courage, and tenacity as an administrator persuaded Empress Anna to launch another, more ambitious effort that ultimately blossomed into the **Great Northern Expedition**, 1732–1742. Bering was promoted to captain commander and put in charge of a monumental enterprise to survey the expanses of Siberia and waters to the north, east, and south. The logistical challenges were again immense and it was another eight years before he could actually undertake the principal aim of the entire endeavor—another voyage in search of America.

Two ships, the *St. Peter* and the *St. Paul*, had been built in Okhotsk by the summer of 1740 and Bering once again crossed to Kamchatka, naming the little settlement in Avacha Bay "Petropavlovsk" in their honor. On 4 June 1741, with Bering in the *St. Peter* and Aleksei Chirikov in the *St. Paul*, the expedition sailed off to the southeast, expecting to find **Gamaland**, which the astronomer **Louis de l'Isle de la Croyère** had persuaded Bering was on the way to America. When this proved illusory they sailed east, but by this time, 20 June, the ships had become separated in a storm. Chirikov made landfall in the **Alexander Archipelago** before turning northwest, rounding the Gulf of Alaska and surveying a number of the **Aleutian Islands**.

Valuable time had been lost searching for the nonexistent Gamaland, but the *St. Peter* finally reached America on 16 July 1741, when

Mount St. Elias was sighted. Landings were made on **Kayak Island** on 20 July and **Georg Wilhelm Steller** undertook the first scientific investigations on the Northwest Coast. The Russians also found evidence of native habitation. Against Steller's advice to winter over in America, Bering decided to move north and west; he skirted the **KenaiPeninsula** and **Kodiak** Island, but did not land. On 2 August the explorers sighted Chirikof Island, named by **George Vancouver** in 1794, and the Semidi Islands on 4 August. After this, however, most of the month was spent battling westerly winds and stormy weather that drove the ship to the southwest.

On 27 August a decision was made to sail north again to try to find land, and on 29 August they sighted a large group of islands. A landing was made the next day on Nagi Island: water was replenished, the sick were taken ashore, and Steller collected plants and made notes about the animals, birds, and fish. On 6 September **Aleut** natives were encountered when they approached the ship and gifts were exchanged. Later, two sailors waded ashore to visit a native village, and the Russians, led by **Sven Waxell**, made detailed observations of the Aleut **kayaks** and clothing. Steller noted the presence of iron knives and deduced that they must have been gained through an inter-native trading system that linked the Aleuts to the Chukchi. Bering called the island group after one of his sailors, Nikita Shumagin, who died and was buried there. The **Shumagin Islands**, therefore, were the site of the first sustained encounter between Europeans and **Native Americans** on the wider Northwest Coast. Continuing southwest, the Russians noted one of the high volcanoes on **Unimak Island**. The *St. Peter* then encountered a period of gale force winds, which drove Bering south and southeast before he could again turn northwest. By the time the expedition was off the Near Islands, Bering and many of the crew were incapacitated from exhaustion and scurvy, and command had effectively passed to Steller and Waxell, who steered the vessel onto **Bering Island** on 15 November. Despite Steller's efforts to prevent his decline, Bering died on 8 December 1741. With him 32 others perished before the survivors, waiting out the winter storms, constructed a new ship from the remains of the *St. Peter* and finally reached Petropavlovsk at the end of August 1742.

Thus ended, in tragic circumstances, Bering's part of the voyage to America. Stretches of America and some of its adjacent islands had been found for the first time, but the distances involved had proven great, the landings limited, the encounters with natives fleeting, and the charts that resulted from the voyage (and that of Chirikov) speculative, leaving more questions unanswered than geography resolved. The most successful aspect of the endeavor proved to be the scientific investigations of Steller. As a result there is no easy, direct line between the Russian state's search for America and its willingness to support the colony of **Russian America**. The immediate result of the voyage was the haphazard advance of the fur-hunting *promyshlenniki* through the Aleutian Islands to the **Alaska Peninsula** and onto the continent proper; it would be another half-century before the Russian government would truly find America and begin to capitalize on Vitus Bering's voyage of discovery.

Bering's death brought an end to a 17-year period of exploration in which he had achieved amazing success as an administrator, crossed Siberia three times, and undertaken two major voyages. By the time he discovered America he had led the Great Northern Expedition for almost a decade, and it is clear that he was mentally and physically exhausted from the responsibility. He was 60 years old in 1741, and his enthusiasm for the task clearly waned as the *St. Peter* struggled to return to Kamchatka and he himself was grievously ill. His reputation has suffered from the biting and unrelenting criticism of Steller, and the suggestion by a number of historians that his actual achievements as an explorer were not particularly noteworthy; **Semen Dezhnev** had preceded him through the Bering Strait, and his voyage round the Gulf of Alaska, which was really in the hands of Waxell and **Sofron Khitrovo** for much of the time, provided only the vaguest possible idea of the shape of the continental coast. Nevertheless, the magnitude of the commissions he undertook and the scope of his activities rank him as one of the most accomplished and courageous members in the pantheon of great explorers.

BERING ISLAND. *See* COMMANDER ISLANDS.

BERING SEA AND BERING STRAIT. The Bering Sea and the Bering Strait, between the Pacific Ocean and Arctic Ocean, separate Asia from America. The strait constituted what was understood in the 16th century, but not actually verified for over 200 years, to be the **Strait**

of Anian. The sea was variously known as the Sea of Alaska, the Sea of Kamchatka, the Mer d'Ormante, the Sleepy Sea, and the Sea of Bobrovoi (Otters) before being formally named after **Vitus Bering** by **Vasilii Golovnin** during his round-the-world voyage, 1817–1819. The strait was navigated by **James Cook** in August 1778, a few days before his search for the **Northwest Passage** ended off **Icy Cape**, and its name appeared for the first time as "Bherings Strait" on the charts from that voyage, as the English navigator accurately defined for the first time the correct relationship between Asia and America.

BERINGIA. Beringia, an ancient land bridge between the Chukotskii Peninsula and **Alaska,** was up to 1,000 miles wide at its largest extent. It existed at two different times, most recently between 25,000 and 10,000 years ago when, as the climate grew warmer, the Bering and Anadyr straits were flooded; Alaska was separated from Siberia; and the **Diomede**, **St. Lawrence**, **Pribilof**, and **Aleutian Islands** were cut off from continental America. The existence of Beringia facilitated human migration from Asia to America, but archaeological evidence also confirms that a marine and land route from Japan to Alaska and the Northwest Coast via the Kurile Islands, **Kamchatka**, and the Aleutians was used.

BERKH, VASILII (1781–1834). Naval officer and historian, Vasilii Berkh came to the Northwest Coast with **Iurii Lisianskii** in the *Neva*. He arrived on **Kodiak** Island in the summer of July 1804 and took part in the second Battle of Sitka in October 1804. The defeat of the **Tlingit** reestablished Russian control of the site. During the winter of 1804–1805 he stayed at Kodiak and researched the early years of **Russian America**, preparing maps and, particularly, tracing the history of the discovery of the **Aleutian Islands** and the upper Northwest Coast of America. His historical interests benefited greatly from his personal contact with **Aleksandr Baranov** and other administrators of the **Russian–American Company**. He later continued his work in various archives in St. Petersburg and, in 1823, published his seminal work, *Khronologicheskaia istoriia otkrytiia Aleutskikh ostrovov, ili podvigi Rossiiskogo kupechestva* (Chronological History of the Discovery of the Aleutian Islands or the Exploits of Russian Merchants).

BILLINGS, JOSEPH (ca. 1758–1806). Joseph Billings enlisted in the Royal Navy a few months before leaving for the Northwest Coast with **James Cook** aboard the *Discovery*. After his return to England he joined the Russian Navy. Despite his young age, his experience impressed the English historian of Russian discoveries, **William Coxe**, who promoted him as a candidate to lead an expedition under discussion during 1784–1785 in response to British, French, and Spanish interest in the North Pacific. In August 1785 he was commissioned to continue the exploration of the Asian and American coasts bordering on the **Bering Sea** and Arctic Ocean, and to explore beyond the **Aleutian Islands** onto the American mainland. He was charged with improving the port facilities at Okhotsk and investigating the establishment of another naval base. The party of nearly 150 land and naval personnel, scientists, and artisans included **Gavriil Sarychev**, the talented writer and artist, who later became an admiral and head of the navy; **Martin Sauer**, who acted as Billings's secretary; and the artist **Luka Voronin**. They arrived in Okhotsk in July 1786.

The first phase of the expedition, while ships were constructed at Okhotsk during the winter of 1786–1787, was spent on the Russian mainland and in an unsuccessful attempt to replicate the voyage of **Semen Dezhnev**. In the summer of 1789 the *Slava Rosii* (Glory of Russia) and *Dobroe Namerenie* (Good Intent) were finally launched, but the latter ran aground and was unsalvageable. This meant that Billings sat out the winter in Petropavlovsk with just one vessel, and it was the *Slava Rosii* alone that set out for the Aleutians in the second major phase of the expedition in May 1790. Billings reached **Unalaska** Island on 1 June. The members of the expedition explored the area, meeting and reporting on the **Aleut** natives, the artists sketching and the naturalist **Carl Heinrich Merck** collecting botanical specimens. They then proceeded to **Kodiak** Island where they stopped over at what had become a substantial trading post established by **Grigorii Shelikhov** at **Three Saints Bay**. One of the tasks Billings had been asked to undertake was an investigation of the charge of brutality towards the natives on Kodiak Island and the inappropriate collection of *iasak*. His report to St. Petersburg was not favorable to the famous merchant.

Sarychev reported that the natives flocked to see the members of the expedition and admired the size of the ship. Sauer noted the presence of about 200 daughters of local chiefs held as hostages for Aleuts enserfed to hunt for furs, and described the establishment in detail. Leaving on 6 July, the *Slava Rosii* sailed for **Prince William Sound**. En route Billings became aware of the presence of the *San Carlos* under **Salvador Fidalgo**, which was exploring **Cook Inlet** and the **Kenai Peninsula**, and sent a message by kayak inviting him to rendezvous in the Sound. But Fidalgo had already set his course for Kodiak and Billings waited in vain. On 30 July he continued exploring southeast, sighting **Kayak Island** and **Mount St. Elias**. By now, however, he was short of supplies and a number of men had scurvy. He turned for home and reached Avacha Bay on 14 October 1790.

During the winter, Billings supervised the construction of a second ship, the *Chernyi Orel* (Black Eagle), which he placed under the command of **Robert Hall** in April 1791. On what was now the third phase of the expedition, the two vessels sailed again to visit various islands in the Aleutian chain en route to Unalaska. Sarychev and Sauer wished to continue east again to complete a survey of the **Alaska Peninsula** and Cook Inlet, but Billings decided to head north into the Bering Sea, where they visited **St. Lawrence Island**, noted King Island, and landed at Cape Rodney. Here Billings went ashore, accompanied by Merck and Voronin. They were the first Russians to set foot in that part of America. Continuing across the Bering Strait and noting the **Diomede Islands**, they landed on the Chukotskii Peninsula in St. Lawrence Bay in early August.

The fourth and final phase of the expedition took place in two areas during the fall and winter of 1791–1792. Billings stayed on the Asian mainland while Sarychev and Hall returned to the Aleutians, the *Slava Rosii* and *Chernyi Orel* sailing south to Unalaska, where they spent a difficult winter.

As soon as they returned to Petropavlovsk in June 1792, the exhaustive efforts of the expedition came to a practical end, and Billings, Sarychev, and Hall set out for St. Petersburg, which they reached on 14 March 1793. Although it rivaled in scope the endeavors of **Vitus Bering**, the Billings Expedition has been regarded as a costly undertaking that actually achieved very few new discoveries. Billings was a cautious explorer, but he was always more interested in eastern Siberia than in the Aleutian Islands and the Gulf of Alaska. Both he and Sarychev were very young men when they set out, and the fact that the expedition implemented a cohesive plan over a period of seven years speaks to his success as an administrator. His expedition was important in upholding Russian sovereignty, and impressing upon the natives of the eastern Aleutian Islands that Russia intended to maintain authority over the region. The journals, maps, and botanical and ethnographic collections also constituted a vast treasure trove of valuable information.

BISHOP, CHARLES (fl. 1760s–1809). English trader Charles Bishop sailed in the Pacific from 1794 to 1797. On the *Ruby* he traded for furs on the Northwest Coast during the summer and fall of 1795. He visited the **Columbia River** and then was driven by stormy weather past **Vancouver Island** to the **Queen Charlotte Islands**, where he traded on the east coast of Moresby Island in Cumshewa Inlet. He then crossed to the mainland in the vicinity of Banks Island before moving up the coast to the entrance to the Portland Canal and over to Prince of Wales Island and the southern reaches of the **Alexander Archipelago**. In this way he was working on parts of the coast frequented by the American **"Boston Men."** He later visited **Nootka Sound** and **Barkley Sound** before returning to the Columbia and arriving in **Hawaii** in early 1796. Bishop never again came to the Northwest Coast although he had hoped to do so. His importance lies in his detailed journal in which he gives a perceptive and detailed account of the **fur trade** experience, interacting with the **natives** and encountering fellow traders. He showed that it was a very tough business, and the tension of the situation he found himself in was ever-present; he respected and relied on the natives, but was always fearful of them, and he recorded how it was necessary to learn from and communicate with other ships and men on the coast.

BLIGH, WILLIAM (1754–1817). British naval officer and cartographer William Bligh was appointed to the *Resolution* in 1776 to accompany **James Cook** on his Third Voyage to the Pacific. As master he was responsible not only for the navigation of the ship, but also any surveys ordered by Cook.

In the North Pacific during 1778 and 1779, Bligh was the author of a general chart with illustrated insets, and a number of fine coastal views. The surveys attributed to **Henry Roberts** were also based on his original work (and that of Cook), as Roberts worked under Bligh as his draughtsman, and made the fair copies of Bligh's surveys. There is no evidence that Roberts himself actually carried out any surveys. After the voyage, Bligh was justifiably incensed when the initial title page of the first edition of Cook's journal stated: "Illustrated with Maps and Charts from Original Drawings made by Lieut. Henry Roberts. . . ." He wrote on the Admiralty copy that "None of the Maps and Charts in this publication are from original drawings . . . [by] . . . Roberts, he did no more than copy the original ones from Captain Cook, who besides myself was the only person that surveyed & laid the Coast down. . . ." The reference to Roberts, therefore, was removed before the first edition was printed for distribution. It appears from an entry in the journal of the log of the *Bounty*, of which he was given command in 1787, that Bligh left onboard, at the time of the famous mutiny, a number of "general surveys of the West Coast of America." Sadly, these manuscripts were never recovered.

After his return to England Bligh was elected a Fellow of the **Royal Society** in 1781 in recognition of his contribution to the success of Cook's voyage of exploration. Whatever his later troubles aboard the *Bounty* and in New South Wales might have displayed about his character, he was a superb navigator and surveyor. His work in the North Pacific was a remarkable achievement, undertaken when he was still a very young man. It provided the direction for, and set a standard unsurpassed by, those who followed him to the coasts of America. *See also* CARTOGRAPHY.

BLONDELA (fl. 1774–1788). Lieutenant Blondela came to the Northwest Coast in 1786 on the *Astrolabe* as a member of the **Jean François de La Pérouse** Expedition. He had previously distinguished himself in the American War of Independence, serving in five different ships-of-the-line, and being involved in nine separate naval engagements, 1777–1782.

La Pérouse highly valued his skill as a draughtsman, and 15 of his drawings were engraved for the atlas accompanying the published journal of the voyage in 1797. These included three executed at **Port des Français (Lituya Bay)** in **Alaska**—a view of a **Tlingit** fishing camp; the frame of a skin-covered canoe on land; and a canoe at sea containing 14 natives. A fourth drawing, not engraved, shows the ships at anchor in the outer basin of the bay, with Frenchmen in a small boat trading with a party of local natives in a canoe. The scene in this drawing formed the basis of the engraving by Nicolas Ozane, which was included in the atlas and which depicted the tragic boat accident at the entrance to the bay that drowned 21 members of the expedition.

BOCHAROV, DMITRII (fl. 1774–1793). A navigator in the Russian **fur trade**, Dmitrii Bocharov's first voyage seems to have been from Okhotsk to the Kurile Islands in the *Prokopti* in 1774. He moved on from there to the **Commander Islands**, returning home in 1778 with a rich cargo of furs. He entered the employ of **Grigorii Shelikhov** and, commanding the *Simeon and Anna*, sailed in company with **Gerasim Izmailov** who commanded the *Three Saints* to take Shelik-hov and his party of settlers to **Kodiak** Island in 1783–1784. In the summer of 1788 he and Izmailov made their celebrated, pioneering voyage of exploration along the north shore of the Gulf of Alaska from the entrance to **Cook Inlet**, southeast down the coast to **Lituya Bay** and **Cross Sound**. They wrote a report of their travels with a description of the native peoples encountered, and the locations in which they buried possession plates to establish Russian sovereignty over the area. It was published in the 1792 edition of Shelikhov's *Voyage to America*. In 1790 he set out with **Aleksandr Baranov** from Okhotsk to Kodiak, but their vessel, the *Three Saints*, was wrecked and they wintered over on **Unalaska** Island. Baranov pro-ceeded to **Three Saints Bay** in 1791, but Bocharov did not go with him; instead he explored the north coast of the **Alaska Peninsula** by *baidarka* and then pioneered the overland route between Bristol Bay and Shelikhov Strait.

BODEGA BAY AND TOMALES BAY. A substantial bay enclosed by Bodega Head and Tomales Point, north of Point Reyes, Bodega Bay is also the entrance (at its southern end) to Tomales Bay, a nar-row, 16-mile-long body of water formed by the San Andreas Fault. The entrance to this latter bay was seen by the *Tres Reyes*, one of the ships of the expedition led by **Sebastián Vizcaíno** at the beginning of January 1603, and called the Rio Grande de San Sebastian on Enrico Martínez's map of the area. Tomales Bay was explored on 3 October

1775 by **Juan Francisco de la Bodega y Quadra** in the *Sonora* on his return from Alaska, and his ship was nearly engulfed by the bay's notorious tidal bore. He called it Puerto de la Bodega but this name was transferred to the larger, outside bay in 1793. This was three years after the Englishman **James Colnett** had visited the location, and when the Spanish were becoming increasingly concerned about English activity on the coast, particularly that of **George Vancouver**. Juan Bautista Matute was sent by the viceroy, the **Count of Revillagigedo**, in the spring of 1793 to explore and colonize the area as a preventive measure against foreign settlement, but nothing came of this initiative, and navigational difficulties forced the Spaniards to approach the bays overland from **San Francisco**. Later that same year, **Juan Martínez y Zayas**, under orders from the viceroy to explore the coast south from the **Strait of Juan de Fuca** to **San Francisco**, drew a chart of Bodega Bay. Russians were active in the area from 1808 onwards as part of the effort of the **Russian–American Company** to found an agricultural settlement in **California**. This led to the building of **Fort Ross** in 1812.

BODEGA Y QUADRA, JUAN FRANCISCO DE LA (1744–1794).
Over a period of 20 years Juan Francisco de la Bodega y Quadra became arguably the most experienced and knowledgeable European mariner on the subject of the Northwest Coast. He arrived in **New Spain** in 1774 with a group of young officers selected and trained to add strength to the **California** supply requirements of the Naval Department of **San Blas**, and to push forward northern exploration.

As a member of the **Bruno de Hezeta** Expedition, 1775, he made an epic voyage to southern **Alaska** in the tiny schooner *Sonora*. After witnessing the tragic loss of six men during a landing at Point Elizabeth in **Washington**, and fearing that Hezeta was about to terminate the voyage, Bodega and his pilot **Francisco Mourelle** separated from Hezeta near the **Strait of Juan de Fuca**. In a clearly unsatisfactory vessel with an untried crew of fourteen farmhands, only four of whom had ever been to sea before, they headed into uncharted waters. They were short of water and there was only enough food for reduced rations. It was a huge gamble. Landfall was made on 15 August at about 57° N, high in the **Alexander Archipelago**, where **Mount Edgecumbe** was named San Jacinto. They anchored in Sea Lion Cove, named Puerto de Nuestra Señora de los Remedios, at the northern end of Kruzof Island, took possession and made the first sustained European encounter with the **Tlingit**. Late summer storms prevented further progress. Turning south Bodega discovered **Bucareli Bay** off Prince William Island. After a two-day stopover the *Sonora* hurried south battling heavy seas, and scurvy amongst her crew. This did not stop Bodega's interest in exploration, however; he searched unsuccessfully for the **Rio de Martín de Aguilar** but recognized **Cape Blanco**, and later entered **Bodega Bay**, which in fact he did not name, and Tomales Bay, which confusingly he did name, after himself. When the schooner reached **Monterey** on 7 October, all on board were so weak that they had to be carried ashore. This remarkable voyage resulted in a chart that presented the first realistic delineation and trend of the coast to 58° N, and led to Bodega and Mourelle's participation in the next northern voyage, the 1779 expedition led by **Ignacio de Arteaga**, during which, in the *Favorita*, he returned to Bucareli Bay before exploring the entrance to **Prince William Sound** and along the **Kenai Peninsula** to Afognak Island.

After an uneventful period in Cuba and Spain, 1783–1789, Bodega returned to the Pacific as commandant at **San Blas** and, with the new viceroy, the **Count of Revillagigedo**, became involved in the aftermath of the **Nootka Crisis** and Spain's response to the first **Nootka Convention** of 1790. He assisted with the planning, management, and work of various Spanish exploring expeditions, notably that of **Alejandro Malaspina** in 1791, but most importantly he himself led the Limits Expedition to **Nootka** in 1792. This thrust him into a diplomatic role. He met with **George Vancouver** in an inconclusive attempt to settle the terms of the treaty under which Spain had agreed to cede to England its establishment at **Friendly Cove**, and tried to settle a northern boundary (or limits) between **Alta California** and English interests on the coast. The expedition also proved to be the final chapter in an intense period of Spanish exploration on the Northwest Coast during 1788–1792.

As plans were being formulated for the expedition, Viceroy Revillagigedo became convinced that Nootka should be abandoned in favor of a new settlement in the **Strait of Juan de Fuca**. Further exploration of Fuca was handed off to **Dionisio Alcalá Galiano** and **Cayetano Valdés** of the Malaspina Expedition. And, with Bodega at Nootka, **Salvador Fidalgo** was instructed to establish the settlement in Fuca (Nuñez Gaona in **Neah Bay**), and **Jacinto Caamaño** was chosen to search for the entrance to the Strait of **Bartholomew de Fonte**. The four ships of the expedition left **San Blas** at different times in February and March 1792. With Bodega in the *Santa Gertrudis* were the scientists **José Mariano Moziño** and **José María Maldonado**, and the artist **Atanásio Echeverría**. These men left an important scientific and artistic legacy from their time at Nootka. Maldonado also accompanied Caamaño to southern Alaska.

Bodega arrived in **Friendly Cove** in April. Although he expected to hand over the establishment, he was happy to bring the warm and outgoing culture of his Lima upbringing to the wilds of the North Pacific, and to provide the best of hospitality to a fellow naval officer who had sailed half way around the world to meet him. Vancouver was not the only beneficiary. The summer of 1792 at Nootka proved to be a remarkable experience for all who visited the port. Regardless of nationality, **fur trade** commanders and officers were welcomed to the Commandant's House, where the multicourse dinners were served on his personal silver plate, and Chief **Maquinna** was an honored guest. Instead of an expected cool reception, Vancouver found Bodega a genuinely warm and generous host: the settlement's facilities were put at his disposal, a building was provided for his stores, his ships were careened, and fresh meat, vegetables, fruit, and milk were delivered to his ships.

Vancouver did not arrive until late August, as a result of which Bodega was able to rethink the Spanish position. He came to appreciate the value of Nootka as a port, and Chief Maquinna confirmed what the American fur traders **Robert Gray** and **Joseph Ingraham** had told him—that **John Meares** had purchased no land, and had only set up a shack in a small cove adjacent to the Mowachaht village of Yuquot. When he added this to his own knowledge that **James Colnett** and his men had been well treated at San Blas, set free and their wages paid in full, and a report from **Alcalá Galiano** that Neah Bay was a poor substitute for Nootka as a base, he determined to argue, if he could not get Vancouver to agree on the Strait of Juan de Fuca as a boundary, that all Spanish rights at Nootka should be retained. When, early in their discussions, Vancouver made it known that he considered the coast open to the English north of **San Francisco**, Bodega was further emboldened to hold on to at least a part of Friendly Cove. As Vancouver maintained that he had no authority to determine boundaries or to do anything but take over the entire establishment, there was soon a stalemate in the discussions, a situation that did not change despite their cordial and respectful relationship and a joint excursion to Chief Maquinna's winter village at Tahsis. With no agreement possible, the commissioners agreed to submit separate reports on the situation to Madrid and London respectively.

The summer's major exploring initiative, Caamaño's search for the strait of Fonte, took place between 13 June and 7 September. Although not as comprehensive as Vancouver's survey in 1793, Caamaño's work essentially disproved the Fonte myth as far as the Spaniards were concerned. Caamaño shared the details of his surveys with Vancouver on his return to Nootka. As a result, the English explorer, the next year, retained a number of Spanish place names on his own charts.

Bodega left Nootka on 12 October and visited Fidalgo, who was preparing to leave the short-lived establishment of Nuñez Gaona prior to spending a miserable winter at Nootka. He then proceeded to Monterey and more meetings with Vancouver. When he finally returned to New Spain, with an extensive journal and reports about Nootka and the Northwest Coast and **Alta California**, he encountered a relieved viceroy, who had received orders from Madrid that Nootka was not to be abandoned despite the treaty with England, and an appreciative Spanish government, which was delighted at Bodega's actions in upholding its sovereignty. Hindsight shows that his efforts were ultimately in vain as Spain was soon to withdraw from the **Pacific Northwest**, but at the time the Limits Expedition, with its negotiations at Nootka and explorations north of **Vancouver Island**, was an important defense of Spain's interests in the region, and ensured that its ultimate retreat would take place in 1819 in a context more of its own choosing.

BOIT, JOHN (1774–1829). As a teenager, American fur trader and explorer John Boit sailed with **Robert Gray** on the second voyage of the *Columbia*. He contributed a short but important journal to the record of the expedition in which he described the discovery of the **Columbia River**, considering it "a fine place for to sett up a *Factory*."

While he was still only 19, Boit was given command of the sloop *Union* on which he made a second voyage to the Northwest Coast. It was a great tribute to his ability as a sailor, and to his administrative skills, that the expedition was a commercial success. After trading along the west coast of **Vancouver Island**, he sailed to Chief **Koyah**'s harbor at the southern end of the **Queen Charlotte Islands**, where he survived a ferocious native attack on his ship. Recalling his positive opinion of the Columbia River, he then sailed south but was unable to cross the bar, thus forfeiting what he expected to be the collection of "many capitall sea otter skins." After sale of its cargo of furs in Canton, the *Union* sailed home to Boston via the Cape of Good Hope, thus achieving a remarkable circumnavigation.

BOLAÑOS, FRANCISCO (fl. 1540–1541). Spanish navigator Francisco Bolaños commanded the fleet of the conquistador Pedro de Alvarado that came from Guatemala to the northwestern coast of **New Spain** in 1540. The purpose was to find a sea route to the fabulous Seven Cities of Cíbola, reported to exist in the desert of present-day New Mexico. An attempt to find this route was already being undertaken by ships under the command of **Hernando de Alarcón**, sponsored by Viceroy Antonio de Mendoza. With the death of Alvarado in 1541, Mendoza inherited his ships and dispatched Bolaños to ascertain if any river existed on the ocean coast explored by **Francisco de Ulloa** in 1539–1540. Some way up the west coast of **Baja California**, probably not much farther than Punta de Abreojos, a storm drove the expedition back, but not before Bolaños had explored Bahia Magdalena, which he called Puerto de San Pedro, and Bahia de Ballenas, which he called San Mateo. This was the Puerto de Santiago of **Juan Rodríguez Cabrillo**, who followed Bolañas up the same coast a few months later. On his way north, Bolaños found a small bay, under the southernmost point of the peninsula. He called it Puerto de San Lucas on the saint's feast-day, 18 October 1541, and this is the origin of name **Cabo San Lucas**.

BOLTS, WILLIAM (1739–1808). William Bolts was one of the most energetic, well informed, and well connected of the merchant adventurers whose dreams and schemes for commercial success in the later years of the 18th century prompted governments to sponsor directly, or support in other ways, voyages of exploration and trade. During the 1760s he was a prominent official with the **East India Company** (EIC). After he had run afoul of the company in the 1770s he transferred his allegiance and knowledge of India to the Empress of Austria and Hungary, traveling to India to set up a commercial enterprise in direct competition with the EIC. Problems with his bankers and disagreements as how best to develop the China trade, however, ultimately doomed this relationship.

By 1780 Bolts had learned of the success of **James Cook**'s men in trading Northwest Coast furs in China and determined to organize a voyage, initially trying to recruit some of Cook's men such as **George Dixon**. But he had no capital. After discussions with the Austrian emperor failed to reconcile the problems of mounting a commercial and scientific voyage as an all-in-one initiative, Bolts shared his ideas with the Russian court of **Catherine II** through the vice-chancellor Count Ivan Andrévitch Ostermann. When this also came to naught he extended his interests into the world of **John Henry Cox**. He was likely the inspiration of, and had an interest in, the first post-Cook trading voyage to the Northwest Coast, that of **James Hanna** in 1785. By this time he had also contacted the French, entering into conversations with Claret de Fleurieu, the director of Ports and Arsenals. Louis XVI and his ministers soon pursued the concept of a voyage aimed at the Northwest Coast, that of **Jean François de La Pérouse**, but not a relationship with Bolts. All this activity stirred the Russians and led directly to the Empress Catherine's plans for the voyages of Grigorii **Mulovskii** and **Joseph Billings**. Bolts is interesting not only in his own right but because, in pressing nations and corporations into action, his activities and influence touched the Northwest Coast in a distinctive way in the era of exploration.

"BOSTON MEN." Natives and other traders referred to Americans who engaged in the Northwest Coast maritime **fur trade** as "Boston Men." It was Boston investors and New England merchants and mariners who pioneered the engagement of the United States in the trade. They were ready to do so because Boson had no commercial hinterland, unlike New York or Philadelphia, and the successful American Revolution had robbed them of their central position in the lucrative colonial trading system. Bostonians came to dominate the fur trade so completely that until well into the 19th century "Boston Men" and "American" essentially became synonymous in the North Pacific.

BRAGIN, DIMITRII (fl. 1760s–1770s). Fur trader and explorer in the **Aleutian Islands** in the 1760s and 1770s, Dimitrii Bragin made a voyage to **Unalaska** in 1762 and was in charge of a group of hunters operating on the island until he had to escape from hostile **Aleuts** in 1764. In 1773 he sailed from **Kamchatka** to Bering Island, then in 1774 on to Unalaska Bay where he stayed for two years. In mid-1776 he voyaged on up the **Alaska Peninsula** to **Kodiak** Island, but soon returned to Unalaska and then continued west to Atka. This island was used as a base from which to explore and hunt in other islands in the Andreanoff group until the summer of 1777. The importance of Bragin's voyages lies in his communication with the scholar **Peter Simon Pallas**, who was developing for Russian authorities, through his writings, a clearer picture of the Aleutian Islands and the evolving **fur trade**. Bragin wrote an account of the voyage for Pallas, who produced an important map in 1780 from this and other contacts with the *promyshlenniki*. The voyages also demonstrated the length and range of these early hunting and exploring expeditions.

BRISTOL BAY. An arm of the **Bering Sea**, Bristol Bay's shoreline forms part of the **Alaska Peninsula** in southwest Alaska. It was explored and named on 16 July 1778 by **James Cook** after his friend Augustus John Hervey, the third Earl of Bristol. In the 1780s traders and hunters working for **Pavel Lebedev-Lastochkin** roamed over the entire area of the upper **Alaska Peninsula**, using the rivers and lakes to establish an important connection between Bristol Bay and Kamishak Bay on **Cook Inlet**.

BRITISH COLUMBIA. Canada's Pacific edge, today the province of British Columbia, encompasses the central portion of the Northwest Coast of America from the **Strait of Juan de Fuca** in the south to **Dixon Entrance** and the Nass River in the north. The province extends much farther to the north, but is cut off from the ocean by the Alaska Panhandle, the southern portion of the former **Russian America**.

The coast of British Columbia includes **Vancouver Island** and the **Queen Charlotte Islands**. As such, it was the landing place, in

Nootka Sound, of James Cook in 1778 and was descended upon by maritime fur traders who, in the decade after 1785, explored and traded along the continental coast among the islands north of 51° N. After Spain established a short-lived military post at Nootka in 1790, her mariners began to chart the coast of the island and to enter the Strait of Juan de Fuca. The island was circumnavigated by **Dionisio Alcalá Galiano** and **George Vancouver** in 1792. The province's coast was also the scene of **Alexander Mackenzie**'s cross continental trek that same year, and of the descent of the **Fraser River** by **Simon Fraser** in 1808.

The lower Fraser River became the location of a key **Hudson's Bay Company** trading post at Fort Langley in 1827, and it was at this fort's third site, close by, that the mainland Crown Colony of British Columbia was proclaimed in 1858. It was united to the Crown Colony of Vancouver Island in 1866 and the whole became a province of Canada in 1871. *See also* DOUGLAS, JAMES.

BROBDINGNAG. This fictional country on the Northwest Coast of America provides an example of how unknown and inaccessible islands and coastlines of the Pacific Ocean, with hints of real people, places, voyages, and events, provided writers of satirical and fantastical travel accounts with attractive and mysterious settings for their work. In 1726 Jonathan Swift published *Travels into Several Remote Nations of the World by Lemuel Gulliver*, in which his hero visited a land of giants in 1703. Depicted on a map accompanying the tale as a huge peninsula, Brobdingnag was placed safely northwest of Monterey, Port Sir Francis Drake, Cape Mendocino, New Albion, Cape Blanco, and the "Streights of Annian." In *Gulliver's Travels* Swift parodied the numerous and popular travel accounts of his age, and exploited the Pacific as a region outside the sphere of reality, approachable only in fiction and satire, as indeed it remained for another generation.

BROUGHTON, WILLIAM (1762–1821). As commander of the *Chatham*, William Broughton accompanied **George Vancouver** in the *Discovery* to the Pacific, 1791–1792. Broughton participated in Vancouver's first season of exploration on the Northwest Coast (April–December 1792), after which he was sent home to England with **Zachary Mudge** from **Monterey** via **San Blas** and Veracruz. He carried Vancouver's secret dispatches concerning the inconclusive diplomatic negotiations with **Juan Francisco de la Bodega y Quadra** at **Nootka Sound**, as well as reports and charts on the progress of the voyage's explorations to date. During the summer spent proving the insularity of **Vancouver Island**, Broughton explored the San Juan Islands and Knight Inlet and took part in a number of small boat excursions. His most important contribution, however, was his exploration of the lower reaches of the **Columbia River**. The *Chatham* crossed the bar on 21 October 1792 and anchored within the tidal estuary. Broughton then took to the boats to explore the river proper and ascended for over 100 miles to what is now Point Vancouver. At nearby Possession Point he took possession of the country in the name of George III. He subsequently took his chart of the river, which he called the "Oregan," with him to England.

After submitting his reports to the authorities in London, Broughton took command of the *Providence* in October 1793. However, he did not leave England to rejoin Vancouver on the Northwest Coast until early in 1795. After a very slow voyage, he arrived at Nootka in March 1796 only to find that Vancouver had completed his survey of the coast and that England and Spain, now allies against republican France, had abandoned any idea of maintaining a permanent presence in the North Pacific.

BROWN, WILLIAM (fl. 1792–1795). British fur trader William Brown was trading on the Northwest Coast in the early 1790s with a fleet of three ships. He served on the *Butterworth* and in the *Jackal*, spending the winters in **Hawaii** and crossing to Canton in 1793. In July 1793 he met **George Vancouver**'s *Discovery* in Chatham Sound and provided information about the local waters. Vancouver named Brown Passage north of Stephens Island in his honor. A year later he met Vancouver off Yakutat and accompanied him into **Cross Sound**, where he gave the English commander the "melancholy intelligence" of the excesses of the French Revolution and the death of Louis XVI. Earlier at Yakutat he had met **Peter Puget** in the *Chatham* and helped **Egor Purtov** to recover a group of Kodiak islanders who had been captured by the local **Tlingit**. The surgeon-artist **Sigismund Bacstrom** served on the *Butterworth* and found Brown to be brutal and unscrupulous in dealing with his crew and particularly the native peoples he encountered. After a summer of trading in 1792, Bacstrom left the ship at Nootka Sound "on account of the ill and mean usage" he received from his captain. Brown was killed by natives in Hawaii in January 1795.

BUACHE, PHILIPPE (1700–1773). Philippe Buache was made geographer to the king at the age of 29, and in 1730 was elected to the Academy of Sciences. Noted for his theory that the earth, including both land and sea, was divided into basins separated by chains of mountains, his importance to the evolving geography of the Northwest Coast came from his involvement with mid-century promotion of the fictional voyage of **Bartholomew de Fonte**. In 1750 he produced a fanciful map to accompany a lecture in Paris by his nephew, **Joseph Nicolas de l'Isle**. The map was published in 1752 along with de l'Isle's memoir, but because it did not actually conform to the Fonte narrative—it placed the entrance to the Rio de los Reyes at 63° N rather than at 53° N—his map was less influential than one published a little later by de l'Isle himself. Buache maintained his belief in the apocryphal Fonte voyage account in his *Considérations Géographiques et Physiques sur les Nouvelles Découvertes au Nord de la Grand Mer* (1753), in which he also stated his conviction about open water in the polar sea, a notion shared by **Samuel Engel**. His stature as one of the most important geographers of his time ensured that belief in the false Fonte account endured for another 40 years. *See also* NORTHWEST PASSAGE.

BUACHE DE LA NEUVILLE, JEAN-NICOLAS (1741–1825). French hydrographer and geographer and nephew of the celebrated **Philippe Buache**, Jean-Nicolas Buache de la Neuville became head of the Dépôt de Cartes et Plans for the hydrographic service of the Navy, a member of the Academy of Sciences, and later geographer royal to Louis XVI. He shared his uncle's fascination with the idea of a navigable passage across the top of North America, and particularly with the voyage of **Bartholomew de Fonte**, whose fictional tale he tried to reconcile with the explorations of **James Cook**. In 1781 he produced his Carte de la Partie Septentrionale du Globe, in which he presented waterways leading east from Sandwich Sound (**Prince**

William Sound) and **Cook Inlet**. Conscious of the British explorations in Baffin Bay and Hudson Bay, however, he left vague their precise Atlantic entrances.

Despite his highly speculative views about the Northwest Coast, which continued until a remarkably late date with his endorsement in 1790 of the veracity of another fictitious tale, that of **Ferrer Maldonado**, he was an experienced, respected, and talented cartographer as demonstrated by his production of five sets of three large charts of the Pacific Ocean to assist the preparations of the **Jean François de La Pérouse** Expedition. These provided La Pérouse with a fine cartographic summary of the ocean as it was understood to exist in the mid-1780s. To the charts he attached tables of latitude and longitude, and drew up a list of questions to guide the expedition's exploratory activities and to address some unresolved geographical issues.

Undaunted by La Pérouse's inability to find anything approaching Fonte's passage, and the explorer's open disdain for European cabinet geographers' belief in any such waterway, Bauche was quick to support, and introduce to a wider public, the story of the fictional voyage of Ferrer Maldonado, of which he had been made aware in 1789. On 13 November 1790 he read an extensive memoir to the Academy of Sciences in Paris in which he concluded that the Spanish navigator had left him in "no doubt . . . about the communication from Hudson Bay to the Frozen Sea. . . . I believe that we may accept as a constant fact the discovery . . . of that **Northwest Passage**, which has been sought for such a long time." As a result of Buache's presentation, Spain's Navy Minister, Antonio Valdés, ordered **Alejandro Malaspina** to explore the Northwest Coast in the summer of 1791.

BUCARELI BAY. Bucareli Bay, a significant water passage between Baker and Suemez Islands off the west coast of Prince of Wales Island in the **Alexander Archipelago**, was named by **Juan Francisco de la Bodega y Quadra** in honor of the viceroy of **New Spain**, **Antonio María de Bucareli** on 25 August 1775. After **Aleksei Chirikov**'s nearby landfall in 1741, Bodega was the first European to come anywhere near this part of the Northwest Coast, preceding **James Cook** by three years. He anchored in Puerto Santa Cruz, on the west coast of Suemez Island, made a chart and recorded the first descriptions of the **natives** of the area. Bodega and **Francisco**

Mourelle returned to the bay in May 1779 as members of the **Ignacio de Arteaga** Expedition. During an extended stopover of over six weeks, Mourelle undertook a small boat excursion that charted the entire sound, its principal islands and main arm, Trocadero Bay. He also ventured north into the Gulf of Esquibel. Of particular importance from the visit are the accounts of the Spaniards' relationship with the native peoples. They provide a unique record of contact because Bucareli Bay was the dividing line between the territories of the Kaigani **Haida** and the southern **Tlingit**, and members of both groups visited the Spanish ships in large numbers. The British traders **John Meares** and William Douglas were in the area in 1787 and, in August 1794, **George Vancouver** noted Cape Bartolome at the southern tip of Baker Island as signifying the entrance of the port "discovered by Senr. Quadra in 1775."

BUCARELI Y URSA, ANTONIO MARÍA DE (1717–1779). Spanish army officer and viceroy of **New Spain**, Antonio María de Bucareli arrived in America as **José de Gálvez** was preparing to leave, and throughout his tenure he shared the visionary royal inspector's concern for the defense of the viceroyalty's northern frontier and particularly for strengthening **Alta California**. His *Reglamento* of 1773 provided a framework of government for the new province. He sponsored the two expeditions of **Juan Bautista de Anza** that pioneered an overland route to the coast from Sonora; sent **Juan Manuel de Ayala** to explore **San Francisco** Bay; and encouraged a regular schedule of supply ships from **San Blas**.

Although supply of **California** was always his priority, he also oversaw the departure of three expeditions to the Northwest Coast— those of **Juan Pérez** in 1774; **Bruno de Hezeta** and **Juan Francisco de la Bodega y Quadra** in 1775; and **Ignacio de Arteaga** and Bodega in 1779. His long and precise instructions to Pérez became a model for orders issued to the commanders of all subsequent voyages. They covered the management of the ship and the keeping of "an exact logbook of all the navigational details." They also dealt with such subjects as how to handle meetings with foreign ships, the need to land and take possession, the identification of natural resources, and rules of engagement with native people. The latter were to be treated "affectionately and given . . . articles," their customs were to be noted, and any evidence of their paying tribute to a foreign power reported. Under no circumstances, except in self-defense, was force to be used against them, and Pérez was explicitly told not to "antagonize the Indians or forcibly take possession of their land." The only order missing was any clear requirement of Pérez and his officers to record their coastal observations on charts, which probably accounts for the lack of such maps (with one confusing exception, created after the voyage) from this first Spanish foray into the high northern latitudes.

BURNEY, JAMES (1750–1821). British naval officer, surveyor, and author, James Burney served on both the *Resolution* and the *Adventure* during **James Cook**'s Second Voyage to the Pacific. He kept a journal and became trained in surveying and cartography. This served him well on the Northwest Coast in 1778 and 1779 as a participant in Cook's Third Voyage in the *Discovery* under **Charles Clerke**. He transferred to the *Resolution* as first lieutenant on Clerke's death at Petropavlovsk in August 1779, shortly before the expedition ended its work in the North Pacific. By this time Burney had been responsible for numerous surveys, including charts of the entrance to **Nootka Sound** around Bligh Island, Sandwich Sound (**Prince William Sound**), and **Cook Inlet**. There are also rough charts of the expedition's progress toward the eastern **Aleutian Islands**, and the Alaskan coast in the **Bering Sea** from the **Alaska Peninsula** to beyond Cape Newnham. A more detailed sketch of the northwest part of **Unalaska** Island shows the June 1778 anchorage in Samgoonoodha Bay. Burney was also responsible for a significant amount of surveying in the Bering Sea from **Norton Sound**, through the **Bering Strait** and into the Arctic Ocean.

After his return to England, serious illness and his openly held republican views effectively ended his active naval career. He turned his attention to writing, and his major accomplishments were a five-volume *Chronological History of the Discoveries in the South Seas or Pacific Ocean* (1803–1817), and *A Chronological History of the North-Eastern Voyages of Discovery; and of the Early Eastern Navigations of the Russians* (1819). In the latter he sketched the story of the Russian advance across the continent, probing the Arctic Ocean and moving into the North Pacific. He covered much of the ground already covered by **William Coxe**, and his narrative ends with the **Joseph Billings** Expedition.

BUSTAMANTE Y GUERRA, JOSÉ (1759–1825). José Bustamante coauthored, with **Alejandro Malaspina**, the 1788 "Plan for
a Voyage" that became the Malaspina Expedition. Subsequently, he
commanded the *Atrevida* for the entire voyage and left a substantial
journal. It essentially confirms the Malaspina account found in his
journal and allied reports. On the Northwest Coast he showed a legitimate interest in the **native** people, their culture and activities, at
both Mulgrave and Nootka. At **Yakutat Bay** he was praised by his
colleagues for restraining himself from using force or causing blood-
shed in responding to local **Tlingit** provocation (stealing, attacks
on individuals, and hostage-taking). He wrote: "my every step was
guided by the principles of humanity and compassion," and he was
correct in suggesting that relations with the natives were hampered
by the Spaniards' lack of understanding of the complexities of their
society and customs.

– C –

CAAMAÑO, JACINTO (?–1759). Jacinto Caamaño came to **New
Spain** in 1789 with **Juan Francisco de la Bodega y Quadra** and
other officers to serve at the Naval Department of **San Blas**; they
were expected to strengthen the corps of officers and pilots engaged
in supply voyages to the Californias, and to undertake further exploration and uphold Spanish sovereignty on the Northwest Coast.

Only in San Blas for a few months, Caamaño sailed north on 15
April 1790 to support the reoccupation of **Friendly Cove** in **Nootka
Sound** by **Francisco de Eliza**. His time at Nootka appears uneventful
and he did not take part in the explorations into the **Strait of Juan de
Fuca** in either 1790 or 1791. In 1792, however, Caamaño was placed
in command of the *Aránzazu* and sailed north to Nootka as part of
Bodega's Limits Expedition. He was destined to undertake a final
search for the archipelago of San Lazaro and the Rio de los Reyes at
the entrance to the strait of the legendary **Bartholomew de Fonte**.

Bodega's instructions were disarmingly straightforward. Caamaño
was to sail to **Bucareli Bay**, explore its various inlets and then examine the coast between it and Nootka, taking care to explore all the principal channels and to determine the actual positions of the Estrecho

del Almirante Fonte. In his journal Caamaño observed that this strait was "considered by recent opinion as doubtful, even imaginary."

The *Aránzazu* set out from Nootka on 13 June 1792. Caamaño was accompanied by the experienced pilot **Juan Pantoja y Arriaga**, who had already been at Bucareli Bay in 1779, and the naturalist **José María Maldonado**. Pantoja y Arriaga improved some aspects of **Francisco Mourelle**'s chart of Bucareli Bay in a launch survey, which also proved that Fonte's passage could not be reached from that location. Caamaño then sailed down the west coast of Dall Island and across **Dixon Entrance** to Langara and Graham Island, where he made a chart and performed the **Act of Possession** in Parry Passage. He recrossed Dixon Entrance to Cabo de Muñoz Gocens (Cape Muzon) and, proceeding east, discovered Cordova Bay. Rounding Cape Chacon he entered the broad expanse of the Canal de Nuestra Señora del Carmen (Clarence Strait) and sailed north beyond 55° before fog, rain, and adverse winds forced him back; he was two degrees north of where Fonte had located the Rio de los Reyes and so considered his search was going nowhere. After a third crossing of Dixon Entrance to the **Queen Charlotte Islands**, where he sailed into McIntyre Bay before rounding the tip of Graham Island at Rose Point, he crossed Hecate Strait in search of the Canal de Principe between Banks and Pitt Islands, which **James Colnett** in 1787 had believed led into the Strait of Fonte. Emerging from Nepean Sound he entered Douglas Channel, Bocas y Brazos de Moniño, and was confident that this might well have been the long-searched-for passage until his second pilot, **Juan Martínez y Zayas**, who took the longboat on an excursion of over 50 miles, reported otherwise. With the summer season now advanced and the weather deteriorating, Caamaño decided to head for Nootka. Sailing inside Campania and Aristazabal Islands and out into Queen Charlotte Sound he concluded, as evidenced by an "Opinion" appended to his journal, that Fonte's tale of a passage was an absurdity and without foundation; there was "no hope of finding it in the archipelago between the parallels of 51° and 54° 46′ of latitude." He arrived at Nootka on 7 September.

Caamaño had undertaken an extensive survey in a ship completely unsuited to the task, but judicious use of the longboats ensured that the summer had been a success. His journal is extensive and his charts added much to Spanish knowledge of the coast. Also the work and observations of José Maldonado ensured a very important ethnographic and scientific legacy. Meeting with Caamaño at Nootka, **George Vancouver** received copies of the charts, and repaid the kindness by retaining or modifying most of Caamaño's place names when he surveyed the same area in 1793. Bodega was pleased with the voyage's results and considered the case of Fonte closed.

CABO SAN LUCAS. Cabo San Lucas is the southernmost point of **Baja California**. **Francisco de Ulloa** had rounded it for the first time on 7 November 1539 without giving it a name, but **Juan Rodríguez Cabrillo** referred to it as Punta de California as he negotiated it three years later, a reference to the use of that name as a joke by the men with Ulloa as they compared the barren landscape at **Hernán Cortés**'s Santa Cruz with the "earthly paradise" imagined in a popular Spanish novel. **Francisco Gali** introduced the name in 1584, taking it from a bay inside the point named by **Francisco Bolaños** in 1541.

CABRILLO, JUAN RODRÍGUEZ (ca. 1498–1543). Discoverer of the coast of **Alta California**, Juan Rodríguez Cabrillo led an expedition of two ships, the *San Salvador* and the *Victoria*, from **New Spain** during 1542. He thus extended north the coastal exploration of **Baja California** begun by **Francisco de Ulloa** two years earlier. His was one of a number of land and sea expeditions sent out after the conquest of the Aztec Empire to find the fabled Otro México (Other Mexico), a land of golden cities and unsurpassed wealth. There was also interest in the trend of the coast, but no expectation of finding a passage from the Pacific to the Atlantic, as the concept of a **Strait of Anian** had yet to be developed.

After service under **Hernán Cortés**, Cabrillo became a leading henchman of Pedro de Alvarado in the province of Guatemala stretching from southern Mexico to Panama. In 1536 Alvarado was given the responsibility of building ships for exploration in the Pacific, and in 1540 he arrived in Acapulco with a fleet of 13 vessels. Viceroy Antonio de Mendoza and Alvarado decided to divide the fleet to explore west into the Pacific (the voyage of López de Villalobos) and north along the coast.

After the death of Alvarado in battle against insurgent natives in 1541, Cabrillo was assigned by Mendoza for the northern voyage, setting sail from Navidad, near present-day Manzanillo, on 27 June 1542. By mid-September he had reached the Bay of Ensenada. On 28 September he sailed into San Diego Bay where he was met by friendly natives, who indicated that they had heard of other white men traveling far inland, presumably members of the Coronado expedition. After sighting the islands of San Clemente and Santa Catalina and entering Santa Monica Bay, Cabrillo proceeded through the Santa Barbara Channel past the islands of Santa Cruz and Santa Rosa as far as Point Conception. There adverse winds caused a retreat to San Miguel Island, named Isla de la Posesión, where Cabrillo injured himself jumping from a launch onto the rocky beach, fracturing his shoulder and leg. Sailing north again the ships reached Cape San Martin, where they became separated in a storm. Meeting up again somewhere north of **Monterey** on 15 November, in the vicinity of Point Año Neuvo, they finally turned back, noting Monterey Bay and Point Pinos before safely returning to San Miguel Island on 23 November. Six weeks later, on 3 January 1543, Cabrillo died of gangrene from his earlier injuries, but not before he had instructed his senior pilot **Bartolomé Ferrer** to continue the northern reconnaissance. He was buried on the island, which was immediately renamed Isla de Juan Rodríguez in his honor.

CALIFORNIA. When **Fortún Jiménez**, exploring for **Hernán Cortés**, landed in the bay of La Paz in 1533, he believed that he was on an island. Within a few years Spanish mariners were jokingly referring to the barren place as "California," a fictional island "at the right hand of the Indies, close to earthly paradise," described in a popular 16th-century romance of chivalry, *Las Sergas de Esplandían*, published perhaps as early as 1508 and readily available in Seville. Thereafter, the name was applied to the known coast and north into the unknown. When Spanish explorers reached **Alaska** at the end of the 18th century they referred to the entire littoral as the Costa Septentrional de California. Even though **Francisco de Ulloa** had explored to the head of the **Gulf of California** in 1539 and rounded **Cabo San Lucas** in 1540, thus proving that California was not an island, **Baja California** remained as such on some maps published as late as 1784.

In 1542 **Juan Rodríguez Cabrillo** entered San Diego Bay and became the first European to land on the coast of today's state of

California. Thirty-seven years later **Francis Drake** landed north of **San Francisco** and claimed **New Albion** for Elizabeth I. The initial period of coastal exploration ended with the voyage of **Sebastián Vizcaíno** in 1602–1603. Although he urged colonization of the region, settlement did not begin until the **Sacred Expedition** led by Gaspar de Portolá reached **San Diego** in 1769 and **Junípero Serra** founded the first mission. By 1823 the Franciscans had built a chain of 21 such missions as far north as Sonoma.

California became a province of independent Mexico in 1822, but central control over the area was never strong, and **Alta California** was conquered by the United States in the U.S.–Mexican War of 1846–1848. Gold was discovered in 1848, leading to a Gold Rush the next year and the entry of California into the Union as the 31st state in 1850.

CAMACHO Y BRENES, JOSÉ (?–1795). A senior pilot in Cadiz before coming to **San Blas** in 1778, José Camacho immediately commanded supply voyages to **Alta California**. He was then appointed to **Ignacio de Arteaga**'s *Princesa* for the 1779 expedition to the Northwest Coast. At **Bucareli Bay**, Camacho was in charge of one of the launches that undertook an extensive survey of the area. His diary demonstrates a particular interest in the **native** people encountered, and on his finished chart he made a little drawing (with an accompanying description) of **Tlingit** paddling a large canoe, the first documented Spanish image of ethnological interest from the coast. This chart was one of a series prepared for **Juan Francisco de la Bodega y Quadra** following the voyage that also included two general maps of the Northwest Coast, and detailed charts of the ports of Santiago (today **Port Etches** on **Hinchinbrook Island**) and Nuestra Señora de la Regla (today Port Chatham on the **Kenai Peninsula**). On the Santiago chart is another drawing and description, this time of two **Aleut/Alutiiq kayaks**.

Bodega was impressed by Camacho and selected him for a voyage to Peru, 1781–1782. For a time during the American Revolutionary War Camacho acted as commandant at San Blas, and was considered to lead the expedition that took **Esteban José Martínez** and **Gonzalo López de Haro** to Alaska in 1788. Thought too old for that assignment, he nevertheless commanded a voyage to the Philippines in 1793.

CAMPA COS, MIGUEL DE LA (fl. 1775). Franciscan priest at the College of San Fernando in Mexico City, Miguel de la Campa Cos was seconded as chaplain for the voyage of **Bruno de Hezeta** to the Northwest Coast in 1775. He sailed in the *Santiago* and left a substantial diary of the expedition. This diary is almost word for word the same as that of the second chaplain on the ship, **Benito de la Sierra**, except in one important section, and it is likely they wrote the account together. The unique section concerns a description of the **natives** in **Trinidad Bay**. Many of the entries relate to the progress of the ship, but there is a good description of activities in Trinidad Bay, including the **Act of Possession**, and at the Rada de Bucareli (Grenville Bay), the first documented landing in the state of **Washington**. He also recorded the discovery of the "beautiful large bay" which proved to be the mouth of the **Columbia River**, and mentioned the general consensus that it signified "some great river."

CAMPBELL, ROBERT (1808–1894). In the 1830s and 1840s the **Hudson's Bay Company** (HBC) made a concerted effort to expand westward from the Mackenzie River to blunt the advance of Russian competition from the coast of the Alaska Panhandle. In 1838 fur trader and explorer Robert Campbell crossed from the Dease/Liard watershed to the Stikine River where he attended a trade fair and met officials of the **Russian–American Company** (RAC) and their **Tlingit** allies. When an HBC/RAC agreement in 1839 gave the former access to the coast, Governor **George Simpson** directed Campbell to focus his activities on the northern branches of the Liard system, which ultimately led him to the Pelly River (1840) and in 1843 to its junction with the Lewes (now the Yukon). So confusing was the situation in the Rocky Mountain trench, Campbell thought initially that the Pelly must be the Colville River that flowed into the Arctic, but later conjectured that it might be the **Copper River** or even the legendary Cook's River. Unaware that his discovery would prove to be the great western-flowing river in the northwest of the continent, Campbell was reluctant to overextend his supply lines and to work in hostile territory. It was not until 1848 that he established Fort Selkirk at the Pelly/Lewes (Yukon) confluence. Finally from there, in 1851, he made his famous descent of the Yukon River to Fort Yukon, thus proving that his Pelly and **John Bell**'s Porcupine were tributaries of the same great river that flowed west through **Russian America** into the **Bering Sea**.

CAÑIZARES, JOSÉ (?–1793). José Cañizares came to **New Spain** in 1765, worked on the staff of **José de Gálvez**, and participated in the Sonora campaign to secure the northern perimeter of the viceroyalty. With the establishment of the Naval Department of **San Blas** in 1768, Cañizares began a career at the base that lasted for 25 years. During that time he made numerous supply voyages to **Alta California**, sailed to Peru and Manila, and was a member of the Spanish voyage of 1779 to the Northwest Coast.

He had hardly established himself at San Blas before he traveled to **Baja California** and then overland to Alta California as a member of the **Sacred Expedition**. Cañizares was later the first Spaniard to enter San Francisco Bay from the sea. In a launch he guided the *San Carlos* of **Juan Manuel de Ayala** through the Golden Gate on the night of 5 August 1775. He then proceeded to take a leading role in the survey of the bay and created the official chart. Ayala gave him full credit, even though the Plano del Puerto de San Francisco bears Ayala's name as commander of the expedition. In 1776 Cañizares returned to the bay for further survey work in support of the founding of San Francisco's presidio and mission.

In 1777 **Juan Francisco de la Bodega y Quadra** selected Cañizares to go with him to Peru to secure a ship for a voyage to the Northwest Coast and then, having been impressed by his competence, named him to the *Favorita* for the expedition that set out under **Ignacio de Arteaga** in 1779. Cañizares kept a full and useful record of the voyage, which is interesting in its description of the Spaniards' contacts with the **native** peoples, particularly the **Aleut/Alutiiq** of **Prince William Sound** where he and **Juan Pantoja y Arriaga** were directed by Arteaga to explore what was the northwest coast of **Hinchinbrook Island** during the expedition's stopover in Puerto de Santiago (**Port Etches**). From their reports Arteaga rightly concluded that the barrier formed by the Chugach Mountains offered no hope of a passage to the north exiting from the sound.

After the expedition's return to San Blas, Cañizares never again participated in a voyage to the far north. In 1793 Bodega wrote to the viceroy in support of a promotion for one whose services on the supply ships had "never been adequately compensated."

CANNIBALISM. Explorers and traders on the Northwest Coast brought with them preconceived ideas about savage life and civilized behavior. By and large they found the **natives** crude, untrustworthy, and ferocious, and their disgust with the "other" was symbolized by a universal distaste for the disfiguring **labret** of the northern tribes. Comments in over two dozen accounts, from **James Cook** and **John Meares** to **Esteban José Martínez**, **Alexander Walker**, and **Camille-Joseph de Roquefeuil**, also raise the specter of cannibalism, but the evidence appears circumstantial at best and was based largely upon the repetition of rumor, and the false assumption that the presence of human body parts proved gustatory practices. Whereas most of the visitors believed the natives of **Nootka Sound** to be cannibals (**Alejandro Malaspina** was an exception), the two Europeans who lived among them for a period of time, **John Mackay** and **John Jewitt**, made no such assertion. In general the visitors saw what they expected to find, but heads and cooked hands and arms were war trophies, preserved and put on display for dramatic effect.

Nevertheless, there remains clearer evidence in later 19th-century observations and anthropological studies, and a rereading of the 18th-century accounts, that the natives of the Northwest Coast did in fact engage in a profoundly spiritual ritualistic cannibalism in their dances and religious practices. But such a concept would have been foreign to the earlier, transient visitors of the exploration and fur-trading period, who were quick to accuse and condemn but were not equipped by either experience or linguistic ability to probe the depths and nuances of native culture and belief.

CAPE BLANCO. The westernmost point of the state of **Oregon**, the cape owes its name (not finally conferred upon the present point until the 19th century) to the Cabo Blanco de San Sebastián, reportedly seen at 42° N on 19 January 1603 by **Sebastián Vizcaíno** in the *San Diego*—"a cape of white earth close to some high sierras covered with snow," and to the Cabo Blanco recorded in Father **Antonio de la Ascensión**'s second-hand account of the second ship on the voyage, the *Tres Reyes*. Although the latter report noted that the coast trended to the east beyond the cape, which it does slightly, thus giving the sighting some credibility, there remains some dispute among scholars as to which headlands were actually seen by the crews on the two ships. **Bruno de Hezeta** reported seeing Cabo Blanco de San Sebastián on 20 August 1775, and **Juan Francisco de la Bodega y Quadra**, returning from southern Alaska in the *Sonora*, gave the name Cabo de los Diligencias to the present Cape Blanco on 27 September of the same year. **George Vancouver** called it Cape Orford on 24 April 1792.

CAPE FLATTERY. The northernmost point of the contiguous United States, Cape Flattery guards the southern entrance to the **Strait of Juan de Fuca** and was named by **James Cook** on 22 March 1778 as he sailed north from his landfall in **Oregon**. He was looking for a safe harbor, but the coast in winter, notorious in the days of sail for its stormy and hazardous conditions, offered him little hope of coming near to shore. Nevertheless, off Cape Flattery he was able to come close enough to see an island (Tatoosh Island) between which "and the northern extreme of the land, there appeared to be a small opening, which flattered us with the hope of finding a harbour. These hopes were lessened as we drew nearer. . . . On this account I called the point of land to the north of it Cape Flattery."

There was some confusion amongst subsequent explorers as to what headland Cook had actually identified. This was largely because fur trader **Charles Duncan** called it Cape Classet (the name for the **Makah** natives of the area) on his chart made in August 1788. The name Flattery was transferred some 15 miles down the coast to what is now Cape Alava. Duncan also made a drawing of the cape in which he identified Pinnacle Rock and Green (Tatoosh) Island. This discovery led many to identify it with the "exceeding high Pinacle or spired Rocke" described by **Juan de Fuca**, although Fuca placed his rock on the northern side of the strait. In 1792 **George Vancouver**, who had been with Cook, "anxiously looked out for the point which Captain Cook had distinguished by the name of Cape Flattery," and determined that "Classet is the point, with an island lying off it." This landmark has since retained the name Flattery.

CAPE MENDOCINO. The most westerly point of North America in the lower latitudes, Cape Mendocino served for almost 200 years as the dividing line between the known reality of the coast of **California** to the south, and speculative geography to the north.

Cabo Mendocino appears on the map Americae Sive Nove Orbis published by **Abraham Ortelius** in his atlas *Theatrum Orbis Terrarum* in 1587. The coast beyond the cape turns dramatically to the east to create a passage between the Pacific and the Atlantic. On subsequent maps of this early period, the cape was placed variously between latitudes 41° and 43° N and was confused with Trinidad Head, which was the case with **Sebastián Rodríguez Cermeño** in 1595. Cape Mendocino is the oldest name of any geographical feature on the Northwest Coast to have survived in the same general location, although its position was not fixed with any precision until **Alejandro Malaspina** recorded it at latitude 40° 29' N on 6 September, 1791, a mere 2' off its actual location.

The origin of the name is shrouded in mystery, although Father **Antonio de la Ascensión**, who sailed with **Sebastián Vizcaíno** (1602–1603), maintained that it was named after the first viceroy of **New Spain**, Antonio de Mendoza, as early as the 1540s. Given that the name did not appear on maps of the coast for another 40 years, however, this seems unlikely. A more obvious vice regal candidate is Lorenzo Suárez de Mendoza (1580–1583) but use of the adjective form of his name makes even this opinion suspect.

CAPE PRINCE OF WALES. Named on 9 August 1778 by **James Cook** as "being the western extremity of all America hitherto known," Cape Prince of Wales is at the end of the Seward Peninsula, **Alaska**. Fog prevented it from being seen by **Vitus Bering** when, in August 1728, he negotiated what is today the **Bering Strait** during the first **Kamchatka Expedition**.

CARDERO, JOSÉ (1766–ca. 1810). As a result of two visits to the Northwest Coast in 1791 and 1792 with the **Alejandro Malaspina** Expedition, mariner and artist José Cardero arguably made the most significant contribution to the artistic record of the region during the last quarter of the 18th century. There are over 50 drawings from **California** to **Alaska**—general views, portraits of **natives**, **artifacts** and coastal profiles.

Cardero never seems to have had any formal artistic education and he joined the expedition as a servant to the officers on the *Descubierta*. A talent for drawing was recognized and increasingly appreciated, however, as the expedition reached Ecuador and moved towards **New Spain**. When one of the professional **artists** left the ships in Peru and the other would only execute botanical drawings, Cardero was pressed into service to draw general views as well as birds and fish. He had completed over 60 drawings before the expedition reached Acapulco. Malaspina sent word to Spain for two replacement artists, but as these could not arrive in time for the expedition's northern excursion in the summer of 1791, **Tomás de Suría** was recruited from the Academy of San Carlos in Mexico City, and Cardero was assigned to continue his role as *dibuxante*, someone who draws but who is not a trained artist. The influence of Suría on Cardero is difficult to gauge but the difference between them is obvious. Suría was a skilled artist who took artistic license to make his work more interesting; Cardero was less confident and more of a draughtsman, but his work has an authenticity about it that gives it great credibility, as he recorded faithfully, with much detail, what he saw. As a result his views, such as those of the ships at anchor at **Mulgrave** in 1791 and of **Alcalá Galiano**'s ships in the San Juan Islands, in 1792, are almost photographic in nature.

In Alaska in 1791 he drew a dozen pictures including two different **Tlingit** burial sites. His "Sculpture and Graves of the Chief's family in the Port of Mulgrave" is particularly important for ethnologists and was praised by Malaspina. But his images of people are much weaker than those of Suría. On the Canadian west coast, Cardero's "Port of Nootka" gives **historians** an excellent view of the battery and settlement, and his two portraits of native women, one entitled "Woman of Nutka," are very fine and a vast improvement over what he had accomplished at Mulgrave. His full-length "Indian Man and Woman, Chiefs of Nootka" is probably a portrait of Chief **Maquinna** and his wife, and contrasts well with the better-known drawing by Suría. From the stopover in **Monterey** 16 drawings by Cardero have survived; they include descriptive views of the presidio, a copy of the "Reception of the Count of La Pérouse" at the **Carmel Mission** by **Gaspard Duché de Vancy**, a portrait of a soldier and his wife, and a number of birds.

When Malaspina and the viceroy, the **Count of Revillagigedo**, decided that an expedition to continue the exploration of the **Strait of Juan de Fuca** was necessary in 1792, Cardero was assigned to the *Sutil* under **Cayetano Valdés**. He left an extant legacy more varied than that of the artists from the **Vancouver Expedition**. It included views such as those of the small boat surveys in Knight and Loughborough Inlets, the notable "Settlement of Majoa" at the northern end of **Vancouver Island**, and various portraits of the natives encountered. The "Chief of the Point of Langara" and the "Indian of the Northwest Coast" are particularly impressive, and all of the portraits display an attention to detail important to ethnologists. Of special interest also are the drawings of a wooden plank, whose hieroglyphics might represent a tide chart, found in Toba Inlet, and the prayer box of Chief Maquinna of Nootka Sound, in which the chief incarcerated himself to commune with the supernatural in preparation for a whale hunt. The distinctive Malaspina Gallery on Gabriola Island off Vancouver Island, near present-day Nanaimo, was obviously drawn by Cardero because it was later "improved" for engraving by Fernando Brambila, but the original has not survived. In 2004 a previously unknown view of the ships in the islands north of Desolation Sound was found in Seville, suggesting that other drawings from Cardero's visits to the Northwest Coast might still exist. After this return to Spain and a brief period in Madrid working on preparation of the drawings of the Malaspina Expedition for publication, he undertook administrative duties in the Navy and never again seems to have employed his skills as an artist.

CARMEL MISSION. Junípero Serra founded the second of the **Alta California** missions at **Monterey** on 3 June 1770, naming it San Carlos Borromeo. The following year he moved it to the nearby Carmel River valley to escape from what he regarded as interference in religious affairs by the commander of the presidio, **Pedro Fages**. The original church in Monterey, rebuilt in 1775 and replaced again in 1794, continued to be served by the Carmel Franciscans. Used by the royal governors, it was known as the Royal Chapel of Monterey.

The fine example of mission architecture existing today in Carmel is a far cry from the collection of adobe buildings visited by **Juan Francisco de la Bodega y Quadra** in 1775 and 1779, and members of the **Jean François de La Pérouse**, **Alejandro Malaspina**, and

George Vancouver expeditions in 1786, 1791, and 1792 respectively. Their journals provide interesting descriptions of the little settlement, and the drawings of **José Cardero** and **John Sykes** show the various structures around a central square with native dwellings beyond. A large cross stood in front of the church. The earliest known drawing was by **Gaspard Duché de Vancy** in 1786; it showed the fathers greeting La Pérouse. The original was lost in the 19th century, but both Cardero and **Tomás de Suría** copied it and their drawings still exist.

CARRASCO, JUAN (fl. 1784–1800). He came to the Naval Department of **San Blas** in 1784 from the Philippines, and was listed as a junior pilot when he accompanied **Esteban José Martínez** to establish an outpost in **Nootka Sound** in 1789. That summer he went with **José María Narváez** to look for the **Strait of Juan de Fuca** as a result of which **Barkley Sound** on the west coast of **Vancouver Island** was originally named Puerto de Carrasco.

In 1790 he returned to the Northwest Coast and was an active participant in the 1790–1791 explorations into the Strait of Juan de Fuca. Carrasco set out from Nootka with **Manuel Quimper** on 31 May 1790, and it was he, sent out in a longboat from Dungeness, who discovered Puerto de la Bodega y Quadra, present-day Port Discovery, and Protection Island, which was initially named after him. These names were changed by **George Vancouver**. On the same trip he did not go far enough east to identify the opening to **Puget Sound**, but later, with **Gonzalo López de Haro**, he undertook the survey of Puerto de Cordova, now Esquimalt Bay. In 1791 Carrasco accompanied Narváez in the *Santa Saturnina* as part of the **Francisco de Eliza** Expedition. They were responsible for a chart of **Clayoquot Sound**, and a further survey of Barkley Sound. Their most important contribution, however, was their exploration into the present-day Gulf of Georgia, called the Gran Canal de la Nuestra Señora del Rosario, which resulted in the creation of the notable *Carta que comprehende los interiors y veril de la Costa desde los 48° de Latitud N. hasta los 50° examinados escrupulosamente por el Teniente de Navio de la Real Armada Don Francisco Eliza, Comandante del Paquebot des SM San Carlos . . . y Goleta Santa Saturnina . . . .*, one of the most important charts of early Northwest Coast exploration.

After this significant contribution, Carrasco returned to San Blas. In 1792 he was assigned to sail north again with orders from the viceroy, the **Count of Revillagigedo**, to tell **Juan Francisco de la Bodega y Quadra** not to consider a retreat from Nootka in his meetings with George Vancouver. Carrasco only got the message to Bodega in **Monterey**, however; fortunately for the viceroy, Bodega had actually refused to surrender Nootka. Until well into the 19th century, Carrasco worked as a pilot in San Blas, surveying the Pacific Coast of **New Spain** and commanding supply vessels to the **California** provinces.

CARTOGRAPHY. In 1731 the French cartographer **Joseph Nicolas de l'Isle** presented a map to the Russian government that represented what he knew about the North Pacific and the relationship of Asia to America. It was drawn to help **Vitus Bering** find his way to America, but the expansive blank between **California**, which had recently regained its peninsular status, and the east coast of Siberia and **Kamchatka**, also shown correctly, would have done little to help the Danish-born navigator. It did reflect, however, a realistic portrait of the Northwest Coast; nothing was known about it.

A map drawn by **Sven Waxell**, based on Bering's voyage and dating from 1742–1743, was able to establish the relationship of Bering's landfall at **Kayak Island** to **Bering Island** and Kamchatka, but confusingly continued the continental shore that is the **Alaska Peninsula** too far west along the **Aleutian Islands**. A little more accurate in this respect was the map from **Aleksei Chirikov**, and it is not difficult to find in these maps—and others circulating in St. Petersburg in the 1740s—the origin of **Gerhardt Friedrich Müller**'s famous map, drawn in 1753 and published in 1754, with its large bulbous peninsula. This remarkably accurate map—given that much of the western Alaska coast up to the location of the sighting of America in the **Bering Strait** by **Mikhail Gvozdev** in 1732 is drawn in a dotted line as speculative—was produced to refute the extraordinarily "fanciful" maps of de l'Isle and **Philippe Buache**, produced in 1752. These creations, designed to promote the so-called truth of the fictional voyage of **Bartholomew de Fonte** in the context of Russian discoveries, gained credence when they were used by another French mapmaker, Robert de Vaugondy, to illustrate Denis Diderot's *Encyclopédie*.

By the end of the 1770s, the fur-hunting voyages to the Aleutians, particularly that of **Stepan Glotov** during the years 1759–1762 (which had produced the map of **Petr Shishkin**) and the voyage of **Petr Krenitsyn** and **Mikhail Levashov**, 1767–1768, had developed for the Russians a clear idea of the Aleutians and their relationship to Kamchatka and the Northwest Coast visited by Bering and Chirikov. This understanding is reflected in a map published by **Peter Simon Pallas** in 1781, which was the first to make use of information also received by the Russians from **James Cook**. By combining his own surveys with knowledge received from the Russians, Cook's own charts, published in 1784, gave the coastlines of Alaska a completely new and authoritative definition.

Taking Cook's chart together with those of **Juan Francisco de la Bodega y Quadra** and **Francisco Mourelle** and **Bruno de Hezeta** from 1775 and 1779, it is clear that the main outlines of the coast had now been fixed, although this was not fully appreciated until Mourelle's 1775 chart, published by **Daines Barrington** in 1781, could be used in conjunction with those published in Cook's atlas.

The fur traders who arrived on the Northwest Coast in the 1780s tended not to provide particularly illuminating maps, although **George Dixon** and **James Colnett** were an exception. **John Meares** reported the insularity of **Kodiak** Island, **Charles Barkley** found the **Strait of Juan de Fuca** and **Robert Gray** the **Columbia River**. Working south to the **Queen Charlotte Islands** and probing the **Alexander Archipelago**, **James Shields** produced an excellent summary map of the northern coast for **Aleksandr Baranov** in 1797. As information filtered back into the hands of **Alexander Dalrymple** and others, the foremost mapmaker of the day, **Aaron Arrowsmith**, was able to publish, in 1794, an updated version of his massive world map initially produced in 1790. It included an accurate representation of the Northwest Coast as it appeared before the final efforts of the Spanish explorers and **George Vancouver** around **Vancouver Island**, and the work of the English navigator in the Alexander Archipelago could become known.

From their base at **Nootka Sound** the Spanish explored the **Strait of Juan de Fuca** during 1790–1792 and proved the insularity of Vancouver Island. **Manuel Quimper**'s 1790 map drawn by **Gonzalo López de Haro** and the large Carta de Comprehende reflecting the discoveries of **José María Narváez** and the **Francisco de Eliza** Expedition of 1791, paved the way for **Dionisio Alcalá Galiano** and **George Vancouver** in 1792. Colored manuscript maps by both explorers exist to show the nature of their cooperation that summer, something that was lost in the publication of the charts in 1798 (Vancouver) and 1802 (Alcalá Galiano). The Vancouver Expedition's meticulous work in 1793 and 1794 continued to reveal the details of the coast, and his surveys of the Alexander Archipelago preceded those begun a few years later by the Russians.

There remained numerous little details to be filled in but the publication of Vancouver charts, which incorporated the sum total of experiences of so many navigators, spectacularly ended the first era of discovery and exploration that began so bleakly with Joseph Nicolas de l'Isle some 67 years earlier. When studied with the maps of the discoveries of **Alexander Mackenzie** (1798–1801), **Lewis and Clark** (1810–1814), and **David Thompson** (1813–1814), Vancouver's charts provide a clear picture of the last temperate coast to be placed on the world map and its relationship to Asia and the rest of the North American continent. *See also* NAVIGATION; RUNNING SURVEY.

CATHERINE II (1729–1796). Empress of Russia from 1762, Catherine II combined a devotion to art, literature, science and politics with some liberal reforms. One of Europe's enlightened despots, she founded the Academy of Letters in 1763 and encouraged the Academy of Sciences to sponsor publications that celebrated Russian history.

Very early in her reign she demonstrated an interest in the new discoveries in the North Pacific. She supported the Chichagov expedition (1765) that sought a Northeast Passage to Japan and China, and maintained an abiding interest in expanding trade with both nations. In order to consolidate the advances made by Russian fur traders in the **Aleutian Islands**, with their promise of annexation of new lands with new subjects, she dispatched the **Petr Krenitsyn** and **Mikhail Levashov** Expedition to explore the region. After the publication of **James Cook**'s journal and charts, which she immediately ordered translated and published in Russian, Catherine took a series of steps to maintain Russian sovereignty in the area. The aborted **Mulovskii Expedition** and the **Joseph Billings** Expedition, and the provision of possession plaques to be placed along the coast by Russian fur traders citing "prior discovery" were the most obvious of these. Catherine lavished honors on the leading traders, allowing them access to government stores and deferment of payment until their ships returned home. Her belief in laissez-faire economics, however, caused her to reject the pleadings of **Grigorii Shelikhov** for a monopoly over the American trade to facilitate settlement and colonization. Until she died in 1796, the Empress preferred the benefits of trade to the financial burdens of actual occupation.

CAVENDISH, THOMAS (1560–1592). English navigator and buccaneer, Thomas Cavendish circumnavigated the globe in the years 1586–1588. In 1587 he ravaged Spanish shipping off the Pacific coast of the Americas, as **Francis Drake** had done a decade earlier. Off the Mexican coast in the autumn, he learned of the imminent arrival of the **Manila galleon** *Santa Ana*, said to be carrying an abundance of gold in addition to her regular cargo of silk and other valuable commodities. Cavendish's *Desire* and *Content* cruised the coast off **Cabo San Lucas** until they finally intercepted the 700-gun vessel on 14 November 1587. The capture took six hours and looting went on for six days. As Cavendish headed across the Pacific in the *Desire* (the *Content* sailed north along the coast of **Baja California**, never to be heard from again), the survivors of the *Santa Ana*, who had been put ashore, rescued the ship and repaired her enough to reach Acapulco. This proven threat of English piracy encouraged the authorities in Mexico City to reinterest themselves in finding safe harbors along the **California** coast for galleon use in an emergency, and led to the explorations of **Sebastián Rodríguez Cermeño**, 1595, and **Sebastián Vizcaíno**, 1602–1603.

CERMEÑO, SEBASTIÁN RODRÍGUEZ. Having survived the looting of the *Santa Ana* by **Thomas Cavendish** in 1587, Cermeño assumed command of the **Manila galleon**, *San Agustín*, in 1595 with orders to search for safe harbors on the **California** coast. Sighting land near Trinidad Head, but discouraged by the rocky shoreline, he sailed south and anchored in **Drake's Bay**, north of **San Francisco**. Fearful of taking the clumsy galleon too close to shore, he used a launch to expedite further exploration. Nevertheless, a severe storm drove the *San Agustín* aground on 30 November 1595, spilling her precious cargo of beeswax, ceramics, and crates of silk. The crew explored the immediate vicinity of the bay, but found nothing of note. Hastily christening an enlarged launch *Santa Buenaventura*, Cermeño boarded the survivors and headed south surveying and mapping as he went, despite the considerable protests of his companions. On 9 December 1595 he was the first navigator, seven years before **Sebastián Vizcaíno**, to note **Monterey** Bay, naming it Bahia de San Pedro. When the group reached the Isla de Cedros, scurvy had begun to take hold, forcing Cermeño to stop his survey and sail directly to Acapulco. Despite his useful survey work, Cermeño was reprimanded for losing the *San Agustín*, and a result of his tale of misery and survival was a royal order prohibiting Manila galleons from being used for exploration.

CEVALLOS, CIRIACO (1764–1816). After service in the American Revolutionary War in the early 1780s, Ciriaco Cevallos showed an unusual aptitude for astronomical and geodesic observation during the 1788–1789 expedition of Antonio de Córdoba to the Straits of Magellan. This experience gained him an invitation to join the **Alejandro Malaspina** Expedition.

In early 1791, joining the voyage late at Acapulco, Cevallos traveled with **José Espinosa** and brought two new Arnold chronometers and a fixed Ellicot pendulum to undertake gravity experiments. He was just in time to join **José Bustamante** in the *Atrevida* for the Northwest Coast campaign. His skill and experience in astronomy and mathematics proved invaluable during the summer of 1791, as it did for the rest of the voyage. Cevallos worked with Malaspina himself with the pendulum both at Port **Mulgrave** and at **Nootka Sound**. Later, in South America, the artist Juan Ravenet drew a picture of the two of them involved in one of their many gravity experiments aimed at substantiating the fact that gravitational force increased with latitude from the Equator. At Nootka, Malaspina entrusted Cevallos and Espinosa with an important survey of the entire sound, its various waterways, and links to the open sea. The result of their work was the definitive Spanish chart of the region. At the end of the voyage Cevallos was one of three officers presented to Carlos IV in the company of Malaspina and Bustamante, and he was invited to help

Felipe Bauza in organizing the mass of documents and astronomical calculations that were needed to accompany the narrative and artistic legacy of the voyage.

CHAMISSO, ADELBERT VON (1781–1838). As a naturalist and ethnographer on the **Otto von Kotzebue** Expedition that visited **Alaska** (1816 and 1817) and **California** (1816), Adelbert von Chamisso's descriptions of **native** peoples on the Northwest Coast and Pacific Islands, and his work on their languages remain extremely important. His research also extended to zoology, geology, and observations on climate. His encounters with the peoples of the Pacific were profoundly influenced by Jean-Jacques Rousseau; as a result he reserved a special sympathy for the Aleuts, whose **Russian–American Company** overlords he wrote "disregard, according to established custom, the rights of a defenseless people to their native liberty." He wrote of their wretched slavery and poverty, and felt that they would soon be extinct.

In addition to his interest in Eskimo and **Aleut** culture, his Alaskan experience resulted in the collection of botanical specimens and descriptions of whales in the **Bering Sea**. He returned from the voyage with a collection of approximately 2,500 plants, including 69 from the area around San Francisco Bay. His work on this collection established his reputation as a scientist, and in 1819 he was awarded an honorary doctorate at the University of Berlin and became director of the Royal Botanical Garden in that city. At his death his personal herbarium amounted to over 10,000 species. Today it is mostly to be found in the St. Petersburg Academy of Sciences. Chamisso Island, in **Kotzebue Sound**, is now a nature reserve.

Although his "Remarks and Observations" were published in Volume Two of Kotzebue's *Voyage of Discovery*, Chamisso never felt that they adequately reflected his work. His own account, *Voyage around the World*, appeared in German in 1836, but in English not until 150 years later. Chamisso was widely acknowledged in his day for his contributions to science by such luminaries as Charles Darwin, Georges de Cuvier and Alexander von Humboldt.

CHINOOK. At the time of contact with the Chinook, the **Native Americans** who make up a number of tribes in the region of the lower **Columbia River,** estimates put their number at about 2,000. They are part of the Coast Salish language family with strong cultural links to the people of **Puget Sound** and the Gulf of Georgia. Like other Northwest Coast native groups theirs was a hierarchical society with chiefs, commoners, and slaves, and the importance of fishing and preserving salmon was central to their annual activities, ceremonies, and mythologies. The topography and climate led to a less harsh existence than that of the northern tribes. Dwellings were partly subterranean, cedar-planked, multifamily homes, and the surrounding countryside provided a good assortment of roots, berries, and animals to supplement their diet of fish. The Chinook had long used their position at the mouth of the Columbia, and upriver as far as The Dalles, to become the middlemen traders of the region, and the link between the coast and the interior. Increasingly, in the years following the visits of the **Lewis and Clark Expedition** and **David Thompson**, they became a key component in the trading system that brought an exchange of articles from as far east as the edge of the Great Plains and the upper Northwest Coast in Alaska. However, the men of the **Hudson's Bay Company** were continually frustrated by their lack of success in turning the Chinook into hunters or farmers.

CHIRIKOV, ALEKSEI (1703–1748). A participant in both of the **Kamchatka Expeditions** of **Vitus Bering** and a key assistant to Bering in organizing the ambitious **Great Northern Expedition**, Aleksei Chirikov taught navigation at the Naval Academy in St. Petersburg before being assigned to Bering's first expedition in January 1725. He was aboard the *St. Gabriel* when, in 1728, Bering sailed through the **Bering Strait**, and crossed the Arctic Circle. Chirikov challenged Bering's decision to turn around when they reached 67°18′ N, wishing to see if the coast tended towards the east—towards America—or towards the west, which would take them to the mouth of the Kolyma River. Nevertheless, he remained close to Bering and returned to St. Petersburg with him in 1730.

Chirikov accompanied Bering as he made his way across Siberia in 1733–1736. In 1740 he asked for command of the sloop *Bolsheretsk*, on which **Martin Spanberg** had sailed to Japan the previous year, to search for the American coast north and east from **Kamchatka**. But Bering refused, preferring Chirikov's involvement in planning the voyage Bering himself intended to make the following year. On 8 September 1740, commanding the *St. Paul*, Chirikov left Okhotsk for Avacha Bay accompanied by Bering in the *St. Peter*. They arrived a month later and sat out the winter.

The *St. Peter* and *St. Paul* sailed in search of America on 4 June 1741. Chirikov's complement of men included the expedition's astronomer, **Louis de l'Isle de la Croyère**. After a fruitless search for the fictional island of **Gamaland** the two ships were separated by stormy and foggy weather at approximately 50° N, 178° E. Thereafter, Chirikov proceeded to make his own way to America. He reached the coast off Baronoff Island on 15 July. Sailing north with the intention of making "a careful survey of a part of the American coast" he searched for safe anchorage. On 17 July near Yakobi Island he sent an 11-man party ashore carrying gifts for any **natives** they might encounter. The group did not return and neither did another of four men sent out six days later. Chirikov was unsuccessful in communicating effectively with two native canoes that approached the *St. Paul*, and the loss of the ship's launches meant that no more landings were possible. The Russians were probably killed or captured by the **Tlingit**. In later years stories were told about blond, blue-eyed natives on the coast, but exactly what happened no one will ever know.

Depressed by his misfortune, Chirikov consulted his fellow officers and the decision was made to head home to Kamchatka. While coasting off Baronoff and Kruzov Islands Chirikov had seen the dramatic cone of **Mount Edgecumbe**, which he named Mount St. Lazaria, and north of **Cross Sound** he sighted the Fairweather Range. On 27 July he was off **Yakutat Bay** and on 1 August sighted the **Kenai Peninsula** and the entrance to **Cook Inlet**. Sailing southwest he passed all the major landmarks—Afgonak Island, **Kodiak** Island, and the **Shumagin** group off the **Alaska Peninsula**. Past the eastern **Aleutian Islands** Chirikov anchored off Adak Island on 9 September and encountered **Aleut** natives, whom he felt resembled Tartars, and engaged in trade. He noted that they drove a hard bargain and were particularly interested in knives.

As they continued, heavy seas, fog, rain, and snow made progress difficult and the **health** of many men deteriorated daily. In the last month before they landed in Avacha Bay on 10 October, six men died, including de l'Isle de la Croyère. Chirikov was so ill he had to be carried ashore. On 18 October, however, he completed his report to the Admiralty with its first descriptions of the Northwest Coast and the Aleuts. Commenting on the Aleutian Islands, he stated that the rocky shores and constant fog made **navigation** extremely hazardous.

In May 1742 Chirikov sailed east again, determined to continue his explorations and to find Bering, who had not returned to Kamchatka as expected. He crossed through the Aleutians perhaps as far east as Amchitka in the Rat Islands group, and set his course for home north of the Aleutian chain. Unknown to him the survivors from the *St. Peter* were busy building their escape ship when Chirikov passed **Bering Island** on 22/23 June. At the beginning of July Chirikov returned to Petropavlovsk and by August 1742 he was in Okhotsk, where he assumed that Bering was lost and took command of the expedition. The next year word came from St. Petersburg that there were to be no more voyages and so the Great Northern Expedition came to an end. In poor health Chirikov returned to the capital in 1746 and died in Moscow two years later.

CHORIS, LOUIS (1795–1828). An artist with the round-the-world expedition led by **Otto von Kotzebue** in the *Riurik*, 1815–1818, Choris was one of the most prolific **artists** who visited the **Aleutian Islands** and the **Bering Sea**, and his work is particularly admired for its originality and realism. He was only 20 years old and recently enrolled at the Academy of Fine Arts in St. Petersburg when invited to join the expedition. The *Riurik* reached **Kamchatka** in July 1816, proceeded through the **Bering Strait** and penetrated **Kotzebue Sound**. Choris produced portraits of individual and family groups of natives on the Chukotskii Peninsula and **St. Lawrence Island**, as well as drawings of **artifacts**. He sketched the northern fur seal rookeries in the **Pribilof Islands**. Most important, however, are his drawings from **Unalaska Island**—his fine portraits of **Aleut** natives (with great attention to costume detail), artifacts and kayaks, birds, coastal profiles, and two views of Unalaska Bay looking both out from and towards the village of Illiuliuk. Choris was there in both 1816 and 1817. Important also are his 11 drawings from his visit to **San Francisco** in October 1816; they include the mission and presidio, a sea lion, a grizzly bear, native portraits, and a native boat in the harbor. After the voyage he lived in Paris and became a skilled lithographer, preparing his drawings for two publications: *Voyage pittoresque autour du monde* (1822) and *Vues et paysages des regions equinoxiales* (1826). A third, *Receuil de têtes et de costumes des habitants de la Russie*, was published after his death.

CLARK, WILLIAM. *See* LEWIS AND CLARK EXPEDITION.

CLAYOQUOT SOUND. The population of Clayoquot Sound, the large, island-filled bay on the west coast of **Vancouver Island**, probably numbered over 4,000 at the time of contact. It was the home of the powerful chief **Wickaninnish**, who was one of the dominant figures in the maritime **fur trade** at the end of the 18th century. The village of Opitsat on Meares Island, opposite the present-day settlement of Tofino, was considered the largest native settlement on the entire Northwest Coast. The sound was first visited in 1786 by fur trader **James Hanna** on his second voyage to America. **Charles William Barkley** traded in the sound in July 1787, and **John Meares** described his visit to Wickaninnish in June 1788 in his *Voyages Made in the Years 1788 and 1789, from China to the North West Coast of America*. Meares referred to his anchorage as Port Cox in recognition of his sponsor, **John Henry Cox**, of Macao, and it is for this reason that this name appears in the conventions that settled the **Nootka Crisis**.

Once established in nearby **Nootka Sound** in 1790 the Spanish quickly became familiar with the sound and its powerful chief. In 1789 **José María Narváez** visited the place en route to investigate the entrance to **Juan de Fuca Strait**, and in 1790 **Manuel Quimper** did the same thing. In 1791 the Archipielago de Clayocuat was surveyed in detail by **Francisco de Eliza**, who created a comprehensive summary chart.

CLERKE, CHARLES (1741–1779). A member of John Byron's expedition around the world, 1764–1766, Charles Clerke sailed on all three of **James Cook**'s voyages to the Pacific. Clerke's description of the natives at the southern tip of South America from the Byron voyage spawned the legend of Patagonia as a land of giants.

On his return from Cook's Second Voyage Clerke was advanced to the rank of commander, and a year later appointed to take charge of the *Discovery*. Leaving England on 1 August 1776 he caught up with the *Resolution* at Cape Town in November. Thereafter, the two ships sailed together, crossing the South Pacific en route to the Northwest Coast and the **Bering Sea**. Following the death of Cook in **Hawaii** on 14 February 1779, Clerke assumed command of the expedition and led it back to the Arctic to test again whether or not there was a route home via the elusive **Northwest Passage**. By this time he was a dying man and he did not survive the two-month voyage from **Kamchatka** to **Icy Cape**—the ships reached latitude 70°33′ N—and back to Petropavlovsk (19 June–24 August). He died at sea on 22 August 1779 but was buried ashore with full military honors in the cemetery of the Russian settlement. In 1787 **Jean François de La Pérouse** replaced the plaque affixed to a tree at the site with an engraved copper plate, and in 1805 the Russian circumnavigator, **Ivan Kruzenshtern**, also paid his respects by erecting a small monument.

COLNETT, JAMES (ca. 1752–1806). James Colnett was one of the earliest and most important fur traders on the Northwest Coast. He had sailed on **James Cook**'s Second Voyage to the Pacific. In 1786, after the American Revolutionary War, he received the Admiralty's permission to assume command of the *Prince of Wales* belonging to **Richard Cadman Etches**'s King George's Sound Company. His officers included surgeon-botanist **Archibald Menzies** and **James Johnstone**, both of whom would later play a central role in the **George Vancouver** Expedition. Colnett accompanied **Charles Duncan** in the *Princess Royal* to trade for furs on the Northwest Coast and spent the summer of 1787 working his way south from **Prince William Sound** (PWS) to the **Queen Charlotte Islands**, making rough charts and learning that the most effective way to trade was to hold off the coast and let the natives bring their canoes and precious furs out to the ship. After meeting up in **Nootka Sound** with Duncan, who had concentrated on the lower coast, and wintering over in the **Sandwich Islands**, Colnett returned to PWS and ran down the coast for more work in the Queen Charlotte Islands. Exploring off the **Alexander Archipelago** and later in Hecate Strait he became so aware of the numerous islands off the mainland that he rightly doubted that he had seen the continent at all.

Colnett reached Canton in November 1788. There, over the winter 1788–1789, he became involved with **John Meares** and with the formation of a new company, the Associated Merchants of London and India Trading to the Northwest Coast of America, in which Meares joined forces with Etches. When his ship was sent home to England with a cargo of tea, another, the *Argonaut*, was purchased, and Colnett was instructed to take her, in company with the *Princess Royal*, to Nootka Sound. He had on board enough Chinese artisans, equipment, and supplies to build ships and establish a permanent settlement (to be called Fort Pitt) as a base for fur-trading operations. On arrival at Nootka in early July 1789, Colnett found **Esteban José Martínez** already well-established in **Friendly Cove** and willing to confront the English traders in defense of Spanish sovereignty. Their subsequent clash resulted in the arrest of the trading vessels and Colnett being taken to **San Blas** where he was held in nearby Tépic until July 1791.

Although under the terms of his release Colnett promised not to resume his trading activities, he did just that by returning to **Vancouver Island**. He gathered over 1,000 furs in **Clayoquot Sound** and Nootka Sound, where he effectively deceived **Francisco de Eliza** the Spanish commandant. Finding China closed to fur traders he attempted with very limited success to open a market with Japan, the first Englishman to do so for over a century. He was finally obliged to bring most of his cargo home to England where he sold it to the **East India Company**.

COLUMBIA RIVER. The mightiest river of western North America, the Columbia River rises in the Selkirk Mountains of **British Columbia** and flows over 1200 miles to the Pacific Ocean at **Astoria** in **Oregon**. Near its mouth it is close to six miles wide.

The Spanish explorer **Bruno de Hezeta** is credited with realizing that there was a major river emptying into what, on 17 August 1775, he called the Bahía de la Asunción. Although he did not enter the bay between the headlands of Cabo San Roque (Cape Disappointment) and Cabo Frondoso (Cape Adams), Spanish charts soon reflected his discovery as the **Entrada de Hezeta**.

It was the American fur trader **Robert Gray** in the *Columbia Rediviva* who, on 11 May 1792, first crossed the bar and explored the lowest reaches of the river he named "Columbia" after his ship. On 20 October, **William Broughton** in the *Chatham*, sailing south from **Nootka Sound** in consort with **George Vancouver**, also managed to cross the bar (Vancouver in the *Discovery* was unable to do so) and spent three weeks surveying the lower reaches of a river he called the "Oregan," advancing over 125 miles from Cape Disappointment to the beginning of the Columbia Gorge where he performed an **act of possession**. The American **Lewis and Clark Expedition** reached the mouth of the Columbia River and wintered at Fort Clatsop in 1805–1806. The first survey of the entire river was completed by the English fur trader **David Thompson** between the years 1807 and 1811. John Jacob Astor supported the founding of Fort Astoria in 1811. As British and American traders moved into the region, their nations' claims to the Columbia Basin were based on these early discoveries and explorations.

COMMANDER ISLANDS. The Commander Islands represent the last distant link between America and Asia, 200 nautical miles from Attu, the nearest island in the **Aleutian Islands** chain, and 132 nautical miles from **Kamchatka**. They take their name from captain-commander **Vitus Bering**, whose ship the *St. Peter* was wrecked on the largest island, Bering Island, in 1741. During their stay on the island, from November 1741 to August 1742, the survivors of Bering's expedition were terrorized by foxes, later hunted for their valuable fur. **Georg Wilhelm Steller** undertook important scientific investigations and identified his famous sea cow, *Hydrodamalis gigas*, which was soon hunted to extinction. The second of the four islands, Mednoi Island, was discovered by **Emel'ian Basov**, in 1744. In 1747 copper was discovered which gave the island its name, and a description of it was published by **Peter S. Pallas** in 1781 in an early volume of his *Neue nordische Beyträge*. Mining, however, never became economically viable, and the hunting of sea mammals was always more successful and remains so today.

In August 1991 Bering's grave was located by a party of Russian and Danish archaeologists. What were considered to be Bering's remains were removed to Petropavlovsk for identification. With the identity confirmed, they were reburied on the island on 15 September 1992, close to the high steel Latin cross which had been erected in June 1966 by the residents of Kamchatka to honor Bering.

CONCHA, JUAN GUTIÉRREZ DE LA (1760–1810). Juan Gutiérrez de la Concha sailed on the **Alejandro Malaspina** Expedition in the *Atrevida*. He was a talented mathematician and astronomer and a valued member of the scientific corps that worked under the direction of **Felipe Bauza** in creating the extensive cartographic record of the voyage. He was also the author of an extensive *Extracto* or Summary of the expedition's Northwest Coast campaign in the summer of 1791. It complements the official account of Malaspina but has an official tone, less personal in its comments than the diaries of **Tomás de Suría** or even **Antonio de Tova**. Nevertheless it is a valuable text, significant portions of which deal with the Spaniards' interaction with the **native** people encountered. At **Mulgrave** he commented on an underlying aggressive nature within **Tlingit** life: "Their manner, their music, their dances, everything reflects a bellicose character, and nothing is guarded more jealously than their military reputation." From the visit to **Nootka Sound** he describes the home of Chief **Maquinna** and reflects on the customs and beliefs of the Mowachaht from interviews conducted by the Spanish officers with some of the younger chiefs.

COOK, JAMES (1728–1779). James Cook had already commanded two successful expeditions to the South Pacific, 1768–1771 and 1772–1775, when he assumed command of a Third Voyage in 1776. This time he sailed to the northern hemisphere to solve one of the more enduring mysteries of the age—the question of a **Northwest Passage**. Despite **Samuel Hearne**'s trek to the Coppermine River, 1771–1772, many cabinet geographers were still convinced that a navigable passage existed across the top of North America in the temperate latitudes. Cook was therefore instructed to search for its Pacific entrance, to take advantage of a sailing season that lasted four months longer than that in Hudson Bay. Russian charts suggested ice-free access to a passage between 60° and 65° N that would bring him back to the Atlantic. Cook was appointed to the *Resolution*, whose master was **William Bligh;** he was also assisted by the cartographer **James King** and accompanied by the artist **John Webber**. **Charles Clerke** commanded the *Discovery*, whose complement included astronomer **William Bayly** and midshipman **George Vancouver**. Rounding Cape Horn, the ships moved from Kerguelen Island to Tasmania and on to New Zealand. From there they headed north, making a giant sweep through the island groups of the western South Pacific before Cook discovered the western portion of the islands of **Hawaii**, which he named after the Earl of Sandwich, and where he explored for two weeks from 18 January to 2 February 1778.

Landfall was made on the **Oregon** coast at 41°13′ near Cape Foulweather on 7 March, and between then and 18 August, the two ships made a **running survey** of over 4,000 miles of coastline, from **Cape Blanco** to the Gulf of Alaska, into the **Aleutian Islands**, and through the **Bering Strait** to **Icy Cape** at 71°40′ N. Missing the **Strait of Juan de Fuca** because of poor weather, Cook doubted its existence, and hurried on to his first anchorage in **Nootka Sound**, where he stayed for most of April to prepare his ships for their northern journey. There were extensive and largely friendly contacts with the local Mowachaht and Muchalaht natives, who were found to be shrewd and experienced traders; but the people and harsh environment stood in strong contrast to what the Englishmen had experienced over the years in the South Pacific. The Northwest Coast was a very different place—rugged, stormy, and clearly not the home of the "noble savage." At Nootka launches undertook detailed surveys of the outer sound, Webber began work on his remarkable artistic portfolio of people and places, and the officers wrote journal entries of great value to ethnographers. Trade in **artifacts** and furs, which brought such unexpected results in Russia and China in 1779, was brisk, particularly in exchange for metal.

As Cook sailed north the coast tended towards the west and in early May he found himself in the area where **Vitus Bering** had landed 37 years earlier. The stopover in what Cook named Sandwich Sound, later changed to **Prince William Sound**, was reminiscent of Nootka, although the snow-capped mountains were much higher. It offered the chance to meet and trade with the **Aleut/Alutiiq** natives, and to survey and draw the surroundings, although **David Samwell** found these "very desolate and dreary." There was no hint of a viable passage to the east. Initially **Cook Inlet**, which **John Gore** named the Gulf of Good Hope, held out some promise, but Turnagain Arm aptly described Cook's experience, made all the more frustrating by the completely misleading Russian map of **Jacob von Stählin**. There was no alternative but to follow the coast, which now turned dramatically southwest, in the hope of finding the promised opening leading north. Cook was still a long way from the 65° N set out in his instructions. For most of June he skirted the southern coast of **Kodiak** Island, assuming that it was part of the mainland, and ran down the **Alaska Peninsula**. Off the **Shumagin Islands** the *Discovery* was approached by a native man who bowed to the Englishmen in the "European manner" and gave them an indecipherable note, no doubt in Russian. Cook, inexplicably, had not brought with him an interpreter familiar with Russian. He passed to the south of **Unimak** Island with its dramatic volcanoes, but missed Unimak Pass that would have taken him into the **Bering Sea**. A day later, however, on 26 June, he sighted a large opening and headed for it but, as fog and darkness rolled in, he was lucky not to have run aground on rocks off Sedanka Island. Finally, on 27 June, he anchored safely in Samgoonoodha Harbour, today English Bay, on the northeastern tip of **Unalaska** Island from which he could see open water to the north. A welcome rest for a few days allowed Webber to draw his famous Aleut portraits and the officers to comment favorably on the politeness of the natives.

After running along the northern coast of the Alaska Peninsula, Cook named **Bristol Bay**, visited Bering's **St. Matthew Island**, without realizing, from his continuing problems with the Russian charts, where he was, and then named Sledge Island before reaching **Cape Prince of Wales**. The winds propelled him west and he was obliged to anchor in St. Lawrence Bay where his unarmed approach, bearing gifts to the Chukchi—restraint that had served him well in the south seas—allowed him to meet, on their own terms, people who had shown open hostility to the Russians. Again Cook was not clear on his location: on the Chukotskii Peninsula or "the island of Alashchka laid down by Mr. Staehlin's Map"? But he rightly surmised from reference to **Gerhardt Friedrich Müller**'s *Voyages from Asia to America* (1761) that he was in the "Country of the Tchuktschians explored by Behring in 1728." He was more than happy to pay respect to his great predecessor by naming "Behrings Straits" after the celebrated navigator, and was relieved after negotiating Cape Lisburne that the coast tended to the east. Any optimism, however, was short-lived when the ships were met by an impenetrable wall of ice. Cook spent a day cruising along its edge, but thanks to such treatises as **Samuel Engel**'s *Mémoires et observations géographiques*, which postulated that the sea never froze close to land, the ships were not equipped to work in an ice field. Fear was soon added to disillusionment. Sailing west, Cook searched briefly for a route home above Asia, but this also proved futile. Retreating back through the Bering Strait, the ships explored **Norton Sound** before stopping over at Samgoonoodha en route to the warmth of a Hawaiian winter. On Unalaska they met **Gerasim Izmailov**, who provided maps and other valuable information about Russian discoveries.

It is a tribute to the determination and professionalism of the officers and men that, after the devastating murder of Cook on 14 February 1779, and the growing incapacity and ultimate death off **Kamchatka** of **Charles Clerke**, who had assumed command on Cook's death, they continued with the plan set out for the summer—a return to the arctic earlier in the season to see if the ice conditions were any different. Using Petropavlovsk as a base, the ships left for the region of **Icy Cape** on 19 June. Before they did so, however, King, Gore, and Webber crossed Kamchatka to visit Governor **Magnus Behm**. He returned with them to the ships and, as he was about to leave for St. Petersburg, Clerke entrusted him with letters and journals that brought the first news of the explorations of 1778 and 1779, and the death of Cook, to England. Once back in the far north, the ships battled drift ice from off Point Hope and finally turned back at 70°33′, some fifteen miles short of their achievement the year before. The ships arrived back in Kamchatka on 24 August 1779 and sailed for home on 9 October via the Cape of Good Hope. They arrived in the Thames almost exactly one year later on 4 October 1780. The last section of the voyage was uneventful save for the remarkable prices received in Canton for the furs so casually acquired at Nootka, which led directly to the maritime fur trade of the 1780s and a new round of exploration on the Northwest Coast.

In charting an outline of the coast in some detail, particularly around the great sweep of the Gulf of Alaska, in the Bering Sea, and through the Bering Strait, Cook had laid down for the first time a recognizable shape for the entire region, adding substantially to Russian exploration in the north and linking it to Spanish exploration in the south. Through publication of his journal and atlas with its charts and engravings in 1784, the European world became aware of the nature and scope of the expedition's incredible achievement—where it had been and what its members had encountered, from dramatic mountain scenery to strange native peoples, stormy seas, "confounded fog," and the impenetrable ice that robbed them of the glory of finding a Northwest Passage.

COOK INLET. Estuary to the west of the **Kenai Peninsula**, Cook Inlet extends 30 miles wide and over 200 miles long. It was surveyed by **James Cook** in June 1778. His manuscript charts refer to it as the Gulf of Good Hope, and he thought that it might be the entrance to a river. The Earl of Sandwich, First Lord of the Admiralty, had the publication of Cook's charts refer to it as Cook's River. In 1785 the legendary **North West Company** trader **Peter Pond**, familiar with the great expanse of lakes in northern Canada, drew his famous speculative map identifying this "river" draining from Lake Athabaska. After they had established themselves on **Kodiak** Island in the early 1780s, Russian fur traders penetrated the inlet, which they knew as Kenai Bay. It was also visited in 1786 by the English fur traders **George Dixon**, **Nathaniel Portlock**, and **John Meares**. In the late 1780s, Russians working for **Pavel Lebedev-Lastochkin** had control of Kamishak Bay with its easy portage to Iliamna Lake, and there was an outpost, Fort St. George, on the Kasilov River on the coast of the Kenai Peninsula as early as 1787. By the mid-1790s Russian hunters and traders controlled Knik Arm and Turnagain Arm. **Salvador Fidalgo**, visiting in July 1790, commented on the Russian establishments and activities, but still performed an **act of possession** near Kachemak Bay. In May 1794 **George Vancouver** completed his definitive survey of the entire area and consequently changed the name from Cook's "River" to "Inlet."

COPPER RIVER. The Copper River flows 250 miles through the Chugach Mountains to enter the Gulf of Alaska through a wide delta. The first ships to have come near it were those of the **Ignacio de Arteaga** Expedition in 1779 but, passing Kayak Island on their way to **Prince William Sound** (PWS), they did not attempt to make a survey. **Juan Francisco de la Bodega y Quadra** alleged later to have been aware that they were off a large river, and the maps of the expedition delineate a large opening in the coast, which is referred to as Puerto y Rio de los Perdidos. As this is not explained and there is no mention of it in the accounts of the voyage, it is not clear what the

Spaniards actually saw. The discoverer of the river is generally recognized to have been the fur trader **Leontii Nagaev**. In 1783 he found the river when, after coming to PWS with **Potap Zaikov** and Filipp Mukhoplev, he explored farther down the coast. The first serious exploration of the river was not undertaken until 1797 by **Dimitrii Tarkhanov** as the Russians were establishing themselves in **Yakutat Bay**. In 1803 and again in 1805 it was reported that **Aleksandr Baranov** sent a fur hunter named Bazenhov to explore the river, and that he brought back samples of the copper, which had given the river its name from Tarkhanov's reports. He returned to **Kodiak** by portaging to **Cook Inlet**.

CORNEY, PETER (fl. 1813–1835). An English mariner and veteran of the West Indies trade, Peter Corney spent the summers of 1814–1818 on the Northwest Coast, wintering in **Hawaii** and leaving a fascinating journal, published many years later as *Voyages in the North Pacific*, but initially serialized in the *London Literary Gazette* in 1821. In 1813 he left London in the **North West Company**'s schooner *Columbia*, which during 1814 established a successful trade route between Fort George on the **Columbia River** and **New Archangel**, that he repeated in subsequent years.

In 1815 his travels took him to Canton, and in 1816 he ventured as far west as **Unalaska** and explored the lower reaches of the Columbia River, where he found the **Chinook** natives friendly and accommodating but uninterested in agriculture. That winter in Hawaii, he witnessed the disastrous attempt by **Georg Schaeffer** to establish Russian influence in the islands. In 1817 he was back for another trading season on the coast, during which he also visited **Fort Ross** and **Trinidad Bay**, where he identified (as had **Archibald Menzies** in 1792) the cross left by **Bruno de Hezeta** on one of the earliest Spanish expeditions in 1775.

Corney's next year, however, did not involve trade. In Hawaii during the winter of 1817–1818, he was given command of the schooner *Santa Rosa*, which acted as consort to the frigate *Argentina*, which was engaged in rebellion against Spain in support of independence for her American colonies. That summer, after a visit to Fort Ross, the two ships bombarded and plundered the coast of **Alta California** and attacked **Monterey**. After an eventful seven-year absence during which his recorded experiences provided a valuable contribution to the evolving history of Pacific North America, particularly the earliest days of settlement at the mouth of the Columbia River, and of the Hawaiian Islands, where he became known to King Kamehameha, he reached London in early 1820.

Although his memoir ends at this time, he is known to have been back on the coast at least twice working on **Hudson's Bay Company** (HBC) vessels in 1830 and in 1834. In the latter year he visited **Fort Vancouver**. He died at sea in a new, recently launched *Columbia*, coming out to the Pacific to act as an HBC supply vessel, and escorting the company's SS *Beaver*, destined to be the first steamship on the Canadian west coast.

CORTÉS, HERNÁN (1485–1547). Hernán Cortés initiated the earliest exploration of the Pacific Coast of **New Spain** shortly after his conquest of the Aztec Empire. By 1522 he had built shipyards on the coasts of Michoacan and Oaxaca. Initial exploration was to the south looking for a strait between the Gulf of Mexico and the Pacific. It was not until 1532, acting on rumors of pearl beds, that he dispatched a northern reconnaissance, which discovered the Tres Marías Islands and sailed inside the **Gulf of California**. The next year he launched another expedition and **Fortún Jiménez** discovered **Baja California**, where he anchored in the Bahia de la Paz. In 1535 Cortés himself sailed into the same bay, arriving on Holy Cross Day, 3 May, and naming the place Santa Cruz. He performed an **act of possession**. By land and sea the Spanish explored the south coast of the peninsula believing they were on an island. In 1539 a small map showing their discoveries and their relationship to the numerous ports that were springing up on the continental mainland, was filed as part of the documentation in one of Cortés's innumerable lawsuits against royal officials and rivals in New Spain. The settlement struggled to survive in the arid environment against native hostility, and food supplies had to be shipped across the gulf. By the end of 1536 it had been abandoned.

Despite the failure at Santa Cruz, Cortés's initiatives in 1532–1536 greatly expanded geographical knowledge of the coast of New Spain. In 1539 hoping perhaps that the Seven Cities of Gold of Alvar Nuñez Cabeza de Vaca might be reached successfully from the sea, he sponsored his fourth and final expedition commanded by

Francisco de Ulloa. This led to further discoveries and continued a process of exploration that would finally reveal the Northwest Coast at the end of the 18th century.

COX, JOHN HENRY (fl. 1781–1791). The son of a celebrated London watchmaker, John Henry Cox received permission from the **East India Company** (EIC) to travel to Canton for reasons of health but he actually went to attend to problems with the family business. Once there he engaged in "country trading" between China and India, contrary to the interests of the EIC, but he survived the threat of expulsion in 1783 and founded a trading company with partners John Reid and Daniel Beale.

The publication of the journal of **James Cook**'s Third Voyage, with **James King**'s practical suggestions for prosecuting a **fur trade** between the Northwest Coast and China, caused Cox's company to change the direction of its sponsorship. For the balance of the decade it became involved in whole or in part in every British voyage that traded and explored on the Northwest Coast, with the exception of that of **James Strange**. Specifically, Cox sponsored **James Hanna**'s pioneering voyage in 1785, invested in those of **John Meares** and **Charles Barkley**, and joined with **Richard Cadman Etches** to send four ships under **James Colnett** to **Nootka Sound** in 1789. His activities, clearly undermining the monopoly of the EIC, led to his expulsion from China in 1787, but the work of his company carried on in Canton and through his personal activities in London.

In 1789 Cox embarked on a voyage to the South Pacific, **Hawaii**, the Northwest Coast, and the eastern **Aleutian Islands**, where he surveyed the strait between **Unalaska** and Sedanka Island before sailing to China. Once there he oversaw the sponsorship of another voyage to America in 1790 under the command of Thomas Barnett.

An interesting aspect of Cox's involvement with Northwest Coast commerce and exploration was his friendship with **Alexander Dalrymple** with whom he shared traders' information about a coast that, even post-Cook, was still largely unexplored. Dalrymple still believed that the reported voyage of **Bartholomew de Fonte** might well be true and in 1789 he published part of Hanna's 1786 journal in his *Plan for Promoting the Fur Trade*. That same year he also published a series of charts that included one of Bucareli Bay in Alaska from Spanish sources and two charts by Hanna, including one of the trip of the *Sea Otter* into Queen Charlotte Sound that identified Fitzhugh Sound. Each was provided to him by Cox.

COXE, WILLIAM (1747–1828). Traveler and historian, William Coxe made two visits to Russia in 1778 and 1785–1786. These led to a number of studies, including four editions of an *Account of the Russian Discoveries between Asia and America* (1780–1803). A supplement, *A Comparative View of the Russian Discoveries with those made by Captains Cook and Clerke*, was added to the 1787 edition. The first edition of the *Account* gave the English-speaking world its first clear indication of the extent of Russian activity in the North Pacific at a time when the ships of **James Cook**'s Third Voyage had yet to return to England. **Gerhardt Friedrich Müller**'s *Voyages from Asia to America* (1761) had brought the story to 1745, and Coxe continued it into the 1770s by translating an anonymous German treatise that summarized, in Part I, 24 voyages of Russian hunters and merchants as far as **Kodiak** Island. Because of its related importance, Part II discussed the fur trade with China. Perhaps most importantly, Part III included an abstract of the journals of the **Petr Krenitsyn** and **Mikhail Levashov** expedition, a revelation even to many Russian scholars because of its secrecy. The volume included four engraved maps and an illustration of the Chinese frontier town of Maimatschin (opposite the Russian post of Kiakhta), where trade was conducted. A fourth edition of the *Account* in 1803 continued the story through 1792, but the mysteries of the geography of the Northwest Coast had already been revealed in the journal and charts of **George Vancouver** in 1798.

CRESPÍ, JUAN (1721–1782). Juan Crespí came to **New Spain** with **Junípero Serra** and like his mentor became associated with the missionary College of San Fernando in Mexico City. He went with Serra to **Baja California**, and accompanied the **Sacred Expedition** to **Alta California** in 1769. After reaching **San Diego**, he proceeded north with Gaspar de Portolá in search of **Monterey** and was in the detachment that discovered San Francisco Bay, which he described as a "very large and fine harbor." He later recorded his exploration of the bay area with **Pedro Fages**, and it is as a diarist that he is particularly important to the earliest recorded history of **California**. He alone was in all the initial exploring expeditions—from Baja California to San Diego, from San Diego to Monterey and **San Francisco**, from Monterey to the San Joaquin Valley, and from Monterey by sea to the **British Columbia** border with **Alaska**.

In May 1774 Serra gained permission to send a priest on the maritime expedition of **Juan Pérez** directed at the Northwest Coast. Crespí was appointed with **Tomás de la Peña** as his companion aboard the *Santiago*. Both priests were charged to keep diaries and there was obvious collaboration between them as some repetition can be noted. The ship sailed from Monterey on 6 June 1774 and Crespí's journal follows its progress to north of the **Queen Charlotte Islands**; he describes the coast and notes latitudinal information provided by Pérez or **Esteban José Martínez**, the weather—particularly the storms during which he suffered seasickness, and the masses said by him and Peña. He was also at pains to record the earliest descriptions of the very different **native** peoples encountered along the way: he noted their canoes, demeanor, clothing including hats (he was the first to describe the famous painted Nootka whaling hats whose "conical crown ends in a ball like a little pear"), tools, arms, baskets, mats, bowls, spoons, and ornaments.

Returning to Monterey on 27 September 1774, Crespí finished a good copy of his remarkable diary at the **Carmel Mission** on 5 October, and transmitted it to Serra. Thereafter, he spent the eight remaining years of his life at Carmel where he is buried.

CROSS SOUND. A passage between Icy Strait and Glacier Bay and the Gulf of Alaska, Cross Sound creates a distinct separation between the **Alexander Archipelago** to the south and the Fairweather Range and coastal plain of the continental coast of **Alaska** to the north. It was named by **James Cook** on Holy Cross Day, 3 May 1778.

CUMSHEWA. A **Haida** village on the eastern side of the **Queen Charlotte Islands,** Cumshewa was named after its chief. It became a favorite port of call for a generation of American fur traders from 1791 to at least 1821, despite being the site of a good deal of **violence**. It was on the north side of an inlet, above Louise Island, which today bears the village's name.

CUNNEAH (fl. 1789–1801). Cunneah was the **Haida** chief whose village at the northwestern tip of Graham Island in the **Queen Charlotte Islands** became an important center for acquiring prime **sea otter** skins in the early years of the **fur trade**. **George Dixon** was the first to visit the area in 1787 and he called the inlet where he traded "Cloak Bay." He was followed by a succession of **"Boston Men,"** one of whom described the chief as "humane" and "friendly." Cunneah seems to have avoided the violence that plagued the relationship of many traders with another Haida chief, **Koyah**. **Sigismund Bacstrom** drew a picture of Cunneah's eldest daughter Koota-Hilslinga in 1793.

– D –

DAGELET, JOSEPH LEPAUTE (1751–1788). Joseph Dagelet was the senior astronomer on the **Jean François de La Pérouse** Expedition. Born into a family of clock and instrument makers he became fascinated by astronomy when he met and studied under Joseph-Jérôme Lefrançais Lalande, France's leading astronomer of the 18th century and later director of the Paris Observatory. Dagelet had sailed with Yves-Joseph Kerguelen across the bottom of the world from the Ile de France towards Australia in 1773–1774, and was recommended to La Pérouse by Lalande. He served on the *Boussole*. Serious-minded, modest, and hardworking, his natural curiosity caused him to explore Port des Français (**Lituya Bay**) by scrambling up a glacier and climbing up the mountainsides. He was responsible for the basic survey work upon which the plans of the port were drawn by **Paul Monneron**, Gérault-Sébastien Bernizet, and Lieutenant **Blondela**. He was also responsible for the navigational instruments and for the work done in the observatories set up at the major stopping places including Lituya Bay and **Monterey**. Working with **Paul-Antoine Fleuriot de Langle** in the *Astrolabe* he directed the fixing (as much as the fog would allow) of the latitudes and longitudes of the principal features of the coast as the expedition sailed from **Alaska** to **California**. The methods used for determining these were the same as those used by **James Cook**: calculations by the lunar distance method and use of chronometers.

DALL, WILLIAM HEALEY (1845–1927). As a young scientist in 1865, American naturalist William Healey Dall was invited to join the Western Union International Telegraph Expedition to **Russian America**. Its leader was Robert Kennicott, curator of the Northwestern University Museum of Natural History, and its goal was to explore the possibility of a cable link to Europe across the **Bering Strait**. When Kennicott died unexpectedly in 1866, Dall became the head of the expedition. Although the cable plan was made redundant by the success of an Atlantic cable route, Dall's explorations in **Alaska**, particularly in the Yukon River Basin, resulted in important collections and geographical research. In 1868 he left Alaska to join the staff of the Smithsonian Institution and to write his seminal work, *Alaska and Its Resources* (1870). In 1871 he was appointed to work with the U.S. Coast and Geodetic Survey, and each summer until 1884 spent a portion of the year in Alaska. Dall's *Pacific Coast Pilot: Coasts and Islands of Alaska* was published in 1879. Thereafter, he visited Alaska on a number of occasions, notably as a member of the privately financed scientific reconnaissance, the Harriman Alaska Expedition of 1899. Dall Island at the southern end of the **Alexander Archipelago** on **Dixon Entrance** is named after him.

DALRYMPLE, ALEXANDER (1737–1808). A student of the history of discoveries, and cartographic scholar and publisher, Alexander Dalrymple was one of the foremost speculative geographers of his time, and a fervent advocate, before they were disproved, of the existence of a southern continent and a **Northwest Passage**. Long associated with the **East India Company** (EIC) and the **Royal Society**, he believed that opening the Pacific would lead to undreamed-of commercial expansion and future prosperity for the British nation.

He used his early years in the service of the EIC in Madras to make voyages to the Philippines and Borneo. In London in the mid-1760s he pursued his interest in a southern continent and published, in 1767, *An Account of the Discoveries Made in the South Pacifick Ocean Previous to 1764*. Despite his unfortunate decision not to accompany **James Cook** on his First Voyage to the Pacific, he influenced its preparations and those for the Second Voyage. During the years 1769–1771 he published in two volumes *An Historical Collection of the Several Voyages and Discoveries in the South Pacific Ocean*. In

1779 the EIC appointed him keeper and scholar-in-residence of the journals and charts accumulated by the company. He subsequently published numerous charts along with nautical instructions, plans of ports, and coastal views.

Although he did not share in its preparations, Dalrymple's connections with Sir **Joseph Banks** and the Royal Society meant that he was privy to the results of **James Cook**'s Third Voyage well before the unauthorized accounts of the expedition appeared (1781–1784) and long before the official account was published (1784). This led him to focus attention on the fur-trading opportunities presented to the EIC and he promoted an amalgamation between it and the **Hudson's Bay Company** (HBC) to build and operate a vast trading network stretching from Hudson Bay across North America to posts and factories on the Northwest Coast, and from there across the ocean to China. His ideas culminated in a *Plan for Promoting the Fur Trade and Securing It to This Country by Uniting the Operations of the East India Company and the Hudson's Bay Company* (1789). While nothing ultimately came of this particular idea, Dalrymple was indefatigable in seeking out those traders, such as **George Dixon**, who had sailed to the coast in the second half of the 1780s. He studied their charts and journals, along with the accounts of traders and explorers pushing west overland across northern Canada, and maps like those of **Peter Pond**. He became convinced, like **Arthur Dobbs** and **Daines Barrington** before him, that there had to be a **Northwest Passage** and that this would make his idea of a vast northern trading empire viable. To this end he produced "A Map of the lands around the North Pole," also in 1789. Skillfully combining the role of scholarly investigator and promoter, and using Banks's interest in a fur-trading establishment on Dixon's **Queen Charlotte Islands** or in **Nootka Sound**, Dalrymple effectively championed the idea of a full-blown naval expedition to the Northwest Coast. This ultimately became the voyage of **George Vancouver**, designed to confirm William Pitt's victory over Spain in the **Nootka Crisis** and to make a thorough survey of the coast. On the other side of the continent, his pressure on the HBC led it to sponsor a land expedition by Dixon (never undertaken) and the voyages of **Charles Duncan** in 1790 and 1791–1792 to continue the search for the passage on the western side of Hudson Bay.

The solving of America's great northern mystery by Vancouver did nothing to diminish Dalrymple's enthusiasm for the publication of geographical information. In 1795 he became hydrographer to the Admiralty, concurrently with his position at the EIC. There he undertook the invaluable work of organizing a rapidly growing collection of charts, using them to compile information for both naval and commercial ships that his reputation, earned over 50 years of study, had already obliged him to provide.

DAURKIN, NIKOLAI (ca. 1730–1792). Nikolai Daurkin was an explorer of the Asian and American coasts of the **Bering Sea**. A Chukchi native, he was captured, baptized, and educated as a young man by the Russians at Iakutsk, and was recruited by the governor of Siberia, **Fedor Soimonov**, to improve Russian–Chukchi relations. In the early 1760s he worked with **Friedrich Plenisner**, the commandant at Anadyrsk and a veteran of **Vitus Bering**'s voyage to America in 1741, to explore and write reports on the Chukotskii Peninsula and its adjacent seas. In 1763 he went by *baidarka* to **St. Lawrence Island** and drew one of the earliest maps of the northern Bering Sea and Strait from his own investigations and what he was told by others. This included the **Diomede Islands** and the western portions of the Seward Peninsula. He also reported on a settlement on the coast of **Norton Sound** that spawned rumors of descendants of shipwrecked Russians.

In 1787 he joined the **Joseph Billings** Expedition with **Ivan Kobelev**, to act as a guide and interpreter to prepare the Russians for visits to the lands of the Chukchi. Prior to linking up with Billings for his overland trip to the Kolyma River in the fall of 1791, Daurkin and Kobelev spent the earlier part of the year visiting the coast of America, reaching the Kheuveren River. They were not able to throw any new light on the story of the supposed Russian settlement in the area, as a result of which the myth of the "lost colony of Novgorod" persisted into the 19th century. It was finally proven fictitious in the 1940s.

DAVIDSON, GEORGE (1768–1801). The Boston-born George Davidson joined **Robert Gray**'s *Columbia* as a "painter" for its second voyage to the Northwest Coast, 1790–1793. During two summers he visited much of the central coast, including **Vancouver Island**, the **Queen Charlotte Islands**, southern **Alaska**, and the mouth of the **Columbia River**, but sadly only a few examples of his artwork are still extant. His drawing of Gray's Fort Defiance in **Clayoquot Sound**, established during the winter of 1791–1792, and the building of the sloop *Adventure*, shows a fine attention to detail. Gray's time on the coast involved a number of skirmishes with the natives, and Davidson recorded two of them, one in the **Strait of Juan de Fuca** and the other, a night scene in Gray's Cove (Nasparti Inlet on the west coast of Vancouver Island), which demonstrate a flair for the dramatic. Davidson made a second voyage to the Northwest Coast, 1799–1800, but neither memoir nor drawings have been found. He died at sea when the ship he was commanding, the *Rover*, was seemingly caught in a typhoon carrying its cargo of furs to Canton after a stopover in **Hawaii**.

DAVIDSON, GEORGE (1825–1911). An influential geographer and astronomer, George Davidson was on the staff of the U.S. Coast and Geodetic Survey from 1845 to 1895. Although many others participated in the work, his name became synonymous with the pioneer survey of the coastline of the Pacific states for navigational purposes during the 1850s. This stemmed largely from his *Directory for the Pacific Coast of the United States* (1858). Davidson and his colleagues visited every nook and cranny along the full extent of the coast from **San Diego** to **Puget Sound**, determined geographic positions, observed thousands of angles in conducting primary and secondary triangulation, mapped much of the shoreline, and cast the lead thousands of times to determine water depth. They also found time to record their observations of the geography of the lands they saw and the **native** peoples they encountered, leaving an invaluable record for future generations. Based on his earlier publication, *Pacific Coast: Coast Pilot of California, Oregon and Washington Territory* appeared in 1869. After the purchase of **Alaska** in 1867, Davidson worked in the north and his *Pacific Coast: Coast Pilot of Alaska* also appeared in 1869. In 1879 he built the first observatory on the Pacific coast in **San Francisco**. Davidson was a keen student of the discovery and early exploration period on the Northwest Coast, and his historical/geographical writings included: *An Examination of some of the early Voyages of Discovery and Exploration on the Northwest*

Coast from 1539–1603 (1887); *The Tracks and Landfalls of Bering and Chirikof* (1901); *The Discovery of San Francisco Bay* (1907); and *Francis Drake on the Northwest Coast* (1908). He also wrote *The Alaska Boundary*, a history of the controversial American/British/Canadian negotiation of the Alaska boundary in 1903.

DAVYDOV, GAVRIIL (1784–1809). Naval officer, explorer, and perceptive reporter on **Russian America**, Gavriil Davydov's short life and career were assisted by the fact that **Nikolai Rezanov** was one of his mentors. Davydov made his first visit to **Kodiak** at the end of 1802. Wintering over, he used his time to explore the island and its coast in a *baidarka*, noting his observations and describing the **Aleut/Alutiiq** people he encountered.

In 1804 he accepted a renewed offer of employment with the **Russian–American Company** but only reached as far as Petropavlovsk, where in June 1805 he met up with Rezanov, harboring resentment from his recent disastrous diplomatic failure in Japan. Davydov and a fellow officer Nikolai Khvostov took Rezanov and **Georg Langsdorff**, who had detached himself from the **Ivan Kruzenshtern** Expedition, to Russian America, making important (in terms of the artistic and descriptive record) visits to the **Pribilof Islands**, **Unalaska**, and Kodiak before arriving in the fledgling settlement of **New Archangel**. They immediately turned round to fetch food supplies and women from Kodiak to support **Aleksandr Baranov**'s struggling colonial capital. Davydov spent the winter of 1805–1806 there, again writing down his observations, and gaining respect for his concern for the welfare of the company's employees and the Aleuts who had been forcibly transported to the settlement. In the spring of 1806, he and Khvostov took Rezanov and Langsdorff on a voyage to **California** to collect supplies. In 1807 apparently fulfilling orders from Rezanov, the two naval friends destroyed Japanese establishments in the southern Kurile Islands. For this they were arrested but later freed though not exonerated. At the time of his death in St. Petersburg, Davydov had been encouraged to write up his observations on Russian America, and had finished an account of his first visit to Kodiak in 1802–1803. A friend wrote up a second section from his letters and this covered his experiences during his second, more extensive visit to the colony in 1805–1806; it includes observations important to ethnographers and a small Russian–Tlingit dictionary. Published in St. Petersburg in 1810–1812, the two-part account appeared in English translation in 1977.

DELAROV, EVSTRAT IVANOV (ca. 1740–1806). A pioneer in the Russian **fur trade** in the North Pacific, Evstrat Delarov first sailed to the **Aleutian Islands** in 1764. He graduated from laborer to navigator and part owner of various ships, becoming wealthy enough to become a merchant in his own right in the 1770s. During the 1780s he became closely connected with the commercial activities of **Grigorii Shelikhov**.

Between the summer of 1781 and fall of 1786 he was in command of the *St. Aleksei* on an extended voyage that took him to **Unimak** Island and then onto Unga Island in the Shumagin group. This became his base for forays further north and east. During 1782 and 1783 he worked with another experienced navigator and fur trader, **Potap Zaikov**, in opening up **Prince William Sound** (PWS). In 1787 he met Shelikhov in Irkutsk and was persuaded to become chief manager of the establishment in **Three Saints Bay** on **Kodiak** Island. From there, that same year, he sailed into Shelikhov Strait, familiar from earlier voyages, and established an outpost at Karluk (on Kodiak) and explored Katmai, the location of a major **native** trading fair on the **Alaska Peninsula**. He also hunted in **Cook Inlet**. In 1788 he dispatched **Gerasim Izmailov** and **Dmitrii Bocharov** bearing official possession plaques and crests to sail southeast along the coast from PWS to **Cross Sound**. The one left at **Yakutat Bay** is now in the collection of the Smithsonian Institution. Also in 1788 he was visited by the Spanish explorer **Gonzalo López de Haro**, in conversations with whom he exaggerated the extent and strength of Russian settlements around the Gulf of Alaska, and hinted at the imminent arrival of a naval expedition (the planned-but-never-launched **Mulovskii Expedition**) which he reported was designed to secure the coast from **Nootka Sound** to Cook Inlet. This information coupled with Zaikov's discussions with **Esteban José Martínez** on **Unalaska**, prompted Spanish authorities to occupy Nootka in the summer of 1789.

DE L'ISLE, JOSEPH NICOLAS (1688–1768). French astronomer Joseph Nicolas de L'Isle was also a cartographer, and his brother

Guillaume (1675–1726) was the leading geographer of his time. While still a teenager de l'Isle produced some perceptive new observations of a solar eclipse and launched his career as an influential astronomer. In 1717 he met **Peter the Great** during the czar's visit to Paris. This visit promoted close links between the scientific communities in France and Russia and in 1726 de l'Isle arrived in St. Petersburg to become a member of the Academy of Sciences, to inaugurate the recently built observatory and educate aspiring astronomers, and to work with Russian cartographers on production of a national atlas. De l'Isle is sometimes blamed for the delay in the publication of the *Atlas Russicus* (1745) because of his insistence that the maps be based on astronomically determined points, the desired number and accuracy of which were almost impossible to produce at that time. Another controversial matter was his transmittal to Paris of important information about Russia circulating in St. Petersburg, particularly about its secret exploratory expeditions and the maps that resulted from them; it is estimated that copies of over 300 maps made their way to France as a result of his 21 years in Russia. He always maintained that communication with Paris was a condition of his employment, but the nature and extent of this espionage was likely never understood by his hosts.

Despite his important work as an astronomer and geographer, de l'Isle's influence on the emerging geography of the Northwest Coast proved to be decidedly misleading. In 1731 he produced a map of Russia's Pacific coast, of which a second version was created in 1733, drawing attention to **Gamaland**, a nonexistent island of considerable size south and east of **Kamchatka**. At **Vitus Bering**'s famous meeting in Avacha Bay in May 1741 to determine the final route of his second voyage, there seems to have been a third version, brought to the meeting by Joseph Nicolas's brother, **Louis de l'Isle de la Croyère**, that placed Gamaland farther to the east and therefore more likely to be on the way to America. This map is usually blamed for the expedition wasting precious time searching for the fictional island.

De l'Isle's second foray into the geography of the North Pacific was a major contribution to the mid-century speculation spawned by the reemergence of the story of the apocryphal voyage of **Bartholomew de Fonte**. This story came to his attention before he returned to France in 1747, and had received wide currency due to its promotion in 1744 by **Arthur Dobbs**, a critic of the **Hudson's Bay Company** and a firm believer in a **Northwest Passage**. In 1750 de l'Isle read a paper in Paris about Russian discoveries in the North Pacific. Obviously more important than his garbled version of Bering's second **Kamchatka Expedition** was his introduction of a manuscript map by **Philippe Buache** that superimposed Fonte's passage from the Pacific towards Hudson Bay upon northwestern North America. Both paper and map were published in 1752. Later that year, de l'Isle published his own map that brought Fonte's passage a more "credible" ten degrees farther south than Buache had placed it, making the link between it and Hudson Bay more obvious. In the next few years there were many variants of this map and the so-called facts that it presented. Although a number of cartographers remained highly skeptical of the Fonte fiction, so influential were the French cartographers, who also produced an atlas of maps based upon Fonte's discoveries in 1753, that their view of the geography of the Northwest Coast was largely accepted for another 30 years, and it was 40 years before the bogus Fonte voyage was finally disproved by **Jacinto Caamaño** and **George Vancouver**.

DE L'ISLE DE LA CROYÈRE, LOUIS (1690–1741). French scientist and astronomer, Louis de l'Isle de la Croyère came to St. Petersburg with his more famous brother **Joseph Nicolas de l'Isle** in 1726. Joseph Nicolas had come to Russia to join the Academy of Sciences and to set up an observatory. Louis also became a member of the academy and taught astronomy, and he undertook travels and observations in Siberia with his brother. In 1732 he was appointed to **Vitus Bering**'s second **Kamchatka Expedition** as its astronomer, and continued his scientific work as the expedition members made their way across the country. He arrived in Okhotsk in 1740, subsequently crossing to **Kamchatka** and participating in the voyage to America in the *St. Paul*, commanded by **Aleksei Chirikov**. His importance lies less in his scientific acumen, which seems to have been largely discounted by his contemporaries, than in the influence he exerted over Bering and his companions at a crucial meeting held in Avacha Bay in May 1741 to determine the route of the expedition. Over the winter Bering and Chirikov had thought that it would be best to head east/northeast and explore between 50° and 65° N. Bering would have been aware of the maps of Joseph Nicolas de l'Isle of 1731 and 1733, with depictions of **Gamaland**, but it seems that de l'Isle de la Croyère brought to the meeting a more recent map, showing this land farther to the south and to the east than had previously been assumed. As a result the expedition sailed much farther south than was planned, everyone agreeing that finding this land and determining its relationship to America to be a worthy undertaking. Later, when the *St. Peter* under Bering never reached home in 1741, and the *St. Paul* ran into trouble getting back to Kamchatka before winter set in, much of the blame was placed on de l'Isle de la Croyère, notably by **Sven Waxell**, for wasting the expedition's time in the futile search for Gamaland. This appears harsh in light of the agreement before the ships set out, but ironically the delay also cost de l'Isle de la Croyère his life; he died of scurvy just as the *St. Paul* reentered the Avacha Bay on 11 October 1741.

DEZHNEV, SEMEN (ca. 1605–1673). Cossack leader and Arctic navigator Semen Dezhnev was the first to sail around the northeastern edge of Asia, now Cape Dezhnev, and through what was later named **Bering Strait**.

During the 1630s, in state service, he was in Siberia collecting tribute from the natives. In the early 1640s he took part in several expeditions aimed at exploring rivers flowing into the Arctic Ocean, and in 1647 participated in an expedition with the trader Fedot Popov to sail, in search of walrus for their ivory, from the Kolyma River to the Anadyr River on the Pacific Coast. The expedition was defeated by ice, but in 1648 set out again with 90 men in seven *kochi* (specially designed ships with rounded hulls for operating in ice). Four were wrecked, but the remaining three navigated the Great Rocky Cape in August and sailed south. Another boat was lost and then Popov's boat disappeared in stormy seas. By now it was October, but winds continued to carry Dezhnev forward and he finally landed south of the mouth of the Anadyr, which he reached overland by the end of the year. In the spring he ascended the river and established the settlement of Anadyrsk. In the years that followed he explored the Gulf of Anadyr and stayed in the region until 1662. Although his remarkable coastal reconnaissance in 1648 made Dezhnev the discoverer of the waters separating Asia from America, there is no evidence that he had any idea of the continent to his east.

Despite his visits to Moscow, news of the expedition never seems to have entered into general knowledge about maritime Siberia, but there is little doubt that information inherited from Dezhnev was incorporated into European maps at the end of the 17th century, and that it sustained Russian interest in the possibility of reaching Japan, China, and India via a Northeast Passage. Neither **Peter the Great** nor **Vitus Bering** knew any specifics about the voyage when the latter was commissioned to undertake the first of his **Kamchatka Expeditions** in late 1724, although Bering became more aware of what were still only vague rumors about it around the time of his own voyage through the same strait in 1728. More definite information became available in 1736, when **Gerhardt Friedrich Müller** located relevant documents in the archives in Iakutsk.

DIOMEDE ISLANDS. Two islands located in the **Bering Strait**, the Diomede Islands would presumably have been seen by **Semen Dezhnev** when he became the first European in recorded history to negotiate the strait at the end of September 1648. Indeed, as he reported landing on an island at that time, he probably visited the larger of the two. Rediscovered by **Vitus Bering** on 16 August 1728 and named for St. Diomede, whose day was being celebrated, they are also referred to as the Gvozdev Islands, after **Mikhail Gvozdev**, who explored the strait and found America in 1732. The international boundary between Russia and the United States now passes between the two islands.

DISEASE. Once explorers and traders arrived on the Northwest Coast in earnest in the 1770s and 1780s, **native health** was undermined by sexually transmitted diseases, alcoholism, dietary change, tuberculosis, and particularly smallpox. The spread of disease was also aided by communal living arrangements in less than sanitary conditions, and general mortality levels were increased by the introduction of firearms. Venereal disease was introduced to **Nootka Sound** by **James Cook**'s men in 1778, but by the time the expedition reached **Unalaska** the sickness had already arrived via the Russians. Epidemics of smallpox, the most virulent and devastating of all the diseases, periodically swept the coast and reduced particular communities by up to 50 percent at any one time. Definitive evidence about the introduction and spread of this disease is lacking, but the results are clear. **George Vancouver** reported village depopulation and signs of smallpox once he entered the **Strait of Juan de Fuca** in 1792, and journals of the period are replete with similar observations. In the north it probably arrived with the Russians from **Kamchatka**; in the south from trading vessels coming from Asia. Record-keeping about shipboard health on naval vessels suggests that none carried active smallpox and that they were probably not the prime culprits. However, they could have unwittingly carried the virus that later burst into the open. It was really the fur traders, who ranged up and down the coast in great numbers during the years 1785–1805, who brought the sustained contact necessary to maintain the presence of all kinds of disease, and once cross-continent contacts were added to the scene the natives were exposed to an even wider world and sources of the problem. In the century 1774–1874 it has been estimated that the native population of the Northwest Coast fell by up to 80 percent from 188,000 to 38,000.

DIXON, GEORGE (fl. 1776–1791). George Dixon's participation in **James Cook**'s Third Voyage to the Pacific as an armourer in the *Discovery* sparked in him an ongoing interest in exploration and discovery. Convinced that the search for the **Northwest Passage** remained incomplete, he urged Sir **Joseph Banks** in 1784 to sponsor an overland expedition from Québec to the Northwest Coast. Nothing came of this idea, but the publication of Cook's journal that same year created intense interest in England in a maritime **fur trade** between America and China. In May 1785 Dixon and a colleague from Cook's voyage, **Nathaniel Portlock**, were engaged by **Richard Cadman Etches** to prosecute this trade under license from the South Sea Company.

With Portlock commanding the *King George*, and Dixon in the *Queen Charlotte*, the expedition left England in August 1785. After rounding Cape Horn and touching briefly at the **Sandwich Islands**, the ships were off **Cook Inlet** (still known as Cook's River) on 18 July 1786. They entered and remained inside the inlet for close to a month, anchoring at four separate places, initially in present-day English Bay (Port Graham), which they called Coal Harbour when Portlock found veins of coal. However, they were unnerved by the presence of Russians, men of **Grigorii Shelikhov**'s company busy establishing the trading post of Aleksandrovskoe, so they proceeded farther into the inlet. They noted the difference between their method of commerce—trading directly with **natives**—and that of the Russians who were accompanied by their own **Aleut** hunters. Anchoring briefly off **Prince William Sound** (PWS), they did not enter, preferring to sail south towards **Nootka Sound**. Adverse winds prevented their entry and so they moved on to winter in **Hawaii**.

In the spring of 1787 the ships were again off PWS and, on 24 April, anchored in Port Chalmers on the northwest side of **Montague Island**. During a stopover of three weeks Dixon and Portlock encountered **John Meares**, who was trading illegally and whose party was in desperate straits having wintered over. Learning that another vessel from Meares's syndicate was due to visit Nootka Sound, Dixon effected a previously planned separation from Portlock and sailed southwards to trade and intercept it.

His first port of call was **Yakutat Bay**, which he entered on 23 May, almost a year after it was seen by **Jean François de La Pérouse**. The *Queen Charlotte* anchored in Port Mulgrave, named after the arctic explorer Constantine John Phipps, the second Baron Mulgrave. Trade was brisk and important descriptions of the area and its native people were recorded. Dixon then continued south beyond **Cross Sound** to Norfolk Sound (today **Sitka Sound**) where he stayed from 12–23 June, and then on to Port Banks (today Whale Bay) on the southwest coast of Baronof Island. He next proceeded to the **Queen Charlotte Islands**, which he named after his vessel, in its turn named for the consort of George III. James Cook and **Juan Francisco de la Bodega y Quadra** had determined the general outline of the coast; now others were beginning to fill in some of the details, and Dixon's pioneering work in the Queen Charlottes, where he found "a greater quantity of furs than perhaps anywhere hitherto known," was especially important. However, his prime concern was trade not exploration and so, although he rightly claimed to have made considerable additions to an understanding of the geography of the coast, he was quite content to leave further discoveries to others. He cruised the outer coast before sailing up the east coast as far as Louise Island. His names for Cloak Bay, Hippa

Island, Rennell's Sound, and Cape St. James have all survived. Off Nootka he met **James Colnett** and was advised that there were no furs in the area, so he moved on to Hawaii and Macao, where he met up with Portlock. They sold their furs and returned to England in September 1788.

Dixon retained a keen interest in the Northwest Coast and his advice was sought by politicians and interested traders after the **Nootka Crisis** of 1789–1790. He supported **Alexander Dalrymple**'s plan for a settlement to thwart Russian, Spanish, and American efforts to establish themselves on the coast, and was in consultation with Banks and others in the early stages of what became the **George Vancouver** expedition.

In 1789 Dixon's account of his expedition was published in London as *A Voyage round the World; but more particularly to the North-West Coast of America.* He wrote an introduction and two appendices dealing with natural history, the progress of the ships, and his astronomical and meteorological observations. The text consists of a series of 49 letters written by William Beresford, the supercargo on the *Queen Charlotte.* Dixon's *Voyage* contains a general chart of the coast from Cook Inlet to Nootka Sound, plans of anchorages, notably Port Mulgrave, and coastal views. In addition there are engravings presenting the Alaskan volcano, Mount Iliamna, **Mount Edgecumbe**, Hippa Island, and a portrait of a young woman of Queen Charlotte Islands wearing the distinctive **labret**.

When John Meares published the accounts of his voyages to the Northwest Coast in 1786–1787 and 1788–1789, Dixon wrote a pamphlet criticizing his inaccuracies and claims of discovery. There followed a pamphlet war from which Dixon emerged victorious.

DIXON ENTRANCE. A broad passage, some 40 miles wide, it forms a natural separation between the **Alexander Archipelago** in the north and the **Queen Charlotte Islands** in the south. It was named by Sir **Joseph Banks** after the explorer and fur trader **George Dixon**, who was on that part of the coast in 1787. Apparently when Dixon presented his manuscript chart of the North Pacific to Banks in 1788 he invited Banks to name a number of features to which names had not yet been assigned. Thus "Dixon Straits" appeared on the general chart published in Dixon's *Voyage* in 1789.

In July 1774 the Spanish navigator **Juan Pérez** crossed the opening of the entrance to 54°40′ N, and his countryman **Jacinto Caamaño**, exploring the area extensively in the summer of 1792, recognized this first discovery by calling the passage Entrada de Juan Pérez. In the early part of the 19th century Dixon Entrance became the boundary between **Russian America** and the **Oregon Territory**, all of which was claimed by the United States as its inheritance of Spanish "rights, claims and pretensions" on the coast north of 42° N following the **Transcontinental Treaty** of 1819. In the wake of the "54/40 or fight" presidential election of 1844, the Treaty of Washington established the 49° parallel as the northern boundary of the United States in 1846; this secured the central Northwest Coast for Britain and ultimately Canada, and Dixon Entrance became the boundary between first, **British Columbia** and Russian America, and then, after 1867, British Columbia and **Alaska**.

DOBBS, ARTHUR (1689–1765). A member of the British parliament and advocate of free trade, Arthur Dobbs became a critic of the **Hudson's Bay Company**, not only because of its monopoly status, but also for what he considered its lethargic approach towards the expansion of trading activities in northern Canada, and its lack of any enthusiasm in the search for the **Northwest Passage**. In the 1720s he became convinced of the passage's existence and the geopolitical dangers posed if France were able to find and control it. In 1731 he published a memorial, in which he placed this belief into a historical context, and made reference to the story of **Juan de Fuca**. Despite strong evidence to the contrary raised by the voyage of Charles Middleton to Hudson Bay in 1741–1742 Dobbs maintained his belief in the passage and in 1744 published *An Account of the Countries adjoining Hudson's Bay, in the Northwest Part of America*, in which he maintained as credible the long-forgotten and discredited story of **Bartholomew de Fonte**. In 1745 this enthusiasm led to a Parliamentary offer of £20,000 to any British vessel that successfully negotiated the waterway; it also persuaded French cartographers **Joseph Nicolas de l'Isle** and **Philippe Buache** to take the possible existence of a passage seriously, and to produce their speculative and erroneous, but influential memorials and maps. Dobbs died believing that Britain's conquest of New France would at last lead to the discovery of the passage.

DOUGLAS, JAMES (1803–1877). Following the merger of the **Hudson's Bay Company** (HBC) and **North West Company**, James Douglas worked in the New Caledonia region of central **British Columbia**. In 1830 he transferred to **Fort Vancouver** where, as chief factor, he played a leading role in establishing the company's exploration and domination of the coastal trade from the **Columbia River** to **Russian America**. In 1842–1843 he established **Fort Victoria** at the southern end of **Vancouver Island** to replace the northern forts, and it gradually became the center of HBC activities after 1846 with the acceptance by Britain and the United States of the 49° parallel as the international boundary in the **Pacific Northwest**. In 1849 Douglas moved to the fort when the island was leased by the British government to the HBC, and in 1851 became governor of the crown colony of Vancouver Island. In 1858, resigning his position with the HBC, he also became governor of the mainland colony of British Columbia and oversaw dramatic developments and settlement precipitated by the Fraser River Gold Rush. He had retired from both positions by 1864.

DRAKE, FRANCIS (ca. 1540–1596). Francis Drake's circumnavigation of the globe in the years 1577–1580 challenged Spanish and Portuguese power and made him the first English explorer in the Pacific Ocean. In the summer of 1579 he visited the coasts of **Oregon** and **California** and searched for the **Strait of Anian**.

Between 1566 and 1573 his piratical activities in the Caribbean were thinly veiled military escapades aimed at harassing Spain's shipping and disrupting its flow of riches from the New World. In 1572 he crossed the Isthmus of Panama, saw the Pacific, and determined to realize the Elizabethan dream of penetrating the ocean. After rounding Cape Horn in September 1578, the *Golden Hind* raided coastal settlements in South America and captured two Spanish merchantmen off Peru. Laden with booty, Drake followed a preconceived plan to return to England via the passage from the Pacific to the Atlantic suggested by the maps of **Abraham Ortelius**.

How far Drake sailed north and the location of any landings he made has been the subject of intense debate, made all the more intriguing by the inset "Portus Novae Albionis" on Jodocus Hondius's Drake Broadside map published around 1595. It seems highly unlikely that he reached the coast of **Vancouver Island**, and the suggestion that he sailed as far as present-day Alaska is purely speculative and, given the difficulties of sailing north against wind and current, and the timelines involved, impractical and improbable. More realistic is the suggestion that he was off **Oregon** around latitude 44° N in the first days of June 1579 and sought shelter in one of a number of possible bays there or in northern California before deciding, with the coast having failed to turn east in any distinctive way, to sail south and careen his ship for urgent repairs before setting out across the Pacific. Many scholars are persuaded by the work of the Drake Navigator's Guild that he rounded **Point Reyes**, north of **San Francisco** in latitude 38° N, entered Drake's Bay on 17 June and set up camp in the *estero* inside the bay, which provided wood and water and a safe place to work on his ship. However, many others dispute the apparent *fait accompli* proposed by the Guild. Wherever he did land, he enjoyed cordial relations with the local natives, whom ethnographers believe were the Coast Miwok people, although we can be sure that they would not have understood, or appreciated, his claim to have taken "possession of this kingdom, whose king and people freely resign their right and title in the whole land unto Her Majesty's keeping now named by me and to be known unto all men as Nova Albion." Drake left **New Albion** on 23 July and reached England in September 1580.

DRAKE'S BAY. *See* POINT REYES AND DRAKE'S BAY.

DUCHÉ DE VANCY, GASPARD (1756–1788). Gaspard Duché de Vancy was the senior artist on the **Jean François de La Pérouse** **Expedition.** Three of his Northwest Coast drawings have survived, one a dramatic general scene of the ships at anchor in Port des Français (**Lituya Bay**); a group of **natives;** and a native woman wearing the **labret**. The latter two were engraved and printed in the atlas of maps and drawings published with the La Pérouse journal in 1797, along with 10 other plates based on his drawings of people and places visited by the expedition, including his famous view of the statues at Easter Island. La Pérouse consistently praised his work.

Duché de Vancy was brought up in Vienna, studied in Paris, and was attached to the royal court, where he is said to have painted a portrait of Marie Antoinette. Before joining the expedition he had traveled in Italy and lived briefly in London where his paintings were exhibited at the Royal Academy.

DUFLOT DE MOFRAS, EUGÈNE (1810–1884). While serving as a diplomat in Mexico City, Eugène Duflot de Mofras made a visit to **California** and the **Oregon** Territory during 1840–1842, producing a perceptive description and analysis of the region in a historical context. He visited **Astoria** and **Fort Vancouver** on the **Columbia River**, and came as far north as **Puget Sound**, the San Juan Islands, and the **Fraser River**. Duflot de Mofras's *Exploration du Territoire de l'Oregon, des Californies et de la mer Vermeille* (1844) is considered by many scholars to be the most important work on the Pacific coast of North America at a time when the whole region was in dispute—between Spain and the United States in the south, and Britain and the United States farther north.

DUFRESNE (fl. 1785–1787). A naturalist with the **Jean François de La Pérouse** Expedition, Dufresne supervised the expedition's trade in furs on the Northwest Coast and their sale in Macao. He also brought home from China a report on the prospects of a successful commerce and four of the finest furs and two pieces of cloth "made by the Indians of **Port des Français**" for Queen Marie Antoinette.

DUNCAN, CHARLES (fl. 1786–1792). In 1786 Charles Duncan, who had reached the rank of master in the Royal Navy, was given command of the *Princess Royal* by **Richard Cadman Etches**'s King George's Sound Company to lead a trading expedition to the Northwest Coast with **James Colnett**. During the summer of 1787 he traded in **Nootka Sound** and on the west coast of **Vancouver Island** before wintering in the **Sandwich Islands**.

The next year, 1788, he proved that so unknown were many of the geographical details of the coast that the earliest traders inevitably found themselves exploring waters previously unseen by other Europeans. On the recommendation of **George Dixon**, he headed initially for the **Queen Charlotte Islands** entering **Dixon Entrance** and sailing south through Hecate Strait, thus completing the first circumnavigation of the islands and conclusively proving their suspected insularity. He concentrated on the continental coast, trading with the

natives as he worked his way down the offshore islands, which he named the Princess Royal Islands, from the Skeena River to Calvert Island, which he also named. **George Vancouver** recognized both these names on his charts in 1792. Duncan then sailed south to trade in **Clayoquot Sound** before continuing on as far as the entrance to the **Strait of Juan de Fuca**, discovered by **Charles Barkley** the previous year. He visited the **Makah** natives at Cape Classet (**James Cook**'s **Cape Flattery**) and drew a fine chart with a coastal profile that identified as Pinnacle Rock the pillar reported by the legendary Greek pilot **Juan de Fuca**. From the Makah, Duncan learned about a "Great Sea" inside the strait that stretched from north (the **Strait of Georgia**) to south (**Puget Sound**), and he convinced himself, and others when he returned to England, that this must be the **Sea of the West** and part of the waterway system that eventually led to Hudson Bay. Despite the history of repeated failure to find the eastern entrance to the **Northwest Passage** in this bay, Duncan became fanatical about the idea of a navigable passage. Consequently, as others such as the influential **Alexander Dalrymple** shared his enthusiasm, he was chosen to lead two voyages to northern Canada in 1790 and 1791. After he started too late in the first year, the second effort also ended in inevitable failure, after which the apparently distraught Duncan faded from the historical record.

– E –

EAST INDIA COMPANY (EIC). The Company of Merchants of London Trading into the East Indies was chartered as a monopoly in 1601 to exploit trade with East and Southeast Asia and India. It came to wield supreme political and economic power in India, acting as an agent of British imperialism from the early 18th century until the mid-19th century. In addition, its activities in China served as the catalyst for the expansion of British influence in that region. The opening of the Pacific in the latter half of the 18th century threatened to undermine the company's monopoly, and no more so than following **James Cook**'s Third Voyage, which promised a lucrative **fur trade** between the Northwest Coast and China. Indeed, despite **James King**'s assertion that such a trade must necessarily involve or receive the consent of the EIC, and this was the case with the pioneering voyages of **James Hanna**, **Nathaniel Portlock**, **George Dixon**, and **James Strange**, the ships of other early traders such as **John Meares** and **Charles Barkley** sailed with the express purpose of flouting the EIC's monopoly. In order to combat the problem, **Alexander Dalrymple** suggested that the EIC and **Hudson's Bay Company** join forces to control the blossoming trade from northern Canada, on the coast and across the North Pacific to China. Neither this plan, nor the proposal for the EIC to build a depot at **Nootka Sound** and to have one ship on the coast to collect furs and another crossing the Pacific to trade them, was pursued. This latter idea was also floated by others, but the high risk and cost involved, plus American displacement of British traders for a generation and the exhaustion of the fur resource itself, rather than any overt action by the EIC, ultimately solved its problem.

ECHEVERRÍA, ATANÁSIO (1770–?). A botanical illustrator and artist with the Royal Scientific Expedition to **New Spain**, Atanásio Echeverría was described by his colleague **José Mariano Moziño** as "one of the best artists on our expedition." Vancouver's naturalist **Archibald Menzies** agreed that Echeverría had "great merit," and Alexander von Humboldt wrote that his work competed "with the most perfect which Europe has produced." Late in 1791 Viceroy **Revillagigedo** and **Juan Francisco de la Bodega y Quadra** added Echeverria, Moziño, and another scientist **José María Maldonado** to the Limits Expedition bound for **Nootka Sound**.

At Nootka during the summer of 1792, Echeverría executed botanical and zoological drawings and sketched a number of general views and **native** people. He continued drawing in **Monterey** on the way home to Mexico City where he turned his originals over to other **artists** at the Academy of San Carlos for the creation of a number of reproductions. It was customary at that time for artists to lend their work to teachers and capable students to finish or improve them for engraving or to produce multiple copies. In the process, although a set of 43 drawings was included in the folio volume of Bodega's *Viaje a la Costa NO* [Noroeste] *de la América Septentrional*, Echeverría's originals were lost. One of his most famous images is the "Interior View of Maquinna's House at Tahsis" showing Chief

Maquinna dancing for his guests, Bodega and **George Vancouver**, in September 1792.

EDGAR, THOMAS (1745–1801). Thomas Edgar joined *Discovery* under **Charles Clerke** as master for **James Cook**'s Third Voyage to the Pacific Ocean. He served on her for the entire voyage, assuming responsibility for the navigation of the vessel and her survey work. As a result he was directly responsible for numerous surveys on the Northwest Coast, including a chart of **Nootka Sound** with informative plans of Ship Cove and **Friendly Cove**; A Plan of Sandwich Sound (**Prince William Sound**) that includes the tracks of *Discovery* to Snug Cove and their relationship to **Hinchinbrook Island** and **Montague Island**; and plans of Providence Bay and Samgoonoodha (English) Bay on **Unalaska** Island.

ELIZA, FRANCISCO DE (1759–1825). Francisco de Eliza arrived in **New Spain** in 1789 to bolster the corps of officers at the Naval Department of **San Blas**. His experience and seniority immediately gave him command of a flotilla of three ships sent early in 1790 to reoccupy **Friendly Cove** in **Nootka Sound**, abandoned by **Esteban José Martínez** the previous fall. He brought with him soldiers under **Pedro de Alberni**, and spent two miserable winters, 1790–1791, on the rain-soaked west coast of **Vancouver Island**. His instructions were wide-ranging: he was not only ordered to develop a settlement, expel any foreigners, and trade for furs, but also to report on the climate, flora and fauna, mineral deposits, and the culture and society of the **native** people. As a result Eliza reported extensively on Nootka Sound and its potential usefulness to Spain. In addition, he oversaw exploratory activity that sent **Salvador Fidalgo** to **Alaska** and **Manuel Quimper** into the **Strait of Juan de Fuca** in 1790.

After the return of Fidalgo and Quimper to **San Blas** in the fall of 1790, the viceroy, the **Count of Revillagigedo**, determined to continue the exploration of the Northwest Coast in defense of Spanish sovereignty. As a result the commandant at San Blas, **Juan Francisco de la Bodega y Quadra**, sent instructions and a new general chart of the coast to Eliza at Nootka. He was to undertake an ambitious survey of the coast from **Mount St. Elias** to **California**, examining the many openings known to exist such as the one seen by **Juan Pérez** in 1774 (Dixon Entrance) as well as the Strait of Juan de Fuca and the **Río de Martín de Aguilar**, which had never been properly located and explored. For the voyage, Eliza decided to use the packet boat *San Carlos* and the schooner *Santa Saturnina*, commanded by **José María Narváez**.

The ships left Nootka on 4 May. It was already late in the season and as soon as he ran into the difficult northwest winds, Eliza quickly turned back, deciding to forget about Alaska and concentrate on the coast south of Nootka. He took the *San Carlos* into **Clayoquot Sound** where he met the noted native fur trader Chief **Wickaninnish**. He was joined there by Narváez who, with Eliza's pilot **Juan Pantoja y Arriaga**, undertook surveys that explored the various inlets and passages of the sound and improved the charts from 1789 and 1790. On 22 May Eliza sailed directly for Quimper's Puerto de Córdoba (Esquimalt Harbour) directing Narváez to meet him there after undertaking further surveys in the Archipielago de Nitinat o Carassco (Barkley Sound). It was on this occasion that Narváez named the Canal de Alberny (the Alberni Canal) in honor of the garrison commander at Nootka.

Once at Córdoba, Eliza immediately decided to undertake the exploration of Quimper's Canal de López de Haro (Haro Strait). This was done initially by **José Antonio Verdía** and then by the schooner and Pantoja in a longboat. They discovered the northern part of the San Juan Islands and were the first Europeans to see the vast expanse of the Gran Canal de Nuestra Señora del Rosario de Marinera (the **Strait of Georgia**). Eliza then transferred his base of operations to the south shore to Quimper's Puerto de Bodega y Quadra (Port Discovery) and dispatched Narváez and the *Santa Saturnina* with **Juan Carrasco** in the longboat to continue the exploration. Narváez entered the Strait of Georgia via what is today Rosario Strait and undertook one of the great pioneering explorations of the early history of the entire Northwest Coast. He was away from 1 to 22 July and during a remarkable voyage generally explored the continental coast to beyond Texada Island and returned along the southeast coast of Vancouver Island. His activities were recorded on a giant chart—the *Carta que comprehende los interiors y veril de la Costa desde los 48° de Latitud N. hasta los 50°*. When he received Narváez's report and saw the shape of the field charts, Eliza seems to have formed the opinion that Nootka was on the western side of a giant island, which it is; but more importantly he wrote in his journal that "the Passage to the Atlantic Ocean, which foreign nations search for with such diligence on this coast, cannot in my opinion, if there be one, be found in any other part; it is either, I think, by this great canal, or it is continent."

While he awaited the return of Narváez it is somewhat surprising that Eliza did not undertake further exploration of Quimper's Ensenada de Caamaño, identified by Juan Carassco the year before. As he had headed north, Narváez had considered it an inlet worthy of more investigation, and determined to explore it further on his return. However, he was short of supplies after his journey and did not do so. Considering that the Spaniards had native information indicating that there was a waterway stretching to the south at the end of the Strait of Juan de Fuca, Eliza's disinterest meant that **George Vancouver** would receive the credit for discovering Admiralty Inlet (**Puget Sound**) and the Hood Canal. The large Spanish map that recorded the explorations of the summer of 1791, however, added the word "boca" (inlet) to "ensenada" (bay), which clearly demonstrated Narváez's belief that what he had seen did indeed stretch deeper into the continent.

The expedition headed back to Nootka on 25 July. Eliza brought Narváez on board the *San Carlos* to work on the charts and put Carrasco in command of the schooner. On the way out of the strait they discovered Port Angeles, which Quimper had missed, and then visited **Neah Bay**. He reached Nootka on 30 August after struggling against adverse winds. The delay robbed him, by two days, of the chance to show his charts to **Alejandro Malaspina**, whose ships he saw as he neared Nootka Sound. Although he himself was a less than energetic or curious explorer, the activities of his young subordinates Narváez, Pantoja, Carrasco, and Verdía ensured that the expedition was a success with its discovery and charting of the Strait of Georgia.

The *Santa Saturnina* never made it to Nootka. A shortage of water persuaded Carrasco to head to **Monterey** and San Blas. When the viceroy and Malaspina were briefed on the results of the expedition, they agreed that another voyage was warranted. This became the **Dionisio Alcalá Galiano** and **Cayetano Valdés** Expedition of 1792.

In the spring of 1792 Eliza and Alberni briefed Bodega when he arrived to meet with **George Vancouver**. Eliza then left for San Blas where he served as commandant following the death of Bodega in 1794, and undertook surveying voyages to continue the improvement of the charts of the Mexican and Californian coasts.

ELLIS, WILLIAM WEBB (?–1785). Appointed surgeon's mate on **Charles Clerke**'s *Discovery* for **James Cook**'s Third Voyage to the Pacific Ocean, William Webb Ellis became, after **John Webber,** the most prolific of the **artists** on the expedition. Working mostly in pencil and watercolor, Ellis drew coastal views, landscapes, **native** people, and natural history subjects. Clerke no doubt encouraged the latter, as he collected specimens and **artifacts** for Sir **Joseph Banks**, with whom he had become friends on Cook's First Voyage. At **Nootka Sound** Ellis drew workmanlike views of the ships at anchor and "Astronomer's Rock" in which he demonstrated his interest in the natural environment. There exists also an interesting little sketch of a white-headed or bald eagle. From **Prince William Sound** two of his views have survived, as have views of the **Shumagin Islands** and the harbor of Samgoonoodha on **Unalaska** Island. Important also are his painting of native "Huts at Unalaska" and his sketch of the "Inside of a Hut at Unalaska."

After the voyage, Ellis presented a portfolio of 150 natural history drawings (90 of them birds) to Banks. Without permission from the Admiralty, which had a rule that all journals must be handed over at the end of a voyage, Ellis published his *Authentic Narrative* (1782), which contained among various scenes, four rather poor engravings of natives from Nootka and Prince William Sounds and Unalaska, for which the original drawings seem to have been lost. His unauthorized publication cost him any hope of serving again in the Royal Navy, and strained his relationships with Banks and his former companions.

ENGEL, SAMUEL (1702–1784). Swiss writer and bibliophile, Samuel Engel published various works on exploration and believed that the polar seas were free of ice away from the coasts. In a *memoire* and accompanying maps published in 1765, he developed this theory in the context of Russian discoveries and the speculative geography of the 1740s and 1750s. His was one of the misleading books that **James Cook** brought with him to the Northwest Coast in 1778. A map depicting the seas and lands east of **Kamchatka** were so sketchy and problematic that they were of no use whatever to the celebrated navigator.

ENTRADA DE HEZETA. The delta of the **Columbia River**, the Entrada de Hezeta was discovered by **Bruno de Hezeta** on 17 August 1775, soon after he had become separated from **Juan Francisco de la Bodega y Quadra** and had abandoned, off lower **Vancouver Island**, his voyage north and was returning to **Monterey**. He named the significant opening in the coast Bahia de la Asunción de Nuestra Señora in recognition of the feast day of the Assumption of Our Lady on 15 August. This name appears on Hezeta's chart but the general chart of the coast, prepared by Bodega and **Francisco Mourelle** after their voyage to southern **Alaska**, uses the term "Entrada descubierta por Dn Bruno Ezeta," and this became standard on subsequent maps.

ESCHSCHOLTZ, JOHANN (1793–1831). Physician and naturalist Johann Eschscholtz joined the brig *Riurik* for the Russian expedition of **Otto von Kotzebue** to **Russian America**, 1815–1818. With his colleague **Adelbert von Chamisso** he was one of the first and most important **scientists** to visit the **Bering Sea**, **Aleutian Islands**, and **California**. They worked well and effectively together; Chamisso was the botanist who collected a second specimen for Eschscholtz whenever possible; Eschscholtz was in charge of collecting insects, birds, and animals. In a bay named after him in **Kotzebue Sound**, he uncovered a significant deposit of prehistoric animal bones, the first such recorded discovery in Russian America. In California, Chamisso named a poppy he found in the countryside around **Fort Ross** after his friend; it is still known as *Eschscholtzia californica*, and is the state flower of California. In 1823–1826 he joined von Kotzebue for a second circumnavigation in the *Predpriyatiye*. In Patagonia and the South Pacific Eschscholtz discovered a number of new bird and reptile species. When the ship reached **New Archangel** after visiting **Kamchatka**, he continued his earlier studies and collecting, describing animals and marine invertebrates. Although he did produce two works, *System der Akalephen* and notably his *Zoologischer Atlas*, he was never able to adequately publish his research before his untimely death at the age of 38.

ESPINOSA Y TELLO, JOSÉ (1763–1815). An officer with the **Alejandro Malaspina** Expedition, José Espinosa came to the Northwest Coast in the summer of 1791. In 1783 he began work with Vicente Tofiño on his survey of the coasts of the Iberian Peninsula. This also involved study under Tofiño at the Royal Observatory in Cadiz, where he became familiar with the most up-to-date instruments of **navigation** and surveying, and practical work in the field. It was at this time that he met both Alejandro Malaspina and **Dionisio Alcalá Galiano**. Shortly after Malaspina had gained royal approval for his voyage to the Pacific, he added Espinosa to his officer corps. During the preparation period it was Espinosa, researching for documents in the Archives of the Indies in Seville that might offer information useful to the expedition, who found and brought to Malaspina's attention the report by **Ferrer Maldonado** about his supposed trip through the **Northwest Passage**. The discovery of this document (although the general details of the apocryphal voyage were already known at the time) would later have profound implications for the expedition and brought it to **Alaska** in 1791. Due to illness Espinosa was unable to sail with the expedition in 1789, but he joined the ships in Acapulco early in 1791, bringing with him a number of navigational instruments including four chronometers, and the most recent copies of the Nautical Almanac through 1794.

As a result of his time in Alaska, Espinosa compiled a lengthy entry in his journal describing the visit to Port **Mulgrave**. He discussed the expedition's encounters with the **Tlingit**, the skill of the **natives** as traders and the tension of the dangerous swarming of some sailors that had to be met with force by **José Bustamante**. He described their physical appearance and dress, customs, and religion. He praised them as industrious and clever, having valor, even ferocity, and a great sense of patriotism. Espinosa visited the impressive burial site drawn by **José Cardero**, describing it in detail. He also assisted **Felipe Bauza** with the survey of the port and its surroundings and authored a set of observations, 8 May to 8 August, "to determine the longitude of Port Mulgrave."

At Nootka, Espinosa with **Ciriaco Cevallos** undertook a detailed survey of the entire sound and its various canals. The trip lasted eight days and resulted in a definitive map of the region. Native villages were located on their chart, which has proven important in present-day treaty negotiations between the Mowachaht people and the Canadian government. An important goal of the expedition, a visit to Chief **Maquinna** in his winter village, was successfully undertaken and resulted in his coming to the ships to meet with Malaspina. Espinosa's notes on the natives encountered were reflected in Malaspina's analysis of the country and people of Nootka as outlined in his official "Description of the Northwest Coast of America."

After the expedition's voyage across the South Pacific, Espinosa disembarked at Callao (the port of Lima) and with Bauza made a trip across the continent to Buenos Aires and Montevideo. Together they produced a remarkable map of their entire journey. Espinosa was later director of the Hydrographic Office and published his seminal work *Memoria sobre las Observaciones Astronomicas hechas por los Navigantes Españoles en Distinos Lugares del Globo* (1809). During the period of the French occupation of Spain he went to England where he continued to work on the publication of Spanish charts. On his return to Spain he reestablished himself at the Hydrographic Department.

ETCHES, RICHARD CADMAN (fl. 1785–1817). Merchant and shipowner Richard Cadman Etches was the leading figure in a London-based syndicate—the King George's Sound Company—formed specifically to develop a fur trade between **Nootka Sound** and China, as suggested by **James King** in the published journal (1784) of **James Cook**'s Third Voyage to the Pacific. The group fitted out two expeditions, that of **Nathaniel Portlock** and **George Dixon** (1785) and another commanded by **James Colnett** (1789). As a result of a short-lived partnership between the Etches syndicate and **John Meares**, who had returned to Macao from America in late 1788 with dreams of founding a commercial empire based on the link between an establishment in Nootka Sound and China, Colnett became commodore of a five-ship assault on the Northwest Coast in 1789. The "United Merchants" (Etches and Meares) was formed specifically to counter the perceived threat posed by American traders **Robert Gray** and **John Kendrick**, whom Meares had encountered at Nootka in the fall of 1788. But Colnett ran into more than Americans when he reached Nootka, his clash with the Spaniard **Esteban José Martínez** sparking the **Nootka Sound Incident**. This effectively robbed Etches and his partners of any profits from their expected commercial success in the North Pacific.

By this time (1789), however, Etches had turned his attention to Europe and become a Danish citizen. He entered the employ of Empress **Catherine II** in the hopes of effecting an imperial alliance between Britain and Russia in the Pacific, but only succeeded in arousing the suspicion of the government in London. During the 1790s he became a spy for Britain on the continent in its struggle with republican France, and helped engineer the escape of two naval officers from imprisonment in Paris in 1795. Later, in 1804, he advised the government on how best to disrupt Napoleon's plans for the invasion of England.

ETHOLEN, ADOLF (1799–1876). Assigned to work for the **Russian–American Company** in 1817, after graduation from the naval academy, Adolf Etholen commanded many company vessels and undertook numerous voyages that took him from north and south of **Sitka** to Okhotsk, **Kamchatka**, the Kurile and Near Islands, the **Aleutian Islands**, and **Kodiak**, as well as to **California** on at least five occasions. Of particular importance were two voyages he made into the **Bering Sea** in 1821–1822, and again in 1830.

On the first occasion, commanding the cutter *Baranov*, with **Vasilii Khromchenko** in the brig *Golovnin*, he undertook a detailed two-season survey along the coast north from **Bristol Bay** to **Norton Sound**. The purpose was not only to lay down the first detailed charts of the area, but also to make direct contact and instigate trade with the native tribes living along the coast. He named Hagemeister Strait and Island, explored the lower reaches of both the Nushagak and Kuskokwim rivers, and surveyed Nunivak Island. He and Khromchenko, who left an important journal with descriptions of his encounters with the Yup'ik and Cup'ik people, were followed by the interior explorations of **Ivan I. Vasil'ev** and **Fedor Kolmakov**, 1829–1832, which brought the natives of the Nushagak and Kuskokwim river basins into the sphere of influence of the Aleksandrovskii Redoubt in Bristol Bay.

In 1830 Etholen ventured north again in the *Chichagov* after the appearance of **Frederick Beechey** in the Arctic Ocean in 1826. Concern about this British voyage, and Etholen's observations north of the **Bering Strait** and subsequent recommendations, led to the establishment in 1833 of the Mikhailovskii Redoubt in Norton Sound, which opened the way for Russian penetration of the Yukon River basin before the end of the decade.

The **Native American** contacts and information provided by these expeditions laid the foundation for relations that proved highly profitable to the Russian–American Company, ultimately opening up all of southwest **Alaska** for the **fur trade**.

During the 1830s Etholen resumed his voyaging that ranged in a giant arc from Okhotsk to California. A valued assistant to the company's chief manager **Ferdinand Wrangell**, he also explored extensively in the **Alexander Archipelago**. In 1838 he was designated chief manager of the Russian colony to succeed Wrangell and assumed his duties at Sitka in May 1840. His time in office was marked by improvements to the physical infrastructure of the settlements at **New Archangel** and **Kodiak**, improved relations with the **Hudson's Bay Company**, and an attempt to better the lot of the **Tlingit** natives trading at Sitka by curbing the excesses of the liquor trade and introducing new regulations to prevent abuse by employees of the company.

EVREINOV, IVAN (?–1724). With Fedor Luzhin, a fellow geodesist and navigator, Ivan Evreinov was sent by **Peter the Great** on a secret expedition to **Kamchatka** in 1719. Interest in the Kamchatka and Chukotskii peninsulas, and the relationship of the eastern coast of Russia to Japan and America, had grown in St. Petersburg since the turn of the century. At that time a shipwrecked Japanese sailor had been taken to meet the czar and provided information about Japan and the Kurile Islands. In 1702 an outpost had been established at Bol'sheettsk on the Bol'shaia River, and in 1716 a sea route was pioneered from Okhotsk to the Tigel River. That same year a large expedition to study the Kamchatka and Chukotskii coasts was authorized. It never materialized, but was later realized in the initiatives of Evreinov and Luzhin and **Vitus Bering**.

The ambitious instructions for the 1719 expedition were "to travel to Kamchatka and beyond," to chart new lands, and to determine "whether Asia and America are joined by land"; also to examine areas "not only south but east and west, and to place everything on a map." It seems that the primary goal of the expedition was to explore the Kurile Islands, where the Japanese were understood to have found silver. Evreinov and Luzhin sailed south from Nizhne-Kamchatsk on 22 May 1721, progressing as far as Simushir, placing 14 islands onto a map, and thus updating Russian knowledge about the coast of Kamchatka and its relationship to the Kurile Islands and the Siberian coast. They had not settled the question of Asia's relationship to America, but had demonstrated that, if there was a connection, it was to the north. This determined the focus of further exploration; Bering's first **Kamchatka Expedition** (1728) and the subsequent voyage of **Mikhail Gvozdev** and Ivan Fedorov (1732) both sailed in that direction.

– F –

FAGES, PEDRO (1734–1794). Arriving in **New Spain** in 1767, Pedro Fages distinguished himself in the Sonora campaign and came to the attention of **José de Gálvez**, who chose him to lead a contingent of Catalonian Volunteers on the sea arm of the **Sacred Expedition** to found **Alta California** in 1769. He was in Portolá's party that set out to find **Sebastián Vizcaíno's Monterey** in the summer of that year, and reached the area of **San Francisco** Bay. After Monterey was finally established in 1770, Fages undertook another expedition to the Bay area. Proceeding down the Santa Clara Valley he explored the eastern shore of the bay and on 28 November was the first to see its entrance—the Golden Gate. In the spring of 1772 he followed the same route, but this time proceeded farther north and then east along Carquines Strait.

From 1770 until 1774 Fages was commander of the presidio in Monterey and governor of Alta California. As such he oversaw the development of the fledgling settlement and established harmonious relations with the **natives**. But he clashed with Father **Junípero Serra**, who accused him of meddling in mission affairs and retarding mission expansion by not providing military and other support for new establishments. Gathering support from a number of disaffected soldiers, who bristled under Fages's authoritarian style of leadership, Serra successfully engineered his removal from Monterey. He spent 1775 in Mexico City writing a detailed report on the natural and human history of California, which was particularly important for its extensive references to the native people.

In 1782 Fages returned to Monterey as governor of **California** and held this position until 1791. In 1786 he welcomed the **Jean François de La Pérouse** Expedition to Monterey as the first foreign visitors to the Californian capital. La Pérouse praised him for his courtesy and generosity in supplying the ships with daily milk, meat, fruits, and vegetables, and was impressed by his knowledge of the country and achievements in New Spain. Indian fighter, explorer, and administrator, Pedro Fages was an important figure in the early history of California.

FERRER, BARTOLOMÉ (fl. 1540s). Bartolomé Ferrer was the chief pilot on the expedition of **Juan Rodríguez Cabrillo** that explored the **California** coast in 1542–1543. Before Cabrillo died early in 1543 on San Miguel Island, he ordered Ferrer to continue the coastal reconnaissance. Leaving the Channel Islands, the *San Salvador* and *La Victoria* passed **Monterey** and reached beyond the latitude of **San Francisco** as far as Punta de Arena, which they named Cabo de Fortunas. As the wind and waves increased in intensity, they continued north but the narrative of the voyage makes it impossible to determine the extent of Ferrer's progress. He thought that he had reached as high as 44° N on 28 February, but historians agree that he was at least two degrees off in his calculations, which would have put him off the California–Oregon border. He was probably lower than this because he never suggested a landmark that can be equated to **Cape Mendocino** after which there is a dramatic change in the direction of the coastline.

Turning for home, the men were increasingly weakened from scurvy and exposure to the elements. The group limped into its home port of Navidad on 14 April 1543. Although it was a remarkable achievement, no fabulous cities had been found to excite the interest of Viceroy Antonio de Mendoza. As a result no new voyages were planned, and it was left to the **Manila galleons**, seeking potential safe harbors for use in an emergency, to undertake, sporadically, the next round of exploration on the coast.

FERRER MALDONADO, LORENZO (ca. 1550–1625). Ferrer Maldonado had a life that often appears more mystery than reality.

• Described as a man of great genius, he was also considered a manipulative charlatan. Towards the end of the first decade of the 17th century he had gained a certain standing at the royal court as an experienced navigator and respected cosmographer. At this time he submitted ideas on various subjects to officials, competed for a royal prize aimed at solving the problem of measuring longitude at sea, and most famously circulated a memoir, "Relación del descubrimiento del Estrecho de Anian," in 1609, in which he claimed to have discovered and sailed through the **Northwest Passage** in 1588. Dismissed at the time as an obvious fraud, the story resurfaced at the end of the 18th century to cause a brief flurry of interest at a time when European exploration on the Northwest Coast was finally confirming the truth that no such navigable passage existed.

Maldonado's fantastic tale was a curious mixture of fact and fiction. He may indeed have made a voyage to northern Europe and so experienced life at sea, and the Atlantic portion of the voyage account seems to have leaned heavily on the 1587 experiences of John Davis, which were published in 1595. Davis had pushed up the strait that bears his name into Baffin Bay. Thereafter the supposed voyage descends into pure fiction with the frozen sea described as being conveniently navigable until the **Strait of Anian** was reached, entering the Pacific at 60° N. The strait, separating America from Asia, was the subject of several views and maps, and Maldonado reported finding a harbor capable of holding 500 ships. There he also met Hanseatic merchants whose vessels were full of "articles similar to those of China, such as brocades, silks, porcelain, feathers, chests, precious stones, pearls and gold." The whole fiction was a not-so-subtle attempt to move Spanish authorities in Madrid and **New Spain** to take seriously the need to secure and defend a strait that was still widely assumed to exist and which, it was believed, the English had probably found. But the reality of English experiences in searching for the passage, and a lack of interest in New Spain in the coast north of **California** following the voyage of **Sebastián Vizcaíno**, led to the quick dismissal of the whole deception.

Its relevance to late-18th-century exploration in the North Pacific arises from its reemergence, first in 1781, and then again in 1789 on the eve of the departure of the **Alejandro Malaspina** Expedition from Cadiz. For 300 years accounts and rumors of voyages through a Northwest Passage had fired varying periods of enthusiasm for finding a definitive answer to the age-old question of its existence. The 1740s and 1750s were one such period, and the 1770s and 1780s were another, with the expeditions of **James Cook**, the Spanish, and **Jean François de La Pérouse** fuelling speculation yet gradually addressing the problem more precisely. In the summer of 1791 **Alejandro Malaspina** duly disposed of the Maldonado fantasy with his visit to **Yakutat Bay**.

FIDALGO, SALVADOR (1756–1803). Salvador Fidalgo came to America in 1789 to strengthen the officer corps at the Naval Department of **San Blas**. After the **Nootka Sound Incident** in 1789, Spanish authorities were determined to maintain their establishment there, and to bolster their presence on the Northwest Coast as a whole. This meant continuing to find out more about Russian activity. As a result, shortly after arriving in **Nootka Sound** with **Francisco de Eliza** in the spring of 1790, Fidalgo set out on 4 May on a voyage to the far north in the packet boat *San Carlos*. He was instructed to concentrate his activities on **Prince William Sound** (PWS) and **Cook Inlet**. As he expected to encounter Russian fur traders he was accompanied by junior pilot **Esteban Mondofía**, who spoke Russian, and 14 soldiers detached from the corps at Nootka.

Fidalgo entered PWS on 24 May, anchoring off Puerto de Santiago (**Port Etches**) and later in Anderson Bay or Double Bay on the north coast of **Hinchinbrook Island**. An **act of possession** was performed on 3 June at the entrance to Orca Bay, which he called Bahia de Córdova. Remarkably, **James Johnstone** of the **George Vancouver** Expedition still found the cross in place four years later. **Aleut/Alutiiq** natives visited the ship looking to trade for iron, but were disappointed in the Spanish gifts of clothing, beads, and offers of copper. The Spaniards continued their exploration, and two more acts of possession were performed before they encountered the ice field of the Columbia Glacier. They were amazed to see a giant block of ice calving off the glacier "with a great subterranean Thundercap." Faced with a wall of mountains, they realized—as had **James Cook** and **Ignacio de Arteaga** before them—that the sound was closed and there was no navigable passage to the northern sea. The bay of Valdez Arm was named after Navy minister Antonio Valdés.

Despite **Esteban José Martínez**'s report that the Russians had already reached PWS, Fidalgo did not encounter any, even as he negotiated himself down the western side of **Montague Island** where an outpost had existed as early as 1783. As July began, Fidalgo made his way along the **Kenai Peninsula** and entered **Cook Inlet** on 4 July where he did meet Russians at Port Graham at the mouth of English Bay (Puerto de Revillagigedo) and at the second Russian fort in the area, the larger Fort George. Before he left the inlet, Fidalgo ignored the obvious presence of another European power and performed yet another act of possession in English Bay on 15 July. The presence of the Spanish vessel had not gone unnoticed by **Joseph Billings**, who was in the area to expel foreign ships and who sent a native canoe with a letter for Fidalgo inviting him to rendezvous in PWS. But Fidalgo was on his way to **Kodiak Island** and **Three Saints Bay** and had no particular interest in retracing his route to encounter a Russian warship. His brief stopover at the Russian trading establishment, 15–16 August, allowed him to meet **Evstrat Delarov** and undertake a little polite espionage. Heading back to Nootka he was prevented by a severe storm from entering that port, so he proceeded on to Monterey and San Blas, which was reached on 13 November.

For what was expected of it, his expedition was a success, although Fidalgo reported back with little new information. He had improved on Spanish cartographic knowledge of the region, had made a further assessment of the Russian advance along the coasts of North America, and had performed four important acts of possession. At a time when the attention of Mexico City and Madrid was increasingly drawn to the lower Northwest Coast, the threat to Nootka and the California settlements, so strongly suggested by Martínez in 1788, was not yet proving to be a serious problem.

As part of the **Limits Expedition** (1792) commanded by **Juan Francisco de la Bodega y Quadra**, Fidalgo established the short-lived establishment of Nuñez Gaona at **Neah Bay**, the first nonnative settlement in the state of **Washington**. The site had been visited by **Manuel Quimper** in 1790 and Francisco de Eliza in 1791. He stayed over at Nootka as commandant for a miserable winter, 1792–1793, and was relieved in April 1793 when George Vancouver's new second-in-command, **Peter Puget**, arrived on the *Chatham* from Hawaii with supplies that successfully combated the scurvy and other ailments rampant in the settlement. It was on this occasion that **Thomas Manby** regretted that he could only communicate with the Spaniards through a translator or sign language, because he found Fidalgo to be "a man of learning, science and great abilities." Following a final voyage to Nootka in 1794, Fidalgo was based at San Blas for the rest of his career.

FONTE, BARTHOLOMEW DE. The account of fictional mariner Bartholomew de Fonte's imaginary voyage into a passage linking the Pacific with the Atlantic appeared in the age of Daniel Defoe and Jonathan Swift, when the recounting of fabulous journeys was a recognized genre. The importance of the Fonte story, which was ignored at the time of its initial publication, lies in the fact that it was taken seriously in the mid-18th century and became the subject of fanciful but influential maps, as well as intense debate.

In 1708 an anonymous letter was published in London in an obscure and short-lived magazine, the *Monthly Miscellany or Memoirs for the Curious*, edited by James Petiver. It outlined in great detail the adventure of "Admiral Bartholomew de Fonte, then Admiral of New Spain and Peru, and now Prince of Chili" who, in 1640, had sailed north from Lima and found a river he called Rio de los Reyes in latitude 53° N, and a series of crooked channels and islands called the Archipelagos de St. Lazarus. Proceeding northeast he neared Hudson Bay where he met two merchantmen out of Boston and received from a Captain Shapley a set of fine charts and journals. Concluding that his meeting with the east coast ships meant that there was indeed a navigable passage to the Atlantic, he retraced his route and returned safely to Peru.

Some 36 years later, in 1744, a wealthy Irish Member of Parliament and critic of the **Hudson's Bay Company**, **Arthur Dobbs**, plucked the tale from obscurity and made it a genuine hoax. The fact that two voyages into Hudson Bay, 1741–1742 and 1746–1747, failed to find the entrance to any passage leading southwest, shifted attention to its supposed Pacific entrance. In 1749 T. S. Drage, who had been on the 1746 voyage, published *An Account of a Voyage for the Discovery of a North-West Passage*, which included "A Chart for the better understanding of de Fonte's Letter," by Edward Holding, and identified Fonte's passage with the **Strait of Anian**. This brought the story to the attention of the renowned French cartographers **Joseph Nicolas de l'Isle** and **Philippe Buache**, and led to the 1752 publication of a series of speculative maps.

In 1757 the director of the Spanish royal archives and libraries, Father Andrés Marcos Burriel, appended a translation of the letter to his edition of the *Noticia de la California* by the Mexican Jesuit, Miguel Venegas. When Burriel's work was translated into English, French, German, and Dutch, however, his detailed, destructive critique of the whole fable was missing. And, despite the overland journey of **Samuel Hearne** from Hudson Bay to the Coppermine River in 1771, and the descriptions of the Northwest Coast by **Juan Francisco de la Bodega y Quadra**'s pilot **Francisco Mourelle** as well as by **James Cook**, published in English in the early 1780s from their 1775 and 1778 reconnaissances, belief in the apocryphal voyage survived until the work of **Jacinto Caamaño** (1792) and **George Vancouver** (1794) finally exposed the hoax and removed the doubts.

FORT NISQUALLY. The first European settlement on **Puget Sound**, this **Hudson's Bay Company** (HBC) fort was built in 1833–1843. The name derived from the name given by French-Canadian explorers to the local Coast Salish Indians, "nez quarré," meaning "square-nosed." The reason for its construction was to capture and control the **fur trade** in the sound being carried on by American ships. Within a few years under William Tolmie the fort grew to be an important establishment, extending its reach far into the eastern mountains between the **Fraser River** and the **Columbia River**. It enjoyed good relations with the natives, and its activities included the final exploration and survey of the sound. In 1839 Governor **George Simpson** created the Puget Sound Agricultural Company to encourage farming and expand settlement in the area, and Tolmie later put thousands of acres of land under cultivation and developed herds of cattle and sheep. As the number of settlers in the surrounding area increased dramatically in the 1850s following the **Oregon Treaty**, 1846, and profits from the fur trade decreased through overhunting that effectively cut the supply of pelts, the economic value of the fort and reason for its existence declined. It finally closed in 1869 when the United States government compensated the HBC for the fort and its agricultural lands.

FORT ROSS. A Russian hunting, trading, and supply post on the coast of **California**, Fort Ross was established by **Ivan Kuskov** in 1812, north of **San Francisco**. In keeping with an audacious plan promoted by **Nikolai Rezanov**, the building of Fort Ross followed a decade of Russian activity on the coast south of **Alaska**. This was designed to extend the reach of the **sea otter** hunt, establish settlements that could provide much needed food supplies for **New Archangel**, and act as a beachhead in support of eventual Russian sovereignty north of latitude 38°. With Britain and Spain allied in a titanic struggle against Napoleon in Europe, and **New Spain** suffering the aftermath of a revolt that would ultimately lead to Mexican independence, the Russians acted almost with impunity in a coastal region that had been under Spanish control for over 150 years. In the end it was the problem of distance, limited ships and men, an agreement with the **Hudson's Bay Company** in 1839 to provide New Archangel with provisions from its settlements in present-day **Washington** and **Oregon**, and a need to consolidate its hold on the Alaskan coast that prevented Russia from making a more serious advance south of latitude 55° N.

In the early years, the abundance of available sea otters and the skill of **Aleut** hunters proved exceedingly valuable to the **Russian–American Company**. But during the 1820s and 1830s Fort Ross and its surrounding village of natives became an increasingly isolated outpost, separated from its Alaskan base by an Oregon Territory coveted by both Britain and the United States. Within a few years of its establishment, unrestricted hunting had depleted the sea otter population, and agriculture and ranching became its prime occupations. However, it was never able to produce a surplus of supply and was abandoned in 1842.

FORT VANCOUVER. A major fur-trading fort, Fort Vancouver was established in 1824–1825 by the **Hudson's Bay Company** (HBC) on the northern bank of the **Columbia River**, some six miles above its junction with the Willamette River. For 20 years it was the headquarters of the HBC's Columbia Department and its chief trading post, supply depot, and settlement in the **Pacific Northwest**. In 1845 the supply depot was moved to **Fort Victoria** on the southern tip of **Vancouver Island**, and the headquarters followed in 1849 in the wake of the **Oregon Treaty**, 1846, which had settled the Canada–United

States boundary at the 49° parallel. The company finally abandoned the post in 1860. *See also* MCLOUGHLIN, JOHN.

FORT VICTORIA. Establishment of this fort at the southern end of **Vancouver Island** in 1843 reflected a view of future economic and political realities in the **Pacific Northwest** held by **Hudson's Bay Company** (HBC) governor **George Simpson**. Although the Columbia Department had reached its greatest territorial extent, operating from **San Francisco** to the Lynn Canal, the supply of furs in the center of **Oregon** was diminishing and American settlers were pouring into the region over the Oregon Trail. Simpson felt that the HBC's future lay to the north, on **Vancouver Island** and farther up the continental coast; in addition to furs there were seemingly abundant agricultural and other natural resources available for export. He determined that Fort Victoria should take over from **Fort Vancouver** as a new HBC headquarters, a reality that was confirmed after the new international border had been set at the 49° parallel in 1846. Fort Victoria was well located to meet the needs of a general ocean-borne trade, and its development marked the beginning of a new phase of British maritime commerce in the North Pacific. Until the emergence of the city of Vancouver, Victoria remained the principal settlement on the coast of **British Columbia** for the next 50 years.

FRANCHÈRE, GABRIEL (1786–1863). Montreal-born fur trader and merchant Gabriel Franchère is best known for his participation as a young man in the short-lived **Astoria** enterprise at the mouth of the **Columbia River.** Hearing about John Jacob Astor's plans to enter the Pacific fur trade, he signed on as a clerk, sailed to the **Oregon** Country on the *Tonquin* in 1810–1811, and assisted in the establishment of Fort Astoria. He kept a journal in which he recorded his impressions of native life and the events that saw the sale and takeover of the post by the **North West Company** in 1813. His French-Canadian background and facility in the local native language encouraged the Nor'westers to employ him for a number of months before he left in April 1814 with the first overland brigade, arriving in Montreal in September. Subsequently employed as Astor's agent in Montreal for 20 years and later in Sault Ste. Marie until 1842, he worked in St. Louis before establishing his own company in New York.

Encouraged to share his reminiscences of Astoria, he sought help from a respected journalist Michel Bibaud, and his *Relation d'un voyage à la côte du Nord-Ouest de l'Amérique septentrionale, dans les années 1810,11,12,13 et 14* was published in 1820. The best single account of Astor's ill-fated initiative, it became the central source for Washington Irving's *Astoria* (1836) and played a minor role in debates in the U.S. Congress over the Oregon Question in the 1840s. As a result it was translated and published in English in 1854.

FRASER, SIMON (1776–1862). Fur trader and explorer Simon Fraser discovered the Fraser River. In 1801 he became a partner in the **North West Company** and was subsequently placed in charge of developing the trade beyond the Rocky Mountains in a region he called New Caledonia. This part of central **British Columbia** had been crossed by **Alexander Mackenzie** in 1793. After establishing a number of forts he set out from Fort George (1807) on 22 May 1808 to explore the large river flowing south, believing it to be the **Columbia River**. When he reached the Pacific he was bitterly disappointed to find that this was not the case and that the perilous navigation of the river made it impossible for use as a trading route to the coast. Nevertheless, when added to the explorations of Mackenzie and **David Thompson**, Fraser's activities served to strengthen the position of the North West Company on the coast, so that in the years of the 1820s and 1830s, following the merger with the **Hudson's Bay Company**, it was Britain that came to dominate the **fur trade** and to further the exploration of the coast south of **Russian America**.

FRASER RIVER. The longest river in **British Columbia** (875 miles), the Fraser River's middle section was explored by fur trader **Alexander Mackenzie** as he made his way to the Pacific Ocean "from Canada by land" in 1792. In 1808 another **North West Company** trader, **Simon Fraser**, who had been exploring and establishing trading posts (1805–1807) in the New Caledonia region of what is today central British Columbia, descended the river to the sea. Its spectacular 168-mile canyon meant that it was unusable as a trade route to and from the Pacific into the interior, but in 1827 the **Hudson's Bay Company**, drawn by the agricultural potential of its wide valley in the lower reaches, established Fort Langley, some 30 miles upstream from the Strait of Georgia. It was named after Fraser by **David Thompson**.

FRIENDLY COVE. A small but well-sheltered harbor at the entrance to **Nootka Sound**, Friendly Cove has been the site of the Mowachaht village of Yuquot for over 4,000 years. The early explorers and fur traders knew it as the summer home of Chief **Maquinna**. **James Cook** visited the natives there in April 1778 and was received with "demonstrations of friendship." As a result of this comment in Cook's journal, the fur trader **James Strange** named the place Friendly Cove and the first plan of it identified as such appeared in **John Meares**'s *Voyages* in 1790. In 1789 it was the scene of the **Nootka Sound Incident** involving the arrest of British fur-trading vessels by **Esteban José Martínez**, and the Spanish occupied the site in 1790–1795. It was visited by the **Alejandro Malaspina** and **George Vancouver** expeditions in the early 1790s; as a result the environs and its native inhabitants were well documented in charts, reports, and artwork.

FUCA, JUAN DE (1536–1602). Also known by his Greek name Apostolos Valerianos, Juan de Fuca informed a leading English merchant, Michael Lok, in Venice in 1596 that he had served the king of Spain as a pilot in the Americas for 40 years. In the late 1580s, he asserted, he had been in the Pacific on the **Manila galleon** *Santa Ana* when it was sacked by **Thomas Cavendish** in 1587. At a time when there was a renewed interest in **New Spain** in the **California** coast as a source of wealth from the pearl fishery and as a location for safe harbors for the galleons, Juan de Fuca stated that he had been on a voyage, cut short by a mutiny, to discover the **Strait of Anian**, and to fortify it against the English. He then maintained that he had been commissioned by the viceroy to sail north in 1592 to complete this mission, a venture that had met with success when, between latitudes 47° and 48° N, he found a broad inlet which he followed for 20 days until he came to the North Sea (Atlantic Ocean) whereupon he turned back and sailed home to New Spain. Fuca also reported that during the voyage he had made several land excursions during which he found people clad in beast skins, and that the land was "very fruitfull, and rich of gold, Silver, Pearle and other things like Nova Spania."

When he failed to receive any reward for his discovery in either New Spain or Spain itself, Fuca turned to the English, offering to navigate the strait again if Queen Elizabeth would furnish a ship, and he persuaded Lok to write to Sir Walter Raleigh and Richard Hakluyt to ask them to engage his services. Lok's account, which also mentions that Fuca was dead or dying by 1602, was published in London in 1625 by Samuel Purchas in *Hakluytus Postumus, or, Purchas His Pilgrimes: Contayning a History of the World in Sea Voyages and Lande Travells by Englishmen and Others*.

Geographical realities, uncovered in the 1790s, proved that Fuca's account of a passage through North America was pure fabrication, and there is now broad consensus that the whole story was probably made up by Michael Lok, who wanted to promote the idea of a **Northwest Passage**, and who had already sponsored the three voyages of Martin Frobisher in the 1570s. While there is no reason to doubt that Lok and Fuca actually met in Venice, or that the old Greek pilot had served on the Pacific coast of New Spain in the 1580s and 1590s, Lok had a motive for exaggerating into the realm of fantasy, and there has been, as yet, no evidence of a voyage to the Northwest Coast in 1592 uncovered in Spanish sources. There was activity during that time on the lower coast of California, but nothing to suggest a voyage farther north. The tale, however, still resonates. Tantalizing details like "Fuca's Pillar" at the entrance to a strait in latitude 49° N remain intriguing to many scholars and, if the Spanish had received direct evidence of a large opening, they would certainly have taken great pains to bury it to prevent such knowledge from reaching the English. The reference to gold, silver, and pearls can be put down to the age's tendency for exaggeration in even authenticated accounts of exploration, where truth and fiction often intertwined. Apocryphal though Michael Lok's story of Juan de Fuca's voyage through America may be, the idea of a Spanish voyage to the far north at the end of the 16th century is not entirely outside the realm of possibility. *See also* STRAIT OF JUAN DE FUCA.

FUCA, STRAIT OF JUAN DE. *See* STRAIT OF JUAN DE FUCA.

FUR TRADE. Three distinct coastal fur trades, each exploiting an apparently insatiable demand for fur in China, combined to push forward the exploration of the Northwest Coast in the wake of discoveries by **Vitus Bering** and **Aleksei Chirikov** (1741) and **James Cook** (1778).

From the mid-1740s Russian *promyshlenniki* (hunters) followed the trail of foxes, fur seals, and sea otters across the **Aleutian Islands** onto the American continent. Enslaving **Aleut** natives to man the hunt, a number of companies consolidated their position on the **Alaska Peninsula** and round the Gulf of Alaska in the 1780s and 1790s. In the early 19th century the **Russian–American Company**, continuing to use the skill of Aleut hunters, established itself in the **Alexander Archipelago** and extended its reach to Spanish **California**. Russian furs were exported to Okhotsk and then taken to the trading market at Kiakhta on the Siberia–Mongolia border. Beginning in the 1760s official naval voyages followed the traders; thus from an early time exploration of the coast was recorded on official maps.

The classic "maritime fur trade" was almost exclusively in sea otter skins. It took place on the Northwest Coast in the period 1785–1825 and followed the accidental discovery by Cook's men of the value of furs collected at Nootka when sold later in Petropavlovsk and Canton. This port, and Macao, became the market for first British then American traders. Many British merchants such as **John Meares** sailed to the coast under flags of convenience to avoid the monopoly of the **East India Company**; others such as **George Dixon** obtained a license to do so. All contributed greatly to coastal exploration in the period 1785–1795 when no less than 35 vessels visited **Oregon**, **Vancouver Island**, the **Queen Charlotte Islands**, the islands of northern **British Columbia** and southeast Alaska, and the continental coast farther north. Likewise **"Boston Men"** (15 vessels in the same decade) such as **Robert Gray** and **William Sturgis** soon came to dominate the trade for a generation. Unencumbered by the problems of monopoly and an almost constant state of war in Europe following the French Revolution, the Americans established a lucrative commerce based on taking furs from the Northwest Coast to China and importing Oriental goods to New England. In the period 1795–1814 American vessels outnumbered the British 90 to 12 and, particularly in the late 1780s and early 1790s, American officers made important geographical discoveries and published key journals and charts.

A third coastal fur trade resulted from the exploits of **Alexander Mackenzie** (1793), **Simon Fraser** (1808), and **David Thompson** (1811), and the merger of the **North West Company** and the

Hudson's Bay Company (HBC) in 1821. This was an extension of the land-based fur trade onto the coast through the aggressive activities of the HBC's Columbia Department and the establishment of a string of forts as far north as **Russian America**. During the 25-year period of 1821–1846, HBC vessels continued the exploration of the Northwest Coast's islands, bays, and fjords as the company gradually diversified the commerce beyond furs. While it sent these to London, it also shipped salmon and lumber to **Hawaii** and foodstuff to **Sitka**, receiving in return sugar, tobacco, and salt from Asia and Hawaii, and retail goods from England.

FUSANG. Fusang is a kingdom reputed to have been found on the west coast of North America by a Buddhist monk, Hui Shen, who returned to China from a long voyage in the sea "where the sun rises" in 499 AD. His story was entered into the great Chinese Encyclopedia compiled by court historians of the Liang emperors, 502–556 AD. Fusang was described as a civilized place whose inhabitants lived in well-organized communities, mined copper, used horses and knew how to write. The account was found and translated into French in the early 18th century and debated in the 19th century. Some scholars argued that the distances attributed to Hui Shen placed Fusang on the northwest coast of Mexico and that the name derived from the maguey plant found there. Others maintained that any North American link was pure fabrication and that the kingdom, if the voyage was ever made, was in Japan or on the island of Sakhalin. In his apocryphal map of northwest America in 1752, **Philippe Buache** placed Fusang in **British Columbia** along with such other regional fantasies as **Quivira**, the **Sea of the West**, the entrance to the **Strait of Juan de Fuca** and the Archipelago of St. Lazarus of the mythical **Bartholomew de Fonte**. As a version of Buache's map was later included in Denis Diderot's *Encyclopédie*, however, these features were given wide circulation and much authority. *See also* ASIAN VOYAGES.

– G –

GALI, FRANCISCO (?–1586). Spanish navigator and cosmographer Francisco Gali became experienced on the **Manila galleon** run between the Philippines and **New Spain**. Responding to interest in finding a safe haven for the galleons in the north Pacific en route to Acapulco, Gali, who had sailed to Manila in early 1583, made a much wider sweep northward than was normal on the return voyage, 1583–1584. Reaching perhaps as high as latitude 50° N he reported experiencing a strong outflow current for much of the middle part of the voyage, which he speculated as evidence of the **Strait of Anian**. Approaching the coast of North America he reported seeing forests, an abundance of sea life, and evidence of many bays and rivers. This sparked renewed interest in the strait and the coast above **Baja California** where, in light of the threat of English piracy following the exploits of **Francis Drake** and **Thomas Cavendish**, the Spanish were keen to locate safe harbors for galleon protection and supplies. Galleon commanders **Pedro de Unamuno** (1587) and **Sebastián Rodríguez Cermeño** (1595) both landed on the coast of **Alta California**, and they were followed in 1602 by the exploring expedition of **Sebastián Vizcaíno**.

GALIANO. *See* ALCALÁ GALIANO, DIONISIO.

GÁLVEZ, JOSÉ DE (1720–1787). *Visitador-general* or royal inspector to **New Spain**, 1765–1771, José de Gálvez initiated economic reforms to maximize tax revenue, supervised the expulsion of the Jesuits (1767) and the putting down of uprisings that followed, and attended to a massive reorganization of the political infrastructure and military operations on the northern frontier. As a result, he emerged as the person most responsible for the colonization of **Alta California** and the extension of Spanish activities to the Northwest Coast. He also initiated the founding of the Naval Department of **San Blas**, and personally oversaw the departure of the **Sacred Expedition** to California in 1769.

Later, as a member of the Council of the Indies, Minister of the Indies, and member of the Council of State, he never lost his interest in the northern perimeter of New Spain and his larger vision of extending and consolidating Spanish control over much of western North America and its Pacific Coast. His energetic leadership, many years after Spain had first become aware of Russian activities on the northern coast, led directly to the Spanish voyages of the 1770s. He closely followed the progress of each expedition and, in defense of Spanish sovereignty, ordered the interception and arrest of **James Cook**, once news of his intended voyage into the North Pacific reached Madrid.

GAMALAND. The mythical Gamaland was believed either to have existed between **Kamchatka** and America, or to have been part of the American continent. It was reportedly seen by the Portuguese navigator, Joaõ da Gama, north of Japan as he was sailing (1589–1590) from Malacca to Acapulco. During the next 150 years, contradictory maps depicted a jumble of real or imagined islands between Hokkaido and Kamchatka, confusing the existing Kurile Islands with Company Land, State Island, Terra Esonis, and Gamaland.

Sometime around 1731, the Russian Admiralty College requested the Academy of Sciences to prepare a map of the North Pacific. **Joseph Nicolas de l'Isle** prepared the map and an accompanying *mémoire* based on work done by his elder brother Guillaume. This showed the three islands mentioned above and the "Land seen by Dom Juan de Gama," which trails off in the direction of America. When the route of the second voyage of **Vitus Bering** was determined in Petropavlovsk in May 1741, this map or another based on it clearly influenced the choice. *See also* DE L'ISLE DE LA CROYÈRE, LOUIS.

GLAZUNOV, ANDREI (?–1846). A Creole navigator, Andrei Glazunov joined the **Russian–American Company** (RAC) in 1826 and saw service on various vessels in the **Alexander Archipelago**, the **Aleutian Islands**, the **Bering Sea**, and on a voyage in 1832 to **California**. During the 1830s he became one of the most persistent pioneer explorers in southwest **Alaska**, as the RAC moved into that region to search for new sources of fur. In 1833 he explored the Unalakleet River, which flows into **Norton Sound**, in an attempt to find a route to the central Yukon. More important was his remarkable journey in the winter of 1833–1834, during which he explored and roughly mapped portions of the lower Yukon and central Kuskokwim rivers. In 1835 he again explored the lower Yukon to select a trading post site, which was then established at Ikogmiut (today Russian Mission), and continued his travels and mapping activity on the river and its tributaries in 1836. In 1837 he explored the headwaters of the Unalakleet and successfully portaged over to the Yukon.

GLOTOV, STEPAN (?–1769). Early fur trader and explorer in the **Aleutian Islands**, Stepan Glotov captained the *St. Julian* from

Kamchatka in September 1758, wintering over on Mednoi Island in the **Commander Islands** group, where he collected **sea otter** and blue fox pelts. In the summer of 1759 the ship progressed as far as **Umnak Island**. The party collected furs both there and on **Unalaska** Island for a period of three years, during which time, after an initial clash, they maintained friendly relations with the **Aleut** natives; and a Cossack named Ponomarev, who was on board as a government representative, collected *iasak*. Glotov baptized and became godfather to the nephew of a local chief on Umnak, naming him Ivan Stcpanovich Glotov. The 12-year-old boy retained his faith for the remainder of his life and later built a chapel at Nikolski, where Stepan Glotov had originally erected a cross to mark the introduction of Christianity into the eastern Aleutians. Ivan returned to Kamchatka with Glotov in 1762. He perfected his Russian and was a valued interpreter on Glotov's subsequent ventures.

The successful hunt for furs, along with the reports of new islands and a map produced by Ponomarev, created a good deal of interest in Kamchatka. Especially noted were reports of lands further to the east, which confirmed the discoveries of the expedition sponsored by Ivan Bechevin, which had wintered over on the **Alaska Peninsula**, 1761–1762. Almost immediately, Glotov was sponsored to undertake another voyage, and he sailed again for the east on the *Andreian I Natal'ia* in October. Wintering over on Mednoi Island for a second time, he also sent men to **Bering Island** where they salvaged iron, lead, copper, planks, and trade goods from the remains of **Vitus Bering**'s *St. Peter*. At the end of July 1763 Glotov proceeded beyond Unalaska and explored numerous islands before landing on **Kodiak** Island in **Three Saints Bay**. The Russians survived a number of native attacks and, in the spring of 1764, established a fur-trading relationship. They also collected **artifacts** that subsequently made their way back to St. Petersburg where they were displayed at the Academy of Sciences. After leaving Kodiak Glotov landed on Umnak Island where he became involved in the aftermath of the Aleut-Russian War of 1763. He spent the next two years gathering furs, finally arriving home in 1766.

In 1767 he came to the attention of **Petr Krenitsyn**, who had arrived in Kamchatka to launch his secret voyage to the Aleutians. Glotov was one of the numerous pioneer voyagers to the east who were interviewed by Krenitsyn and subsequently recruited for the expedition. Also enlisted was Glotov's godson to serve as an interpreter. Sailing from Kamchatka in the summer of 1768, the expedition lost over 30 men from hunger and scurvy, including Glotov, during the terrible winter of 1768–1769 on **Unimak Island**.

GOLOVNIN, VASILII (1776–1831). Vasilii Golovnin was an influential Russian naval officer and critic of the **Russian–American Company** (RAC). In 1807 he set out on the navy's third round-the-world-voyage to **Russian America**, and the first of his two voyages to the North Pacific. He made a visit to **Sitka** in 1810, where he verified the excellent charts of **Ivan F. Vasil'ev**, but was disturbed by the weaknesses of the RAC's administration, and the threats to Russian interests posed by American fur traders.

Returning to St. Petersburg in 1814, Golovnin joined a growing number of voices that had developed as a result of reports from the voyages of **Ivan Kruzenshtern** and **Iurii Lisianskii** (1803–1806) and **Ludwig von Hagemeister** (1806–1810). They felt that the navy had to play a much greater role in the affairs of the RAC and the protection of Russian interests in the North Pacific if Russian America was going to survive as a colony. In 1816 Hagemeister left on his second voyage to investigate affairs further and, if necessary, to replace **Aleksandr Baranov**, which he did on 11 January 1818. Golovnin's second voyage had three specific goals: to bring supplies to Okhotsk and Kamchatka, to inspect the two major settlements in Russian America, and to explore those parts of the coast of America in the Bering and Arctic Seas which **James Cook** had not been able to survey. The latter task was made redundant by the **Otto von Kotzebue** Expedition, and so interest has centered on Golovnin's visits to **Kodiak** and **New Archangel**, **Fort Ross** and **Monterey** in the summer and fall of 1818. Further hydrographic work was done at Pavlovsk Harbor (Kodiak) and in Sitka Sound, and the artist **Mikhail Tikhanov** made a series of drawings of **natives** that have proven extremely important to ethnographers. Golovnin's main task was to report on the living and working conditions of the employees of the RAC and their relations with the **Tlingit**. On his return to St. Petersburg in September 1819 he was scathing in his criticism of the RAC's affairs in these areas and of its general administrative practices. He also left the government in no doubt that the RAC had been negligent in not reporting forcefully enough the dangers posed to Russian sovereignty by American traders.

The results of the voyages and inspections carried out by Golovnin and Hagemeister were twofold. First, although the charter of the RAC was renewed in 1821, the colony would now be governed by a high-ranking naval officer, accountable first and foremost to the government, not to the directors, and concerned primarily with the interests of the state not commerce; and second, the unilateral decision by the czar to ban foreign vessels from doing business with the colony and to set its southern boundary at 51° N. Because Russian America could never be self-sufficient without an agricultural economy, and supplies from Fort Ross were inadequate for this purpose, the result of the trading ban was catastrophic; the boundary decision brought hostile reaction from both Britain and the United States. Both of these decisions were reversed in 1825. *See also* RUSSIAN AMERICA BOUNDARY CONVENTIONS.

GORE, JOHN (ca. 1730–1790). John Gore had already made two round-the-world voyages with John Byron (1764–1766) and Samuel Wallis (1766–1768) when he joined **James Cook** for a third on the *Endeavour*, 1768–1771. He rejoined Cook for the Third Voyage, and left England with him on the *Resolution* in 1776. Solid and reliable but unimaginative and somewhat dour, he matched Cook in experience but was by nature a dependable subordinate rather than a leader. Nevertheless, on Cook's death he took command of the *Discovery* when **Charles Clerke** transferred to the *Resolution*, and later in **Kamchatka** he took over command of the whole expedition when, on Clerke's death, he returned to the *Resolution* in August 1779.

Gore kept a log of the voyage in which, uncharacteristically, he sometimes gave imaginative names to specific features on the coast: thus **Mount Edgecumbe** became Mount Beautiful; **Mount St. Elias** became Mount Pommel because it reminded him of a pommel at the front of a saddle; the west coast of the **Kenai Peninsula** became the Land of Good Prospect in the Gulf of Good Hope (**Cook Inlet**); and farther up Cook Inlet, the East and West Forelands became Gore's Head and Nancy's Head in honor of a favorite female acquaintance. Cook named **St. Matthew Island** in the **Bering Sea** after Gore, but later changed it back to its original name given by **Ivan Sindt** in 1766.

GRAY, ROBERT (1755–1806). American fur trader and explorer Robert Gray pioneered the entry of "**Boston Men**" into the maritime **fur trade** with voyages to the Northwest Coast in 1787–1788 and 1790–1793. He is best remembered for crossing the bar of the **Columbia River** in 1792 and discovering that the **Entrada de Hezeta** was the entrance to a great river.

A veteran of the American Revolutionary War, Gray was operating as a merchant seaman in New England when engaged to command the *Lady Washington* on a fur-trading voyage led by **John Kendrick** in the *Columbia Rediviva*. The ships reached **Nootka Sound** in September 1788, but not before Gray had stopped on the **Oregon** coast in the vicinity of Tillamook Bay, where he engaged in trade and where also one of his sailors was murdered. They wintered over at Nootka until the spring of 1789. While Kendrick stayed put, Gray explored and traded to the south to **Clayoquot Sound**, **Cape Flattery**, and into the **Strait of Juan de Fuca**. After returning to Nootka he sailed to the north, deep into Queen Charlotte Sound as far as the mainland islands and, after some brisk trading, explored up Hecate Strait. Crossing **Dixon Entrance** the expedition became the first from the United States to encounter the **Haida**. Gray named the land before him Washington Island (today the bottom of Prince of Wales Island at the southern end of the **Alexander Archipelago**). The explorers were convinced that enough openings to the north and east such as Revillagigedo Channel and Clarence Strait, gave credence to the tale of **Bartholomew de Fonte**. Off Dall Island the *Lady Washington* was nearly lost in high seas before Gray sailed south to trade in Parry Passage between Langara and Graham Islands and to continue on to Nootka. The haul of furs was then transferred to the *Columbia* and, on 30 July, Gray left with them for China where the skins were traded for tea and fine china. Rounding the Cape of Good Hope and crossing the Atlantic Ocean, the *Columbia* made a triumphant return to Boston on 10 August 1790, completing the first American circumnavigation of the globe and inaugurating a relationship between New England and the Northwest Coast that would endure and dominate the fur trade for another 30 years.

Despite the fact that the voyage had been a financial disappointment, there was enough support in Boston for another expedition and, on 28 September 1790, Gray and the *Columbia* left again for the North Pacific. Clayoquot Sound was reached on 5 June 1791 and the subsequent months were spent trading for furs along the coast from the Strait of Juan de Fuca to southern Alaska. After a short cruise to the south, Gray headed for Hecate Strait where he again explored and traded amongst the islands and at **Cumshewa** Inlet on the eastern shore of Graham Island, one of the best areas for sea otter skins in the **Queen Charlotte Islands**. Gray sailed on deep into Clarence Strait before retracing his route down the eastern coast of the Queen Charlottes and back to **Vancouver Island**. By late September he had settled down in Clayoquot Sound for the winter, meeting up again with John Kendrick. They constructed Fort Defiance as their camp and built the sloop *Adventure*. She was launched in February 1792, used for the trading season and then sold to the Spanish. Relations with Chief **Wickaninnish** and the local **natives** gradually deteriorated, and when Gray seemingly uncovered a plot to seize the *Columbia* he retaliated by burning down the village of Opitsat. It was one of the most violent acts ever perpetrated upon the original inhabitants of the Northwest Coast.

Heading south, Gray encountered **George Vancouver** on 29 April off **Washington** State before, on 7 May 1792, discovering and naming Gray's Harbor. A few days later on 11 May came the climax of his substantial exploring activity during three seasons on the coast—his discovery of the Columbia River. As recorded by **John Boit**, rounding John Meares's Cape Disappointment, which he named Cape Hancock, Gray "saw an appearance of a spacious harbor abrest the Ship, hauled our wind for itt, observed two sand bars making off, with a passage between them to a fine river." Following the ship's boat over the bar, in water made deeper by the river being in flood with the spring freshets, Gray found that "the River extended to the NE as far as eye cou'd reach, and water fit to drink as far down as the Bars, at the Entrance. We directed our course up this noble river in search of a Village. The beach was lin'd with Natives, who ran along shore following the Ship." The *Columbia* anchored in a small bay on the north side of the river some 15 miles upstream and stayed until 20 May. Contrary to later assertions Gray never took formal possession of the region, and it was some days before he decided to name his discovery "Columbia" after his ship. Conscious that the primary purpose of his voyage was gathering furs, Gray headed north again into Queen Charlotte Sound where he had had so much previous success.

However, his summer is more noteworthy for his continued problems with the natives and a near disaster when *Columbia* ran aground off the mainland below Hecate Strait. Gray's daring, even recklessness, in searching for furs in remote bays left him open to both native attack and sudden changes in the weather on an uncharted, rock-strewn coast. Returning to Nootka, he informed George Vancouver of his discovery of the Columbia River and left him a sketch of its estuary. As a result **William Broughton** made his survey a few weeks later.

Returning to Boston via China, Gray reached New England on 26 July 1793. A prominent figure in the early history of the Northwest Coast, Gray proved himself an intrepid explorer and a tenacious trader. Above all, his discovery of the Columbia River gave to the young United States a legitimate claim to the Oregon country.

GRAY'S HARBOR. A large bay on the coast of **Washington**, Gray's Harbor was discovered by **Robert Gray** on 7 May 1792, and originally named Bulfinch's Harbor in honor of Charles Bulfinch of Boston, one of the partners in his ship, the *Columbia Rediviva*. It was surveyed by **Joseph Whidbey** of the **George Vancouver** Expedition in October of the same year. He renamed the harbor after its discoverer and this name survived due principally to the publication in 1798 of the journal and charts of Vancouver's voyage. In the summer of 1793, **Juan Martínez y Zayas**, engaged in the last formal Spanish exploration on the coast, entered the harbor and named it Puerto Grek, presumably a corruption of Gray's name.

GREAT NORTHERN EXPEDITION. The Great Northern Expedition was the most extensive and costly exploration initiative of the 18th century, 1733–1743. Two years after his return to St. Petersburg, **Vitus Bering** had persuaded the Admiralty College, the Senate, and Empress Anna to launch yet another expedition to the far north and east. This soon blossomed into a vast undertaking involving at least 13 ships and thousands of men, including **scientists**, engineers, surveyors, and **artists**. It aimed to increase the geographical knowledge of Siberia, its human and natural resources, and included three principal maritime endeavors, each of which met with a good deal of success. First were a series of remarkable surveys of the

Arctic coast that included a reconnaissance of the region between the Ob and Yenisy rivers by Dimitri Ovtsvyn, and Dimitrii Laptev's exploration of the coast east from the Lena River to beyond the mouth of the Kolyma; secondly, the reconnaissance of the Kurile Islands and northern Japan by **Martin Spanberg**; and thirdly, the voyages to America by Bering and **Aleksei Chirikov**.

Although Bering was placed in overall command of the expedition, much of the work was inevitably undertaken beyond his control while he focused on the miracles of logistical organization that allowed him to launch his own second **Kamchatka Expedition**, another voyage in search of America. Directing events as best he could, it took him eight years to reach Okhotsk, across four mountain ranges, and up and down numerous rivers with the necessary equipment to establish shipbuilding facilities. He finally crossed to **Kamchatka** in the spring of 1741.

GULF OF CALIFORNIA. The Gulf of California, 700 miles long and up to 100 miles wide, separates the peninsula of **Baja California** from the mainland of Mexico. Although crossings were made to the peninsula by **Fortún Jiménez** and **Hernán Cortés** in the early 1530s, it was a few more years before the coastline of the entire gulf was thoroughly explored through the efforts of **Francisco de Ulloa** and **Hernando de Alarcón**. The work of these two navigators was first reflected on a world map in the Pacific Ocean part of Battista Agnese's influential parchment map from about 1543, now in the collection of the Medicea-Laurenziana Library in Florence. On the maps of **Abraham Ortelius**, published in successive editions of his atlas *Theatrum Orbis Terrarum* from 1570, the gulf is named Mar Vermejo (Bermejo) after Ulloa's reference to the red color of the water at the mouth of the Colorado River.

In the early years of the 17th century, as interest was renewed in its pearl fishery, the true geographical nature of the gulf was forgotten and the old, short-lived idea of the "Isla de California" was reinvented and became common currency thanks to the writings of the influential **Antonio de la Ascensión**. This fiction lasted about 100 years.

GVOZDEV, MIKHAIL (fl. 1727–1759). Mikhail Gvozdev was appointed in 1727 to a major expedition to subdue the Chukchi natives, and to investigate their reports of a "great land" of forests and high mountains beyond the Chukotskii Peninsula. When the military campaign proved inconclusive, attention shifted to the search for this land. It finally took place in 1732 using **Vitus Bering**'s *St. Gabriel* and involved Ivan Fedorov, a junior naval officer, with Gvozdev responsible for scientific matters.

Sailing from Anadyr to **St. Lawrence Island** and the **Bering Strait**, they visited the **Diomede Islands**. On 21 August they sighted land in the vicinity of **Cape Prince of Wales**, but seeing no sign of human life skirted the coast in a southerly direction. When evidence of habitation was seen, shallow water and adverse winds prevented a landing and pushed them offshore where they found another island and met an Alaskan native in a *baidarka*. This was probably King Island, named in August 1778 by **James Cook**. With the navigation season shortening, supplies running low, and the ship leaking, Fedorov sailed for Kamchatka where they arrived on 28 September.

Neither the logbook nor any report survived. Fedorov died in 1733 and Gvozdev was imprisoned following a complaint from a sailor on the voyage. A further decade had passed before **Martin Spanberg** visited Okhotsk and local officials were showing some interest in the voyage. When Gvozdev petitioned for promotion, Spanberg made it a condition that he write an account of the expedition and provide information for a map. Although Gvozdev probably believed that he and Fedorov had discovered the "great land," Spanberg's map did not identify it as such. Thus the significance of the 1732 discovery—that the "land" of Gvozdev was part of America—was not fully realized for a number of years. Further exploration was undertaken by **Ivan Sindt** in the late 1760s, but the real shape of the coast was not confirmed until James Cook's survey in 1778. Gvozdev's pioneering voyage, therefore, is only important in hindsight; certainly it had no immediate contemporary consequence, as Bering's 1741 voyage was directed not north, but south of the **Aleutian Islands**.

– H –

HAENKE, TADEO (1761–1816). Bohemian-born naturalist and scholar, Tadeo Haenke was the botanist on the **Alejandro Malaspina**

Expedition. A true renaissance man Haenke used to good purpose, during the voyage, his general knowledge of botany, geology, zoology, and music, and developed a keen interest in the emerging field of ethnology.

In the summer of 1791 as Malaspina's ships moved north along the coast of southern **Alaska**, Haenke analyzed the air quality using a eudiometer and described fish, birds, and mollusks. Once they arrived at Port Mulgrave inside **Yakutat Bay**, he botanized assiduously and his talent as a musicologist allowed him to transcribe a melody—El canto de la Paz (Song of Peace)—a unique jewel of early Alaskan native folklore. With **Felipe Bauza** and **José Espinosa** he made notes on native customs and created a small dictionary of the **Tlingit** language. He also made a personal collection of **artifacts** separate from the official collection for the royal cabinet in Madrid.

At **Nootka Sound** Haenke transcribed another piece of native music—El canto de la Alegria (Song of Happiness), collected plants, and recorded a thorough description of the area. He determined that most of the plants, later catalogued by his fellow botanist Luis Née, could not be found in Europe, but were known on the other side of North America. Haenke recorded details about the rocky reefs, the soils, and the different grasses. Among the few birds he saw were crows, herons, woodpeckers, and hawks. He described a number of varieties of fish and different colored starfish, as well as insects, butterflies, and beetles. During his time on the voyage, Malaspina constantly praised his work.

One of the most interesting of the thousands of science-related documents that have survived from the expedition, and which Haenke carried with him, is a notebook in his own handwriting entitled *Systema Colorum Tabulae atque comparativum pro expeditiori plantarum cum vivis coloribus adumbratione in itinere cum hispanais navibus circa Globum Terraqueum annis 1789–1793*. It consists of 16 pages, a dozen of which contain more than 2,500 differently numbered watercolor "shades" for artists who might want to paint botanical specimens, along with the pigments that had to be mixed to build up the color groupings. There is also a page in which Haenke describes how to draw a plant. His commitment to precise observation and recording, and to the scientific methodology of the age of Linnaeus is nowhere more apparent than in this notebook.

HAGEMEISTER, LUDWIG VON (1780–1833). Russian naval officer Ludwig von Hagemeister first visited **Russian America** in 1807 in the *Neva*, which also brought the noted cartographer **Ivan F. Vasil'ev** to **New Archangel**. Hagemeister visited **Kodiak** during the winter of 1807–1808, and in 1808–1809 made a voyage to the Hawaiian Islands to purchase supplies. He met King Kamehameha, and surveyed Maui, Oahu, and Kauai so as to allow his government the option of extending its influence to **Hawaii** in support of her American colony.

On his second voyage to Russian America, 1816–1819, Hagemeister commanded the *Kutuzov* and initiated the practice of naval officers being placed in control of the colony with his removal of **Aleksandr Baranov** as manager of the **Russian–American Company** (RAC). He instituted more rigorous administrative procedures over the RAC's affairs, went to California in the fall of 1818, and authorized the expedition of **Petr Korsakovskii** to begin a more precise exploration of the coast of southwest **Alaska**, north from **Bristol Bay**. This ultimately opened both coast and interior to the traders of the RAC. Before he departed **Sitka** at the end of 1818, he had ordered the establishment of the Novo Aleksandrovskii Redoubt at the mouth of the Nushagak River (Bristol Bay), and had begun a renewed Russian interest in the **Copper River**, which led to the explorations of **Afansii Klimovskii** in 1819.

In the years 1828–1830 he made his third voyage to Kamchatka and Russian America during which he undertook hydrographic work in the Pacific Ocean, particularly in the Marshall Islands. During his visits to America he made numerous observations, but to date scholars have not adequately studied his voluminous journals.

HAIDA. The native nation of Haida numbered about 9,800 at contact and occupied the **Queen Charlotte Islands** and the southern tip of Prince of Wales Island—the Kaigani Haida—in the **Alexander Archipelago**. Even more than their **Tlingit** neighbors, their existence essentially depended on the sea—salmon and halibut for food, sea lions and seals for fur. Autonomous villages were noteworthy for their large plank buildings and sea-going canoes drawn up onto the beach. The Haida are divided into two matrilineal clans—Raven and Eagle—whose households retain rights to certain lands, names, songs, dances, and crests. They developed a high level of artistic creativity, especially in woodworking for ceremonial articles. The Haida system of potlatch underlay a structure of social hierarchy based on heredity and acquired wealth, and maintained a culture by which wealth was redistributed in the community. They were seasoned traders and, once the **fur trade** began in the late 1780s, places like **Cunneah**'s Harbor (**George Dixon**'s Cloak Bay at the northern end of the islands, opposite Langara Island, where **Juan Pérez** had sailed in 1774), **Koyah**'s Village on Anthony Island in the south, and **Cumshewa**'s Harbor on the east coast developed quickly as important centers. Although wealth and increased status gained in the trade affirmed the power of the village chiefs, and the introduction of new tools led directly to the 19th-century tradition of master carvers, **violence** and **disease** decimated the population.

HALL, ROBERT (1761–1844). The English-born Robert Hall entered Russian naval service in 1774. In 1785 he joined the **Joseph Billings** Expedition. He played an important role in moving men and equipment across Siberia, and in building two ships—the *Slava Rossii* (Glory of Russia) and *Dobroe Namerenie* (Good Intent)—in Okhotsk. However, in September 1789 the *Dobroe Namerenie*, with Hall in command, was taken out to sea and subsequently floundered. In Nizhekamchatsk during 1789–1791 Hall built and launched another ship, the *Chernyi Orel* (Black Eagle), and sailed her with Billings in the *Slava Rossii* among the **Aleutian Islands** as far as **Unalaska**. Rather than moving on to the American continent for further exploration, the expedition headed into the **Bering Sea**, visiting **St. Lawrence Island** and in August entering St. Lawrence Bay on the Chukotskii Peninsula. From here Hall returned to Unalaska with **Gavriil Sarychev** and wintered over, 1791–1792, at the settlement of Illiuliuk. They had a difficult time; 17 men died of scurvy and most of the others became too unfit to handle the ship for a summer of exploration. Hall, therefore, came back to Kamchatka and undertook no further activities related to the expedition. Although he was a key figure in the overall Billings initiative, and important as a shipbuilder, Hall's two voyages to Unalaska barely advanced Russian knowledge of the area or contributed to the scientific work of the enterprise.

HANNA, JAMES (fl. 1785–1787). As captain of the *Sea Otter*, James Hanna pioneered British entry into the maritime **fur trade** between the Northwest Coast and China. Hanna was sponsored by a British trader resident in Canton, **John Henry Cox**, and backed by other gentlemen in commerce who had connections to the **East India Company**. Setting out from Macao on 15 April 1785, he caught the prevailing winds and current off Japan that brought him to **Nootka Sound** on 8 August. Although there was one violent altercation in which a number of **natives** lost their lives, Hanna was successful in trading for furs and returned to Macao with 560 pelts worth over 20,000 Spanish dollars.

Encouraged by this financial success Hanna's backers sponsored a second voyage in 1786. Leaving Macao in May he again reached Nootka in August. He had been preceded by an expedition led by **James Strange**, however, as a result of which he was able to purchase only 50 skins. Sailing north he discovered and named a number of inlets and islands on the west coast of **Vancouver Island**. Examples include Sea Otter Cove in what Hanna originally named St. Patrick's Bay (now San Josef Bay), Cox Island in the Scott group, and the Sea Otter Islands in Queen Charlotte Sound. Seeing land to the north, which was probably the islands off the continent or even Kunghit Island, the southernmost of the **Queen Charlotte Islands**, Hanna named it Nova Hibernia. He constructed a rough chart used by **George Dixon**, **John Meares**, and **George Vancouver**; and **Alexander Dalrymple** later referred to his activities when seeking to advance British claims to the coast and his argument about goverment obligations to promote the fur trade. Hanna then moved south to **Clayoquot Sound** where he continued his explorations and visited Chief Cleaskinah (later known as "Captain Hanna") at Ahousat, then on Vargas Island. But his success in trading for pelts was limited, and shortly after his arrival in Macao in early 1787 he died before he was able to make a planned third voyage to America.

HASWELL, ROBERT (1768–1801). Robert Haswell was still a teenager when he joined the *Columbia Rediviva* under **John Kendrick** bound for the Northwest Coast out of Boston in 1787. He transferred to the *Lady Washington* and, after wintering over at **Nootka Sound**, traded in her as second officer under **Robert Gray** during the summer of 1789. The expedition ranged from the **Strait of Juan de Fuca** in the south to **Dixon Entrance** in the north, and Haswell's presence proved vital because his journal is the only full account of the voyage. With Gray, and back on the *Columbia*, he sold the furs in China and returned triumphantly to Boston in August 1790.

For the second voyage of the *Columbia*, Gray was the captain and Haswell sailed as first officer. During his time on the coast, 1791–1792, he wrote another important journal, made sketches, and drew little maps. After arriving in June 1791, Gray again sailed up and down the coast, and Haswell sketched the ship in Hancock's River (Masset Sound) in the "Washington Islands" (**Queen Charlotte Islands**). At the end of the summer the *Columbia* wintered over in **Clayoquot Sound**, where the sloop *Adventure* was built and launched on 23 March 1792. Haswell was given command and his is the only extant account of her trading activities that summer. From Clayoquot Sound he sailed north, stopping in Checleset Bay west of Kyuquot Sound, where he draw a small map, before heading for the rich trading grounds of the Queen Charlotte Islands. He worked up the western coast of the islands exploring many of the inlets discovered by **George Dixon**; he then traded on the upper east side before retracing his route back south to **Koyah**'s Harbor at the southern end of Moresby Island.

After moving up the eastern coast of the islands to complete a circumnavigation, Haswell sailed the *Adventure* over to the islands off the continental coast, which he explored before sailing to Dall Island, and then back south along the continental islands to the west coast of **Vancouver Island**. After a meeting with Gray and the *Columbia* in June, Haswell again sailed north to the Queen Charlotte Islands before extending his voyage into the **Alexander Archipelago**, where he visited Dixon's Port Banks, of which he drew a map, and **Sitka Sound**, the farthest north reached by an American trader at that time. Haswell's remarkably active and successful summer of exploring and trading ended when he met up again with Gray in the Queen Charlotte Islands and returned to Nootka. Haswell resumed his position on the *Columbia* after the *Adventure* had been sold to Spanish captain **Juan Francisco de la Bodega y Quadra** at **Neah Bay**. Via China he sailed home to Boston arriving in July 1793.

Haswell continued the life of a mariner and spent two years in the U.S. Navy. In 1801 he died at sea, commanding the *Louisa* out of Boston en route to the Northwest Coast on another fur-trading voyage. An important and energetic figure in the early history of the coast, he was only 33 years old.

HAWAII. Although other navigators had probably seen some of the islands in the Hawaiian archipelago, their formal discovery is rightly credited to **James Cook** who sighted Oahu on 18 January 1778 and landed on Kauai the next day. He returned from the Arctic Circle and **Bering Sea** to see Maui and land on Hawaii almost exactly one year later. He thus inaugurated a tradition among Northwest Coast explorers and traders to stop at what he called the Sandwich Islands coming to or from America, like **Jean François de La Pérouse**; or wintering over, as did Cook himself, **George Dixon** and **Nathaniel Portlock**, **George Vancouver**, and **Otto von Kotzebue**. In 1794 Vancouver negotiated the cession of the islands to Britain but his negotiations with King Kamehameha I were never followed up, and the deal lapsed along with Cook's name for the islands which were united as the Kingdom of Hawaii in 1810. In 1815–1817 without proper official backing a self-styled adventurer named **Georg Schaeffer** tried to establish a formal Russian presence in the islands, but was spectacularly unsuccessful.

HEALTH. The captains of naval and merchant ships coming to the Northwest Coast in the 18th century were acutely aware that the success of their endeavors depended as much upon the health of their men as upon their own skill as navigators, the design of their ships or the effectiveness of their navigational instruments. A crew's good health—always under threat from poor food and water, and damp, crowded conditions, which encouraged dysentery, diarrhea, arthritis, and the general spread of viral infections such as colds and influenza—was vital in operating a ship. Throughout the second half of the 18th century venereal **disease** was a constant companion to sailors from all nations, with calamitous results for the **native** peoples, as demonstrated in **Hawaii** and at **Nootka Sound** in 1778. That same year Cook's men contracted a Russian strain of gonorrhea in **Unalaska**. The famous British naval surgeon and fleet physician, Thomas Trotter, maintained that the real problems of seaman resulted from the particular nature of sea life: laborious duty, changes of climate, and inclement weather. As a result, he wrote: "few of them live to be very old." The issue of health on board, however, was perhaps more complicated than that, although the sheer physical strain involved in manning the sails and such tasks as raising an anchor with a capstan were daunting. On the Northwest Coast the effects of long small-boat sorties for exploration and surveying, that lasted daily from before dawn to dusk, often in very poor weather, cannot be overestimated. **Charles Clerke** in 1778 wrote of the "confounded fog" that plagued all ships operating in the summer months; **Francisco Mourelle** battled constant rain in his 1779 survey of **Bucareli Bay,** and navigating the coast in 1786 the ships of **Jean François de La Pérouse** were continually drenched from the rain and mist.

The catastrophic loss of life experienced by the voyage of George Anson (1740–1744) highlighted the fact that scurvy, caused by Vitamin C deficiency, was the central problem for long voyages. It had plagued the progress of the **Manila galleons** since the 16th century. Although James Lind had written *A Treatise of the Scurvy* in 1753, publicizing the known facts about the disease and recommending the solution to the problem—a regular and frequent use of citrus fruit juices, particularly lemon—it was not until 1795 that the British Royal Navy mandated the full-scale introduction of lemon juice into its rations. Although **James Cook** realized that fruit juice appeared helpful as an anti-scorbutic, he was skeptical of its true value because he relied on its thickened essence to reduce its bulk, thus robbing it of much of its Vitamin C content. He was much more positive about the need for regular fresh provisions, which in fact proved extremely effective; on the other hand, his belief in the value of malt and sauerkraut was largely misplaced. In the South Pacific, he also came to appreciate the value of coconut juice. Although Cook's underestimation of fruit juices retarded their ready acceptance as a cure for scurvy, his obsession with keeping his ships clean, as dry as possible through lighting stoves, and well aired had a profound influence on his successors, La Pérouse, **Alejandro Malaspina**, and **George Vancouver**. All four commanders issued heavier, warmer clothing and their men also used local furs to combat the colder weather found in the northern latitudes. During their three summers on the Northwest Coast Vancouver's men, particularly, benefited from fresh meat and fish, vegetables, and berries found at their anchorages. The stopovers also provided the brewers with an opportunity to use molasses as a substrate and spruce needles as a flavoring agent to create a palatable beer that contained enough ascorbic acid to top up the men's bodily stores for a number of weeks. All four major expeditions benefited from the genuine concern of their commanders for shipboard health, and from the presence of knowledgeable doctors and naturalists. At Nootka in 1791, Malaspina's surgeon Francisco Flores "took charge of the production . . . of beer from spruce needles . . . to serve both as a preservation of health and to show those in the [Spanish] establishment how to make it, as an efficacious and agreeable remedy during the coming winter. . . ." The recipe was provided by Malaspina's other surgeon, Pedro María Gonzalez, who later (1805) wrote an important treatise on maintaining the health of sailors at sea. A little earlier, towards the end of the five-week trip from Yakutat Bay to Nootka, the artist **Tomás de Suría** recorded that surgeon Flores had given the officers and men rations of lemonade to reward them for their good work and "to keep them away from the scurvy which was insidiously threatening them." By the time Vancouver was on the coast in 1792, a mere six years after the experience of **John Meares** over the winter of 1786–1787 had demonstrated how disastrous ignorance of scurvy and its treatment could be, there was a lively and informed concern about the importance of diet in preserving general health. Not one of the five men lost by Vancouver from a complement of nearly 200 died of scurvy.

HEARNE, SAMUEL (1745–1792). Native reports of a large river, copper mines, and an abundance of furs persuaded the **Hudson's Bay Company** (HBC) to send Samuel Hearne, who was based at Fort Prince of Wales on the Churchill River, to explore in the far northwest of the continent in the late 1760s. On his third journey (1770–1772) he reached the mouth of the Coppermine River, which effectively and finally disproved the existence of a navigable **Northwest Passage** running west from Hudson Bay. As a result **James Cook**, on his Third Voyage to the Pacific, was instructed not to begin a serious search for the western entrance to the passage until he reached 65° N. Hearne was commanding Fort Prince of Wales when it was surrendered to a French force under **Jean François de La Pérouse** in 1782. Thus the Frenchman also came to know, before his Pacific voyage, that there was no passage in the lower latitudes. La

Pérouse allowed Hearne to keep his journal after extracting a promise that it would be published. However, *A Journey . . . to the Northern Ocean* did not appear until 1795.

HEDDINGTON, THOMAS (1774–1852). Thomas Heddington joined the George Vancouver Expedition on the *Chatham* as its youngest midshipman, and contributed to the achievements of the voyage as an **artist**; four of his sketches were engraved for the publication of the official journal, and there are also eight of his coastal profiles in the atlas. During the 1792 circumnavigation of **Vancouver Island**, Heddington drew important sketches of two native villages—"Village of the Friendly Indians at the entrance of Bute's Canal" and "Cheslakee's Village in Johnstone Straits." Also published were his panoramic views of "Salmon Cove, Observatory Inlet" (1793) and "Icy Bay and Mount St. Elias" (1794).

HEZETA, BRUNO DE (ca. 1744–1807). Bruno de Hezeta came to America in 1774 with five other officers to strengthen the Naval Department of **San Blas**. Following the significant but inconclusive results of the expedition of **Juan Pérez** to the Northwest Coast in 1774, Viceroy **Antonio María de Bucareli** was keen to launch another northern voyage. Hezeta was placed in command of a fleet of three ships, the frigate *Santiago*, whose second captain was Pérez, the schooner *Sonora*, and the packet-boat *San Carlos*. The plan was for the first two ships to head north to reach latitude 65° N, to survey the coast and perform **Acts of Possession**, to make detailed reports on the **natives** encountered, and to note any evidence of exploitable natural resources. The latter vessel was to bring supplies to **Monterey** and then explore the bay reported to exist in the vicinity of **San Francisco**. The expedition left San Blas on 16 March 1774. When the chosen captain of the *San Carlos* became delusional, Hezeta decided to put **Juan Manuel de Ayala** in charge of the ship to take him back to San Blas and then resume the voyage to **California**, and to place **Juan Francisco de la Bodega y Quadra** in command of the *Sonora*.

The little *Sonora* was a poor sailer, and progress was slow in poor weather. On 9 June they discovered **Trinidad Bay**, just north of **Cape Mendocino**. During a 10-day stopover, possession was taken, the harbor was surveyed, and there was extensive contact with the Yurok Indians. Important descriptions of their culture and activities were recorded by both **Miguel de la Campa Cos**, and Bodega. The expedition then pressed on, sailing far out to sea before making landfall again on 11 July off the coast of **Washington**. Anchorage was found on 13 July in the vicinity of Cape Elizabeth and Point Grenville, and Hezeta named the roadstead Rada de Bucareli in honor of the viceroy. Again the act of possession was performed, descriptions of the surroundings were recorded, and gifts were given to the Quinault Indians who brought fish, meat, and vegetables to the *Sonora*. But her anchorage was among shoals and, while waiting for the tide, Bodega sent a party ashore to fetch water. It was attacked and all were lost.

It was already 14 July and Hezeta was becoming increasingly concerned about the ability of the *Sonora* to continue; also scurvy had appeared among her crew. Bodega and his pilot **Francisco Mourelle** persuaded him to sail on, but were not confident that he would do so for very long. On the night of 29/30 July, therefore, they purposely separated from the *Santiago*, and Bodega launched his remarkable voyage to southern Alaska. Hezeta hoped that his lost consort would make it safely back to **Monterey** while he himself sailed on north. On 11 August he had reached close to 50° N, just south of the Brooks Peninsula on the west coast of **Vancouver Island**, where canoes came out to meet him to trade sea otter pelts. Sailing south Hezeta followed the coast closely as directed by his instructions, but missed the opening of the **Strait of Juan de Fuca** as **James Cook** would also do three years later. Moving on he sighted, on 17 August, a large bay between two capes; it was the mouth of the **Columbia River**, one of the great discoveries of the period, but one not exploited by the Spanish and therefore lost to their credit. Nevertheless, Hezeta considered the bay to be "the mouth of some great river, or some passage to another sea." He seems to have considered it **Juan de Fuca**'s strait as he had not found that waterway in a higher latitude and thought that the legendary Greek mariner had miscalculated his position. By the time he reached **Monterey** on 29 August Hezeta had successfully identified **Sebastián Vizcaíno**'s **Cape Blanco** de San Sebastián, which he called Cape Diligencias, but had been unable to negotiate his way into San Francisco Bay as he had intended.

Hezeta had been in Monterey for five weeks before Bodega and Mourelle appeared. He was relieved to see them alive but they were so sick that departure for San Blas was delayed. They finally reached their destination on 20 November. The journals were rushed to the viceroy and on to Madrid, where **José de Gálvez** was delighted with the results; no sign of encroachment on **New Spain**'s northern perimeter had been detected, and four Acts of Possession had secured Spanish sovereignty over the coast.

Recognition of Hezeta's achievement suffered in comparison with that of Bodega, whose daring voyage was the highlight of the summer and was later publicized through the publication of Mourelle's journal in English in 1781. Nevertheless, both men had made important discoveries, and Hezeta's careful pioneering survey of the lower Northwest Coast now merits much praise. His charting of the estuary of the Columbia River and fixing of the position of Cape Blanco are finally being recognized to his credit. He never again sailed on the Northwest Coast as an explorer, but he stayed in the Pacific for another few years serving as commandant at San Blas from 1777 to 1780.

HILL, SAMUEL (1777–1825). After experience as a merchant seaman and captain sailing from New England to Europe, South America, and the East Indies, Samuel Hill commanded the *Lydia* on a fur-trading voyage to the Northwest Coast, 1804–1807. During the early summer of 1805 he arrived on the **Columbia River** from **Hawaii**. In July he put into **Nootka Sound** where he rescued **John Jewitt** and John Thompson, sole survivors from the Mowachaht attack on the *Boston* two years earlier. Heading north to the **Alexander Archipelago**, he wintered over before heading back down the coast to the Columbia River in 1806. There, he was given a letter that had been left with the natives by the **Lewis and Clark Expedition** before exploring upstream for over 100 miles. He took the letter to Canton and sent it home to America.

The *Lydia* was never a happy ship as Hill proved himself a brutal and mentally unstable captain. Nevertheless, he was given another command, this time of the brig *Otter*, for a second voyage, 1809–1812. He traded in the islands of southeast Alaska and his time on the coast was notable for two serious confrontations. In the first, south of

Sitka, he supported local natives in driving off two rival trading vessels that were operating under the direction of **Russian–American Company** official **Ivan Kuskov**. In the process eight **Aleut** hunters were murdered. In the second, his own ship was attacked by Chilkat **Tlingit**; two men were killed and six others wounded. Sailing to Canton via Hawaii, Hill sold his cargo of furs and sandalwood before heading home to Boston.

HINCHINBROOK ISLAND. Straddling the southeast entrance to **Prince William Sound**, Hinchinbrook Island was discovered and named after Viscount Hinchinbrooke, father of the Earl of Sandwich, by **James Cook** on 12 May 1778. Cook anchored briefly in **Port Etches**, a large sheltered bay at the western end of the island. This became the Puerto de Santiago of **Ignacio de Arteaga** in 1779 and was known as Nuchek to the Russians who built a trading post there—Fort Konstantin—in 1793. This was visited by **James Johnstone** of the **George Vancouver** Expedition in June 1794, during his survey of that part of the sound. Despite being given a variety of names in the early exploration period—Isla de la Magdalena by Arteaga, Khtagaliuk Island by **Leontii Nagaev** (1783), and Rose Island by **John Meares** (1788), it was Cook's original name that survived.

HISTORIANS. The discovery, exploration, and early history of the Northwest Coast were given their first narrative by Robert Greenhow, a historian at the U.S. State Department. In 1844, he published the fruits of his research into the American position on the Oregon question as *The History of Oregon and California & the Other Territories of the Northwest Coast of America.*

This narrative was carried forward in the late 19th century by bibliophile and publisher Hubert Howe Bancroft, who used his huge library and archives to employ a team of researchers and writers, principal among whom was Henry L. Oak, to prepare a series of histories of the Pacific coast and western states from Mexico to Alaska. They ran to a set of 39 volumes. His two-volume *History of the Northwest Coast* (1884) preceded individual volumes on **Alaska**, **British Columbia**, **Washington**, **Oregon**, and **California**. Although now dated by the breadth and depth of modern analytical scholarship, Bancroft's achievement was immense.

Two historians working in the early 20th century developed important strands of Bancroft's narrative. Vancouver's Frederic W. "Judge" Howay spent most of his adult life researching the maritime **fur trade**, which resulted in his seminal "A List of Trading Vessels in the Maritime Fur Trade" first published in the *Transactions of the Royal Society of Canada*, 1930–1934, and gathered together in one volume only in 1973. With his steady output of mostly articles on every aspect of British Columbia's early coastal history, Howay strove to give the province a history and to place it firmly in the imperial landscape of the British Empire. In the south, retired mining engineer Henry Raup Wagner, who had lived in London, Mexico, and Chile before retiring to a life of book-collecting, research, and writing in California, used his knowledge of Spanish to publish key works on Spain's role on the Californian and Northwest coasts from the 16th to the 18th centuries, including *Spanish Voyages to the Northwest Coast of America in the Sixteenth Century* (1929), *Spanish Explorations in the Strait of Juan de Fuca* (1933), and his monumental *The Cartography of the Northwest Coast of America to 1800* (1937).

Wagner's mantle in this context was assumed in the second half of the century by Donald Cutter. He taught and mentored many historians who contributed to a better appreciation of Spain's influence in the history of the American west. Much of his personal research focused on California and the Spanish exploration of the north Pacific coast following the publication of his pioneering *Malaspina in California* (1960). A key figure in the revival of the Spanish presence was Canadian Christon Archer, not only for his own work, but for his encouragement of other scholars. In British Columbia, Howay's work was carried forward by W. Kaye Lamb, first provincial and later Dominion archivist, who capped a productive career with publication of a standard-setting four-volume edition of Vancouver's journal, *The Voyage of George Vancouver* (1984). Another scholar who continues to make a long-standing contribution is Glyndwr Williams, whose work on Pacific exploration in general and the search for the Northwest Passage in particular came together on the Northwest Coast of America with studies on Cook and Vancouver. His comprehensive narrative *Voyages of Delusion: The Search for the Northwest Passage* was published in 2002. The study of key aspects of British history on the Northwest Coast has also been carried forward by Canadian historian Barry Gough, while important work on the activities of the Russians in Alaska, and on the maritime fur trade and relations between the **Russian–American Company** and the **Hudson's Bay Company** has been undertaken by James R. Gibson. American historian Richard Pierce made a major contribution to the study of Russian America by founding the Limestone Press in the 1960s, through which he and a host of other colleagues translated and edited both documents and key works by Russian scholars.

HOOD CANAL. *See* PUGET SOUND AND HOOD CANAL.

HUDSON'S BAY COMPANY. The British Hudson's Bay Company (HBC) was given a commercial, executive, judicial, and legislative monopoly in 1670 to operate trading along the lakes and rivers flowing into Hudson Bay. It was not until the Treaty of Utrecht (1713) had officially transferred lands in eastern and northern Canada from France that the HBC was able to expand its activities from the Great Lakes to the Rocky Mountains. As one of the company's obligations was to search for the **Northwest Passage**, it was criticized during this period of increasing interest in such a waterway for its inaction and lukewarm support for exploratory expeditions. After the Treaty of Paris (1763) gave New France to Britain, French-Canadian traders continued to seek furs over much of the center of the continent and, in 1779, combined their activities with a predominantly Scottish association of fur-trading merchants in Montreal to form the **North West Company** and challenge the monopoly of the HBC. The "Nor'westers" consistently out-fought and out-traded the HBC but ultimately became overextended and were forced into a merger in 1821. The end of the bitter and wasteful rivalry meant that the HBC inherited the North West Company–inspired explorations of **Alexander Mackenzie**, **Simon Fraser**, and **David Thompson**, and its ambitious but still nascent dream of a great trading empire beyond the mountains that would link British North America directly with China. This legacy also gave the HBC a number of trading posts west of the Rockies, including Fort George (1812) at **Astoria**, the Northwest Coast's principal link to Asia. Consequently the HBC was able to move quickly to establish and consolidate its Columbia Department, encompassing the **Oregon** Territory as defined in 1818 from the 42° parallel south of the **Columbia River** to **Russian America**. For a brief period between 1821 and 1843, the HBC successfully eliminated American and Russian competition and developed a system of trans-Pacific commerce that took the natural resources of the Northwest Coast (salmon and lumber as well as fur) to Asia.

The dream of developing the Columbia Department belonged to Governor **George Simpson**, who visited the coast in 1824–1825 and 1828–1829. It was carried out by **John McLoughlin** from its center at **Fort Vancouver** (1825) on the Columbia River. By creating a series of other coastal forts—Fort Langley (1827) on the Fraser River; Fort Simpson (1831) at the mouth of the Nass River on the edge of Russian America; Fort McLoughlin (1833) on Milbanke Sound; Fort Nisqually (1833) on Puget Sound; and Fort Stikine (1839) inside Russian America—the HBC finally tied together the surveys of **George Vancouver** and the expeditions of Mackenzie and Fraser. In doing so it reinvigorated British coastal exploration with such sailing ships as the *Cadboro* and *Vancouver*, and the introduction of the *Beaver*, the first steamship on the coast, which arrived in 1836. Thereafter it plied the waters of the coast, furthering an understanding of its intricacies and advancing its economic value to the British Empire. *See also* OGDEN, PETER SKENE.

HUMPHRYS, HENRY (1774–1799). Artist on the **George Vancouver** Expedition, Henry Humphrys enrolled as a midshipman on the *Discovery* in 1790. Two of his sketches were engraved to illustrate Vancouver's published journal: first, his famous "A View of Friendly Cove in Nootka Sound" which shows the extent of the Spanish establishment and the cove from which **John Meares**'s men launched the *Northwest America* in 1788; and secondly a view of "Port Dick, near Cook's Inlet" (on the southwestern edge of the **Kenai Peninsula** in Alaska). Humphrys also contributed eight coastal profiles for the atlas. In 1794 as the expedition was preparing to leave **Monterey** for the voyage home to England, he was transferred to the *Chatham* as master, a highly responsible position for a young man of 20.

HUNT, WILSON PRICE (1783–1842). Businessman, fur trader, and explorer, Wilson Price Hunt was in business in St. Louis when contracted by John Jacob Astor to lead a land expedition to meet up with the *Tonquin* out of New York at the mouth of the **Columbia River**. He was to found and command the fur-trading post of Fort **Astoria**. The party left St. Louis in October 1810 and finally made the fifth crossing of the continent, following **Alexander Mackenzie**, **Lewis and Clark**, **Simon Fraser**, and **David Thompson**. By choosing to deviate from Lewis and Clark's route, Hunt trapped himself with the nearly impossible task of navigating the treacherous Snake River and stumbled into Astoria in February 1812. Historians have condemned him for his inexperience, the death of two men, and the abandonment of his horses in favor of taking to boats on the Snake, but his expedition did pioneer a short-cut route between the Snake and Columbia rivers that later became an important section of the Oregon Trail. In establishing the Astor enterprise he visited **Russian America** and **Hawaii**, before being obliged by pressure from the **North West Company** during the War of 1812 to conclude the sale of Fort Astoria to that company in 1814.

– I –

IASAK. Iasak was a tribute or tax paid in kind by non-Russian peoples engaged in hunting during the expansion of Russia across Siberia. In theory it meant that as long as they paid the *iasak*, **natives** would be regarded as citizens and their property and way of life left unmolested. The concept, if rarely the reality, was carried into the **Aleutian Islands**. As early as 1745 a Cossack from **Kamchatka** was assigned aboard a Russian hunting ship to summon inhabitants of any newly discovered islands "in a kindly and friendly manner" to become subjects, and to "collect *iasak*, which might benefit the treasury." Unfortunately the general history of ***promyshlenniki***–native relationships on the islands was so unkind and unfriendly that the contract implicit in *iasak* was often undermined and the tribute could not be collected. Nevertheless, in the early days of the **fur trade**, navigators and ship owners knew that permission and support for another voyage were more forthcoming with a delivery of furs to pay *iasak*. As a result of abuse in the gathering and payment of the tribute in Russia, however, collection without the authority of special *Iasak* Commissions set up by the new regime of Empress **Catherine II** in

1764, was prohibited. At the end of the 1780s, one of the tasks of the naval expedition of **Joseph Billings** was to investigate not only the charges of brutality and murder against the natives on **Kodiak** Island by **Grigorii Shelikhov**, but also his illegal collection of *iasak*. During her reign Catherine was always interested in a census of native populations in Siberia and the new lands in the North Pacific so that, at a later date, her commissions could establish formal *iasak* payments according to law.

ICY CAPE. Icy Cape is the name of a promontory high on the northwest coast of **Alaska**. Proceeding through the **Bering Strait** into the Arctic Ocean and beyond 70° N, **James Cook** found that the coast ran to the east. On 15 August 1778 he identified "a point that was much encumbered with ice" which became the northern limit of his explorations.

INGRAHAM, JOSEPH (1762–1800). American fur trader and explorer Joseph Ingraham first came to the Northwest Coast with **John Kendrick** aboard the *Columbia*, which pioneered the appearance of **"Boston Men"** in the region in 1788. With **Robert Gray** commanding the ship he took a cargo of furs to China and then completed the first American circumnavigation of the globe in 1790. Once back in Boston he took command of the *Hope* and sailed again for the North Pacific. He made discoveries in the Marquesas Islands and visited **Hawaii** before heading for the **Queen Charlotte Islands**. After selling his furs in China with great difficulty, due to an embargo, Ingraham returned to the coast for the summer of 1792 during which he again visited the Queen Charlottes as well as Dall Island and the southeast of Prince of Wales Island in the **Alexander Archipelago**. The natives' desire for changing trade goods as well as competition from other traders proved difficult. Later, at Nootka, he visited **Juan Francisco de la Bodega y Quadra**, who described him as "an active young man, very talented . . . full [of] information about his extensive explorations . . . [and] possessed [of] great knowledge of the coast." As he had also witnessed the **Nootka Sound Incident** in 1789, Bodega gained valuable information in advance of his meeting with **George Vancouver**. After a visit to **Neah Bay** in the **Strait of Juan de Fuca**, Ingraham left for China, where his difficulty in selling his furs continued; on his return to Boston, his voyage had proven to be a financial disaster.

Nevertheless, Ingraham's well-written journal of the *Hope*'s trading and exploration activities was accompanied by important charts and numerous insightful drawings. He displayed a legitimate interest in the native people, and left one of the earliest descriptions of two **Haida** totem poles "about 40 feet in height carved in a very curious manner indeed—representing men, Toads, & the whole of which I thot did great credit to the naturale genius of these people." He also described a house front with the door "through the mouth of one of the images."

IZMAILOV, GERASIM (1745–ca. 1796). Gerasim Izmailov trained as a navigator on the **Ivan Sindt** and **Petr Krenitsyn** and **Mikhail Levashov** expeditions, which sailed in the **Bering Sea** and **Aleutian Islands** during the 1760s. He became one of the most experienced mariners in the North Pacific, and enjoyed a long and varied career in **Russian America**.

In 1775 he mapped the west coast of **Kamchatka**. A year later he was directed to hunt and trade for an extended period of time in the eastern Aleutians from a base at Illiuliuk on **Unalaska** Island. It was during this time that he met **James Cook** during his second stopover at Samgoonoondha Bay in 1778; he gave the celebrated English explorer some up-to-date charts and information about the Aleutian Islands and **Alaska Peninsula**, as well as a letter of introduction to **Magnus Behm**, the governor of Kamchatka. Cook, in turn, gave Izmailov, "a sensible and intelligent man," a letter to be forwarded to the Admiralty and a Hadley's octant, an instrument with which the Russian was not acquainted but whose use and value he quickly appreciated.

In 1781 Izmailov returned to Okhotsk with a valuable cargo of furs and *iasak*. In 1783 he took **Grigorii Shelikhov** to **Kodiak** Island arriving in 1784. Before they left to return to Russia in May 1786, Izmailov circumnavigated and charted Kodiak Island and its adjacent islands, and surveyed the outer waters of **Cook Inlet**. In 1787 he was back on Kodiak, having transported Shelikhov's new manager, **Evstrat Delarov**, to **Three Saints Bay**. A year later, in 1788, he met the Spanish explorer **Gonzalo López de Haro** and was sent south along the coast from **Prince William Sound** to **Cross Sound** with

Dmitrii Bocharov to explore, and to leave possession plates at significant places like **Yakutat Bay** and **Lituya Bay**. Thereafter, he was active exploring Cook Inlet, the southern coast of the **Kenai Peninsula**, and **Prince William Sound**, supporting **Aleksandr Baranov** to move aggressively into those locations after the establishment of a new settlement in St. Paul's Harbor on the northeast coast of Kodiak Island in 1792. In June 1792 Izmailov helped Baranov fend off a Chugach/Tlingit native attack on his temporary encampment in Prince William Sound, and that same year saw him in the Bering Sea visiting the Pribilof Islands. After a voyage from Kodiak to Okhotsk via Unalaska in 1793–1794, Shelikhov accused him of dealing with another company, offering transport to their men and selling furs for his own profit. As navigators with his experience were not easily found, however, he was re-engaged by Shelikhov to sail back to Kodiak, this time carrying a religious mission group, whose members were immediately assigned to posts as far apart as Unalaska, Kodiak, and Yakutat Bay.

– J –

JEFFERSON, THOMAS (1743–1826). Scholar, statesman, and president of the United States, 1801–1809, Thomas Jefferson's interest in western North America was twofold: he saw space in which an agrarian society could best preserve republican values, and he worried about sharing the best part of the continent with Spain and particularly Britain, preferring to dream, without appreciating the size and complexity of a country no American had yet seen, of his republic "as the nest from which all America, North and South is to be peopled." He also epitomized the intellectual curiosity of the age in its fascination with geography, botany, and **native** peoples.

In 1781 before the American Revolutionary War was over, he tried to sponsor an expedition to explore the west and seek a water route to the Pacific, confident that the river systems would make it possible in a land whose mountains he thought were a western version of the Blue Ridge Mountains with which he was familiar. While Ambassador to France, 1784–1789, he read the account of **James Cook**'s last voyage and followed closely the preparations and progress of the **Jean François de La Pérouse** Expedition, fretting as to whether France might entertain establishment of a new colony to compensate for the loss of Québec. He befriended **John Ledyard**, whose plan to cross Russia, sail to the Northwest Coast and return to the United States across the continent he enthusiastically supported. He also collected information on Spanish Louisiana for future reference. Back in America, he was undaunted by Ledyard's failure to achieve his plan, and in 1793 drew up instructions for another expedition, later abandoned, by the French botanist André Michaud to ascend the Missouri and cross to the Pacific.

In August 1802, now president, Jefferson read **Alexander Mackenzie**'s *Voyages from Montreal*. Fascinated by the achievement, he was disturbed by the relentless progress of the British **fur trade**, which was conquering the northern part of the continent. It was the challenge he needed to launch the **Lewis and Clark Expedition**, which would explore the west and link, practically, the United States with **Robert Gray**'s **Columbia River**. Shortly before the expedition departed St. Louis, his government happily negotiated the Louisiana Purchase, thus addressing his two long-identified concerns—space for expansion and ridding the immediate West of foreign powers. In the wake of Lewis and Clark's successful crossing, Jefferson continued the challenge to Britain by supporting the Northwest Coast enterprise of John Jacob Astor. The consistency of his dream for a pan-American nation never wavered and, with the retreat of Spain from the **Pacific Northwest** in 1819, he continued to expect that the **Oregon** Country would indeed provide the nation with its window onto the Pacific, and all the economic benefits that would flow from such an achievement.

JEFFERYS, THOMAS (ca. 1719–1771). English cartographer, engraver, and publisher, Thomas Jefferys is noted particularly for some of the most important and detailed maps of British and French North America in the years before and after the Seven Years' War (1756–1763). He was appointed geographer royal to George III in 1760. In his shop he carried maps and prints from all over Europe and was the leading supplier of his day, contributing greatly to London's reputation as a center of cartographic scholarship. In addition to his own publications, he also produced maps for books and magazines and other geographers and commentators. Thus he found himself involved on both sides of the mid-18th century **Bartholomew de Fonte** controversy, publishing in 1753 the *Remarks* and chart of Bradock Mead (John Green) that denounced the fiction; and yet, in 1768, the work of Thomas Drage, *The Great Probability of a North West Passage: Deduced from Observations on the Letter of Admiral De Fonte*, for which he produced the maps that continued to give the notion of a passage an element of respectability. In 1768 he published an English version of **Gerhardt Friedrich Müller**'s map of Russian discoveries in the North Pacific, thus bringing it to a wider English-speaking public. In the years before his death he was concerned with a series of maps that dealt with North America from the Caribbean Sea to the northern ocean, published as *A General Topography of North America and the West Indies* (1768) and posthumously used in *The American Atlas: or A Geographical Description of the Whole Continent of America* (1775), that included depictions of the explored and unexplored reaches of Canada, the Northwest Coast, and northeast Russia. Later editions brought the discoveries of **Juan Francisco de la Bodega y Quadra's** voyage to southern Alaska in 1775 to the attention of the public with "A Chart Containing the Coasts of California, New Albion and Russian Discoveries to the North, with the Peninsula of Kamschatka, Asia. And Islands dispersed over the Pacific Ocean to the North of the Line."

JEWITT, JOHN (1783–1821). In 1802 the English-born John Jewitt joined the crew of the *Boston*, a trading vessel out of New England, as a blacksmith and arrived at **Nootka Sound** in March 1803. Subsequently he and sailmaker John Thompson were the only survivors of a **native** attack and massacre of the entire company and the burning of the ship. The two men lived among the Mowachaht people under Chief **Maquinna** for over two years before being rescued by another American trader, the *Lydia*, under **Samuel Hill**. Shortly after his return to Boston in 1807, Jewitt published a short account of his experiences as *A Journal kept at Nootka Sound*. Some years later, with the assistance of a local author, he published his more detailed *A Narrative of the Adventures and Sufferings of John R. Jewitt, Captive of Maquinna* (1815) which gained him local attention. As one of three outsiders who lived with the Nootka natives for an extended period of time during early contact, Jewitt was the only one to write about it, making his account particularly valuable.

JIMÉNEZ, FORTÚN (?–1533). The discoverer of **Baja California**, Fortún Jiménez was pilot on the *Concepción*, under Diego de Becerra, sent from Tehuantepec to Jalisco in the fall of 1533 to recover a ship captured by Nuño de Guzmán, a rival of **Hernán Cortés**. Apparently fearful of the assignment, Jiménez and the crew mutinied and killed Becerra. After landing the wounded on the coast of Michoacán, he did not abandon the voyage, but rather guided the ship northwest across the entrance of the **Gulf of California** finally bringing it into a bay which he called La Paz, an unfortunate misnomer as, when he went ashore, he and a number of his companions were killed by the local natives. The survivors managed to sail back to Jalisco, where one escaped capture by Guzmán, and was able to inform Cortés of the discovery of a "great island," rich with gold and pearls. Thus was born the legend of the "Island of California." *See also* CALIFORNIA.

JOHNSTONE, JAMES (fl. 1778–1818). A key member of the **George Vancouver** Expedition, James Johnstone first came to the Northwest Coast during 1787–1788. He was a shipmate of **Archibald Menzies** in the *Prince of Wales* on a fur-trading voyage led by **James Colnett**, and it was he who brought the ship home from China. Appointed master of the *Chatham* his experience and competence as a surveyor were soon appreciated, and Vancouver used him to lead a large number of the small boat excursions that characterized the expedition and were central to its success.

In 1792 Johnstone worked in **Puget Sound**. From Desolation Sound he explored Bute Inlet and negotiated the Arran Rapids to discover Loughborough Inlet and the strait that now bears his name. His work proved to Vancouver that the expedition could exit to the ocean without retracing its route to the **Strait of Juan de Fuca**. He ended the first survey season in Burke Channel. The next year, from Restoration Cove, Johnstone completed his survey of this channel and the two Bentinck Arms and surveyed the length of Mathieson Channel; he worked in Nepean Sound and Grenville Channel, and from Observatory Inlet surveyed Portland Inlet before heading north into Clarence Strait, where he worked in Ernest Sound and reached

Sumner Strait. During the final season of 1794 he worked the east coast of **Prince William Sound** and then in the *Chatham* southeast down the continental coast to Cape Suckling and **Yakutat Bay**, and on to **Cross Sound**. His major and final survey of the summer was in the **Alexander Archipelago**, to the southeast of Baranof Island, from Cape Decision to Frederick Sound and from there into Keku Sound. Johnstone shared the leadership of the small boat surveys with **Joseph Whidbey** and, as the survey came to an end, Vancouver praised them both "on whom the execution of that laborious and dangerous service principally fell, and to whom I feel myself indebted for the zeal with which they engaged in it on all occasions."

– K –

KAMCHATKA. Extending south some 1,000 miles from northeastern Siberia, the Kamchatka Peninsula provided the Russians with a springboard for their exploration of the North Pacific Ocean and the discovery of America. It was known to the Russians from the mid-17th century but not really conquered until 1731. The growth of Okhotsk into a naval port in 1711 led to the establishment of shipbuilding capabilities on direct orders from the czar, and the pioneering of a sea route to the peninsula. The first round trip from Okhotsk to Bol'sheretsk on the west coast of the peninsula took place in 1716–1717. On the east coast, the fort at Nizhne-Kamchatsk became the leading port in the north, and it was here that **Vitus Bering** built the *St. Gabriel* and launched the first **Kamchatka Expedition** in 1728. In the south, Bering named the little settlement in the magnificent natural harbor of Avacha Bay "Petropavlovsk" in 1740, and it was from here that he set out for America on the second Kamchatka Expedition in 1741. Both of these ports were vital to the Russian exploration of the **Aleutian Islands** and **Bering Sea**, and to the founding of **Russian America**. Under the command of **Charles Clerke**, **James Cook**'s Third Expedition to the Pacific visited Avacha Bay in 1779, and in 1787 the **Jean François de La Pérouse** Expedition also visited Petropavlovsk.

KAMCHATKA EXPEDITIONS. Vitus Bering in 1728–1729 and 1741–1742 commanded the two voyages known as the Kamchatka

Expeditions. Their purpose was to discover America and to claim sovereignty over its resources before what today is the Northwest Coast could be reached from the south and the east by Spain and England respectively. They were part of a major program of exploration and conquest that grew into the **Great Northern Expedition** (1733–1742). Initially launched by **Peter the Great** and carried on after his death (1725), the program was designed to extend Russian control over north and eastern Siberia, to map the arctic coast and to undertake voyages in the Pacific directed towards Japan and America. Political and economic control may have been the goal, but scientific knowledge was one of the principal results of this imperial ambition. Ultimately, towards the end of the 18th century, it led to the establishment of **Russian America**.

KASHEVAROV, ALEKSANDR (1808–1866). A Creole, Aleksandr Kashevarov was sent to St. Petersburg and later graduated from the navigation school at Kronstadt. After briefly returning to **Russian America** in 1829, he came back for an extended period, 1832–1843, during which he commanded **Russian–American Company** ships sailing between **Sitka** and **Kodiak**, and between Sitka and **California**.

In 1834 Kashevarov explored the Pastolik River that linked **Norton Sound**, in the vicinity of the Mikhailovskii Redoubt, with the delta of the Yukon River. He provided excellent maps, reported on the abundance of salmon and native seal and whale hunting, described the local trading networks, and provided some of the earliest, detailed ethnographic descriptions of northern Yup'ik culture.

During the summer of 1838 he was put in command of a hydrographic expedition that proceeded from Sitka to Mikhailovskii Redoubt, and through the **Bering Strait** as far as Cape Lisburne. The purpose was to complete a survey of the last stretch of arctic coast not reached in the mid-1820s by **Frederick Beechey** from the west, or by John Franklin from the east. Using a *baidara* and five *baidarkas*, the party left Cape Lisburne on 5 July, passing Point Barrow on 23 July and discovering today's Iko Bay and Dease Inlet. But some 50 kilometers beyond Point Barrow, with the season advancing and the local natives increasingly hostile, Kashevarov reluctantly turned back.

Unbeknownst to him the **Hudson's Bay Company** had sent an expedition the previous year to survey the exact same piece of unexplored coast, and Thomas Simpson had in fact "bridged the gap" on foot, arriving at Point Barrow from the Mackenzie River in early August. Kashevarov's contribution to an early understanding of northwestern **Alaska** was very important for its detailed description of the coast and its native people. He was the first Russian explorer to take an Iñupiaq interpreter with him into the region.

In 1843 Kashevarov returned to St. Petersburg where he joined the Navy Ministry's Hydrographic Department to work on charts for an *Atlas of the Eastern Ocean including the Okhotsk and Bering Seas*. It was published in 1850.

KATLEYAN (fl. 1801–1818). In 1802, the **Tlingit** chief Katleyan planned and led the successful destruction of the first **New Archangel** in **Sitka Sound**. For many years he lived at Kake (Point Macartney) in Frederick Sound at the northern end of Kupreanof Island, and is understood to have controlled other fortified villages in Chatham Strait. In 1818 the chief, who was respected by **Aleksandr Baranov** for his "intelligence and bravery," came to New Archangel to make his peace with the Russian governor. On this occasion the noted artist **Mikhail Tikhanov** painted a famous portrait.

KAYAK. See *BAIDARKA*.

KAYAK ISLAND. A small island, northwest of **Yakutat Bay**, where the Gulf of Alaska begins to curve west towards the **Alaska Peninsula**. It is noted as the landing place on 20 July 1741 of **Georg Wilhelm Steller** and other members of **Vitus Bering**'s second **Kamchatka Expedition**. Bering named it Saint Elias Island in recognition of the saint's day, a name that was later transferred to the giant mountain nearby. **Sofron Khitrovo** explored the surrounding waters and drew the earliest map of the island and its relationship to the mainland. Although he had the shape of the island right, he missed recording Okalee Spit, extending north from Cape Suckling. **James Cook**'s expedition visited on 12 May 1778 and named it Kaye's Island after Richard Kaye, chaplain to King George III, who had given Cook some coins, which were buried there. A year later, on 16 July 1779, **Ignacio de Arteaga**, marked another saint's day by naming it Isla de la Nuestra Señora del Carmen. It was given its current name in the 1820s by **Gavriil Sarychev**, when he was hydrographer-general of the Russian Navy. He thought it resembled a kayak.

KELLETT, HENRY (1806–1875). Kellett is best known for his explorations in the Arctic in search of Sir John Franklin. On two occasions in the 1830s and again in the 1840s, however, he undertook extensive surveys on the Northwest Coast. In the summer of 1837 in command of the *Starling* he supported **Edward Belcher**'s hydrographic work in **Russian America**, including the waters around **Prince William Sound** and **Sitka**. On that occasion he established the precise position of **Mount St. Elias**. The two ships also visited **Nootka Sound** and **San Francisco**, where they charted the Sacramento River. In 1839 Kellett surveyed the bar and entrance to the **Columbia River** to aid a later entry by Belcher, who arrived from **Alaska**. In 1846 commanding the *Herald* (with James Wood in the *Pandora*) Kellett was responsible for surveys at the southern end of **Vancouver Island**, including Victoria Harbour, and in the **Strait of Juan de Fuca**. Between 1847 and 1850 he made three Arctic voyages, negotiating the **Bering Strait** and exploring both **Kotzebue Sound** and **Norton Sound**.

KENAI PENINSULA. The Kenai Peninsula separates **Prince William Sound** from **Cook Inlet**, south of Turnagain Arm, and its configuration was determined by **James Cook** in 1778. The Spanish expedition of **Ignacio de Arteaga** charted its southwest corner in the area of Port Chatham in 1779. Russian fur traders were active along its coastlines in the early 1780s. Blying Sound, a large bight on its southern coast facing the Gulf of Alaska, contains Resurrection Bay, where **James Shields** established a shipyard for **Aleksandr Baranov** in 1792. **Nathaniel Portlock** had called it Port Andrews in 1787.

KENDRICK, JOHN (ca. 1740–1794). One of the original **"Boston Men,"** John Kendrick was given command of an expedition to the Northwest Coast in 1787. He sailed in the *Columbia Rediviva* accompanied by **Robert Gray** in the *Lady Washington*. The ships reached **Nootka Sound** in September 1788 and wintered over.

The next year Kendrick proved to be more interested in establishing a settlement and relations with Chief **Maquinna** than in trading. He bought land from the chief and while Gray was away established

"Fort Washington" in Marvinas Bay. When Gray returned in July, Kendrick transferred the *Columbia* to his colleague and sent him to China with a cargo of furs, and then on to New England. During this year of the **Nootka Sound Incident**, Kendrick's diplomatic skills allowed him to persuade **Esteban José Martínez** that the American presence was no threat to Spanish sovereignty; in fact he supported the Spaniard's arrest of the British ships, which conveniently eliminated his trading rivals and encouraged him to take the *Lady Washington* up the coast to the **Queen Charlotte Islands** where he traded with the **Haida**. He then proceeded to China via **Hawaii**.

Kendrick did not return to the coast until 1791, arriving via Japan where he was disappointed in the lack of a market for **sea otter** skins. On 13 June the *Lady Washington* anchored off **Koyah**'s Village at the southern end of the Queen Charlotte Islands, where she suffered an attack that was only repulsed with a heavy loss of native life. Unsettled, Kendrick sought refuge in Nootka Sound where he renewed his friendship with the Mowachaht by paying high prices for their furs and gained more land from Chief Maquinna. He also initiated the sale of guns to the natives, thus bringing a new level of **violence** into the **fur trade** and native warfare. He then sailed south to **Clayoquot Sound** where he obtained more furs and met up with Gray before departing for China.

Kendrick spent two further summers on the Northwest Coast in 1793 and 1794. Arriving in December 1794 in Hawaii, where he wanted to continue exploration of the potential of a profitable trade in pearls and sandalwood, he was killed in an accident. Kendrick lacked Gray's passion for the fur trade, and his expeditions added little to an understanding of the geography of the coast. But his activities did serve to underscore the passion of New England entrepreneurs in the trade, even if he was unable to secure the support of the American government to found a colony of settlers on the land he had acquired at Nootka.

KHITROVO, SOFRON (?–1756). Sofron Khitrovo sailed in both of **Vitus Bering**'s **Kamchatka Expeditions**. As fleet master in 1741 he was responsible for gathering together supplies over the winter and spring, 1740–1741. His competence was questioned by **Georg Wilhelm Steller**, who blamed him for delaying the departure of the expedition, and was openly hostile to him throughout the voyage.

When the *St. Peter* reached the Northwest Coast, Khitrovo was in charge of a survey of **Kayak Island**. He reported on a native fish-processing camp on the island, where he found structures for drying and storage, tools, baskets, and net weights. In the **Shumagin Islands** he undertook more small boat trips and met and traded with the **Aleuts**. The logs of the voyage and comments by Waxell suggest that Khitrovo was a well-trained and experienced mariner valued for his abilities. He was also a talented cartographer who made an important contribution to the visual record of the expedition, and who verified its maps in St. Petersburg in 1746. Although he suffered badly from scurvy, he survived the winter of 1741–1742 on **Bering Island**, and it was he and Waxell who signed the official log of the voyage that was subsequently turned in to the Admiralty.

KHLEBNIKOV, KIRILL (1785–1838). Official and historian of the **Russian–American Company** (RAC), Kirill Khlebnikov first worked for the company in Okhotsk and then went to **Kamchatka** for a decade from 1803 to 1813. He traveled extensively and met and assisted the influential **Vasilii Golovnin** during the winter of 1809–1810. He was later offered the position of office manager at **New Archangel** in the expectation that he would play a key role in the administration of the colony upon the retirement of **Aleksandr Baranov**. This became his destiny. He sailed for **Russian America** with **Ludwig von Hagemeister** and between 1817 and 1832 diligently served a succession of governors as an administrator, trader, and diplomat. His work took him to **Kodiak**, the **Aleutian Islands**, and the **Pribilof Islands** in 1829, but it was to **California** that he made numerous voyages to secure supplies and uphold the position of **Fort Ross** as a vital outpost of the RAC's Alaskan operations. Throughout his career he kept a journal from which he compiled his encyclopedic *Notes on Russian America*, an invaluable record of all aspects of the growth and development of Russian America in the first part of the 19th century. In 1832 after nearly 30 years of service, he left America for St. Petersburg. He was elected to the RAC Board of Directors, and wrote a biography of Baranov.

KHROMCHENKO, VASILII (?–1849). Vasilii Khromchenko was a navigator with the **Otto von Kotzebue** Expedition, 1815–1818. This introduced him to a region of **Russian America** to which he would return on a celebrated two-year voyage of exploration in the company of **Adolf Etholen**, 1821–1822. With Khromchenko in the brig *Golovnin* and Etholen in the cutter *Baranov*, the expedition undertook a precise survey of the east coast of the **Bering Sea** from **Bristol Bay** west to Kuskokwim Bay and then north to **Norton Sound**, whose eastern and northern coasts were explored. En route they surveyed Nunivak Island, discovered two days prior on 21 July 1821 by the round-the-world **Mikhail Vasil'ev** Expedition. The charts of both expeditions were used by **Gavriil Sarychev** in the preparation of his *Atlas of the Northern Parts of the Eastern Ocean* published in 1826.

Geographical exploration, however, was only one of the goals of Khromchenko and Etholen; just as important were the contacts with the natives and an understanding of their commercial relationships and trade routes into the interior. In this the Russians were quite successful. In Norton Sound they entered into a modest trade and Khromchenko received valuable information about a thriving commerce in furs from the interior of **Alaska** to Siberia by way of **St. Lawrence Island** and the **Bering Strait**. The journals of Khromchenko and Etholen for 1821 were never published, and their work is only available from the writings of contemporaries; but Khromchenko's journal for 1822 is an invaluable source for the study of **native** culture in the coastal regions of southwest Alaska in the early contact period. It was first published in edited installments in the magazine *Severnyy Arkhiv* in 1824. The original journal was lost for over a century before being discovered in the papers of **Kirill Khlebnikov** in 1953.

KING, JAMES (1750–1784). James King played a key role in **James Cook**'s Third Voyage to the Pacific after his naval experience, and scientific studies in Paris and Oxford, had brought him to the attention of the Board of Longitude as a competent astronomer. Assigned to the *Resolution* he shared astronomical duties with Cook and **William Bayly**, and his observations were vital to the establishment of geographical positions upon which the charts of the surveys of the coastlines of North America, the **Aleutian Islands**, the **Bering Sea**, the Arctic Ocean, and Siberia were based.

Upon the death of Cook in Hawaii in February 1779, King transferred to the *Discovery* with **Charles Clerke**. When Clerke died on 22

August 1779, he took command of the ship and, with **John Gore** in the *Resolution*, was responsible for bringing the expedition home. From the moment of his command, he kept a running journal until he reached the Cape of Good Hope on 12 April 1780, surmising correctly that, as the most educated officer on the voyage, he would be called upon to write up the account of the voyage from the time of Cook's death. He became intimately involved in the preparation of *A Voyage to the Pacific Ocean* and its atlas of charts and illustrations, actually writing the narrative of the final part of the voyage, which became Volume III.

King's observations from the voyage, along with Cook's and Bayly's, had been published earlier by the Board of Longitude in 1782. He barely lived long enough to see the first edition of the *Voyage* published in June 1784. A fine portrait of King by **John Webber**, signed and dated 1782, hangs in the National Library of Australia.

KING GEORGE'S SOUND. *See* NOOTKA SOUND.

KINO, EUSEBIO FRANCISCO (1645–1711). Jesuit missionary and explorer Eusebio Francisco Kino came to **New Spain** in 1681. Trained in astronomy, he was also an enthusiastic student of **cartography**. Assigned as cosmographer to an expedition that aimed at colonizing **Baja California** in 1683, he founded a mission at La Paz. Although the initiative was abandoned two years later, he was the first to cross the peninsula to the Pacific Ocean.

Kino's activities now shifted to the region of northern Sonora (Pimería Baja) and southern Arizona (Pimería Alta), where he would spend the rest of his life, undertaking over 50 expeditions from his base at the mission of Nuestra Señora de la Dolores in the San Miguel River Valley. He is credited with founding 24 missions. During some of these earlier expeditions, the indefatigable Kino found evidence of plants and shells that he had seen in Baja California, suggesting that it was not an island as then thought despite the early explorations of **Francisco de Ulloa**. He determined to find a route to a region that he still felt held the potential for successful missionary activity. Exploring via the Gila and Colorado rivers during the period 1697–1702, he descended the latter to its mouth in 1702, and proceeded some distance down the east coast of the peninsula. Kino prepared maps, later printed in Europe, which confirmed the geography of Baja California.

But his dream of a viable supply route linking the missions in the pimerías with those established in the peninsula from 1697 was not realized for another 75 years.

KITTLITZ, FRIEDRICH HEINRICH VON (1799–1874). In 1825 Friedrich Heinrich von Kittlitz gained permission to retire from the Prussian army to join **Fedor Litke**'s voyage around the world. He held the position of natural scientist with a specialty in ornithology, and developed his talent as an artist. In 1826 he visited **Sitka Sound**, **Unalaska**, the islands of the **Bering Sea**, and **Kamchatka** where, in 1827, he explored the interior. His principal work was to hunt, collect, study, describe, and illustrate birds, and in the atlas to Litke's journal there is a wonderful drawing of him trapping birds on a cliff in Kamchatka. He made numerous drawings and specialized in detailed drawings of the forests and countryside. When he started the voyage, he was "unacquainted with botany" but was interested enough to draw "portraits and characteristic sketches of the vegetation" he encountered. With his companion **Aleksandr Postels**, he amassed a huge number of specimens and related data; this collection and over 1200 sketches were presented to the Academy of Sciences in St. Petersburg when the expedition returned to Russia in 1829.

Although his illustrated account of the expedition was not published until 1858, he did publish, in 1844, a study of coastal vegetation scenes from the Pacific Islands he had visited which included two views drawn on Baranoff Island in the **Alexander Archipelago**, one on Unalaska and six from Kamchatka. A significant number of his finished drawings relating to **Russian America** and Kamchatka, 17 in all, were also engraved in the Litke atlas, and it is for these that he is best known. Among these images are views of the establishment of **New Archangel**, native figures in panoramic forest scenes, a native habitation in Unalaska, and the best drawing of its kind from the exploration period of two **Aleut** hunters at sea in their *baidarka*s. An important feature of the French edition of the atlas is the extensive description of his drawings provided by Kittlitz, which corrected a number of mistakes in the now extremely rare Russian edition.

KLIMOVSKII, AFANSII (1793–1868). Creole employee of the **Russian–American Company** and explorer, Afansii Klimovskii in

1818 was a member of **Petr Korsakovskii**'s expedition to **Bristol Bay**. His most important contribution, however, was an exploration of the **Copper River** in the summer of 1819. Setting out in *baidara*s from the trading post of Nuchek on **Hinchinbrook Island**, the expedition proceeded some 130 miles upriver to its tributary, the Gulkana. He named Mount Wrangell, then an active volcano, and wrote a description of the river, its glaciers, and **native** peoples. For a brief period in the mid-1820s he was manager at Nuchek, and in 1837–1838 was active in southwest **Alaska**, where he inoculated many natives against a raging smallpox epidemic. In the early 1840s he led a second expedition up the Copper River, producing a valuable map of the region from native accounts, which showed Tazlina Lake. However, the Russians never effectively exploited the Copper River basin and its overland links to **Cook Inlet**.

KOBELEV, IVAN (1739–?). A Cossack officer, Ivan Kobelev may have had a Chukchi mother, which would explain his facility in the language and his value to the Russians as a guide, intermediary, and explorer. In the spring of 1779 Kobelev was sent to the Chukotskii Peninsula and the **Bering Strait**, ostensibly to collect *iasak*, but in reality to check on reports of two foreign vessels seen there the previous summer. These were the ships of **James Cook**. While in the area, he went by *baidarka* to explore the **Diomede Islands**. From the natives he met he heard information about a settlement of "bearded men" on the American mainland, which fuelled the legend of a colony of "lost" Russians, survivors from the **Semen Dezhnev** era over 125 years earlier.

Concern about the implications of Cook's voyage, such as the publication of journals and charts that could lead to foreign encroachment in Russian waters, ultimately led the government to respond in the form of the **Joseph Billings** Expedition, which Kobelev joined in 1787. In the summer of 1789 he and **Nikolai Daurkin** were required to locate the nomadic Chukchi and inform them of the imminent arrival of Billings's party. This arrival, however, was delayed by Billings's inability to descend the Kolyma River and sail round the Chukotskii Peninsula as Dezhnev had done in 1648, and so Kobelev spent at least a year following the Chukchi and reporting to authorities on their nomadic lifecycle.

In the spring of 1791 he and Daurkin met up again and decided to look for the "lost" colony of Russians in America. They visited the largest of the Diomede Islands and reached the Kheuveren River, which crosses the Seward Peninsula before emptying into **Norton Sound**. But they didn't ascend it and found no Russian settlement. On their way home, they stopped at King Island. During the winter of 1791–1792 Kobelev was a key member of the Billings group's overland trek to the Kolyma River and back to Iakutsk.

KODIAK. The name Kodiak has been applied variously to the island and its main settlement of St. Paul, site of the present-day city of Kodiak. The largest island in **Alaska**, Kodiak dominates the southwest part of the Gulf of Alaska and gives its name to an archipelago that reaches from the Barren Islands off the **Kenai Peninsula** to the Chirikov Islands and the Semedi Islands. Afognak Island protects the entrance to St. Paul's Harbor. The island was first reached by **Stepan Glotov**, who wintered over, 1762–1763, in **Three Saints Bay**, despite native hostility. **Potap Zaikov** visited in the mid-1770s and **James Cook**'s expedition skirted the island in poor weather in 1778, unable to distinguish its insularity from the **Alaska Peninsula**. Hunting and trading for furs essentially remained centered in the **Aleutian Islands** until **Grigorii Shelikhov** established a post in Three Saints Bay in 1784 and ruthlessly subdued the Koniag natives. This precipitated the exploration of Shelikhov Strait, the Alaska Peninsula, and **Cook Inlet**, and led to sustained Russian hunting trips into **Prince William Sound** during the 1780s. By summer 1786 **Gerasim Izmailov** had circumnavigated and charted the island. Shortly after his arrival in 1791, **Aleksandr Baranov** determined that Three Saints Bay could not serve as headquarters of the expanding **fur trade**, and within the year he had moved to St. Paul. Baranov directed the affairs of the Shelikhov Company and the **Russian–American Company** from there until 1804 when the capital of **Russian America** was moved to **New Archangel**.

KOLMAKOV, FEDOR (?–1839). Manager of a trading post at Katmai on Shelikhov Strait, Fedor Kolmakov played a key role in establishing the presence of the **Russian–American Company** (RAC) in southwest **Alaska** in the 1820s and 1830s. The region had been rumored, since the activities of the **Pavel Lebedev-Lastochkin** Company on the **Alaska Peninsula** in the 1790s, to abound with beaver. In 1816 he explored the north coast of the peninsula around **Bristol Bay** by *baidarka* and, in 1818, was assigned to an expedition led by **Petr Korsakovskii**, but which relied heavily on his experience. The group crossed the peninsula from **Kodiak** and explored the north coast of Bristol Bay, past Cape Newnham into Kuskokwim Bay. In 1819 Kolmakov founded a redoubt and trading post for the Bristol Bay area, Novo Aleksandrovskii, at the mouth of the Nushagak River. From this base he became one of the most effective local administrators for the RAC by establishing good relations with the natives in the interior, whose chiefs were given special silver medals recognizing them as "Allies of Russia." During the years 1832–1833 he made two important forays into the middle reaches of the Kuskokwim River and its tributaries, again establishing key links with the native tribes and creating a series of seasonal way stations for fur collection.

KORSAKOVSKII, PETR (1799–1831). Russian explorer Petr Korsakovskii was sent from **Kodiak** by **Ludwig von Hagemeister** in 1818 to establish a presence for the **Russian–American Company** (RAC) in southwest **Alaska**. The decline of fur-bearing animals in the traditional hunting areas round the Gulf of Alaska obliged the RAC to turn its attention to the vast coastal and inland areas of the continent north of the **Alaska Peninsula**. The party, which included the energetic and experienced Creole trader **Fedor Kolmakov** and a number of natives from **Kodiak**, crossed the peninsula in the summer of 1818. Traveling by *baidarka* they progressed around **Bristol Bay** and along the coast beyond Cape Newnham; then, retracing their steps, they went inland to Lakes Iliamna and Clark before returning to Kodiak. The next year, 1819, Korsakovskii and Kolmakov established the Novo Aleksandrovskii Redoubt in Bristol Bay and worked their way up the coast as far as the mouth of the Kuskokwim River, while a company vessel charted the coast as far as Cape Newnham, work that was continued north in 1820. All this effort, and particularly the work of Kolmakov out of Aleksandrovskii, soon expanded the company's trading links with the local native populations, and the stage was set for further exploration and expansion with the expedition of **Adolf Etholen** and **Vasilii Khromchenko** in 1821–1822.

KOTZEBUE, OTTO VON (1788–1846). A distant relative of **Ivan Kruzenshtern**, whose round-the-world voyage he had joined as a teenager in 1803, Kotzebue was chosen to lead a privately funded expedition to the Pacific during the period of peace brought on by the defeat of Napoleon. The expedition's sponsor was Count **Nikolai Rumiantsev**, a statesman, patron of the arts and sciences, and a major shareholder in the **Russian–American Company** (RAC). The aims of the voyage were to undertake scientific investigations in the "South Sea," to explore and uphold Russian sovereignty and interests on the Northwest Coast, and particularly to search for an entrance to the **Northwest Passage**.

Aboard the *Riurik* (often anglicized as *Rurik* or *Rurick*) when it left Kronstadt in July 1815 were the German writer and naturalist **Adelbert von Chamisso**, his colleague **Johann Eschscholtz**, and the artist **Louis Choris**. Kotzebue reached **Kamchatka** in early June 1816. Proceeding through the **Bering Strait**, where clear weather allowed him to see both Asia and America, he sailed northeast into an inlet that he initially convinced himself was the long-sought passage for which "fate had chosen me to be the discoverer." His hopes were soon dashed but he named the sound after himself before retreating for a lengthy stopover on **Unalaska**. Here both he and Chamisso roundly condemned the conditions in which **Aleut** natives lived under the so-called protection of the RAC. Kotzebue then guided the *Riurik* south for a visit to **San Francisco**, where the descriptions of Chamisso and the drawings of Choris proved to be an important addition to the early record of the area. After wintering in **Hawaii** the expedition returned to the Aleutians but a fierce storm, during which he was seriously injured, persuaded Kotzebue to abandon further exploration in the north and he headed home via Hawaii, the Gilbert and Marshall Islands, Guam, Manila, and the Cape of Good Hope. While the geographical contributions of the voyage were limited, and the ethnographical work of Chamisso is now regarded as its most important accomplishment, Kotzebue lost only one man during three years of voyaging, and his relations with the native people encountered were generally very productive.

On his return to Russia, the publication of his lively and well-written journal made him something of a celebrity, and he secured the command of a naval expedition in the *Predpriatie* (1823–1826).

This was another round-the-world voyage designed to patrol the Northwest Coast, visit Russian settlements, including **Fort Ross** in **California**, and generally to exercise a Russian presence in the Pacific. This brought Kotzebue to California again in 1823.

KOTZEBUE SOUND. A large bay on the west coast of **Alaska**, north of **Cape Prince of Wales**, Kotzebue Sound was discovered and explored in 1816 by **Otto von Kotzebue** as he tried to find a navigable western entry to the **Northwest Passage**. He prepared a fine chart. On 11 August 1778, **James Cook** crossed the Arctic Circle and for the next few days sailed across the sound's outer waters. Battling rain and poor visibility he did not enter it, deciding instead to push north as far as he could go while still in open water.

KOYAH (fl. 1787–1795). **Haida** Chief Koyah's principal village was on Anthony Island at the southern end of the **Queen Charlotte Islands**. After successful trading with **George Dixon** in 1787, **Charles Duncan** in 1788, and **Robert Gray** in 1789, Koyah became embroiled in a couple of disastrous clashes with **John Kendrick** in 1789 and 1791, the second of which cost many native lives. In 1793 Koyah helped Chief **Cumshewa** capture an American brig, and a year later a British ship, which resulted in the murder of all but one of its crew. In 1795 he participated in an attack on **John Boit**'s *Union*. Despite the **violence** that marked his encounters with the fur traders, his village remained a favorite port of call because of the quantity and quality of the furs available.

KRASHENINNIKOV, STEPAN (1711–1755). Natural scientist and explorer of **Kamchatka**, in 1733 Stepan Krasheninnikov was appointed to **Vitus Bering**'s second **Kamchatka Expedition**, assigned to undertake botanical, zoological, and geological investigations as an assistant to **Gerhardt Friedrich Müller**. In 1737 he sailed for Kamchatka, where he wandered the peninsula making notes and collecting numerous specimens. In 1740 he was joined by **Georg Wilhelm Steller**, but the two never became friendly, and Steller, probably seeing in Krasheninnikov a rival for selection on Bering's upcoming voyage to America, engineered his return to Okhotsk. After Steller's death in 1746, however, he was given access to Steller's field notes from Kamchatka, which he used in conjunction with his own to produce his seminal studies of the peninsula. These were gathered together in *Opisanie Zemli Kamchatki* (Description of the Land of Kamchatka) published in 1755. Of particular interest is chapter 10 of Part I entitled "America" and constructed from Steller's notes from his 1741–1742 voyage with Bering. Although short, it deals with some of the German scientist's natural history observations, **Bering Island**, and comparisons between the natives encountered during the voyage and the itel'men of Kamchatka. It was one of the first published accounts of the earliest impressions of **Alaska** and the **Aleutian Islands**, and was accompanied by the earliest printed picture of an inhabitant of Russian America. While Krasheninnikov never visited America nor its islands, his work was a reference point for studies of the wider region. In 1764 an English medical doctor, John Grieve, translated a much-reduced English edition of the "Description," and **James Cook** brought a copy with him to the North Pacific in 1778.

KRENITSYN, PETR (1728–1770). Twenty years after **Vitus Bering**'s second **Kamchatka Expedition** had led to the exploration of the **Aleutian Islands**, there was a good deal of local knowledge but much that remained mysterious about the seas and lands east of **Kamchatka**. At the same time, the late 1750s and early 1760s were a period of renewed interest in the Northeast Passage from European Russia to the Pacific. In 1764 Empress **Catherine II** approved a two-pronged initiative that would see one expedition led by Admiral Vasilii Chichagov negotiate the route through the polar seas, and a second, under Krenitsyn, explore north from the Aleutian Islands. The plan was for them to rendezvous, exchange information, and cross over, with the former ending his voyage at Okhotsk and the latter returning to Europe via the north.

Krenitsyn and **Mikhail Levashov** left St. Petersburg in July 1764, but progress was slow; there were many delays and it was not until 21 July 1768 that the *St. Catherine* under Krenitsyn and the *St. Paul* under Levashov left Nizhne-Kamchatsk. Sailing east and mapping the islands they found along the Aleutian chain, they arrived separately in **Umnak** Pass and proceeded together to Unalaska Bay (present-day Dutch Harbor) on the north coast of **Unalaska** Island. Continuing east they surveyed **Unimak** Island and both the **Bering Sea** and Pacific Ocean coasts of the eastern end of the **Alaska Peninsula**, which they thought was another large island. Krenitsyn wintered near Isanotski Strait at the eastern end of Unimak Island, where his cautious attitude towards men leaving the camp in search of food, and towards the local **Aleuts**, who were discouraged from coming close, maximized his loss of men from scurvy; over 50 percent of his company of 71 men perished. Levashov, meanwhile, wintered in Captain's Bay in the inner harbor of Unalaska Bay where he lost only three men. In June 1769 he joined Krenitsyn and the expedition headed for home, abandoning any idea of meeting up with Chichagov. The ships arrived separately in late July. Krenitsyn drowned in a **kayak** accident, and it was Levashov who brought the ships back to Okhotsk and took the mass of charts, reports, and ethnographic descriptions back to St. Petersburg. He reported to the Admiralty College in 1771. Much of the material has yet to be analyzed in detail by scholars, and the journals remain unpublished.

Because of the failure to connect with the Chichagov expedition the results of the voyage were undervalued at the time. Nevertheless, it combined the first official survey of the main geographical features of the entire sweep of the Aleutian Islands with the navigational observations of experienced naval officers. A map based on the expedition's work appeared in 1777. Levashov's ethnographical notes and drawings with their detailed information about the Aleuts, their clothing and adornments, tools and arms, housing and watercraft provided a critical snapshot of Aleut culture, as contact with the fur traders was leading to irreversible and often disastrous change.

KRUZENSHTERN, IVAN FEDOROVICH (1770–1846). Russian naval officer Ivan Kruzenshtern was appointed to the proposed voyage of Grigorii **Mulovskii** in 1788. Although it was cancelled Kruzenshtern never lost interest in a major voyage. While in Canton and Macao in the late 1790s he saw first hand the advantages of the Northwest Coast **fur trade** and was convinced that instead of dealing with China through Kiakhta, companies in the emerging **Russian America** should bring their furs directly to Canton and trade them for Chinese goods. Initially there was no support for his idea, but once the **Russian–American Company** (RAC) took control in **Alaska**, he found influential allies in Count **Nikolai Rumiantsev** and **Nikolai Rezanov**.

The result was his appointment in August 1802 to head an expedition along the lines he had long advocated, and the Kruzenshtern and **Iurii Lisianskii** Expedition, 1803–1806, became the Russian navy's first voyage around the world. It was a joint project of the navy (officers and men) and the RAC (ships and supplies) and had three main goals: to chart Russia's Far East coast; to carry and support Nikolai Rezanov in opening diplomatic and trade relations with Japan, responsibility for which had been given to the RAC; and to visit, support, and report on Russian establishments in **Kamchatka**, the **Aleutian Islands**, and mainland America.

Two ships were purchased in England, refitted and dispatched from Kronstadt on 26 July 1803. Kruzenshtern commanded the *Nadezhda* and Lisianskii the *Neva*. They entered the Pacific via Cape Horn. Although Kruzenshtern's scientists returned home with important natural history collections and he undertook valuable surveying work in the Pacific Ocean, particularly in the Marquesas Islands, and published an account of the voyage with a 104-chart atlas depicting the places visited, none of his activities took place on the Northwest Coast. The best part of a year was wasted in supporting Rezanov's fruitless negotiations with the Japanese. It was actually Lisianskii who visited America, helping **Aleksandr Baranov** to reestablish a Russian presence at **New Archangel** after a successful **Tlingit** attack two years earlier, and spending the winter of 1804–1805 on **Kodiak** Island.

The expedition was considered a great success not only because of its considerable overall achievements, but also because of its pioneering nature in establishing a direct link between European Russia and the North Pacific. It demonstrated that it was indeed possible, from northern Europe, to uphold Russian sovereignty on the Northwest Coast despite the proximity of Spanish America and the fact that British and American traders were active in the region. Later, as an adviser to Count Rumiantsev, Kruzenshtern assisted preparations for the **Otto von Kotzebue** Expedition of 1815.

KUSKOV, IVAN (1765–1823). As assistant to **Aleksandr Baranov**, Ivan Kuskov played an important role in establishing Russian hunting and trading activity in **Prince William Sound** during the 1790s, in **Yakutat Bay**, and in the **Alexander Archipelago**. He led many of the large hunting flotillas of *baidarka*s that Baranov sent out to explore and hunt down the coast. For a number of years from 1797 he was based at Nuchek (**Port Etches**) on **Hinchinbrook Island**. At the time of the destruction of the initial Russian settlement in **Sitka Sound** in 1802 he was working along the coast between Yakutat and the islands south of **Cross Sound**. In 1804 while Baranov was away in the Alexander Archipelago determined to recapture **New Archangel** and reestablish it, he was in charge on **Kodiak** Island, where he hosted **Iurii Lisianskii** and later **Nikolai Rezanov**, who was impressed by his energy, honesty, and local knowledge.

After Rezanov had returned from an information-gathering visit to **California** in the spring of 1806, Baranov looked to Kuskov to implement his plan to explore the coast beyond the **Strait of Juan de Fuca**, to expand the company's hunting activities, and to see if agriculture and cattle-breeding for Russian America in a location north of the Spanish settlements might be possible. In 1808 Kuskov left New Archangel and visited **Trinidad Bay** before arriving in **Bodega Bay**. He explored the surrounding region, whose potential to supply food for the Russian settlements impressed him, and returned to Sitka Sound with a rich bounty of furs in 1809. The next year Kuskov was en route to California when, during a hunting stopover in the **Queen Charlotte Islands**, his party was attacked by **Haida** natives supported by the American trader **Samuel Hill**. He lost eight **Aleut** hunters and was forced to abandon his expedition. In late 1811 he set out again, this time with artisans and supplies and a large support group of Aleuts to found an outpost above Bodega Bay. This became **Fort Ross**. The Russian presence was of grave concern to the Spaniards, but they had little way of dislodging their unwelcome visitors; and Kuskov remained in California for 10 largely successful years. He lived in a state of uneasy peace with his Spanish neighbors before returning to Russia in 1822.

– L –

LABRET. A facial adornment worn by adult **Tlingit** women, the labret was a small, well-polished saucer-shaped piece of wood inserted in the lower lip, split at gum level across the mouth. Portraits of women found in the published journals of **George Dixon** and **Jean**

François de La Pérouse show why the European visitors found the practice "hideous" and "revolting." **José Bustamante**, while accepting the fact that there were different concepts of beauty, wondered how a custom that deformed the face could increase a woman's attractiveness. But it was clearly important to the women themselves, for La Pérouse noted that when "on occasion we urged them to take off this ornament, they did so reluctantly, expressing the same embarrassment as a European woman whose breast is bared."

LAMANON, JEAN-HONORÉ-ROBERT PAUL, CHEVALIER DE (1752–1787). A classic 18th-century enlightened amateur—bright, energetic, and well-connected in the mould of a young **Joseph Banks**—Jean-Honoré Lamanon's academic credentials and connections got him appointed to the **Jean François de La Pérouse** Expedition. He and La Pérouse never became close and clashed openly in Macao—the result of an inevitable tension between the pragmatic realist and world-weary sailor and the enthusiastic but dreamy academic, who espoused a belief in the noble savage and never felt his interests received the respect they deserved. He was killed by natives in Samoa, ironically after suggesting that the natives of the Pacific were better men than the French. Throughout the voyage Lamanon worked tirelessly with the other members of the scientific corps, amassing and documenting the collections that tragically were lost when the ships were wrecked. At **Lituya Bay** he climbed one of the surrounding mountain slopes with his fellow naturalists collecting geological specimens; "no stone, no pebble escaped their vigilance" wrote La Pérouse in his journal, "samples . . . of which we are bringing back to Europe." Lamanon also described animals such as a **sea otter** caught by his colleagues, and he himself caught a water rat.

LANGLE, PAUL-ANTOINE FLEURIOT DE (1744–1787). Interested in the development of navigational instruments, Paul-Antoine Fleuriot de Langle became responsible for making compasses for the navy, and in the mid-1770s wrote about the calculation of longitude by the lunar distance method. Towards the end of the American Revolutionary War he was given command of the *Astrée* to accompany **Jean François de La Pérouse** on his daring raid against British forts in Hudson Bay. Along the dangerous, ill-charted coasts of northeastern Canada he more than proved his worth as a skilled navigator.

His successful experience with La Pérouse gained him appointment as second-in-command of the Pacific expedition as commander of the *Astrolabe*. For the first half of the voyage, particularly, including the time spent on the Northwest Coast, he was responsible with **Joseph Dagelet** for making and recording the results of the expedition's astronomical observations and determining how they would be incorporated into the creation of charts. On the Asian coast he took the lead role in navigating through waters little known and inadequately surveyed by European navies of the time. He was killed by natives in Samoa.

An interesting sidelight of his visit to the Northwest Coast is given in a drawing of the ships in Port des Français (**Lituya Bay**) by **Gaspard Duché de Vancy**. On the stern of the *Astrolabe* one can see a windmill, an ingenious construction by de Langle with the help of one of the sailors who had worked as a miller. Persuaded that dried grain kept better than flour, the two men experimented on the voyage north from Maui with the design of a small wheat-grinding mill. The sails were only a limited success and were ultimately replaced by a crank, but the little millstones produced excellent flour. De Langle later donated his mill to the **Carmel Mission** near **Monterey**, where one of the millstones can still be found.

LANGSDORFF, GEORG HEINRICH VON (1774–1852). A German-born physician who had developed an interest in ethnology and natural history, Georg Heinrich von Langsdorff was invited to join the expedition of **Ivan Kruzenshtern** in 1803. He sailed on the *Nadezhda*, keeping an informative journal of the voyage across the Pacific and the abortive attempt of **Nikolai Rezanov** to open diplomatic and trade relations with Japan. In **Kamchatka** in May 1805, he decided not to continue the voyage but to accompany Rezanov on a tour of **Russian America** and down the coast to **California**. He visited the **Pribilof Islands**, **Unalaska**, **Kodiak**, and **New Archangel**. At each stopover he provided valuable descriptions of geographical features and of the **native** people and, just as importantly, made a number of sketches. In **San Francisco** he did the same thing, describing the countryside and harbor, the mission and the natives, and musing about the possibilities of viable commerce for the **Russian–American Company**. He wrote that this could only happen if a colony was established north of the Spanish settlement (as later happened with **Fort Ross**), believing that the climate and resources would bring success.

Langsdorff published his account of the voyage in 1812 with five engravings of his sketches, including a view of the Russian settlement on Unalaska Island, groups of **Tlingit** dancing at New Archangel, and heavily tattooed natives dancing at the mission in San Francisco. Other Alaskan and Californian images are preserved at the Bancroft Library at the University of California. Of particular interest are a view of St. George Island in the **Bering Sea**, detailed plans of Aleut *baidarka*s, a map and view of the reestablished **New Archangel**, and a view of the "Spanish settlement of San Francisco."

LA PÉROUSE, JEAN FRANÇOIS GALAUP DE (1741–1788).

After a distinguished career in war and peace, Jean François de La Pérouse was appointed by Louis XVI in 1785 to lead a major expedition to the Pacific Ocean. It was designed to complement the work of **James Cook** and was expected to bring glory to France in a period of intense imperial rivalry.

The idea for the expedition grew from intense French interest in investigating the potential of a **fur trade** between America and China reported by Cook and **James King**. This commercial venture soon developed into a full-blown naval expedition, a voyage of exploration that would establish France's presence in the north as well as in the South Pacific. The king, a student of geography, became an active and enthusiastic supporter.

The expedition left Brest in August 1785 in two ships, the *Boussole* and the *Astrolabe*. They stopped at La Concepción in Chile after which they sailed on to Easter Island and Maui before heading in the summer of 1786 to the Northwest Coast. Alaska was reached on 23 June and a small boat party landed at the southern entrance to **Yakutat Bay** on 26 June. The weather was poor and foggy so La Pérouse sailed south down the coast until, below Cook's Mount Fairweather, he discovered **Lituya Bay**. He called it Port des Français. The full force of the expedition's energies was brought to bear on the place: taking astronomical observations; collecting natural history specimens; drawing the surroundings; engaging with the **Tlingit**; trading for furs and reporting on the possibilities of establishing a trading settlement. There was also the obligatory **act of possession** and search for a passage to the east, an endeavor that La Pérouse could only enter into lightheartedly when faced with the glaciated Fairweather Range in front of him. He also knew from his discussions with **Samuel Hearne** after he had captured Fort Prince of Wales in Hudson Bay in 1782 during the American Revolutionary War, that no passage to that bay from the Pacific at latitude 59° N could possibly exist.

While the Frenchmen admired the canoes and basketry of the **natives**, and the beautifully woven hats, headdresses, and helmets, they were not generally impressed. La Pérouse found the Tlingit gloomy, dirty, ungrateful, thieving, and quarrelsome. There was no noble savage so much loved by the *philosophes*. He worried about the lack of the civilizing effects of agriculture, and was concerned what the introduction of arms and alcohol might do. His comments were harsh and were likely affected by a mood of melancholy that had overtaken him when 21 men were drowned in a small boat accident. He had been ready to leave, but the tragedy delayed him until 30 July, meaning that he had to hurry his survey of the coast as he sailed south towards **Monterey**.

The weather was damp and foggy and he soon realized the impossibility of any detailed surveying, as was undertaken by **George Vancouver** in 1794. Off the **Alexander Archipelago** he commented on the absurdity of the supposed voyage of **Bartholomew de Fonte**, and fog prevented any visit to **Nootka Sound** or investigation of that other dubious report—of **Juan de Fuca**—whose strait had been found that same summer, but whose voyage was also a fiction. None of La Pérouse's names have survived for, when his atlas was published in 1797, English and Spanish names were entering into common usage, and with the Revolution, France had ceased to be a player in the North Pacific.

The hospitality of the Spaniards in Monterey was welcome after a difficult few months. At the same time, the various reports and drawings of the French visitors have proven a valuable resource for the study of early **California** history. La Pérouse left for Asia on 23 September 1786. Visits to Manila and Macao were followed by the expedition's most important and productive phase of exploration on the China coast before Petropavlovsk in **Kamchatka** was reached on 3 September. Here La Pérouse received orders to investigate the new English establishment in Botany Bay, and so he sailed the entire length of the Pacific to arrive in Australia at the end of January 1788. The final disaster at Vanikoro in the Solomon Islands in June 1788, when the ships were wrecked in a cyclone, meant that many of the expedition's lofty goals were never realized and its substantial achievements were compromised. Fortunately, what was sent home from Kamchatka and Botany Bay added much to an understanding of the opening of the Pacific, and included valuable information about, and unique pictures of, the Northwest Coast.

LEBEDEV-LASTOCHKIN, PAVEL (?–1800). One-time partner with, and later rival to, **Grigorii Shelikhov** and his successors, Pavel Lebedev-Lastochkin established in the 1780s and 1790s one of the most important fur-trading companies to operate in the eastern **Aleutian Islands** and on the Alaskan mainland. His initial interest was in the Kurile Islands and opening up trade with Japan, and he worked closely with Shelikhov during the period 1775–1780. The venture was unsuccessful, so they turned their attention to the Aleutians, helping to finance voyages including the one on which **Gavriil Pribylov** found the rich seal rookeries on the islands in the **Bering Sea** that now bear his name.

With Shelikhov's voyage to establish a settlement on **Kodiak** Island (1783–1786), the interests of the two men diverged, and once **Aleksandr Baranov** arrived on **Kodiak** as the new manager of the Shelikhov-Golikov Company in 1792, the companies engaged in an increasingly bitter fight for control of the Alaskan **fur trade**. Despite Shelikhov's apparent advantage of a base on Kodiak, the Lebedev-Lastochkin Company remained strong in **Unalaska**, and his men were the first to explore and dominate the trade in the upper **Alaska Peninsula**, where they explored and controlled the portages from **Bristol Bay** to **Cook Inlet**. They then explored inland as far as the Yukon-Kuskokwim basin. In 1787 and 1790 he established two forts, St. George and St. Nicholas, on the western side of the **Kenai Peninsula**. By the mid-1790s his men were dominant at the head of Cook Inlet, and controlled the portages between Cook Inlet and **Prince**

William Sound (PWS). They had outposts on **Montague Island**, at Nucek **(Port Etches)** on **Hinchinbrook Island**, and explored down the coast from PWS into the delta of the **Copper River**.

After the death of **Catherine II**, political connections succeeded in securing a charter in 1799 for the Shelikhov Company's successor, the **Russian–American Company**. By this time Pavel Lebedev-Lastochkin had been in trouble for a few years: his company had no strong settlement or management in Alaska, such as Baranov was providing in Kodiak; no ship building facilities; and he was over-extended and unable to provide his men with sufficient supplies and reinforcements. His company lacked the clarity of purpose required to confront Baranov. When he refused to join other Shelikhov company rivals in the United American Company in 1797, it was clear that Lebedev-Lastochkin would become the big loser in the final struggle to control the Alaskan fur trade. But there is no doubt that he was an extremely important figure in the initial period of Alaskan exploration and establishment of Russian control around the Gulf of Alaska.

LEDYARD, JOHN (1751–1789). American-born adventurer and traveler, John Ledyard enlisted in the British army and then as sergeant of marines on the *Resolution* for **James Cook**'s Third Voyage to the Pacific. This brought him to the Northwest Coast in 1778 and, although he never returned, he became obsessed by the idea of capitalizing on the **fur trade**. After the voyage he returned to Hartford and used the account of **John Rickman** as the basis for his own memoir, published as *Journal of Captain Cook's Last Voyage to the Pacific Ocean* (1783). It was one of four accounts that predated the official version of 1784.

Despite his best efforts in New England, Ledyard was unable to get backing for a voyage to the North Pacific. In 1785 he was in Paris where he met Benjamin Franklin and then **Thomas Jefferson** and John Paul Jones. The **Jean François de La Pérouse** expedition was setting out with exploration and investigation of fur trade possibilities on the Northwest Coast as one of its tasks. Jefferson was suspicious of French designs on America and he provided encouragement as Ledyard and Jones devised an elaborate plan, which they were ultimately unable to finance, to establish a fur-trading post in the **Pacific Northwest**, which the former would manage while the latter sailed to and from the Orient. Concurrently, Jefferson and Ledyard discussed another idea: the linking of the Northwest Coast with the eastern United States through an overland exploring expedition. He wished to do this from the Pacific, but for Jefferson the seeds had already been sown for what eventually became the **Lewis and Clark Expedition**.

Disappointed in his inability to mount a seaborne expedition to the Northwest Coast, Ledyard decided in 1786 on an ambitious plan to reach the North Pacific and America by crossing Russia, and then continuing east by crossing the then unexplored Pacific Northwest. When a visa was refused by the Empress Catherine, he continued with his plan anyway, sharing it with Sir **Joseph Banks**, whose continuing interest in the Northwest Coast had been kept alive by **George Dixon**. Ledyard entered Russia and by sheer coincidence met his old shipmate on the *Resolution*, **Joseph Billings**, in Siberia. But this friendship was unable to prevent his arrest and expulsion in 1788; clearly the Russian authorities were not keen to have a well-connected American reporting on their activities east of **Kamchatka**.

Back in London Ledyard was again received by Banks and became fascinated by the idea of opening up Africa, but he died in Cairo en route to join an expedition to cross the continent. Though he was distracted by this African adventure, the Northwest Coast always remained his prime interest. Writing to James Madison in 1788, Jefferson noted that Ledyard had promised on his return to "go to Kentucky [*sic*] and endeavour to penetrate westwardly from thence to the South Sea." Ledyard never gave up the dream of bringing the Northwest Coast into the sphere of influence of the United States, and kindled in his mentor and benefactor, later the third president of the United States, the same belief and enthusiasm.

LESSEPS, JEAN-BAPTISTE BARTHÉLÉMY DE (1766–?). A Frenchman raised in St. Petersburg, Jean-Baptiste Barthélémy de Lesseps was appointed to the **Jean François de La Pérouse** Expedition as "Russian interpreter." Knowing that the expedition might have contact with fur traders, and with plans to visit **Kamchatka**, the French were determined to learn from **James Cook**'s mistake in not taking on board anyone who spoke Russian. De Lesseps sailed on **Paul-Antoine Fleuriot de Langle**'s *Astrolabe*.

After the La Pérouse visit to Petropavlovsk in September 1787, de Lesseps was directed to return to France across Siberia to carry reports of the progress of the expedition to date. It took him a full year to reach Paris. After he had delivered his precious packages, including La Pérouse's journal, reports on the Northwest Coast, and charts, plans, and drawings to the authorities, he was presented to Louis XVI, who eagerly listened to the details of the great voyage and his adventures. The account of his travels was ordered published and *Journal historique de M. de Lesseps, Consul de France, employé dans l'expédition de M. Compte de la Pérouse* appeared in 1790. It was immediately translated into English as *Travels in Kamptschatka during the years 1787 and 1788*.

LEVASHOV, MIKHAIL (1738–ca. 1775). In 1764 Mikhail Levashov was made second in command of the secret expedition to the North Pacific led by **Petr Krenitsyn**. Historians and ethnographers have come to appreciate the contribution made by Levashov to their understanding of the eastern **Aleutian Islands**. He was not only a talented cartographer and draughtsman, but also a curious explorer, interesting diarist, and careful artist. His drawings, notes, and observations of the **Aleuts**, their costume, habitations, and material culture are of inestimable value to students of the contact period. When Krenitsyn died in a kayak accident in Kamchatka in 1770, Levashov took over command of the expedition. He brought the ships safely to Okhotsk and delivered the journals and charts of the voyage to the Admiralty in St. Petersburg in the fall of 1771.

LEWIS, MERIWETHER. *See* LEWIS AND CLARK EXPEDITION.

LEWIS AND CLARK EXPEDITION, 1804–1806. The first overland expedition to the Pacific Ocean from the eastern United States, it was launched by **Thomas Jefferson**, who had dreamed of such a project since the early 1780s. Assuming the presidency in 1801, and fully aware of the recent history of the Northwest Coast, Jefferson now had the opportunity to make happen what he increasingly considered an undertaking vital to long-term U.S. interests—an expansion of the nation's authority over much of the continent, including an outlet on the Pacific Ocean. He also saw it as a scientific undertaking that would make a record of all aspects of the country explored—its native peoples, geography, and natural history. In 1803 as his administration negotiated the Louisiana Purchase and sought the support of Congress for the expedition, he received a copy of **Alexander Mackenzie**'s account of his trek to the Pacific some 10 years earlier, along with its **Aaron Arrowsmith** map of western North America. A response from the United States was now more pressing than ever.

The expedition was placed under the command of Jefferson's private secretary, army captain Meriwether Lewis, who chose William Clark as coleader. Lewis set out for the west on 5 July 1803 and, via the Ohio and Mississippi rivers, reached the mouth of the Missouri. Here he organized supplies, recruited and trained men, and collected information from traders who had already been some way up the Missouri River.

The Corps of Discovery began its journey upriver on 14 May 1804. They wintered over at Fort Mandan in present-day North Dakota during which they received vital information about the route west from Minnetaree natives. From April to November 1805 the explorers crossed the Rocky Mountains and pressed on until they were able to descend the Clearwater and lower Snake rivers to the **Columbia River**, which took them to the ocean. On 18 November Clark wrote that the "Men appeared much Satisfied with their trip beholding with estonishment . . . this emence Ocian." Hoping to enjoy the winter at Fort Clatsop, south of present-day **Astoria**, in a climate milder than the previous year, the corps actually suffered months of incessant rain, thieving natives, and poor hunting. They began their return trip on 23 March 1806, arriving in St. Louis exactly six months later.

The expedition was a great success; its gathering and recording of information about the western country and its aboriginal inhabitants was a remarkable achievement. The immediate results for United States interests were less certain: Spain still claimed the **Pacific Northwest**, and British fur traders and explorers were poised to dominate the region in the immediate future. Nevertheless, after Spain's withdrawal in 1819 and the struggle for **Oregon** was engaged in earnest in the 1830s and 1840s, the fact that Lewis and Clark's "first crossing" south of the 49° parallel could be cited, along with **Robert Gray**'s "first discovery" of the Columbia River, was vital in helping to secure, permanently, the southern portion of the **Oregon Territory** for the United States in 1846.

LIMITS EXPEDITION. *See* BODEGA Y QUADRA, JUAN FRANCISCO DE LA.

LISIANSKII, IURII (1773–1837). In 1802 Iurii Lisianskii was invited by **Ivan Kruzenshtern** to become second-in-command of Russia's first round-the-world voyage to the North Pacific. He captained the *Neva* and during the period 1804–1805 made visits to **Kodiak** and **Sitka Sound** that were vital in securing Russian sovereignty on the Northwest Coast, expanding the early **cartography** of the coastlines of **Russian America**, and contributing to the ethnographic record of the colony.

Rounding Cape Horn, the *Neva* sailed to Easter Island and the Marquesas Islands before Lisianskii moved on to **Hawaii**. There he learned about the destruction of **New Archangel** by the **Tlingit** in 1802. As the voyage was partly sponsored by the **Russian–American Company** (RAC), Lisianskii sailed to Kodiak and then hurried on to Sitka where he met **Aleksandr Baranov**, who was hunting in the **Alexander Archipelago**, and formulating a plan to attack the fortified Tlingit settlement that had replaced his establishment. Lisianskii's presence proved crucial to Baranov's success in the face of fierce native resistance, the guns of the *Neva* largely determining the outcome of the battle in October 1804. Lisianskii and his men wintered over on Kodiak Island, and then returned to New Archangel for the summer of 1805. The *Neva* then left for Macao for a rendezvous with Kruzenshtern, carrying a large cargo of RAC furs. After trading these at Canton, the expedition headed for home and a rapturous welcome in August 1806.

Lisianskii's lengthy journal was published in 1812. An English edition appeared in 1814. It is full of information about Kodiak Island and southeast Alaska. His fine charts remained the best available for those parts of Russian America for many years to come. There are also excellent illustrations of the harbors of "St. Paul in the Island of Cadiak [Kodiak]" and "New Archangel in Sitka or Norfolk Sound" engraved from his own sketches. Lisianskii's curiosity extended to climbing Mt. Edgecumbe and to providing detailed descriptions of native life. His journal included vocabularies of the various native languages he encountered, and he executed excellent interpretive drawings of the **artifacts** he collected. Engraved sketches of Tlingit armor, masks, headdresses, fishing tackle, a rattle, and a pendant are particularly noteworthy.

LITKE, FEDOR PETROVICH (1797–1882). Also known by his German name Friedrich Lütke, in the years 1826–1829 Fedor Petrovich Litke led one of the most scientifically important of all of the European voyages to the North Pacific. Family connections had gained him appointment to **Vasilii Golovnin**'s expedition to **Kamchatka, Russian America**, and **California** in 1817–1819. This and a number of survey voyages in the Arctic made him the obvious choice for an expedition in the mid-1820s to undertake new surveys of the coasts of Asia and Russian America. Commanding the *Seniavin*, with **Mikhail Staniukovich** in the *Moller*, Litke left Kronstadt in August 1826. On reaching the Pacific, however, the ships operated independently.

Litke anchored in **Sitka Sound** in June 1827 for a five-week visit. He delivered supplies and equipment, and recorded detailed observations of the establishment. His journal also deals at some length with the peoples, places, and operations of the entire colony, complementing the information supplied by earlier expeditions. Surveys were made of the surrounding waters. Taking on board two **Aleut** hunters, their *baidarka*s, and a cargo of wheat, the *Seniavin* set off for **Unalaska**, arriving in August for a 10-day stopover. He then undertook new and detailed surveys of St. George Island in the **Pribilof Islands**, and of **St. Matthew Island**, completing a very busy and productive summer with a survey of **Bering Island** and a visit to Petropavlovsk.

During 1828 Litke returned to Kamchatka and embarked upon a summer season of surveying its east coast and the Chukotskii Peninsula south of the **Bering Strait**. He arrived back in Kronstadt in August 1829. Coming as it did shortly after Russia had concluded treaties with Britain and the United States to set the maritime boundaries of Russian America in the south and to stabilize the colony's trading relationships with foreigners, the voyage was able to be less concerned with issues of sovereignty and supply. It is noteworthy for the range and quality of its hydrographic and related marine surveys and for its spirit of enquiry. The observations recorded in Litke's journal, and the scientific and artistic work of **Friedrich Heinrich von Kittlitz, Aleksandr Postels,** and **Karl-Heinrich Mertens** meant that it was one of the most fruitful voyages to the North Pacific in the early 19th century. Certainly it gained for Litke a reputation of high standing in European naval and scientific circles. Russian and French editions of his account appeared in the mid-1830s in three volumes, plus an atlas that included the impressive drawings of Kittlitz.

LITUYA BAY. A long, narrow bay between **Yakutat Bay** and **Cross Sound**, Lituya Bay is surrounded by the high, snow-capped mountains of the Fairweather Range. It was discovered by the French explorer **Jean François de La Pérouse** on 2 July 1786. He referred to it as "perhaps the most extraordinary place in the world" and stayed there for a month during which he performed an **act of possession**.

The **natives** encountered were the **Tlingit**, temporarily installed in summer encampments not far from their more permanent villages in **Cross Sound**. Lieutenant **Blondela** executed a fine chart of the bay, which was engraved for the atlas accompanying La Pérouse's published journal. There are two drawings that give a good impression of the bay: a view looking down from the mountain slopes on the southern side to the ships lying in the inner basin by **Gaspard Duché de Vancy**, and a view looking up the bay from its entrance towards Cenotaph Island by Blondela.

In July 1788 the Russian navigators **Gerasim Izmailov** and **Dmitrii Bocharov** visited the bay on their voyage of exploration down the coast from Kodiak, during which they left possession plates in various significant locations. Plate 19 was left at Lituya.

As La Pérouse found out, the entrance to the bay is treacherous, and in 1796 **James Shields** reported to **Aleksandr Baranov** that "The mouth of L'tua Bay is very dangerous; the current is fast and beats against underwater rocks, making it like rapids . . . in bad weather . . . it is still more frightening." Tlingit oral tradition confirms their awareness of the danger. American naval officer George Emmons, who was stationed in Alaska at the end of the 19th century, recorded the Tlingit legend of Kah Lituya, a monster of the deep who dwelled in ocean caverns near the entrance to the bay; he resented any approach to his domain and captured those who came near. As his slaves, they became bears and roamed the slopes of the Fairweather mountains warning their master of the approach of canoes. Then, with him, they grasped the surface of the water and shook it, causing great waves to engulf their enemies. In fact, due to the Fairweather fault that runs across the little inlets at the rear of the bay, earthquakes do indeed cause the "giant waves of Lituya." In 1853, and spectacularly in 1958, they have caused huge tidal waves that rush down the bay, carrying all before them. The La Pérouse drawings show a trim line along the mountain slopes consistent with the height of such a wave, suggesting that this had happened before as well as after 1786.

LÓPEZ DE HARO, GONZALO (?–1823). He played an important role in Spanish exploration of the Northwest Coast, 1788–1792. Appointed to the Naval Department of **San Blas** in 1787 to take part in a new expedition directed at **Alaska**, he accompanied **Esteban José Martínez** on a voyage in 1788 that visited **Prince William Sound**, **Kodiak**, and **Unalaska**. He commanded the *San Carlos*. At **Three Saints Bay** he encountered the Russian fur trader **Evstrat Delarov** from whom he received an exaggerated account of Russian activities on the islands and coastlines around the Gulf of Alaska. His journal provides a detailed account of the Russian settlement. Leaving Kodiak Island for Unalaska, he explored the Trinity Islands.

In 1789, despite their quarrels during the previous year's voyage, he went with Martínez to occupy **Nootka Sound**. He was thus a witness to the **Nootka Sound Incident**, and escorted the captured *Princess Royal* to **Monterey**. Next he was part of the Spanish force under **Francisco de Eliza** that came to reoccupy Nootka in 1790. He was assigned with **Manuel Quimper** to undertake the first major exploration deep into the **Strait of Juan de Fuca**. He played a crucial role in the small boat surveying activities of that voyage, and was responsible for the plans of various ports including San Juan, Revilla Gigedo (Sooke), Cordova (Esquimalt), Bodega y Quadra (Port Discovery), and Nuñez Gaona (**Neah Bay**) as well as the larger charts that resulted from the expedition. López de Haro visited Nootka for a third time with the **Limits Expedition** of **Juan Francisco de la Bodega y Quadra** in 1792. That fall he commanded the *Adventure*, renamed *Orcasitas*, purchased by Bodega from **Robert Gray**, from Neah Bay to Monterey, and then immediately back to Nootka before the end of the year, taking supplies and instructions to **Salvador Fidalgo** that ordered him to exclude all foreigners from the port except the British.

LOVTSOV, VASILII (fl. 1760s–1780s). Navigator Lovtsov sailed on the Okhotsk–Kamchatka run for 30 years from the 1760s, and would have been familiar with the maritime endeavors of the period from the **Petr Krenitsyn** and **Mikhail Levashov** voyage to **Joseph Billings**'s Expedition, as well as the numerous fur-trading initiatives during the 1770s and 1780s.

He is of interest because of an elaborate atlas of 21 hand-drawn, colored charts produced in **Kamchatka** in 1782. It includes charts from Japan in the west to the coast north of **Vancouver Island** in the east. With the exception of the one involving the **Alaska Peninsula** and **Kodiak Island**, those from the **Bering Strait** through the **Aleutian Islands** and southeast down the coast of North America are very sketchy indeed, and likely relied almost totally on information received from Cook's officers in 1779. As a snapshot at a particular point in time, just before the activities of **Grigorii Shelikhov** and others in the 1780s quickly revealed the geography of the eastern Aleutians and the American coast, it shows that the Russians were keen to access and record the evolving knowledge of the North Pacific, no matter what the source. *See also* CARTOGRAPHY.

LÜTKE, FREDERIC VON. *See* LITKE, FEDOR PETROVICH.

– M –

MACKAY, JOHN (fl. 1785–1788). Soldier and assistant surgeon on the voyage of **James Strange** to the Northwest Coast, John Mackay was left at **Nootka Sound** for a year, 1786–1787, to record details of native life and customs. However, he proved inadequate for the task and lost the confidence of Chief **Maquinna**, so that the chance for a good deal of information gathered at the time of contact was squandered. He provided some comments to **Alexander Walker**, who wrote a journal of the Strange voyage, and whom he met later in India, but the only notable thing that he accomplished was helping

Charles Barkley to collect a good cargo of furs in June 1787, and to inform him that Nootka was on an island. As a result, later that summer, Barkley discovered the **Strait of Juan de Fuca**.

MACKENZIE, ALEXANDER (1762–1820). Scottish-born fur trader and explorer, Alexander Mackenzie was the first European to travel overland to the Pacific from eastern America. In 1779 he entered the **fur trade**, subsequently becoming a partner in a company absorbed into the **North West Company** in 1787. By that time his activities had already stretched into the Athabasca country, and a year later he succeeded **Peter Pond** in charge of that department, and as an explorer.

On 3 June 1789 he set out from Fort Chipewyan to explore the great river flowing out of Great Slave Lake, believing it to be Pond's "Cook's River" that would take him to the Pacific. Instead, what is now called the Mackenzie River took him to the Arctic Ocean by 12 July. Returning to Lake Athabasca in 1792 he began his ascent of the Peace River as far as its confluence with the Smoky River. From here at Fort Fork on 9 May 1793 he continued up the Peace. Supported by native advice he negotiated the Parsnip River before portaging to a tributary of the Fraser. After following the Fraser until he realized that it would lead him south rather than west, Mackenzie went up the West Road River before crossing the mountains to the Dean. He reached tidewater on 20 July on the North Bentinck Arm of Burke Channel with the aid of a canoe provided to him earlier at a Nuxalk settlement. He proceeded into Dean Channel where on a rock he used a mixture of vermilion and bear grease to write his famous message: "Alex. Mackenzie from Canada by land 22^d July 1793." The next day he began his return journey and reached Fort Chipewyan on 24 August.

Mackenzie had just missed meeting **George Vancouver**, who explored Dean Channel six weeks earlier, but their respective discoveries would later prove vital to establishing Britain's claim to the central portion of the Northwest Coast. The **Lewis and Clark Expedition** did not reach the mouth of the **Columbia River** for another 10 years. Mackenzie's achievement added a huge amount of new information to the maps of northern North America. It was less important for the fur trade, however, which came to concentrate on the routes pioneered by **Simon Fraser** and particularly **David Thompson**.

Mackenzie's journals were published in 1801 as *Voyages from Montreal . . . through the continent of America to the Frozen Sea and Pacific Oceans*. He became a strong advocate for Britain's use of the overland route to establish a commercial link between England and Canada, the Pacific and Asia. He was unsuccessful, but his dream was later achieved through the activities of the **Hudson's Bay Company**'s Columbia Department.

MAKAH. A native tribe located around **Cape Flattery**. Historically they are part of the Nootka people of the west coast of **Vancouver Island**, with whom they shared a highly developed skill for whale hunting in large ocean-going dugout canoes. *See* NEAH BAY.

MALASPINA, ALEJANDRO (1754–1810). Commander of a major political and scientific voyage to the Pacific, 1789–1794. Although modeled on the imperial/scientific voyages of **James Cook** and **Jean François de La Pérouse**, the expedition's prime goals were actually colonial investigation—political, social, economic, and scientific—and the creation of new coastal charts. Too late and too distracted by other aims, it was not a voyage of discovery or indeed of much exploration. But its visit to the Northwest Coast in 1791 (and the adjunct voyage of **Dionisio Alcalá Galiano** and **Cayetano Valdés** in 1792) resulted in abundant, and valuable documentation—cartographic and geographical, visual and ethnographic. Malaspina had just completed a round-the-world voyage when, in 1788, he and **José Bustamante** proposed to use his previous experience in the Pacific and of its Spanish possessions in leading a new voyage of investigation. It was meticulously planned. Two purpose-built ships were constructed and staffed with the most competent young officers. Its scientific corps matched those of its English and French precursors.

The *Descubierta* and *Atrevida* departed Cadiz on 30 July 1789. A great deal of effort was expended visiting and surveying the coasts and settlements of South America before the expedition arrived in **New Spain** in early 1791. Malaspina's initial intention to visit the Northwest Coast had never been more than vague. Despite a brief flurry of interest in a report on the supposed passage of **Ferrer Maldonaldo** before the expedition left Spain, Malaspina was unconvinced. A Royal Order changed everything. **Jean-Nicolas Buache de**

la Neuville, France's leading geographer, had expressed his belief in the Maldonado story in late 1790, and so Malaspina was directed to sail north to 60° to find the passage. At the same time the recent crisis at **Nootka Sound** suggested that a visit and report on the situation at the Spanish establishment there would also be timely. Consequently the full resources of another major European expedition, with skilled cartographers, **scientists**, and **artists**, were directed towards exploration on the Northwest Coast. The ships left Acapulco on 1 May 1791 and made landfall near **Mount Edgecumbe**. Malaspina's journal is full of references to the activities of other navigators from **Juan Francisco de la Bodega y Quadra** and **Francisco Mourelle** to James Cook and **George Dixon**.

The ships anchored in Port Mulgrave inside **Yakutat Bay** on 27 June. The visit lasted until 6 July and allowed for extensive interaction with the local **Tlingit**. The Spaniards found them experienced traders. Although they were increasingly impatient with the natives' propensity for theft, and the scientists and artists were obliged to move about with armed escorts, the encounters were essentially peaceful until Malaspina and a survey party left to explore the head of the bay and there was a nasty altercation between Bustamante and the natives, reminiscent of the attack on La Pérouse's men in Samoa. Fortunately, the Spaniards avoided the French tragedy primarily because their ships were close enough to open fire. This scene and other drawings of people and places were faithfully recorded by artists **Tomás de Suría** and **José Cardero**; and **Tadeo Haenke** collected natural history specimens and transcribed music. By the time they left, the visitors had also acquired numerous artifacts. Malaspina's search for Maldonado's passage proved to be short. **Felipe Bauza** drew a plan of the head of the bay, Puerto de Desengaño, today Disenchantment Bay, where they were stopped by the Hubbard Glacier; he also made a drawing of the scene, which was later developed into a fine colored painting by Juan Ravenet. An **act of possession** was performed before they returned to Mulgrave. As the voyage continued to the northwest, Malaspina viewed the snow-capped cordillera in front of him. Reminded of the surveys of Cook (1779), Martínez (1788), and Fidalgo (1790), he was fully persuaded that no passage existed and that the whole Maldonado story was a cruel hoax.

The stopover at Nootka lasted from 13 to 27 August. The artists and scientists were again active. Artisans were employed and supplies handed over to help the little settlement, and Malaspina himself made a determined effort to strengthen the Spaniards' uneasy relationship with the ranking Mowachaht chief, **Maquinna**. Extensive reports were compiled about the natives' way of life, culture, and beliefs, and Malaspina authored one in which he doubted that the local natives practiced **cannibalism**. Plans were drawn of **Friendly Cove** and other specific locations, and **José Espinosa** and **Ciriaco Cevallos** undertook an extensive mapping of the waterways of the sound and their relationship to the ocean. Following a visit to **Monterey** the ships returned to Acapulco on 18 October.

The oceanic phase of the voyage began two months later. Malaspina visited Guam and Manila and Bustamante went to Macao. It was then south to New Zealand and Australia, where Malaspina undertook a little polite espionage in the British settlement at Port Jackson. After an examination of the Friendly Islands of Tonga, Malaspina decided not to return to Spain via the Cape of Good Hope. He had wearied of the great enterprise and, disillusioned, even harbored fears of a mutiny. The ships made their way to Peru. Subsequently rounding Cape Horn, they arrived in Cadiz on 21 September 1794.

Unfortunately during 1795, as a result of his triumphant return, Malaspina allowed his political interests and connections to distract him from the task at hand—the preparation of a publication to surpass Cook's journal and atlas. Seemingly immune to the dangers involved in court politics and providing unwanted advice, he suffered a dramatic fall from grace with arrest and imprisonment. The immediate consequence was that the voluminous collection of documents including reports and letters, diaries, scientific papers, statistical records, drawings, and charts that ran to many thousands of items were dispersed or locked away. Any hope of a grand publication disappeared. Although parts of the record were used in a published account of the Alcalá Galiano voyage, and some charts and diaries also found their way into the public domain, it was close to 100 years before Pedro Novo y Colson produced an edited version of the journal and related documents in 1885, and promptly reburied them again in a folio of 681 pages, 573 of them double-columned with no index. Thus the Malaspina Expedition became the least known of all the great Pacific voyages. It was not until the period approaching and encompassing the bicentennial years of the voyage at the end of the 20th century that the true scope and nature and value of the expedition to the history of the Pacific, and particularly to the exploration period on the Northwest Coast, were finally fully appreciated. A full English edition of Malaspina's journal was published 2000–2004.

MALDONADO, JOSÉ MARÍA (fl. 1791–1793). A member of the Royal Scientific Expedition to New Spain, José María Maldonado joined fellow scientist **José Mariano Moziño** and artist **Atanásio Echeverría** on the **Limits Expedition** under **Juan Francisco de la Bodega y Quadra** in the summer and fall of 1792. This brought him to **Nootka Sound**, **Alaska** and **California** where he worked closely with the others in gathering, cataloguing, describing, and illustrating numerous plants as well as identifying many animals and birds, and generally observing the different landscapes. He also helped Moziño with his research on the Mowachaht and Muchalaht people (**Nootka**) of **Vancouver Island**.

Between 13 June and 7 September Maldonado accompanied **Jacinto Caamaño** on his voyage of exploration to the area of **Dixon Entrance**, the southern **Alexander Archipelago**, the northern **Queen Charlotte Islands**, and the adjacent continental coast. In addition to the cartographic achievements of the voyage there was a substantial scientific legacy. Nothing written directly by Maldonado has survived, but the lists of plants, animals, fish, and birds included in Caamaño's journal would have been compiled by Maldonado, and the same goes for the geographical descriptions of the places they surveyed that included the trees and vegetation and observations on the climate. We can also be certain that he and Caamaño's pilot **Juan Pantoja y Arriaga** discussed at length the **native** people—the **Tlingit**, Tsimshian, and **Haida**—they encountered. The descriptions, particularly from **Bucareli Bay**, are much more extensive than those of **George Vancouver**, who was in the Alexander Archipelago in 1793–1794. The descriptions include the natives' physical appearance and demeanor, clothing and ornaments, daily living arrangements, economy and trading practices, weapons and protective armor, and what information could be gleaned about marriage customs, religious beliefs, and government. The Spaniards were impressed by the natives' handling of canoes and their use of iron to make knives but, like other visitors, they were taken aback by the women's use of the **labret**.

MALDONADO, LORENZO FERRER. *See* **FERRER MALDO-NADO**.

MANBY, THOMAS (1769–1834). During the **George Vancouver** Expedition Thomas Manby served successively as midshipman on the *Discovery*, master of the *Chatham*, and as 3rd lieutenant on the *Discovery*. Although he kept an official log, which was handed in to the Admiralty at the end of the voyage, he also kept, secretly, a journal in the form of a series of letter-like articles, which he described as "the scribble of a plain blunt seaman."

The journal is in two parts: the first covers the voyage from England to its landfall in **New Albion** in April 1792; the second covers the first survey season of 1792, the winter of 1792–1793 in **Hawaii**, and the second survey season until the end of June 1793. Manby was no friend of Vancouver and never forgave him for the reprimand meted out when, towards the end of the small boat excursion that explored the coast in the **Strait of Georgia** from Birch Bay, including Burrard Inlet and Howe Sound, his launch became separated from that of the commander. Nevertheless, Manby produced an interesting and perceptive account that complements the official version, discussing the nature of the surveys; the native people, whom he did not particularly care for; the meeting with **Juan Francisco de la Bodega y Quadra** at **Nootka Sound** in which he expressed the opinion that the Spanish commissioner had been unduly influenced by the American traders **Robert Gray** and **Joseph Ingraham**; **William Broughton**'s ascent of the **Columbia River;** and the visit to **Monterey** and the **Carmel Mission**. In 1793, before the second survey season started, the *Chatham* visited Nootka, where Manby was fulsome in his praise for the support received from **Salvador Fidalgo**. Shortly afterwards, when the ships were on the central **British Columbia** coast off Princess Royal Island, the account ends abruptly with the visit to the ship of a number of Tsimshian natives, and a harsh description of the women—"uncouth and horrid beyond description."

MANILA GALLEONS. The establishment of Spanish rule in the Philippines in the 1560s resulted in development of the world's longest-lasting continuous trade route between Manila and Acapulco during the period 1571–1815. When neither agriculture nor mining proved promising, the Philippine economy was saved by exploitation of the wealth of the Chinese empire. Rich goods from the Orient, especially silk, were exchanged for European products and Mexican silver, and the galleons became the most significant vehicle for commercial and cultural interchange between Europe and Asia.

The navigation—some 9,000 nautical miles in each direction—was particularly difficult on the outward journey from Manila. As a result, in the earlier years, the idea of exploring the coast of **California** for possible way stations was considered. After the attacks on Spanish shipping by **Francis Drake** and **Thomas Cavendish**, such an idea gained more currency, but the experiences of **Pedro de Unamuno** and **Sebastián Rodríguez Cermeño** proved that galleons were unsuitable for close coastal reconnaissance. They were thus forbidden to undertake exploratory work. Instead, the voyage of **Sebastián Vizcaíno** (1602–1603) was launched to undertake a major survey, but his enthusiastic support for the bay of **Monterey** as a location for galleon stopovers was dismissed, and this ended the brief suggestion that California might play a role in assisting the galleon trade route.

Three galleons were wrecked on the American coast. Of these, the one on the Nehelam spit near Tillamook, **Oregon**, the so-called "beeswax wreck" (wax for candles was an important component of all the galleons' cargo) is the most interesting. There were survivors who seem to have been absorbed into the native tribes of the region, and who thus became the first-known outside visitors to the Northwest Coast above **Cape Mendocino**. The galleon may have been the *Santo Cristo de Burgos* lost in 1692, or the *San Francisco Xavier*, which disappeared in 1704. The other two wrecks are lower on the coast: the *San Agustín* of Cermeño wrecked in 1595 in Drake's Bay just north of **San Francisco**, and the oldest of the three, the *San Felipe*, which was wrecked on the coast of **Baja California** in 1576.

MAQUINNA (fl. 1788–1818). Principal chief of the Mowachaht in **Nootka Sound**, Maquinna met many of the earliest explorers and fur traders including **Alejandro Malaspina, Juan Francisco de la Bo-**

dega y Quadra, George Vancouver, Dionisio Alcalá Galiano, John Meares, James Colnett, and Alexander Walker and is frequently mentioned in their journals. He was noted for his prowess in the whale hunt. Nootka Sound contained a family of individual chiefs who each owned, and jealously guarded, territorial rights, houses, and various other privileges. Maquinna's growing influence and wealth resulted primarily from his relationship with the Europeans who made **Friendly Cove**, the site of his village of Yuquot, their main anchorage, particularly during the Spanish occupation, 1790–1795. He benefited greatly from his control of the early **fur trade** and from the deference and gifts he received from the Europeans, which served to advance his status.

The name "Maquinna" is held by successive Mowachaht chiefs, and the chief who met **James Cook** in 1778 would appear to have been the father of the chief who met with Alejandro Malaspina in 1791, and dined with Bodega and Vancouver, entertaining them at his winter village at Tahsis in 1792. John Meares who met him in 1788 put his age at about 30 years. A report that he had died in 1795 does not seem to have been correct, as the Maquinna who captured and held **John Jewitt** between 1803–1805, regaled him with stories of the early fur trade, and the French navigator **Camille-Joseph de Roquefeuil**, who met him in both 1817 and 1818, wrote of the "old Chief" who remembered fondly the Spanish and English who came to Nootka in the early 1790s.

Maquinna skillfully used the early years of the fur trade to establish the Mowachaht as the wealthiest group in Nootka Sound, and his diplomatic interactions with the Europeans ensured that he gained a position of power with the visitors to the detriment of the other chiefs in the immediate area. As the maritime fur trade declined and with it the wealth that he and his people had enjoyed, he was faced with the onerous task of trying to maintain their prosperity in relation to his rivals and neighbors. Although Jewitt reported a potlatch held by Maquinna in which he distributed a considerable amount of property, including muskets and gunpowder, his later years would have witnessed a return to the earliest years of his leadership, fraught with difficulty and the tensions that came from almost constant warfare.

MARCHAND, ETIENNE (1755–1793). A French navigator in merchant service, Etienne Marchand had a chance meeting with **Nathaniel**

Portlock in St. Helena in 1788 as the English fur trader was returning home from the Northwest Coast. The information he obtained persuaded him to seek the support of the Baux Company of Marseilles to finance an expedition to the North Pacific. On 14 December 1790 he left France in the *Solide* with a plan to shuttle twice across the Pacific to Canton, using proceeds from his first and second cargoes to buy trade goods before finally returning home from China with tea and silk.

Sailing via Cape Horn and the Marquesas Islands, Marchand reached the Northwest Coast, entering Norfolk Sound **(Sitka Sound)** on the west coast of Baranof Island on 7 August 1791. After a couple of weeks trading he headed for Cloak Bay at the northern end of the **Queen Charlotte Islands** where he found the **Haida** intelligent and clever traders, and was particularly impressed with their giant sculptures (totem poles and house fronts) and their canoes. In his journal he commented extensively on Haida culture. After exploring the various harbors on the west coast of the islands, he headed south where, anchoring off **Vancouver Island**, he encountered other trading ships. As he expected to return to the coast, he decided not to enter either **Nootka Sound** or **Barkley Sound** but to go directly to China. Once there, however, he found Macao and Canton closed to the fur trade and was obliged to return, not to the Northwest Coast but to France. The furs were stored in Lyons to wait out revolutionary turmoil engulfing the nation but were destroyed by vermin.

Thus one of the most efficiently planned and implemented of the late-18th-century trading voyages, and fastest circumnavigation of the globe to date, ended in financial disaster. But the voyage itself and Marchand's reputation were celebrated in a lavishly produced account edited by the influential naval administrator Charles Pierre Claret de Fleurieu.

MARTÍNEZ, ESTEBAN JOSÉ (1742–1798). Esteban José Martínez was one of the more interesting and controversial figures in the early exploration period on the Northwest Coast. A graduate of the pilot-training academy of San Telmo in Seville, he sailed in both the Atlantic and the Pacific oceans before arriving at the Naval Department of **San Blas** in 1773.

Appointed second-in-command of the expedition of **Juan Pérez** in 1774, he made the first of four voyages to the coast north of

California. His *diario* provides a full account of the voyage and details meetings with the **Haida** natives of the **Queen Charlotte Islands**. Later, to prove Spain's first discovery and to bolster its claims of sovereignty over the coast, he maintained that two silver spoons, given to a member of **James Cook**'s Expedition in 1778, were pilfered by the natives off **Nootka Sound**. He also maintained that he had been aware during the return journey of what was later discovered as the **Strait of Juan de Fuca** in the mid-1780s. Both stories would appear to be fabrications.

Martínez never lost his interest in the Northwest Coast after 1774, and years later exhibited an almost messianic desire personally to secure Spanish rights to the region. In 1790 shortly after his actions had precipitated the **Nootka Crisis**, he petitioned the viceroy to allow him to return and prove that Juan de Fuca's strait opened up either into the fabled passage to the Atlantic, whose control he would guarantee for Spain, or into a strategically important link with the Mississippi River and Gulf of Mexico. Then, in 1793, he petitioned the King himself to fund an expedition of ships and soldiers by which he would assert Spanish sovereignty over the coast from the Strait of Juan de Fuca south to California.

Between 1775 and 1788 Martínez was occupied almost annually with supply voyages to the Spanish settlements in **Baja** and **Alta California**. In 1786 a chance meeting in **Monterey** with the French explorer **Jean François de La Pérouse** alerted him to what seemed an aggressive advance by the Russians towards California. He believed from the Frenchman's information, erroneously as it turned out, that the Russians had occupied Nootka Sound. Nevertheless his report to the viceroy was enough to complement other rumors about the Russians that had reached Madrid and Mexico City to give him command of a full expedition. The Martínez and **Gonzalo López de Haro** Expedition of 1788 sailed north to make a reconnaissance of the situation. Visits were made to **Montague Island** at the entrance to **Prince William Sound**, **Three Saints Bay** on **Kodiak** Island, and **Unalaska**. In this latter location Martínez learned that a Russian squadron (the **Mulovskii Expedition**) was expected on the coast and that a settlement at Nootka was in the plan.

Viceroy Manuel Antonio Flórez was convinced by the reports of Martínez and López de Haro that it was necessary to preempt this

Russian move; such a foreign settlement so low on the coast would seriously imperil Spanish interests. Despite his comparatively low rank and a record of conflict with his colleagues, Martínez was the most experienced officer available and consequently was appointed to command the expedition to Nootka to set up a temporary post and fly the flag, a gesture felt sufficient to guarantee Spanish sovereignty. The expedition arrived at Nootka on 5 May and discovered a number of trading vessels at anchor in **Friendly Cove**. While Martínez was persuaded that the American traders had no long-term designs on the port, the English presence troubled him, with its vessels flying the Portuguese flag as an easily discernible ruse. When **James Colnett** arrived with plans to establish a settlement, Martínez provoked the **Nootka Sound Incident** by arresting him, detaining two English ships and sending them to San Blas. In a separate incident, an argument with an influential native chief, Callicum, led to the latter's murder, an event that made Martínez feared and hated by the local **natives**, and which remained a source of much of the distrust that marked Spanish-Indian relations for as long as they permanently occupied Friendly Cove, 1790–1795.

Martínez was obliged by a vice regal order to abandon Nootka in the fall of 1789 only to see it reoccupied the next spring. Within a year the arrest of the English ships had precipitated the **Nootka Crisis**. Martínez's actions, instead of making him the hero he had hoped to be—the man who had prevented the establishment of an English foothold on the coast, and had formulated a bold plan to link Nootka with **New Spain** and the **Sandwich Islands** in a trans-Pacific trading system—made him, instead, the scapegoat for a full-blown international dispute. He had been instructed to act with "prudent firmness, tact and civility" and to avoid "precipitating harsh expression" towards any Englishmen or Russians; clearly in hindsight his character, noted for its erratic and hotheaded behavior, had served neither him nor his country well. A new viceroy, the **Count of Revillagigedo** (1789), would refer to his handling of the affair as "ill-founded."

Though he was a fine seaman, Martínez was someone whose personality was probably ill-suited to the demands of anything but straightforward command. Embittered when his actions and ideas about the Northwest Coast were not viewed in a positive light, he nevertheless came north again with **Francisco de Eliza** in 1790, after which he largely disappeared from view, going to Spain before returning to San Blas in 1795 and resuming supply vessel duties servicing California.

MARTÍNEZ Y ZAYAS, JUAN (fl. 1788–1793). Juan Martínez y Zayas served as pilot on the *San Carlos* under **Gonzalo López de Haro** during the 1788 Spanish expedition to **Alaska**. In **Prince William Sound** he was transferred to the *Princesa*, commanded by **Esteban José Martínez**, and with him made an extended stopover at **Unalaska**, being entertained by the Russian *promyshlenniki*, **Potap Zaikov**.

In 1792 he participated in the **Limits Expedition** under **Juan Francisco de la Bodega y Quadra**, sailing first to **Nootka Sound** and then exploring as far north as southern Alaska with **Jacinto Caamaño**. During this voyage he made a lengthy small boat reconnaissance of Douglas Channel in northern **British Columbia**, only to confirm that it was not part of the fictional strait of **Bartholomew de Fonte**. Following up the information that resulted from the Limits Expedition, **Robert Gray**'s discovery of the **Columbia River**, and **William Broughton**'s ascent of that river, all in 1792, Viceroy **Revillagigedo** decided to concentrate any further exploration activity on the lower coast, south of the **Strait of Juan de Fuca**, and to occupy **Bodega Bay**, north of **San Francisco**. Although **Bruno de Hezeta** had roughly surveyed it in 1775, the lower coast had been largely overlooked since the occupation of Nootka Sound in 1789–1790. **Francisco de Eliza** and Martínez y Zayas were given this assignment in 1793. The two soon became separated, but while Eliza accomplished very little of value, Martínez y Zayas completed a detailed survey of the entire coastline between Fuca and San Francisco. He entered **Gray's Harbor**, crossed the bar of the Columbia River, charted Bodega Bay, and fixed the position of all the major headlands, recording his efforts on a remarkably accurate map. His was one of the most impressive of all the Spanish surveys, undertaken in a small vessel, the *Mexicana*, on a rugged coastline in seas made difficult by the constantly changing winds.

MCLOUGHLIN, JOHN (1784–1857). John McLoughlin entered the service of the **North West Company** in 1803 but, despite his fierce partisanship, became reconciled to the merger with the **Hudson's**

Bay Company (HBC) in 1821. Governor **George Simpson** appointed him chief factor of the Columbia Department in 1824 and, for over two decades operating from **Fort Vancouver**, he was the major figure in the early history of the **Pacific Northwest**. He was later referred to as the "Father of **Oregon**." Agricultural developments soon made the district independent of outside provisions; McLoughlin reorganized trapping expeditions on the Snake River, and used the schooner *Cadboro* to found Fort Langley on the Fraser River and to open trade with **California** and **Hawaii**. After Simpson's visit in 1828 he implemented the plan to construct a series of coastal trading posts that contributed to the final exploration of the Northwest Coast in the first half of the 19th century. The distance of the Pacific from HBC decision makers in Lower Fort Garry and London meant that he wielded dictatorial, though largely benevolent, authority. His generous support of American settlers arriving overland to the Willamette Valley in the 1830s, coupled with Simpson's decision to abandon most of the coastal posts in favor of increased shipping capacity after an agreement with the **Russian–American Company** in 1839, and the governor's lack of support in investigating the murder of McLoughlin's son at Fort Stikine, ultimately alienated him from his HBC superiors. After the **Oregon Treaty** of 1846 he never left the Columbia region but retired from the HBC and in 1851 became an American citizen.

MEARES, JOHN (1756–1809). John Meares was one of the earliest fur traders on the Northwest Coast. As principal operator of the Bengal Fur Company, he sailed to **Alaska** in 1786 in the *Nootka* with **William Tipping** in the *Sea Otter*. In doing so he flouted the monopolies of the **East India** and South Sea Companies and Russian claims of sovereignty in the North Pacific. With **James Cook**'s journal and atlas as his guide, Meares arrived off the **Shumagin Islands** in late August. Trading all the way, he proceeded into **Cook Inlet** via Shelikhov Strait between **Kodiak** Island and the **Alaska Peninsula**. He was the first English navigator to sail in these waters, as they had not been discovered by Cook. In Cook Inlet he found Russian rivalry and influence with the natives against him, so he moved on to **Prince William Sound**. With the *Sea Otter* having departed for China, he prepared to winter over. It was a disastrous decision as everyone suffered mightily and 23 men died of scurvy. In May 1787 he was found by members of the **Nathaniel Portlock** and **George Dixon** Expedition. They were trading legally for the King George's Sound Company and assisted him only when he promised to quit the coast and sail directly to Macao, a promise he promptly ignored.

In 1788 Meares returned to America flying Portuguese colors, a ruse that allowed him to pay lower custom duties at Macao. He also felt that it might protect him from the suspicions of other British traders trading legally, and any Spanish ships that might be encountered. He reached **Nootka Sound** on 13 May. Setting up a camp near the native village of Yuquot in **Friendly Cove**, he later maintained that Chief **Maquinna** had sold him the land. He traded for furs and his men began to build the *Northwest America*, the first European ship constructed on the Northwest Coast. On 11 June Meares left Nootka to explore the coast south. He was particularly interested in the **Strait of Juan de Fuca**, having obtained the charts and papers of **Charles Barkley** in China, and the rumored **Entrada de Hezeta**. His first stopover was in **Clayoquot Sound**, which he named Port Cox after his sponsor. He explored parts of the sound and was much impressed by the size of Chief **Wickaninnish**'s village at Opitsat on the island that now bears his name. Continuing south he visited the **Makah** Indians at **Cape Flattery**, but was unable to find a good anchorage and so did not stay; fear of the natives also seems to have prevented him from entering the strait, which, he noted, extended "as far as the eye could see." He later published a fine panorama drawing of the scene.

Moving on he saw and named Mount Olympus (the Santa Rosalía of **Juan Pérez)** but to his great disappointment in early July he was unable to find any evidence of the river suspected by Hezeta. Meares was not the first mariner to miss the mouth of the **Columbia River**, but his failure to do so with excellent visibility delayed its formal discovery by four years. Convinced that "no such river exists" he named the wide expanse of water before him Deception Bay. Nevertheless, Meares's survey of the **Oregon** coast was remarkably accurate; passing Tillamook Head he sailed across the opening of Tillamook Bay as far as a prominent headland, which he called Cape Lookout. He drew an excellent picture titled "The Country of New Albion" which shows what today are Cape Meares and Three Arch Rocks. By 26 July Meares had retraced his route and was again in Nootka Sound. A further visit was made to Clayoquot Sound and at Nootka the *Northwest America* was launched on 20 September. Before he departed, he promised Chief Maquinna that he would return the next year to expand his establishment. He never actually made another voyage to the Northwest Coast, but his sponsorship of **James Colnett** in 1789 would have far-reaching ramifications when it resulted in the **Nootka Sound Incident** and the subsequent **Nootka Crisis**.

Meares's *Voyages Made in the Years 1788 and 1789, from China to the Northwest Coast of America* was published in 1790. It was immediately attacked by George Dixon and others for the apparent exaggeration of its author's activities on the American coast—his achievements as both a trader and explorer. While its illustrations and some of the charts are informative, as are his comments about the native people, his large chart presented as a Sketch of the Track of the American sloop *Washington* in the Autumn of 1789, stretching from the Strait of Juan de Fuca to southern Alaska, was largely a fabrication. His weak response to Dixon; the obviously exaggerated claims made in his famous *Memorial* following the Nootka Sound Incident; the view of Chief Maquinna who referred to him as "liar Meares"; and the comments of American traders that he was "untruthful" and "by no means a gentleman" have damaged his reputation in the eyes of **historians**. With his shameless self-promotion and disregard for the truth, and his aggressive entrepreneurship, Meares seems to have made enemies easily. Nevertheless, while he remains a controversial figure, his two voyages, coming as early as they did, and covering the coast from Alaska to **Oregon**, were a substantial achievement.

MENZIES, ARCHIBALD (1754–1842). Archibald Menzies combined his medical studies with a complementary interest in plants. The opportunities for collecting provided by service in the Royal Navy brought him to the attention of Sir **Joseph Banks**, which led to his appointment as surgeon on a fur-trading voyage to the Northwest Coast under **James Colnett**. During the summer of 1787 he collected his first botanical specimens in the region in **Nootka Sound** (including species of the Coastal *Penstemon*, one of which was later named for him) and later on the **Queen Charlotte Islands**. The next year he made his first visit to southern **Alaska** before, again in the Queen Charlotte Islands, he found an unusual burnet with a large crimson flower. It was later recognized as a new species and named *sanguisorba menziesii* in his honor.

Menzies was sponsored by Banks to join the **George Vancouver** Expedition and he sailed on the *Discovery* as naturalist. Largely because of his closeness to Banks, who was no friend of Vancouver, he suffered an uneasy relationship with his commander. This finally deteriorated into a tense squabble over Vancouver's seemingly cavalier attitude to the plants that Menzies was keeping in a special frame on the quarter-deck and which were damaged in a rainstorm; and then a power struggle (won by Menzies despite the threat of a court martial) over the disposition of his journal. He maintained that it was personal and scientific and not subject to naval regulations, which mandated its surrender at the end of the voyage; rather he wished to deliver it to Banks. The expedition's three summers on the American coast from the **Strait of Juan de Fuca** to **Cook Inlet** afforded Menzies a unique opportunity to work as a naturalist. As a result he identified and collected hundreds of plants, many of whose taxa celebrate his achievement in the epithet *menziesii*. He also proved to be a skilled botanical artist. In Port Discovery, the expedition's first anchorage, he found over 30 trees and shrubs including the madroño tree later named *arbutus menziesii*, and the Pacific rhododendron which has since been adopted as the official flower of **Washington** State.

Given the scope of his work, Menzies's published research was disappointingly limited, and his plant collections were not formally described and named until many years after his return from the Pacific. Nevertheless, his importance to science lives on through his specimens represented in the herbaria of the British Museum of Natural History, the Royal Botanical Garden in Edinburgh, and the Linnaean Society in London.

MERCK, CARL HEINRICH (1761–1799). A German-born physician, Carl Heinrich Merck was invited to join the **Joseph Billings** Expedition as its naturalist in early 1786. Although not a trained scientist he had met as a young man many of the leading savants of his time including **Peter Simon Pallas**. Recruited as a doctor to work in Russia, he was chosen by Billings to replace the appointed naturalist who was unable to serve, and a potentially more qualified candidate who was too old. Given the rigors of the expedition experienced by

Merck and other senior members of the party in Siberia, the **Aleutian Islands**, and around the Gulf of Alaska, he exhibited a good deal of stamina and not a little courage in undertaking an eclectic amount of research and amassing collections.

Merck received detailed instructions from Pallas about the botanical and zoological specimens to be collected and the ethnographic and linguistic investigations to be undertaken. The principal part of Merck's work related to Siberia, but he was on the *Slava Rossii* (Glory of Russia) for Billings's voyage in 1790 to **Unalaska**, **Kodiak**, and the Northwest Coast as far as **Kayak Island**. In 1791 he again accompanied Billings to Unalaska, but instead of coming farther east, the expedition turned north exploring the principal islands of the Bering Sea and the Seward Peninsula (Cape Rodney) before landing in St. Lawrence Bay on the Chukotskii Peninsula.

Merck shared his notes, maps, and collections with the Admiralty College and the Academy of Sciences where, with the collections of Pallas from Siberia and the Caucasus, they formed the foundation of one of Russia's most important museums. His work had benefited greatly from the genuine interest and support of Billings himself, and the scientific achievements of the expedition surpassed its exploratory value, although not its political importance to the cause of Russian sovereignty. Merck certainly proved himself competent, in the tradition of the 18th-century encyclopedists, in ethnology, ornithology, ichthyology, botany, and zoology; he was somewhat less interested in geology. Pallas used Merck's work in compiling his *Zoologia Rosso-Asiatica*, but Merck's larger journal and other related documents, although entrusted to Pallas, were lost until 1935. They were published in English in 1980.

MERTENS, KARL-HEINRICH (1796–1830). A medical doctor and botanist, the German-born Karl-Heinrich Mertens traveled to St. Petersburg in 1823 in the hope of joining the second **Otto von Kotzebue** Expedition. Finding that all the appointments had been made, he resolved to remain in Russia, learn the language, continue his research, and await another voyage.

With the support of the influential **Ivan Kruzenshtern**, he was named in 1826 as naturalist on the *Seniavin* under **Fedor Litke**, which proved one of the most productive voyages of scientific discovery sent out by any country in the 19th century. In addition to its survey work on the Asian and American coasts, and in the Caroline Islands, the scientific corps of Mertens, ornithologist **Friedrich Heinrich von Kittlitz**, and mineralogist **Aleksandr Postels** established an excellent working relationship that led to the description of over 1,000 new species of insects, fish, birds, and other animals, and more than 2,500 different types of plants, algae, and rocks. Mertens seems to have paid particular attention to the collection and study of mollusks. Together the trio made more than 1,250 sketches of their findings, 350 of which were attributed to Mertens. In addition, they also collected valuable ethnographic **artifacts**. The collections and drawings were all deposited in the museum of the Academy of Sciences in St. Petersburg.

In the French edition of the atlas to Litke's journal there is a long dissertation on the vegetation of Baranof Island by Mertens to accompany a drawing by Postels of the forest near **New Archangel**; he also commented on the difficulties of collecting in such dense and steep terrain while accompanied by the "hostile conduct of the natives." Many species of plant carrying the epithet *mertensiana* or *sitchensis* are a direct result of his pioneering work in **Russian America**, such as the Leafy Bluebell—*mertensiana oblongifolia*, and the Mountain Hemlock—*tsuga mertensiana*. Unfortunately the scope of his achievement could never be fully appreciated because, although he had begun to write up his investigations after the expedition's return to St. Petersburg, in 1830 he caught a fever on a voyage into the North Atlantic, again with Litke, from which he died; much of the information in his head, or left in undecipherable notes, was lost forever.

METCALFE, SIMON (fl. 1784–1795). Merchant sailor and fur trader, and captain of the brig *Eleanora* out of New York, Simon Metcalfe seems to have been the first American on the Northwest Coast, trading there in the summer of 1788 before the arrival that fall of **John Kendrick** and **Robert Gray**. He had learned of the potential of the **fur trade** from reading the journal of **James Cook**, speaking with **John Ledyard**, meeting English merchants in India, and visiting Macao, where in 1787 he probably met **John Henry Cox**. The evidence is not clear but it may well have been Cox who sponsored his voyage to the Northwest Coast in 1788. Exactly where he went is not known but he seems to have returned to Canton via **Hawaii**. In Manila in early 1789 Metcalfe purchased a small schooner to accompany the *Eleanora*. She was named the *Fair American*. Both ships sailed for the Northwest Coast, where Metcalfe met Kendrick while trading in the **Dixon Entrance/Queen Charlotte Islands** section of the coast. The schooner visited **Unalaska** and then sailed down the coast to Nootka, where she was detained by **Esteban José Martínez**—a victim of the Spaniard's clash with English traders that became known as the **Nootka Sound Incident**. Metcalfe made three more voyages to the Northwest Coast in 1790, 1791, and 1795. During the latter he was killed in a native attack on his last vessel, the *Ino*, at **Koyah**'s Village at the southern end of the Queen Charlotte Islands. Despite his five voyages to the Northwest Coast little is known about Metcalfe; no journal has survived, and no maps to indicate where he went to trade or explore, although it seems certain that he joined other American vessels north of Vancouver Island and in southern Alaska.

MIKHAILOV, PAVEL (1786–1840). Elected as a member of the Academy of Fine Arts in 1815, Pavel Mikhailov was appointed three years later as official artist on the sloop *Vostok*, for a round-the-world voyage commanded by Fabian von Bellingshausen. The expedition crossed the Antarctic Circle in late January 1820 (the first to do so since **James Cook** in 1773) and was credited with discovering the mainland of the continent of Antarctica. The work of Mikhailov recorded this achievement and the progress of the expedition through many unknown islands in the South Pacific. Many of his watercolor sketches appeared in 1831 in the atlas accompanying the publication of Bellingshausen's journal.

Mikhailov joined the expedition of **Mikhail Staniukovich** and **Fedor Litke** aimed at **Kamchatka** and **Russian America** in 1826. As a result of his presence on the *Moller* (under Staniukovich), posterity is the recipient of a number of valuable images for the history and ethnology of **Alaska**. He sketched both general views, for example **New Archangel** in 1827, and detailed portraits of **Aleuts** from **Unalaska**, natives on the north coast of the **Alaska Peninsula**, and a unique portrait of a Creole employee of the **Russian–American Company** at **Sitka**. It is unfortunate that Mikhailov did not sail with the much more energetic Litke on the *Seniavin*, where he would have had the benefit of working in a more engaging environment with that commander's trio of scientist-artists, **Friedrich Heinrich von Kittlitz**, **Aleksandr Postels**, and **Karl-Heinrich Mertens**.

MONDOFÍA, ESTEBAN. A pilot in the Spanish navy, Esteban Mondofía hailed from the republic of Dubrovnik on the Dalmatian coast, now in Croatia. He accompanied **Esteban José Martínez** to **Alaska** in 1788, and returned to the far north again in 1790 with **Salvador Fidalgo**. His Slavic origin was considered useful in that he could act as a translator in any encounters with the Russians, and this indeed proved to be the case, although the Russians apparently found him very difficult to understand. At the settlement on **Unalaska** they were more impressed with his participation in their religious devotions. In his journal Martínez records a meeting with an **Aleut** in a canoe off Unalaska, who spoke enough Russian to provide Mondofía with important information about Russian settlements and commercial activity. It is clear that Martínez's visit to Unalaska where he met and "asked many leading questions" of **Potap Zaikov** was successful and very informative due to the presence of Mondofía "who served as my interpreter of the Russian language." Mondofía himself left an informative diary about his experiences and, of the meetings with Zaikov he wrote: "(he) communicated different things that I reported to the Commander since I understood the language." In 1789 Mondofía was again with Martínez, this time on the expedition sent to occupy Nootka Sound; as a result he was a witness to the **Nootka Sound Incident**. Unfortunately, the diary Mondofía wrote about the Fidalgo Expedition the next year, 1790, has not survived, but Fidalgo himself refers to his value as an interpreter in the encounters with Russians in **Cook Inlet** and on **Kodiak** Island.

MONNERON, PAUL (1748–1788). A French military engineer, Paul Monneron was a friend and confidant of **Jean François de La Pérouse** and played a key role in the preparations for his expedition. In April 1785 he was entrusted with a semi-secret five-day visit to London to find out what details he could about **James Cook**'s last voyage, particularly as they related to the prevention of scurvy. He was also ordered to buy navigational instruments, which he did from

Jesse Ramsden and Nairne and Blunt, the two leading makers of the period, and books for the expedition's library. Monneron had his portrait painted by **John Webber**, who showed him his drawings of the Northwest Coast and allowed himself to be quizzed about Cook's voyage, including details of its encounters with the **native** people and the sort of trade goods that should be taken on board—not just trinkets but axes, fish hooks, nails, and knives. He was received by Sir **Joseph Banks**, who was openly helpful with advice, and interceded with the Board of Longitude to lend the expedition two dipping needles, which Cook himself had used. La Pérouse later received these "with a religious feeling of respect towards the memory of that great man."

As the leading member of the scientific corps on the *Boussole*, Monneron worked closely with La Pérouse (and **Paul-Antoine Fleuriot de Langle** and **Joseph Dagelet** on the *Astrolabe*) and supervised the activities of his surveyor-geographer assistant, Gérault-Sébastien Bernizet, with whom he drew charts, plans, and coastal profiles. The two of them constructed a fine plan of Port des Français (**Lituya Bay**). He was responsible for recording his impressions of the military preparedness and drawing plans of the various Spanish settlements visited by the expedition, including **Monterey**.

MONTAGUE ISLAND. Fifty miles long, Montague Island lies across the southwest entrance to **Prince William Sound**. It was discovered as the ships of **James Cook**'s Third Voyage to the Pacific entered the sound through Hinchinbrook Entrance on 12 May 1778. It was named by Cook on 18 May to honor John Montagu, the 4th Earl of Sandwich and 1st Lord of the Admiralty, 1771–1782. Adjacent **Hinchinbrook Island** was named after the earl's father. A year later, the Spanish explorer **Ignacio de Arteaga** called it Isla de Quiros. It was reached from the west in 1783 by the Russian fur traders **Potap Zaikov**, Filipp Mukhoplev, and **Leontii Nagaev**, the discoverer of the **Copper River**. Despite sustained **Aleut/Alutiiq** hostility the Russians wintered over in a deep bay at the north end of the island. Five years later **José María Narváez**, a pilot with the **Esteban José Martínez** and **Gonzalo López de Haro** Expedition, which had anchored in Port Chalmers on the west side, undertook a launch survey of its northern coast and found Zaikov's camp.

MONTEREY. The bay of Monterey was discovered on 16 November 1542 by **Juan Rodríguez Cabrillo**. He named the wide body of water and its southern point Bahía de los Pinos and Cabo de Pinos respectively. Exploring the coast south from Drake's Bay in 1595, after the disastrous wreck of the galleon *San Agustín*, **Sebastián Rodríguez Cermeño** crossed the bay and named it San Pedro in honor of the feast day of St. Peter, 9 December. The most important of the early visitors was **Sebastián Vizcaíno** whose expedition arrived on 16 December 1602. He called it Puerto de Monterey in honor of the viceroy of **New Spain**. The Spaniards stayed in the area until 3 January 1603 working on the ships and setting up an encampment on shore. They also explored the Carmel River valley. Vizcaíno described the **natives** as peaceable, friendly and generous, and was fulsome in his praise for the sheltered harbor, a dubious assessment for which he later received no credit. As Spanish interest in the **California** coast receded in favor of Central and South America and the western Pacific, Monterey was forgotten for 166 years. When, in the late 1760s, it was decided to colonize **Alta California**, the **Sacred Expedition** was commissioned to find Vizcaíno's harbor, but on his first attempt Gaspar de Portolá was unable to locate it, and it was not until the summer of 1770 that it was recognized, and a presidio and mission founded with formal ceremonies of possession and establishment.

The garrison at Monterey was dependent on supply ships from **San Blas**. When they failed to arrive in both 1772 and 1773 there was famine, only somewhat alleviated by hunting and Indian generosity. Once **Juan Bautista de Anza** had pioneered the overland route from Sonora in 1774, and the roads to **San Diego** and other missions founded in the 1770s and 1780s became more well traveled, however, the outpost at Monterey grew and became less isolated, by land and by sea, from the other California settlements. In 1777 it became the capital of "Las Californias," and as such was visited by three of the great exploring expeditions of the late 18th century—those of **Jean François de La Pérouse** (1786), **Alejandro Malaspina** (1791), and **George Vancouver** (1792, 1793, and 1794). Each left detailed descriptions in various diaries and journals, and the Frenchman's reports of daily milk and the gardens of the governor and mission "filled with an infinity of vegetables" suggests a level of stability had been attained. Vancouver was less than complimentary about the state of military defense. This matter so bothered **Juan Francisco de la Bodega y Quadra** in 1792, that he wrote a special report to the viceroy about the problem. La Pérouse's Atlas (Plate 34) contains a fine plan of the bay showing the location of the presidio, as well as the mission at nearby Carmel. **José Cardero** made some important, revealing drawings of the presidio and mission, and local natives; and his portraits of a soldier and his wife are particularly noteworthy. **John Sykes**, master's mate on Vancouver's *Discovery*, sketched a "View of Monterey" from the ship in 1792, which placed the presidio beside the bay in the context of the surrounding hills.

Although some outlying ranches were established by retired soldiers, particularly in the Salinas Valley, in the 1790s, the majority of the approximately 500 people living on the Monterey peninsula at the turn of the 19th century resided in the presidio and mission. A mid-1820s drawing by **William Smyth**, artist on the voyage, of **Frederick Beechey** shows a small, scattered settlement. The town of Monterey did not really begin to take any formal shape until the 1840s. Never more than an imperial outpost, despite its role as a colonial capital, Monterey remained lonely and uninteresting with no noticeable trade or enterprise. It "ill accorded," wrote Vancouver, "with the ideas we had conceived of the sumptuous manner in which the Spaniards lived on this side of the globe."

MONTEREY SHELLS. The colorful shells of the rock-clinging mollusk, abalone, were often brought to the Northwest Coast by Spanish sailors. Abalone are found in abundance along the **California** coast, and their flattened shell with its lining of mother-of-pearl became a source of adornment, currency, and fishing lures for the **natives**. They were much prized in the contact period. **Alejandro Malaspina**'s artist, **Tomás de Suría**, recorded in his *diario* that, on arrival at Nootka in 1791, the natives approached the ships and "the first thing they asked for was shells with the words *pachitle conchi*—give us shells!"

MONTI, ANNE-GEORGES-AUGUSTIN, CHEVALIER DE (1753– 1788). French naval officer Anne-Georges-Augustin de Monti joined the **Jean François de La Pérouse** Expedition on the *Astrolabe*. When the expedition arrived off the Northwest Coast on 26 June 1786, Monti led a small boat party to the beach on Phipps Peninsula that, in the south, defines the entrance to **Yakutat Bay**. He was the first European to land, "with great difficulty" according to La Pérouse, on this part of the coast. Although the boats rounded Ocean Cape and were able to view the expanse of the bay, the weather was deteriorating and he did not proceed far enough to find the harbor, which a year later would provide **George Dixon** with the fine anchorage of Port Mulgrave. La Pérouse named Yakutat Bay Monti Bay in recognition of his efforts but Dixon changed it to Admiralty Bay. However, Monti's name was retained by **Alejandro Malaspina** (1791) for the bay leading into the Mulgrave roadstead, and it survives to this day. At Port des Français (**Lituya Bay**), Monti and **Paul-Antoine Fleuriot de Langle** and **Joseph Dagelet** climbed onto the glacier cascading down from Mount Fairweather and later, after the tragic boat accident that drowned 21 men, searched for the body of one of them with the local **Tlingit**. La Pérouse seems to have held Monti's abilities as an officer in high regard for, after the second tragedy in Samoa in which de Langle was killed, he left him in command of the *Astrolabe* until the expedition reached Botany Bay.

MOUNT EDGECUMBE. A distinctive volcanic cone on south central Kruzof Island in the **Alexander Archipelago**, Mount Edgecumbe acts as a sentinel at the entrance to **Sitka Sound**. It was first seen by **Aleksei Chirikov** in the middle of July 1741, as he moved up the coast from his landfall west of present-day Ketchikan towards Yakobi Island and the tragic loss of his 2 boats and 15 men. He named it, and the nearby cape, St. Lazarus, which was retained by **Gavriil Sarychev** in his atlas of 1826. The current name was given to both features by **James Cook** on 2 May 1778, no doubt after the First Earl of Edgecumbe, commander-in-chief of the English port of Plymouth in 1773, who already had the mountain overlooking that harbor named after him. Cook's artist **John Webber** drew a fine picture of the mountain. An engraving published in **George Dixon**'s journal provides an excellent panorama of the scene from within Norfolk Sound (Sitka Sound).

MOUNT ST. ELIAS. On the northwest edge of **Yakutat Bay** in southern Alaska, Mount St. Elias's sighting by **Vitus Bering** on

16 July 1741 traditionally marks the European discovery of the Northwest Coast. It is 18,008 feet high and became one of the most important reference points for mariners exploring and trading on the coast in the late 18th century. The massive size of the mountain, "majestically conspicuous in regions of perpetual frost" in the words of **George Vancouver**, can be appreciated from early drawings, one made in 1791, probably by **Felipe Bauza** but attributed to **Tomás de Suría**, both members of the **Alejandro Malaspina** Expedition, the other in 1794 by **Thomas Heddington**, who was with Vancouver.

MOURELLE DE LA RUA, FRANCISCO (1750–1820). A pioneer explorer on the Northwest Coast, Francisco Mourelle rose from the post of humble pilot at the Naval Department of **San Blas** to the highest ranks of the Navy and is buried in the Pantheon of Illustrious Mariners near Cadiz.

Mourelle first came to **New Spain** in 1775 to strengthen the supply of the **California** provinces and to undertake exploration on the coast. Within a few weeks he was sailing north in the expedition commanded by **Bruno de Hezeta**.

He had volunteered to serve on the tiny *Sonora* and thus began a fruitful friendship with **Juan Francisco de la Bodega y Quadra**. He and Bodega shared a zeal for adventure, as well as a genuine desire to fulfill the mandate of the expedition, when they allowed their vessel to drift away from Hezeta's *Santiago* off the **Strait of Juan de Fuca** so that they could continue the voyage independently. They reached close to 58° N and discovered **Bucareli Bay** in the **Alexander Archipelago**. Mourelle kept a complete journal of the voyage in which, in addition to matters navigational, he showed a keen interest in geography and the **native** peoples encountered. His comments on this voyage and his next one in 1779 are of great value to ethnologists. Mourelle's account of the 1775 voyage was published in English by **Daines Barrington** in 1781; this brought his name, and one of the bravest voyages in the history of the Spanish Navy, to a wider European public. On his return to San Blas, Mourelle was commissioned as a junior officer and commanded supply vessels to **California**, until he and Bodega again sailed together in the next expedition to the Northwest Coast in 1779. They were in the *Favorita* with the commander **Ignacio de Arteaga** in the *Princesa*. At Bucareli Bay (2 May–1 July),

Mourelle was chosen to make what was the first detailed exploration of a section of the Northwest Coast undertaken by European mariners. His 26-day survey of the bays, inlets, and islands around Bucareli in almost incessant rain was a major achievement, particularly as the launches were constantly shadowed by **Tlingit** canoes, encounters with which always involved thefts, threats, and a general level of tension that could easily have deteriorated into **violence**. The rest of the voyage, with its survey work at anchorages in **Prince William Sound** and off the tip of the **Kenai Peninsula**, was uneventful for Mourelle, but he recorded in a journal his views about native activity. He admired greatly the **kayaks** and the **Aleut/Alutiiq** harpoons with their carefully fashioned tips of bone and lines of gut secured to a float to stop the hunted **sea otter** or seal from sinking. Like Bodega, Mourelle was highly critical of Arteaga's decision to abort the voyage off Afognak Island, writing later that his reasons had "little substance."

In 1780–1781 Mourelle undertook a voyage from Manila to **New Spain** in which he discovered and explored a number of islands in the South Pacific. A good deal of Mourelle's reputation in Spanish naval history rests on this voyage, which produced charts and ethnological collections and observations of immense importance. After more Pacific crossings to Manila and Canton and a brief period as commandant at San Blas, he was commissioned in the fall of 1791 by the viceroy, the **Count of Revillagigedo**, to undertake an expedition to follow up Spanish explorations in the **Strait of Juan de Fuca**, specifically those of **José María Narváez**. As it turned out he never made the voyage because **Alejandro Malaspina** insisted that it belonged to his mandate and should be undertaken by his officers. Thus it was not Mourelle but **Dionisio Alcalá Galiano** and **Cayetano Valdés** who gained the credit for circumnavigating **Vancouver Island** in the summer of 1792. Instead, Mourelle was assigned by the viceroy to undertake a special research project to bolster Spain's case against England following the **Nootka Crisis**. This was to compile a compendium, with commentary, of all the Spanish voyages to the Northwest Coast with their records of **Acts of Possession**. The result was his lengthy *Diarios de los descubrimientos hechos por los españoles en las costas de América.*

MOZIÑO, JOSÉ MARIANO (1757–1820). In 1787, the year in which José Mariano Moziño gained a medical degree, Spain launched the Royal Scientific Expedition to **New Spain**. As the study of botany was closely allied to medicine because of the curative properties of plants, Moziño attended courses in botany offered by members of the Expedition at the Royal Botanical Garden in Mexico City. He demonstrated such an aptitude for botanical research that he was immediately chosen to participate in the work of the Expedition, and during 1790–1791 was joined by a former classmate, **José María Maldonado**; he also worked with the artist **Atanásio Echeverría**. In 1791 there were financial difficulties within the Expedition and rather than see the men lost to botanical work, **Juan Francisco de la Bodega y Quadra** agreed to take them on his **Limits Expedition** due to depart for **Nootka Sound** in early 1792.

The trio arrived in Nootka at the end of April 1792. Moziño used his four-month visit to **Vancouver Island** to undertake a comprehensive survey of the area's history, ethnography, botany, and zoology. He and Maldonado prepared a catalogue of more than 400 species of plants, animals, fish, and birds. He made a particular point of researching **native** life, culture, and beliefs and compiled a Brief Dictionary of the Terms that Could be Learned of the Language of the Natives of Nootka. Although this was only Moziño's second field-work assignment and his first ethnographic study, the results were the remarkable achievement captured in his *Noticias de Nutka*. It was not published until 1913. Moziño's studies constitute a major source of knowledge and understanding of the natives of Nootka in the contact period. *Noticias de Nutka*, written as 12 articles, includes a history of the Spanish presence and European voyages to the sound, and offers a unique insight into how contact with Europeans was impacting the natives' way of life. Although over the years Spanish naval officers had recorded a good deal of information, inevitably their views were highly subjective. Moziño brought his training as a scientist and philosopher to Nootka and his linguistic abilities meant that his numerous interviews were more focused and productive. Toward the end of his stay the Spanish scientists were joined by **Archibald Menzies**, naturalist with the **George Vancouver** Expedition, with whom they enjoyed a mutually useful collaboration.

Back in Mexico, Moziño continued his work with the Royal Scientific Expedition, and from 1799 to 1803 worked with its leader

Martin Sessé to catalogue a collection of over 10,000 specimens. Today it is preserved in the Real Jardín Botanico in Madrid.

MUDGE, ZACHARY (1770–1852). Zachary Mudge was an officer on the **George Vancouver** Expedition, with which he spent the first season of 1792 on the Northwest Coast. After participating in the circumnavigation of **Vancouver Island** he went home to England with **William Broughton** carrying the charts of the expedition's discoveries to date and Vancouver's report on his inconclusive negotiations with **Juan Francisco de la Bodega y Quadra**. This included an explanatory drawing of **Friendly Cove** by **Henry Humphrys**, and a request for further instructions. He returned to Nootka with Broughton in March 1796 only to find that Vancouver had completed his survey of the coast and that Spain and England, now allies against republican France, had settled their differences. During the summer of 1792, Mudge kept a journal to which he added his own sketches; one of these was later engraved for the official account of the voyage—the dramatic "The *Discovery* on the Rocks in Queen Charlotte's Sound," which shows Vancouver's ship in a precarious position as he neared completion of his exploration of the waters behind Vancouver Island.

MULGRAVE. *See* YAKUTAT BAY.

MÜLLER, GERHARDT FRIEDRICH (1705–1783). German-born historian Gerhardt Friedrich Müller went to St. Petersburg in 1725 to teach in the school attached to the Academy of Sciences. During a visit to London in 1730 he was elected to the Royal Society.

In 1733 he was appointed to the **Great Northern Expedition** under **Vitus Bering**, one of a group of academics that included the naturalists Johann Georg Gmelin and **Stepan Krasheninnikov**, and the scientist and astronomer **Louis de l'Isle de la Croyère**. By 1736 he had based himself in Yakutsk where he uncovered a mass of documentation on the history of Siberia that later formed the basis for his seminal work *Opisaniye Sibirskago tsarstva*. He returned to St. Petersburg in 1743.

In *Nachrichten von Seereisen und zur See gemachten Entdeckungen*, published in the Russian capital in 1758, Müller documented the maritime expeditions aimed at America with a relatively detailed account of Bering's two **Kamchatka Expeditions**. On the accompanying map Müller sketched a picture of North America, which speculated that the landfalls of Bering and Chirikov in 1741 and of the **Mikhail Gvozdev** and Ivan Fedorov Expedition in 1732, were all part of the same continental land mass. As a result he produced a coastline that extended a huge **Alaska Peninsula** far to the west. The narrative was published in London in 1761 under the title *Voyages from Asia to America for completing the Discoveries of the North West Coast of America* by **Thomas Jefferys**, the royal geographer, and the map was also republished as A Map of the Discoveries made by the Russians on the North West Coast of America. Both book and map were taken by **James Cook** on his voyage to the North Pacific. He soon found them totally unreliable in assisting the close coastal survey upon which he was embarked, and was somewhat unfairly scathing in his denunciation of Müller's work, writing in his journal: "the account of that [Bering's] voyage is so very much abridged and the Chart so extremely inaccurate, that it is hardly possible by either the one or the other, or both together, to find out any one place that that Navigator either saw or touched at."

MULOVSKII EXPEDITION. The Mulovskii Expedition was authorized by Empress **Catherine II** in 1786 to sail to the Pacific Ocean in response to the arrival of British fur traders on the Northwest Coast, and the departure of the **Jean François de La Pérouse** Expedition, 1785, aimed in the same direction. The ambitious goals of the voyage were to uphold Russia's sovereignty over the territories discovered by its mariners, to explore and survey the coast in order to make new discoveries, to open trade with Japan, and to bring supplies to Okhotsk and **Kamchatka**. It was to be a major show of force; four heavily armed ships-of-the-line were as well manned, equipped, and prepared as any peacetime flotilla dispatched by the empress or her predecessors. The orders given to her experienced commander, Grigorii Mulovskii, were to claim the coast north of **Nootka Sound** to Baranof Island where **Aleksei Chirikov** had made landfall in 1741, if no other power was occupying it, and to chase away any foreigners north of that point, destroying any installations or markers left by them. Just as preparations were in their final stages in the fall of 1787, however, the empress reluctantly canceled the expedition because war had broken out between Russia and Turkey and Sweden, and the focus of naval resources was demanded elsewhere. There is little doubt that had the expedition sailed, it would have had far-reaching effects on the future of the coast. The **Joseph Billings** Expedition, which was planned as part of the "Mulovskii program" to uphold Russian rights in American waters, arrived on the Northwest Coast proper only in 1790 and then reached only as far south as **Yakutat Bay**. It was hardly the show of force originally planned by the authorities in St. Petersburg. Nevertheless, the news that the Russians intended to occupy **Nootka Sound** was received by **Esteban José Martínez** at **Unalaska** in 1788, during his northern voyage, and was enough to cause the Spanish authorities to order a preemptive move of their own in that direction. This resulted in the **Nootka Sound Incident** (1789) and the establishment of a Spanish base there in 1790.

– N –

NAGAEV, LEONTII (fl. 1780–1797). A merchant from **Kamchatka**, Leontii Nagaev participated in two long-range hunting and trading voyages (1780–1786, 1790–1797) to the **Aleutian Islands** and the **Alaska** mainland. His claim to fame resulted from his ship, the *St. Michael*, joining a flotilla of vessels led by **Potap Zaikov**, who was working for **Pavel Lebedev-Lastochkin**, to move beyond **Kodiak** and Afognak Islands in 1783 to **Prince William Sound**. During that same year Nagaev ventured south, out of the sound, and discovered the **Copper River**.

NARVÁEZ, JOSÉ MARÍA (1765–1840). José María Narváez arrived at the Naval Department of **San Blas** in 1787 and immediately sailed on supply missions to **California**. A year later he began an intense few years as an explorer on the Northwest Coast as pilot on the *San Carlos* with the **Esteban José Martínez** and **Gonzalo López de Haro** Expedition to **Alaska**. He left a substantial account of the voyage. At **Montague Island** in **Prince William Sound** he undertook a survey of the island's west coast in the vicinity of Green

Island; rounding its northern tip he entered a bay in which he found evidence of the Russian camp where Russian trader **Potap Zaikov** had wintered over 1783–1784. Like other commentators he wrote extensively on the **kayak**s and hunting weapons of the **Aleut/Alutiiq**, noting particularly their skilled use of iron and flint. It was Narváez in a launch that first approached the Russian establishment in **Three Saints Bay** on **Kodiak** Island, and his journal includes an extended commentary on the settlement and the native people of the area.

In 1789 Narváez again sailed north with López de Haro in the *San Carlos*. They were accompanying Martínez to establish a post in **Nootka Sound**. He was a witness to the **Nootka Sound Incident** that summer, but more significantly was sent by Martínez in the confiscated *North West America*—renamed *Santa Gertrudis*—on the first Spanish exploration along the west coast of **Vancouver Island** towards the **Strait of Juan de Fuca**. He briefly visited Barkley Sound and sailed some distance beyond Port San Juan, returning with 75 **sea otter** pelts to tell Martínez that he had seen the opening to a strait about which rumors were circulating among the fur traders at Nootka. In 1790 **Manuel Quimper** continued the exploration, making use of the rough chart drawn by Narváez.

He did not participate in Quimper's expedition, but in the spring of 1791 was back at Nootka and was chosen by **Francisco de Eliza** to command the schooner *Santa Saturnina* on an expedition whose principal aim was to explore Quimper's Canal de Haro exiting to the north out of the Strait of Juan de Fuca. Narváez left Nootka with Eliza on 4 May. En route stopovers were made in both **Clayoquot Sound** and Barkley Sound where further surveys were undertaken to improve the charts of the previous two years. On 1 July he left Eliza in Puerto de Bodega y Quadra (Port Discovery) and, with **Juan Carrasco** in the longboat, negotiated Rosario Strait to begin a three-week expedition into the Gran Canal de Nuestra Señora Rosario de Marinera (the **Strait of Georgia**). No log book from the voyage has survived but its achievement can best be appreciated by reference to the great chart that resulted from the survey. Often referred to as the Narváez Chart or Eliza Chart, its official title is *Carta que comprehende los interiors y veril de la Costa desde los 48° de Latitud N. hasta los 50° examinados escrupulosamente por el Teniente de Navio de la Real Armada Don Francisco Eliza, Comandante del Paquebot* *des SM San Carlos . . . y Goleta Santa Saturnina. . . .* Nine different copies of this master chart exist.

Narváez sailed up the east coast of the strait, visiting Bellingham Bay, Birch Bay, and Boundary Bay. He considered Point Roberts (Isla de Cepeda) and Point Grey (Islas de Lángara) to be islands, an error corrected the following year by **Dionisio Alcalá Galiano**. However, he noted the existence of fresh water in this location, surmising correctly that it was the mouth of a great river. This was the **Fraser River**, named in 1808 by **Simon Fraser**. Many of Narváez's place names were changed by **George Vancouver** and the English ones have survived; for example, Bocas de Carmelo became Howe Sound in 1792. Nevertheless, two Spanish names did survive the English survey—Texada Island and Lasqueti Island—which also happened to mark the northernmost point of the expedition. The view north as the schooner turned southwest allowed Narváez to note the Islas de Lerena (Hornby and Denman islands), and Punta de Laso de la Vega has retained its name in the vicinity of Comox. Crossing the strait Narváez and Carrasco appear to have hugged the coast of Vancouver Island as they made their way south to what is today Saturna Island. They noted the opening to Nanaimo Harbour (Boca de Winthuysen) and also Porlier Pass (Boca de Porliel) but they were not able to distinguish between the islands of Gabriola, Valdés, and Galiano.

The importance of the discoveries of the expedition was immense, and proved that Narváez exhibited that intangible sense of energy and curiosity common to all natural explorers. But his work was almost immediately superseded by the more sophisticated surveys of Alcalá Galiano and **Cayetano Valdés** and George Vancouver in 1792. From the trend of the coast on the field charts, and Narváez's own view that the whales he encountered had come into the Strait of Georgia by a route other than the Strait of Juan de Fuca, Eliza determined that Nootka was probably on the west side of a large island. He also wrote in his journal that the long-sought-after passage to the Atlantic, if it existed, would likely be found exiting to the cast of the Gran Canal. This prompted both the Viceroy, the **Count of Revillagigedo**, and **Alejandro Malaspina** to agree in November 1791 that a follow-up voyage was required. At the beginning of the expedition Narváez had noted an inlet to be surveyed on the way back; this was Admiralty Inlet, the entrance to **Puget Sound**. Unfortunately he was short of supplies as he returned to Port Discovery, so the discovery of this sound and the Hood Canal was not achieved by Spain and fell to the credit of Vancouver the next year. Eliza transferred Narváez to the *San Carlos* for the return to Nootka so that he, **Juan Pantoja y Arriaga** and **José Antonio Verdía** could work on the charts.

After his return to San Blas in 1791, he never again returned to the Northwest Coast. In 1792 he made a voyage to the Philippines with **Jacinto Caamaño** after which he returned to commanding supply vessels to the Californias. In 1822 **Kirill Khlebnikov**, the historian of the **Russian–American Company**, met him in **Monterey** and wrote that he still recalled "with pleasure" the experience of his 1788 voyage to Alaska.

NATIVE AMERICANS OF THE NORTHWEST COAST. Occupying the coast from southeastern **Alaska** to northern **California**, the aboriginal peoples of North Pacific America developed a distinctive culture unlike any other on the continent. It owed nothing to the strong cultural influences that radiated from Mexico; rather it was an extension of the cultures of eastern Asia from where the first migrations originated. Its almost exclusively maritime focus meant that there was an overall unity to the culture—a similarity in subsistence practices, the use of technology and wood, belief systems, and socio-economic organization based on hierarchy and the distribution of wealth—that overlaid local and regional differences. Nevertheless, these regional differences have led to a classification into three geographical areas.

In the North what is often referred to as the classic Northwest Coast culture involved the **Tlingit**, who occupied the coast and islands from **Yakutat Bay** to the bottom of the **Alexander Archipelago**; the **Haida** almost exclusively confined to the **Queen Charlotte Islands**; and the Tsimshian on the lower reaches of the Skeena River, the adjacent coast, and offshore islands. The Central area was dominated by the Kwakwaka'wakw (Kwakiutl) peoples, who straddled Queen Charlotte Sound between the continent and northeastern **Vancouver Island**, and the Nootka (now the Nuu-Chah-Nulth First Nations in **British Columbia**) on the west coast of the island and on the north coast of the Olympic Peninsula, home of one of the area's subgroups, the **Makah**.

These two areas presented three classic features. First, an economy based almost exclusively on salmon and other fish, and to a lesser extent on sea mammals (whales and seals), shellfish, and birds. Land hunting for deer, mountain sheep, goats, and other fur-bearing animals was not significant but it did provide antlers, horn, and bones for use in the fashioning of wood. The socioeconomic unit became the village, based on language and kinship and related to salmon runs through which community effort produced a long-term supply of food. Abundance spawned a density of population unknown anywhere else on the continent north of Mexico. A surplus of fish oil also opened up trade with interior tribes, where it was in great demand. It was traded for furs, copper, and rare stones, which flowed back along the grease trails and canoe routes to the houses of the coastal chiefs. The second key feature was the availability of wood, especially the soft cedar, which gave the Northwest Coast a distinctive flavor. It allowed the natives to build solid planked houses, often painted or carved, as well as elaborate dugout canoes, which in turn created the ability for whale hunting and deep-sea fishing. Wood was used for food storage and cooking containers. Clothing was made of bark and combined with wool to make robes and blankets. Wood was also used to create carved masks and religious objects, and totem poles told stories and preserved family history. Thirdly, the reality of abundance and surplus, which meant that native religion highly honored such elements of the natural world as salmon and wood, translated into the concept of wealth. Prestige and status and the dissemination of property were all bound up with a culture of feasting; the potlatch—"gift giving"—served to advance status. Wealth was inherited and society was ordered between chiefs and commoners. Another result was constant feuding between families, and warfare between villages and tribes, which introduced slavery as a major feature of Northwest Coast life.

The Southern area of coast included the Coast Salish tribes around the Gulf of Georgia and Puget Sound, the **Chinook** to the north and south of the **Columbia River**, the Tillamook in **Oregon** and the Hula and Chilcan in northwestern California. All these peoples shared the salient features of Northwest Coast culture, but in the south they were increasingly modified by the less rugged topography and gentler climate, and the river valleys and mountain passes that made communication with tribes in the interior more prevalent. For example, in **California** the plank houses could be less well constructed, the distribution of wealth was less important than hoarding, shells were the unit of currency and a sign of wealth, and feuding and warfare were less obvious.

Archaeological investigation over the last 50 years at sites such as Ozette on the Olympic Peninsula in **Washington**, have begun to piece together enough cumulative data to trace the evolution of the culture now identifiable as "Northwest Coast." It was this culture whose vitality and uniqueness was encountered and recorded by the explorers and traders of the 18th century. Their written and artistic legacy has led to a greater understanding of a culture that included some of the wealthiest hunter-gatherer communities the world has ever known. *See also* DISEASE; VIOLENCE.

NAVIGATION. Prior to the middle of the 18th century there had been, literally for centuries, little substantive change in determining the position of ships at sea. This made it impossible to develop truly accurate charts. In the 1740s and 1750s, compasses, telescopes, cross-staffs, sand glasses, and the log and line were still the basic instruments in use. Although determination of latitude had long been reasonably accurate, and was made more so by the general use of quadrants and then sextants from mid-century, it was the introduction of two methods for establishing longitude that created revolutionary change in the 1760s. The first relied on the measurement of lunar distances based on the annual publication of accurate astronomical information associated with British astronomer royal, Neil Maskelyne. This was the *Nautical Almanac* and its use was much aided by ongoing improvements in the sextant. The second was the introduction of the marine chronometer, basically a watch with a compensating balance that mitigated the problems of ship movement. The increasingly sophisticated scientific instrument industry in London developed the quality and accuracy of a wide range of navigational instruments of which the chronometer, invented by John Harrison in the 1730s, proved to be by far the most important. Chronometers came to the Northwest Coast with the four major naval expeditions of the late 18th century—those of **James Cook**, **Jean François de La Pérouse**, **Alejandro Malaspina** and **George Vancouver**—and their use, complemented by astronomical observation, aided on land by such instruments as the Ramsden quadrant, resulted in remarkably accurate, detailed charts. As important as the instruments, the well-trained officers on board the ships were knowledgeable in astronomy and mathematics, and skilled in the use of the instruments available to them. Almanac, sextant, and chronometer—these were the friends of the navigator that allowed him to produce reliable maps of the coastlines of the North Pacific. *See also* CARTOGRAPHY.

NEAH BAY. The site of a **Makah** village on the south side of the entrance to the **Strait of Juan de Fuca**, Neah Bay was visited by **Manuel Quimper** in July 1790. When he performed the **act of possession** on 1 August, he named it Bahia de Nuñez Gaona after a leading Spanish admiral. In the summer of 1792 it became the site of the first nonnative community in **Washington** State when **Salvador Fidalgo** established a short-lived Spanish settlement.

NEW ALBION. Between 17 June and 23 July 1579, **Francis Drake** anchored the *Golden Hind* in a bay north of San Francisco, taking possession of the surrounding country for England and naming it Noua Albion. This was the first formal challenge to Spanish authority on the Pacific coast of the Americas, and was intended as the foundation of a British Empire in North America. The claim was never abandoned until the **Oregon Treaty** of 1846. Although Drake's maps have disappeared, two engraved contemporary charts by Nicola van Sype (1583) and Jodocus Hondius (ca. 1595) present the route of Drake's circumnavigation of the globe and specifically identify Nova Albio [*sic*] and Nova Albion respectively. It was an undefined territory on the northwest coast of New Spain, north of the **California** peninsula. New Albion also features prominently on the charts of both **James Cook** and **George Vancouver** created in 1778 and 1792.

NEW ARCHANGEL. The Russian settlement of New Archangel was founded on the west coast of Baranof Island in the **Alexander Archipelago** in 1799. During the 1790s **Aleksandr Baranov** extended the fur-hunting and trading activities of the Shelikhov Company down the coast from **Prince William Sound**. Despite the opposition of the **Tlingit**, long-distance hunting parties from **Kodiak** Island soon reached the rich fur-bearing waters of the Alexander Archipelago, and **Sitka Sound** became a regular port of call. In 1796 **James Shields** undertook an initial survey of the area, and in 1798 Gavriil Talin charted the sound and its adjacent waterways with the view to a permanent settlement being established.

In the summer of 1799 Baranov arrived and negotiated with the local chiefs, persuading himself that they were agreeable to the creation of an establishment in return for trading arrangements and the promise of an alliance against their enemies. Construction was begun and the settlement was named Novo-Arkhangel'sk (New Archangel) after an old seafaring center on the White Sea. Although Baranov had left before a formal ceremony was held in the spring of 1800 to mark and celebrate Russian possession of the land upon which Mikhailovskii Redoubt (Fort St. Michael) was built, he had earlier taken pains, with limited success, to cultivate the friendship of the local chiefs and had presented an imperial crest and document to Chief Skautlel't. This stated that the territory in question had been freely ceded to the Russians for appropriate compensation. In addition to the fort, there were barracks, a communal gathering hall, a blacksmith's shop, and warehouses.

The presence of British and American trading vessels provided a less than stable situation for the Russians, and Baranov himself could have been under no illusions that the presence of the settlement was anything but anathema to the Tlingit. His concern about the balance of power in Sitka Sound was justified when, following a series of attacks on hunting parties, a coordinated attack involving natives from all over the archipelago destroyed it on 20 June 1802. The Russians were convinced that without British and American agitation and threats to cease trading with the local Tlingit, including supplying arms, the natives would not have launched the attack. Nevertheless, a British trader, Henry Barber, in the *Unicorn* rescued a number of Russian and **Aleut** survivors and brought them to **Kodiak**, where Baranov paid a sizable ransom to secure their release.

A permanent base in Sitka Sound was far too important in his long-term plans for Baranov to allow this setback to last for very long. Immediately he planned to retake the site and rebuild New Archangel. Two ships were built at Yakutat and, in the summer of 1804, Baranov planned a showdown with the natives involving three ships and a flotilla of 300 **kayak**s. When he arrived at Sitka on September 2, 1804, he was surprised and relieved to find the frigate *Neva* under the command of **Iurii Lisianskii** on hand to help him. Although the Tlingit repulsed the initial attack, the final outcome was never in doubt. After protracted negotiations the natives abandoned their encampment on 7 October. The Russian victory led to a formal negotiated truce in which the Tlingit retained independence and autonomy over their affairs, and the Russians gained acceptance of their presence and a permanent trading partner. New Archangel was rebuilt on a new site a few miles away, around a new fort that became a favorite scene for visiting **artists**. A lithograph based on a drawing by Lisianskii in 1805 shows the settlement in its formative years; another by **Friedrich Heinrich von Kittlitz** in 1827 presents the substantial fortification, which dominated a large settlement that contained a church, shipyard and warehouses, and buildings to accommodate the **Russian–American Company**. In 1804 Baranov moved from Kodiak to New Archangel to make it the capital of the colony. With the purchase of Alaska by the United States in 1867, New Archangel, with a population of 968, was renamed Sitka.

NEW SPAIN. After the conquest of the Aztec Empire (1519–1521), which gave the Spaniards control over the densely populated Mexican highlands, **Hernán Cortés**, his fellow conquistadors, and royal officials quickly spread their influence, if not their complete authority, over all of present-day Mexico and Central America as far south as the present-day border of Costa Rica and Panama. This vast territory defined what became, within a few years, the viceroyalty of New Spain. In the north, although the Spanish soon ventured into Texas, Colorado, New Mexico, and Arizona, and authority was assumed over much of western North America and the far coastal regions of the **Pacific Northwest**, the northern frontier was never formally established until the **Transcontinental Treaty** in 1819. **Baja California** was discovered in 1534, but settlement did not take root until the end of the 17th century; **Alta California** was not settled until the 1770s.

Although Cortés was named governor and captain-general of New Spain in 1522, King Carlos I (Charles V of the Holy Roman Empire) and his officials moved quickly to establish their own authority. Royal appointees arrived in Mexico in 1524 to assert financial control by staffing a branch of the royal treasury. In the same year, adminis-trative, legislative, and judicial authority was vested in a Council of the Indies, which met at court and whose meetings usually involved the king himself. The audiencia of Mexico, a judicial tribunal, was established in 1527 to implement the rule of law, but political and legal stability did not really arrive until the viceroyalty was formally created in 1535 and Antonio de Mendoza took up his vice-regal du-ties. Answerable to the Council of the Indies, the viceroy and his suc-cessors presided over a political and military system that, for all of its documented deficiencies, maintained the authority of the crown over the most important jurisdiction in Spain's American empire.

Opposition to Spanish rule in the 18th century was centered in the Creole class of American-born Spaniards and, taking its cue from the successes of the American and French revolutions, finally erupted in 1810. Independence from Spain was secured by Mexico in 1821, but its inheritance of New Spain was reduced when the southern border with Guatemala was established in 1823 and, more significantly, when it lost fully 30 percent of its territory in a war with the United States, 1846–1848, and the Gadsden Purchase of 1853.

NOOTKA, THE. The name "Nootka" was given by 19th-century anthropologists to identify a number of native tribes, now the Nuu-Chal-Nulth First Nations, who live on the west coast of **Vancouver Island**. The Nootka were renowned as intrepid whalers; the hunt demanded the construction of large cedar canoes, great bravery, strength, and skill, and an understanding of ritual. Due to **Nootka Sound** becoming a focus of Spanish, British, and American attention in the aftermath of the visit of **James Cook** in 1778, the natives of this part of the Northwest Coast had earlier and more sustained con-tact with explorers and traders than did any other. As a result, journal descriptions of numerous encounters and many drawings provide a rich legacy describing the Nootkan people and their culture from the moment of contact. Both Nootka Sound, with its Spanish settlement, and nearby **Clayoquot Sound** became centers of the maritime **fur trade**, increasing the status and wealth of local chiefs **Maquinna** and **Wickaninnish**.

The Nootka lived in permanent winter villages made up of large cedar-planked houses in which a number of families lived. Local chiefs enjoyed a good deal of independence and headed societies divided into several classes: slaves, commoners, a middle class including warriors and hunters, and a nobility that included the ranking chief, whose position derived from inherited wealth and primogeniture. His authority was sustained by potlatches that served to distribute wealth within the community. The ever-present cedar was used to fashion baskets and clothing. Over thousands of winters the natives developed a rich mythology linked to the spirit world. In the spring and summer they emerged from the deep inlets or protected bays to establish summer villages and camps. They traded along the coast and into the **Strait of Juan de Fuca**, and Maquinna's people had a well-established trade route across Vancouver Island.

NOOTKA CONVENTIONS, 1790–1794. The first Nootka Convention to settle the dispute between England and Spain was signed at San Lorenzo del Escorial on 28 October 1790. The key articles allowed for: compensation for **John Meares** and restoration of the land, acquired in 1788, of which he had supposedly been dispossessed, thus giving England its first formal foothold on the Northwest Coast; the ability for English ships to land and trade on coasts not occupied in the Pacific, which essentially confirmed Spain's abandonment of its claim for sole use of the ocean's trade routes and the sovereignty given to it by the **Treaty of Tordesillas**; and the right of both countries to trade on the Northwest Coast, north of Spanish California, into any settlement established by the other. The convention was, however, drawn up by people who had no knowledge of the region or of what had happened at Nootka in the years 1788 and 1789. This was made clear when **Juan Francisco de la Bodega y Quadra** and **George Vancouver** met in 1792 to settle the handover of Meares's "buildings and tracts of land." The commissioners could only agree to refer their disagreement to their governments.

The second convention was signed in London on 12 February 1793. It did not touch on the problems experienced by Bodega and Vancouver, news of which had not yet reached Europe. Instead it dealt with the level of compensation for Meares.

The third and final convention, however, did deal with the question of which nation possessed the clearest title to Nootka. The answer was that both had legitimate rights. Against a background of republican upheavals in France that had temporarily made the two countries allies, they agreed that both would have the right to use the port, and that neither would establish a permanent settlement. Suddenly, with the existence of a Northwest Passage finally disproved by Vancouver's meticulous survey, Nootka Sound was no longer very important. For Mexico City and Madrid, the retention of an establishment was an unnecessary expense; for London exclusive ownership appeared simply unnecessary. The Convention for the Mutual Abandonment of Nootka was signed on 11 January 1794.

In January 1795 two new commissioners, José Manuel de Alava and Thomas Pierce met in **Monterey**. They sailed to Nootka together, arriving on 16 March. The fort was dismantled, and by 28 March the Spanish were ready to abandon their settlement. Alava and Pierce took part in a ceremony in which the British flag was raised over the cove where Meares's men had built the *North West America*, lowered and given to Chief **Maquinna** for safe-keeping. The rights of the Mowachaht people were thus restored at **Friendly Cove** six years after they had been dispossessed—years of imperial maneuvering in which their aboriginal interests had been conspicuously ignored.

NOOTKA CRISIS, 1790. In the wake of the **Nootka Sound Incident**, the former crewmembers of the English trading vessel *North West America*, detained on the Northwest Coast by **Esteban José Martínez**, were transported to Canton by the American **Robert Gray** in the *Columbia*. There they informed **John Meares** of what had transpired and gave him letters from **James Colnett**, which they had managed to smuggle out of **Friendly Cove**. He immediately returned to London where he produced an inflammatory and exaggerated *Memorial*. He lobbied the government of William Pitt for redress of his grievances and compensation for his losses, and was able to garner a good deal of public sympathy. Although dubious about Meares's more extravagant claims, Pitt was facing an election and was under pressure from the commercial community to assert vigorously the doctrine of freedom of the seas and England's right to trade anywhere not specifically settled by a foreign power. He seized the chance to challenge Spain's theoretical and outdated claim to sovereignty over the Pacific Ocean, and mobilized for war. Spain, robbed of the support of its traditional ally by the upheavals of the French Revolution, and informed by the new viceroy of **New Spain**, the **Count of Revillagigedo**, of crucial weaknesses in the economy and naval defenses in the Americas after the strains of the American Revolutionary War, was finally forced to back down. Nevertheless, the defeat, which some scholars have argued heralded the end of the Spanish Empire in the Americas, undoubtedly appears greater in retrospect than it did at the time. Spain's retreat from North America was anything but precipitous and the independence movements of the 19th century were still many years away.

NOOTKA SOUND. A large opening of bays, islands, channels, and inlets on the west central coast of **Vancouver Island**. It was named Surgidero de San Lorenzo by **Juan Pérez**, who anchored off the sound's outer bay in August 1774. The sound was first entered by **James Cook**'s expedition to the North Pacific, which arrived at the end of March 1778. At first Cook called it King George's Sound, but this was later changed to Nootka based on the native word meaning "go around" that Cook mistook for the name of the place. The Mowachaht-Muchalaht people have been the principal occupants of the sound for thousands of years.

Due to the prices received by Cook's men in Russia and China for furs collected at Nootka, the site of Chief **Maquinna**'s village of Yuquot in **Friendly Cove** became the initial focus of the maritime **fur trade** after 1785. In his *Voyages made in the Years 1788 and 1789, from China to the North West Coast* (1790) trader **John Meares** published a map entitled Sketch of Friendly Cove in Nootka Sound, which identified the village and the English Factory, a somewhat grandiose name for the shacks he set up in an adjacent cove.

In the summer of 1789, Spaniards under **Esteban José Martínez** established a military outpost at Yuquot, which became permanent in 1790–1795. It was the scene of the **Nootka Sound Incident** that nearly caused a European war. Drawings by **José Cardero**, **Felipe Bauza**, and **Henry Humphrys**, 1791–1792, and charts drawn by the **Alejandro Malaspina** Expedition, 1791, provide an excellent idea of the nature of the establishment. In March 1795, due to successive **Nootka Conventions**, Spain abandoned her settlement. The Mowachaht demolished the Spanish buildings, and Friendly Cove returned to its previous appearance.

Cook and a number of fur traders, as well as the resident Spaniards, ventured into parts of the sound near its entrance, but the first complete survey was not completed until 1791 by Malaspina's officers, **José Espinosa** and **Ciriaco Cevallos**. The most important early descriptions of the Nootka people and the area's natural resources are in the journals from the Cook expedition, in the records of the Malaspina expedition, and in **José Mariano Moziño**'s *Noticias de Nutka*. Fur trader journals, such as those of **Alexander Walker** and **Joseph Ingraham**, are also valuable.

NOOTKA SOUND INCIDENT, 1789. What began as a local dispute, the Nootka Sound Incident created a diplomatic crisis in Europe, and very nearly led to war between England and Spain in 1790. It involved the arrest of an English fur-trading vessel under the command of **James Colnett** by **Esteban José Martínez**. This incident, which had been preceded by the detention of other English vessels, one permanently, and the subsequent arrest of a third one, took place in **Friendly Cove**, **Nootka Sound** over two days, 2–3 July 1789.

Martínez and **Gonzalo López de Haro** had arrived from **San Blas** to establish a post at Nootka on 5 May. The purpose was to forestall a presumed Russian occupation, but there was also concern about potential English or American settlement and fur-trading activity. This proved to be well founded because, once he reached Nootka, Martínez found ships from both nations, although the English vessel, the *Iphengenia Nubiana*, was engaged in a disguise by flying Portuguese colors. She, and two other ships that also arrived in Friendly Cove, the *North West America* and the *Princess Royal*, belonged to a commercial syndicate operated by **John Meares**. All three ships were detained by Martínez, who rightly determined that the English presence was much more sinister than that of the Americans **Robert Gray**, **John Kendrick**, and **Joseph Ingraham**, who appeared deferential to Spanish authority and persuaded him that their interests on the coast were merely transitory. During May and June, the Spanish commander set about consolidating his hold on the site and formally performed an **act of possession** on 24 June. By this time two of the English ships had been released on a promise that they would leave the coast, but the *North West America* was retained.

On 2 July Colnett arrived in the *Argonaut* to be informed by Martínez that Nootka Sound belonged to Spain by virtue of prior discovery by **Juan Pérez** in 1774. Colnett countered by telling the Spaniard that Nootka was English by virtue of **James Cook**'s visit in 1778 and the occupation of Friendly Cove by Meares in 1788, and that he had come to set up a trading post and to be commander of the port. Although the initial exchanges between the two men were respectful, their relationship quickly deteriorated and Martínez arrested Colnett and forcibly took control of the *Argonaut*. When the *Princess Royal* inadvisably returned from trading, she too, and her crew and captain, Thomas Hudson, were immediately detained. The Englishmen and ships, sailed by Spanish officers, were promptly dispatched to San Blas, where they were held until July 1790. The *North West America* was kept at Nootka, where she was used for coastal exploration.

NORTH WEST COMPANY. An association of Montreal-based fur-trading merchants, mostly Scots, and *canadien* labor and experience, the North West Company was formed in 1776–1779 to challenge the **Hudson's Bay Company** (HBC). Through the energetic work of **Peter Pond** and **Alexander Mackenzie** its reach extended northwest beyond the Great Lakes into the Athabasca region by the mid-1780s. In 1789 Mackenzie traveled to the mouth of the river that bears his name and in 1793 reached the Pacific. Building on ideas promoted in London by such influential men as **Alexander Dalrymple**, Mackenzie advocated linking the overland trade to the Northwest Coast with the Orient. With the publication of an account and map of his travels in 1801, the North West Company was persuaded to become the first to explore and trade aggressively beyond the mountains. It sponsored activity in two districts, that of **Simon Fraser** in New Caledonia and **David Thompson** in the upper Columbia. Locked in a fierce struggle with the HBC east of the Rockies, which finally led the British government to force a merger in 1821, the North West Company nevertheless created the necessary environment for the new company to realize the age-old dream of linking Europe with Asia via northern North America.

NORTHWEST PASSAGE. A navigable waterway across the top of North America between the Atlantic and the Pacific oceans, the

Northwest Passage proved to be a persuasive illusion for over 300 years. As such it became one the most enduring mysteries in the approaches to and the exploration of the Northwest Coast.

It did not take long for merchants and geographers in Europe to realize that the lands on the other side of the Atlantic discovered at the beginning of the 16th century were not the Cathay of Marco Polo. Rather, it quickly became obvious that a great continent stood between Europe and the riches of the East. **Hernán Cortés** found that there was no way through Central America, and the Spaniards were obliged to sail far south to the Strait of Magellan to find a direct way into the Pacific. This led to the belief in an open passage across the top of North America, one that persisted until the final years of the 18th century. Then, explorers and traders on the Northwest Coast, beginning with **Juan Pérez** and **Juan Francisco de la Bodega y Quadra** in the mid-1770s, and **James Cook**, who sailed north from **Oregon** into the Arctic Ocean in 1778, and finally **George Vancouver**, who completed his survey between 1792 and 1794, proved conclusively that there was no navigable waterway in the temperate latitudes.

The earliest attempts to find the passage from the North Atlantic, which took place over a period of more than 50 years beginning in 1576, were a study in frustration and disappointment. But rumors persisted, and in **New Spain** there was a general assumption, fuelled by such tales as those of **Juan de Fuca** and **Ferrer Maldonado**, that somewhere in the north the **Strait of Anian** led to the passage. As the 18th century unfolded, English exploration in Hudson Bay led to a revival of interest in the tale of the fictional **Bartholomew de Fonte**. This encouraged French cartographers **Philippe Buache** and **Joseph Nicolas de l'Isle** to link the story of his apocryphal voyage with vaguely understood Russian discoveries in the North Pacific, and to produce highly speculative and erroneous, but influential, maps at the beginning of the 1750s.

In 1771 **Samuel Hearne**, trading and exploring for the **Hudson's Bay Company**, trekked as far north as the mouth of the Coppermine River, effectively proving that no passage existed through the continent anywhere below 68° N. But his discovery was not widely appreciated, and **Peter Pond**, as late as the end of the 1780s, was asserting that Great Slave Lake was the center of a system of rivers linking **Cook Inlet** and the Arctic Ocean with Lake Winnipeg, Hudson Bay, and the Great Lakes. In 1786 and 1791 the highly skeptical navigators **Jean François de La Pérouse** and **Alejandro Malaspina** commanded major naval expeditions with instructions to search for the Pacific entrance to the passage.

As the reality of the explorers' nondiscovery became apparent, it was understood that only a successful battle with the ice that had thwarted the initial efforts of Martin Frobisher, John Davis, Henry Hudson, William Baffin, and Luke Foxe would solve the problem. The struggle lasted for the best part of the 19th century as slowly the nature of the ice-bound islands, bays, and straits of the Canadian arctic were revealed. An uncertain and by no means regular ice-free period for ships during a few weeks in August and September was finally reported, but it was not enough to realize the age-old dream of a commercially viable waterway. Between 1904 and 1906, and not in one season, the Northwest Passage was finally traversed east to west by the Norwegian explorer Roald Amundsen in his tiny ship the *Gjøa*. Between 1940 and 1942 Henry Larsen in the *RCMP St. Roch* navigated the passage from the Pacific. *See also* CARTOGRAPHY.

NORTON SOUND. A large gulf extending east from the **Bering Sea** into mainland **Alaska**, south of the Seward Peninsula, Norton Sound was named by **James Cook** in honor of Sir Fletcher Norton, the 1st Baron Grantly, and explored for 10 days in September 1778 on his return from the Arctic Ocean. It was his final effort to find a navigable entrance into the **Northwest Passage**.

NUÑEZ GAONA. *See* NEAH BAY.

– O –

OGDEN, PETER SKENE (1794–1854). Fur trader, hunter, and explorer, Peter Skene Ogden served the **Hudson's Bay Company** (HBC) in the Columbia Department, 1824–1830; on the Northwest Coast, 1831–1834; in New Caledonia, 1835–1844, and then back on the **Columbia River**, 1845–1854.

It was in the 1820s that, under orders from Governor **George Simpson**, he trapped the Snake River country bare, turning it into a "fur desert" to discourage American hunter/traders. Undertaking six major expeditions he explored most of the interior of the **Pacific Northwest** south of the Columbia River, and northern **California**. He discovered and traced the route of the Humboldt River, which later became the main immigrant route to California, and disproved the myth of the "Bonaventura River" said to flow from Great Salt Lake to the Pacific. His last trek took him south from **Oregon** across the Great Basin to the Colorado River, which he followed to the **Gulf of California**. He returned to the Columbia by crossing the Sierra Nevada to explore the San Joaquin and Sacramento valleys of central California. The new information from his reports and maps soon reached England and France via the HBC, and was incorporated into the maps of **Aaron Arrowsmith** and Adrien Brué.

Transferred to the north coast in 1830, Ogden established Fort Simpson near the mouth of the Nass River from where he successfully competed with American traders and the **Russian–American Company**, and continued exploration using the HBC schooners C*adboro* and *Vancouver*. His attempt in 1834 to create a fort on the Stikine River sparked an international incident, but negotiations later allowed Governor Simpson to exact trading privileges on the Alaskan coast beneficial to the HBC.

OREGON. The name Oregon comes from "Ouregon Country," an undefined region west of the Great Lakes first mentioned in London in 1765 by an English army officer, Robert Rogers. He was petitioning for support of an exploring expedition. Between 1766 and 1768 Jonathon Carver, an American veteran of the French and Indian Wars, traveled into the area and in his published account (1778) wrote of the "River Oregon or River of the West, that falls into the Pacific Ocean." His map shows it north of the headwaters of the Missouri River.

By the early years of the 19th century the term Oregon Country was being used to define the coastal and inland region south of the **Strait of Juan de Fuca** to below the recently discovered "River Oregon" or **Columbia River**, and **Thomas Jefferson** used the term in his instructions to the **Lewis and Clark Expedition**. But after the formal retreat of Spain from the region in 1819, and separate agreements between Russia and the United States and Britain in 1825, what became increasingly referred to as the Oregon Territory formally stretched between 42° latitude in the south to 54°40′ in the north. By convention in 1818, renewed in 1827, the United States and Britain agreed on joint occupancy of an area that now encompasses the American **Pacific Northwest** and the Canadian province of **British Columbia**.

Charts in both countries, particularly in America, which reflected an increasingly jingoistic belief in Manifest Destiny, showed the territory as a legitimate part of their respective nations. However, as long as the **Hudson's Bay Company** (HBC) held sway in the Columbia Department, Britain's claim remained strong. As late as 1845, long after increased American settlement and the British government's disinclination to uphold the interests of the monopolistic company had fatally weakened the British position, James Wyld in London was able to publish a map and booklet entitled *Comparative Chronological Statement of the Events connected with the Rights of Great Britain and the Claims of the United States to the Oregon Territory*. The sentiments expressed in this publication, and on the opposite side in a bill introduced into the United States Senate in 1841 by Senator Lewis Linn of Missouri, aimed at authorizing the occupation of the Oregon Territory from 42° to 54°40′, demonstrate the passions aroused in the growing controversy about sovereignty over the region. Many believed that it would lead to war. Cooler heads prevailed, however, and the **Oregon Treaty**, 1846, divided the territory along the 49° parallel. The real debate had been over the land between the Fraser River in the north and the Columbia River in the south. In the end the Americans were successful in getting most of this territory, but Britain received **Vancouver Island** in its entirety. Although the term Oregon Territory had been widely used in official circles in the United States since the early 1830s, it was never officially constituted as such until proclaimed by President James Polk in 1848. In 1853 **Washington**, north of the Columbia River, broke away from the territory, and in the years 1859–1864 the present-day boundaries of Oregon were defined, initially with Washington, and then with Idaho. The state of Oregon was admitted into the union in 1859.

It is likely that **Bartolomé Ferrer** (1543), **Francis Drake** (1579) and **Martín Aguilar** (1603) all sighted the southwest coast of Oregon, but the first European to actually explore the coast was **Bruno de Hezeta**, sailing south from **Vancouver Island** in the summer of

1775, during which he identified the mouth of the **Columbia River**. **James Cook** ran the coast of **New Albion**, as he called it in 1778, and in 1792 the American fur trader **Robert Gray** crossed the bar of the Columbia, and **William Broughton** explored it. The Lewis and Clark Expedition was the first to come overland in 1804–1805. In 1811 access from the north down the Columbia River was accomplished by **David Thompson**. South of the river the trailblazers were **Wilson Price Hunt** (1811), **Robert Stuart**, who in 1812 pioneered the route that was to become the Oregon Trail of the 1840s, Jedediah Smith (1827–1828), **Peter Skene Ogden** (1824–1830), Nathaniel Wyeth (1832), Benjamin Bonneville (1833–1834), and finally John C. Frémont (1843–1844). Despite the individual achievements of these expeditions they were more important for future American interests; between 1820 and 1846 the Oregon Territory was the preserve of the HBC managed from **Fort Vancouver**, where **John McLoughlin** played the role of benevolent dictator to traders, settlers, and natives alike. But the HBC's favored position did not last as the beaver population dwindled from overhunting, and American settlers who, inspired by Hal J. Kelley's American Society for Encouraging Settlement of the Oregon Territory, began moving into the Willamette Valley opposite Fort Vancouver. As the HBC looked to the government in London for a favorable boundary line, only to be met with indifference, McLoughlin was obliged by policy and humanitarian concerns to aid American settlement. As the number of Americans began to increase dramatically in the 1840s, and American interests were underlined by the visit of the **Charles Wilkes** Expedition in 1841, the stage was set for resolution of a rapidly advancing dispute with Britain, and for Oregon to become part of the United States *See also* ASTORIA; RUSSIAN AMERICA BOUNDARY CONVENTIONS; TRANSCONTINENTAL TREATY.

OREGON TREATY, 1846. Also known as the Treaty of Washington, the Oregon Treaty, 1846, fixed the Canada–United States boundary between the Rocky Mountains and the Pacific coast. It was signed in Washington, D.C., on 15 June 1846.

    With Spain and Russia formally surrendering their claims, in 1819 and 1825 respectively, to what became known as the Oregon Territory, an Anglo-American Convention had agreed to temporary joint occupation in 1818. Subsequently the Americans favored an extension of the 49° parallel that existed to the Rocky Mountains west of the Great Lakes, but the British held out for a southern boundary along the **Columbia River**, basing their claim on **Hudson's Bay Company** (HBC) control in the region.

Despite renewal of the joint occupancy agreement in 1827, the British position gradually weakened as a result of a steady influx of American settlers into the disputed area, and the London government's cool attitude towards the interests of the HBC. In the 1844 presidential election, Democratic candidate James Polk campaigned on the extreme position of "54°40′ or fight" but, after winning the presidency, backed away from the threat of war with England, knowing that a more potentially advantageous one with Mexico would be necessary to secure a southern boundary for the United States. His administration was also reluctant, in the final analysis, to challenge the power of the Royal Navy. The boundary in the north was set at the 49° parallel from the Rocky Mountains to the Coast, southward through the Gulf Islands, and then mid-point through the **Strait of Juan de Fuca** to the Pacific Ocean. Navigation in the islands and the strait was assured for both nations. While the United States achieved the resolution it had been seeking for a generation, Britain retained all of **Vancouver Island**.

Nevertheless, the ambiguous wording of the treaty ensured that the question of the San Juan Islands and the boundary through the adjacent islands north of the Strait of Juan de Fuca would remain unresolved. Americans settled there and the HBC was also active. In 1859, the **San Juan Boundary Dispute**, also known as the Pig War, brought matters to a head, but the issue was not resolved until an international arbitration panel fixed the boundary in Haro Strait and awarded the San Juan Islands to the United States.

ORTELIUS, ABRAHAM (1527–1598). Aside from Gerard Mercator, Abraham Ortelius was the greatest geographer of his age. An engraver, colorer, and salesman of maps he traveled extensively in Europe, gradually becoming more interested in scientific geography and in preparing maps of his own. In 1564 he produced an eight-sheet *mappemonde*, which later appeared in the world's first modern atlas, his 53-map *Theatrum Orbis Terrarum*—a systematically organized and uniformly sized collection that was non-Ptolemaic (based entirely on contemporary knowledge). There were 42 regular editions of the atlas published between 1570 and 1612, and 31 reduced-format editions had appeared before the end of the 17th century. His work was hugely influential and essentially resulted in a codification, for two centuries, of the idea that the Northwest Coast of America ended in a narrow sea, the **Strait of Anian**, separating Asia from America and leading into a navigable waterway across the top of the world.

– P –

PACIFIC NORTHWEST. The term Pacific Northwest has been used since the middle of the 19th century to identify that area of the **Oregon** Territory, made up of the present-day states of Oregon, **Washington**, and Idaho, which was absorbed into the United States of America under the terms of the **Oregon Treaty**, 1846.

PALLAS, PETER SIMON (1741–1811). Naturalist, geographer, and explorer Peter Simon Pallas was an energetic and influential member of the Academy of Sciences during the reign of Empress **Catherine II**. Between 1769 and 1774 he led an expedition to Siberia, which harvested a significant collection of natural history specimens. Thereafter, he became increasingly interested in the discoveries of the ***promyshlenniki*** in the Far East and North Pacific, and began to research and write on the subject. His contribution to the study of the Aleutian **fur trade** and **Russian America** is contained in a series of articles collected in his *Neue nordische Beyträge zur physikalischen und geographischen Erd-und Völkerbeschreibung, Naturgeschichte, und Oekonomie*, published in seven volumes, 1781–1796. In the first four volumes he wrote a commentary on **William Coxe**'s *Account of the Russian Discoveries between Asia and America*. In Volume I he published a remarkably accurate Map of the Discoveries between Siberia and America to the Year 1780, which included the eastern **Aleutian Islands**, **Kodiak** Island, and **Cook Inlet**, and he detailed the exploits of trading voyages, by Ivan Solov'ev to the **Alaska Peninsula**, 1770–1775; **Dimitrii Bragin** to Kodiak, 1772–1777; and **Potap Zaikov** to **Unimak Island**, 1772–1778. In Volume III he published a map of the Aleutian Islands based upon the observations of these voyages, and of the **Petr Krenitsyn** and **Mikhail Levashov** Expedition of the late 1760s; it provides a very clear idea of the eastern Aleutians, Alaska Peninsula, and Kodiak Island. When the Empress Catherine decided to launch the ultimately cancelled **Mulovskii Expedition** to the Northwest Coast in 1786, Pallas was appointed historiographer and was directed to assemble the scientific corps.

PANTOJA Y ARRIAGA, JUAN (ca. 1755–?). The Spanish pilot Juan Pantoja y Arriaga was involved in three voyages to the Northwest Coast—in 1779, 1791, and 1792. He met **Juan Francisco de la Bodega y Quadra** in Peru in 1777 and returned with him to **New Spain**. Bodega formed a good opinion of Pantoja and recommended him for the next northern expedition, as a result of which Pantoja served on the *Princesa* under **Ignacio de Arteaga**.

Pantoja proved to be a talented cartographer and a perceptive chronicler of the expedition. His journal is uncommonly well written and like other participants he recorded in some detail his impressions of the **natives** encountered in **Bucareli Bay** and **Prince William Sound** (PWS). At the former he wrote about the welcome they received with the natives gathering in their canoes around the ships, throwing feathers on the water and singing continually. He described the men and women, their clothing and use of white, blue, red, and black colors to paint themselves. He suggested that only married women wore the **labret**. He also wrote about the trading relationship that developed including the purchase of a number of children. Pantoja was one of the pilots who participated in the survey of the environs of Bucareli Bay led by **Francisco Mourelle**, and his manuscript journal contains his map of the area. Approaching PWS the *Princesa* was met by two **Aleut/Alutiiq** *baidarka*s, which fascinated him, and he was especially impressed by the tunics worn by the men and their hunting harpoons or *atlatl*. At the end of the **Kenai Peninsula**, it was Pantoja who surveyed the waters surrounding Elizabeth Island, the first European to do so, and to create a chart.

On his return to New Spain, Pantoja joined the regular corps of pilots at **San Blas** and commanded supply missions to **Alta California**. In 1791 he sailed to Nootka on the *San Carlos* under Ramón Saavedra. Again he proved to be an astute observer of his surroundings and the natives he met. Understanding that they built their houses in sheltered coves with beaches, he recognized that **Friendly Cove**, the location of the Spanish establishment, was a coveted site. While many Spanish officers suggested that the Mowachaht were happy and accepting of their presence, Pantoja wrote, "they are continually asking when we are going to leave, the eagerness with which they solicit this being noteworthy." That summer he played an important role in the expedition of **Francisco de Eliza** into the **Strait of Juan de Fuca**. Pantoja contributed a major diary and worked with **José María Narváez** and **José Antonio Verdía** to produce "the many charts which had to be made." He was responsible for an excursion in one of the launches to survey Haro Strait, the lower Gulf Islands off the east coast of **Vancouver Island**, and the waters north of San Juan Island. It was he who gave the name Gran Canal de Nuestra Señora del Rosario la Marinera to what **George Vancouver** would call the Gulf of Georgia the following year.

In 1792 he came north again, participating in Bodega's **Limits Expedition** on board the *Aránzazu* commanded by **Jacinto Caamaño**. With Caamaño in southern Alaska he was instrumental in improving Francisco Mourelle's 1779 chart of **Bucareli Bay** and assisting with the survey of the continental coast that essentially disproved the existence of the passage of **Bartholomew de Fonte**.

PEÑA, TOMÁS DE LA (1743–1806). Father Peña arrived in **New Spain** in 1770. He served at missions in both **Baja California** and **Alta California** before, in 1774, he found himself at the **Carmel Mission** near **Monterey**. Here he was assigned by **Junípero Serra** to accompany **Juan Crespí** as a chaplain on the expedition to the far Northwest Coast under the command of **Juan Pérez** in the *Santiago*.

Peña left a detailed diary of the voyage, on which he proved to be a better sailor than Crespí. His grasp of nautical terminology and the operation of the ship was also superior, and he made notes on the progress of the voyage through a good working relationship with **Esteban José Martínez**. At their farthest point north, off the **Queen Charlotte Islands**, he noted the trend of the coast towards the northwest and later, off **Nootka Sound**, wrote that it had been the intention of Pérez to make a landing and take possession of the land. This was never achieved but Peña did describe the **native** visitors to the ships, their canoes, and their interest in trading for the colorful **Monterey shells**. When Serra received his journal he immediately sent it to Viceroy **Antonio María de Bucareli**.

PÉREZ, JUAN (ca. 1725–1775). Juan Pérez was a key player in supporting the early settlement of **Alta California;** also, in 1774, he led Spain's first official voyage to the Northwest Coast since the early 1600s.

A veteran pilot on the **Manila galleons**, Pérez was in the newly established Naval Department of **San Blas** in the summer of 1768. In October, as preparations were underway to launch the **Sacred Expedition** to Alta California, **José de Gálvez** assigned Pérez to command the *San Antonio*. He sailed to **San Diego**, arriving in April 1769; his subsequent return to **New Spain** for supplies, which were delivered in March 1770, helped ensure the fledgling settlement's survival. Pérez then sailed on to **Monterey** in support of Gaspar de Portolá's second overland attempt to locate that harbor, and was thus the first mariner to enter both San Diego and Monterey bays since **Sebastián Vizcaíno**'s historic voyage in 1602. In the years that followed, he established himself as a dependable sailing master on the **California** supply ships.

When Viceroy **Antonio María de Bucareli** was ordered to send an expedition to the Northwest Coast to look for any evidence of a Russian advance towards New Spain, he turned to Pérez to lead it. Other more highly trained officers had been appointed to the base but had not yet arrived from Spain. In the recently constructed frigate *Santiago*, Pérez left San Blas on 24 January 1774 with a daunting array of instructions. In addition to delivering supplies and **Junípero Serra** and a number of settlers to Monterey, Pérez was ordered to proceed as far north as 60° N (the latitude of **Prince William Sound**), explore the entire coast—never losing sight of it, recording detailed navigational observations, looking for potential settlement sites, taking note of any useful resources from metallic ores to spices (a somewhat ambitious expectation), landing and taking possession, and meeting with and describing the culture of the **natives**. Second in command was **Esteban José Martínez**; also on board were the priests **Juan Crespí** and **Tomás de la Peña**. All four left written accounts of the voyage.

The expedition left Monterey on 6 June. Pérez set a northwesterly course until he reached 50° N at which point he sailed due north expecting to find the coast, which had been visited by **Vitus Bering** in 1741, close to the 60° required of him. Almost immediately, however, he veered northeast to reach the coast sooner, worried that the direction of the winds would make a return difficult, that his men were exhibiting weakness from the cold and general sickness, and that he needed to replenish his water supply. On 19 July they were off Langara Island (Santa Margarita), the most northerly of the **Queen Charlotte Islands**. Here they encountered canoes of **Haida**, with whom they traded beads, bits of metal, clothing, and **Monterey shells** for furs, capes, baskets, and beautifully woven and decorated blankets that amazed the court when they were later exhibited in Madrid. What is now the earliest remaining Spanish **artifact** collected in the contact period—a small bird figure, made from the ivory tooth of a sperm whale—was acquired: it is in the collection of the Museo de América in Madrid. The *Santiago* stayed in the area for a few days and ventured as far north as 54°30′, seeing Cape Muzon (Punta Santa Magdelena) on Dall Island at the bottom of the Alaska Archipelago. But adverse winds and currents and the prospect of a rocky shore prevented an easy landing.

Turning south, the expedition was soon off **Vancouver Island**, 7 August, and anchored at the southern entrance to **Nootka Sound** (Surgidero de San Lorenzo) where they again encountered canoes full of natives keen to trade. Later, in an attempt to bolster Spain's claim of sovereignty, Martínez would make the controversial assertion that during this encounter silver spoons, later purchased by a member of the **James Cook** Expedition in March 1778, were stolen from the ship. Again any hope of landing was thwarted by the arrival of a strong westerly wind. As she continued south, the *Santiago* sailed past the entrance to the **Strait of Juan de Fuca** without the Spaniards recognizing what it was. Martínez again asserted later that he had seen "an entrance," but his account is unsubstantiated and it would be difficult to believe that, if this were true, Pérez would not have investigated further, the approximate latitude of Fuca's supposed strait having been reflected on speculative maps of the coast for many years. Pérez noted Mount Olympus (Santa Rosalía) in **Washington** State before the clear weather turned into fog and signs of scurvy appeared among the crew. As the expedition hurried south there was one more opportunity to see the coast, in central Oregon in the vicinity of Yaquina Head, before Pérez and his companions sailed into Monterey Bay on 28 August. The *Santiago* reached San Blas on 5 November. She had been away from home for 285 days.

Pérez participated in the subsequent **Bruno de Hezeta** and **Juan Francisco de la Bodega y Quadra** Expedition in 1775, although there is evidence that he was not in good health. His journal for that voyage has a number of gaps, suggesting that he was too ill at times to record the usual daily entry. He died on 2 November 1775 as his old ship, the *Santiago*, this time commanded by Hezeta, was sailing towards San Blas after a stopover in Monterey.

Although recent historians have been more charitable to Pérez than those who wrote earlier accounts of his 1774 voyage to the Northwest Coast, recognizing that the gap between expectations and results was not entirely his fault—that his fateful inability to land and take possession was not for want of trying, and that the requirement to visit Monterey on the way north robbed him of precious time and better weather—the suspicion remains that he lacked that essential element of courage, desire, and tenacity to push an exploration forward. The one resulting chart, although interesting, was not particularly detailed and was made after the event by **José Cañizares**, who had not even been on the voyage. It was soon rendered redundant by the work of Hezeta and Bodega in 1775.

PETER THE GREAT (1672–1725). Peter the Great was the emperor of Russia remembered for his efforts, from 1685–1725, to modernize the institutions of government, to establish Russia as a military and naval power, and to end her cultural isolation from the rest of Europe. His successful war against Sweden gave him access to the Baltic and allowed him to build a new capital, St. Petersburg, but his sweeping economic and political reforms and military adventures required him to enlarge his tax base and its administration. An important element in organizing his expanding empire was better geographical knowledge based on modern surveying and charting. The survey program initiated by the czar, which extended the far-eastern boundaries of Russia through the conquest of **Kamchatka** and the annexation of the Kurile Islands, ultimately formed the basis for the *Atlas Russicus* published by **Joseph Nicolas de l'Isle** in 1745.

It also propelled Peter to search for America not, as sometimes asserted, to solve an apparent mystery of whether Asia and America were joined (he knew they were not) but rather to satisfy his imperial ambition to control its resources. Evidence suggests that, from the time of his visit to Amsterdam in 1697, Peter was intrigued by the idea of a northeast passage across the top of Russia to the Pacific, and whether or not the separation of the continents by the **Strait of Anian** would allow for a route to China and India. His sponsorship of the **Ivan Evreinov** Expedition to Kamchatka in 1719 also suggests a keen interest in determining the relationship of this region to America. By 1722 he would have been familiar with the maps of Kamchatka that depicted, to the east, a great, unnamed land. He seems to have grasped the potential gains to be made by advancing from Russia's Pacific ports not just south to Japan and the Philippines, but on to America and down its west coast to **California**. There is a direct connection between this appreciation of the potential of America and Peter's commissioning of **Vitus Bering** in late 1724, on the eve of his death, to prepare his first **Kamchatka Expedition**.

PLENISNER, FRIEDRICH (?–1778). Personal clerk to **Vitus Bering** and artist on his voyage in search of America in 1741, Friedrich Plenisner's importance lies in his friendship with the naturalist **Georg Wilhelm Steller** for whom he drew a number of illustrations, such as those found in *De bestiis marinis*. After helping Steller with his reports during the winter of 1742–1743, he rose to become commandant of Okhotsk.

Working under the influential governor of Siberia, **Fedor Soimonov**, Plenisner was appointed to administer the region of Anadyr in 1762. Here he became involved in the exploration of the Chukotskii Peninsula and was at the forefront of a determined Russian effort to gather information about the Asian coast and islands in the **Bering Sea** and Arctic Ocean, and about the still-mysterious Great Land to the east. Under orders from Soimonov he directed the explorations of **Ivan Sindt**, aimed at America; sent an expedition from the mouth of the Kolyma River to search for the Great Land; and, in 1764, dispatched the Chukchi cossack **Nikolai Daurkin** to explore the coast of the peninsula and to find out from local natives their knowledge of the **Bering Strait** and the American shore. In the mid-1760s he mysteriously withheld his cooperation from the planning underway in Okhotsk for the secret **Petr Krenitsyn** and **Mikhail Levashov** Expedition, and thereafter his fortunes and influence seem to have waned, although in 1766 he initiated a small expedition to explore the Kurile Islands. In 1776 he moved to St. Petersburg and a year later made a presentation to the Academy of Sciences based on the map and reports about Chukotka and America gleaned from the work of Daurkin.

POINT REYES AND DRAKE'S BAY. The southwest point of this distinctive peninsula, some 30 miles north of San Francisco, was named Punta de los Reyes in honor of the Feast Day of the Three Kings by **Sebastián Vizcaíno** on 5 January 1603. It encloses the northern section of Drake's Bay, in whose *estero* many scholars believe **Francis Drake** careened the *Golden Hind* in 1579. The **Manila galleon** *San Agustín*, under the command of **Sebastián Rodríguez Cermeño**, was wrecked there on 30 November 1595.

POND, PETER (1739–1807). New England–born fur trader, explorer, and mapmaker, Peter Pond was a veteran of the French and Indian Wars. He entered the **fur trade** in 1765 and by the late 1770s had ventured north to explore and trade in the vast Tabasco region. In the 1780s, aligned with the **North West Company**, he pushed farther west and learned information from the natives that led to the construction of his celebrated grand map in the winter of 1784–1785. This showed what was later identified as the Mackenzie River flowing into the Arctic Ocean. It offered the possibility not only of new avenues of commerce, but also of a lake and river route that many cabinet geographers still thought could provide a way into the **Bering Sea**, and thus the Pacific Ocean. Later versions of Pond's map, inspired by his visits to Great Slave Lake in 1786–1787, his knowledge of **James Cook**'s apparent discovery of "Cook's River," and more information from natives who claimed to have actually seen and traded with Cook's ships, included a more southerly river with access from Great Slave Lake directly to the ocean. It would not be many more years before the two crucial inaccuracies of Pond's otherwise remarkable maps—his problem with longitude that put Great Slave Lake much closer to the Pacific than is actually the case, and his ignorance of the Mackenzie Mountains that essentially block any possibility of a "Cook's

River"—were revealed. Meanwhile, in the late 1780s, his maps were pored over by such enthusiasts as Sir **Joseph Banks** and **Alexander Dalrymple**, who retained the hope that some kind of transcontinental passage might still exist. They also served to focus attention on the maritime and overland endeavors that were pressing forward to solve the riddle of this great northern mystery.

PORT DES FRANÇAIS. *See* LITUYA BAY.

PORT ETCHES. A large bay on the west side of **Hinchinbrook Island** at the entrance to **Prince William Sound**, Port Etches provided an obvious anchorage for ships entering the sound between Hinchinbrook and **Montague** islands. It was discovered by **James Cook** on 12 May 1778, and provided him with his first stable anchorage since leaving **Nootka Sound** at the end of April. He called the place Nuchek, which he understood to be its native name. A year later, on 22 July 1779, the **Ignacio de Arteaga** and **Juan Francisco de la Bodega y Quadra** Expedition dropped anchor and called the place Puerto de Santiago in honor of Spain's patron saint. It was the English fur trader **Nathaniel Portlock** who, in the summer of 1787, visiting the bay in which he had been with Cook eight years earlier, gave it its present name after his patron, **Richard Cadman Etches**. Thereafter, the port became one of the bases for Russian hunting and fur trading in the sound, and the launching area for forays southeast down the coast to the delta of the **Copper River** and **Yakutat Bay**.

PORTLOCK, NATHANIEL (1749–1817). The American-born Nathaniel Portlock was already an experienced mariner when he joined the Royal Navy in 1771. In 1776 he sailed as master's mate on the *Discovery* under **Charles Clerke** in **James Cook**'s Third Voyage to the Pacific, visiting the Northwest Coast for the first time. In August 1779 he transferred to the *Resolution*, but when she reached the Cape of Good Hope he was sent ahead to England in a faster ship, carrying the journals, drawings, and observations from the voyage for the Admiralty.

In 1785 Portlock was appointed by the King George's Sound Company, headed by **Richard Cadman Etches**, to command the *King George* and lead an expedition to develop a **fur trade** between the Northwest Coast and China. He was accompanied by **George Dixon** in the *Queen Charlotte*. On 18 July 1786 the ships arrived in **Cook Inlet**, where they traded for furs during a lengthy stay and encountered Russians who were busy establishing permanent posts in the area. In Portlock's journal there is an engraving of his ship in Coal Harbour (today English Bay), so named because "in these hills are beds of coal." Moving east to the entrance to **Prince William Sound** (PWS) the ships did not enter but sailed south towards **Nootka Sound**, which the two commanders had also visited with Cook in 1778 and where they had agreed to winter over. But adverse weather conditions denied them entry and forced them farther south to a more pleasant resting place in **Hawaii**.

By April of the following year they were back off PWS and anchored in Port Graham on the west side of **Montague Island** for three weeks. They engaged in trade and later encountered **John Meares**, who had spent a miserable winter in the sound in his ship the *Nootka*. Portlock provided assistance, but not before extracting a promise from Meares, who was trading without a license from the **East India Company**, that he would cease trading and quit the region. After leaving Montague Island, Portlock and Dixon separated, the latter heading south to **Yakutat Bay** and the **Queen Charlotte Islands**. Portlock moved over to **Hinchinbrook Island** where he named **Port Etches** after his sponsor. Portlock then sailed south down the coast as far as Chichagof Island where, in early August, he entered what is still known today as Portlock's Harbour and traded with the local **Tlingit**. Portlock left the coast on 23 August, journeying to Hawaii before meeting up with Dixon in Macao in November 1787. Here they sold their combined cargo of 2,252 skins for the huge sum of $54,857. They reached England in August 1788.

Portlock published his *Voyage* (often confused with Dixon's account because it has the same title) in 1789. It contains his portrait as a frontispiece and is dedicated to the king. There is a general chart of the tracks of the ships in the Gulf of Alaska in both 1786 and 1787, and small charts of all of Portlock's anchorages. In addition to engravings of views in the harbor in Cook Inlet and on Chichagof Island, there is a full appendix with details of Portlock's route and observations taken from the *King George*, as well as a "List of Plants, Birds and Fossils seen in Cook's River."

PORTOLÁ, GASPAR DE (ca. 1723–1786). *See* SACRED EXPEDITION.

POSTELS, ALEKSANDR FILIPPOVICH (1801–1871). Scientist, educator, and artist, Aleksandr Filippovich Postels was appointed to accompany **Fedor Litke** to the North Pacific Ocean in 1826. His particular expertise was mineralogy, and he developed a collection of over 300 mineral specimens. He also worked closely with the naturalist **Karl-Heinrich Mertens** and the ornithologist, **Friedrich Heinrich von Kittlitz**, helping them with their collections, and acting as an artist to Mertens for whom he drew hundreds of plants and fish. In all, he made over a thousand sketches, some of which were published 30 years after the expedition returned to Europe. Like Kittlitz, he became adept at executing views that detailed precisely the vegetation of a forest or a body of water. A forest scene near Sitka, in **Russian America**, was published in the atlas to Litke's journal in 1836; also portraits of individual **Tlingit**, and a group in a "Kaloche cabin, Sitkha [*sic*] Island." Most of his drawings in the Academy of Sciences in St. Petersburg remain unpublished.

PRIBILOF ISLANDS. *See* PRIBYLOV, GAVRIIL.

PRIBYLOV, GAVRIIL (?–1796). Navigator and fur trader, Pribylov was active along the **Aleutian Islands** during the 1780s in the service of the early **Pavel Lebedev-Lastochkin** and **Grigorii Shelikhov** partnership. On **Unalaska** Island during the winter of 1785–1786 he noted a large number of young fur seals arriving from the north and concluded that they must be coming from another island. In June 1786 he discovered St. George, one of four islands in the Pribilof group, finding it swarming with seals. Returning in 1787 he found that the *promyshlenniki* he had left on the island the previous year had seen another island further north, which was investigated and named St. Paul. The abundance of animals in these rich seal rookeries caused Pribylov to stay and harvest furs throughout the summer of 1790, when he returned to Petropavlovsk.

He was then appointed pilot of the *Slava Rossii* (Glory of Russia) and took part in the Northwest Coast expedition of **Joseph Billings**. Later in the 1790s he became closely allied with **Aleksandr**

Baranov, who was openly at war with the Lebedev-Lastochkin organization. Pribylov commanded ships that explored the coast and gathered furs from the Gulf of Alaska south to **Yakutat Bay** and the **Queen Charlotte Islands**.

PRINCE WILLIAM SOUND. The large gulf, Prince William Sound, 70 miles wide and 30 miles long, extends north from the Gulf of Alaska. Its entrance is guarded by two substantial islands—**Montague** and **Hinchinbrook**. Although Russian traders had reached **Kodiak** Island and the south coast of the **Alaska Peninsula** in the early 1760s, and had consolidated their presence there during the 1770s, they did not venture as far as Prince William Sound (or Chugatskaya as they called it after the **native** name) until after it had been entered and surveyed by **James Cook**, whose expedition spent eight days there, anchoring in English Bay at the entrance to **Port Etches**, and then in Snug Corner Cove at the entrance to present-day Port Fidalgo. **Artists John Webber** and **William Ellis** were the first to provide visual images of the place and its people. Cook called it Sandwich Sound to honor the first lord of the Admiralty, but the earl himself had the name changed to Prince William after the third son of George III, and this is how it appeared in the atlas accompanying Cook's journal in 1784. In 1779 it was visited by **Ignacio de Arteaga** and **Juan Francisco de la Bodega y Quadra**, whose brief survey, like that of Cook, determined that there was no passage through the surrounding high mountains. In 1780 and 1781, armed with information from Cook received at **Unalaska** and in **Kamchatka**, the first Russian fur-hunting expeditions formally entered the sound. Thereafter it became the scene of increasing competition between the employees of **Grigorii Shelikhov** and **Pavel Lebedev-Lastochkin**. The Spanish navigator **Salvador Fidalgo** stayed in the sound in 1790, and the modern settlement names of Cordova and Valdez result from his visit. As Russian traders increasingly frequented the sound, **George Vancouver** completed his definitive survey in 1794.

PROMYSHLENNIKI. *Promyshlenniki* is the Russian name for private hunters that, like *coureurs de bois* in Canada, became synonymous with trapping for and gathering furs. They obtained their furs at the source either directly through their own efforts or from natives through trade or extortion. By the very nature of their activities they were the great explorers of Siberia, and then led the Russian advance through the **Aleutian Islands** of the far North Pacific Ocean onto the mainland coast of Northwest America. On the Northwest Coast after the 1760s their individualism became more and more absorbed into organized companies, and by 1800 they were controlled by the **Russian–American Company**. *See also* FUR TRADE.

PUGET, PETER (1765–1822). Chosen by **George Vancouver** to serve as 2nd Lieutenant on the *Discovery*, Peter Puget made a significant contribution to the success of the Vancouver Expedition. When **William Broughton** returned to England after the first of Vancouver's three seasons on the coast, Puget was named commander of the *Chatham*. Cape Puget at the southwest entrance to **Prince William Sound** (PWS), and **Puget Sound** in **Washington** State, the location of the city of Seattle, were both named in his honor. In 1792 he explored the intricate channels of the latter, as well as the Hood Canal, in a series of small boat excursions, and then accompanied Vancouver from the ships' anchorage in Birch Bay that brought them to Jervis Inlet and Burrard Inlet, the site of the present-day city of Vancouver. Later, he was the first to explore Discovery Passage, which allowed Vancouver to bring his ships north into Queen Charlotte Sound and out into the Pacific. During the second season (1793) Puget continued to participate in the small boat sorties that made it possible for the expedition to complete its remarkably accurate survey of the Northwest Coast; he accompanied **Joseph Whidbey** in the exploration of Douglas Channel and later worked with Vancouver in the Behm Canal, where his prompt reaction to an attack by the **Tlingit** averted a disaster that could have cost Vancouver his life. In 1794 the *Chatham* explored the western shore of **Cook Inlet**, and Puget had a number of encounters with Russian fur traders and visited an establishment belonging to the **Lebedev-Lastochkin Company** on the North Foreland opposite Turnagain Arm. Coming south from PWS, Puget explored the coast beyond the **Copper River** delta and surveyed **Yakutat Bay** where he again encountered **Egor Purtov**, a senior assistant to **Aleksandr Baranov**, whom he had previously met in Cook Inlet. From Purtov he learned much about the hunting methods of the Russians who did little trading with the local natives, preferring to rely on their own **Aleut**

hunters. Vancouver relied on Puget's log books, which Kaye Lamb has described as "the most interesting and valuable of all the official logs, and in great part a journal . . . personal and outspoken," when editing his *Voyage of George Vancouver*; they were particularly important in describing the work of the expedition when the *Discovery* and *Chatham* were separated.

PUGET SOUND AND HOOD CANAL. Two long channels extending south from the eastern end of the **Strait of Juan de Fuca**, Puget Sound and Hood Canal are accessed by a large opening named Admiralty Inlet by **George Vancouver** and discovered by him on 7 May 1792. It had been identified as a bay in 1790 by **Juan Carrasco** but left unexplored. In 1791 **José María Narváez** had considered the bay more significant but did not have time to explore it. From his expedition's two ships, *Discovery* and *Chatham* anchored in Port Discovery, Vancouver set out with **Peter Puget**, **Joseph Whidbey**, and **Archibald Menzies** to explore the coast eastwards by small boat. After discovering Port Townsend they entered Hood Canal and surveyed it before returning to the ships on 15 May. Vancouver named it Hood's Channel after Lord Hood, a member of the Board of Admiralty, but it appeared on his charts as Hood's Canal. On 18 May the ships entered Admiralty Inlet, which was the original name of the upper portion of Puget Sound. This name, which now applies to the whole body of water above Vashon Island, was given by Vancouver to the southern section in recognition of the intricate survey work undertaken by Puget and Whidbey, 20–27 May. They spent over a week in the channels, bays, and islands in the southernmost part of the region reached through The Narrows, west of the present-day city of Tacoma.

PUNTA DE LOS MÁRTIRES. Cape Elizabeth in the State of **Washington**, north of **Gray's Harbor**, is also known as Punta de los Mártires (Martyrs' Point). On 13 July 1775 **Juan Francisco de la Bodega y Quadra** in the schooner *Sonora* sailed under the cape and anchored in the bay between it and Point Grenville, south of which **Bruno de Hezeta** had taken the *Santiago*. The next day, as Bodega was waiting for the tide to rise to extricate his ship from the shoals guarding the northern beach of the bay, seven sailors went ashore to fetch water and were immediately attacked by **natives** on the beach near the Quinault River. Five were killed and two drowned as they tried to swim back to the ship. It was the first violent encounter between natives and Europeans on the coast north of **Alta California** and south of **Russian America**. Although there has been some scholarly disagreement on the exact location of the tragedy, and which of the two headlands was named in memory of the murdered seamen, Hezeta's map of the area makes it clear that the "punta" is Cape Elizabeth.

PURTOV, EGOR (fl. 1792–1793). Russian *promyshlennik* Egor Purtov worked closely with **Aleksandr Baranov** and was entrusted by him in 1792 to initiate the practice of sending huge flotillas of *baidarkas* with **Aleut** hunters down the coast from **Prince William Sound** to **Yakutat Bay** and beyond. The experiment was repeated in 1794 with the result that the Russians subsequently extended their exploration of the coast and hunting activities into the **Alexander Archipelago**. That same year Purtov met **Peter Puget** and the *Chatham* in both **Cook Inlet** and at Yakutat, and provided him with information about Russian activities, discoveries, and settlements.

PUSHKAREV, GAVRIIL (fl. 1758–1762). In 1757 an Irkutsk merchant Ivan Bechevin received official encouragement to mount an expedition to the North Pacific Ocean. The voyage would then swing back to the Gulf of Anadyr, proceed through the **Bering Strait**, and follow the coast west to the Lena River. Bechevin never carried out this ambitious plan but the next year organized navigator Pushkarev to sail from **Kamchatka** to the **Aleutian Islands**. It is not clear whether Bechevin himself was on board. Arriving at Atka Island in the Andreanoff group in September 1758, Pushkarev found another trading vessel under attack from the **Aleuts**. He raised the siege and the two crews joined forces to winter over and hunt. They stayed in the region of Atka and Amelia Islands until the summer of 1761, at which point Pushkarev continued to sail east.

He reached the **Alaska Peninsula** without knowing he had discovered continental America and, trading with the **natives**, prepared to winter over at Protassov Bay opposite the Shumagin Islands. In January 1762 the Russians violated Aleut women on Unga Island, which led to a series of native attacks. A number of Russians were killed and wounded and their encampment burned. They retreated to Umnak Island, where they seized several islanders and obliged them to take them to other islands; but the ship was caught in a storm and driven westward, ultimately to Kamchatka. There tragedy befell the hostages who were still on board; over 20 men, women, girls, and boys were reported murdered or committed suicide. The brutal misdeeds of the Russians are what is best remembered from the voyage, but their reports from the eastern Aleutians and coast of the Alaska Peninsula provided new and important information about the geography of the region.

– Q –

QUEEN CHARLOTTE ISLANDS. Because they were initially approached from the west, the Queen Charlotte Islands were thought to be one large island during the exploration period. But there are two main islands—Graham and Moresby, with Langara off the north coast, and Kunghit at the southern end. In addition there are numerous small islands off the east coast. They are now usually referred to by their native name Haida Gwaii.

They were discovered by **Juan Pérez** on 18 July 1774, and he traded with the **Haida** off Langara Island. In 1786 the English trader **James Strange** saw them on his way from Nootka to **Prince William Sound**. **George Dixon** in July 1787 finally named them, after his ship, which had been named in honor of the consort of George III. Dixon sailed at close quarters down the entire west coast and halfway up the east coast as far as Louise Island, experiencing great success in trading for furs. His general chart was the first serious attempt to provide an outline of the islands. Thereafter, by word of mouth, and particularly following the publication in 1789 of the account of his voyage, the islands became a favorite target of British and American traders, despite the Haida's reputation for hostility. In 1792 **Jacinto Caamaño** performed a late **act of possession** on Graham Island, and explored around the islands, across **Dixon Entrance** into southern **Alaska**, and in the numerous bays, islands, and fjords off the adjacent continental coast. His chart, which he shared with **George Vancouver** at Nootka in September 1792, was a marked improvement upon that of Dixon. Vancouver explored the west coast of the islands in September 1793.

Impressed by stories of success in the **fur trade**, both **Alexander Menzies** and **Joseph Whidbey** advocated British settlement on the Islands to lay claim to sovereignty on the Northwest Coast.

QUIMPER, MANUEL (ca. 1750–1844). A Peruvian-born Spanish naval officer, Manuel Quimper found himself traveling from Spain to **New Spain** in 1789 in the same ship as **Juan Francisco de la Bodega y Quadra**, who quickly had him assigned to the Naval Department of **San Blas**.

He was given command of the *Princesa Real*, captured during the **Nootka Sound Incident**, and joined **Francisco de Eliza**'s expedition to reoccupy **Nootka Sound** in 1790. The ship was to be returned to her former captain, but when he did not arrive Eliza assigned Quimper to explore the **Strait of Juan de Fuca**, approached in 1789 by **José María Narváez**. He set out on 31 May with the pilots **Gonzalo López de Haro** and **Juan Carrasco**. First they explored **Clayoquot Sound**, then more briefly Barkley Sound and Port San Juan. López de Haro began to construct his fine chart of the voyage.

The party soon entered Sooke Harbour, which Quimper named Puerto de Revilla Gigedo in honor of the viceroy. He performed the **act of possession**. Proceeding eastwards another possession ceremony was performed at Rada de Valdés y Bazan, today Royal Roads, and named after Navy Minister Antonio Valdés. Here Quimper learned from **natives** that farther east channels led off to the north, but he decided to explore the southern shore. The spit at Dungeness, named by **George Vancouver** in 1792, was named Bahia y Puerto de Quimper, and Vancouver's Port Discovery was called Puerto de la Bodega y Quadra. As the *Princesa Real* sailed northeast, pilot Carrasco charted the entrance to Admiralty Inlet as a large bay, thus missing the discovery of **Puget Sound**. As he wanted to be back at Nootka by 15 August to hand over the ship, Quimper was pressed for time. Thus he was loath to follow any channels off the larger strait. He did, however, note the entrance to Rosario Strait, which he named Boca de Fidalgo after his fellow officer, named Mount Baker the Gran Montaña de Carmelo and then discovered a more impressive channel leading north. Today it retains the name Canal de López de Haro or Haro Strait. Sailing west, he took the time to explore the harbor at Esquimalt, naming it Puerto de Córdova, before crossing the strait once again to resume his survey of its southern shore.

On 1 August he was at **Neah Bay**, Bahia de Nuñez Gaona, an important discovery as his favorable report led to its selection as a possible new post if Nootka had to be abandoned. But his analysis of the site was flawed; Neah Bay is wide and open to westerly winds. From Neah Bay, where he performed his fifth act of possession, Quimper sailed out into the Pacific, on 4 August, thus ending the first sustained exploration of the Strait of Juan de Fuca. Fog, winds, and adverse currents prevented a return to Nootka, so he went south to **Monterey**. His chart is in the Archivo Histórico Nacional in Madrid.

Quimper's homecoming to San Blas caused concern about the return of the *Princesa Real*, so he was ordered to go to Manila, where the governor could hand her over to **James Colnett**. En route he would explore the Sandwich Islands (**Hawaii**) and report on conditions that might be useful to Spanish navigation. He sighted the large island of Hawaii on 20 March 1791. He charted both it and Maui, and met King Kamehameha. In Hawaii Quimper also encountered Colnett, who demanded that the *Princesa Real* be handed over immediately. After some tense moments they negotiated a truce and he was able to continue surveying and to proceed to Manila as planned.

QUIVIRA. Quivira identifies that part of the California coast that predates the **New Albion** of **Francis Drake**. It appears on the copperplate map *Typus Orbis Terrarum* by **Abraham Ortelius**, 1564, published six years later in his *Theatrum Orbis Terrarum* (1570). The name derived from stories of a rich city, Gran Quivira, located much farther east, which drew members of the Francisco Vázquez Coronado expedition (1540–1542) to the edge of the Great Plains in Kansas. The mythical community was later described in the *Hispania Victrix* (1553) of Francisco López de Gómara, an early but highly unreliable historian, who never visited the New World, but had become chaplain to **Hernán Cortés** in 1540.

– R –

REVILLAGIGEDO, COUNT OF (1740–1799). As viceroy of **New Spain**, 1789–1794, the Count of Revillagigedo inherited problems arising from the **Nootka Sound Incident**. Although he persuaded himself that England had no case against Spain, he was little interested in maintaining a Spanish presence north of the **Strait of Juan de Fuca**, considering it unproductive, indefensible, and expensive. This conviction increased as he presided over the last intensive period of Spanish exploration in 1790–1792 (**Manuel Quimper**; **Francisco de Eliza** and **José María Narváez**; **Alejandro Malaspina**; **Dionisio Alcalá Galiano**; and **Júan Francisco de la Bodega y Quadra** and **Jacinto Caamaño**) that disproved the theories about a navigable **Northwest Passage**. For a short time he harbored unrealistic hopes of limiting British access to the coast overland from the east by proposing a line directly north from Fuca to 60° N, but even abandoned this idea in favor of a retreat to **San Francisco**. In this he was at odds with the view from Madrid, and Spain continued to occupy **Friendly Cove** in **Nootka Sound** until 1795.

REZANOV, NIKOLAI (1764–1807). Army officer and courtier, Nikolai Rezanov was an important figure in the early history of the **Russian–American Company** (RAC). In 1794 he met **Grigorii Shelikhov** and subsequently married his daughter, Anna. From this time on, although his father-in-law died in 1795, Rezanov became intimately associated with Shelikhov's dream of a commercial empire in the North Pacific. With **Natalia Shelikhov**, he cultivated their influential contacts in St. Petersburg. The opportunity offered by the death of **Catherine II**, and their links to the new czar, allowed him to pursue the long-desired Shelikhov goal of monopoly control over the American **fur trade**. It took a few years, but the political decision was ultimately made in their favor, and the RAC was given the first of its three charters as the century came to a close. Many government and court officials became shareholders, and its affairs became closely linked with government policy in the Far East and North Pacific.

After Anna's untimely death in 1802, Rezanov became involved with **Ivan Kruzenshtern**'s idea of round-the-world voyages to support and supply **Russian America**, and to promote trade with China and India. With the crucial support of one of his more influential patrons, **Nikolai Rumiantsev**, the minister of commerce, Rezanov worked with Kruzenshtern to plan the pioneering voyage that set out in 1803. To its tasks was added the transportation of Rezanov to Japan in an attempt to open up trade with America. This was a total failure, but when Kruzenshtern in the *Nadezhda* returned to **Kamchatka** in May 1805,

Rezanov left the expedition and took a RAC ship to **Sitka Sound** where he found **Aleksandr Baranov** building up the settlement of the second **New Archangel**. Rezanov's many discussions with Baranov, and his own observations, resulted in a number of reports to the government about how the fledgling colony in North America might be improved. While he appreciated what Baranov had achieved since 1791, he was not impressed by the RAC's state of affairs, and in one report asked the czar to authorize naval vessels to come and expel American fur traders from the coast. He also put a stop, at least for a short time, to Baranov's dealings with the traders for the benefit of his settlement. Concerned as he was about the present, Rezanov also articulated a wider vision—to push the Russian presence farther south, an idea that Baranov shared. Both agreed that access to the resources of the more temperate lands on **Vancouver Island** or beyond was indispensable to future success, and they dreamed of prosperous settlements in **Nootka Sound**, at the mouth of the **Columbia River**, and in northern **California**.

In the spring of 1806 Rezanov sailed for California. He tried unsuccessfully to cross the bar of the **Columbia River** to survey sites for a possible settlement, but his sojourn in **San Francisco** confirmed an almost complete absence of Spanish control over the area north of that settlement. Rezanov became excited about the prospect of bringing the whole of the central and northern coast of America under Russian control, and immediately recommended the establishment of the outpost that later became **Fort Ross**. During the years before it was built in 1812, the Russians began to ferry **Aleuts** to California, where they hunted at will, even inside the Golden Gate. Demonstrating the value of a direct link with California, Rezanov returned to Sitka with a cargo of meat and grain.

Before leaving America, Rezanov bombarded Baranov with another round of orders for the development of the colony, with plans ranging from sponsoring agriculture and industry to aggressively moving south along the coast. But his dream of empire was never fulfilled; he died before he could reach St. Petersburg to advocate for an expansion of Russian sovereignty and trade to a position of absolute dominance in the North Pacific.

RICHARDS, GEORGE HENRY (1820–1896). Marine surveyor and hydrographer George Henry Richards entered the Royal Navy in 1833, and served worldwide, including in the Arctic with **Edward Belcher**, searching for the ill-fated expedition of Sir John Franklin. In 1856 he took command of HMS *Plumper* to undertake a detailed survey of **Vancouver Island** and the southern coast of **British Columbia**. He arrived at the naval base at Esquimalt in 1857 and, in subsequent years, acted as a commissioner for the San Juan Boundary Commission, formed to survey the waters and islands along the disputed boundary between Canada and the United States at the southern end of the **Strait of Georgia**. It had been left unclear by the terms of the **Oregon Treaty**, 1846. Between 1857 and 1860 Richards conducted a succession of meticulous surveys of the coasts and islands in the waters between southeast Vancouver Island and the continent, including Burrard Inlet, the site of the future city of Vancouver. In 1857 he fixed the exact location of the 49° parallel in Semiahmoo Bay. In 1860 the *Plumper* was replaced by the paddle wheeler *Hecate* in which Richards completed his survey of the entire coastline of Vancouver Island. The majority of the place names in the region date from his work, in which he respected both the Spanish and English heritage of the area. *See also* SAN JUAN BOUNDARY DISPUTE.

RICKMAN, JOHN (?–1818). John Rickman sailed on the *Discovery* with **James Cook** on his Third Voyage to the Pacific, 1776–1780. In completing the official journal, **James King** insinuated that the murder of an important chief by a boat party under Rickman in another part of Kealakekula Bay had fermented the fateful melee on the beach on 14 February 1779 that led to Cook's murder. Other eyewitnesses discounted this interpretation, but King's antagonism to Rickman in an attempt to find a scapegoat in defense of Cook's reputation likely encouraged him to publish, in 1781, his own account of the voyage and perspective on the tragedy. He did so anonymously because of strict naval regulations, which stated that all reports and journals written during a voyage had to be transmitted to the Admiralty. Initially it was thought that **John Ledyard** was the author because it bore a strong resemblance to his account published in 1783, but this is because Ledyard used Rickman's factual data to expand his own recollections. Rickman's journal was the first to be published in English and confirmed the rumors already circulating in England, and beyond, about the potential for a rich **fur trade** between the Northwest Coast and China. It thus contributed to the buildup (along with the other early accounts by **Heinrich Zimmermann**, **William Ellis**, and Ledyard) to the rush to the North Pacific unleashed in 1784–1785.

RIOBO, JUAN ANTONIO GARCÍA (1740–?). Juan Antonio García Riobo sailed as chaplain on the *Princesa* with **Ignacio de Arteaga** in 1779. He had arrived in **New Spain** in 1769 and was attached to the College of San Fernando, which trained and dispatched missionaries in the viceroyalty. His journal is a small gem in the literature of Northwest Coast exploration. Quite short at eight folios, it is full of details about the progress of the voyage and descriptions of the nature and culture of the **native** peoples Riobo encountered, notably at **Bucareli Bay**. The manuscript was found in the library of the Mission of Santa Clara near San Francisco in 1851.

On the voyage north, Riobo describes a storm "of great fury . . . the frigate was tossed about violently. . . ." He reported that it abated when the commander made a vow to the Blessed Virgin, who thereafter gave the voyage "her powerful protection." His descriptions of interactions with the natives at Bucareli take up as much as 20 percent of the narrative. Riobo noted their almost obsessive desire to trade, especially for iron when they could not steal it. He was fascinated with their arms and armor, and recorded the difficulties encountered, and the fear aroused, by the high number of canoes that stalked the small boat survey excursion of **Francisco Mourelle**. He was impressed with the fine features of the women, but was repulsed by their use of the **labret**. In the Gulf of Alaska he recognized that the **Aleut/Alutiiq** led a quite different existence from the **Tlingit** and, as did all foreigners, he remarked favorably on their *baidarka*s and how, in their tunics, they fitted into them so tightly. He found them friendly and described the bone ornamentation worn by both men and women. At Puerto de Santiago (**Port Etches**) the natives were "very much inclined to steal, and they are very cunning in doing it." Where the expedition landed he also commented on nature: the flowering plants at Bucareli, the stunted trees in **Prince William Sound**, and a great deal of grass but few trees on the **Kenai Peninsula**.

RIO DE MARTÍN DE AGUILAR. The Rio de Martín de Aguilar was discovered by the crew of the *Tres Reyes*, sailing in the **Sebastián**

Vizcaíno Expedition, 1602–1603. Accounts of the voyage were based on the recollections of second pilot Esteban López, and the identification of the "voluminous river" whose "force of current defeated the attempts of the explorers to enter it" has always been unclear. After separating from Vizcaíno's *San Diego* in the vicinity of **Cape Mendocino**, the *Tres Reyes* under Martín de Aguilar and pilot Antonio Flores was driven by a storm beyond the current **California–Oregon** boundary at 42° N, and probably as far north as **Cape Blanco**. Close by they saw a river, probably the Rogue River in southern Oregon. A second account records that after reaching latitude 43° N on 19 January 1603 the explorers discovered a bay full of **native** canoes and another river south of Cape Mendocino.

Both Aguilar and Flores perished on the northern coast and it was left to López to bring the ship and the tale of their adventures back to **New Spain**. In 1615 Juan de Torquemada's *Monarchia Indiana* placed the Rio de Martín de Aguilar at 43° N, north of Cape Blanco, where it became a feature of maps of the Northwest Coast for another 175 years. For most of that time there was no European exploration in the region, and maps based on the ideas of French cartographer Guillaume de l'Isle (1675–1726) were constructed from accounts of explorers pushing into the middle of the continent from the east and north. Native information about a great river led to the cartographic construction of a **River of the West**, and de l'Isle and others linked this to the river seen by the Spanish mariners in 1603, long before an actual great river, the **Columbia River**, was discovered farther north in the late 18th century. Aguilar's river was also shown on speculative maps as late as the 1780s as an outlet to the Pacific of another of the more interesting creations of Europe's cabinet geographers, an inland **Sea of the West** that wandered cartographically across the continent from early in the 16th century.

RIOU, EDWARD (1762–1801). Two years after entering the navy at the age of 12, Edward Riou was appointed as a midshipman on **James Cook**'s *Discovery* on 22 February 1776. As a member of the scientific corps, he drew a number of competent charts including, on the Northwest Coast, of **Nootka Sound** and **Prince William Sound**. His chart of **Unalaska** Island includes an inset of Samgoonoodha Harbour (English Bay). A chart of Avacha Bay (Petropavlovsk, **Kam-**

chatka) with an inset plan and view is particularly fine. The sketch provides a vista looking past the observatories and ships at anchor to a Russian galliot, recently arrived from Okhotsk (September 1779), and buildings on the shore to Mount A'wantchka in the distance.

RIVER OF THE WEST. Historians of the **Pacific Northwest** have tended to assume that the name River of the West applied to the **Columbia River** long before it was discovered or explored. But this is simplistic. The use of the term by Jesuit missionaries in the Great Lakes region, and particularly its connection with the explorations of Pierre Gaultier de La Vérendrye west of Lake Superior, would appear to make the link tenuous at best. That far east, many rivers offering a route west would have been candidates for the title and, based upon which natives were being encountered, it could have been any one of a number of rivers at any given time. The "Rivière de l'Ouest" first appears on a La Vérendrye map dating from 1730. It was based on a drawing made for him by an Assiniboine chief in 1728. Although the original has not survived, the image still exists from a tracing taken by **Philippe Buache**, and published by him in 1754. Using this information, the French cartographer Jean Nicolas Bellin (1703–1772) published, in 1743, a map with the river heading west from Lake Winnipeg.

There was much room for speculation. Early- and mid-18th-century French and English cartographers usually presented the river flowing across the unexplored western part of the continent into the Pacific directly or via a large inland **Sea of the West**, a remarkably persistent feature that also graced many speculative maps of western North America. Although some mapmakers connected it to the strait supposedly discovered by **Juan de Fuca**, the River of the West reached the ocean more often than not at the "Entrance discovered by Martín de Aguilar in 1603" north of **Cape Blanco**. This is most clearly shown in the **Gerhardt Friedrich Müller** map of 1754, and in the map published to illustrate Jonathan Carver's *Travels through the Interior parts of North America in the Years 1766, 1767 and 1768*. It is the proximity of the unidentified **Rio de Martín de Aguilar** to the Columbia River that probably accounts for the River of the West's connection with the greatest river on the Northwest Coast, but with the orientation coming from east to west, this would seem to be more coincidence than anything else. *See also* CARTOGRAPHY.

ROBERTS, HENRY (1757–1796). He joined the *Resolution* for **James Cook**'s Second Voyage to the Pacific (1772–1776), coming under the influence of the **artist** William Hodges, and exhibiting talent as a draughtsman by copying charts and coastal views. On the *Resolution* again, as master's mate for Cook's Third Voyage to the North Pacific, he worked closely with Cook and **William Bligh**, and amply fulfilled his earlier promise as an artist and draughtsman. Roberts's sketches of **Nootka Sound** demonstrate his meticulous approach, as do his fine charts of **Prince William Sound** and **Cook Inlet**, the harbor at Samgoonooda Bay, **Unalaska**, **Norton Sound**, and Avacha Bay in **Kamchatka**.

Shortly after the voyage began Roberts started to work with Cook on a chart of the world upon which the tracks of his ships and the discoveries of his three expeditions could be recorded. The result of their collaboration was A General Chart: Exhibiting the Discoveries made by Captn Cook in this and his two previous Voyages; with the Tracks of the Ships under his Command, which was engraved for the atlas that accompanied publication of the journal of the Third Voyage in 1784.

After the expedition's return in 1780, Roberts went to sea again briefly before settling down to prepare the charts of the voyage for publication. This took the best part of four years, 1781–1784, and led to an unfortunate dispute with **William Bligh**. Although he did indeed prepare the charts, and they were engraved from his "original" drawings, it is very unlikely that he himself did any of the initial survey sketches, which were the work of Cook and Bligh. Bligh complained about the credit given to Roberts on the title page of the final draft of the first edition of Cook's *Voyage* with the result that Roberts's name was removed. It was technically correct that Roberts had not been responsible for the surveys, but the removal of his name also robbed him of proper recognition for his significant contribution to the publication.

In late 1789 Roberts was appointed to command a new *Discovery*, named in Cook's honor, for an expedition to search for bases for English whalers in the South Pacific and fur traders on the Northwest

Coast. But the **Nootka Sound Incident** caused a postponement, and other plans ultimately resulted in Roberts receiving a new command that took him to the West Indies. The Pacific expedition, redesigned into an exhaustive survey of the Pacific coast of North America, with an important diplomatic element, was given to **George Vancouver**.

ROQUEFEUIL, CAMILLE-JOSEPH, MARQUIS DE (1781–1831).

After the turmoil of revolution and Napoleonic adventure, France regained its interest in the Pacific and the commercial possibilities of the Northwest Coast, dormant since the era of **Jean François de La Pérouse** and **Etienne Marchand**. A voyage was sponsored by the Bordeaux trading firm of Balguerie, with the support of the French navy, which provided charts and a chronometer. The expectation was that commerce and exploration in the national interest would result.

Commanding *Le Bordelais*, Roquefeuil sailed the entire length of the Northwest Coast from Spanish **California** to **Russian America** in 1817–1819. His journal is important for the wealth of information about the **native** peoples and its commentary on European settlements. Roquefeuil traveled to **San Francisco** and **Fort Ross**, to **Nootka Sound** (where he met an aged **Maquinna** remembering the halcyon days of **Juan Francisco de la Bodega y Quadra** and **George Vancouver**), to **New Archangel** (where he encountered **Ludwig von Hagemeister**), to **Kodiak**, and to the **Queen Charlotte Islands**. Among the islands of the **Alexander Archipelago** he undertook extensive exploration, and participated in trading partnerships with employees of the **Russian–American Company** during which he added comments to Vancouver's hydrographic observations and survived an attack by **Tlingit** natives. The commercial success of the voyage was limited by American competition, the inadequacy of French trade goods, and the lone nature of the initiative, but it gave French authorities up-to-date information about the Northwest Coast, and suggested that success in the **fur trade** might be possible with a series of well-organized expeditions. But France had actually lost contact with the North Pacific, in which others now enjoyed the ascendancy, and its commercial interests ultimately became focused elsewhere.

ROYAL SOCIETY. Granted its charter in 1662, although its members had already been meeting for some time, the Royal Society of London for the Improvement of Natural Knowledge is the oldest learned society in Britain. It brought together "worthy persons, inquisitive into natural philosophy and other parts of human learning," and its *Philosophical Transactions* (1664) is the oldest continuous scientific publication in the world. Historically the society has been called upon by the British government for advice on scientific matters and potential undertakings of national importance; likewise the society has often urged support of the government for matters it deems worthy of attention.

In the mid-18th century the society was essentially a forum for gentlemen with mutual interests, and any influence stemmed more from individual connections and the wealth of its officers and fellows, than it did from its strength as an organization. The latter only really took shape during the long presidency of Sir **Joseph Banks**, 1778–1820, when administration was improved and fellowship made more difficult to attain.

In the world of 18th-century geographical discovery and exploration, the most obvious confluence of interest between the society and government can be found in the voyages of **James Cook** to observe the Transit of Venus, and to search for the southern continent and a Northwest Passage; also in the work of the Royal Observatory at Greenwich with its related interest in the improvement of instruments of **navigation** and the correct determination of longitude. In 1775 Cook was elected a fellow, and a year later was awarded the Society's Copley Medal for the research for his paper on methods of preserving the **health** of men at sea. From before the period of Cook's involvement with the Royal Society in the 1770s, there existed a complementary organization, the Royal Society Club, a dining club that offered fellows the chance to meet more informally. The presence at these gatherings of Banks and such influential members as **Alexander Dalrymple**, the astronomer royal Nevil Maskelyne and the jurist **Daines Barrington**, all keenly interested in the emerging geography of the Northwest Coast and the promise of a Northwest Passage, would have meant regular discussion of these matters. After all, it was Barrington, well-connected to the Admiralty through his friendship with the first lord, the Earl of Sandwich, who as early as 1774 had received society support for a proposal for "a Ship or Ships . . . to run to the Northern Parts of New Albion . . . proceed up the North western side of that continent, so as to discover whether there is passage into the European Seas"—the genesis of Cook's Third Voyage. In the wake of that voyage, the rise of the Northwest Coast maritime **fur trade** and the **Nootka Crisis**, the dining club and wider society's interest in, and support for, what became **George Vancouver's** voyage would have been obvious.

RUMIANTSEV, NIKOLAI (1754–1826). An influential Russian statesman and patron of the arts and sciences, Nikolai Rumiantsev developed an abiding interest in **Russian America**, and became a major shareholder in the **Russian–American Company** (RAC). In 1802 he became minister of commerce and was especially keen to promote trade in the far east and to expand Russia's influence in the North Pacific. He was convinced that the role of the RAC was crucial, a conviction shared by the RAC's principal lobbyist in St. Petersburg, **Nikolai Rezanov**. In 1800 Czar Paul I had decreed that all attempts to establish a diplomatic and trading relationship with Japan should flow through the RAC. Rumiantsev and Rezanov both supported **Ivan Kruzenshtern**'s idea that a regular naval presence was necessary in the North Pacific to help the RAC establish a strong colony, built on an effective trading relationship with China and Japan. Rumiantsev used his influence to have the Kruzenshtern and **Iurii Lisianskii** Expedition launched in 1803 as the first of regular round-the-world voyages of sovereignty and supply. It was largely paid for by the RAC, but sailed under the flag of the Navy. In terms of establishing Russian America, the interests of the state and the RAC became totally intertwined. He also supported the subsequent expedition and voyages of **Ludwig von Hagemeister**, 1806–1810. In 1808 Rumiantsev became minister of foreign affairs and in 1810 chairman of the State Council. Ill health at the time of Napoleon's invasion of Russia (1812) forced him to retire, but during the peace that followed he used his own extensive wealth to finance the **Otto von Kotzebue** Expedition, with its principal goal being the discovery of the **Northwest Passage** from the Pacific/Arctic coast of **Alaska** to Hudson Bay. When this dream failed, he pursued the idea of financing, with the RAC, an expedition to the Mackenzie River to link up with an official English expedition under the command of John Franklin, who 20 years later would lose his life in a spectacularly unsuccessful search for the great passage.

RUNNING SURVEY. The method of coastal surveying used by **James Cook**, **Jean François de La Pérouse**, and **Alejandro Malaspina**, running survey provided a general and preliminary idea of the Northwest Coast. After determining the latitude and longitude of their offshore position, the explorers took the bearing of a prominent coastal feature, keeping the ship as stationary as possible. They would then move the vessel to another position and take a new bearing of the same feature. The distance between the two positions was then calculated by using a log to measure the distance traveled. Once this baseline was established and the angles measured, the latitude and longitude of the feature could also be calculated. By running surveys the explorers fixed the bearings of numerous features, moving on to new promontories while continuing to take bearings of all the points passed. It was thus possible to construct accurate, general maps, but until the Russians and **George Vancouver** undertook small boat surveys, more complex features like the **Alexander Archipelago** could not be revealed. *See also* CARTOGRAPHY; NAVIGATION.

RUSSIAN AMERICA. The colony known as Russian America emerged in the far northwest coastal region of North America over a period of 50 years following **Vitus Bering's** second **Kamchatka Expedition** in 1741. At first undefined as fur traders advanced through the **Aleutian Islands** and onto the **Alaska Peninsula**, it became clearer when Czar Paul I permitted the **Russian–American Company** to form a commercial monopoly in 1798–1799, and **Aleksandr Baranov**—who had arrived on the coast in 1791 to direct the affairs of its predecessor Shelikhov Company—was able to sustain his advance into the **Alexander Archipelago** with the founding of **New Archangel**, 1799–1804. Although other major European powers explored the Northwest Coast north of 55° N and entertained ideas of establishing commercial settlements, none was ultimately interested enough or able to do so in any significant way, with the brief exception of the **Hudson's Bay Company**. Continuous ship contact with Kamchatka and Okhotsk and regular naval voyages to the North Pacific served to maintain Russian sovereignty.

In 1824–1825 the southern boundary of the colony was fixed at latitude 54°40′ by treaties with the United States and Britain. The Anglo-Russian treaty also attempted to determine the coastal boundary north.

Simply put, the line of demarcation went up the Portland Canal; then parallel to the coast following the summits of the mountains as far as longitude 141° W; and then due north to the "Frozen Ocean." It was this territory that was sold to the United States in 1867 and became **Alaska**. The final fixing of the boundary of the Alaska Panhandle was the subject of a bitter late-19th-century dispute between the United States and Canada and Britain, and was only determined by a controversial settlement in 1903. *See* RUSSIAN AMERICA BOUNDARY CONVENTIONS.

RUSSIAN AMERICA BOUNDARY CONVENTIONS, 1824 & 1825. The southern boundary of **Russian America** was fixed at 54°40′ N by treaties between the government of Czar Alexander I and the United States of America on 17 April 1824, and with Britain on 28 February 1825. These were influenced by two events: the agreement between the United States and Great Britain in 1818 to establish joint control over the **Oregon** country, which both assumed stretched north to **Dixon Entrance** at 54°40′ N, and secondly by the 1821 Russian decision to ban all trade by foreigners with Russian America, whose southern boundary St. Petersburg unilaterally fixed at 51° N, off the northern end of **Vancouver Island**. As well as concern in both countries about freedom of trade and the idea of Russian expansion south along the coast, the United States was also alarmed by the fact that the czar was prepared, however impractical the reality, to assist Spain in the recovery of its former colonies in Latin America. This was a clear challenge to America's growing self-confidence and recently proclaimed Monroe Doctrine (1821). In addition, the **Hudson's Bay Company** and the **Russian-America Company** were feuding over trading territory, the former claiming rights on the coast due to the voyage of **George Vancouver**, 1792–1794 (before the Russians moved in earnest out of **Prince William Sound**), the latter securely ensconced at **New Archangel**. Thus aroused, the United States and Britain challenged Russia's assumptions about the coast, and the treaties rolled back the boundary to 54°40′ N, and reopened trade with its colony.

RUSSIAN–AMERICAN COMPANY. Founded in 1798 and formally established a year later by a *ukase* of Czar Paul I, the Russian–American Company (RAC) charter granted the company a monopoly over trade in Russia's American possessions for 20 years and effectively gave it complete political autonomy. In this way it mirrored the **Hudson's Bay Company**. The charter was renewed with few changes in 1821 and 1842. The RAC was still the dominant economic and political force when the United States purchased **Alaska** in 1867, despite the fact that there had been no third renewal of its charter. The RAC was liquidated in 1881.

The RAC was the ultimate survivor of numerous trading companies formed from the 1740s onwards to sponsor fur-trading voyages, exploring and hunting into the Commander, Kurile, Aleutian, and Pribilof islands. Overhunting gradually necessitated longer voyages and better ships which, by the 1780s, had begun to reach mainland America bordering the Gulf of Alaska. Fierce competition gradually reduced the number of viable companies; in 1781 there were seven, by 1795 only three—the Northeastern American Company of **Grigorii Shelikhov** and Ivan Golikov based on **Kodiak** Island; the Irkutsk Company in **Prince William Sound**; and the **Pavel Lebedev-Lastochkin** Company on the **Kenai Peninsula** and in **Cook Inlet**. In 1797 the first two combined to form the United American Company, and when its remaining rival essentially collapsed in 1798, it became the nucleus of the Russian–American Company that same year.

The affairs of the RAC were overseen by a Board of Directors in St. Petersburg, but the governors general, most notably **Aleksandr Baranov** from 1799 to 1818, directed matters in the colony from its capital **New Archangel**, exercising immense power and influence. Between its twin headquarters, the RAC maintained other important offices, principally in Irkutsk and Okhotsk, until 1844 when port operations were moved to Aian. Through these two locations passed the furs for Europe and for sale into China at Kiakhta on the Mongolian border (the Russians were excluded from Canton), and the all-important mail between St. Petersburg and New Archangel.

Although its priority was the procurement of furs, the RAC undertook detailed exploration of the Alaskan coast and introduced agriculture, cattle farming, and the trades. It extended Russian rule over the **native** populations and established and strengthened Imperial Russia's strategic position in the North Pacific. In the long run, however, the RAC failed to maintain a sustainable food economy or to attract sufficient colonists to give **Russian America** the sort of permanence necessary to ensure continued interest in its future by the government in far-off St. Petersburg.

RUSSIAN ORTHODOX CHURCH. The introduction of Christianity via the Russian Orthodox Church was an important feature of the advance of the *promyshlenniki* through the **Aleutian Islands** between 1750 and 1780. These laymen brought the symbols of their faith aboard their saint-named ships, regularly conducted prayer services in which the **natives** were invited to participate, and established godparent relationships with young **Aleuts**. The best-documented example of the latter is **Stepan Glotov**'s ties to Ivan Stepanovich Glotov, a native of **Umnak Island**, who was educated in Russia and became a valued interpreter living on **Unimak Island**. The adoption of Christianity by the Aleuts, and later by the Alutiiq, Chugach, **Tlingit**, and Yup'it, did not result from traditional missionary activity with its culturally destructive demands of use of the colonial language, abandonment of native customs, and a change in lifestyle. From the start, the monks and priests who soon followed the laymen, and the natives who themselves spread the faith into areas where there was no sustained Russian presence, spoke in native languages. Especially in the Aleutians, round the Gulf of Alaska, and on the **Bering Sea** coast, they built on similarities between the new faith and traditional beliefs: acceptance of a creator; use of water as a medium of healing and transformation; the practice of fasting; and the concept of confession.

The first formal mission came to **Kodiak** in 1794, and the presence of priests and monks helped to mitigate the worst types of abuse of the natives by their Russian conquerors. It was a constant battle, not appreciated by **Aleksandr Baranov** and his contemporaries. The first church in **Alaska** was built at St. Paul's Harbor in 1796. The influence of the venerated monk German (St. Herman of Alaska) and Hieromonk Gideon consolidated Orthodoxy in the Kodiak region. The latter was also important because his papers reveal much about the ethnography of the Alutiiq-speaking natives of Kodiak, and about the **Ivan Kruzenshtern** and **Iurii Lisianskii** Expedition, which brought him to the fledgling colony. During his time in **Russian America** (1804–1807) he not only traveled around the islands of the region by *baidarka*, but also taught school in St. Paul, and compiled the first Alutiiq-Russian dictionary.

By the second decade of the 19th century the gradual spread of Christianity in the colony had led to a demand for priests in several areas of Alaska, notably in **Unalaska**, Kodiak, and **New Archangel**, where a chapel dedicated to St. Michael had been built in 1804. The **Russian–American Company** brought the first priest to the capital in 1816. The 1820s were important for the future of the church as the government, in renewing the RAC's charter in 1821, stipulated that a number of health, educational, and religious services be maintained. In 1824, the legendary **Ioann Veniaminov** arrived to serve the eastern Aleutians from Illiuliuk on Unalaska.

– S –

SACRED EXPEDITION, 1769. When he decided to settle **Alta California** to defend the northwest frontier of **New Spain**, **José de Gálvez** determined that it would be a spiritual as well as a military initiative; the foundation of missions was to be as important as the establishment of presidios. In this way the principal method of extending Spanish authority in **Baja California** was continued in the north.

Gálvez planned a two-pronged—maritime and land—approach for the expedition to **San Diego** and beyond. Two packetboats, the *San Antonio* and the *San Carlos*, sailed from La Paz at the beginning of 1769. The former was commanded by **Juan Pérez**, who arrived in **San Diego** on 11 April; the *San Carlos* followed on 29 April. The land contingent consisted of two detachments under Gaspar de Portolá, governor of Baja California and overall commander of the expedition, and Fernando de Rivera y Moncada. The latter, accompanied by Father **Juan Crespí**, reached San Diego towards the end of May; Portolá did not arrive with Father **Junípero Serra** until July. Because so many of the expeditionaries were overcome with sickness and many had died, the *San Antonio* was sent back to La Paz for reinforcements and supplies, while the *San Carlos* and Portolá set out to find **Monterey**, the "desirable port" of **Sebastián Vizcaíno** (1602). The search failed that summer because, although the expedition reached the right location, Portolá did not believe that the great, wide-open bay matched Vizcaíno's positive description. He pushed on and, in November, some members of his party were the first to reach **San Francisco** Bay and see **Point Reyes**. Realizing that he had somehow passed Monterey, Portolá retraced his steps and arrived back in San Diego on 24 January 1770. Ironically, other members of his group, who were exploring away from the main expedition, planted a cross on the still unrecognized shore of Monterey Bay on 9 December 1769.

In March Portolá was ready to abandon the expedition because of the sorry state of affairs at San Diego, but the arrival of supplies with the *San Antonio* allowed him to plan a return to what he now realized must have been Monterey Bay. The expedition set out in mid-April 1770, determined to establish a presidio and mission. It arrived on 24 May, followed by the *San Antonio* on 31 May. On 3 June ceremonies of possession and establishment were conducted, and the presidio and mission were formally founded.

SALAMANCA, SECUNDINO (ca. 1768–1839). After working under the famous hydrographer Vicente Tofiño in the Azores Islands, Secundino Salamanca joined the **Alejandro Malaspina** Expedition, sailing from Cadiz in the *Descubierta* in 1789. He first came to the Northwest Coast, visiting **Yakutat Bay** and **Nootka Sound**, in the summer of 1791. During his time at Nootka he wrote a long dissertation about the lifestyle and customs of the **native** people. It was his work with **Dionisio Alcalá Galiano** during the circumnavigation of **Vancouver Island** in 1792, however, that was particularly important. He was detached from the main expedition to serve on the *Sutil*, and he was almost constantly involved in the expedition's small boat surveys and visits to native villages. Alcalá Galiano named Loughborough Inlet Canal de Salamanca after him, and there is a drawing by **José Cardero** of Salamanca working in a launch in those waters.

SAMWELL, DAVID (1751–1798). While sailing on **James Cook**'s voyage to the North Pacific as a doctor, David Samwell wrote what is arguably the most important journal of the voyage after the official Cook/King account. *Some Account of a Voyage to the South Sea's in 1776–1777–1778* covered the entire voyage, and his detailed eyewitness account of Cook's death is widely quoted; many historians consider it the most reliable. Samwell probably received his medical training at sea, and he is known to have been on a voyage to

Greenland in 1771. In 1776 Cook appointed him assistant surgeon to William Anderson on the *Resolution*. When Anderson died in 1778, he was replaced by John Law and Samwell became surgeon on the *Discovery*.

The well-rounded and detailed descriptions of the **natives** encountered at **Nootka Sound**, **Prince William Sound**, and on the island of **Unalaska**, are especially important to ethnographers. Samwell was a curious observer and not only described the natives' language, appearance, dress, and food, but also their habitations, tools, and artistic efforts and, especially at Nootka, their interest in trade, particularly for iron. At Samgoonoodah Harbor he noted that the **Aleuts** were in a "state of subjection to the Russians" and that there was no real trade because they had stripped the place of all its available furs.

SAN BLAS. The Naval Department of San Blas on the Pacific Coast of **New Spain** was established in 1768. The initial motivation for founding the port was military not naval, as **José de Gálvez** was interested in the transport of soldiers, ammunition, and supplies by sea, rather than overland, for his campaign against the natives of Sonora. But once established, its development as a naval department in supplying the presidios and missions of **Alta California**, and supporting exploration and the supply of the establishment in **Nootka Sound** became predominant.

It was never a popular place for those who had to live and work there, and from the early 1770s there were endless debates about investing in improvements or relocation. Although a decision was finally made in 1794 to shift operations to Acapulco, this did not take place until well into the 19th century. Once a complex of buildings was constructed on the bluff overlooking the waterfront, and the naval officers were permitted to set up living quarters in the inland town of Tepic, maintaining the operation rather than actually relocating it was always the easier option.

The problem was the humid climate from May to October, which, although responsible for the abundance of hardwoods that made the site attractive for ship construction, brought plagues of mosquitoes from the surrounding swamps. Also the harbor was never more than a tidal channel that required constant dredging. Other benefits were a good supply of fresh water, the proximity to Guadalajara, and the shortness of voyages to Loreto in **Baja California** and to negotiate Cabo St. Lucas en route to the northern coast. Over a period of 30 years San Blas grew into a bustling hive of activity and in the early 1790s, at the height of official interest in Alta California and the Northwest Coast, had a population of 20,000 people of whom over 700 were officials involved in naval operations.

SAN DIEGO. The bay on which San Diego now stands was discovered on 28 September 1542 by **Juan Rodríguez Cabrillo**, and named Bahia de San Miguel. This was changed to San Diego by **Sebastián Vizcaíno**, who named it after his flagship, the *St. Didacus*, in 1602. It was settled following the arrival of the **Sacred Expedition** of 1769, which founded a presidio and mission. San Diego never grew and prospered in the Spanish period as much as **Monterey**, which became the capital of the two Californias in 1776. At the end of the 18th century, there were less than 200 nonnative settlers.

SAN FRANCISCO. In 1592 the name "San Francisco" appeared on a Dutch map by Peter Plancius to signify a cape south of **Cape Mendocino** in almost exactly the same latitude as the present-day city. Although this is now considered to belong to the realm of imaginary geography, the name Bahia de San Francisco was given to Drake's Bay by **Sebastián Rodríguez Cermeño** when he anchored there in 1595.

At the end of October 1769 a detachment from the **Sacred Expedition** of Gaspar de Portolá saw the wide sweep of the Gulf of the Farallones and believed that they had rediscovered Cermeño's bay. A few days later they saw what is now San Francisco Bay but considered it an estuary to the main bay. The Puerto and Estero de San Francisco appeared on a map by Miguel Costansó printed in Madrid in 1772, the same year that Father **Juan Crespí** made a sketch of the estuary. In 1774 Viceroy **Antonio María de Bucareli** decided to occupy the port, which led to **Juan Manuel de Ayala** sailing the *San Carlos* through the Golden Gate on 4 August 1775; he and the pilots **José Cañizares** and Juan Bautista Aguirre undertook the first proper marine survey of the area, and Cañizares drew a map that identified the bay as the Puerto de San Francisco. The arrival overland of **Juan Bautista de Anza** in March 1776 led to the dedication of the mission of Saint Francis on 29 June 1776 (five days before the American

Declaration of Independence) and the dedication of the presidio on 17 September. In 1779 **Esteban José Martínez** provided an extensive description of San Francisco Bay and the fledgling Spanish settlement during a coastal voyage that also took him to **Monterey** and **San Diego**. Later that year **José Camacho**, serving on the **Ignacio de Arteaga** and **Juan Francisco de la Bodega y Quadra** Expedition, which made a visit during its return to **New Spain** from **Alaska**, updated earlier maps by identifying the sites of the presidio and mission.

SAN JUAN BOUNDARY DISPUTE. In the San Juan Boundary Dispute, a controversy between the United States and Great Britain over the U.S.–Canada maritime boundary in southern **British Columbia,** the problem arose from the inexact wording of the **Oregon Treaty,** 1846, which established the northern boundary of the Oregon Territory. That agreement set the boundary in the **Strait of Georgia** south of 49° N as a line through the middle of the channel between the mainland and **Vancouver Island** and westward into the Pacific Ocean via the **Strait of Juan de Fuca**. But at its southern end the former strait breaks into several channels, and between the two larger ones—Haro Strait and Rosario Strait—lie the San Juan Islands. Ownership of the islands, especially San Juan Island, was disputed. The lack of clarity created a crisis in 1859 when an American settler Lyman Cutler shot a pig belonging to the **Hudson's Bay Company** because it was trespassing on his land. When U.S. troops occupied the island, British warships rushed to the scene. Before a so-called Pig War could erupt, cooler heads prevailed and joint occupation of the island was arranged pending a final decision. Attempts to appoint a neutral arbitrator were frustrated until the Washington Treaty of 1871 dealt with a number of irritants between the two countries. They agreed to submit the dispute to an arbitration panel headed by Emperor William I of Germany. The Americans, as inheritors of Spanish rights, used the chart of the 1791 **Francisco de Eliza** Expedition to argue prior discovery—that Haro Strait should be the boundary and that the islands rightfully belonged to them. The panel agreed and gave the San Juan archipelago to the United States.

SANDWICH ISLANDS. *See* HAWAII.

SANDWICH SOUND. *See* PRINCE WILLIAM SOUND.

SANTA MARÍA, VICENTE (1742–1806). Vicente Santa María came to **New Spain** in 1769 and was attached to the College of San Fernando, the seminary for missionaries in Mexico City from where he was seconded to serve as chaplain on the *San Carlos* in 1775. While **Bruno de Hezeta** and **Juan Francisco de la Bodega y Quadra** headed for the coast north of **California**, Father Vicente accompanied **Juan Manuel de Ayala** to **Monterey** with supplies and then participated in the first naval visit to **San Francisco**. His "Journal of Events in the discovery of the Harbor of San Francisco" was published in English in 1971, and shows that he was more interested in his encounters with the **natives** of the area than in the marine surveys being undertaken by his naval colleagues. He spent a good deal of time on shore and describes visits to two different villages, as well as a visit by a group of natives to the ship. In submitting his report to his superior, he expressed the opinion that sustained missionary activity could be successful. The next year he again served as chaplain when the *San Carlos* made a return visit to San Francisco to support the founding of the presidio and mission, and to undertake further surveys. In 1793 he was serving at San Buenaventura, south of Santa Barbara, when he was visited by **George Vancouver** en route to **Hawaii** after his second season on the Northwest Coast. Vancouver wrote that "the garden at Buena Ventura far exceeded anything . . . I had before met in these regions, both in respect to the quality, quantity and variety of its excellent productions." When Vicente visited the ships he brought 10 sheep for their voyage and 20 donkeys loaded with fresh fruits and vegetables. As Vancouver commented: "having crossed the ocean more than once himself, he was well aware how valuable the fresh productions of the shores were to persons in our situation." He named the southern point of Santa Monica Bay after his benefactor "Father Vincente [sic]." Point Vicente today retains this name as a reminder of the meeting between the English navigator and the generous Franciscan.

SARYCHEV, GAVRIIL (1763–1831). Naval officer, explorer, and hydrographer Gavriil Sarychev was assigned to the **Joseph Billings** Expedition in 1785. Contemporaries **Martin Sauer** and **Ivan**

Kruzenshtern were fulsome in their praise of his skills and contribution to the expedition, to the extent that they suggested, perhaps unfairly to Billings, that what accomplishments it achieved were largely due to him.

Crossing Siberia with Billings and Sauer in 1786, Sarychev navigated down the Kolyma River to the East Siberian Sea from which he accompanied Billings on a voyage to the east that was frustrated by ice. Returning to Okhotsk he explored the coast to the north in a *baidarka* before embarking with Billings in the *Slava Rossii* (Glory of Russia) to go to **Unalaska** and to spend the summer of 1790 on the Northwest Coast. During this voyage he visited **Prince William Sound** and the coast southeast to **Mount St. Elias**. The next year he was again on the same ship returning to Unalaska before heading north into the **Bering Sea**. Here the expedition discovered Hall Island and surveyed the strait between it and **St. Matthew Island**, naming it after Sarychev. It then surveyed **St. Lawrence Island**, the east side of the **Bering Strait**, and the **Diomede Islands**.

In August 1791 Billings gave him command of the ship with orders to return to Unalaska for the winter. Sarychev was joined there by **Robert Hall** in the *Chernyi Orel* (Black Eagle), and the two officers reinforced Russian authority over the **Aleuts**. In January 1792 Sarychev directed one of his officers to explore the islands east of Unalaska, which led to the discovery and naming of the Khudiakov Islands off the north coast of the **Alaska Peninsula**. In February he took to a *baidarka* again and embarked on a detailed exploration of the north and west coasts of Unalaska during which, except on one occasion when an attack was foiled, he enjoyed excellent relations with the Aleuts. At this time also, he gathered important information about the number of Aleuts on Unalaska, **Umnak**, and in the present-day Krenitzin Islands, estimating that there were about 4,500 people living in 40 villages that included 916 able-bodied men. In May the ships left the islands for home and reached Petropavlovsk the following month. Returning to Okhotsk, Sarychev stayed there a year before accompanying Billings back to St. Petersburg. He received the first of a series of promotions in an illustrious naval career that lasted until his death, by which time he was a full admiral and had been commander of the naval base at Kronstadt, hydrographer-general of the navy, acting commandant of the naval staff, and acting minister of the navy.

In 1802 Sarychev published a journal of the expedition with an accompanying atlas, notable for its drawings, coastal profiles, and charts. In 1811 he published another account of the expedition that added information from Hall's journal. In 1826 he was responsible for the production of an important atlas, which contained twenty-six maps and plans, and summarized the work of a number of explorers and navigators. It was particularly important for its contribution to the toponyms of the northern and eastern coasts of continental Russia and the coast of **Russian America**.

SAUER, MARTIN (fl. 1785–1806). An English civil servant who knew Russian, French, and German, Martin Sauer became acquainted with **Joseph Billings** in St. Petersburg in the 1780s. He agreed to join Billings's expedition as his secretary and interpreter. It was agreed that he would write the official account, but there is some controversy about his activities when he returned to St. Petersburg in 1794. It has been suggested that he left hurriedly for England with much of the important archival material from the voyage, including diaries and secret reports, so that he could publish a record of the expedition before Russian authorities and scholars in the Academy of Sciences could review its details. Given this opinion, it is somewhat odd that he was back in the capital in 1806, four years after the publication appeared. Sauer's *An Account of a Geographical and Astronomical Expedition to the Northern Parts of Russia . . . performed by command of Her Imperial Majesty Catherine the Second . . . by Commodore Joseph Billings in the years 1785 . . . 1794* was published in London in 1802. It contains an abundance of detail about eastern Siberia and the **Aleutian Islands**, and records the expedition's visits to **Kodiak** Island, **Prince William Sound**, and the coast south as far as **Yakutat Bay**. The chart was made by **Aaron Arrowsmith** from Sauer's notes and Billings's observations, and the whole complements well the other contemporary accounts of the expedition by the cartographer **Gavriil Sarychev** and the naturalist **Carl Heinrich Merck**.

SCHAEFFER, GEORG (1779–1836). A German-born doctor, Georg Schaeffer went to Russia in 1808 and worked as an army surgeon. In 1814 he arrived in **New Archangel** as the physician on one of the round-the-world supply ships of the **Russian–American Company**

(RAC). At this point **Aleksandr Baranov** recruited him to go to **Hawaii** and represent Russian interests, promoting the sandalwood trade and negotiating the release of a cargo of furs that had been appropriated by one of the local rulers, King Kaumualii. Baranov was keen to establish a Hawaiian connection to forge supply and commercial links that could benefit the RAC's fledgling colony, but Schaeffer was a self-important adventurer and quite the wrong person to be entrusted with a diplomatic assignment. When he arrived on the island of Oahu in late 1815, he quickly undermined Baranov's directives and alienated King Kamehameha by defiling a *morai* and erecting a fort. The next year he moved on to Kauai where he aligned himself with Kamehameha's rival, Kaumualii, promising him the protection of the Russian emperor and support of the Russian navy in return for a promise to restore the furs, a pledge of allegiance to the czar, an exclusive trading relationship with the RAC, and permission for the company to build factories. Schaeffer himself built a grand fort and established plantations.

The whole initiative fell apart when **Otto von Kotzebue** arrived on Oahu in November 1816 and informed Kamehameha that under no circumstance did the Russian government support Schaeffer's antics. When the king threatened war on his rival, Kaumualii expelled Schaeffer from Kauai. He left Hawaii in disgrace, returning to St. Petersburg, where he was conspicuously unsuccessful in persuading the RAC's directors to compound the expensive disaster by trying to assert Russian authority in Hawaii. Any expectations by Baranov that Hawaii might be useful to the RAC and come within Russia's sphere of influence came to naught through Schaeffer's arrogance and bumbling miscalculation of Hawaiian politics. In 1818 the czar, receiving strong naval advice, confirmed that Russia could see no benefits in bringing the Hawaiian Islands under imperial protection.

SCIENTISTS. The intellectual revolution that characterized the 18th-century enlightenment and "age of reason" had at its center the concept of naturalism—a belief that the study and observation of reality, both human and natural, would reveal truths that would continue to challenge, effectively, the wisdom of ancient authority and the superstitions that often accompanied it. Jean-Jacques Rousseau believed that much could be learned from the "noble savage" and simpler societies to redirect the sorry state of the human condition as found in Europe; and natural scientists were as keen to document the natural world as governments were to discover new lands to expand commercial interests and thus strengthen the state. To serve the enthusiasm for new knowledge, Denis Diderot published the multivolume *Encyclopédie* (1751–1776) as a major reference work of the arts and sciences, explaining the new sciences of physics and cosmology and introducing the new philosophies of naturalism and humanism.

In this context, naval voyages of exploration for imperial advantage, as well as purely commercial enterprise, offered valuable platforms for research. Although voyage journals (with their accompanying charts and geographical reports, **artifact** collections and the significant contributions of many **artists**) are replete with descriptions of the native peoples encountered in the Pacific, and thus contributed to the nascent discipline of anthropology that would flourish in the later 19th century, there was a special interest at the end of the 18th century in how voyages might serve the interests of natural science. The reasons for this were essentially practical—the identification of plants with medicinal properties, of woods for shipbuilding, and of minerals such as iron ore and copper. An additional reason was the existence of a series of major works of nomenclature produced by mid-century by the Swedish botanist Carolus Linnaeus (1707–1778), that gave the scientists who traveled to the Northwest Coast, as elsewhere, a classification system within which to work.

After his experience on **James Cook**'s First Voyage, Sir **Joseph Banks** became the chief proponent of the value of voyages to develop scientific enquiry. Much of the voyage-related artistic work produced in the period was to illustrate flora and fauna, birds and fish. David Nelson continued the Banks tradition on Cook's Third Voyage, but by far the most important naturalists on the coast at the end of the 18th century, following the very early pioneering work of **Georg Wilhelm Steller** in the 1740s, were **Tadeo Haenke**, **Archibald Menzies**, **José Mariano Moziño**, **José Maldonado**, and **Carl Heinrich Merck**. Sadly, the core work done by **Jean-Honoré Lamanon** and his colleagues was lost with the shipwreck of the **La Pérouse** Expedition, but the Frenchman did leave a remarkable picture of the experience of the voyager-scientist: "The pleasures I enjoy are great. I work more than 12 hours a day, yet can never finish my work: fish to dissect, quadrupeds to describe, insects to catch; shells to classify, events to record, mountains to measure, stones to collect, languages to study, new experiences to have, a journal to keep, nature to contemplate. I wish for all this that I could expand my life 20 times." Under the general direction of the Academy of Sciences, scientists on the Russian naval voyages of the 19th century more than carried forward the work of their Russian, British, Spanish, and French precursors. Particularly significant were the contributions of **Adelbert Chamisso**, **Johann Eschscholtz**, **Aleksandr Postels**, **Karl-Heinrich Mertens**, and **Friedrich Heinrich von Kittlitz**. Although he came on the scene late, perhaps the most distinguished and important scientist of all was the Russian scholar, naturalist, and ethnographer **Il'ia Voznesenskii**, who worked in both **Russian America** and **California**.

Much of the results of the collecting activity of the scientists who worked on the Northwest Coast of America still survives in museums and botanical gardens from St. Petersburg and Berlin, to Paris, London, Edinburgh, and Madrid, and in the Americas in Washington, D.C., and Mexico City. These collections of specimens, field notes, and reports are a testament to the courage, dedication, enthusiasm, and energy of the Northwest Coast's pioneer scientists.

SCURVY. *See* HEALTH.

SEA OF THE WEST. A mythical sea in the heart of North America, the Sea of the West had its origin in Giovanni Verrazano's sighting, in 1524, of Pamlico Sound behind Cape Hatteras on the coast of present-day North Carolina. His report of open water held out the promise of a link to the Pacific Ocean. As explorers from New France, notably Robert La Salle in the 1680s, traveled southwest into the interior of the continent, the "Sea of Verrazano" was pushed to the west. A few years later, a map constructed by the most celebrated mapmaker of his day, Guillaume de l'Isle, but kept secret by French authorities, identified a huge "Mer de l'Ouest" beyond the Mississippi River and opening out into the Pacific. De l'Isle's maps and memoirs, however, survived his death in 1726 and the Sea of the West became popularized, along with the Strait of **Bartholomew de Fonte** on the maps of **Philippe Buache** and **Joseph Nicolas de l'Isle**

in 1752. They showed it exiting to the Pacific through the **Rio de Martín Aguilar** and the **Strait of Juan de Fuca**. Coastal and interior exploration finally disposed of this, and other enduring geographical myths, in the years 1790–1812. *See also* RIVER OF THE WEST.

SEA OTTERS. Marine mammals, sea otters rely on their thick fur coats rather than blubber to keep themselves warm. In response to demands for this fur in China, and later in Europe, sea otter pelts were sought by Russian *promyshlenniki* in the **Aleutian Islands** in the decades following **Vitus Bering**'s second **Kamchatka Expedition**, 1741–1742. The accidental discovery of the value of sea otter pelts in China acquired at Nootka by members of **James Cook**'s Third Voyage to the Pacific in 1778 led directly to European commercial and imperial rivalry on the Northwest Coast beginning in 1785, which hastened its final discovery and general exploration before the end of the 18th century.

SERRA, JUNÍPERO (1713–1784). Junípero Serra came to **New Spain** in 1749 to pursue his vocation of bringing Christianity to its native peoples. He was noted for his enthusiasm, energy, and unfailing dedication to the cause. After a decade in the field, he taught at the College of San Fernando, the Franciscan seminary in Mexico City, worked in villages near the capital, and traveled throughout the viceroyalty as a commissioner for the Inquisition.

Following the expulsion of the Jesuits (1767), he was named, in 1768, father-president of the missions in **Baja California**, which were transferred to the Franciscan Order, but within a year had been appointed by **José de Gálvez** to lead the spiritual mission to **Alta California**. He thus joined the **Sacred Expedition** in 1769. That summer he founded the mission of San Diego de Alcalá, the first of nine established during his lifetime. In 1770 he traveled to **Monterey**, where the second mission, dedicated to San Carlos Borromeo, was founded and became his headquarters. A year later he moved it to nearby Carmel to escape perceived interference by Governor **Pedro Fages** at the presidio, who opposed his restless zeal to establish more missions than could be protected, and his insistence that he be consulted on all decisions affecting relations with the **natives**. Over the years more missions were founded, and in moving constantly between them, up and down the coast, Serra and his companions explored the region and paved the way for its future settlement.

SHELIKHOV, GRIGORII (1748–1795). A leading merchant in the Aleutian **fur trade**, Grigorii Shelikhov founded the first permanent settlement in **Alaska**, and was a partner in the company that, after his death, gained a monopoly over the economic and political fortunes of **Russian America**.

In the 1770s he attached himself to another merchant, Ivan Golikov, and together they entered the highly profitable but fiercely competitive fur trade in the North Pacific. In 1762 **Catherine the Great** had rescinded the state monopoly on trade with China, and in 1774 abolished the 10 percent tax on furs. These developments brought new, large-scale, and politically well-connected entrepreneurs and capital into the trade, and gradually squeezed smaller companies out of business. Shelikhov and Golikov formed the American, Northeastern, North and Kurile Company that brought a new level of organization and efficiency to hunting and trading in the **Aleutian Islands**.

In August 1784 Shelikhov founded a settlement at **Three Saints Bay** on the southwest coast of **Kodiak** Island. Almost immediately, and in contravention to the law, he found a reason to attack the hostile natives. The result was swift, brutal, and effective; hundreds of Koniags were killed by the well-armed Russians, and many were taken hostage. It was a defining moment in the exploration of the northern Northwest Coast. The little settlement survived a harsh winter, and a small fort was built on Afognak Island. During 1786 Shelikhov's men reached **James Cook**'s Barren Islands before exploring outer **Cook Inlet** and establishing a post on the **Kenai Peninsula** at Nan walek (English Bay). **Gerasim Izmailov** charted the entire coastline of Kodiak Island, and in 1787 **Evstrat Delarov**, who had already been to **Prince William Sound** from a base on Unga in the **Shumagin Islands**, established an outpost at Karluk on the Shelikhov Strait side of Kodiak. From the Shumagins the company's activities had quickly moved west to **Unalaska**. In 1786 and 1787 the two **Pribilof Islands** were discovered. In order to find more men and supplies for his establishments, Shelikhov returned to Okhotsk in 1786. The instructions to those left behind were to maintain the network of outposts and, humanely but firmly, to impress the natives into the service of the company. Once reinforcements arrived and the established posts were strengthened, exploration was undertaken to create new ones beyond the Kenai Peninsula on **Hinchinbrook Island** at Nuchek (**Port Etches**), in **Prince William Sound**, and down the coast to **Yakutat**. In 1788 Izmailov sailed beyond **Lituya Bay** as far as **Cross Sound**.

Shelikhov went back to Irkutsk in 1787 to submit a number of reports to the governor of Siberia. One of these described his experiences and was published in St. Petersburg in 1791; it was immediately translated into English as *A Voyage to America, 1783–1786*. A second edition appeared in 1792 with excerpts from Izmailov's 1788 journal.

For the remainder of his life Shelikhov relentlessly pursued his dream to strengthen his operations in America and to use his company as an instrument for extending the reach of the Russian Empire. His efforts took two forms. First, he set about building viable settlements on the ground. Before he left Kodiak Island, he had founded a school where native boys would be taught the Russian language, crafts such as woodworking and blacksmithing, the fundamentals of navigation, and the basics of Christianity. He enlisted the support of Golikov to press the government to sponsor a spiritual mission, which finally arrived in 1794 and took over responsibility for **Aleut/Alutiiq** education. Ships left Russia with seeds and animals to develop an agricultural infrastructure, and Shelikhov laid plans to develop shipbuilding facilities for which he later recruited the English shipbuilder **James Shields**. He envisioned an America with cities, vibrant with economic and cultural activity.

The second direction for his efforts was to impress upon the empress the need for a monopoly to create this reality, one backed by government loans and soldiers to create an effective military presence. Through his company, he argued, Russia would be able to exercise and extend its political, commercial, and military power throughout the North Pacific, keeping foreigners away from the coast while establishing profitable trading relationships in a great arc from the Philippines, Korea, and Japan to **New Spain**. For this ambitious program, Shelikhov successfully lobbied the support of successive governors of Siberia, but he failed to persuade the empress. Although by no means uninterested in the American adventure, as demonstrated by her willingness to send the **Joseph Billings** and Grigorii

Mulovskii expeditions halfway round the world, Catherine was more interested in trade than sovereignty. When Shelikhov arrived in the capital at the end of 1788, Russia was at war with Turkey and Sweden and there were no resources for empire building on the Northwest Coast of America. In addition, he was fighting off serious (and warranted) charges of mistreating the natives on Kodiak and Afognak Islands and was never able to shake off this blot on his reputation.

Nevertheless, Shelikhov was able during these years to deliver a masterstroke for the future. This was his appointment in 1790 of **Aleksandr Baranov** to manage his American establishments. Shelikhov died in 1795 but Baranov was to live for another 24 years. When the new czar proved open to the idea of a monopoly along the lines of the **Hudson's Bay Company**, Baranov demonstrated the skill, energy, and foresight to realize, at least in part, Shelikhov's ambitions for a "Russian" America.

SHELIKHOV, NATALIA (?–1810). Wife of **Grigorii Shelikhov**, Natalia Shelikhov provided strong support for her ambitious and energetic husband as he laid the foundations of his commercial power and influence during the 1780s. She accompanied him to **Kodiak** Island in 1784. After his early death, she was instrumental in carrying forward his dream of a commercial empire in America, and emerged in the late 1790s as the most powerful force, supported by her well-connected son-in-law **Nikolai Rezanov**, in the formation and development of the **Russian–American Company**.

SHIELDS, JAMES (?–1799). British naval officer and shipbuilder, he came to Russia in the late 1780s under the auspices of Colonel Samuel Bentham, a promoter of British–Russian cooperation, who knew **Grigorii Shelikhov** and of his desire to build ships for work in the North Pacific. He was sent to Okhotsk, where he built the *Severo-vostochnyi Orel* (Northeastern Eagle) for service among the fur-trading posts of the **Aleutian Islands**, and on the continent. Thereafter, Shields remained in Pacific waters and was a key figure in the expansion of Shelikhov's operations on the American coast.

In 1792 Shelikhov sent him in the *Orel* with a load of shipbuilding supplies to **Kodiak** Island. He took orders to **Aleksandr Baranov** to develop a shipbuilding industry using native labor. But the native situation was too unstable and the island was unable to sustain such a project. Baranov, who had personally explored the coast of the **Kenai Peninsula** and **Prince William Sound** during the summer of 1792, decided to send Shields to the mainland where a shipyard was established in 1793 at the head of Resurrection Bay, in the vicinity of present-day Seward. Here he built a frigate, the *Phoenix*, completed in 1794. He drew a couple of sketches of the establishment at the time of her launch. That summer Shields received news that **George Vancouver** was on the coast, and sent him a letter via Russian traders who delivered it off **Yakutat Bay**. It invited Vancouver to make use of his facilities and asked for any reading material with news of England. But neither the *Chatham* nor *Discovery* was able to visit as they were heading down the coast rather than north and west. During the winter of 1794–1795, Shields built two small vessels near St. Paul's Harbor (Kodiak), and in 1795 sailed one of them to provide Baranov with a survey of the coast north from the **Queen Charlotte Islands**. This was in direct response to Vancouver's presence in Alaskan waters. He visited **Bucareli Bay**, **Sitka Sound**, and **Yakutat Bay**.

Baranov reported that Shields next wanted to explore the Alaskan coast side of the Bering Sea from the Alaska Peninsula to the Bering Strait, hoping to find the still-rumored passage to Hudson Bay. But he disallowed the venture, feeling uncertain about Shields's loyalty to Russia. Instead, Shields sailed southeast again in 1796, navigating the Lynn Canal and surveying potential harbors on Sitka Island. From his various voyages Shields created a chart of the coast from Kodiak to 56° N.

In 1798 he sailed the *Phoenix* to Okhotsk, but on the return voyage the ship was lost at sea. Providing a decade of service to Shelikhov and Baranov, Shields proved himself a valuable shipbuilder and explorer at a time when the Russians were seeking to advance down the coast towards **Dixon Entrance** in the face of the increasingly aggressive presence of English and American fur traders.

SHISHKIN, PETR (fl. 1750s–1760s). Petr Shishkin was an early Russian navigator, fur trader, and mapmaker. The voyages of the *promyshlenniki* from Okhotsk and **Kamchatka** reached the eastern **Aleutian Islands** and the **Alaska Peninsula** during the late 1750s and early 1760s. Using their experience as explorers, exploiting the knowledge of the natives they met, and gaining their help to undertake island coastal surveys by *baidarka*, the Russians compiled the first maps of the islands, and the coasts of the "Great Land."

One of the most revealing charts to have survived is by Shishkin, who sailed with **Stepan Glotov** in 1762. The map, which probably dates from the mid-1760s and could have had earlier incarnations, shows northeast Siberia and **Kamchatka**, the **Commander Islands** and the **Diomede Islands**. The names of many **Aleutian Islands** are present, including **Umnak** and **Unalaska**. **Kodiak** Island reflects the voyages of Glotov, and the **Alaska Peninsula** appears from the early explorations of **Gavriil Pushkarev**.

Shishkin's work was studied closely by the Admiralty and shown to the Empress **Catherine**. She had already become interested in the progress of the fur hunters largely as a result of the arrival in St. Petersburg in 1762 of the knowledgeable and influential **Fedor Soimonov**. As early as 1763, acting on his advice, she approved the placement of naval officers on the hunting vessels to keep journals, make descriptions of the people and places encountered, draw charts, and ensure just treatment of the natives. The rapid and detailed revelation of islands and the "Great Land" of America in the North Pacific impressed upon the empress the need to send an official expedition to the area. This became the **Petr Krenitsyn** and **Mikhail Levashov** Expedition of 1768–1769, a major undertaking at the time of **James Cook**'s First Voyage in the South Pacific. In this context the value of the hunting voyages and the production of maps like that of Shishkin cannot be overestimated.

SHUMAGIN ISLANDS. An archipelago containing about 50 islands, the Shumagin Islands lie south of the lower section of the **Alaska Peninsula**. **Vitus Bering** named one of them, Nagai, after Nikita Shumagin, a crew member of the *St. Peter* who died of scurvy and was buried there in 1741. It was the only occasion in either of his two **Kamchatka Expeditions** that Bering did not name a place in accordance with the church calendar. Later the sailor's name was transferred to the entire island group. Bering's men explored and landed on various islands and **Georg Wilhelm Steller** gathered up a collection of plants. The next visitors were **Stepan Glotov** and **Gavriil Pushkarev** in the early 1760s, as they passed through to reach **Kodiak** Island and the Alaska Peninsula. **James Cook** negotiated the islands in June 1778, and his chart distinguished them clearly from the continent.

SIERRA, BENITO DE LA (?–1778). With another priest, **Miguel de la Campa Cos**, Benito de la Sierra was seconded to serve as a chaplain on the voyage of **Bruno de Hezeta** to the Northwest Coast in 1775. He and Campa produced almost identical diaries detailing the progress of the expedition. His account surfaced in the 1920s and was then translated into English. In his introduction to the text, Henry Wagner states that Sierra also made two voyages to **Monterey** from **San Blas** in 1776 and 1777, as chaplain on supply vessels.

SIMPSON, GEORGE (ca. 1787–1860). Governor of the **Hudson's Bay Company** (HBC), first of its Columbia and Northern Departments, then in 1826 of the entire operation, George Simpson made three visits to the Pacific Coast, in 1824, 1828, and 1841. Beginning with **Fort Vancouver** on the **Columbia River** in 1825, he directed the establishment of a series of coastal trading forts (Langley, Simpson, McLoughlin, Stikine, and Taku during the period 1827–1840) that effectively ended American domination of the maritime **fur trade** and, through the activities of trading vessels such as the *William & Ann*, *Cadboro*, and *SS Beaver*, extended the detailed exploration of the coast inherited by the HBC from **George Vancouver**. After his last visit, the number of posts was reduced. Activity was consolidated around Forts Langley, Simpson, and Victoria, but coastal shipping increased.

SINDT, IVAN (fl. 1741–1779). Early in his career Ivan Sindt sailed with **Vitus Bering** to America. He survived the winter of 1741–1742 on **Bering Island**. Under the direction of **Fedor Soimonov**, governor of Siberia, and an experienced naval officer and cartographer, Sindt became involved in survey work on the coasts of the Sea of Okhotsk and **Kamchatka**, 1761–1765. By 1766 his efforts were directed towards the **Bering Strait** and the coast of North America opposite the Chukotskii Peninsula. He sighted **St. Lawrence Island**, which he reported as many separate islands, and undertook an accurate survey of the **Diomede Islands**. Running the American coast as far as Cape

Rodney at the northern entrance to **Norton Sound**, he discovered **St. Matthew Island** in September 1766 en route for Avacha Bay. A number of scholars believe that Sindt's expedition was linked to the more ambitious voyage of Vasilii Chichagov, who unsuccessfully tried to pioneer a polar route to the Pacific in 1766, and to the **Petr Krenitsyn** and **Mikhail Levashov** Expedition, whose delayed undertaking charted the **Aleutian Islands** between 1768 and 1770. If so, no connection was made and Sindt's failure to survey the coast south of the Bering Strait meant the Russians had to await information from **James Cook** in 1778 to understand better the continental coast between it and the **Alaska Peninsula**.

SITKA. *See* NEW ARCHANGEL.

SITKA SOUND. The large open water off the west coast of Baranof Island, separating it from Kruzof Island, is Sitka Sound. Its entrance is dominated by **Mount Edgecumbe**. **Aleksei Chirikov** made his landfall in this latitude in 1741, and **Juan Francisco de la Bodega y Quadra** in 1775 gave it a name—Ensenada del Susto or Bay of Terrors (which he did not explain). **George Dixon** had an extended stopover in June 1787; he called it Norfolk Sound after the Duke of Norfolk, and this was the name adopted by **George Vancouver** in 1794. But it was the Russian name Sitka (after the **Tlingit** word for "by the sea") that prevailed after **Aleksandr Baranov** established the fort and settlement of **New Archangel** there in 1799–1804.

SMYTH, WILLIAM (1800–1877). British naval officer and artist William Smyth came to the North Pacific with **Frederick Beechey** in the *Blossom*. Visiting **California** and the Arctic Ocean in 1826–1827, he left behind a number of drawings of these regions of the larger Northwest Coast. His work includes a fine sketch of Iñupiaq natives in **Kotzebue Sound** and views of the ship's barge working its way to Point Barrow, which, Beechey noted, was "the most northerly point yet discovered on the continent of America." Smyth eschewed drawing artifacts or animals or plants: he was more interested in general views presented in picturesque detail. Thus among his eight extant California sketches are watercolors of **Monterey** and the nearby **Carmel Mission** of San Carlos Borremeo.

SOIMONOV, FEDOR (1692–1780). Hydrographer and statesman. As governor-general of Siberia, 1757–1762, Fedor Soimonov was one of the key figures in the support and facilitation of the Russian advance towards America. Under the previous governor in the 1750s, he had supported the establishment of a navigational school in Irkutsk; in 1765 as an influential senator in St. Petersburg he promoted the opening of another school in Iakutsk. He made it his business to absorb all the information he could get from the navigator-hunters who had pushed into the eastern **Aleutian Islands**, and he was particularly interested in recording Russian discoveries with proper charts. To this end, in the 1760s, he compiled and supervised the creation of some of the earliest maps of the islands, and he dispatched **Ivan Sindt** to the **Bering Strait**. In the capital he campaigned for an official voyage to chart and document the newly discovered islands. This ultimately transpired in the **Petr Krenitsyn** and **Mikhail Levashov** Expedition of 1764–1771. The Empress **Catherine II** was aware of his work and influence, and in 1770 he produced for her a general chart of the North Pacific in which he attempted to detail the relationship to Asia of the emerging America.

SPANBERG, MARTIN (?–1761). A Danish-born navigator, Martin Spanberg participated in the first **Kamchatka Expedition** of **Vitus Bering**, playing a key role in the movement of the expedition across Siberia to the Pacific, and sailing with Bering and **Aleksei Chirikov** through the **Bering Strait** into the polar sea.

Between 1731 and 1744 he played an increasingly important role in the **Great Northern Expedition** and was responsible for a good deal of shipbuilding activity in Okhotsk. He is most closely associated with a series of voyages, in 1738, 1739, and 1742, from **Kamchatka** towards Japan, and produced a fine map of the Kurile Islands. Although he reached the main Japanese islands of Hokkaido and Honshu, he was unsuccessful in establishing any permanent contacts. He also searched in vain for **Gamaland** in 1739.

When news reached Kamchatka in 1742 that Bering had died, Spanberg became the ranking officer in change of the expedition. In this capacity he wrapped up its work and returned to St. Petersburg in 1745.

A final note of interest: Spanberg's chance meeting with **Ivan Gvozdev** in Okhotsk in 1743 led to the preparation of a report and the drawing of a map of the latter's voyage to the **Bering Strait** in 1732. While the map accurately depicted **Cape Prince of Wales**, it remained vague about the "Great Land" and betrayed a reluctance to identify it as America. In any event it was too late to affect plans for Bering's second voyage and after his discoveries in the **Aleutian Islands**, future expeditions concentrated in that area.

ST. LAWRENCE ISLAND. A large island 95 miles long and 25 miles wide, St. Lawrence guards the southern entrance to the **Bering Strait**. It may have been seen, even visited, by **Semen Dezhnev** in 1648, as he is known to have landed on an island while coming south from the cape that bears his name. It was named by **Vitus Bering**, who sailed close to it on the saint's day, 10 August 1728, during the first **Kamchatka Expedition**. It was visited by **Nikolai Daurkin** during his exploration of the northern **Bering Sea** and **Norton Sound** region in 1763, and noted by **Ivan Sindt**, who seems to have identified it as more than one island during his voyage in 1766. This problem also plagued **James Cook**, who ended up giving the same island three different names. Sailing towards the Bering Strait in early August 1778, he did not identify it with the island Bering had named, and called it Anderson Island in memory of William Anderson, his surgeon on the *Resolution* who had just died. Then, coming south from the Bering Strait in early September, he correctly recognized it as Bering's St. Lawrence Island. However, exiting **Norton Sound** later that month, he mistook it for yet another new island and named it Clerke's Island after the commander of the *Discovery*. During the years 1816–1817 the expedition of **Otto von Kotzebue** made three separate landings on the island, and the artist **Louis Choris** drew portraits of the natives and their habitations. Further descriptions of the natives were provided by **Frederick Beechey**, who visited the island in the summer of 1826.

ST. MATTHEW ISLAND. A significant island in the **Bering Sea**, 35 miles long and rising to an elevation of 1,500 feet at its southern point, St. Matthew was discovered by **Ivan Sindt** on 4 September 1766. The historian **William Coxe** recorded the name on the chart in the first edition of his *Account of the Russian Discoveries* (1780), suggesting that the name was given because of the closeness of the sighting to the saint's day, 21 September. **James Cook** identified it twice, first naming it Bird Island as he sailed north in July 1778, due to the large number of seabirds, but later, in September, naming it Pinnacles Island. Later, in Cook's chart it is named after **John Gore**, first lieutenant on the *Resolution*. Cook considered the island "wholy unknown to the Russians . . . consequently a new discovery" but this was not the case, and Sindt's original designation survived, essentially because it was reflected on maps in the atlases of **Gavriil Sarychev** (1826) and **Mikhail Teben'kov** (1852) compiled when **Alaska** was still **Russian America**.

STÄHLIN, JACOB VON (1709–1785). A founder and director of the Academy of Fine Arts in St. Petersburg, Jacob von Stählin possessed an intellectual arrogance that caused him to express himself on almost any subject. In the early 1770s he published an account of the geography of the northern seas between Asia and America. Purported to improve upon the work of **Gerhardt Friedrich Müller**, it also claimed to present previously unpublished discoveries by **Ivan Sindt** and Russian traders active in the **Aleutian Islands**. Brief and out of date, but widely accepted because of his position in academic circles, and despite criticism from Müller, the account was much less important than the accompanying map. A Map of the New Northern Archipelago was published in London in 1774 and was on board the *Resolution* when **James Cook** rounded the Gulf of Alaska in June 1778. Cook put a certain amount of trust in the map because it suggested easy access to the polar sea, a primary purpose of his voyage. The map depicted the **Alaska Peninsula** as a large island, with a convenient strait leading north between it and the mainland to the east. Although Cook finally managed to negotiate his way through the islands blocking his way into the **Bering Sea**, it was with no help from Stählin. "What could induce him," he wrote, "to publish so erroneous a map, in which many of the islands are jumbled together in regular confusion, without the least regard to the truth . . . ?" So wildly inaccurate was this map for the date it was published, that some scholars believe the whole project was purposely false to confuse the other European powers at a time when Russia, after the **Petr Krenitsyn** and **Mikhail Levashov** Expedition, sought to consolidate its own position in the North Pacific. *See also* CARTOGRAPHY.

STANIUKOVICH, MIKHAIL (ca. 1785–1869). In 1826 Mikhail Staniukovich was given command of the sloop *Moller* for an expedition to **Kamchatka** and **Russian America** with **Fedor Litke**. The two separated rounding Cape Horn and never actually worked together. Because his journal was never published, Staniukovich's reputation suffered in comparison to the energetic Litke and the achievements of his scientist-artist companions. After a visit to Petropavlovsk, the *Moller* arrived on **Unalaska** Island. No serious surveying was done because of poor weather and, after an uneventful visit to **New Archangel**, Staniukovich wintered over in **Hawaii**. The *Moller* again visited Petropavlovsk before cruising among the **Aleutian Islands**, arriving again off Unalaska in April 1828. Rating his chronometers and taking on board a *baidara*, he sailed along the north coast of Unimak Island and on 3 June began a precise exploration of the **Bering Sea** side of the **Alaska Peninsula**, from Isanotski Strait to the mouth of the Naknek River emptying into **Bristol Bay**. He charted Port Moller, naming it after his ship. After a visit to Amak Island on 13 July, bad weather forced the *Moller* to the south side of Unimak Island. Staniukovich decided to abandon any more surveying, headed for Unalaska and then back to Petropavlovsk. Apart from his work on the north side of the Alaska Peninsula, which Litke reported on in the Nautical Section of his journal, little exploring had been done, and the voyage is now best remembered for the artistic work of **Pavel Mikhailov**.

STELLER, GEORG WILHELM (1709–1746). German scholar, naturalist, and botanist, Georg Wilhelm Steller is best remembered for his pioneering fieldwork as a member of the second **Kamchatka Expedition** to America in 1741, commanded by **Vitus Bering**.

In 1734 Steller arrived in St. Petersburg and attached himself to the Botanical Garden. He became an adjunct professor at the Academy of Sciences, and successfully applied to join the **Great Northern Expedition**, setting out for Siberia in 1738. Working alongside **Gerhardt Friedrich Müller** and Johann Gmelin, he collected numerous specimens and wrote reports that were sent to St. Petersburg. After meeting Bering in Okhotsk in August 1740, he moved on to **Kamchatka** to supervise the work of **Stepan Krasheninnikov**, and was engaged in this duty when Bering summoned him to Petropavlovsk to take part in the voyage to America as assistant to the appointed physician. Most of the doctors on the early voyages of exploration were naturalists, because so much of medicine at that time involved an understanding of plants. Although Steller was not a doctor, his knowledge of botany and his guidance on diet later saved the lives of many of Bering's men on **Bering Island** during the winter of 1741–1742.

Highly intelligent but impetuous, stubborn, and often belligerent, Steller did not initially endear himself to the officers of the *St. Peter*. He was particularly harsh in his criticism of Bering who, increasingly ill and worried about the progress of the expedition as the voyage wore on, at first refused to allow him to explore **Kayak Island** in the shadow of **Mount St. Elias**, when the expedition landed on the Northwest Coast. The commander relented, however, and on 20 July Steller went ashore with a watering party. In a few frantic hours he made notes about the climate, soil, and plants, identifying the salmon berry later classified as *Rubus Spectabilis*, and an herb called sweet grass, now the Alaskan wild celery or *Heracleum lanatum*. He also noted the animals, including the red fox, and birds such as the blue jay later named *Cyanocittus stelleri* or Steller's Jay. The men also found evidence of human habitation including smoldering fires, trails, and tasty smoked fish. There was evidence of meat being boiled by the hot stone method, and a fire drill was found similar to those used by the natives in Kamchatka. Steller found a grass-covered storage pit with sweet grass and other plants and bundles of bark, along with some arrows. He made a collection of items and, in payment, Bering ordered that cloth, knives, tobacco, and beads be left behind.

Steller's next opportunity for fieldwork was on Nagi Island in the **Shumagin Islands**. He recorded the presence of slate, and collected many plants, at least one of which had antiscorbutic properties; he made notes about the animals—foxes, marmots, squirrels, and wolf, whose presence he deduced from tracks—and fish—cod, char, halibut, and salmon—which were similar to those found in Kamchatka. He also noted fur seals swimming offshore. When the ship was moved to a safer anchorage Steller accompanied **Sofron Khitrovo** and **Sven Waxell** on small boat excursions, during which the Russians became the first Europeans to encounter **Aleut** natives. For this purpose they had carried gifts of tobacco and pipes, mirrors, knives, beads, and cloth. The first contact took place with natives in

kayaks and there was an exchange of gifts. On a second occasion the heavy waves made a general landing impossible, but three of the party waded ashore to visit a native habitation, and the Aleuts visited the Russian longboat in their kayaks. Finally a small flotilla of native kayaks approached the *St. Peter*; gifts, including needles and cloth and a kettle were exchanged over the side, but the Aleuts would not come on board. The importance to ethnographers, however, of the descriptions of the Aleuts in the journals of Steller and Waxell cannot be overestimated. Their accounts complement each other and provide vital details about appearance, clothing, the kayaks, and armament.

When the expedition wintered over on **Bering Island**, Steller assumed a leadership role. He helped dig caves and build shelters, he hunted and cooked and prepared various plant concoctions to stave off scurvy. Although Bering and others died, many lived because of Steller's efforts, and they later showed their appreciation by signing over to him a share of the valuable pelts they had collected on the voyage. The extended stopover on Bering Island allowed Steller a unique opportunity for fieldwork. He reported on the geographical features of the island; described and sketched the spectacled cormorant, *Phalacrocorax perspicillatus* and sea eagle; made detailed notes on the seals, sea otters, and sea lions, *Eumetopias jubata*; and most famously he documented the sea cow or northern manatee, *Hydrodamalis gigas*, that was soon hunted to extinction as Russian *promyshlenniki* moved through the **Aleutian Islands** in the 1750s and 1760s. He returned to Kamchatka with a collection of over 200 plant species. It was a remarkable achievement of scientific research.

Steller remains one of the most important figures of the exploration and discovery of the Northwest Coast While his journal is invariably self-serving, and needs to be balanced with a study of Waxell's account, the great value of his descriptions and insights cannot be denied, and the scope of his scientific investigations was monumental.

STRAIT OF ANIAN. The early name for the narrow waterway separating Asia from America, the Strait of Anian was thought to provide access from the Pacific to a Northwest Passage across the top of America and a Northeast Passage across the top of Russia. The existence of the strait was accepted by cartographers from the mid-1560s, although it was unproven before the voyage of **Semen Dezhnev** in

1648 and essentially unknown until the results of **Vitus Bering**'s first **Kamchatka Expedition** in 1728 were disseminated in the 1730s.

In 1561 Giacomo Gastaldi published a map in Venice showing a strait and region called "Ania Pro[vincia]" on the far eastern edge of Asia. A year later in his pamphlet *La Universale Descrittione del Mundo*, he confirmed his belief that Asia and America were separated. Gastaldi's map influenced another by **Abraham Ortelius** in 1564, upon which "Ania" became "Anian" and had been shifted from the Asian side of the strait to the extreme northwest corner of America. The term "Streto de Anian" first appeared on a map by Bolognini Zaltieri of Nova Franza (1566) and was copied by Gerard Mercator in 1569.

Following the publication of Ortelius's atlas *Theatrum Orbis Terrarum* in 1570, the strait entered the realm of accepted truth, but it was not until **James Cook**'s reconnaissance in 1778 that the promised access through it to a **Northwest Passage** was proven false.

STRAIT OF GEORGIA. A large inland sea between southern **Vancouver Island** and the Lower Mainland of **British Columbia**, the Strait of Georgia is joined to the Pacific Ocean by Haro and Rosario Straits and the **Strait of Juan de Fuca**. It was discovered and given its first name by pilot **Juan Pantoja y Arriaga** on the **Francisco de Eliza** Expedition on 15 June 1791. He called it the Gran Canal de Nuestra Señora del Rosario la Marinera after a famous image in Seville. The Virgen de Rosario was patron saint of Francisco de Eliza's ship, the *San Carlos*. Approximately 140 miles in length from the San Juan Islands to Quadra Island, and up to 25 miles wide, the strait was first explored, essentially in its entirety, by **José María Narváez** and **Juan Carrasco**, also pilots with Eliza, during the month of July 1791.

The next year, 1792, the eastern coast of the strait was explored more precisely by the **Dionisio Alcalá Galiano** and **Cayetano Valdés** Expedition and by **George Vancouver**. The latter improved the Narváez chart by finding **Puget Sound**, Burrard Inlet, and Howe Sound, and both Spanish and English surveys identified Point Roberts (Punta de Cepeda) and Point Grey (Punta de Lángara) as part of the mainland instead of groups of islands. Spanish artist **José Cardero** drew the first portraits of native people of the strait with his chiefs of Winthuysen (Nanaimo), Descanso (Gabriola Island), and Lángara (Point Grey).

Vancouver named the strait the Gulf of Georgia in honor of King George III, but this was changed to Strait of Georgia by **George Henry Richards** on the charts that emerged from his surveying activities in 1857–1860. This is its formal name, but it is still often referred to by the name given to it by Vancouver.

STRAIT OF JUAN DE FUCA. The Strait of Juan de Fuca, a large strait at 48° N, 125° W, leads to the entrance of the **Strait of Georgia** and the eastern coast of **Vancouver Island**. It creates the southern edge of Vancouver Island and today marks the international boundary between Canada (**British Columbia**) and the United States (**Washington**). It was named for **Juan de Fuca**, a Greek pilot in Spanish service reputed to have found, in 1592, between latitude 47° and 48° N, the Pacific entrance to the **Strait of Anian** and the **Northwest Passage**.

In March 1778 **James Cook** ran past the entrance at night in a gale. He wrote disdainfully: "It is in this very latitude . . . geographers have placed the pretended Strait of Juan de Fuca, but we saw nothing like it, nor is there the least probability that iver any such thing exhisted." Nevertheless, towards the end of July 1787, acting on information provided by **John Mackay**, who had been left in **Nootka Sound** by the fur trader **James Strange**, **Charles Barkley** left Nootka and cruised the coast south beyond the sound that today bears his name. "To our great astonishment," wrote his wife Frances Barkley, "we arrived off a large opening extending to the eastward," which they "immediately recognized as the long lost Strait of Juan de Fuca." Barkley gave this opening the name of its "original discoverer" and placed it on his chart. In June 1788 another British trader, **John Meares,** who had received information about Barkley's discovery in China and had inherited his papers, sailed past the entrance of the strait and sketched a fine drawing that was published in 1790 in his *Voyages Made in the Years 1788 and 1789, from China to the North West Coast of America*. But the correctness of Meares's chart, which showed that an American trading vessel had sailed far into the strait in 1789 and, in a giant arc, had circumnavigated Vancouver Island, exiting near the **Queen Charlotte Islands**, was denied by **Robert Gray** and denounced as false by his contemporaries. The American trader had indeed penetrated the strait that year for a distance of about 25 miles and confirmed that it broadened in the east into a "large sea," but he had gone no farther. In August 1788, shortly after Meares's visit, yet another trader, **Charles Duncan**, sketched the opening and learned from the **Makah** natives of **Cape Flattery** that it was the entrance to "a Great Sea" that ran "a great way up to the Northward [the **Strait of Georgia**]; and down to the Southward [**Puget Sound**]". In April 1790 **Aaron Arrowsmith** published a chart in London that reflected Duncan's information.

In 1789 viceroy Manuel Antonio Flórez had sent **Esteban José Martínez** to occupy **Nootka Sound**. In the midst of his clash with British traders that sparked the **Nootka Crisis**, Martínez dispatched **José María Narváez** to confirm the existence of the strait that the American traders were talking about. This was duly reported to him, and he wrote in his journal about the division of the strait "which they call Juan de Fuca" into two branches, and his belief that the southern one "has a communication with the Mississippi River, towards the east-southeast. . . ." Keen to uphold Spain's sovereignty in the region, Martínez would also report that he had seen the opening to the strait as early as 1774, when he was on the coast with **Juan Pérez**, but this has been largely discounted as it is unlikely that Pérez, had he known of the sighting, would not have investigated and reported on it himself, and that Martínez would not have encouraged him to do so.

When the Spaniards under **Francisco de Eliza** returned to Nootka again in 1790, **Manuel Quimper** and his pilot **Gonzalo López de Haro** were dispatched to explore and follow the opening of "Fuca." Retracing the route taken by Narváez they explored the entire strait as far as the entrance to Puget Sound, which they did not find, and the southern coasts of the San Juan Islands with the enticing channels leading north. It was obvious these merited further exploration. The result was the Eliza Expedition of 1791 that took José María Narváez beyond the islands to the head of the Strait of Georgia. His report in turn precipitated the voyage of **Dionisio Alcalá Galiano** and **Cayetano Valdés** in 1792, during which the Spanish explorers met **George Vancouver** off the present-day city that bears his name. *See also* CARTOGRAPHY.

STRANGE, JAMES (1753–1840). An official with the **East India Company** (EIC), James Strange was already aware of **William**

Coxe's account of Russian discoveries in the North Pacific when he became acquainted, during 1785, with the journal of **James Cook**. He enlisted EIC support for a private-venture voyage to the Northwest Coast in 1786. Although exploration was a goal of the expedition of the *Captain Cook* and the *Experiment*, its primary objective was commerce. Neither was achieved with much success, for Strange was a cautious trader and an unadventurous explorer. He arrived in **Nootka Sound** in June, met Chief **Maquinna** and engaged in trade, but did not find the **natives** particularly accommodating. By keeping the ships together for security purposes his initial haul of furs was not as great as it would have been had one of them been sent off into other inlets. In July the ships made their way north and the expedition was responsible for naming Cape Scott in honor of their sponsor, David Scott, as well as Queen Charlotte Sound. But trading was slow so the expedition made haste for another Cook anchorage in **Prince William Sound** only to be met by a rival trader **William Tipping**, a colleague of **John Meares**. The Englishmen traded for furs but their explorations added nothing new to an understanding of the geography or natural history of the sound. Strange hoped that the *Captain Cook* would be able to investigate the copper deposits on Mednoi Island on the way back to China, but this was prevented by stormy weather. Both ships arrived in Macao in mid-November. Although they had secured a profitable 600 pelts, the expedition was a financial failure. It is now best remembered for the extensive observations of native life found in the journal of **Alexander Walker**, and for leaving at Nootka the surgeon **John Mackay**. He subsequently "resided upwards of a year among the American Savages" and provided Walker with "an account of their manners and of his own adventures."

STUART, ROBERT (1785–1848). One of the Astorians, Robert Stuart arrived at the mouth of the **Columbia River** on the *Tonquin* in March 1811 and assisted in establishing Fort **Astoria**. In June 1812 he set out in command of a small party to return to New York with dispatches for John Jacob Astor. In crossing the Continental Divide he discovered South Pass in the Wind River Range of Wyoming, the easiest route found to date. It later became a crucial part of the Oregon Trail in the 1840s.

STURGIS, WILLIAM (1782–1863). William Sturgis was one of the most important and influential **"Boston Men"** to come to the Northwest Coast. He made the first of his four successful voyages in 1799 aboard the *Eliza*, which moved between trading centers in the **Queen Charlotte Islands** and the **Alexander Archipelago**. During this voyage, in which he transferred to the *Ulysses* as an officer, he wrote a journal noteworthy for its impressions of life at sea, **fur trade** practices, and encounters with the **native** people with whom he developed a series of highly successful trading relationships. He began to learn their languages, which stood him in good stead during subsequent voyages, and became adroit at bringing to the coast articles for trade—such as ermine on his third voyage—that would be attractive to them. His other voyages were in the *Caroline*, 1800–1803 and 1803–1806, and the *Atahualpa*, 1806–1808.

These fur trade voyages and two others to Canton made Sturgis a wealthy man and an experienced merchant, all before he was 30 years old. In 1810 he entered into the partnership of Bryant, Sturgis & Co., continuing in the Asian trade before pursuing opportunities in banking, manufacturing, and transportation. Although his life as a seaman had ended, Sturgis retained a personal interest in the Northwest Coast and the fur trade, and discussed these and promoted American interests in the region with published lectures that covered the claims of the Russians and "The Oregon Question." In striking contrast to most visitors to the North Pacific, he cherished his contacts with the natives and lamented the deplorable way in which they had been treated, and their rights to life and property almost completely disregarded by those who thought themselves civilized and Christian.

SURÍA, TOMÁS DE (1761–ca. 1835). Tomás de Suría was the artist on the **Alejandro Malaspina** Expedition during its visit to the Northwest Coast in 1791. As a student in Madrid, Suría was mentored by Jeronimo Antonio Gil, particularly in the art of engraving. When Gil became director of the Academy of San Carlos in Mexico City, Suría followed him to **New Spain** in 1778.

Upon his arrival in Mexico in early 1791, **Alejandro Malaspina** sent an urgent appeal to the viceroy, the **Count of Revillagigedo**, to find an artist for his Northwest Coast campaign. When approached for help, Gil nominated Suría, then working as an engraver at the

Mexican mint. Before he left Acapulco for the north on the *Descubierta*, Suría executed a number of drawings of fish and birds for the chief natural historian, Antonio Pineda. Two general scenes, a cockfight and a view of the bay, have also survived.

Suría made a major contribution to the expedition. In addition to his drawings, most notably of native people, he kept a journal/sketchbook, which provides a fascinating, nonofficial, account of the voyage interspersed with little sketches, some of which were worked up into finished drawings. Unfortunately, Suría's account ends abruptly during the stay at **Nootka Sound**, and the fact that the extant document attributed to him is marked "Notebook 1" suggests that one or more other notebooks have been lost. This opinion is supported by the fact that only three of his drawings have survived from the southern leg of the journey, and its stopover at **Monterey** on the way to Acapulco.

Suría's finished drawings such as his "Chief of the Port of Mulgrave named Ankaiui," "Tlupanamabu, chief of Nootka," and "Principal chief of Nutka named **Maquinna**" are testaments to his skill. His "Plebian woman at Mulgrave" and two sketches, a close-up and a full-length study, both entitled "Woman of Nutka" are particularly noteworthy. In addition, his numerous little sketches, especially one called "Armed Indian" (a Tlingit at Yakutat Bay), are of great interest to ethnographers.

Suría's journal is equally important. He wrote about life at sea from a nonmariner's perspective and was especially animated when discussing a terrifying storm off the **Queen Charlotte Islands**. It barely merited attention in Malaspina's journal. The extensive comments describing the natives, especially in **Alaska**, and their interaction with the Spaniards, show that Suría was fascinated by the adventure of the voyage, the new people and the magnificent mountain vistas. At Nootka, he recorded a "political speech" by Chief Tlupanamabu, which demonstrated the latter's interest in gaining more influence with the Spaniards than his rival in the area, Chief Maquinna.

Malaspina was well-pleased with Suría's efforts. In a letter to Navy Minister Antonio Valdés he wrote: ". . . our collections for the Royal Cabinet have been very numerous and very interesting, inasmuch as Don Tomas Suría has depicted with the greatest faithfulness to nature all that merits the help of the engraver's art, so as to secure a better understanding of the historical narrative of this voyage." Suría later developed a career as an artist, achieving recognition for religious paintings and portraits.

SYKES, JOHN (1774–1858). A former shipmate of **George Vancouver**, John Sykes joined the *Discovery* when the **Nootka Crisis** was settled and the Admiralty's plan for a voyage to the Northwest Coast was resurrected in 1790. He served as master's mate under **Joseph Whidbey**.

His importance lies in his artistic contribution to the expedition. Along with other "young gentlemen of the quarterdeck," **Henry Humphrys** and **Thomas Heddington**, he produced topographical views, and all but one of the engraved illustrations in the official account of the voyage were produced by this trio, including Sykes's "Mount Rainier from the South Part of Admiralty Inlet," "Cheslakee's Village in Johnstone Strait" and "The New Eddystone in Behm's Canal." They produced, however, no portraits or drawings of artifacts or natural history specimens. Sykes was the most prolific of Vancouver's **artists**, and many unengraved original sketches survive in the British Hydrographic Office in Taunton, Somerset. Of particular interest are the watercolor sketch of the surveying encampment, "View of Observatory Point," drawn shortly after the expedition entered the **Strait of Juan de Fuca** in 1792, showing tents set up on the beach; the "View of the Indian Village on Cape Mudge" at the head of the Gulf of Georgia; a small boat party in "View from the anchorage of the head of Port Protection" on the northern tip of **Prince of Wales Island** in the southern **Alexander Archipelago**; and the distinctive "View of Volcano Mount, Cook's River." Valuable too are his views of the presidio at **Monterey** and of the nearby **Carmel Mission**, two of which were engraved for inclusion in Vancouver's *Voyage*.

– T –

TARKHANOV, DIMITRII (fl. 1790s). An officer in the Corps of Mining Engineers, Dimitrii Tarkhanov visited Russian America between 1794 and 1798. He spent the winter of 1795–1796 as a hostage of the **Tlingit** in **Yakutat Bay**, and the winter of 1796–1797 in an

Eyak village on the Kaliakh River between Icy Bay and Controller Bay. His travels took him to the lower reaches of the **Copper River** in the spring of 1797, which meant that he undertook the first sustained land exploration of a significant portion of the Northwest Coast.

In September 1796 he set out on snowshoes to travel along the coast from Yakutat to explore the Copper River. It was an exhausting journey through rugged terrain, crossing numerous rivers. After resting at the Eyak village he was guided by the **natives** as far as the Bering River from which the Mednovtsy Indians, whose homeland was the lower sections of the Copper River and its delta, took him overland to that river and up it as far as the settlement of Takekat at its junction with the Tiekel River. There he became something of a celebrity among people who had never before seen a European. Poor health prevented him from proceeding further, but the Mednovtsy drew sketches for him of the central and upper Copper River and he was able to record information about their trading relationship with the Ahtna, the Athabaskan group of that region, who themselves traded with the natives of **Cook Inlet** via Lake Tazlina and the Susitna River. Before he left by *baidarka* in May 1797 he had come to appreciate the copper resources of the area and the profitable trade in the metal conducted downstream by his hosts. In June he was back on **Kodiak** Island and reporting his findings to **Aleksandr Baranov**.

Tarkhanov's *Journal of the Wanderings and Travels for Mining Science* is a gem of early exploration literature. It not only records the progress of his journey, but also provides a detailed ethnographic survey of the Yakutat Tlingit especially, and to a lesser extent the Eyaks and the Mednovtsy. His is the first account of the economic cycle of life among the Tlingit; he writes about their houses, clothing, ornamentation, and weapons, and also describes the performance of a shaman. His work complements the earlier descriptions recorded by **George Dixon** in 1787 and the **Alejandro Malaspina** Expedition in 1791. Tarkhanov was especially impressed by the gentle and gracious nature of the Mednovtsy, which stood in strong contrast to the demeanor of the coastal natives and those he met on Kodiak Island.

TEBEN'KOV, MIKHAIL (1802–1872). Naval officer and colonial administrator, Mikhail Teben'kov joined the **Russian–America**

Company (RAC) in 1825. He gained a solid reputation for skilled command of a number of ships on the American coast, and between the years 1829 and 1831 undertook hydrographic surveys in **Norton Sound** and the **Alexander Archipelago**. In 1833 chief manager **Ferdinand Wrangell** set him to establish Mikhailovskii (St. Michael) Redoubt in **Norton Sound**, and it soon became the base for extensive exploration in central southwest **Alaska**.

After a short period in St. Petersburg and more time in **Russian America**, 1835–1840, he was appointed chief manager at **New Archangel** in 1844. The 1840s were a period of expansion for the RAC and Teben'kov's earlier interest and experience in exploration and hydrography led him to organize a number of expeditions to chart and describe the coast north from the capital, round the Gulf of Alaska and along the **Aleutian Islands**. Particularly noteworthy were new surveys in 1846 of **Cook Inlet**, **Prince William Sound**, and around **Kodiak** Island by **Illarion Arkhimandritov**. Less successful was a fateful expedition sent to the **Copper River** in 1848, where the natives killed four men. Other notable aspects of his administration were the creation of successful commercial links with **Hawaii**; improved relations with the Tlingit due to the inauguration of an annual trading fair; and improvements to the infrastructure of the capital including construction of a sawmill and flour mill, and the beginning of a new cathedral.

During his governorship Teben'kov began to compile the charts necessary to produce a comprehensive atlas of Russia's American territories and adjacent regions. Upon his return to St. Petersburg in 1851, this was prepared for publication as the *Atlas of the Northwest Coast of America from Bering Strait to Cape Corrientes and the Aleutian Islands with several sheets on the Northwest Coast of Asia* (1852). Of particular value were his complementary Hydrographic Notes, with a historical context and commentary written for each sheet. The atlas consists of 38 charts covering all the coasts of Russian America, except **Kotzebue Sound** and the far north coast of arctic Alaska. Although now curiosities, they represented a great advance in their day and provided **George Davidson** (1825–1911) with a vital reference point for the production of his *Coast Pilot of Alaska* (1869), the first guide to the coast after the United States purchased the territory.

THOMPSON, DAVID (1770–1857). Perhaps the greatest of all North American explorer-geographers, David Thompson unraveled the complexities of the **Columbia River** drainage basin in the early years of the 19th century before being the first explorer to travel the entire length of the great river in 1810–1811.

Thompson apprenticed to the **Hudson's Bay Company** (HBC) in 1784. During the winter of 1789–1790 he came under the tutelage of the noted surveyor Philip Tumor and, at York Factory in the early 1790s, pursued his interest in surveying and astronomy to the extent that his work impressed his superiors. In subsequent years he became a valued leader of HBC surveying and trading activities as far west as Lake Athabasca.

In 1797 Thompson left the HBC to join the **North West Company**, for which he made numerous surveying expeditions across western Canada and into northern sections of the Louisiana Territory. In 1798 he surveyed the northern source of the Mississippi River and created a map that was later used by the **Lewis and Clark Expedition**. Trading activities had to be balanced with surveying, but by the turn of the century he had worked his way into the Rocky Mountains. He had become increasingly interested in finding a viable route across the continent by determining from how far inland the rivers feeding into the Columbia River could offer him a route to the Pacific. In 1804 he became a partner in the North West Company and by June 1807 had crossed the Rockies to reach Kootenay Lake, which he realized only later was actually the headwaters of the Columbia. Surveying an area that offered rich possibilities for trade delayed his final descent of the river, and he did not reach the ocean until 15 July 1811. There he found Americans of John Jacob Astor's Pacific Fur Company busy establishing Fort **Astoria**. Nevertheless, he had effectively linked the Great Lakes to the Northwest Coast across the continent north of the 49° parallel, and in the process had surveyed with remarkable accuracy the entire length of the Columbia.

Thompson retired in 1812 and devoted himself to preparing a huge map of western Canada from Lake Superior to the **Oregon** Country (1814). Now in the collection of the Archives of Ontario, it stands as a monument to the unparalleled achievements of an explorer whose travels of over 50,000 miles by canoe, horse, and foot finally brought him to the coast of **Bruno de Hezeta, John Meares, Robert Gray, George Vancouver,** and **William Broughton.**

THREE SAINTS BAY. The deep Three Saints Bay on the southwest coast of **Kodiak** Island was discovered by **Stepan Glotov** in 1762. **Grigorii Shelikhov** established a trading settlement there in 1784. It had grown into a substantial establishment by the time the Spaniard **Gonzalo López de Haro** visited in 1788, and it was drawn by **Luka Voronin** and described by members of the **Joseph Billings** Expedition in 1790. In 1788, however, an earthquake changed the nature of the inner bay, making it a poor anchorage, and ships often used nearby Old Harbor. The area also lacked an adequate supply of timber for shipbuilding and general construction. So **Aleksandr Baranov** abandoned it in favor of St. Paul's Bay at the northeast end of Kodiak in 1792–1793.

TIKHANOV, MIKHAIL (1789–1862). Artist on the round-the-world voyage of **Vasilii Golovnin,** which visited **Russian America** and **California** in 1818, Mikhail Tikhanov was born into serfdom. Tikhanov was fortunate to have his artistic talent recognized by his noble master and to be given a scholarship to the Academy of Fine Arts in St. Petersburg. An outstanding student, he graduated and received his freedom in 1815. In 1817 the director recommended him to Golovnin, who encouraged the young artist to complement the written descriptions of people and places with his drawings. An album of 43 watercolors has survived in the collection of the Academy; there are 19 images devoted to **Alaska** and the **Aleutian Islands** and five from California. Tikhanov's work is bold and arresting, his portraits of native peoples iconographic in their precision. In most of these he displayed an original technique, drawing and painting his subjects in full-face and in profile in the same picture. His attention to detail—the natives' tattoos and face painting, clothing, ornamentation, and arms—makes his work extremely valuable to ethnographers. Of particular importance are his portraits of "Pannioiak," a woman of Kodiak; the chief "Nankok" also of Kodiak Island; a man from the Copper River delta; and the "Tlingit chief Kotlean from Sitka Island," who was celebrated amongst his people for leading the successful destruction of **New Archangel** in 1802, and who came to be much admired by **Aleksandr Baranov** for his intelligence and bravery. One of Tikhanov's best-known portraits is that of Baranov himself. The California subjects are all Bodega Miwok Indians, drawn while the expedition visited **Fort Ross**.

TIKHMENEV, PETR (ca. 1825–1888). Naval officer and official historian of the **Russian–America Company** (RAC), Petr Tikhmenev was engaged in 1857 to write the history of the RAC, an assignment that proved timely because of its demise a decade later. The end of Russian America in 1867 led to the destruction, dispersal, and loss of valuable archival material that had provided Tikhmenev with information about the development of the colony in America, and which would otherwise have been unavailable to scholars today. His work appeared in two volumes between 1861 and 1863—a narrative, and a priceless collection of supporting documents. They were published in English in 1978–1979.

TIPPING, WILLIAM (fl. 1785–1786). William Tipping joined the Bengal Fur Company in 1785 and commanded the *Sea Otter* to explore and trade on the Northwest Coast with **John Meares** in the *Nootka*. He was thus one of the earliest trader-explorers on the coast. The ships set out separately in February 1786 and never actually worked together for, when Meares reached **Prince William Sound** in October, he found evidence that Tipping had already been there and had left with "plenty of skins." In fact rival trader **James Strange** reported meeting with Tipping in Prince William Sound on 5 September and that he had come to America after running the coasts of Japan and visiting various places in the **Aleutian Islands**. Hearing from Strange that the coast south had been "traded out," Tipping made for **Cook Inlet** en route to China. Writing the introductory chapter of his *Voyages* (1790) Meares reported that there had been no further news of Tipping or his ship and that he could only "conclude therefore that she and her people have perished beneath the waves."

TLINGIT. A significant native nation, estimated at about 10,000 people at the time of contact, the Tlingit occupy the coastal region of southeast **Alaska** from **Yakutat Bay** to the bottom of the **Alexander Archipelago**. The stability of their ocean food supply and an abundance of wood allowed them to build numerous large villages, dominated by large plank dwellings, and to develop a complex social system, founded on two clans, the Raven and the Wolf, with a community life rich in ceremony, mythology, and artistic creativity. The Tlingit were great traders both inland and along the coast. The earliest explorers and traders to make any sustained contact, **George Dixon**, **Jean François de La Pérouse**, and **James Colnett** commented on their magnificent canoes and seafaring skill, as well as their experience in bartering.

The Tlingit were regarded as the most militaristic of the Northwest Coast peoples. Well organized, tactically astute, armed with bows and arrows, spears and clubs, and protective armor and helmets, they proved to be formidable opponents. Once they acquired firearms in the maritime **fur trade** they became even more so. Although the Russians occupied a good deal of their territory for nearly 70 years, they exercised no real control; the Tlingit (known as Koloshes to the Russians) maintained their culture, protected ownership of their land by refusing to enter into treaties, and essentially sought communication only to benefit from technology and economic opportunity. Under Chief **Katleyan** the Tlingit successfully destroyed the first **New Archangel** in 1802 and, in 1805, moved against the Russian post at Yakutat. Traders operating in Tlingit waters were usually met with hostility unless their presence was seen to be specifically advantageous. In the early years of the 19th century the Russians often had to employ their **Aleut** hunters, whom the Tlingit particularly resented, as soldiers, and in 1818, after a large party of Aleuts had been ambushed and murdered, the Russians always had a naval vessel on patrol in **Sitka Sound**.

TOLSTYKH, ANDREAN (?–1765). Russian merchant, explorer, and fur trader, Andrean Tolstykh was one of the earliest and most persistent *promyshlenniki* to exploit the **Aleutian Islands**. By 1746 he and other merchants joined forces to build a ship and sail to **Bering Island**, returning again in 1747. He set out again in 1749, wintered on Bering Island, and then spent two years on Attu in the Near Islands, where he introduced foxes for later hunting. He made another two-year voyage between 1753 and 1755. In 1756 he built a new ship and hunted for the next three years primarily on Attu, where he enjoyed good relations with the natives, and introduced the ancient practice of netting sea mammals.

Between 1760 and 1764 he not only visited his favorite islands, but also sailed farther east and explored and visited a group in the central Aleutians, including Atka, which were subsequently named "Andreanof" in recognition of his discovery. In 1765 Tolstykh set out on a voyage to the Kurile Islands and to search for the fabled **Gamaland** before heading to the Aleutians for further hunting and trade; however, the crew became sick and on the return to **Kamchatka** the ship was wrecked in a storm and he and most of his companions were drowned. The historian **Vasilii Berkh** wrote that Tolstykh was esteemed for his "many successful voyages that brought him universal praise and profits," and suggested that had he lived he may well have occupied, at an earlier date, the place in history now occupied by the famous **Grigorii Shelikhov**.

TOMALES BAY. *See* BODEGA BAY AND TOMALES BAY.

TOVA Y ARREDONDO, ANTONIO DE (1760–1825). Antonio de Tova was a participant in the **Alejandro Malaspina** Expedition during which he served as first officer of the *Atrevida* under **José Bustamante**. He owes his importance today to the survival of his journal, which was not found until the middle of the 20th century. It records many details about the voyage and its surveying tasks at the various ports of call, not found in other accounts, but is particularly noteworthy because of the author's interest in the **native** peoples he encountered, whether in Patagonia, Chile, or Tonga or on the Northwest Coast. He covers extensively the expedition's visits to Port Mulgrave (**Yakutat Bay**), during which he commanded one of the two launches that explored as far as the Hubbard Glacier, and to **Nootka Sound**. At Mulgrave he noted the local Tlingit's keen interest and obvious experience in trade and their desire to break into song whenever they saw it might advance their interests: ". . . they gave us several vocal concerts. The choirmaster kept time with a little paddle and sang his solos, subsequently singing in unison with the rest in an outstanding way. . . . The Mulgrave songs pleased everyone. Nevertheless, though their music was designed to seek or demonstrate peace, it in fact reflects a savage character and is more appropriate to arousing martial passions than exciting sweet and tender feelings."

At Nootka, Tova was one of the officers who engaged in long conversations with the young chief Natzape and recorded his insights into the natives' customs, religion, and trading relationships.

TRANSCONTINENTAL TREATY, 1819. The Transcontinental Treaty between Spain and the United States, also known as the Adams–Onís Treaty, signaled Spain's formal withdrawal from much of the Northwest Coast. In reality it confirmed a retreat that had begun with the abandonment of the establishment in **Nootka Sound** in 1795, and Spain's growing disinterest in the coast north of **San Francisco** as the 19th century began. Indeed, the **Pacific Northwest** had never been more to Spain than the "coast north of **California**," and once it was proven that a passage to the Atlantic did not exist, Mexico City and Madrid could only imagine their continued presence in the north to mean endless expenditure, international disputes and risk of war, and the hardships of a cold climate.

In a context in which Spain was keen to secure an eastern border with the expansionist United States, the actual boundary in the north was much less important. Nevertheless, still officially battling the Mexican revolution, and negotiating through its minister in Washington, Luís de Onís, Madrid wished to put as much coast as possible between California and Britons and Americans on the **Columbia River**. American Secretary of State John Quincy Adams was equally determined to protect the opening to the Pacific Ocean provided by **Robert Gray's** discovery of the Columbia River (1792), the **Lewis and Clark Expedition** (1804–1806), and the activities of American fur traders at **Astoria** (1811) and in the Columbia River basin.

After negotiations in the fall of 1818, particularly over the ceding of Florida and the northeastern boundary of **New Spain** in the center of the continent, the frontier in the **Pacific Northwest** was accepted by both sides at the 42° parallel, today the dividing line between the states of California, Nevada, and Utah in the south, and **Oregon** and Idaho in the north. The treaty was signed in Washington on 22 February 1819.

TRAPEZNIKOV, NIKIFOR (ca. 1740–1785). Nikifor Trapeznikov was a pioneer in the Aleutian **fur trade**. After the successful 1743–1745 voyage of **Emel'ian Basov** to Bering Island, Trapeznikov immediately supported another expedition, which had equally sensational results. Thereafter, for the next 17 years, he sent out vessels of his own and financially sponsored others. He himself went to the islands only once between 1749 and 1752. In 1756, along with two other merchants he helped back the *Adreian I Natal'ia*, which hunted in the Near Islands out of Attu and recorded the most financially successful haul of furs in the earliest years of the trade. In 1762 he was a partner in a flotilla of four vessels, one of which was his own, that set out to the eastern Aleutians not only to hunt but also to undertake a full survey of the islands and to identify the best hunting grounds. But the expedition got caught in the Aleut–Russian War of 1763, and although his ship escaped, the others were destroyed and he suffered a major financial loss. At this time Empress **Catherine II** initiated a reform that began to change the nature of the fur trade; she rescinded the state monopoly on trade with China, which brought larger merchant houses into the picture. With his personal losses, Trapeznikov faded from the scene. In 1774 his major role in initiating the trade and the discovery and exploration of the **Aleutian Islands** and others off the **Alaska Peninsula**, and bringing them under Russian control, earned him one of 12 gold medals given to fur trade entrepreneurs by the empress.

TREATY OF TORDESILLAS. An agreement between Spain and Portugal, 1493–1494, the Treaty of Tordesillas created a line of demarcation dividing the discovered world between them. It was set about 1,300 miles west of the Cape Verde Islands. Lands to the east were claimed by Portugal, to the west by Spain. Thus Spain claimed most of the Pacific Ocean as a "Spanish Lake" and the treaty was the basis for the Laws of the Indies under which she claimed sovereignty over the Northwest Coast. As other maritime powers ignored the treaty, however, this claim was never realistically upheld and was successfully challenged in the 18th century.

TRINIDAD BAY. North of **Cape Mendocino**, Trinidad Bay was discovered by **Bruno de Hezeta** and **Juan Francisco de la Bodega y Quadra** in June 1775. During their nine-day stay, the Spaniards visited the local Yurok Indians and provided detailed descriptions of their way of life, clothing, and armaments. On 11 June, the day of the "ineffable mystery of the Most Blessed Holy Trinity," the **act of possession** was performed, the first north of **San Francisco**, which was being explored and established in the same period, 1774–1776. The wooden cross set up on Trinidad Head was visited by **Archibald Menzies**, during the **George Vancouver** Expedition's stopover in May 1793. Menzies was still able to make out the inscription "Carolus III. Dei. G. Hyspaniarum. Rex." The English mariner **Peter Corney** confirmed that it was still there in 1817. In 1913 a large granite cross was erected on the same spot with the same Latin inscription referring to King Charles III.

– U –

ULLOA, FRANCISCO DE. A Spanish navigator, Francisco de Ulloa's explorations during 1539–1540 established the nature of the **Gulf of California** and the southwest coast of **Baja California**. The earliest explorations of Sonora and Baja California were not promising in terms of finding gold, but when Alvar Nuñez Cabeza de Vaca returned to Mexico City in 1536, after years of wandering in what is today the southern United States and northern Mexico, with stories of golden cities, interest in the north was rekindled. Both Viceroy Antonio de Mendoza and **Hernán Cortés** responded with plans for new expeditions that resulted in the exploration activities of Marcos de Niza, Francisco de Ulloa, **Hernando de Alarcón**, and Francisco Vásquez de Coronado.

Cortés appointed Ulloa to command three ships, which left Acapulco on 8 July 1539. One was wrecked in the gulf but the *Santa Agueda* and the *Trinidad* reached La Paz on the east coast of Baja California where Ulloa had earlier been in charge of Cortés's short-lived settlement. Recrossing the gulf to the mainland shore, Ulloa proceeded north past present-day Guaymas to see if access to the golden cities could be gained from the sea. Reaching the swift running waters and violent seas at the mouth of the Colorado River, and surveying the bleak landscape, he retreated down the west coast of the peninsula, becoming the first person to realize that Baja California was not an island. Despite this discovery, which was initially reflected in 16th-century maps, the old idea of the "island of California" resurfaced in the 17th century, and continued to appear on maps well into the 18th century. Passing La Paz and rounding **Cabo San Lucas** he sailed up the outer coast. In January 1540 he discovered the Isla de Cedros and may have reached Punta Canoas before retreating to the island in the face of strong winds. He then sent the *Santa Agueda* back to Acapulco with an account of the expedition and continued his exploration northward in the *Trinidad*. How far he sailed is open to conjecture, but it could have been as far as Punta San Antonio near latitude 30° N.

Two narratives of the early part of the voyage, by Ulloa himself and by Francisco Preciado, and two maps by the pilots Juan de Castellon and Pedro de Bermes have survived. The latter formed the basis of the influential maps of Battista Agnese in 1542 and Sebastian Cabot in 1544. Both show clearly the Sea of Cortés or Gulf of California and that Ulloa's voyage had effectively established the shape of lower Baja California.

UMNAK. The third largest island in the **Aleutian Islands** chain, Umnak was reached by **Stepan Glotov** in September 1759 and recorded by its **Aleut** name in the reports of the **Petr Krenitsyn** and **Mikhail Levashov** Expedition, 1768. It had earlier been a battleground in the Aleut–Russian War of 1763. **James Cook** gave it the name "Oomanak" in 1778. The first **Russian Orthodox** chapel in the eastern Aleutians was built at the village of Recheshnoe (Nikolski) in 1806 by the Aleut leader Ivan Glotov to recognize his baptism by his godfather Stepan Glotov in 1759.

UNALASKA. The second largest of the **Aleutian Islands** (after **Unimak**), Unalaska was probably seen by **Aleksei Chirikov** in 1741, but was not reached by Russian *promyshlenniki* until 1760. Here, at the end of the deep, natural harbor of Unalaska Bay, **Stepan Glotov** visited the village of Iliuliuk and encountered the descendants of the Unangan (**Aleut**) people who had lived around the bay for over 9,000 years. The Russians later referred to the place as "Dutch Harbor," believing that it had been discovered by a Dutch vessel. The island was explored in part by **Mikhail Levashov**, who spent the winter of 1768–1769 in an interior inlet of the bay. He made the first drawings depicting the native people of the area, their dwellings, and material culture.

In 1778 **James Cook** visited nearby Samgoonoodha Bay (English Bay) on two occasions. He referred to the island as "Oonalaska." On the second visit he established cordial relations with the navigator-hunter **Gerasim Izmailov**, who was living at the hunting/trading post set up at Iliuliuk. He corrected Cook's charts and provided information about coasts unknown to the Englishman. It was on Unalaska that **John Webber** drew his compelling portraits of native men and women, and also the interior of a semi-subterranean house. In 1791–1792 **Gavriil Sarychev** spent the winter in Unalaska Bay. He undertook further exploration and placed "Illyulyuk" on a map dated 1792, which was later published in his Atlas (1826). The Spanish expedition of **Esteban José Martínez** and **Gonzalo López de Haro** met the Russian trader **Potap Zaikov** in Unalaska Bay in 1788 and, despite Russian prior discovery, secretly performed an **act of possession**.

UNAMUNO, PEDRO DE (fl. 1587). Pedro de Unamuno commanded the **Manila galleon** *Nuestra Señora de Esperanza* from the Philippines in 1587, and was ordered to search for the mythical islands of Rica de Oro and Rica de Plata, believed to exist east of Japan. Unamuno was predictably unsuccessful in this quest, but he partially fulfilled a second command—to explore the **California** coast for a safe harbor. On 18 October he entered what was long thought to be Morro Bay near San Luis Obispo but which, from its latitude and description, was more likely Santa Cruz Bay farther north. Naming it San Lucas in recognition of the saint's day, he claimed the region with an **act of possession**. An inland reconnaissance was abandoned in the face of native hostility. The result of this encounter was an official order prohibiting inland exploration, which temporarily deterred interest in colonization on **New Spain**'s northern frontier. Effective exploration down the rest of the coast was hampered by persistent fog, but this poor weather probably saved the galleon from attack by the English buccaneer **Thomas Cavendish**, who was cruising the coast off **Cabo San Lucas** and who, a few days later, successfully intercepted and looted the great *Santa Ana*.

UNIMAK. The largest of the **Aleutian Islands**, Unimak sits immediately southwest of the **Alaska Peninsula**. It was likely discovered by **Stepan Glotov** in 1760 and was also visited by **Gavriil Pushkarev** as he headed towards **Alaska**. *Promyshlenniki* under Dmitrii Pankov spent the winter of 1761–1762 on the island. In the summer of 1775 **Potap Zaikov** made the island his base for three years, hunting as far east as **Kodiak** Island. On Unimak he enjoyed good relations with the local natives and collected valuable information about their lives and culture. The name of the island derives from "Ooneemak" recorded by **James Cook** in 1778 after his visit to nearby **Unalaska**. He had earlier passed to the south, noting "some hills," which dominate the island ". . . whose elevated summits were seen towering above the clouds to a most stupendious height. The most South westerly was discovered to be a Volcano which continually threw out a vast column of smoke." This was likely Mt. Shisaldin, the other Mt. Isanotski, both of which were sketched by **William Ellis**. In June 1778 Cook had no reason to believe that he had come to the end of the continent, but his charts show that passing north of the island in early July, and receiving information from the Russians who visited him later during his second visit to Unalaska, he had rightly surmised that it was not part of continental America.

URDANETA, ANDRÉS DE (1508–1568). Andrés de Urdaneta came to **New Spain** in 1538. For 20 years he served as an advisor to Viceroy Antonio de Mendoza and gained a reputation as a geographer. At the request of Philip II in 1559, he was asked to command an expedition to the Philippines to secure the islands for Spain, but because he was by then a priest he recommended that it be led by Miguel López de Legazpi, with himself as navigator. Five ships left Navidad in November 1564. While conquest of the Philippines was the chief aim of the expedition, Urdaneta also wanted to test his theory that a return voyage could be made from the western Pacific by sailing far to the north and catching the prevailing winds that would bring a ship eastwards. This was the longed-for *tournaviaje* that would obviate the necessity of Spanish ships returning to the Atlantic through the Portuguese-dominated seas of the world. Although the first return voyage was credited to another ship in the Legazpi expedition, the *San Lucas* of Alonso Arrellano, navigated by his pilot Lope Martín, Urdaneta on the *San Pedro* left the Philippines on 1 June 1565, crossed the Pacific in a wide arc by sailing as far north as 42° and reached Acapulco on 18 September. Though he followed Arrellano by six weeks, Urdaneta is regarded as the true pioneer of the trans-Pacific route because it was his theory that was proven correct, and it was he who provided a guide for future sailors to develop the commercial revolution that was the **Manila galleon**. It was the introduction of this trade route that rekindled interest in the coast of **California** and led to the first approaches to **Oregon**.

– V –

VALDÉS Y FLORES, CAYETANO (1767–1835). Cayetano Valdés was only 22 years old when selected to participate in the **Alejandro Malaspina** Expedition, on which he visited **Yakutat Bay** and the Spanish establishment at Nootka in 1791. Valdés never completed the voyage around the Pacific Ocean because he was appointed by Malaspina to command the *Mexicana* and accompany **Dionisio Alcalá Galiano** in the *Sutil* to explore the interior channels of the **Strait of Juan de Fuca** and the **Strait of Georgia** in the summer of 1792. He thus met with **George Vancouver** and achieved the first nonnative circumnavigation of **Vancouver Island**, exploring the long continental fiords and islands that separate it from the mainland. He returned to Spain via Mexico in 1793. Thereafter, he enjoyed a distinguished but turbulent career in the navy and politics.

VANCOUVER, GEORGE (1757–1798). Vancouver sailed aboard the *Resolution* on **James Cook**'s Second Voyage to the Pacific, during which he studied under the noted astronomer William Wales as the expedition searched for the legendary southern continent. In 1776 he was appointed to the *Discovery* for Cook's Third Voyage in search of the Pacific entrance to the **Northwest Passage**. Vancouver's lengthy apprenticeship under Cook provided him with a unique learning opportunity in seamanship and surveying, and allowed him to experience the leadership of the greatest navigator of his age.

In 1789 the Spanish expulsion of British whalers in Patagonia, and London's growing interest in establishing a settlement on the Northwest Coast to develop the **fur trade** with China, caused the Admiralty to plan the dispatch of a naval vessel to show the flag in the South Atlantic en route to the North Pacific. **Henry Roberts**, a veteran of Cook's last two voyages, was appointed commander with Vancouver as his second in command. Mobilization of the British fleet following the **Nootka Sound Incident** cancelled the departure of the newly-built *Discovery*, but with the signing of the first **Nootka Convention** in 1790 the plan was resurrected. With Roberts under consideration for another assignment, Vancouver was given command of the *Discovery* with instructions to undertake a thorough survey of a coast over much of which the Convention had unexpectedly given England equal authority to Spain. He was also to meet with a Spanish commissioner at Nootka to receive back the lands taken from English traders in 1789.

It was a more complex task than previously contemplated when a settlement was the prime goal, and the result was that the brig *Chatham* commanded by **William Broughton** was added to the expedition. It was expected that Vancouver would finally solve the continuing mystery of the existence of a Northwest Passage and formally establish an English presence on the Northwest Coast.

Vancouver's remarkable survey of 10,000 miles of coastline over three summers, 1792–1794, was as heroic and successful a hydrographic initiative as ever undertaken by the Royal Navy. Much of the work was done in small boats. During the voyage, Vancouver also negotiated, unsuccessfully, with **Juan Francisco de la Bodega y Quadra** concerning the return of the lands in **Nootka Sound**, but successfully with King Kamehameha in **Hawaii** to cede to Britain the islands whose unification he promoted over three visits.

The expedition sailed on 1 April 1791. Proceeding to the Pacific via the Cape of Good Hope, Vancouver examined the southwest coast of Australia and visited New Zealand, Tahiti, and Hawaii before landfall was made on the coast of **New Albion**, some 115 miles above **San Francisco** on 16 April 1792. Sailing north with a plan to explore the **Strait of Juan de Fuca**, Vancouver began the first of three seasons surveying the coast. Once in Fuca, he established a modus operandi for the entire campaign made necessary by the intricate nature of the shoreline, and the *Chatham*'s unsuitability for close inshore work. He became convinced that the bulk of the exploring would have to be done in small boats. The ships were anchored as they moved north, therefore, at various locations for an extended period of time. These anchorages—for example initially in Port Discovery, Birch Bay, and Desolation Sound—became the bases from which the small boat parties set out on their exploration sorties. The key figures in these parties soon became **Joseph Whidbey** and **James Johnstone**, although both Vancouver (before he became too ill) and **Peter Puget** made important contributions. In addition, at each anchorage, an observatory was set up to provide the basic readings for the survey's overall framework. In 1793 **Thomas Heddington** captured such a scene in his panoramic view of "Salmon Cove, Observatory Inlet."

The summer of 1792 was spent circumnavigating **Vancouver Island**, with the expedition proving conclusively that the Strait of Juan de Fuca offered no entrance to a passage across the continent. An important discovery was **Puget Sound**, the survey of which put to rest any idea of a water link with the Mississippi River. Broughton explored the San Juan Islands, and Vancouver himself headed a small boat party that explored Burrard Inlet—the site of the city that now bears his name, Howe Sound, and Jervis Inlet. This was a prelude to his encounter on 22 June with the Spaniards **Dionisio Alcalá Galiano** and **Cayetano Valdés** off Point Grey in the **Strait of Georgia**. The meeting was cordial and the two commanders shared their survey results and agreed to work together, which they did for a short time until the limitations of the Spanish ships and Vancouver's determination to make sure that his boats explored all the inlets, even those discovered by the Spaniards, hastened his departure towards Nootka. This he had been keen to do once he had been informed by Alcalá Galiano that the Spanish commissioner, Bodega y Quadra, was awaiting his arrival, and by the work of Whidbey, Puget, and Johnstone, which suggested that the Arran Rapids and the narrow channels, Discovery Passage and Johnstone Strait, tending towards the west, ultimately led back into the Pacific. Nevertheless, before he ended the season and headed down the west coast of Vancouver Island, Vancouver took time to move beyond Queen Charlotte Sound to explore the continental coast as far north as Burke Channel. At Nootka, while he appreciated the hospitality of Bodega, he was frustrated by the Spaniard's refusal to hand over the port as expected, and he certainly wanted nothing to do with Bodega's suggestion that he negotiate a boundary between English and Spanish interests at the Strait of Juan de Fuca. He left the Spaniards in charge at **Friendly Cove** while he sought further instructions from London. After its sojourn at Nootka (28 August–12 October) the expedition continued its investigations as it sailed south; on the way to **Monterey**, Whidbey investigated **Gray's Harbor** and Broughton in the *Chatham* managed to cross the bar of the **Columbia River** and chart its lower reaches.

After wintering in **Hawaii**, the expedition resumed the survey in May 1793 with Puget commanding the *Chatham* after Broughton had returned to England. The summer was largely spent among the labyrinthine channels, islands, and inlets that make up the coast of **British Columbia**. In June, when Vancouver explored Dean Channel, he had narrowly missed what would have been a remarkable meeting with **Alexander Mackenzie**, who ended his trek across the continent there some six weeks after Vancouver's visit. Although he retained a few of the names that appeared on **Jacinto Caamaño**'s chart shared with him at Nootka in 1792, Vancouver's toponyms naturally reflected his own heritage—King Island, Fitzhugh Sound, Princess Royal Island, Douglas, Gardner and Grenville Channels, Portland Canal, Dixon Entrance, Clarence Strait, and Prince of Wales Archipelago. The expedition ended its season on 21 September, slightly above 56° N at Port Protection, which opens onto Sumner Strait at the top of Prince of Wales Island. But this was not achieved before Vancouver had come close to being killed when his boat came under attack from a party of hostile **Tlingit** in Behm Canal. After running down the west coast of the **Queen Charlotte Islands**, Vancouver retraced his steps to Nootka Sound and then proceeded on to Monterey and **San Diego**, finishing the year's survey efforts on the northern coast of **Baja California**.

The final season, 1794, began in early April off **Kodiak** Island and in "Cook's River." It did not take long to prove that neither Knik Arm nor Turnagain Arm provided river access, let alone a passage leading to Hudson Bay. Moving east Vancouver explored the waters of **Prince William Sound**, by now well traveled by the Russians, English traders, and the Spanish, while Puget moved south exploring **Yakutat Bay** and the adjacent coast. The *Discovery* and *Chatham* then met up in **Cross Sound** to complete their survey of the **Alexander Archipelago**. The pattern of small boat excursions to achieve the precision required was continued, and the work was often made more exacting by poor weather, the hostility of the local Tlingit, and the intricate maze of channels, bays, straits, and inlets. Joseph Whidbey began with an exploration of Cross Sound, Icy Strait, and the Lynn Canal, before proceeding down Chatham Strait and seeing the open ocean beyond Cape Decision (1793) and Cape Ommaney. He retraced his steps to the ships and Cross Sound, after which Vancouver moved his base to Port Conclusion on the southeast corner of Baranof Island, from where the final boat trips under Whidbey and Johnstone explored Frederick Sound, Stephens Passage and Taku Inlet, and Chatham and Keku Straits. Meeting up in Frederick Sound, the two boat crews performed an **act of possession** ceremony before returning to the ships on 18 August. On completion of the survey Vancouver felt confident enough to write: "I trust the precision with which the survey of the coast . . . has been carried into effect, will remove every doubt, and set aside every opinion of a Northwest Passage. . . ."

Before quitting the coast Vancouver made a final visit to Nootka Sound to see if further instructions might have arrived to allow him to settle matters with the Spanish. They had not, and he proceeded to Monterey with the same thought in mind. But no new dispatches had arrived there either and so, refreshed for the final time by Spanish hospitality, he left for home on 2 December 1794. The expedition formally ended with the arrival of the *Discovery* in the Thames on 20 October 1795.

Vancouver's achievement was never adequately recognized at the time. Only in recent years has his reputation as a great navigator and explorer become enhanced, and his personal courage in the face of a debilitating illness associated with kidney disease fully appreciated. It is often overlooked that he was already a very sick man before the end of the 1793 survey season. Disproving something like the Northwest Passage, while useful and necessary, could never be the same as an important discovery. England's rapprochement with Spain and the looming crisis with France soon diverted the government's attention far from the North Pacific. Vancouver was also dogged by reports that he had been an irascible and harsh commander. His difficulties with **Archibald Menzies** and Sir **Joseph Banks** froze him out of a wide circle of people whose respect and support he might have enjoyed. And his clash with the psychotic midshipman Thomas Pitt, later Lord Camelford, whom he punished severely and finally sent home during the voyage, robbed him of any sympathy from another circle of government contacts. He spent his final years working on his journal; it was unfinished at his death and had to be completed by his brother John. *A Voyage of Discovery to the North Pacific Ocean and round the World* was published in 1798 in an attractive edition of three quarto volumes with an accompanying atlas.

VANCOUVER ISLAND. The largest island on the Northwest Coast, Vancouver Island was formed by the partial submergence of the outer edge of the coastal cordillera. It is separated in the north by Queen Charlotte Strait from the islands of the same name, and in the south from the State of **Washington** by the **Strait of Juan de Fuca**. A rugged spine of mountains separates the deeply indented west coast, whose abundant marine and forest resources supported the rich cultural life of the **Nootka** (now the Nuu-Chal-Nulth First Nations) for thousands of years, from the climatically milder coastal lowlands on the eastern side, where Coast Salish nations at the time of contact enjoyed mixed marine and agricultural economies.

When **Juan Pérez** saw, and **James Cook** visited, the outer coast in 1774 and 1778 respectively, they had no way of knowing that they had found an island; indeed, for the first few years following the beginning of the maritime **fur trade** (1785) and the creation of a Spanish establishment at **Friendly Cove** in **Nootka Sound** (1789), the insularity of the encountered land mass could not be easily appreciated. This began to change as fur traders began to probe the Strait of Juan de Fuca in the late 1780s, and Spanish naval officers followed with three consecutive summers of exploration, 1790–1792. In the last year, **Dionisio Alcalá Galiano** and **Cayetano Valdés** were joined by **George Vancouver** and **William Broughton** in completing the first circumnavigations.

During his visit to the Tahsis Inlet village of Chief **Maquinna** with **Juan Francisco de la Bodega y Quadra** in September 1792, Vancouver proposed that the "tract of land that had first been navigated by us" be named "the island of Quadra and Vancouver." Bodega was (according to Vancouver) "highly pleased" with this suggestion and the double name appeared on both English and Spanish charts until Spain's influence in the **Pacific Northwest** declined and "Quadra" was dropped. By 1824 the **Hudson's Bay Company** (HBC) was referring to "Vancouver's Island" in official correspondence, and its influential position on the coast ensured that this would become the standard for future charts and maps. Sometime later the apostrophe ending was eliminated and the island took on its present name.

Permanent European settlement did not take place until 1843 when **James Douglas** was directed by the HBC to select the site of a fort that might replace **Fort Vancouver** on the Columbia River if the disputed Oregon Territory was lost to the United States. He chose Fort Victoria and, when the Oregon Treaty confirmed the island as British territory in 1846, Victoria became the capital of the Colony of Vancouver Island, 1849–1866. During 1864, merchants and scientists undertook the Vancouver Island Exploring Expedition, looking for major coal and gold deposits. They were disappointed, but they described several parts of the island previously unknown. In 1866 the colony was combined with the mainland Colony of British Columbia and, united, they entered the Dominion of Canada as **British Columbia** in 1871.

VASIL'EV, IVAN FILIPPOVICH (1776–1812). Navigator, cartographer, and artist, Ivan Filippovich Vasil'ev served in the Baltic Sea until a request to join the **Russian–American Company** led to his appointment on the *Neva* to sail to the North Pacific with **Ludwig von Hagemeister** in 1806. During the years 1807–1811 he was responsible for producing a series of superb charts of the area around **Sitka Sound** and **New Archangel**, and of Pavlovsk Harbor and other parts of the coast of **Kodiak** Island. These were highly praised by the influential naval officer **Vasilii Golovnin**, when he visited **Russian America** in 1810, and Vasil'ev's notes and cartographic surveys were used by **Gavriil Sarychev** in compiling his atlas published in 1826. Vasil'ev also made a number of sketches of the settlements at both Sitka and Kodiak. After returning to Petropavlovsk in 1811, he sailed in the company's brigantine, *Novaia Finlandiia*, in the western **Aleutian Islands** and the **Commander Islands**, bringing relief to *promyshlenniki* there who had been cut off from the world for a number of years. Again he drew excellent charts and made extensive notes of the people and places he encountered; these have since proved valuable to ethnographers studying the early history of Atkha and Attu. He returned to Okhotsk in 1812 but died shortly afterwards in a *baidarka* accident in the harbor.

VASIL'EV, IVAN I. (1797–ca. 1838). From 1822 Ivan I. Vasil'ev served on a variety of **Russian–American Company** ships, sailing from Sitka to **Kodiak** and **Unalaska**, to the **Commander Islands** and Okhotsk, and south to **California**. In 1829 he began two years of interior exploration starting from the Novo-Aleksandrovskii Redoubt established in **Bristol Bay** 10 years earlier. The ultimate purpose was an ambitious one: to explore the interior lakes and rivers lying between that bay, Kuskokwim Bay and ultimately **Norton Sound**; and to get a better understanding of the geography of the interior and the patterns of activity of its native people. In the first year, after crossing the **Alaska Peninsula** from Kodiak, he worked his way up to Lake Aleknagik, retraced his steps and ascended the Nushagak and Nuyakuk rivers back into the lake country. He hoped to cross the mountains into the valley of the Kuskokwim, but could find no native guides to show him the way. He tried again via Lake Aleknagik but without success. In 1830 he traveled again to the mouth of the Nushagnak River from Kodiak; he then proceeded far upriver until he was able to cross over to the Hoholitna that took him down to the Kuskokwim, where he visited a number of native settlements and collected high-quality fox and sable furs. This second expedition was especially important in persuading chief manager **Ferdinand Wrangell** of the potential of the Kuskokwim fur trade, and he ordered establishment of the first permanent trading post on the river. Vasil'ev was the precursor of more expeditions undertaken by **Fedor Kolmakov** (1833) and **Lavrentii Zagoskin** (1842–1844). Back in **New Archangel** in 1833, Vasil'ev undertook some surveying activity in **Sitka Sound** (the Biorka Islands, Olga Strait) and in the waters to the north of Baranof Island (Peril Strait). He left Russian America in 1834.

VASIL'EV, MIKHAIL (1770–1847). Russian naval officer and explorer, Mikhail Vasil'ev led a round-the-world voyage to the **Bering Sea** and Arctic Ocean. This was the northern counterpart to the southern hemisphere voyage of Fabian von Bellingshausen that reached Antarctica in 1820–1821. Its chief task was to probe for the Pacific entrance to the **Northwest Passage**, which had also been the principal goal of the first **Otto von Kotzebue** Expedition. The Russians still held out hope that it was possible to find a way through the ice that had defeated **James Cook** over 40 years earlier. Sailing from **Kamchatka** through the **Bering Strait** in 1820, Vasil'ev explored the **Alaska** coast from Cape Lisburne to **Icy Cape**, and finally reached 71°6′ N, 116°8′ W, 100 miles north of the cape and some 28 miles farther than Cook had been able to sail. The next summer, 1821, the ships explored the continental coast north from **Bristol Bay**

and discovered Nunivak Island off Alaska in latitude 60° N, whose presence had surprisingly eluded earlier explorers. After a survey had been made of **St. Lawrence Island**, the Russians again sailed through the Bering Strait, but were no more successful in making progress through the ice flows than in the previous year. Their two seasons of work had in fact added little to what Cook had learned in 1778, and the Russian navy abandoned hopes of finding a navigable route across the top of America.

VENIAMINOV, IOANN (1797–1871). The most renowned priest in the **Russian Orthodox Church** to serve in **Russian America**, Ioann Veniaminov arrived at the fur-trading settlement of Illiuliuk on **Unalaska** Island in 1824, staying until 1834, when he went to **New Archangel** and later to **Fort Ross** from which he visited the Spanish missions near **San Francisco**. He ended his first tour of duty in America in 1838. Visiting Sitka in 1837, **Edward Belcher** was much impressed by the energetic and intelligent priest and was shown his personal workshop in which he was making an organ and a barometer. While in Unalaska he had recorded daily details of the weather.

On his arrival in Illiuliuk, Veniaminov trained a group of **natives** to replace the original chapel (1812) with a new Church of the Ascension, consecrated in 1826. By this time he had traveled extensively by *baidarka* to visit the outlying islands of his eastern Aleutian parish, which stretched from the **Shumagin Islands** in the east to **Umnak** Island in the west. He quickly mastered the **Aleut** language and began to write both original material and to translate the scriptures and other sacred texts. In this way he made a pioneer contribution to the development of a written Aleut language and to Aleut literacy. His *Indication of the Way to the Kingdom of Heaven*, originally written in Aleut, went into 40 editions in Russian and was translated into all of the major languages of the world. It is still used in the Orthodox Church as an instructional text. More important for **historians** and ethnographers is his *Notes on the Islands of the Unalaska District* published in St. Petersburg in 1840. It provides an exhaustive analysis of the geography of the region and its inhabitants: their character, customs, religious faith, government, food, language, traditions and stories, and music. It also includes a long appendix on the culture and language of the **Tlingit**, information gathered in New Archangel. An

English edition appeared in 1984. He also published an Aleut grammar and dictionary in 1846.

Within two years of his return to Europe, Veniaminov was on his way back to America as the new bishop of **Kamchatka**, the Kurile Islands, and the Aleutians, an immense diocese. Basing himself in Sitka until 1850, he oversaw the consecration of the new cathedral of St. Michael (1848) but perhaps more importantly introduced a special church for the local Tlingit (1849) and a seminary (1845) in which clergy were trained to speak and write at least one native language. He also expanded missionary activity among the Yup'ik of southwest **Alaska**.

In 1850 Veniaminov became archbishop of Iakutsk and left Russian America to concentrate on the vast region of eastern Siberia. In 1868 Czar Alexander II appointed him metropolitan of Moscow and head of the entire Church. Veniaminov's importance to the development of Russian America as parish priest, missionary, administrator, and scholar is indisputable. His genuine concern for its native peoples, respecting their traditional customs and promoting the use of their languages, involved a unique approach to his work, and was the most important legacy of his remarkable stewardship. In 1977 he was glorified as Saint Innocent of Alaska.

VERDÍA, JOSÉ ANTONIO (fl. 1788–1791). José Antonio Verdía participated as a pilot in three expeditions to the Northwest Coast. In 1788 he apprenticed on the **Esteban José Martínez** and **Gonzalo López de Haro** Expedition that explored the Gulf of Alaska and the **Aleutian Islands**; in 1789 he sailed with **Martínez** to occupy **Nootka Sound** and thus witnessed the **Nootka Sound Incident**; and in 1790 he came north again with **Francisco de Eliza** to reoccupy **Friendly Cove** and construct the establishment at Yuquot. Verdía was a valued participant on the *San Carlos* when, in the summer of 1791, Eliza led an important exploring expedition into the **Strait of Juan de Fuca**. Anchoring in what is today Esquimalt Harbour, Eliza sent Verdía in a longboat accompanied by a number of soldiers to explore **Manuel Quimper**'s Canal de López de Haro (1790). It proved to be a short day trip as the boat was constantly menaced by hostile **natives**, whose canoes grew in number despite the soldiers opening fire. They caused Verdía to retreat and it fell to **Juan Pantoja y Arriaga** to explore the strait more fully. However, Verdía commanded an armed longboat that accompanied **José María Narváez** for three weeks on the first European exploration of the **Strait of Georgia**. Later, at Nootka, he worked assiduously with the other pilots to complete the charts of the expedition.

VERNACCI, JUAN (1763–1810). Like a number of other officers recruited for the **Alejandro Malaspina** Expedition Juan Vernacci had worked under the famous Vicente Tofiño in the marine survey of the Iberian Peninsula in the second half of the 1780s. He served on the *Atrevida* and was valued for his knowledge of astronomy, becoming a key member of the group who rated the chronometers and recorded countless celestial observations, especially when a stopover, such as that at Port Mulgrave (**Yakutat Bay**) in **Alaska**, allowed the expedition to set up a proper observatory and use the Ramsden quadrant.

His greatest contribution to exploration came in the summer of 1792 when he was detached from the main expedition to return to the Northwest Coast as second-in-command on the *Mexicana*, under **Cayetano Valdés**, for the **Dionisio Alcalá Galiano** and Valdés Expedition. He played a leading role in the small boat surveys that explored the various inlets, bays, narrows, and islands along the continental coast as the Spanish circumnavigated **Vancouver Island**. These included Burrard Inlet, the site of the city of Vancouver, and a seven-day survey of the extensive Knight Inlet, which Alcalá Galiano named Brazo de Vernacci in his honor, during which the artist **José Cardero** drew his famous picture of a waterfall. Vernacci often had the Arnold chronometer number 344 and an artificial horizon with him to aid his observations and surveying, and his achievement over an intense seven-week period in the maze of islands north of the **Strait of Georgia** was impressive.

VIOLENCE. From their first encounters, violence was part of the Euroamerican/Native American experience on the Northwest Coast. Initially, the loss of sailors in landing parties (**Aleksei Chirikov** in 1741 and **Juan Francisco de la Bodega y Quadra** in 1775) was a **native** response to trespassing and fear of "the other." In general, encounters involving explorers such as **James Cook**, Bodega, **Ignacio de Arteaga**, **Jean François de La Pérouse**, **Alejandro Malaspina**, and **George Vancouver**, though not without moments of tension (such as those experienced by **José Bustamante** at Yakutat in 1791 and Vancouver in the Behm Canal in 1793) were relatively stable. This was due to a basic discipline inherent in naval vessels. The murder of Chief Callicum at Nootka by **Esteban José Martínez** in 1789, and the killing of natives by **Salvador Fidalgo** at **Neah Bay** in 1792 in retaliation for the murder of a Spanish sailor were isolated incidents and must be set against such friendly relationships as that between Bodega and Chief **Maquinna** in 1792.

It was the coming of the fur traders, who introduced competition and aggression into the picture, that caused an almost immediate and rapid decline in relations. The Euroamericans considered themselves socially, economically, and spiritually superior, and their prejudices soon rationalized abuse and violence, especially when faced with an underlying native hostility and desire to steal anything from sailors' clothing to nails from the ship. Only when trade brought advantage was this hostility held in check; tolerance and enmity essentially existed side by side. When deceit, hostage taking, alcohol, guns and revenge for slights real or imagined entered the equation, the ferocity of the exchanges was often horrific. The worst violence occurred when traders encouraged too many natives to surround their ships and then lost control, as in the cases of the *Boston* at Nootka (1803) and the *Tonquin* in Clayoquot Sound (1811), or nearly did so when trading was used to mask a sudden attack; then there was swift retribution that inevitably killed numerous natives. Perhaps the worst act of retaliation was **Robert Gray**'s destruction of the 200-house village of Opitsat in 1792. For many years the **Tlingit** barely tolerated the Russians, destroying the first **New Archangel** (1802) and always threatening to ambush **Aleuts** brought into the **Alexander Archipelago**. Sometimes they were successful and the Russians were obliged to send armed longboats to protect their hunters.

VIZCAÍNO, SEBASTIÁN (ca. 1548–1624). Sebastián Vizcaíno led an official expedition to the coast of **California** at the turn of the 17th century. It was the last Spanish voyage of any consequence towards the Northwest Coast before the 1770s, and ended the initial period of interest in the western maritime frontier of **New Spain** inspired by **Hernán Cortés** in the 1530s.

During the 1580s Vizcaíno was sailing with the **Manila galleons** and he survived the looting of the *Santa Ana* by **Thomas Cavendish** in 1587. In 1595 he received a monopoly on the pearl fishery at Cortés's short-lived establishment at La Paz, but when his party reached **Baja California** storms prevented any fishing, and the arid landscape and native hostility defeated any hope of a settlement. Nevertheless, Vizcaíno's faith in wealth through Californian pearls, gold, and silver coincided with the viceroy's alarm over the loss of the *San Agustin* under **Sebastián Rodriguez Cermeño** in 1595. This allowed him to persuade the Count of Monterrey to receive royal approval for an expedition to explore further the potential of the pearl fishery, and to continue the search for safe harbors for the eastbound galleons.

Vizcaíno left Acapulco on 8 June 1602 with three ships—the *San Diego*, *San Tomás*, and *Tres Reyes*—and orders to undertake "the discovery and charting of ports, bays, and inlets which exist between **Cabo San Lucas** at 22°15′ and **Cape Mendocino** at 42°." To avoid native hostility he was not to undertake sorties inland, and was required to respect the toponyms established by **Juan Rodríguez Cabrillo** in 1542.

The expedition battled its way up the coast of Baja California, taking five months to reach Cabrillo's Bahia de San Miguel on 10 November 1602. Vizcaíno renamed it **San Diego** in honor of the feast day of the saint. By this time he had replaced many of Cabrillo's other names and had even called the great bay north of Isla de Cedros after himself. Leaving San Diego, he landed on Santa Catalina Island before proceeding through the Santa Barbara Channel; he had rounded and named Point Concepción by 8 December. On 16 December the ships anchored off **Monterey**, which Vizcaíno named after the viceroy, describing it as "the best port that could be wished for."

With many sailors suffering from scurvy, and 16 men already dead, Vizcaíno detached the *San Tomás* to return to Acapulco with a report on his progress. Leaving Monterey on 3 January 1603, the *San Diego* and *Tres Reyes* proceeded north reaching Drake's Bay and naming its headland **Point Reyes** on 5 January. On 7 January the ships became separated. Caught in a gale Vizcaíno passed Cape Mendocino, but on 19 January, his crew ravaged by sickness, he turned for home and arrived in Acapulco on 21 March. The *Tres Reyes* under Martín de Aguilar had been driven by the same gale into an anchorage north of Mendocino and was able to continue the voyage. The ship's exact northern progress is unclear, as is its identification of the mysterious **Rio de Martín Aguilar**, but it probably reached the California–Oregon border at 42° N. Having exceeded the expedition's instructions, the *Tres Reyes* turned south and on 23 February 1603 sailed into Acapulco. By then she was manned by only five survivors, and the expedition as a whole had cost the lives of more than 40 men.

No logs or onboard journals have survived, but summaries of the voyage and other records still exist. Its major achievement was the charting of Monterey Bay, but the favorable reports of Vizcaíno and **Antonio de la Ascensión** made their "sheltered harbor" unrecognizable to the **Sacred Expedition** in 1769. More useful were two route maps. One, describing the coast from the north from Cape Mendocino to San Diego and including the Mexican coast, was drawn by the pilot of the *San Diego*, **Francisco Bolaños**; the other, from the south was drawn as far as Monterey by Gerónimo Martín Palacios. The former map was used by galleons approaching the coast for over 125 years.

If searching for the **Strait of Anian** or the fabulous city of **Quivira** had been the unwritten purposes of the expedition, there was disappointment. The Californian coast had once again proven to be rugged and stormy. There were no golden islands, abundant pearl fisheries, or rich civilizations. A new viceroy immediately blocked any suggestion of a settlement at Monterey or further searches for the fabled strait. He reasoned that it was unnecessary for the galleons to stop so close to Acapulco and that discovering a passage to the Atlantic would merely invite interlopers into the Spanish Lake. The first period of active exploration aimed at the Northwest Coast from the south thus came to an end. Vizcaíno did sail once again into the North Pacific. Between 1611 and 1613 he was commissioned to visit Japan and return with a delegation of diplomatic dignitaries. In this he was successful; less so was his fruitless search for the islands of Rica de Oro and Rica de Plata, now thought to be Marcus Island at 154° E, 24° N.

VORONIN, LUKA (1765–?). Artist on the **Joseph Billings** Expedition, Luka Voronin was chosen to sketch the natives' "furs, dresses, arms and manufactures" as well as "the most curious products of nature" and "views of the coast and remarkable objects." A recent graduate of the Academy of Fine Arts in St. Petersburg he set out with Billings, **Gavriil Sarychev**, and **Martin Sauer** on the trans-Siberian journey that would ultimately take him to the **Aleutian Islands** and south along the Northwest Coast, across the **Bering Sea**, and with his commander over the Chukotskii Peninsula to the Kolyma River. Sarychev praised his work, and an engraving of Voronin's fine portrait of a "Woman of Unalaska" is reproduced in the atlas to Sarychev's *Puteshestvie flota Kapitana Sarycheva po severovostochnoi chasti Sibiri* (translated in 1807 as Account of a Voyage to the North-East of Siberia, the Frozen Ocean and the North-East sea). Also engraved is his view of **Grigorii Shelikhov**'s fur-trading establishment in **Three Saints Bay**. Other sketches extant in the Hydrographic Archives of the Ministry of Marine in St. Petersburg include the *Slava Rossii* (Glory of Russia) at anchor in front of the **Aleut** village of Iliuliuk in Unalaska Bay. The illustrations accompanying Martin Sauer's published account of the expedition, by contemporary British engraver William Alexander, inexplicably omit any credit to Voronin as the original artist.

VOZNESENSKII, IL'IA (1816–1871). Scholar, naturalist, and ethnographer, Il'ia Voznesenskii traveled extensively in **Russian America** in the 1840s collecting natural history specimens and ethnographic **artifacts** for the Academy of Sciences. He also gathered numerous duplicates that formed the basis of a collection in **New Archangel**, much of which found its way into the Peabody Museum at Harvard after 1867.

Voznesenskii arrived in New Archangel in 1840 and immediately advised the authorities on the description and cataloguing of existing collections. His first two collecting expeditions, 1841–1842, took him to **Fort Ross** and the environs of **San Francisco**; and then to Loreto in **Baja California**, where he collected representative flora of the peninsula. In late 1842 he went to **Kodiak** and used it as a base to undertake extensive collecting across the **Alaska** and **Kenai** peninsulas. During 1843 he made a long voyage into the **Bering Sea**, visiting **Unalaska**, the **Pribilof Islands**, **Norton Sound**, and **Kotzebue Sound**. After a visit to the Kurile Islands in early 1844, he set off from **Kamchatka** on a voyage that took him to the **Commander Islands** and Attu Island,

and again to the Pribilof Islands before arriving in **Sitka Sound**. He spent the balance of the year exploring and collecting in the **Alexander Archipelago**, before spending another winter, 1844–1845, in New Archangel. After two successful years in Kamchatka, Voznesenskii made a final stopover in New Archangel in late 1848 before leaving for Kronstadt with a remarkable treasure trove of over 3,600 specimens of mammals, birds, fish, mollusks, shells, animal skeletons, and other zoological items; 10,000 insects; over 2,000 dried plants; and hundreds of mineral specimens. In addition, his ethnological collections covered the geographical spectrum from California to the Alexander Archipelago, the Aleutian Islands, the east coast of the Bering and Chukchi Seas, and Kamchatka; they included weapons, clothing and adornments, and domestic utensils. These collections were accompanied by over 150 drawings and voluminous notes, reports, and journals. Returning to St. Petersburg in 1849, Voznesenskii spent the rest of his life documenting his collections: the work he began and the deciphering of his notes still continues.

– W –

WALKER, ALEXANDER (1764–1831). A young soldier in the service of the **East India Company**, Alexander Walker accompanied **James Strange** to **Nootka Sound** in 1786. When the plan to establish a military post and to install a garrison to support the **fur trade** was abandoned, he satisfied his natural curiosity by making a series of astute observations of life at Nootka and later in **Prince William Sound** (PWS).

At Nootka he preceded his contemporary **José Mariano Moziño** by six years and provided an account as important as that of the better-known Spaniard. He visited native villages and his memoir included a vocabulary. He commented on everything from trading practices to appearances, adornment and clothing, manners, cooking, fishing and hunting, and **cannibalism**. He initially thought that this was practiced but later changed his opinion from information provided by **John Mackay**, who was left at Nootka for a year. Walker tended to look upon the natives of Nootka as "noble savages" on their way to civilization; they were more at one with nature than Europeans, but obviously less cultivated and intelligent. The harsh environment and daily struggle with life made them at once aggressive and suspicious, even treacherous and deceitful; warmth and generosity were not among their more obvious traits, although loyalty to the group was present probably because "their safety depends on the strength of their mutual attachment."

In PWS he found the natives simple and timid but still skilled at theft. He wrote that contact with the Russians had not increased their happiness; rather the introduction of arms, alcohol, and **disease** in such a harsh climate had threatened their existence. He marveled at their skill in the *baidarka*, at the quality of manufacture of their hunting equipment, and at the skill with which they used their harpoons, bows, and arrows. He noted their skin clothing and its appropriateness for cold and wet weather, but he was disgusted by the extensive piercing of their faces to wear bone and wood adornments. As at Nootka he compiled a short dictionary.

A cultured man of letters, Walker reconstructed his journal from notes and memories some 30 years after the event because his original manuscript was lost. His writings tend to reflect the recollections of a more mature man, rather than the immediacy of a much younger observer. Nevertheless, they retain great value as one of the earliest accounts of west coast native peoples at the time of contact.

WASHINGTON. The northern part of the **Oregon** Territory, between the **Columbia River** and the **Strait of Juan de Fuca**, Washington became part of the United States under the terms of the **Oregon Treaty**, 1846. It was detached from Oregon to become the Washington Territory in 1853. It became a full state of the Union in 1889.

In 1774 **Juan Pérez** sailed close enough to the coast to name El Cerro de la Santa Rosalia (Mount Olympus) and thus identified Washington's first geographical feature. **Bruno de Hezeta** in 1775 and **James Cook** in 1778 ran the outer coast, but the northern coast, inside the Strait of Juan de Fuca, and **Puget Sound** were not explored until 1790–1792. In 1792 **Robert Gray** discovered **Gray's Harbor** and **William Broughton** explored Gray's Columbia River. In 1811 **David Thompson** navigated down the Columbia from the Rocky Mountains, and the American traders **Wilson Price Hunt** and David Stuart arrived at the Columbia via the Snake River.

Early settlement was almost exclusively centered in the lower Columbia River valley around **Fort Vancouver** until the 1830s and 1840s when settlers moved into Puget Sound and the southeast of the present-day state, where missionaries were also active. The Cowlitz Trail from the Columbia to Puget Sound expanded exploration and settlement in the north after 1845, and settlers came into the territory in the 1850s via the Snake River and the Emigrant Trail, a northern extension of the Oregon Trail from Fort Walla Walla. This served to link the southeast part of the region via the Yakima River to Puget Sound.

WAXELL, SVEN (1701–1762). Sven Waxell sailed with **Vitus Bering** in 1741 as first officer on the *St. Peter*, assuming a good deal of authority for the voyage as it unfolded when Bering spent more and more time in his cabin in poor health. Waxell essentially took over as Bering became almost completely incapacitated as the ship headed southwest out of the Gulf of Alaska along the **Aleutian Islands**. He steered the vessel, battered by almost perpetual storms, onto **Bering Island** in the Commander group in November and took command of the expedition when Bering died a month later. As others also died of scurvy, Waxell's leadership was put to the test, but he managed to maintain morale among the 45 survivors and oversaw the construction of a new ship, a 36-foot sloop, from the remains of the *St. Peter*. He safely navigated this vessel home to Petropavlovsk in August 1742.

Waxell's initial report, with the ship's log books, a chart of the American coast, and sketch maps of the islands of St. Elias (**Kayak Island** and its neighbors), **Shumagin**, and other Aleutian Islands were sent to the Admiralty, arriving in September, 1743. On one of his charts Waxell drew the first image of a native Alaskan, an honest but crude representation of an **Aleut** hunter in his *baidarka*.

Waxell also wrote a fuller account of the voyage. His manuscript, which was lost to the public for many years on different occasions, finally resurfaced in 1938 and was acquired by the Saltykov-Shchredin State Library in Leningrad. It provides details of the progress of the voyage and is an illuminating counterpoint to **Georg Wilhelm Steller**'s narrative, the only other firsthand account of the expedition. It was used by **Gerhardt Friedrich Müller** to construct his summary of the voyage published in 1758. In his account, Waxell emerges as an excellent seaman, a reluctant but prudent leader, conscientious and considerate of his men. Even the hypercritical Steller praised him for his work on Bering Island and his friendly encouragement as he strove to maintain morale. Waxell made it clear in his journal that he blamed the tragic end of the voyage on time lost searching for the nonexistent **Gamaland**, but it seems doubtful that this delay was as defining an issue as he suggested. The stormy weather encountered in the autumn appears much more problematical. More telling perhaps is the fact that Bering himself is barely mentioned, a reflection of Waxell's reluctance to speak critically of a distinguished fellow officer, but also an indication that the commander's inability to meet the challenges of the expedition was also a serious problem.

WEBBER, JOHN (1751–1793). Official artist on **James Cook**'s Third Voyage to the Pacific, John Webber served aboard the *Resolution*. Formally trained in landscape painting and portraiture, he had studied in both Paris and London before two views exhibited at the Royal Academy in 1776 brought him to the attention of the Admiralty.

With over 100 extant original drawings of the region, Webber's importance to the record of the voyage in the North Pacific, and to the exploration and discovery of the Northwest Coast cannot be overestimated. The fine portraits and detailed views created, in most instances, at the very moment of first contact, not only served to illustrate written accounts, but also remain of supreme value to ethnologists. Webber and Cook often planned the artistic work with a view to the future publication of the official journal. He also made a number of drawings of natural history subjects.

On the Northwest Coast, Webber began his work with a panoramic view of "The Resolution and Discovery in Ship Cove" in **Nootka Sound**. The various versions of "Habitations in Nootka Sound" probably represent the village of Yuquot in **Friendly Cove**, likely also the site of his house interior sketches. At Nootka, Webber drew groups of **natives**, detailed sketches of some of the **artifacts** collected, and portraits of men and women notably "A Woman of Nootka Sound" wearing a chief's hat with the distinctive whale hunt motif. One of his most interesting drawings, because of the later unleashing of the maritime **fur trade**, is a full-length drawing of a **sea otter**. The scope of the work done at Nootka was repeated in **Prince William Sound**, where Webber busied himself providing images of the dramatic mountain scenery, and a series of fine portraits of native men and women. From Cook's run along the **Alaskan Peninsula** to **Unalaska** there are drawings of natives in their **kayaks**. During the two visits to Samgoonoondha, Webber drew interiors of the native habitations, but his concentration was on portraits as a result of which there exist a remarkable series of "A Man of Unalaska" and "A Woman of Oonalaska." As Cook pushed beyond the Arctic Circle, Webber drew "Resolution and Discovery among the Ice" and Cook's men "Shooting Sea Horses [walrus] on an Ice Flow."

His association with Cook allowed Webber to paint four portraits of the great navigator. Three have survived: a head and shoulders in the National Portrait Gallery in London, and an almost full-length study now in the National Gallery in Wellington, New Zealand (both from life); the third, painted later, but based on the New Zealand painting, is in the National Portrait Gallery in Canberra, Australia. After the voyage he oversaw production of the 61 engraved plates for the official publication of Cook's journal and atlas in 1784, including a number of unsigned coastal views and profiles. There was a major exhibit of his works from the voyage at the Royal Academy just prior to publication.

WHIDBEY, JOSEPH (1755–1833). Joseph Whidbey played a central role in the surveying achievements of the **George Vancouver** Expedition. A former shipmate of Vancouver in the Caribbean, he was master of the *Discovery*. Throughout the three survey seasons, 1792–1794, Vancouver's deteriorating health caused him to rely on Whidbey's judgment and experience, his quiet competence and dedication to the cause, and his remarkable energy. Whidbey participated in almost all of the more important small boat excursions that produced the raw data needed to create the charts for which the expedition is justly renowned. Once Vancouver realized that only surveying from small boats would allow him to fulfill his instructions successfully, he looked to Whidbey, **James Johnstone**, and **Peter Puget** to undertake the leadership required.

During 1792 Whidbey's name was given to the island in Admiralty Inlet that he surveyed; he later worked with Puget to explore Toba Inlet and then with Vancouver in Queen Charlotte Strait. The next year he worked north from Restoration Cove past the Skeena River, and from Observatory Inlet; he then worked in the Behm Canal and Clarence Strait, finally ending with an exploration of the western shore of Sumner Strait until it opened out into the Pacific. With Vancouver almost totally incapacitated in 1794, he surveyed in **Cook Inlet**, exploring Turnagain Arm; in **Prince William Sound**; and later in the northern sections of the **Alexander Archipelago—Cross Sound**, Chatham Strait, Stephen's Passage, and Frederick Sound.

Whidbey's logbooks have not survived, but Vancouver clearly relied heavily on them in constructing his narrative of the voyage. A portrait of Whidbey by an unknown artist hangs in the office of the Harbour Master in Devonport (Plymouth) in southwest England.

WICKANINNISH. During the exploration period, powerful and wealthy Chief Wickaninnish of **Clayoquot Sound** on the west coast of **Vancouver Island** met Spanish explorers and numerous **fur trade** captains including **John Meares**, **Charles Barkley**, and **Robert Gray**. Although **Nootka Sound** was visited by more European vessels, and became the site of a Spanish establishment and the scene of Spanish–English conflict, he seems to have been more powerful in his domain than his better-known rival **Maquinna**. The fur trade allowed him to enhance his wealth and status, and he learned how to manipulate the competition and control the supply of furs by collecting them from around the sound and preventing outsiders from trading directly with the ships. Meares wrote that it was necessary for traders to establish a relationship with the chief because of his "power and extensive territory." Over the years there were a number of instances of tension and **violence** associated with the traders' visits. In 1792 Robert Gray destroyed the village of Opitsat, and some scholars believe that Wickaninnish was responsible for the destruction of John Jacob Astor's *Tonquin*.

WILKES, CHARLES (1798–1877). Charles Wilkes was Commander of the United States Exploring Expedition to the Pacific, 1838–1842. In the years that followed the early maritime explorations of American fur traders, and the overland trek of the **Lewis and Clark Expedition**, the United States retained a growing interest in the Pacific Coast. By the 1820s there was an emerging consciousness in Washington, D.C., that a successful scientific voyage to examine "the territory of the United States on the seaboard . . . (and) . . . the coast of California" would be in the national interest. Congress finally approved the voyage in 1836. To complement the Wilkes initiative,

John C. Frémont was later sent overland in 1843 to explore new ways to reach **Oregon** and **California**.

Wilkes left Hampton Roads on 18 August 1838 in a flotilla of six ships that included the *Vincennes*, the *Peacock*, and the *Porpoise*. After rounding Cape Horn and exploring extensively in the South Pacific, including Antarctic waters, he went to Sydney, the Fijian Islands, and **Hawaii** before landfall was made on the Northwest Coast, off the **Columbia River** on 28 April 1841. Proceeding north in the *Vincennes* he established a base in **Puget Sound** at **Fort Nisqually** from where overland parties were sent north to the **Fraser River**, east and south. The wreck of the *Peacock* on the treacherous bar of the Columbia River meant that the river (as far as the Snake River) had to be explored by land, and it diverted the *Porpoise* from an intended detailed survey of the **Strait of Georgia** and **Vancouver Island**. An overland party also negotiated the fur traders' trail up the Willamette Valley and south to the Sacramento River. Wilkes's thorough survey of Puget Sound, which led him to praise its harbors in glowing terms, the settlements on the Columbia River, and the ports of California all convinced him that the Oregon Country and northern California "could form a state . . . destined . . . to become a powerful maritime nation, with two of the finest ports in the world—that within the straits of Juan de Fuca, and San Francisco." His opinions were not lost on American politicians who were gearing up for battles with Britain and Mexico for control of that very region.

The expedition's significant cartographic and scientific achievements were somewhat obscured at the time by the nature of the return of the expedition to New York on 13 January 1842. A number of officers were under arrest and Wilkes was being accused of tyrannical leadership. This led to a court martial and subsequent reprimand. However, various artists left an important record of the **Pacific Northwest**, particularly capturing its **native** life. The expedition's scientist James Dana, later appointed professor of Natural History at Yale University, spent 13 years completing his Pacific reports that were published in four huge volumes all with folio atlases full of plates. Of the work of the artists on the coast, "Chinook Lodge" by Alfred Agate, and Joseph Drayton's "Indian Horses near Mount Hood" and other native scenes, and Henry Eld's "A Scene on the Columbia River" are particularly interesting.

WOODCOCK, JOSEPH (1767–?). A student of mathematics and drawing, Joseph Woodcock was engaged by **Nathaniel Portlock** to care for a group of boys who joined the latter's voyage to the Northwest Coast in 1786–1787. He was expected to teach them navigation and chart preparation. Woodcock created some artwork of his own, as three (rather poor) engravings of his original drawings, now no longer extant, are presented in Portlock's *Voyage round the World.* They show the *King George* at anchor in "Coal Harbour" (English Bay, **Cook Inlet**), and two views in "Portlock Harbour" on the west coast of Chichagof Island.

WRANGELL, FERDINAND (1796–1870). Naval officer, arctic explorer, scientist, and writer, Ferdinand Wrangell proved to be one of the ablest managers of the **Russian–American Company** (RAC). He served on the round-the-world voyage of **Vasilii Golovnin** (1817–1819) and was recommended by Golovnin to lead an expedition to explore and chart the coast of northeast Siberia. Wrangell disproved the rumor of a great landmass north of the **Bering Strait**, but failed to find the mountainous island off Siberia reported to him by coastal natives; it was not discovered until 1867 by American whalers, who promptly named it in his honor. After this tour of duty in **Russian America**, Wrangell published an account of his arctic adventures in *Journey on the Northwest Coasts of Siberia and the Arctic Ocean, 1820–1824* (1841). Between 1825 and 1827 he commanded his second round-the-world supply voyage to the north Pacific, spending three weeks at **New Archangel** in the fall of 1826.

In 1828 he was appointed chief manager of the RAC and set out across Siberia to take up the appointment. He reached New Archangel in September 1830. Wrangell proved to be an effective colonial administrator, asserting direct control over the accounts of the company's district offices; attending to the buildings of the capital and the working conditions of his employees; consolidating shipbuilding with an expanded yard in **Sitka Sound**; and stabilizing the **fur trade** by introducing new conservation regulations into the **sea otter** hunt. He cooperated with **Ioann Veniaminov** to establish improved relations with the local **Tlingit**, and made renewed efforts to provide better schools, missions, and medical services to the colony's population. His wife Elizabeth Wrangell introduced a degree of refinement into the social and cultural life of New Archangel with musical evenings, theatrical performances, and dances.

Wrangell's interest in searching for new sources of furs stimulated further exploration in the **Alexander Archipelago**, but particularly in southwest **Alaska**. He pressed forward the exploration efforts of **Fedor Kolmakov** and **Ivan I. Vasil'ev** along the Nushagak River and in the basin of the Kuskokwim River. More important for the future of the RAC's commerce, and both coastal and interior exploration, was his decision to follow up the recommendations of **Adolf Etholen** to establish a major post—Mikhailovskii Redoubt—in **Norton Sound** in 1833. His regular tours of inspection up and down the coast resulted in a plethora of notes, articles, and reports, a number of which were gathered after his return to St. Petersburg into a 1839 publication (in German), *Russian America: Statistical and Ethnographical Information on the Russian Possessions on the Northwest Coast of America.*

Wrangell's determination to advance the interests of the RAC in the face of pressure from the **Hudson's Bay Company** (HBC) in southeast Alaska, led to the establishment of the Dionis'evskii Redoubt at the mouth of the Stikine River in 1834. This led to the *Dryad*/Stikine Affair, and effectively blocked British navigation into the river before he and **George Simpson** could negotiate a settlement that gave the HBC its desired access to the coast, and the Russian colony the vital food supplies it needed. During his final year as chief manager, Wrangell intended to renew his interest in arctic exploration with a voyage through the Bering Strait, but this was thwarted by the affair on the Stikine and concerns about the status of **Fort Ross**, under increasing pressure from the Mexican republic, which Russia had not yet recognized. During the winter of 1835–1836, Wrangell was given permission to make his way home to Russia via Mexico for meetings to formalize the cession to Russia of the territory around Fort Ross. But the Mexicans were less than enthusiastic about negotiating such a prospect, and the discussions were a standoff.

– Y –

YAKUTAT BAY. A large sound in the shadow of **Mount St. Elias**, Yakutat Bay's name derives from the **Tlingit** name "Jacootat" or

"Yacootat" reported by **Iurii Lisianskii** in 1805. It was seen but not entered by **Vitus Bering** in July 1741. As he passed by in 1778 **James Cook** was able to identify Bering's large mountain, and the suggestion remains, amidst modern scholarly debate, that he considered Yakutat to be "Behrings Bay." Certainly **George Vancouver** considered this to be the case. Launches belonging to the **Jean François de La Pérouse** Expedition landed briefly on Ocean Cape (the southwest extremity of the bay) in June 1786, but his ships did not enter, instead moving on to **Lituya Bay**. Had he rounded the cape, La Pérouse would have found a safe anchorage in present-day Monti Bay, subsequently named after one of his officers. It was discovered in May 1787 by **George Dixon**. He called it Port Mulgrave and the larger bay, whose entrance he roughly charted, Admiralty Bay. Mulgrave and the group of islands in the southwest corner of Yakutat Bay were visited by the English fur trader **James Colnett** in 1788, and more importantly by Spain's **Alejandro Malaspina** Expedition in 1791. The latter charted the whole bay as far as the Hubbard Glacier. Prior to 1787 the Russians were concentrating their efforts in **Cook Inlet** and **Prince William Sound**, but they grew increasingly uneasy about English activity in the Gulf of Alaska. As a result **Gerasim Izmailov** and **Dmitrii Bocharov** explored the coast southeast from **Hinchinbrook Island** in 1788, placing possession plates and crests at various locations, including the **Tlingit** village at Yakutat (Mulgrave). Thereafter, Russian traders visited the bay in increasing numbers. **Peter Puget** of Vancouver's expedition reported a huge group under **Egor Purtov** in 1794, the year in which **Aleksandr Baranov** decided to establish a permanent settlement. This plan was implemented during 1795–1796, despite periods of intense Tlingit hostility as the Yakutat natives, as elsewhere down the coast, considered the Russian hunting of **sea otters** in their territory to be a gross violation of their sovereignty.

– Z –

ZAGOSKIN, LAVRENTII (1808–1890). Lavrentii Zagoskin entered the employ of the **Russian–American Company** (RAC) in 1838 and became one of the most important of the early explorers of interior **Alaska**. Arriving in Sitka in 1839, his travels on RAC vessels during

1840–1841 took him as far west as **Kamchatka** and south as **California**. With the support and encouragement of **Adolf Etholen**, who had previously explored in the region, he undertook a three-year expedition, 1842–1844, into the two great river systems of western Alaska. His goal was to find out how the RAC could turn to its advantage the well-established trading system between the people of central Alaska and the Chukchi of Siberia. Zagoskin explored far up the Yukon and Kuskokwim rivers, thus formally pioneering the Russians' move inland from their trading posts on the coast. His work resulted in the first detailed descriptions of the interior tribes and the intricacies of their trading networks, and the amassing of important ethnological collections. Returning to Sitka in the fall of 1844, he worked on his notes and collections before leaving for St. Petersburg. There, **Ferdinand Wrangell** persuaded him to prepare a narrative of his exploits for publication, and his work appeared in two parts in 1847 and 1848 as *The Survey on Foot of Part of the Russian Possessions in America Made in 1842, 1843 and 1844*. It was republished in 1956, and in an English edition in 1967.

ZAIKOV, POTAP (?–1791). Trader and explorer, Potap Zaikov is renowned for two long voyages to the **Aleutian Islands**, and his pioneering activity in **Prince William Sound** (PWS). His first voyage lasted from 1772 to 1779. He worked his way along the islands reaching **Umnak** in the summer of 1775, where he formed an alliance with other traders and moved on to **Unimak** Island. Anchoring in Isanotski Strait, where **Petr Krenitsyn** had wintered in 1768–1769, he spent three years exploring, hunting, and trading among the islands off the **Alaska Peninsula** as far as **Kodiak** Island. By the end of the voyage he had compiled a good deal of important geographical data.

Zaikov's second voyage began in 1781 and initially took him to the eastern Aleutians. In the summer of 1783 he led a flotilla of trading vessels to PWS and ventured as far south as **Kayak Island**. His initial base was Nuchek (**Port Etches**) on **Hinchinbrook Island**, and he wintered over in a bay on the north end of **Montague Island** to continue to trade despite the severe native hostility, which cost a number of Russian lives. Between 1784 and 1788 he was in the Fox Islands, and in August 1788 was at the settlement of Illiuliuk in Unalaska Bay. There he entertained **Esteban José Martínez** and

Gonzalo López de Haro, to whom he gave information about the expected arrival of the **Mulovskii Expedition**. This caused the Spaniards to occupy **Nootka Sound** in 1789 to forestall the Russians and block English trading activities. A year later, still at Illiuliuk, he met the English commercial entrepreneur **John Henry Cox**.

ZAREMBO, DIONYSIUS (1791–?). Dionysius Zarembo was an officer on ships of the **Russian–American Company** for over 30 years. After two early voyages to **Russian America** he spent the years 1827–1839 sailing in the North Pacific out of **New Archangel**. Under orders from **Ferdinand Wrangell**, Zarembo established the St. Dionysius Redoubt in 1834 at the mouth of the Stikine River to forestall the advance of the **Hudson's Bay Company** (HBC) and the building of an HBC fort farther upstream. He commanded the armed brig *Chichagof* that prevented the HBC vessel *Dryad* from entering the river. In building the fort and founding what later became the settlement of Wrangell, he charted the harbor. He later completed a number of surveys in the bays and inlets of southern Admiralty Island in the **Alexander Archipelago**. In particular he surveyed and named Woewodski Harbor (Pybus Bay), and his work was later published by the Russian Hydrographic Department.

ZIMMERMANN, HEINRICH (1741–1805). Heinrich Zimmermann served on board the *Discovery* on **James Cook**'s Third Voyage to the Pacific. His only claim to fame is that he published, in Mannheim in 1781, the first of the unauthorized memoirs of the expedition with news of the remarkable prices fetched for Northwest Coast furs in China. It was translated into French in 1783 and Russian in 1786, but not into English until 1926. This is likely because the journals of **John Rickman** and **William Ellis** were more thorough, and the official account came out in 1784. His section on America is short, but does contain a brief description of the natives in the "beautiful and commodious harbour" of **Nootka Sound**. Zimmermann described their trade practices, dwellings and weapons, and their strong, warlike appearance, and he noted down a few words of their language. His comments from the stopovers on **Unalaska** Island were equally brief; he mentions meeting the Russian hunters, and the Aleuts who were "orderly and well mannered."

Bibliography

CONTENTS

A. INTRODUCTION

The history of the discovery and exploration of the Northwest Coast of America cannot easily be separated from a much wider canvas—the expansion of the European world into the Americas and the Pacific beginning in the 16th century; the Russian conquest of Siberia; the evolution of the geography of the rim of the North Pacific beginning in Asia; the impact of the North American fur trades, both land-based and maritime; and European and American diplomatic maneuvering in the 18th and 19th centuries, when the nature and scope of empires were being decided. While mindful of these larger themes, this bibliography has naturally been developed with a more specific focus and is designed to complement the introductory essay that guides readers into the dictionary itself. The arrangement leads from the general to the specific, quickly arriving in North America and on the Northwest Coast. Many of the books cited include extensive bibliographies of their own, and journal articles are usually extensively footnoted. Thus by assisting access to a number of relevant works, particularly more recent ones, this guide inevitably opens up a much wider world of useful references. Where possible, reference to the most recent edition of a republished work has been included.

The literature on the subject of this volume has expanded enormously in the last generation, particularly with the publication of monographs, exhibition catalogues, and anthologies of specialty conference papers related to bicentennial and other benchmark recognitions. Because of this, there has been much new scholarship related to the lives, times, and achievements of such figures as Vitus Bering, James Cook, Alejandro Malaspina, George Vancouver, Meriwether Lewis, and William Clark, so central to the story under discussion. We are also fortunate that the digital revolution has made publication, and particularly the reproduction of high-quality historical images and maps, so much easier and more efficient. And of course the Internet has, through the search engines now available, opened up access to databases, general information, and the reproduction of the texts of whole books, documents, and articles that would have been inconceivable even a few years ago. Of particular importance is JSTOR, an online journal archive made available to researchers through participating libraries. We can be confident that the high level of service now routinely offered by university libraries and leading public libraries will, happily, only get better. What only a generation ago was being copied onto microfilm is now being scanned for Internet access.

General Reference Works

A number of encyclopedic works related to world exploration or regional and national biography introduce the principal players and events involved in the subject under discussion. The citations in the bibliography are variously useful, but are eclipsed by four works that have now become the standard: the *Dictionary of Canadian Biography* (1966–1999); the *Oxford Dictionary of National Biography* (2004); *American National Biography* (1999–2005); and Raymond John Howgego, *Encyclopedia of Exploration*, 3 vols. The first two volumes, *To the Year 1800* (2003) and *1800 to 1850* (2004) of this "Comprehensive Reference Guide to the History and Literature of Exploration Travel and Colonization" are relevant. The Canadian dictionary comprises a series of chronological volumes related to a specific period, with entries determined by the date of the individual's death; thus volumes 4 to 9 should be consulted.

Other general encyclopedic reference works of value are: David Buisseret, ed., *Oxford Companion to World Exploration* (2007); *Literature of Travel and Exploration: An Encyclopedia*, edited by Jennifer Speake (2003); and Daniel Baker, ed., *Explorers and Discoverers of the World* (1993).

Two general bibliographic guides are of great importance. First, Edward Godfrey Cox, *A Reference Guide to the Literature of Travel including Voyages, Geographical Descriptions, Adventures, Shipwrecks and Expeditions*, vol. 2, *The New World* (1938); the sections entitled "North Pacific" and "North America" are relevant. Secondly, England's National Maritime Museum's five-volume *Catalogue of the Library* (1968–1977).

Pacific and North American Reference Works

Valuable information of a general nature can be found in the four-volume *The Canadian Encyclopedia*, edited by James Marsh (1988, 3rd edition printed in one volume, 1999); the *Encyclopedia of British Columbia*, edited by Daniel Francis (2000); the *Dictionary of Oregon History*, edited by Howard Corning (1956); Michael Gorlay and John Bowman, *North American Exploration* (2003), in which entries are usefully arranged in convenient sections, including "The Spanish Enter the New World, 1492–1635," "Exploring West of the Mississippi, 1635–1800," and "The Arctic and Northernmost Regions, 1576–1992"; Alan Day, *Historical Dictionary of the Discovery and Exploration of the Northwest Passage* (2006); John Dunmore, *Who's Who in Pacific Navigation* (1991); and Clive Holland, *Arctic Exploration and Development* (1994). More expansive treatment of a number of relevant themes can be found in Howard Lamar, *The New Encyclopedia of the American West* (1998); and Richard Pierce, *Russian America: A Biographical Dictionary* (1990), introduces many generally unfamiliar personalities.

Access to selected documents illustrating early Spanish exploration of the Pacific Coast is provided by David B. Quinn, *New American World: A Documentary History of North America to 1612* (1979); and *The Exploration of North America, 1630–1776*, edited by W. P. Cumming, S. E. Hillier, D. B. Quinn, and G. Williams (1974), includes two chapters, "The Fur Trade and Exploration North to the Arctic and West to the Rockies" and "The Pacific Coast," in which essays are followed by excerpts from explorer journals.

The most valuable bibliographic guide is Tina Loo's excellent chapter, "The Pacific Coast," in *Canadian History: A Reader's Guide*, edited by M. Brook Taylor and Douglas Owram (1994). Also see Iris Engstrand and Daniel Tyler, "Hispanic California 1542–1848" in *A Guide to the History of California*, edited by Doyce Nunis and Gloria Lothrop (1989); and Marvin Falk, *Alaska History: An Annotated Bibliography* (2006).

The most important study of Alaskan place names remains Donald Orth, *Dictionary of Alaska Place Names* (1967). *British Columbia Place Names: Their Origin and History* by John Walbran (1909, reprinted 1971) is a classic but must be used with caution. More recent studies of the three west coast Pacific states are: Robert Hitchman, *Place Names of Washington* (1985), *Oregon Geographic Names* by Lewis MacArthur (1992), and *California Place Names: The Origin and Etymology of Current Geographical Names* by Erwin Gudde (now in its 4th edition, revised and enlarged by William Bright, 1998).

Maps and Atlases

Although *The Times Atlas of World Exploration* (1991) and volumes 1 and 2 of the *Historical Atlas of Canada* (1987 and 1994) provide useful maps and commentary of an introductory nature, readers are advised to move quickly to William Goetzman and Glyndwr Williams, *The Atlas of North*

American Exploration: From the Norse Voyages to the Race for the Pole (1992). This fine and comprehensive work of reference and interpretation consists of a series of double-page spreads, each with an introductory text and a modern map on which explorer routes are drawn and explained. The pages are also interspersed with interesting illustrations and quotations from contemporary journals. Part 4, "Ocean to Ocean," contains most of the relevant entries under the general titles "The Northern Fur Trade," "The Pacific Northwest," and "Jeffersonian Pathfinders."

In recent years this excellent work has been complemented by a series of historical atlases in which author Derek Hayes combines illuminating commentary with fine reproductions of contemporary maps and charts, both manuscript and published. Each of Hayes's five North American volumes are worth referencing because some of the same images are re-presented in larger format, but the two that merit particular attention here are: *Historical Atlas of the North Pacific Ocean: Maps of Discovery and Scientific Exploration* (2001) and *Historical Atlas of British Columbia and the Pacific Northwest* (1999).

Three other modern atlases are also valuable: Warren Beck and Ynez Hasse, *Historical Atlas of California* (1974); William Loy and Stuart Allen, *Atlas of Oregon* (2001); and James Scott and Roland DeLorme, *Historical Atlas of Washington* (1988).

Of historical interest is the 37-sheet atlas of North Pacific Asia and America by 19th-century Russian naval officer and cartographer Mikhail Teben'kov, originally published in 1852. It was reproduced, in 1981, as *Atlas of the Northwest Coasts of America*, with a translated introductory text by Richard Pierce.

Finally, although it is not an atlas per se, but remains a classic contribution to the study of American cartography, it is obligatory to mention Henry Raup Wagner's magisterial two-volume *The Cartography of the Northwest Coast of America to 1800* (1937, reprinted in one volume in 1999). With its erudite text and reproduction of many important maps and an extensive catalogue, and place-name checklist, it continues to stand the test of time.

Historical Surveys

The context for the discovery and exploration of the Northwest Coast of America is well provided by Glyndwr Williams, *The Expansion of Europe in the Eighteenth Century: Overseas Rivalry, Discovery and Exploration* (1966), chapter 7. See also Williams's essay "The Pacific: Exploration and Exploitation" in volume 2 of *The Oxford History of the British Empire*, edited by P. J. Marshall (1998). Four books that provide excellent overviews of the early history of the coast from different perspectives are: Warren Cook, *Flood Tide of Empire: Spain and the Pacific Northwest, 1543–1819* (1972); Barry Gough, *The Northwest Coast: British Navigation, Trade and Discoveries to 1812* (1992); Lydia Black, *Russians in Alaska* (2004); and James R. Gibson, *Otter Skins, Boston Ships and China Goods: The Maritime Fur Trade of the Northwest Coast, 1785–1841* (1992). See also Gough's *Fortune's a River* (2007). Less scholarly, but nonetheless useful as a summary of the major themes, personalities, and earliest events is Derek Pethick, *First Approaches to the Northwest Coast* (1976) and *The Nootka Connection: Europe and the Northwest Coast, 1790–1795* (1980), while a fine, more focused, introductory work on an important aspect of the period is John Frazier Henry, *Early Maritime Artists of the Pacific Northwest Coast, 1741–1841* (1984).

Edited by John Logan Allen, the three-volume *North American Exploration* (1997) contains four long and valuable essays, extensively footnoted: "The Early Exploration of the Pacific Coast" by W. Michael Mathes in volume 1, *A New World Discovered*; "The Exploration of the Pacific Coast" by James R. Gibson and "The Canadian Fur Trade and the Exploration of Western North America, 1797–1851" by John L. Allen in volume 2, *A Continent Defined*; and "Exploring the American West in the Age of Jefferson" by James Ronda in volume 3, *A Continent Comprehended*.

The encounter of explorers and fur traders with the native people of the coast has been the subject of numerous books and articles. Volumes 5 (Arctic, 1984), 7 (Northwest Coast, 1990), and 8 (California, 1978) of the *Handbook of North American Indians*, edited respectively by David Damas, Wayne Suttles, and Robert Heizer provide the best overview of a subject fraught with opinion and emotion. Each native group (e.g. Tlingit) is covered in a scholarly essay, and the references to other works are extensive and valuable. Erna Gunther, *Indian Life on the Northwest Coast of America, as Seen by the Early Explorers and Fur Traders during the Last Decade of the Eighteenth Century* (1972) is a pioneer study, but its listing of artifacts in museum collections is now outdated and reference should be made to the other works cited in the bibliography. The effects of contact are treated in Robin Fisher, *Contact and Conflict: Indian–European Relations in British Columbia, 1774–1890* (1977). For a thought-provoking analysis of native and explorer and trader contact that challenges the views and assumptions of many other scholars, see also Daniel W. Clayton, *Islands of Truth: The Imperial Fashioning of Vancouver Island* (2000).

Key Monographs: Books and Articles

The bibliography that follows cites the studies that deserve to be consulted. A few selected highlights, however, merit special attention.

For mythical voyages: Henry R. Wagner, "Apocryphal Voyages to the Northwest Coast of America," *Proceedings of the American Antiquarian Society*, April 1931, and Glyndwr Williams, *Voyages of Delusion: The Northwest Passage in the Age of Reason* (2002).

For the Russians see Raisa Makarova, *Russians on the Pacific, 1743–1799* (1975); James R. Gibson, "A Notable Absence: The Lateness and Lameness of Russian Discovery in the North Pacific Ocean, 1639–1803" in *From Maps to Metaphors: The Pacific World of George Vancouver*, edited by Robin Fisher and Hugh Johnston (1993); Orcutt Frost, *Bering: The Russian Discovery of America* (2003); and Glynn Barratt, *Russia in Pacific Waters, 1715–1825: A Survey of Russia's Naval Presence in the North and South Pacific* (1981).

There were two phases of Spanish exploration. The earlier period is dealt with in Maurice Holmes, *From New Spain by Sea to the Californias* (1963); Henry Kelsey, *Juan Rodríguez Cabrillo* (1986); and W. Michael Mathes, *Sebastián Vizcaíno and Spanish Expansion in the Pacific Ocean* (1968). For the late-18th-century period see especially Christon Archer, "Spain and the Defence of the Pacific Ocean Empire, 1750–1810" in *Canadian Journal of Latin American Studies* 11, no. 21, 1986; Iris Engstrand, *Spanish Scientists in the New World* (1981); Herbert Beals, *Juan Pérez on the Northwest Coast* (1989); Freeman M. Tovell, *At the Far Reaches of Empire: The Life of Juan Francisco de la Bodega y Quadra* (2008); Donald Cutter, *Malaspina and Galiano: Spanish Voyages to the Northwest Coast 1791 & 1792* (1991); and Wallace Olsen, *Through Spanish Eyes: Spanish Voyages to Alaska, 1774–1792* (2002).

For the two principal British explorers on the coast consult John Robson, *Captain Cook's World: Maps of the Life and Voyages of James*

Cook (2000); Andrew David et al., *The Charts and Coastal Views of Captain Cook's Voyages*, volume 3: *The Voyage of the Resolution and Discovery, 1776–1780* (1997); Robin Fisher, *Vancouver's Voyage: Charting the Northwest Coast* (1992); and a number of the excellent essays in two anthologies edited by Robin Fisher and Hugh Johnston, *Captain James Cook and His Times* (1979) and *From Maps to Metaphors: The Pacific World of George Vancouver* (1993).

The voyage of La Pérouse is dealt with by John Dunmore in *Where Fate Beckons: The Life of Jean-François de La Pérouse* (2007), and Robin Inglis, "La Pérouse 1786: A French Naval Visit to Alaska" in *Enlightenment and Exploration in the North Pacific*, edited by Stephen Haycox et al. (1997).

An introduction to the maritime fur trade can be found in an old but useful article by Frederic William Howay, "An Outline Sketch of the Maritime Fur Trade" in the Canadian Historical Association *Annual Report*, 1932; and in James R. Gibson, "Bostonians and Muscovites on the Northwest Coast, 1788–1841" in *The Western Shore: Oregon Country Essays*, edited by Thomas Vaughan (1976). See also Mary Malloy, *Boston Men on the Northwest Coast: The American Maritime Fur Trade, 1788–1844* (1998); Richard Somerset Mackie, *Trading Beyond the Mountains: The British Fur Trade on the Pacific, 1793–1843* (1997), and two books by J. Richard Nokes, *Columbia's River: The Voyages of Robert Gray* (1991) and *Almost a Hero: The Voyages of John Meares R.N. to China, Hawaii and the Northwest Coast* (1998).

For the pioneering overland treks to the Northwest Coast by Alexander Mackenzie and Meriwether Lewis and William Clark, see Derek Hayes, *First Crossing: Alexander Mackenzie, His Expedition across North America, and the Opening of the Continent* (2001); and Stephen E. Ambrose, *Undaunted Courage: Meriwether Lewis, Thomas Jefferson and the Opening of the American West* (1996). James P. Ronda, *Astoria and Empire* (1999), is the authoritative study of John Jacob Astor's short-lived, but vital-for-the-future trading post at the mouth of the Columbia River.

Contemporary Accounts

Historians of the Northwest Coast are fortunate to have so many fascinating original journals to consult. These have been listed by Edward

Eberstadt, *The Northwest Coast, a century of personal narratives of discovery, conquest [and] exploration from Bering's Landfall to Wilkes' surveys, 1741–1841* (1941). A significant number of the accounts have been edited and annotated, sometimes with an extensive introductory essay, by modern scholars and reprinted, often with complementary maps and illustrations. The four major European voyages of exploration to visit the coast—those of James Cook, Jean François de La Pérouse, Alejandro Malaspina, and George Vancouver—have been published by the Hakluyt Society: J. C. Beaglehole, *The Journals of Captain James Cook,* volume 3, *The Voyage of the Resolution and Discovery, 1776–1782,* 2 vols. (1967); John Dunmore, *The Journal of Jean-François de la Pérouse, 1785–1788,* 2 vols. (1994); Andrew David et al. *The Malaspina Expedition, 1789–1794,* 3 vols. (2001–2004); and W. Kaye Lamb, *The Voyage of George Vancouver,* 4 vols. (1984). Other editions of contemporary journals include: Richard Pierce and Marina Ramsey, *A Voyage to America, 1783–1786* by Grigorii Shelikov (1981); Iris Engstrand, *Noticias de Nutka: An Account of Nootka Sound in 1792* by José Mariano Moziño (1991); Robert Galois, *A Voyage to the Northwest Side of America: The Journals of James Colnett, 1786–89* (2004); and Robin Fisher and J. M. Bumsted, *An Account of a Voyage to the Northwest Coast of America in 1785 & 1786* by Alexander Walker (1982).

B. WORLD AND PACIFIC REFERENCE WORKS

Atlases

Farrington, Karen. *Historical Atlas of Exploration.* New York: Checkmark Books, 2000.
Fernández-Armesto, Felipe, ed. *The Times Atlas of World Exploration.* London: Times Books, 1991.
Grimbly, Shona, ed. *Atlas of Exploration.* Chicago: Fitzroy Dearborn, 2001.
McEvedy, Colin. *The Penguin Historical Atlas of the Pacific.* New York: Penguin Books, 1998.

Dictionaries and Encyclopedias

Baker, Daniel B., ed. *Explorers and Discoverers of the World.* Detroit: Gale Research, 1993.
Bohlander, Richard E., ed. *World Explorers and Discoverers.* New York: Macmillan, 1992.

Buisseret, David, ed. *The Oxford Companion to World Exploration*, 2 vols. Volume I: A–L; Volume II: M–Z. New York: Oxford University Press, 2007.

Delpar, Helen, ed. *The Discoverers: An Encyclopedia of Explorers and Exploration*. New York: McGraw Hill, 1980.

Dunmore, John. *Who's Who in Pacific Navigation*. Honolulu: University of Hawaii Press, 1991.

Fulford, Tim. *Travels, Explorations and Empires: Writings from the Era of Imperial Expansion, 1770–1835*. London: Pickering & Chatto, 2001.

Great Soviet Encyclopedia. Translation of the 3rd edition. 31 vols. plus index. New York: Macmillan, 1973–1983.

Hanbury-Tenison, Robin. *The Oxford Book of Exploration*. Oxford: Oxford University Press, 2005.

Howgego, Raymond John. *Encyclopedia of Exploration: From the Earliest Times to 1800*. Sydney: Hordern House, 2003.

———. *Encyclopedia of Exploration: 1800 to 1850*. Sydney: Hordern House, 2004.

Matthew, H. C. G., and B. H. Harrison, eds. *Oxford Dictionary of National Biography*. Oxford: Oxford University Press, 2004.

The Modern Encyclopedia of Russian and Soviet History, 46 vols. plus supplements and indexes. Gulf Breeze, Fl.: Academic International Press, 1976.

Speake, Jennifer, ed. *Literature of Travel and Exploration: An Encyclopedia*. 3 vols. New York: Fitzroy Dearborn, 2003.

Historical Surveys of Exploration

Baugh, Daniel. "Seapower and Science: The Motives for Pacific Exploration." In *Background to Discovery: Pacific Exploration from Dampier to Cook*, ed. Derek Howse. Berkeley: University of California Press, 1990.

Bériot, Agnes. *Grands Voiliers autour du monde: les voyages scientifiques, 1760–1820*. Paris: Éditions du Pont Royal, 1962.

Brosse, Jacques. *Great Voyages of Discovery: Circumnavigators and Scientists, 1764–1843*. Trans. Stanley Hochman. New York: Facts on File, 1983.

Cameron, Ian. *Lost Paradise: The Exploration of the Pacific*. London: Century Hutchinson, 1987.

Morton, Harry. *The Wind Commands: Sailors and Sailing Ships in the Pacific*. Vancouver, B.C.: University of British Columbia Press, 1975.

Rigby, Nigel, Pieter van der Merwe, and Glyndwr Williams. *Pioneers of the Pacific: Voyages of Exploration, 1787–1810*. Fairbanks: University of Alaska Press, 2005.

Spate, O. H. K. *The Pacific since Magellan*. Vol. 3, *Paradise Found and Lost*. Minneapolis: University of Minnesota Press, 1988.

Williams, Glyndwr. *The Expansion of Europe in the Eighteenth Century: Overseas Rivalry, Discovery and Exploitation*, chap. 7. London: Blandford Press, 1966.

———. "The Pacific: Exploration and Exploitation." In *The Oxford History of the British Empire*, ed. P. J. Marshall. Vol. 3, Chapter 25. Oxford: Oxford University Press, 1998.

C. NORTH AMERICA: GENERAL REFERENCE WORKS

Atlases and Cartography

Gentilcore, R. L., ed., and Geoffrey J. Matthews, cartographer. *Historical Atlas of Canada*. Vol. 2, *The Land Transformed, 1800–1891*. Toronto: University of Toronto Press, 1994.

Goetzmann, William H., and Glyndwr Williams. *The Atlas of North American Exploration: From the Norse Voyages to the Race for the Pole*. New York: Prentice Hall, 1992.

Harris, R. Cole, ed., and Geoffrey J. Matthews, cartographer. *Historical Atlas of Canada*. Vol. 1, *From the Beginning to 1800*. Toronto: University of Toronto Press, 1987.

Hayes, Derek. *America Discovered: A Historical Atlas of North American Exploration*. Vancouver, B.C.: Douglas & McIntyre, 2004.

———. *Historical Atlas of the United States*. Berkeley: University of California Press, 2006.

Lewis, G. Malcolm, ed. *Cartographic Encounters: Perspectives on Native American Mapmaking and Map Use*. Chicago: University of Chicago Press, 1998.

McEvedy, Colin. *The Penguin Atlas of North American History to 1870*. London: Penguin, 1988.

Portinaro, Pierluigi, and Franco Knirsch. *The Cartography of North America, 1500–1800*. New York: Crescent Books, 1987.

Verner, Coolie, and Basil Stuart-Stubbs. *The North Part of North America: A Facsimile Atlas of Early Canadian Maps*. Toronto: Academic Press Canada, 1979.

Dictionaries and Encyclopedias

Day, Alan. *Historical Dictionary of the Discovery and Exploration of the Northwest Passage*. Lanham, Md.: Scarecrow Press, 2006.

Dictionary of American Biography. New York: Charles Scribner's & Sons, 1928–1958.

Dictionary of Canadian Biography. Toronto: University of Toronto Press, 1966–1999.

Garraty, J. A., and M. C. Carnes, eds. *American National Biography*. 24 vols. and supplements. New York: Oxford University Press, 1999–2005.

Golay, Michael, and John S. Bowman. *North American Exploration*. Hoboken, N.J.: J. Wiley, 2003.

Holland, Clive. *Arctic Exploration and Development c.500 B.C. to 1915: An Encyclopedia*. New York: Garland, 1994.

Marsh, James H., ed. *The Canadian Encyclopedia*. 2nd edition. Edmonton, Alta.: Hurtig, 1988.

Nuttall, Mark, ed. *Encyclopedia of the Arctic*. 3 vols. London: Routledge, 2005.

Story, Norah, ed. *The Oxford Companion to Canadian History and Literature*. Toronto: Oxford University Press, 1967.

D. THE NORTHWEST COAST OF AMERICA: REFERENCE WORKS

Atlases and Cartography

Beck, Warren A., and Ynez D. Haase. *Historical Atlas of California*. Norman: University of Oklahoma Press, 1974.

———. *Historical Atlas of the American West*. Norman: University of Oklahoma Press, 1989.

David, Andrew. "From Cook to Vancouver: The British Contribution to the Cartography of Alaska." In *Enlightenment and Exploration in the North Pacific, 1741–1805*, ed. Stephen Haycox et al. Seattle: University of Washington Press, 1997.

Davidson, George. *Directory for the Pacific Coast of the United Sates*. Reported to the Superintendent of the United States Coast Survey, 1858. Washington, D.C.: U.S. Government Printing Office, 1859.

Hayes, Derek. *Historical Atlas of British Columbia and the Pacific Northwest*. Vancouver, B.C.: Cavendish Books, 1999.

———. *Historical Atlas of the Arctic*. Seattle: University of Washington Press, 2003.

———. *Historical Atlas of the North Pacific Ocean: Maps of Discovery and Scientific Exploration*. Vancouver, B.C.: Douglas & McIntyre, 2001.

Highsmith, Richard M. *Atlas of the Pacific Northwest: Resources and Development*. Corvallis: Oregon State College, 1957.

Hornbeck, David, Philip Kane, and David Fuller. *California Patterns: A Geographical and Historical Atlas*. Palo Alto, Calif.: Mayfield, 1983.

Loy, William G., and Stuart Allan, eds. *Atlas of Oregon*. Eugene: University of Oregon Press, 2001.

Scott, J. W., and Roland L. DeLorme. *Historical Atlas of Washington*. Norman: University of Oklahoma Press, 1988.

Verner, Coolie. "Maps Relating to Cook's Age." In *Explorations in the History of Canadian Mapping*, ed. Barbara Farrell and Aileen Desbarats. Ottawa: Association of Canadian Map Libraries and Archives, 1988.

Wagner, Henry Raup. *The Cartography of the Northwest Coast of America to the Year 1800*. 2 vols. Berkeley: University of California Press, 1937. Reprinted in Limited Facsimile of the Original Edition, in one volume, by Martino Publishing, Mansfield Centre, Conn., 1999.

Bibliographies and Guides

Allan, Robert V. "Alaska before 1867 in Soviet Literature." *Quarterly Journal of the Library of Congress* 23, no. 3, 1966.

Bond, Mary E., and M. M. Caron. *Canadian Reference Sources*. Vancouver, B.C.: UBC Press and the National Library of Canada, 1996.

Cole, Garold L. *Travels in America: From the Voyages of Discovery to the Present. An Annotated Bibliography of Travel Articles in Periodicals, 1955–1980*. Norman: University of Oklahoma Press, 1984.

Conzen, Michael P., Thomas A. Rumney, and Graeme Wynne. *A Scholar's Guide to Geographical Writing on the American and Canadian Past*. Chicago: University of Chicago Press, 1993.

Cox, Edward Godfrey. *A Reference Guide to the Literature of Travel: Including Voyages, Geographical Descriptions, Adventures, Shipwrecks and Expeditions*. Vol. 2. Seattle: University of Washington Press, 1938.

Day, Alan E. *Search for the Northwest Passage: An Annotated Bibliography*. New York: Garland, 1986.

Eberstadt, Edward. *The Northwest Coast: A Century of Personal Narratives of Discovery, Conquest & Exploration from Bering's Landfall to Wilkes' Surveys, 1741–1841*. New York: Edward Eberstadt and Sons, 1941.

Engstrand, Iris, and Daniel Tyler. "Hispanic California, 1542–1848." In *A Guide to the History of California*, ed. Doyce B. Nunis Jr. and Gloria Ricci Lothrop. New York: Greenwood, 1989.

Falk, Marvin W. *Alaska History: An Annotated Bibliography*. Westport, Conn.: Praeger, 2006.

———. *Alaskan Maps: A Cartobibliography of Alaska to 1900*. New York: Garland, 1983.

Gormley, Mary. "Early Culture Contact on the Northwest Coast, 1774–1795: Analysis of Spanish Source Material." *Northwest Anthropological Research Notes* 11, Spring, 1977.

Hilton-Smith, R. D. "Northwest Approaches: The First Century of Books." *British Columbia Historical Quarterly* 32, 1969.

Medushevskaya, O. M. "Cartographic Sources for the History of Russian Geographical Discoveries in the Pacific Ocean in the Second Half of the 18th Century." Trans. James R. Gibson. *Canadian Cartographer* 9, 1972.

Rey-Tejerina, Arsenio. "The Spanish Exploration of Alaska, 1774–1796: Manuscript Sources." *Alaska History* 3, 1988.

Richards, Kent. "In Search of the Pacific Northwest: The Historiography of Oregon and Washington." *Pacific Historical Review* 50, no. 4, 1981.

Taylor, Martin Brook, and Douglas Owram, eds. *Canadian History: A Reader's Guide: Beginnings to Confederation.* Toronto: University of Toronto Press, 1994.

Dictionaries and Encyclopedias

Corning, Howard McKinley, ed. *Dictionary of Oregon History.* Portland, Ore.: Binfords and Mort, 1956.

Francis, Daniel, ed. *Encyclopedia of British Columbia.* Madeira Park, B.C.: Harbour, 2000.

Hart, James D. *A Companion Guide to California.* New York: Oxford University Press, 1978.

Lamar, Howard R., ed. *The New Encyclopedia of the American West.* New Haven, Conn.: Yale University Press, 1998.

Pierce, Richard A. *Russian America: A Biographical Dictionary.* Kingston, Ont.: Limestone Press, 1990.

Quinn, David B., ed. *New American World: A Documentary History of North America to 1612.* New York: Arno Press, 1979.

Twigg, Alan. *First Invaders: The Literary Origins of British Columbia.* Vancouver, B.C.: Ronsdale Press, 2004.

Place Names and Nomenclature

Akrigg, G. P. V., and Helen B. *British Columbia Place Names.* 3rd ed. Vancouver, B.C.: UBC Press, 1997.

Gudde, Erwin G., and William Bright. *California Place Names: The Origin and Etymology of Current Geographical Names.* 4th ed. Berkeley: University of California Press, 1998.

Harder, Kelsie B., ed. *Illustrated History of Place Names: United States and Canada.* New York: Van Nostrand, Reinhold, 1976.

Hitchman, Robert. *Place Names of Washington.* Tacoma: Washington State Historical Society, 1985.

McArthur, Lewis L., ed. *Oregon Geographic Names*. Portland: Oregon Historical Society Press, 1992.

Middleton, Lynn. *Place Names of the Pacific Northwest Coast*. Victoria, B.C.: Elldee Publishing Co., 1969.

Orth, Donald J. *Dictionary of Alaska Place Names*. Washington, D.C.: United States Department of the Interior, Geological Survey Professional Paper 567, 1967.

Philips, James W. *Alaska–Yukon Place Names*. Seattle: University of Washington Press, 1973.

———. *Washington State Place Names*. Seattle: University of Washington Press, 1971.

Walbran, John T. *British Columbia Place Names: Their Origin and History*. Vancouver, B.C.: Douglas & McIntyre, 1971.

E. THE NORTHWEST COAST OF AMERICA: HISTORICAL SURVEYS

General and Introductory Studies

Allen, John L. "The Canadian Fur Trade and the Exploration of Western North America." In *North American Exploration*, vol. 3, *A Continent Comprehended*, ed. John Logan Allen. Lincoln: University of Nebraska Press, 1997.

Bancroft, Hubert H. *History of Alaska, 1730–1885*. San Francisco: A. L. Bancroft, 1886.

———. *History of British Columbia, 1792–1887*. San Francisco: The History Company, 1887.

———. *History of Oregon*. 2 vols. San Francisco: The History Company, 1886–1888.

———. *History of the Northwest Coast*. 2 vols. San Francisco: A. L. Bancroft, 1884.

Clayton, Daniel W. *Islands of Truth: The Imperial Fashioning of Vancouver Island*. Vancouver, B.C.: UBC Press, 2000.

Frank, Sherry. *Pacific Passions: The European Struggle for Power in the Great Ocean in the Age of Exploration*. New York: William Morrow, 1994.

Fuller, George W. *A History of the Pacific Northwest, with a Special Emphasis on the Inland Empire*. New York: Alfred A. Knopf, 1960.

Gerdts, William. *Art across America: Two Centuries of Regional Painting, 1710–1920*. Vol. 3. New York: Abbeville Press, 1990.

Gibson, James R. "The Exploration of the Pacific Coast." In *North American Exploration*, vol. 2, *A Continent Defined*, ed. John Logan Allen. Lincoln: University of Nebraska Press, 1997.

Greenhow, Robert. *The History of Oregon and California & the other territories of the Northwest Coast of America; accompanied by a geographical view and map of those countries. . . .* Boston: C.C. Little and J. Brown, 1844.

Haycox, Stephen. *Alaska: An American Colony.* Seattle: University of Washington Press, 2002.

Henry, John Frazier. *Early Maritime Artists of the Pacific Northwest Coast, 1741–1841.* Vancouver, B.C.: Douglas & McIntyre, 1984.

Howay, F. W. *A List of Trading Vessels in the Maritime Fur Trade, 1785–1825,* ed. Richard Pierce. Kingston, Ont.: Limestone Press, 1973.

Hunt, William R. *Arctic Passage: The Turbulent History of the Land and People of the Bering Sea, 1697–1975.* New York: Charles Scribner, 1975.

Johansen, Dorothy O. *Empire of the Columbia: A History of the Pacific Northwest.* 2nd ed. New York: Harper and Row, 1967.

Kohl, J. G. *History of Discovery and Exploration on the Coasts of the United States.* Washington, D.C.: U.S. Coast and Geodetic Survey, 1885.

Lower, Arthur J. *Ocean of Destiny: A Concise History of the North Pacific, 1500–1978.* Vancouver, B.C.: University of British Columbia Press, 1978.

Mathes, W. Michael. "The Early Exploration of the Pacific Coast." In *North American Exploration,* vol. 1, *A New World Disclosed,* ed. John Logan Allen. Lincoln: University of Nebraska Press, 1997.

McDougall, Walter A. *Let the Sea Make a Noise: A History of the North Pacific from Magellan to MacArthur.* New York: Harper Collins, 1993.

Nuffield, Edward W. *The Pacific Northwest: Its Discovery and Early Exploration by Sea, Land and River.* Surrey, B.C.: Hancock House, 1990.

Pethick, Derek. *First Approaches to the Northwest Coast.* Seattle: University of Washington Press, 1979.

———. *The Nootka Connection: Europe and the Northwest Coast, 1790–1795.* Vancouver, B.C.: Douglas & McIntyre, 1980.

Ronda, James P. "Exploring the American West in the Age of Jefferson." In *North American Exploration,* vol. 3, *A Continent Comprehended,* ed. John Logan Allen. Lincoln: University of Nebraska Press, 1997.

Schwantes, Carlos Arnaldo. *The Pacific Northwest: An Interpretive History.* Lincoln: University of Nebraska Press, 1996.

Weber, David J. *The Spanish Frontier in North America.* New Haven, Conn.: Yale University Press, 1992.

Spanish Voyages

Archer, Christon. "The Political and Military Context of the Spanish Advance into the Pacific Northwest." In *Spain and the North Pacific Coast: Essays in Recognition of the Bicentennial of the Malaspina Expedition, 1791–1792*, ed. Robin Inglis. Vancouver, B.C.: Vancouver Maritime Museum Society, 1992.

———. "Russians, Indians and Passages: Spanish Voyages to Alaska in the Eighteenth Century." In *Exploration in Alaska: Captain Cook Commemorative Lectures, June–November 1978*, ed. Antoinette Shalkop. Anchorage, Alaska: Cook Inlet Historical Society, 1980.

———. "Spain and the Defence of the Pacific Ocean Empire, 1750–1810." *Canadian Journal of Latin American Studies* 11, no. 21, 1986.

———. "The Transient Presence: A Reappraisal of Spanish Attitudes towards the Northwest Coast in the Eighteenth Century." *BC Studies* 18, Spring, 1973.

Brand, Donald D. "Geographical Exploration by the Spaniards." In *The Pacific Basin: A History of Its Geographical Exploration*, ed. Herman R. Friis. New York: American Geographical Society, 1967.

Cook, Warren L. *Flood Tide of Empire: Spain and the Pacific Northwest, 1543–1819*. New Haven, Conn.: Yale University Press, 1973.

Cutter, Donald C. "California, Training Ground for Spanish Naval Heroes." *California Historical Society Quarterly* 40, no. 2, 1961.

———. "Early Spanish Artists on the Northwest Coast." *Pacific Northwest Quarterly* 54, 1963.

———. "Spain and the Oregon Coast." In *The Western Shore: Oregon Country Essays Honoring the American Revolution*, ed. Thomas Vaughan. Portland: Oregon Historical Society, 1975.

———. "Spanish Scientific Exploration along the Pacific Coast." In *New Spain's Northern Frontier: Essays on Spain in the American West, 1540–1821*, ed. David J. Weber. Albuquerque: University of New Mexico Press, 1979.

Engstrand, Iris H. W. "Images of Reality: Early Spanish Artists on the Pacific Coast." In *Encounters with a Distant Land: Exploration and the Great Northwest*, ed. Carlos Schwantes. Moscow: University of Idaho Press, 1994.

———. *Spanish Scientists in the New World: The Eighteenth Century Expeditions*." Seattle: University of Washington Press, 1981.

Kendrick, John. *The Men with Wooden Feet: The Spanish Exploration of the Pacific Northwest*. Toronto: NC Press, 1986.

Ogden, Adele. "The Californias in Spain's Pacific Otter Trade, 1775–1795." *Pacific Historical Review* 1, no. 1, 1932.

San Pío, María Pilar de. *Expediciones Españolas del Siglo XVIII: El Paso del Noroeste*. Madrid: Editorial Mapfre, 1992.

Tovell, Freeman M. *At the Far Reaches of Empire: The Life of Juan Francisco de la Bodega y Quadra*. Vancouver, B.C.: UBC Press, 2008.

English Voyages

Frost, Alan. *The Global Reach of Empire: Britain's Maritime Expansion in the Indian and Pacific Oceans, 1764–1815*. Carlton, Victoria, Aust.: Miegunyah Press, 2003..

———. "Nootka Sound and the Beginnings of Britain's Imperialism of Free Trade." In *From Maps to Metaphors: The Pacific World of George Vancouver*, ed. Robin Fisher and Hugh Johnston. Vancouver, B.C.: UBC Press, 1993.

Gascoigne, John. *Science in the Service of Empire: Joseph Banks, the British State and the Uses of Science in the Age of Revolution*. Cambridge: Cambridge University Press, 1998

Gough, Barry M. *Distant Dominion: Britain and the Northwest Coast*. Vancouver, B.C.: University of British Columbia Press, 1980.

———. "India-based Expeditions of Trade and Discovery in the North Pacific in the Late Eighteenth Century." *Geographical Journal* 55, no. 2, 1989.

———. *The Northwest Coast: British Navigation, Trade and Discoveries to 1812*. Vancouver, B.C.: UBC Press, 1992.

Harlow, Vincent T. *The Founding of the Second British Empire, 1763–1793*. Vol. 2. London: Longmans, Green, 1952.

Ruggles, Richard I. "Geographical Exploration by the British." In *The Pacific Basin: A History of Its Geographical Exploration*, ed. Herman R. Friis. New York: American Geographical Society, 1967.

Williams, Glyndwr. "The Achievement of the English Voyages, 1600–1800." In *Background to Discovery: Pacific Exploration from Dampier to Cook*, ed. Derek Howse. Berkeley: University of California Press, 1990.

———. "'The Common Center of We Discoverers': Sir Joseph Banks, Exploration and Empire in the Late Eighteenth Century." In *Sir Joseph Banks: A Global Perspective*, ed. R. E. R. Banks et al. Kew, Richmond: Royal Botanic Garden, 1994.

———. *The Great South Sea: English Voyages and Encounters, 1570–1750*. New Haven, Conn.: Yale University Press, 1997.

Russian Voyages

Andreev, Aleksandr I. *Russian Discoveries in the Pacific and in North America in the Eighteenth and Nineteenth Centuries: A Collection of Materials*, trans. and ed. Carl Ginsberg. Ann Arbor, Mich.: J. W. Edwards for the American Council of Learned Societies, 1952.

Barratt, Glynn. *Russia in Pacific Waters, 1715–1825: A Survey of the Origins of Russia's Naval Presence in the North and South Pacific*. Vancouver, B.C.: University of British Columbia Press, 1981.

Black, Lydia. *Russians in Alaska, 1732–1867.* Fairbanks: University of Alaska Press, 2004.

Burney, James. *A Chronological History of the North-Eastern Voyages of Discovery; and of the Early Eastern Navigations of the Russians.* London: Payne and Foss, and John Murray, 1819.

Coxe, William. *Account of the Russian Discoveries between Asia and America.* London: T. Cadell, 1780. Reprinted as *The Russian Discoveries Between Asia and America.* Readex Microprint Corporation, 1966.

Gibson, James R. *Imperial Russia in Frontier America: The Changing Geography of Supply of Russian America, 1784–1867.* New York: Oxford University Press, 1976.

———. "A Notable Absence: The Lateness and Lameness of Russian Discovery and Exploration in the North Pacific, 1639–1803." In *From Maps to Metaphors: The Pacific World of George Vancouver,* ed. Robin Fisher and Hugh Johnston. Vancouver, B.C.: UBC Press, 1993.

Golder, Frank A. *Russian Expansion on the Pacific, 1641–1850: An Account of the earliest and later expeditions made by the Russians along the Pacific coast of Asia and North America. . . .* Cleveland, Ohio: Arthur H. Clark Company, 1914. Reprinted, Gloucester, Mass.: Peter Smith, 1960.

Lebedev, Dimitri M., and Vadim I. Grekov. "Geographical Exploration by the Russians." In *The Pacific Basin: A History of Its Geographical Exploration,* ed. Herman R. Friis. New York: American Geographical Society, 1967.

Müller, Gerhardt Friedrich. *Voyages from Asia to America, for Completing Discoveries of the North West Coast of America.* London: T. Jeffreys, 1761.

Neatby, L. H. *Discovery in Russian and Siberian Waters.* Athens: Ohio University Press, 1973.

O'Grady, Alix. "Russians on the West Coast." *The Beaver,* December 1988–January 1989.

Polevoi, B. P. "The Discovery of Russian America." In *Russia's American Colony, ed. S. Frederick Starr.* Durham, N.C.: Duke University Press, 1987.

French Voyages

Blue, George Verne. "French Interest in Pacific America in the Eighteenth Century." *Pacific Historical Review* 4, no. 3, 1935.

Dunmore, John. *French Explorers in the Pacific.* 2 vols. Oxford: Oxford University Press, 1965–1969.

———. *Pacific Explorer: The Life of Jean François de La Pérouse.* Annapolis, Md.: Naval Institute Press, 1985.

———. *Where Fate Beckons: The Life of Jean François de La Pérouse.* Fairbanks: University of Alaska Press, 2007.

Garry, Robert J. "Geographical Exploration by the French." In *The Pacific Basin: A History of Its Geographical Exploration*, ed. Herman R. Friis. New York: American Geographical Society, 1967.

American Voyages

Bertrand, Kenneth J. "Geographical Exploration by the United States." In *The Pacific Basin: A History of Its Geographical Exploration*, ed. Herman R. Friis. New York: American Geographical Society, 1967.

Bradley, Harold W. "The Hawaiian Islands and the Pacific Fur Trade, 1785–1813." *Pacific Northwest Quarterly* 30, no. 3, 1939.

Busch, Briton C., and Barry M. Gough, eds. *Fur Traders from New England: The Boston Men in the North Pacific, 1787–1800. . . .* Spokane, Wash.: Arthur H. Clark, 1997.

Gibson, James R. *Otter Skins, Boston Ships, and China Goods: The Maritime Fur Trade of the Northwest Coast, 1785–1841.* Seattle: University of Washington Press, 1992.

Malloy, Mary. *"Boston Men" on the Northwest Coast: The American Maritime Fur Trade, 1788–1844.* Kingston, Ont.: Limestone Press, 1998.

Morison, Samuel Eliot. "Boston Traders in [the] Hawaiian Islands, 1789–1823." *Washington Historical Quarterly* 12, no. 3, 1921.

———. *The Maritime History of Massachusetts, 1783–1860.* Chap. 4, "Pioneers of the Pacific, 1784–1792," and chap. 5, "The Northwest Fur Trade, 1788–1812." Cambridge, Mass.: Riverside Press, 1923.

F. COLLECTIONS OF ARTICLES, ESSAYS, AND PAPERS

Allen, James Logan. *North American Exploration.* 3 vols. I. *A New World Discovered*, II. *A Continent Defined*, III. *A Continent Comprehended.* Lincoln: University of Nebraska Press, 1997.

Allen, Mark, and Raymond Starr, eds. *Spain's Legacy in the Pacific.* San Diego, Calif.: Maritime Museum of San Diego, 2006

Bernar, Gabriela, and Santiago Saavedra, eds. *To the Totem Shore: The Spanish Presence on the Northwest Coast.* Madrid: Ediciones El Viso, 1986.

Efrat, Barbara S., and W. J. Langlois, eds. *Nu·tka· Captain Cook and the Spanish Explorers on the Coast.* Sound Heritage, vol. 2, no. 1. Victoria, B.C.: Provincial Archives of British Columbia, 1978.

Farrell, Barbara, and Aileen Desbarats, eds. *Explorations in the History of Canadian Mapping.* Ottawa, Ont.: Association of Canadian Map Libraries and Archives, 1988.

Fisher, Robin, and Hugh Johnston, eds. *Captain James Cook and His Times.* Vancouver, B.C.: Douglas & McIntyre, 1979.

————, eds. *From Maps to Metaphors: The Pacific World of George Vancouver.* Vancouver, B.C.: UBC Press, 1993.

Fitzhugh, William W., and Aron Crowell, eds. *Crossroads of Continents: Cultures of Siberia and Alaska.* Washington, D.C.: Smithsonian Institution, 1988.

Friis, Herman R., ed. *The Pacific Basin: A History of Its Geographical Exploration.* New York: American Geographical Society, 1967.

Frost, Alan, and Jane Samson, eds. *Pacific Empires: Essays in Honour of Glyndwr Williams.* Vancouver, B.C.: UBC Press, 1999.

Haycox, Stephen, James Barnett, and Caedmon Liburd, eds. *Enlightenment and Exploration in the North Pacific, 1741–1805.* Seattle: University of Washington Press, 1997.

Haycox, Stephen W., and Mary Childers Mangusso, eds. *An Alaska Anthology: Interpreting the Past.* Seattle: University of Washington Press, 1996.

Inglis, Robin, ed. *Spain and North Pacific Coast: Essays in Recognition of the Bicentennial of the Malaspina Expedition, 1791–1792.* Vancouver, B.C.: Vancouver Maritime Museum, 1992.

Lincoln, Margarette, ed. *Science and Exploration: European Voyages to the Southern Oceans in the Eighteenth Century.* Woodbridge, Suffolk: Boydell Press, 1998.

Orozco Acuaviva, Antonio, Mercedes Palau Baquero, and Juan M. Castenado y Galán, eds. *Malaspina y Bustamante '94: II Jornadas Internacionales.* Cádiz: Real Academia Hispano-Americana, 1996.

Palau Baquero, Mercedes, ed. *La Expedición Malaspina, 1789–1794: Viaje a América y Oceania de las corbetas "Descubierta" y "Atrevida."* Madrid: Ministerio de Cultura, 1984.

Palau Baquero, Mercedes, and Antonio Orozco Acuaviva, eds. *Malaspina '92: I Jornadas Internacionales.* Cádiz: Real Academia Hispano-Americana, 1994.

Peset, José, ed. *Culturas de la Costa Noroeste de América.* Madrid: Sociedad Estatal Quinto Centenario and Turner Libros S.A., 1989.

Pierce, Richard A., ed. *Russia in North America: Proceedings of the 2nd International Conference on Russian America, Sitka, Alaska, August 19–22, 1987.* Kingston, Ont.: Limestone Press, 1990.

Shalkop, Antoinette, ed. *Exploration in Alaska: Captain Cook Commemorative Lectures, June–November 1978.* Anchorage, Alaska: Cook Inlet Historical Society, 1980.

Starr, S. Frederick, ed. *Russia's American Colony.* Durham, N.C.: Duke University Press, 1987.

Sweetland Smith, Barbara, and Redmond J. Barnett, eds. *Russian America: The Forgotten Frontier.* Tacoma, Wash.: Washington State Historical Society, 1990.

Thrower, Norman J. W., ed. *Sir Francis Drake and the Famous Voyage, 1577–1580: Essays Commemorating the Quadricentennial of Drake's Circumnavigation of the Earth.* Berkeley: University of California Press, 1984.

Vaughan, Thomas, ed. *The Western Shore: Oregon Country Essays Honoring the American Revolution.* Portland: Oregon Historical Society/American Revolution Bicentennial Commission of Oregon, 1975.

Weber, David J., ed. *New Spain's Far Northern Frontier: Essays on Spain in the American West, 1540–1821.* Dallas, Tex.: Southern Methodist University, 1985.

Williams, Glyndwr, ed. *Captain Cook: Explorations and Reassessments.* Woodbridge, Suffolk: Boydell Press, 2004.

G. NATIVE PEOPLES/FIRST NATIONS

General Works

Archer, Christon A. "Cannibalism in the Early History of the Northwest Coast: Enduring Myths and Neglected Realities." *Canadian Historical Review* 61, no. 4, 1980.

———. "The Making of Spanish Indian Policy on the Northwest Coast." *New Mexico Historical Review* 52, 1977.

———. "Seduction before Sovereignty: Spanish Efforts to Manipulate the Natives in Their Claims to the Northwest Coast." In *From Maps to Metaphors: The Pacific World of George Vancouver*, ed. Robin Fisher and Hugh Johnston. Vancouver, B.C.: UBC Press, 1993.

———. "Whose Scourge? Smallpox Epidemics on the Northwest Coast." In *Pacific Empires: Essays in Honour of Glyndwr Williams*, ed. Alan Frost and Jane Samson. Vancouver, B.C.: UBC Press, 1999.

Arima, E. Y. *The West Coast People: The Nootka of Vancouver Island and Cape Flattery.* Victoria: British Columbia Provincial Museum, Special Publications No. 6, 1883.

Barbeau, Marius. "Totem Poles: A By-product of the Fur Trade." *Scientific Monthly*, December, 1942.

Boyd, Robert. *The Coming of the Pestilence: Introduced Infectious Diseases and Population Decline among Northwest Coast Indians, 1774–1874.* Seattle: University of Washington Press, 1999.

———. "Smallpox in the Pacific Northwest: The First Epidemics." *BC Studies* 101, Spring, 1994.

Damas, David, ed. "Arctic." In *Handbook of North American Indians.* Washington, D.C.: Smithsonian Institution, 1984.

Donald, Leland. *Aboriginal Slavery on the Northwest Coast of North America.* Berkeley: University of California Press, 1997.

Drucker, Philip. *Cultures of the North Pacific Coast*. New York: Harper and Row, 1965.

———. *Indians of the Northwest Coast*. New York: American Museum of Natural History, 1963.

Gerber, Peter, and Maximilien Bruggmann. *Indians of the Northwest Coast*. New York: Facts on File, 1989.

Gibson, James R. "Smallpox on the Northwest Coast, 1835–1838." *BC Studies* 56, Winter, 1982–1983.

Gormly, Mary. "Early Culture Contact on the Northwest Coast, 1774–1795." *Northwest Anthropological Research Notes* 11, 1987.

Graves, William, ed. *Indians of North America*. Washington: National Geographic Society, 1990.

Gunther, Erna. *Indian Life on the Northwest Coast of America, as Seen by the Early Explorers and Fur Traders during the Last Decades of the Eighteenth Century*. Chicago: University of Chicago Press, 1972.

Heizer, Robert F., ed. "California." In *Handbook of North American Indians*. Washington, D.C.: Smithsonian Institution, 1978.

———. "The Introduction of Monterey Shells to the Indians of the Northwest Coast." *Pacific Northwest Quarterly* 31, no. 4, 1940.

Howay, F. W. "Indian Attacks upon Maritime Traders of the North-west Coast, 1785–1805." *Canadian Historical Review* 6, no. 4, 1925.

Kroeber, A. L. *Cultural and Natural Areas of Native North America*. Berkeley: University of California Press, 1963.

McDowell, Jim. *Hamatsa: The Enigma of Cannibalism on the Pacific Northwest Coast*. Vancouver, B.C.: Ronsdale Press, 1997.

Scott, Leslie M. "Indian Diseases as Aids to Pacific Northwest Settlement." *Oregon Historical Quarterly* 29, no. 1, 1928.

Suttles, Wayne, ed. "Northwest Coast." In *Handbook of North American Indians*. Washington, D.C.: Smithsonian Institution, 1990.

Trigger, Bruce G., and Wilcomb E. Washburn, eds. "North America," part 2. In *The Cambridge History of the Native Peoples of the Americas*. Cambridge: Cambridge University Press, 1996.

Canada

Dickason, Olive P. *Canada's First Nations: A History of the Founding Peoples from Earliest Times*. Norman: University of Oklahoma Press, 1992.

Duff, Wilson. *The Indian History of British Columbia*, vol. 1. "The Impact of the White Man." Victoria, B.C.: Provincial Museum of Natural History and Anthropology, 1965.

Efrat, Barbara S., and W. J. Langlois. "The Contact Period as Recorded by Indian Oral Tradition." In *Nu·tka· Captain Cook and the Spanish Explorers on the Coast*. Victoria, B.C.: Sound Heritage, vol. 2, no. 1. Victoria, B.C.: Provincial Archives of British Columbia, 1978.

Fisher, Robin. *Contact and Conflict: Indian–European Relations in British Columbia, 1774–1890*. Vancouver, B.C.: University of British Columbia Press, 1977.

Inglis, Robin. "Maquinna of Nootka: Portrait of an Indian Chief on the Edge of the Empire." In *De la Ciencia Illustrada a la Ciencia Romantica*, ed. Alejandro R. Díez Torre, Tomás Mallo and Daniel Pacheco Fernández. Madrid: Doce Calles, 1995.

Mathes, Valerie Sherer. "Wickaninnish: A Clayoquot Chief, as Recorded by Early Travelers." *Pacific Northwest Quarterly* 70, no. 3, 1979.

Moziño, José Mariano. *Noticias de Nutka: An Account of Nootka Sound in 1792*, trans. and ed. Iris H. Wilson Engstrand. Seattle: University of Washington Press, 1991.

United States of America

Crowell, Aron L., Amy F. Steffian, and Gordon Pullar, eds. *Looking Both Ways: Heritage and Identity of the Alutiiq People*. Fairbanks: University of Alaska Press, 2001.

Gibson, James R. "European Dependence upon American Natives: The Case of Russian America." *Ethnohistory* 25, no. 4, 1978.

———. "Russian Dependence upon the Natives of Alaska." In *Russia's American Colony*, ed. S. Frederick Starr. Durham, N.C.: Duke University Press, 1987.

Gormly, Mary. "Tlingits of Bucareli Bay, Alaska, 1774–1792." *Northwest Anthropological Research Notes* 5, no. 2, 1977.

Jonaitis, Aldona. *From the Land of the Totem Poles: The Northwest Coast Art Collection at the American Museum of Natural History*. Seattle: University of Washington Press/American Museum of Natural History, 1988.

Laguna, Frederica de. *Under Mount St. Elias: The History and Culture of the Yakatat Tlingit*. Smithsonian Contributions to Anthropology, vol. 7. Washington, D.C.: Smithsonian Institution, 1972.

Langdon, Steve. *The Native People of Alaska*. Anchorage, Alaska: Greatland, 1993.

Liapunova, R. G. "Relations with the Natives of Russian America." In *Russia's American Colony*, ed. S. Frederick Starr. Durham, N.C.: Duke University Press, 1987.

Olsen, Wallace M. "Encounters between Spaniards and Native Alaskans." In *Spain's Legacy in the Pacific*, ed. Mark Allen and Raymond Starr. San Diego, Calif.: Maritime Museum of San Diego, 2006

Ruby, Robert H., and John A. Brown. *The Chinook Indians: Traders of the Lower Columbia River*. Norman: University of Oklahoma Press, 1976.

———. *A Guide to the Indian Tribes of the Pacific Northwest*. 2nd edition. Norman: University of Oklahoma Press, 1992.

———. *Indians of the Pacific Northwest: A History*. Norman: University of Oklahoma Press, 1981.

Suttles, Wayne. "They recognize no superior chief: the Strait of Juan de Fuca in the 1790s." In *Culturas de la Costa Noroeste de América*, ed. José Peset. Madrid: Sociedad Estatal Quinto Centenario and Turner Libros S.A., 1989.

Collections and Museums

Cabello Carro, Paz. "The Ethnographic Collections: A Special Legacy of the Spanish Presence on the Northwest Coast." In *Spain and the North Pacific Coast: Essays in Recognition of the Bicentennial of the Malaspina Expedition, 1791–1792*, ed. Robin Inglis. Vancouver, B.C.: Vancouver Maritime Museum, 1992.

Cole, Douglas. *Captured Heritage: The Scramble for Northwest Coast Artifacts*. Vancouver, B.C.: Douglas & McIntyre, 1985.

Holm, Bill. "Cultural Change across the Gulf of Alaska: Eigtheenth Century Tlingit and Pacific Eskimo Art in Spain." In *Culturas de la Costa Noroeste de América*. Madrid: Sociedad Estatal Quinto Centenario and Turner Libros S.A., 1989.

Kaeppler, Adrienne L. *"Artificial Curiosities": Being an Exhibition of Native Manufactures Collected on the Three Voyages of Captain James Cook, RN*. Honolulu, Hawaii: Bishop Museum Press, 1978.

King, J. C. H. *Artificial Curiosities from the Northwest Coast of America: Native American Artefacts in the British Museum Collected on the Third Voyage of Captain James Cook. . . .* London: British Museum, 1981.

Lohse, E. S., and Frances Sundt. "History of Research: Museum Collections." In *Handbook of North American Indians*, ed. Wayne Suttles, vol. 7. Washington, D.C.: Smithsonian Institution, 1990.

Malloy, Mary. *Souvenirs of the Fur Trade: Northwest Coast Indian Art and Artifacts Collected by American Mariners, 1788 –1844*. Cambridge, Mass.. Peabody Museum of Archaeology and Ethnology/Harvard University, 2000.

H. ANCIENT ASIAN VOYAGES

Brooks, Charles Wolcott. *Japanese Wrecks, stranded and picked up adrift in the North Pacific Ocean. . . .* San Francisco: [California] Academy [of Sciences], 1876.

———. "Report of Japanese Vessels Wrecked in the North Pacific Ocean from the Earliest Records to the Present Day." In *Proceedings of the California Academy of Sciences* 6, 1876.

Drury, Clifford M. "Early American Contacts with the Japanese." *Pacific Northwest Quarterly* 36, no. 4, 1945.

Leland, Charles Geoffrey. *Fusang, or the Discovery of America by Chinese Buddhist Priests in the Fifth Century.* London: Trübner, 1875.

Mertz, Henriette. *Pale Ink: Two Ancient Records of Chinese Exploration in America.* Chicago: Swallow Press, 1972.

Quimby, George. "Japanese Wrecks, Iron Tools and Prehistoric Indians." *Arctic Anthropology* 22, no. 2, 1985.

Steiner, Stan. *Fusang: The Chinese Who Built America.* New York: Harper and Row, 1979.

Vining, Edward P. *Inglorious Columbus; or, Evidence that Hwai Shan and a Party of Buddhist Monks from Afghanistan Discovered America.* New York: D. Appleton, 1885.

Watson, Douglas S. "Did the Chinese Discover America?" *California Historical Review* 14, no. 1, 1936.

I. MYTHICAL VOYAGES/IMAGINED CARTOGRAPHY

Adams, Percy. *Travelers and Travel Liars, 1660–1800.* Berkeley: University of California Press, 1962.

Barr, William, and Glyndwr Williams, eds. *Voyages to Hudson Bay in Search of a Northwest Passage, 1741–1747.* Vol. 1, *The Voyage of Christopher Middleton, 1741–1742*; vol. 2, *The Voyage of William Moor and Francis Smith, 1746–1747.* London: Hakluyt Society, 1994 and 1995.

Briggs, Henry. *A Treatise of the Northwest Passage to the South Sea through the Continent of Virginia and by Stretum Hudson.* London: 1622. Reprinted in Samuel Purchas, *Hakluytus Postumus; or, His Pilgrimes.* London: 1625–1626.

Chassigneux, E. "Rica de Oro et Rica de Plata." *Toung Pao* 30, 1933.

Delanglez, Jean. "A Mirage: The Sea of the West." *Revue d'Histoire de l'Amérique Française* 1, 1947–1948.

Engel, Samuel. *Mémoires et observations géographiques et critiques sur la situation des pays septentrionaux de l'Asie et l'Amérique. . . .* Lausanne: Antoine Chapius, 1765.

"The Ferrer Maldonado Fantasy." In *The Malaspina Expedition 1789–1794: The Journal of the Voyage by Alejandro Malaspina*, ed. Andrew David, Felipe Fernandez-Armesto, Carlos Novi, and Glyndwr Williams. Vol. 2, appendix 2. London: Hakluyt Society/Museo Naval, Madrid, 2003.

Goldson, William R. *Observations on the passage between the Atlantic and Pacific Oceans, in two memoirs on the Straits of Anian, and the discoveries of De Fonte. Elucidated by a new and original map. To which is prefixed an historical abridgement of discoveries in the north of America.* Portsmouth: W. Mowbray, 1793.

Kendrick, John. "Seas No Mariner Has Sailed." *The Northern Mariner/Le Marin du Nord* 4, no. 3, July 1994.

Kingston, C. S. "Juan de Fuca Strait: Origin of the Name." *Pacific Northwest Quarterly* 36, no. 2, 1945.

Lagarde, Lucie. "Le Passage du Nord-Ouest et la Mer de l'Ouest dans la Cartographie française du 18e Siècle, Contribution à l'Etude de l'Oeuvre des Delisle et Buache." *Imago Mundi* 41, 1989.

Lewis, G. Malcolm. "La Grande Rivière et Fleuvre de l'Ouest: The Realities and Reasons behind a Major Mistake in the Eighteenth Century Cartography of North America." *Cartographica* 28, no. 1, 1991.

Mathes, W. Michael. "The Mythological Geography of California: Origins, Development, Confirmation, and Disappearance." *Américas* 45, 1989.

Navarette, Martin Fernández de, and Eustaquio Fernández de Navarrete. "Examen historico-critico de los viajes y descubrimientos apocrifos del Capitan Lorenzo Ferrer Maldonado, de Juan de Fuca y del Almirante Bartolomé de Fonte." *Colección de documentos inéditos para la historia de España.* Madrid: 1849.

Novo y Colson, Pedro. *Sobre los viajes apócrifos de Juan de Fuca y Lorenzo Ferrer Maldonado.* Madrid: 1881.

Postnikov, Alexei V. "The Search for a Sea Passage from the Atlantic Ocean to the Pacific via North America's Coast: On a History of a Scientific Competition." *Terrae Incognitae* 32, 2000.

Purchas, Samuel, *Hakluytus Postumus; or, Purchas His Pilgrimes Contayning a History of the World in Sea Voyages and Lande Travels.* London: William Stansby, 1625. Reprinted in 20 vols. by J. MacLehouse and Sons, Glasgow, 1905–1907.

Ruggles, Richard I. "The Cartographic Lure of the Northwest Passage: Its Real and Imagined Geography." In *Meta Incognita: A Discourse of Discovery,* ed. Thomas H. B. Symons. Hull, Québec: Canadian Museum of Civilization, 1999.

Staehlin, J. von. *An Account of the New Northern Archipelago, Lately discovered by the Russians in the Seas of Kamtschatka and Anadir.* London: Printed for C. Heydinger, 1774.

Toole, R. V. *California as an Island: A Geographical Misconception Illustrated by 100 Examples from 1625 to 1770.* London: Map Collector's Circle, 1964.

Wagner, Henry R. "Apocryphal Voyages to the Northwest Coast of America." *Proceedings of the American Antiquarian Society,* April, 1931.

Williams, Glyndwr. *The British Search for the Northwest Passage.* London: Royal Commonwealth Society, 1962.

———. "An Eighteenth Century Spanish Investigation into the Apocryphal Voyage of Admiral Fonte." *Pacific Historical Review* 30, 1961.

———. "Myth and Reality: James Cook and the Theoretical Geography of North America." In *Captain James Cook and His Times*, ed. Robin Fisher and Hugh Johnston. Vancouver, B.C.: Douglas & McIntyre, 1979.

———. *Voyages of Delusion: The Northwest Passage in the Age of Reason*. London: HarperCollins, 2002.

J. SPANISH APPROACHES IN THE 16TH AND 17TH CENTURIES

General and Introductory Works

Cutter, Donald, and Iris Engstrand. *Quest for Empire: Spanish Settlement in the Southwest*. Golden, Col.: Fulcrum, 1996.

Hammond, George P. "The Search for the Fabulous in the Settlement of the Southwest." In *New Spain's Far Northern Frontier: Essays on Spain in the American West, 1540–1821*, ed. David J. Weber. Albuquerque: University of New Mexico Press, 1979.

Holmes, Maurice G. *From New Spain by Sea to the Californias, 1519–1668*. Glendale, Calif.: Arthur H. Clark, 1963.

Kelsey, Henry. "Mapping the California Coast: The Voyages of Discovery, 1533–1543." *Arizona and the West* 26, Winter, 1984.

Myers, Paul A. *North to California: The Spanish Voyages of Discovery, 1533–1603*. Coral Spring, Fl.: Lumina Press, 2004.

Philips, Carla Rahn. "Spain and the Pacific: Voyaging into Vastness." In *Spain's Legacy in the Pacific*, ed. Mark Allen and Raymond Starr. San Diego, Calif.: Maritime Museum of San Diego, 2006.

Wagner, Henry R. *Spanish Voyages to the Northwest Coast of America in the Sixteenth Century*. San Francisco: California Historical Society, 1929.

Hernán Cortés and the Discovery of Baja California

"The Expedition of Francisco de Ulloa." In *New American World: A Documentary History of North America to 1612*, ed. David B. Quinn, vol. 1. New York: Arno Press, 1979.

"The Expedition of Hernando de Alarcón." In *New American World: A Documentary History of North America to 1612*, ed. David B. Quinn, vol. 1. New York: Arno Press, 1979.

Mathes, W. Michael, ed. and trans. *The Conquistador in California, 1535: The Voyage of Fernando Cortés to Baja California in Chronicles and Documents*. Los Angeles: Dawson's Book Shop, 1973.

Miller, Robert Ryall. "Cortés and the First Attempt to Colonize California." *California Historical Society Quarterly* 53, no. 1, 1974.

Ulloa, Francisco de. "The Voyage of Francisco de Ulloa." In "California Voyages, 1539–1541," trans. and ed. Henry R. Wagner. *California Historical Society Quarterly* 3, no. 4, 1924. Republished as Wagner, Henry R. *California Voyages, 1539–1541*. San Francisco: John Howell, 1925.

———. "Voyage to the North-west of California." In *Terra Australis Cognita or Voyages to the Terra Australis or Southern Hemisphere in the Sixteenth, Seventeenth and Eighteenth Centuries*, ed. John Callander. Edinburgh: A. Donaldson, 1766–1768. Reprinted by N. Israel, Amsterdam, 1967.

Wagner, Henry Raup. "Francisco de Ulloa Returned." *California Historical Society Quarterly* 19, no. 3, 1940.

Juan Rodríguez Cabrillo

Cabrillo, Juan Rodríguez. "Cabrillo Account." In *Spanish Exploration in the Southwest*, ed. Herbert Eugene Bolton. New York: Charles Scribner's Sons, 1916.

Kelsey, Henry. *Juan Rodríguez Cabrillo*. San Marino, Calif.: Huntington Library, 1986.

Lemke, Nancy. *Cabrillo: First European Explorer of the California Coast*. San Luis Obispo, Calif.: EZ Nature Books, 1991.

Mathes, W. Michael. "The Discoverer of Alta California, João Rodrigues Cabrilho or Juan Rodríguez Cabrillo." *Journal of San Diego History* 19, 1973.

———. "The Expedition of Juan Rodríguez Cabrillo, 1542–1543: An Historiographical Re-examination." *Southern California Quarterly* 76, no. 3, 1994.

Pourade, Richard F. "Juan Rodríguez Cabrillo: Discoverer of California." In *The Spanish Borderlands*, ed. Oakah L. Jones. Los Angeles: Lorrin L. Morrison, 1974.

Reupsch, Carl F., ed. *The Cabrillo Era and His Voyage of Discovery*. San Diego, Calif.: Cabrillo Historical Society, 1982.

"The Voyage of Juan Rodríguez Cabrillo (João Rodrigues Cabrilho) up the Pacific Coast, 1542–1543." In *New American World: A Documentary History of North America to 1612*, ed. David B. Quinn, vol. 1. New York: Arno Press, 1979.

Wagner, Henry Raup. "A Map of Cabrillo's Discoveries." *California Historical Society Quarterly* 11, no. 1, 1932.

The Manila Galleons and California

"Abstract of the Journal of Sebastian Cermeño on His Voyage up the California Coast." In *New American World: A Documentary History of North America to 1612*, ed. David B. Quinn, vol. 5. New York: Arno Press, 1979.

Chapman, Charles Edward. "Gali and Rodríguez Cermenho: Exploration of California." *Southwestern Historical Quarterly* 23, January 1920.

Cutter, Donald C., ed. *The California Coast: A Bilingual Edition of Documents from the Sutro Collection.* Documents no.2, 3, 4, and 5. Norman: University of Oklahoma Press, 1969.

Heizer, Robert. "Archaeological Evidence of Sebastián Rodríguez Cermeño's California Visit in 1595." *California Historical Society Quarterly* 20, no. 4, 1941.

Lyon, Eugene, "Track of the Manila Galleons." *National Geographic* 178, no. 3, September 1990.

Schurz, William Lytle. *The Manila Galleon.* New York: E.P. Dutton and Co. 1939.

"The Manila Galleons and the Forging of the Pacific Rim." *Mains'l Haul* [Maritime Museum of San Diego] 38, nos 1 & 2 , 2002.

Wagner, H. R. "The Voyage of Pedro de Unamuno to California in 1587." *California Historical Society Quarterly* 2, no. 1, 1933.

Baja California

Bolton, Herbert E. *Rim of Christendom: A Biography of Eusebio Francisco Kino, Pacific Coast Pioneer.* Tucson: University of Arizona Press, 1984.

Crosby, Harry. *Antigua California: Mission and Colony on the Peninsular Frontier.* Albuquerque: University of New Mexico Press, 1994.

Dunne, Peter Maston. *Black Robes in Lower California.* Berkeley: University of California Press, 1952.

Leon-Portilla, Miguel, *Cartográfia y cronicas de la Antigua California.* Coyoacán, D.F.: Universidad Nacional Autónoma de México, Fundación de Investigaciones Sociales, 1989.

Mathes, Michael. *Baja California: Textos de su historia.* México, D.F.: Instituto de Investigaciones Dr. José Luis Mora, 1988.

Sebastián Vizcaíno

Ascensión, Antonio de. "Fray Antonio de Ascensión's Account of the Voyage of Sebastián Vizcaíno," trans. and ed. H. R. Wagner. *California Historical Society Quarterly* 8, no. 1, 1929.

———. "Fray António de la Ascension's Brief Report of the Voyage of Sebastián Vizcaíno up the California Coast." In *New American World: A Documentary History of North America to 1612,* ed. David B. Quinn, vol. 5. New York: Arno Press, 1979.

"Letter of Sebastián Vizcaíno to Philip III." In *New American World: A Documentary History of North America to 1612,* ed. David B. Quinn, vol. 5. New York: Arno Press, 1979.

Mathes, W. Michael. "California's First Explorer: Sebastián Vizcaíno." *Pacific History* 25, no. 3, 1980.

———. *Sebastián Vizcaíno and Spanish Expansion in the Pacific Ocean.* San Francisco: California Historical Society, 1968.

Torquemada, Juan de. *The Voyage of Sebastián Vizcaíno to the Coast of California, Together with a Map and Sebastián Vizcaíno's Letter Written at Monterey, December 28, 1603.* San Francisco: Book Club of California, 1933.

Vizcaíno, Sebastián, et al. Various letters. In *The California Coast: A Bilingual Edition of Documents from the Sutro Collection*, ed. Donald C. Cutter. Documents no. 6–15. Norman: University of Oklahoma Press, 1969.

K. ENGLISH APPROACHES IN THE 16TH AND 17TH CENTURIES

General Works

Bawlf, Samuel. *The Secret Voyage of Sir Francis Drake.* Vancouver, B.C.: Douglas & McIntyre, 2003.

Cavendish, Thomas. *The admirable and prosperous voyage of the worshipful Master Thomas Cavendish . . .* In *Principall navigations, voiages, traffiques and discouveries of the English Nation*, ed. Richard Hakluyt, vol. 3. London: G. Bishop, R. Newberie and R. Barker, 1598–1600.

Gonzalez-Aller Hiero, José Ignacio. "La presencia de Drake y Cavendish en la costa américana del Pacífico sur: las incursiones antarticas." *Derroteros de la mar del Sur* 2, 1994.

Kelsey, Harry. *Sir Francis Drake: The Queen's Pirate.* New Haven, Conn.: Yale University Press, 1998.

Morison, Samuel Elliot. *The European Discovery of America: The Southern Voyages, AD 1492–1616.* New York: Oxford University Press, 1974.

Penzer, N. M., ed. *Francis Drake: The World Encompassed and analogous contemporary documents concerning Sir Francis Drake's circumnavigation of the world.* London: Argonaut Press, 1926. Reprinted by N. Israel, Amsterdam, 1991.

Wagner, Henry R. *Sir Francis Drake's Voyage Around the World: Its Aims and Achievements.* San Francisco: John Howell, 1926.

Wallis, Helen. "The Cartography of Drake's Voyage." In *Sir Francis Drake and the Famous Voyage, 1577–1580*, ed. Norman Thrower. Berkeley: University of California Press, 1984.

Francis Drake in Oregon and California

Aker, Raymond, and Edward Von der Porten. *Discovering Francis Drake's California Harbor.* Palo Alto, Calif.: Drake Navigator's Guild, 2000.

Gough, Barry M. "Drake's Portus Novae Albionis: George Davidson's Pursuit of Historical Evidence." In *The North Pacific to 1600: Proceedings of the Great Ocean Conferences*, vol. 1. Portland: Oregon Historical Society, 1990.

Hanna, Warren L. *Lost Harbour: The Controversy over Drake's California Anchorage*. Berkeley: University of California Press, 1979.

Heizer, Robert F. "Francis Drake and the California Indians, 1579." *University of California Publications in American Archaeology and Ethnology* 42, no. 3, 1947.

Martin, N. B. "Portus Novae Albionis: Site of Drake's California Sojourn." *Pacific Historical Review* 48, no. 3, 1979.

Seeler, Oliver. "Drake's Lost Harbour Found Again!" *Map Collector* 54, Spring, 1991.

Taylor, E. G. R. "Master John Dee, Drake and the Straits of Anian." *Mariner's Mirror* 15, 1929.

Thrower, Norman J. W. "Drake on the Pacific Coast of North America." In *European Outthrust and Encounter. The First Phase c. 1400–1700: Essays in Tribute to David Beers Quinn on His 85th Birthday*, ed. Cecil H. Clough and P. E. H. Hair. Liverpool: Liverpool University Press, 1994.

Wallis, Helen, et al. "Further Comments on the Lost Harbour." *Map Collector* 49, Winter, 1989.

Ward, Bob. "Lost Harbour Found! The Truth about Drake and the Pacific." *Map Collector* 45, Winter, 1988.

L. RUSSIA: FROM EUROPE AND SIBERIA TO THE PACIFIC

Dmytryshyn, Basil. "Russian expansion to the Pacific, 1500–1700." *Slavic Studies* 25, 1980.

Dmytryshyn, Basil, E. A. P. Crownhart-Vaughan, and Thomas Vaughan, eds. and trans. *Russian Penetration of the North Pacific Ocean 1700–1797, A Documentary Record. To Siberia and Russian America, Three Centuries of Russian European Expansion*, vol. 2. Portland: Oregon Historical Society Press, 1988.

Fisher, Raymond H. "Dezhnev's Voyage of 1648 in the Light of Soviet Scholarship." *Terrae Incognitae* 5, 1973.

———, ed. *The Voyage of Semen Dezhnev in 1648: Bering's Precursor*. London: Hakluyt Society, 1981.

Gibson, James R. "Russian Expansion in Siberia and America: Critical Contrasts." In *Russia's American Colony*, ed. Raymond Starr. Durham, N.C.: Duke University Press, 1987.

Hughes, Lindsey. *Russia in the Age of Peter the Great*. New Haven, Conn.: Yale University Press, 1998.

Lantzeff, George V., and Richard A. Pierce. *Eastward to Empire: Exploration and Conquest of the Russian Frontier to 1750*. Montreal, Québec.: McGill-Queens University Press, 1973.

Lincoln, W. Bruce. *The Conquest of a Continent: Siberia and the Russians*. New York: Random House, 1994.

M. RUSSIAN VOYAGES, EXPLORATION, AND TRADE, 1725–1799

Vitus Bering, Aleksei Chirikov, and Mikhail Gvozdev

Dall, William H. "A Critical Review of Bering's First Expedition, 1725–30, Together with a Translation of His Original Report on It with a Map." *National Geographic Magazine* 2, 1890.

Davidson, George. *The Tracks and Landfalls of Bering and Chirikof on the Northwest Coast of America*. San Francisco: John Partridge, 1901.

Divin, V. A. *The Great Russian Navigator: A. I. Chirikov*, trans. Raymond H. Fisher. Fairbanks: University of Alaska Press, 1993.

Falk, Marvin W. "Vitus Bering." In *Exploration in Alaska: Captain Cook Commemorative Lectures, June–November, 1978*, ed. Antoinette Shalkop. Anchorage, Alaska: Cook Inlet Historical Society, 1980.

Fisher, Raymond H. *Bering's Voyages: Whither and Why*. Seattle: University of Washington Press, 1977.

———. "Imperial Russia Moves Overseas." In *Russia in North America: Proceedings of the 2nd International Conference on Russian America, Sitka, Alaska, August 1987*, ed. Richard Pierce. Kingston, Ont.: Limestone Press, 1990.

Ford, Corey. *Where the Sea Breaks Its Back: The Epic Story of Early Naturalist Georg Steller and the Russian Exploration of Alaska*. Boston: Brown, Little, 1966.

Frost, O. W., ed. *Bering and Chirikov: The American Voyages and Their Impact*. Anchorage: Alaska Historical Society, 1992.

———. "Getting the Record Straight: Georg Steller's Plant Collecting on Kayak Island, Alaska, 1741." *Pacific Northwest Quarterly* 90, no. 3, 1999.

———. "Vitus Bering and Georg Steller: Their Tragic Conflict during the American Expedition." *Pacific Northwest Quarterly* 86, no. 1, 1995.

Frost, Orcutt. *Bering: The Russian Discovery of America*. New Haven, Conn.: Yale University Press, 2003.

Golder, F. A. *Bering's Voyages*, vol. 1. New York: American Geographical Society, 1922.

Kushnarev, Evgenii G. *Bering's Search for the Strait: The First Kamchatka Expedition, 1725–1730*, trans. and ed. E. A. P. Crownhart-Vaughan. Portland: Oregon Historical Society Press, 1990.

Müller, Gerhard Friedrich. *Bering's Voyages: The Reports from Russia*, trans. and ed. Carol Urness. Fairbanks: University of Alaska Press, 1986.

Report of the Superintendent of the U.S. Coast Guard and Geodetic Survey Showing the Progress of Work During the Fiscal Year Ending June, 1890. Washington, D.C.: Government Printing Office, 1890. Appendix 19 contains "Notes on an Original Manuscript Chart of Bering's Expedition of 1725–1730, and on an Original Manuscript Chart of His Second Expedition; Together with a Summary of a Journal of the First Expedition Kept by Peter Chaplin, and Now First Rendered into English from Bergh's Russian Version.

Smith, J. L. *The First Kamchatka Expedition of Vitus Bering, 1725–1730*. Anchorage, Alaska: White Stone Press, 2002.

———. *Russia's Search for America, 1716–1732*. Anchorage, Alaska: White Stone Press, 2002.

———, ed. *To the American Coast: The Voyages and Explorations of M. S. Gvozdev, the Discoverer of Northwestern America*. Anchorage, Alaska: White Stone Press, 1997.

Stejneger, Leonhard. *Georg Wilhelm Steller: The Pioneer of Alaskan Natural History*. Cambridge, Mass.: Harvard University Press, 1936.

Steller, Georg Wilhelm. *Journal of a Voyage with Bering, 1741–1742*. Ed. and trans. Margritt A. Engel and O. W. Frost. Stanford, Calif.: Stanford University Press, 1988.

Van Horn, Walter. "Vitus Bering: Chronology." In *Exploration in Alaska: Captain Cook Commemorative Lectures, June–November, 1978*, ed. Antoinette Shalkop. Anchorage, Alaska: Cook Inlet Historical Society, 1980.

Waxell, Sven. *The Russian Expedition to America*. Ed. M. A. Michael. New York: Collier, 1962.

The Aleutian Islands: Discoveries, Exploration, and the Fur Trade

Berkh, V. N. *A Chronological History of the Discovery of the Aleutian Islands; or, The Exploits of Russian Merchants with a Supplement of Historical Data on the Fur Trade*, trans. Dmitri Krenov, ed. Richard A. Pierce. Kingston, Ont.: Limestone Press, 1974.

Black, Lydia T. *Atka: An Ethnohistory of the Western Aleutians*. Kingston, Ont.: Limestone Press, 1984.

Fisher, Raymond H. *The Russian Fur Trade, 1550–1700*. Berkeley: University of California Press, 1943.

Henning, Robert, ed. "Islands of the Seals: The Pribilofs." In *Alaska Geographic* 9, no. 3, 1982.

Makarova, R. V. *Russians on the Pacific, 1743–1799*, trans. and ed. Richard A. Pierce and Alton S. Donnelly. Kingston, Ont.: Limestone Press, 1975.

Masterson, James R., and Helen Brower, trans. and ed. *Bering's Successors, 1745–1780: Contribution of Peter Simon Pallas to the History of Russian Exploration towards Alaska*. Seattle: University of Washington Press, 1948.

Müller, Gerhard Friedrich. *Voyages from Asia to America for completing the Discoveries of the North West Coast of America*. London: Thomas Jefferys, 1761.

Rennick, Penny, ed. "Kodiak." *Alaska Geographic* 19, no. 3, 1992.

Smith, J. L. *Russians in the Pribilof Islands, 1786–1787*. Anchorage, Alaska: White Stone Press, 2001.

Smith, J. L., ed., and Svetlana Potton, trans. *The Russian Discovery of the Aleutian and Kodiak Islands*. Anchorage, Alaska: White Stone Press, 2003.

Urness, Carol. "Dmitri Bragin's Voyage in the North Pacific." *Terrae Incognitae* 2, 1970.

Petr Krenitsyn and Mikhail Levashov

Glushankov, I. V. "The Aleutian Expedition of Krenitzen and Levashov," trans. and ed. Mary Sadouski and Richard A. Pierce. *Alaska Journal* 3, no. 4, 1973.

Grigorii Shelikhov and the Early American Fur Trade

Shelikhov, Grigorii I. *A Voyage to America, 1783–1786*, trans. Marina Ramsey, ed. Richard A. Pierce. Kingston, Ont.: Limestone Press, 1981.

Solovjova, Katerina, and Aleksandra Vovnyanko. "The Rise and Decline of the Lebedev-Lastochkin Company: Russian Colonization of South Central Alaska, 1787–1798." *Pacific Northwest Quarterly* 90, no. 4, 1999.

Joseph Billings

Alekseev, A. J. "Joseph Billings." *Geographic Journal* 132, no. 2, 1966.

Merck, Carl Heinrich. *Siberia and Northwestern America, 1788–1792: The Journal of Carl Heinrich Merck, Naturalist with the Russian Scientific Expedition Led by Captains Joseph Billings and Gavriil Sarychev*, trans. Fritz Jaensch, ed. Richard A. Pierce. Kingston, Ont.: Limestone Press, 1980.

Pierce, Richard A., ed. and Z. D. Titova, trans. "Voyage of Mr. Billings from Akhotsk to Kamchatka . . . , 1789–1790–1791." In *Siberia and Northwest-*

ern America, 1788–1792: The Journal of Carl Heinrich Merck, Naturalist with the Russian Scientific Expedition Led by Captains Joseph Billings and Gavriil Sarychev. Appendix. Kingston, Ont.: Limestone Press, 1980.

Sarychev, Gavriil. *An Account of a Voyage of Discovery to the North-east of Siberia, the Frozen Ocean, and the North-east Sea.* London: Barnard, 1806. Reprinted by N. Israel, Amsterdam, 1969.

Sauer, Martin. *An account of a geographical and astronomical expedition to the northern parts of Russia . . . performed by the command of her Imperial Majesty Catherine the Second . . . by commodore Joseph Billings in the years 1785 . . . 1794.* London: T. Cadell and W. Davies, 1802.

Cartography of the Russian Discoveries

Black, Lydia. *The Lovtsov Atlas of the North Pacific Ocean.* Kingston, Ont.: Limestone Press, 1991.

Breitfuss, L. "Early Maps of North-Eastern Asia and of the Lands around the North Pacific: Controversy between G. F. Müller and N. Delisle." *Imago Mundi* 3, 1939.

Efimov, A.V., ed. *Atlas of Geographical Discoveries in Siberia and in Northwest America, XVII–XVIII Centuries.* Moscow: 1964.

Falk, Marvin. "Mapping Russian America." In *Proceedings of the 2nd International Conference on Russian America, Sitka, Alaska, August 19–22, 1987*, ed. Richard A. Pierce. Kingston, Ont.: Limestone Press, 1990.

Longenbaugh, Dee. "From Anian to Alaschka: The Mapping of Alaska to 1778." *Map Collector* 29, 1984.

Postnikov, Alexei V. *The Mapping of Russian America: A History of Russian–American Contacts in Cartography.* Milwaukee, Wis.: American Geographical Society Collection, Special Publication No. 4, 1995.

Urness, Carol. *Bering's First Expedition: A Re-examination Based on Eighteenth-Century Books, Maps and Manuscripts.* New York: Garland, 1987.

———. "Joseph Nicolas Delisle's Map for Bering's Second Kamchatka Expedition." In *Russia in North America: Proceedings of the 2nd International Conference on Russian America, Sitka, Alaska, August 19–22, 1987*, ed. Richard Pierce. Kingston, Ont.: Limestone Press, 1990.

Related Works of Interest

Gibson, James R. "The Abortive First Russian Circumnavigation: Captain Mulovsky's 1787 Expedition to the North Pacific." *Terrae Incognitae* 31, 1999.

N. SPANISH VOYAGES IN THE 1760s and 1770s

Alta California and the Sacred Expedition

Bolton, Herbert E. "The Mission as a Frontier Institution in the Spanish–American Colonies." In *New Spain's Far Northern Frontier: Essays on Spain in the American West, 1540–1821*, ed. David J. Weber. Albuquerque: University of New Mexico Press, 1979.

———. *Outpost of Empire: The Story of the Founding of San Francisco*. New York: Knopf, 1931.

Burus, Ernest J. "Rivera y Moncada: Explorer and Military Commander of Both Californias, in Light of His Diary and Other Contemporary Documents." *Hispanic America Historical Review* 50, November 1970.

Chapman, Charles E. *The Founding of San Francisco*. New York: Macmillan, 1917.

Crespi, Juan. *A Description of Distant Roads: Original Journals of the First Expedition into California, 1769–70*, ed. and trans. Alan K. Brown. San Diego: San Diego State University Press, 2001.

Crosby, Harry. *Gateway to Alta California: The Expedition to San Diego, 1769*. San Diego: Sunbelt Publications, 2003.

Cutter, Donald C. "Plans for the Occupation of Upper California: A New Look at the 'Dark Age' from 1602–1769." *Journal of San Diego History* 24, Winter, 1978.

Ewing, Russell C. *The Founding of the Presidio de San Francisco*. San Francisco: Society of California Pioneers, 1936.

Guest, Francis F. "Mission Colonization and Political Control in Spanish California." *Journal of San Diego History* 24, Winter, 1978.

Hilton, Sylvia L. *La Alta California Española*. Madrid: Editorial Mapfre, 1992.

Johnson, Paul C., ed. *The California Missions: A Pictorial History*. Menlo Park, Calif.: Sunset Books, 1979.

Nuttall, Donald A. "Pedro Fages and the Advance of the Northern Frontier of New Spain, 1767–1782." Ph.D. thesis. University of California, 1964.

Priestly, Herbert Ingram. *José de Gálvez: Visitor General of New Spain, 1765–1771*. Berkeley: University of California Press, 1916.

———, trans. & ed. *A Historical, Political and Natural Description of California by Pedro Fages, Soldier of Spain*. Berkeley: University of California Press, 1937.

Treutlein, Theodore E. *San Francisco Bay: Discovery and Colonization, 1769–1776*. San Francisco: California Historical Society, 1968.

Wagner, Henry Raup. "The Last Spanish Exploration of the Northwest Coast and the Attempt to Colonize Bodega Bay." *California Historical Society Quarterly* 10, no. 4, 1931.

Weber, Francis J. *The California Missions: Bibliography.* Documentary History of the California Missions. vol. 22. Los Angeles: Archdiocese of Los Angeles Archives, 1987.

———. *Prominent Visitors to the California Missions: The Provincial Period 1786–1842.* Santa Barbara, Calif.: McNally & Loftin, 1991.

Juan Pérez

Beals, Herbert K., trans. & annotation. *Juan Pérez on the Northwest Coast: Six Documents of His Expedition in 1774.* Portland: Oregon Historical Society Press, 1989.

———. "The Juan Pérez–Josef de Cañizares Map of the Northwest Coast." *Terrae Incognitae* 27, 1995.

Bolton, Herbert E. *Fray Juan Crespi, Missionary Explorer of the Pacific Coast, 1768–1774.* Berkeley: University of California Press, 1927.

Crespi, Juan. "Diary of the Voyage . . . in His Majesty's frigate called the *Santiago* . . . commanded by Don Juan Pérez. . . ." In *The California Coast: A Bilingual Edition of Documents from the Sutro Collection*, ed. Donald C. Cutter. Document 19. Norman: University of Oklahoma Press, 1969.

Howay, F.W. "The Spanish Discovery of British Columbia in 1774." *Annual Report of the British Columbia Historical Association*, 1923.

Peña, Tomás de la. "Diary . . . of the Voyage of His Majesty's Frigate called *Santiago* . . . commanded by . . . Don Juan Pérez. . . ." In *The California Coast: A Bilingual Edition of Documents from the Sutro Collection*, ed. Donald C. Cutter. Document 18. Norman: University of Oklahoma Press, 1969.

"The Pérez Expedition of 1774: Selections from the Journals." In *Through Spanish Eyes: Spanish Voyages to Alaska, 1774–1792*, ed. Wallace M. Olson. Auke Bay, Alaska: Heritage Research, 2002.

Bruno de Hezeta, Juan Francisco de la Bodega y Quadra, and Juan Manuel de Ayala

Archer, Christon I. "Los Viajes de Juan Francisco de la Bodega y Quadra, 1775 y 1779." *Derroteros de la mar del Sur* 4, 1996.

Beerman, Eric. "Bruno de Heceta: The First European Discoverer of the Columbia River." *The Pacific Historian* 23, no. 1, 1979.

Bodega y Quadra, Juan Francisco de la. "Navegación hecha por Don Francisco de la Bodega y Quadra, Teniente de Fragata de la Real Marina y Comandante de la Goleta *Sonora* a los Descubrimientos de los Mares y Costa Septentrional de California, Año de 1775." In *Juan Francisco de la Bodega y Quadra: El Descubrimiento del Fin del Mundo (1775–1792)*, ed. Salvador Bernabeu Albert. Madrid: Alianza Editorial, 1990.

Campa Cos, Fray Miguel de la. *A Journal of Exploration Northward Along the Coast from Monterey in the Year 1775*, ed. John Galvin. San Francisco: John Howell, 1964.

Caster, J. G. "The Last Days of Don Juan Pérez, the Mallorcan Mariner." *Journal of the West* 2, 1963.

Galvin, John. *The First Spanish Entry into San Francisco Bay, 1775*. San Francisco: John Howell, 1971.

Hezeta, Bruno de. *For Honor and Country: The Diary of Bruno de Hezeta*, trans. and ed. Herbert K. Beals. Portland: Western Imprints, Oregon Historical Society, 1985.

"The Hezeta Expedition of 1775: Selections from the Journals." In *Through Spanish Eyes: Spanish Voyages to Alaska, 1774–1792*, ed. Wallace M. Olson. Auke Bay, Alaska: Heritage Research, 2002.

Landin Carrasco, Amancio. *Mourelle de la Rua: Explorador del Pacífico*. Madrid: Edición Cultural Hispanica, 1971.

Majors, Harry M. "The Hezeta and Bodega Voyage of 1775." *Northwest Discovery* 1, 1980.

Mourelle, Francisco. "Journal of a Spanish Voyage in 1775, to explore the Western Coast of North America." In *Miscellanies*, ed. Daines Barrington. London: J. Nichols, 1781.

Raup, H. F. "The Delayed Discovery of San Francisco Bay." *California Historical Society Quarterly* 27, no. 4, 1948.

Sierra, Benito de la. "Fray Benito de la Sierra's Account of the Hezeta Expedition to the Northwest Coast in 1775," trans. A. J. Baker, ed. Henry R. Wagner. *California Historical Society Quarterly* 9, no. 3, 1930.

Tovell, Freeman M. "The Hezeta–Bodega Voyage of 1775: Its Significance for Spain's Presence in the Pacific Northwest." *Terrae Incognitae* 27, 1995.

Ignacio de Arteaga y Bazan and Juan Francisco de la Bodega y Quadra

Beerman, Eric. "Basque Sailor at Bucareli Bay [Ignacio de Arteaga]." *Alaska Journal* 12, no. 4, 1982.

Bodega y Quadra, Juan Francisco de la. "Navigación y descubrimientos hechos de orden de Su Majestad en la costa septentrional de California desde la latitud en que se halla el Departamento de San Blas. . . ." In *Juan Francisco de la Bodega y Quadra: El Descubrimiento del Fin del Mundo (1775–1792)*, ed. Salvador Bernabeu Albert. Madrid: Alianza Editorial, 1990.

"The Expedition of 1779: Selections from the Journals." In *Through Spanish Eyes: Spanish Voyages to Alaska, 1774–1792*, ed. Wallace M. Olson. Auke Bay, Alaska: Heritage Research, 2002.

Langdon, Stephen J. "Efforts at Humane Engagement: Indian–Spanish Encounters in Bucareli Bay, 1779." In *Enlightenment and Exploration in the North Pacific, 1741–1805*, ed. Stephen Haycox et al. Seattle: University of Washington Press, 1997.

Riobo, Juan. "An Account of the Voyage Made by Father John Riobo as Chaplain of His Majesty's Frigates, *Princesa* and *Favorita* to Discover New Lands and Seas North of the Settlements of the Ports of Monterey and of Our Father San Francisco," trans. and ed. Walter Thornton. *Catholic Historical Review* 4, 1918.

O. JAMES COOK AND THE SEARCH FOR THE NORTHWEST PASSAGE

James Cook and Charles Clerke

Clayton, Daniel. "Captain Cook's Command of Knowledge and Space: Chronicles from Nootka Sound." In *Captain Cook: Explorations and Reassessments*, ed. Glyndwr Williams. Woodbridge, Suffolk, Eng.: Boydell Press, 2004.

Conner, David, and Lorraine Miller. *Master Mariner: Captain Cook and the Peoples of the Pacific*. Vancouver, B.C.: Douglas & McIntyre, 1978.

Cook, James. *The Journals of Captain James Cook*, III, *The Voyage of the Resolution and Discovery, 1776–1780*, ed. J. C. Beaglehole, 2 vols. Cambridge: Hakluyt Society, 1967.

Cook, James, and James King, eds. *A Voyage to the Pacific Ocean in the years 1776, 1777, 1778, 1779, and 1780 undertaken by the command of His Majesty, for making discoveries in the Northern Hemisphere*, 3 vols. and atlas. London: John Douglas, 1784.

David, Andrew, Rüdiger Joppien, and Bernard Smith, eds. *The Charts and Coastal Views of Captain Cook's Voyages*, vol. 3, *The Voyage of the Resolution and Discovery, 1776–1780*. London: Hakluyt Society/Australian Academy of Humanities, 1997.

Ellis, William. *An Authentic Narrative of a Voyage Performed by Captain Cook and Captain Clerke, in His Majesty's ships Resolution and Discovery during the years 1776, 1777, 1778, 1779, and 1780; In search of a North-West Passage. . . .* London: G. Robinson, J. Sewell and J. Debrett, 1782.

Gascoigne, John. *Captain Cook: Voyager between Worlds*. London: Hambledon Continuum, 2007.

Gough, Barry. "Nootka Sound in James Cook's Pacific World." In *Nu·tka· Captain Cook and the Spanish Explorers on the Coast*. Sound Heritage vol. 7, no. 1, ed. Barbara S. Efrat and William J. Langlois. Victoria, B.C.: Provincial Archives of British Columbia, 1978.

Joppien, Rüdiger, and Bernard Smith. *The Art of Captain Cook's Voyages with a descriptive catalogue of all the known original drawings of people, places, artifacts and events, and the original engravings associated with them.* Vol. 3. *The Voyage of the Resolution and Discovery, 1776–1780.* Melbourne: Oxford University Press/Australian Academy of Humanities, 1988.

Ledyard, John. *A Journal of Captain Cook's Last Voyage to the Pacific Ocean, and in Quest of a North-West Passage, between Asia & America; Performed in the Years 1776, 1777, 1778 and 1779.* Hartford, Conn.: Nathaniel Patten, 1783.

Nordyke, Eleanor. *Pacific Images: Views from Captain Cook's Third Voyage.* Honolulu: Hawaiian Historical Society, 1999.

Norris, John. "The Strait of Anian and British Northwest America: Cook's Third Voyage in Perspective." *BC Studies* 36, Winter, 1977–1978.

Rickman, John. *Journal of Captain Cook's last voyage to the Pacific Ocean on Discovery; performed in the years 1776, 1777, 1778, 1779.* London: E. Newberry, 1781.

Robson, John. *The Captain Cook Encyclopedia.* Auckland: Random House New Zealand, 2004.

———. *Captain Cook's World: Maps of the Life and Voyages of James Cook.* Seattle: University of Washington Press, 2000.

Vaughan, Thomas. *Captain Cook R.N., the Resolute Mariner: An International Record of Oceanic Discovery.* Portland: Oregon Historical Society, 1974.

Williams, Glyndwr. "Alaska Revealed: Cook's Explorations in Alaska in 1778." In *Exploration in Alaska: Captain Cook Commemorative Lectures,* ed. A. Shalkop. Anchorage, Alaska: Cook Inlet Historical Society, 1980.

Withey, Lynne. *Voyages of Discovery: Captain Cook and the Exploration of the Pacific.* New York: William Morrow, 1987.

Cook and the Russians

Armstrong, Terence. "Cook's Reputation in Russia." In *Captain James Cook and His Times,* ed. Robin Fisher & Hugh Johnston. Vancouver, B.C.: Douglas & McIntyre, 1979.

Beaglehole, J. C., ed. *Cook and the Russians: An Addendum to the Hakluyt Society's Edition of the Voyage of the* Resolution *and* Discovery, *1776–1780,* trans. Yakov M. Svet. London: Hakluyt Society, 1973.

Crownhart-Vaughan, E. A. P. "Clerke in Kamchatka, 1779." *Oregon Historical Quarterly* 80, no. 2, 1979.

David, Andrew. "Russian Charts and Captain Cook's Third Voyage." *The Map Collector* 52, Autumn, 1990.

Gibson, J. R. "The Significance of Cook's Third Voyage to Russian Tenure in the Pacific." *Pacific Studies* 1, no. 2, 1978.

Svet, Yakov M., and Svetlana G. Fedorova. "Captain Cook and the Russians." *Pacific Studies* 2, no. 1, Fall, 1978.

Werrett, Simon. "Russian Responses to the Voyages of Captain Cook." In *Captain Cook: Explorations and Reassessments*, ed. Glyndwr Williams. Woodbridge, Suffolk, Eng.: Boydell Press, 2004.

P. ENGLAND AND THE BEGINNING OF THE MARITIME FUR TRADE

James Hanna

Galois, R. M. "The Voyages of James Hanna to the Northwest Coast: Two documents. *BC Studies* 103, Autumn, 1994.

Lamb, W. Kaye. "James Hanna and John Henry Cox: A Postscript." *BC Studies* 88, Winter, 1990–1991.

Lamb, W. Kaye, and Tomás Bartroli. "James Hanna and John Henry Cox: The First Maritime Trader and His Sponsor." *BC Studies* 84, Winter, 1989–1990.

Nathaniel Portlock and George Dixon

Dillon, R. H., ed. "Letters of Captain George Dixon in the Banks Collection." *British Columbia Historical Quarterly* 14, no. 3, 1950.

Dixon, George. *A Voyage round the World: but more particularly to the North-West Coast of America: performed in 1785, 1786, 1787 and 1789 in the King George and Queen Charlotte, Captains Portlock and Dixon*. London: Geo. Goulding, 1789.

Letter and Memorandum from Captain George Dixon to Sir Joseph Banks regarding the Fur Trade on the Northwest Coast, 1789. N.p., White Knight Press, 1941.

Portlock, Nathaniel, *A Voyage round the World; but more particularly to the North-West Coast of America: Performed in 1785,1786,1787 and 1788, in the King George and Queen Charlotte, Captains Portlock and Dixon*. London: John Stockdale and George Goulding, 1789.

John Meares

Howay, Frederick W., ed. *The Dixon–Meares Controversy, containing Remarks on the Voyages by John Meares, by George Dixon, An Answer to Mr. George Dixon, by John Meares, and Further Remarks on the Voyage of John Meares, by George Dixon*. Amsterdam: N. Israel, 1969.

Meares, John. *Voyages made in the Years 1788 and 1789, from China to the Northwest Coast of America. To Which Are Prefixed an Introductory*

Narrative of a Voyage Performed in 1786 from Bengal, in the Ship "Nootka";
Observations on the probable Existence of a North West Passage; and some
Account of the Trade between the North West Coast of America and China;
and the Latter Country and Great Britain. London: Logographic Press,
1790. Reprinted by De Capo Press, New York, 1967.

Nokes, J. Richard. *Almost a Hero: The Voyages of John Meares, R.N. to China,*
Hawaii and the Northwest Coast. Pullman, Wash.: Washington State University Press, 1998.

Charles Barkley

Hill, Beth. *The Remarkable World of Frances Barkley: 1769–1845.* Sidney,
B.C.: Gray's Publishing, 1978.

Lamb, W. Kaye. "The Mystery of Mrs. Barkley's Diary: Notes on the Voyages
of the 'Imperial Eagle,' 1786–87." *British Columbia Historical Quarterly* 6,
no. 1, 1942.

James Colnett

Colnett, James. *A Voyage to the Northwest Side of America: The Journals of*
James Colnett, 1786–89, ed. Robert Galois. Vancouver: UBC Press, 2004.

Kuykendall, Ralph S. "James Colnett and the 'Princess Royal'." *Oregon His-*
torical Quarterly 25, no. 1, 1924.

Moeller, Beverley B. "Captain James Colnett and the Tsimshian Indians,
1787." *Pacific Northwest Quarterly* 57, no. 1, 1966.

James Strange

Carey, Charles. "Review of James Strange's Journal of Commercial Expeditions
to the Northwest Coast, 1785–86." *Oregon Historical Quarterly* 30, no. 3,
1929.

Strange, James. *James Strange's Journal and Narrative of the Commercial Expe-*
dition from Bombay to the Northwest Coast of America. Introductory material
by A. V. Venkatarama Ayyar. Fairfield, Washington: Ye Galleon Press, 1982.

Walker, Alexander. *An Account of a Voyage to the North West Coast of*
America in 1785 and 1786, by Alexander Walker, ed. Robin Fisher and J. M.
Bumsted. Seattle: University of Washington Press, 1982.

Britain and the Nootka Incident

Blue, G. V. "Anglo-French Diplomacy during the Critical Phase of the Nootka
Controversy." *Oregon Historical Quarterly.* Volume 39, no. 2, 1938.

Dalrymple, Alexander. *The Spanish Memorial of 4 June Considered.* London:
1790.

————. *The Spanish Pretensions Fairly Discussed*. London: 1790.

Manning, William Ray. "Nootka Sound Controversy." In *American Histori-cal Association: Annual Report for 1904*. Reprinted, New York: University Microfilms/Argonaut Press, 1966.

Meares, John. *Authentic Copy of the Memorial to the Right Honourable Wil-liam Wyndham Grenville, One of His Majesty's Principal Secretaries of State, by Lieutenant John Mears* [sic]*, of the Royal Navy; Dated 30th April, 1790, and Presented to the House of Commons, May 13, 1790. Contain-ing Every Particular Respecting Capture of the Vessels in Nootka Sound*. London: J. Debrett, 1760 [sic, 1790]. Reprinted in Meares, *Voyages*, 1790; Pipes, *The Memorial of John Meares*, 1933; and Nokes, *Almost a Hero*, 1998.

Mills, "The Real Significance of the Nootka Sound Incident." *Canadian His-torical Review* 6, no. 2, 1925.

The Nootka Sound Convention [October 28, 1790]; *The Nootka Claims Con-vention* [February 12, 1793]; *Convention for the Mutual Abandonment of Nootka* [January 11, 1794]. In William Ray Manning, *The Nootka Sound Controversy*. New York: University Microfilms/Argonaut Press, 1966.

Norris, J. M. "The Policy of the British Cabinet in the Nootka Crisis." *English Historical Review* 70, no. 4, 1955.

Pipes, Nellie B., ed. *The Memorial of John Meares to the House of Commons respecting the Capture of Vessels in Nootka Sound*. Portland, Ore.: Metro-politan Press, 1933.

Charles Bishop

Bishop, Charles. *The Journal and Letters of Captain Charles Bishop on the North-West Coast of America, in the Pacific and in New South Wales, 1794–1799*, ed. Michael Roe. Cambridge: Hakluyt Society, 1967.

Related Works of Interest

Cole, Douglas. "Sigismund Bacstrom's Northwest Coast Drawings and an Ac-count of His Curious Career." *B.C. Studies* 46, Summer, 1980.

Cole, Douglas, and Maria Tippett. "Pleasing Diversity and Sublime Desola-tion: The 18th Century British Perception of the Northwest Coast." *Pacific Northwest Quarterly* 65, no. 1, 1974.

Cook, Andrew. "Alexander Dalrymple and the Hydrographic Office." In *Pa-cific Empires: Essays in Honour of Glyndwr Williams*, ed. Alan Frost and Jane Samson. Vancouver, B.C.: UBC Press, 1999.

Dalrymple, Alexander. *Plan for Promoting the Fur Trade and Securing It to This Country by Uniting the Operations of the East India Company and the Hudson's Bay Company*. London: George Bigg, 1789.

Gough, Barry, and Robert J. King. "William Bolts: An Eighteenth Century Merchant Adventurer." In *Archives* 21, no. 112, 2005.

Howay, F. W. "Four Letters from Richard Cadman Etches to Sir Joseph Banks, 1788–92." *British Columbia Historical Quarterly* 6, no. 2, 1942.

———. "Letters Concerning Voyages of British Vessels to the Northwest Coast of America, 1787–1809." *Oregon Historical Quarterly* 39, no. 3, 1938.

Robinson, Sheila P. "Man and Resources on the Northern Northwest Coast of North America, 1785–1840: A Geographical Approach to the Maritime Fur Trade." Ph.D. thesis, University of London, 1983.

Q. FRANCE ON THE NORTHWEST COAST

Jean François Galaup de La Pérouse

Beerman, Eric, and Conchita Beerman. "The Hospitality of the Spanish Governor of Monterey, Pedro Fages to the Ill-fated French Expedition of the Conte [*sic*] de la Pérouse." *Noticias del Puerto de Monterey* 22, no. 2, 1976.

Bellec, François. *La généreuse et tragique expédition Lapérouse*. Rennes: Ouest France, 1985.

Brossard, Maurice de. "Lapérouse's Expedition to the Pacific Northwest, 1785–1788." *Pacific Studies* 2, no. 1, 1978.

Chinard, Gilbert, ed. *Le Voyage de Lapérouse sur les côtes de l'Alaska et de la Californie*. Baltimore, Md.: Johns Hopkins Press, 1937.

Emmons, G. T. "Native Account of the Meeting between La Pérouse and the Tlingit." *American Anthropologist* 12, 1911.

Gaziello, Catherine. *L'Expédition de Lapérouse, 1785–1788: Réplique Française aux Voyages de Cook*. Paris: Comité des Travaux Historiques et Scientifiques, 1984.

Inglis, Robin. "Lapérouse 1786: A French Naval Visit to Alaska." In *Enlightenment and Exploration in the North Pacific 1741–1805*, ed. Stephen Haycox, James Barnett, and Caedmon Liburd. Seattle: University of Washington Press, 1997.

———. *The Lost Voyage of Lapérouse*. Vancouver, B.C.: Vancouver Maritime Museum, 1986.

La Pérouse, Jean François Galaup de. *The Journal of Jean-François Galaup de la Pérouse 1785–1788*, ed. John Dunmore. 2 vols. London: Hakluyt Society, 1994.

———. *Voyage de la Pérouse autour du monde, publié conformément au décret du 22 avril 1791*, redigé par M. L.-A. Milet-Mureau, 4 vols. and atlas. Paris: Imprimerie de la République, an 5 (1797).

———. *Le Voyage de Lapérouse 1785–1788: Récit et documents originaux*, ed. Maurice de Brossard et John Dunmore. Paris: Imprimerie Nationale, 1985.

Lenz, Mary Jane. "Myth and Memory at Lituya Bay." In *Culturas de la Costa Noroeste de América*, ed. José Peset. Madrid: Sociedad Estatal Quinto Centenario and Turner Libros, 1989.

Philips, Henry, and Wright Wenrich. "How the White Men Came to Lituya and What Happened to Yeahlth-kan Who Visited Them: The Tlingit Tradition of La Perouse's Visit." *Alaska Magazine* 1, 1927.

Pinault, Madelaine. "Duché de Vancy, dessinateur de l'expédition Lapérouse." In *Bicentenaire du Voyage de Lapérouse: Colloque Lapérouse Albi, Mars, 1985*. Albi: Association Lapérouse Albi-France, 1988.

Etienne Marchand

Marchand, Etienne. *A Voyage round the World Performed during the years 1790, 1791 and 1792 by Etienne Marchand, preceded by a Historical Introduction and Illustrated by Charts*. Translated from the French of C. P. Claret de Fleurieu. London: T. N. Longman and O. Rees, 1801.

Marchand, Etienne. *Voyage autour du Monde pendant les années 1790, 1791 et 1792 par Etienne Marchand, précédé d'une introduction historique*, par C. P. Claret de Fleurieu. Paris: Imprimerie de la République, an 6 (1798).

R. SPANISH VOYAGES, EXPLORATION, AND SETTLEMENT, 1788–1792

Esteban José Martínez and Gonzalo López de Haro

López de Haro, Gonzalo. "Diary of the voyage which . . . with the undersigned, First Pilot of the Royal Navy and Commander of His Majesty's Packetboat *San Carlos* hopes to make under the command of His Majesty's Frigate the *Princesa*, her Captain, the Ensign and First Pilot of the Navy, Don Estevan José Martínez. . . ." In *Through Spanish Eyes: Spanish Voyages to Alaska, 1774–1792*, ed. Wallace M. Olsen. Auke Bay, Alaska: Heritage Research, 2002.

Martínez, Esteban José. "Diary of the Voyage . . . of the Frigate *Princesa* and the Packetboat *San Carlos*, carried out under the Order of the King . . . and the decree of His Excellency Señor Manuel Antonio Florez, Viceroy of New Spain, from the Naval Base of San Blas to the discoveries of the Northern Coast of the California in the present year of 1788." In *Through Spanish Eyes: Spanish Voyages to Alaska, 1774–1792*, ed. Wallace M. Olsen. Auke Bay, Alaska: Heritage Research, 2002.

Stewart, Charles L. "Martínez and López de Haro on the Northwest Coast, 1788–1789." Ph.D. thesis, University of California, 1937.

Esteban José Martínez and Nootka Sound

Fisher, Vivian C. "Esteban José Martínez: A naval officer who steered Spain to the Edge of War in the Pacific Northwest." *Mains'l Haul* [Maritime Museum of San Diego] 36, no. 1, 2000.

Priestly, Herbert Ingram. "The Log of the *Princesa* by Estevan Martínez: What Does It Contribute to our Knowledge of the Nootka Sound Controversy?" *Oregon Historical Quarterly* 21, no. 1, 1920.

Stewart, C. L. "Why the Spaniards Temporarily Abandoned Nootka Sound in 1789." *Canadian Historical Review* 17, no. 2, 1936.

Spain and the Nootka Crisis

Convenio de San Lorenzo el Real, 1790 [28 de octubre de 1790.] In *Tratados, convenciones y declaraciones de paz y de comercio que han hecho con las potencias extranjeras los Monarcas españoles de la Casa de Borbón.* Madrid, 1843. Also printed in Spanish in Warren Cook, *Flood Tide of Empire: Spain and the Pacific Northwest, 1543–1819.* New Haven, Conn.: Yale University Press, 1972; and in Mercedes Palau et al., *Nutka 1792.* Madrid: Ministerio de Asuntos Exteriores de España, Dirección General de Relaciones Culturales y Científicas, 1998.

Soler Pascual, Emilio. "El lento decliner del Imperio español y la crisis política de Nutka." In *Nutka 1792,* ed. Mercedes Palau, Freeman Tovell, Pamela Sprätz, and Robin Inglis. Madrid: Ministerio de Asuntos Exteriores de España, Dirección General de Relaciones Culturales y Científicas, 1998.

Sota, José de la. "The Nootka Crisis." In *To the Totem Shore: The Spanish Presence on the Northwest Coast,* ed. Gabriela Bernar and Santiago Saavedra. Madrid: Ediciones El Viso, 1986.

Manuel Quimper

Beerman, Eric. "Manuel Quimper y Bodega y Quadra: Dos Limeños al servicio de la Real Armada." In *Nutka 1792,* ed. Mercedes Palau, Freeman Tovell, Pamela Sprätz, and Robin Inglis. Madrid: Ministerio de Asuntos Exteriores de España, Dirección General de Relaciones Culturales y Científicas, 1998.

Quimper, Manuel. "Diary of the Voyage of Don Manuel Quimper." In *Spanish Explorations in the Strait of Juan de Fuca,* trans. and ed. H. R. Wagner. New York: AMS Press, 1933.

Tovell, Freeman. "Manuel Quimper: Exploration of the Strait of Juan de Fuca." *Resolution* [Maritime Museum of British Columbia] 19, 1990.

Tueller, James B. "A Spanish Naval Tourist in Hawai'i: Manuel Quimper." In *Spain's Legacy in the Pacific*, ed. Mark Allen and Raymond Starr. San Diego, Calif.: Maritime Museum of San Diego, 2006.

Salvador Fidalgo

Fidalgo, Salvador. "Journal of the voyage which includes the departure from the port of San Blas to the arrival at Nootka and the stay there until the departure for higher latitudes by the Lieutenant of the Navy and Royal Armada, dn. Salvador Fidalgo, Commander of the Packet boat of His Majesty named the *San Carlos*, 1790." In *Through Spanish Eyes: Spanish Voyages to Alaska, 1774–1792*, ed. Wallace M. Olsen. Auke Bay, Alaska: Heritage Research, 2002.

Nelson Patrick, Elizabeth. "The Salvador Fidalgo Expedition, 1790: The Last Spanish Exploration of the Far North Pacific Ocean." Ph.D. thesis, University of New Mexico, 1981.

Francisco de Eliza, Juan Pantoja y Arriaga, and José María Narváez

Bartroli, Tomás. "Eliza Expedition, 1791." In *Genesis of Vancouver City*. Vancouver, B.C.: Marco Polo Books, 1997.

Crosse, John. "Malaspina and the Eliza Expedition of 1791." In *Malaspina '92: I Jornadas Internacionales*, ed. Mercedes Palau Baquero and Antonio Orozco Acuaviva. Cádiz: Real Academia Hispano-Américana, 1994.

McDowell, Jim. *José Narváez: The Forgotten Explorer*. Spokane, Wash.: Arthur H. Clark, 1998.

Sánchez, Joseph P. "Pedro Alberni and the Spanish Claim to Nootka: The Catalonian Volunteers on the Northwest Coast." *Pacific Northwest Quarterly* 71, no. 2, 1980.

———. *Spanish Bluecoats: The Catalonian Volunteers in Northwestern New Spain, 1767–1810*. Albuquerque: University of New Mexico Press, 1990.

Wagner, Henry R., trans. & ed. "Extract of the navigation made by the pilot Don Juan Pantoja y Arriaga." In *Spanish Explorations in the Strait of Juan de Fuca*, ed. Henry R. Wagner. New York: AMS Press, 1933.

———, trans. & ed. "Extract of the voyage, explorations and discoveries made . . . by Don Francisco Eliza in the year 1791." In *Spanish Explorations in the Strait of Juan de Fuca*, ed. Henry R. Wagner. New York: AMS Press, 1933.

Alejandro Malaspina

Bartroli, Tomás. "The Malaspina Expedition at Nootka." In *Spain and the North Pacific Coast: Essays in Recognition of the Bicentennial of the Malaspina Expedition, 1791–1792*, ed. Robin Inglis. Vancouver, B.C.: Vancouver Maritime Museum, 1992.

Cutter, Donald C. *Malaspina and Galiano: Spanish Voyages to the Northwest Coast, 1791 and 1792*. Vancouver, B.C.: Douglas & McIntyre, 1991.

David, Andrew. "Alejandro Malaspina's Survey Operations on the Northwest Coast, 1791–1792." In *Charting Northern Waters: Essays for the Centenary of the Canadian Hydrographic Service*, ed. William Glover. Montreal & Kingston: McGill-Queens University Press, 2004.

———. "Felipe Bauza and the British Hydrographic Office." In *Malaspina 92: I Jornadas Internacionales*, ed. Mercedes Palau Baquero and Antonio Orozco Acuaviva. Cádiz: Real Academia Hispano-Americana, 1994.

Hart, Catherine Poupeney. "Malaspina at Port Mulgrave: An Examination of the Texts." In *Spain and the North Pacific Coast: Essays in Recognition of the Bicentennial of the Malaspina Expedition, 1791–1792*, ed. Robin Inglis. Vancouver, B.C.: Vancouver Maritime Museum, 1992.

———. *Relations de l'Expédition Malaspina aux confins de l'empire espagnol: L'échec du voyage*. Longueil, Québec: Éditions du Préambule, 1987.

Higueras Rodríguez, Dolores. *Catálago Crítico de los Documentos de la Expedición Malaspina*. 3 vols. Madrid: Museo Naval, 1985–1994.

———. *NW Coast of America: Iconographic Album of the Malaspina Expedition*. Madrid: Museo Naval, 1991.

Kendrick, John. *Alejandro Malaspina: Portrait of a Visionary*. Montreal, Québec: McGill-Queens University Press, 1999.

Kendrick, John, and Robin Inglis. *Enlightened Voyages: Malaspina and Galiano on the Northwest Coast, 1791–1792*. Vancouver, B.C.: Vancouver Maritime Museum, 1991.

Malaspina, Alejandro. *The Malaspina Expedition 1789–1794: The Journal of the Voyage by Alejandro Malaspina*, ed. Andrew David, Felipe Fernandez-Armesto, Carlos Novi, and Glyndwr Williams, 3 vols. London: Hakluyt Society/Museo Naval, Madrid, 2001–2004.

———. *Viaje politico-científico alrededor del mundo por las corbetas* Descubierta *y* Atrevida, *al mando de los capitanes de navío Don Alejandro Malaspina y Don José Bustamante desde 1789 a 1794*, ed. Pedro Novo y Colson. Madrid: Imprenta Abienzo, 1885.

The Malaspina Expedition: In the Pursuit of Knowledge. Santa Fe: Museum of New Mexico Press, 1977.

Manfredi, Dario. *Alessandro Malaspina: A Biography*, trans. Don S. Kirschner and Teresa J. Kirschner, ed. Russell McNeill and John Black. Nanaimo, B.C.: Alexandro Malaspina Research Centre, Malaspina University College, 2001.

———. "An Unknown Episode behind the Search for the Northwest Passage of the Malaspina Expedition?" In *Spain and the North Pacific Coast: Essays in Recognition of the Bicentennial of the Malaspina Expedition, 1791–1792*, ed. Robin Inglis. Vancouver: Vancouver Maritime Museum, 1992.

Martin-Merás, Luisa. "Felipe Bauza y Cañas, un marino liberal para la neuva cartografía de América y el Pacífico." In *Marinos Cartógrafos Españoles*. Madrid: Prosegur y Sociedad Geográfica Española, 2002.

Saiz, Blanca. *Bibliografia sobre Alejandro Malaspina y acerca de la expedición Malaspina y de los marinos y científicos que en ella participaron*. Madrid: Ediciones El Museo Universal, 1992.

Sotos Serrano, Carmen. *Los Pintores de la Expedición de Alejandro Malaspina*. 2 vols. Madrid: Real Academia de Historia, 1982.

Suría, Tomás de. *Journal of Tomás de Suría of His Voyage with Malaspina to the Northwest Coast of America in 1791*, trans. Henry Raup Wagner, ed. Donald C. Cutter. Fairfield, Wash.: Ye Galleon Press, 1980.

———. *Tomás de Suría: a l'expedició Malaspina Alaska, 1791*, ed. Arsenio Rey Tejerina. Valencia: Generalitat Valenciana, 1995.

Tova, Antonio de. *The Diary of Antonio de Tova of the Malaspina Expedition 1789–1794*, ed. Enrique Porruá. Lewiston, N.Y.: Edwin Mellen Press, 2001.

Vaughan, Thomas, E. A. P. Crownhart-Vaughan, and Mercedes Palau. *Voyages of Enlightenment: Malaspina on the Northwest Coast, 1791/1792*. Portland: Oregon Historical Society, 1977.

Dionisio Alcalá Galiano and Cayetano Valdés y Flores

Alcalá Galiano, Dionisio. *California in 1792: A Spanish Naval Visit*, trans. and ed. Donald C. Cutter. Norman: University of Oklahoma Press, 1990.

———. *Relación del Viaje hecho por las goletas* Sutil *y* Mexicana *en el año 1792 para reconocer el Estrecho de Juan de Fuca* (1802), ed. Mª. Dolores Higueras Rodríguez y Mª. Luisa Martín-Merás. Madrid: Museo Naval, 1991.

———. *The Voyage of the* Sutil *and* Mexicana *1792: The Last Spanish Exploration of the Northwest Coast of America*, trans. and ed. John Kendrick. Spokane, Wash.: Arthur H. Clark, 1991.

Higueras, Rodríguez, María Dolores, and María Luisa Martín-Merás. "The Mala-spina Expedition on the Northwest Coast of America in 1791 [and 1792]," trans. and ed. John Kendrick. In *Spain and the North Pacific Coast: Essays in Recognition of the Bicentennial of the Malaspina Expedition, 1791–1792*, ed. Robin Inglis. Vancouver, B.C.: Vancouver Maritime Museum, 1992.

Juan Francisco de la Bodega y Quadra and the Limits Expedition

Archer, Christon I. "Retreat from the North: Spain's Withdrawal from Nootka Sound." *BC Studies* 37, Spring, 1978.

Bodega y Quadra, Juan Francisco de la. "Viaje a la Costa Noroeste de la América Septenrional por don Juan Francisco de la Bodega y Cuadra, del Orden de Santiago, capítan de navío de la Real Armada y comandante del Departamento de San Blas, en las fragatas de su mando, *Santa Gertrudis*, *Aránzazu*, *Princesa* y goleta *Activa*. Año de 1792," notes, Freeman Tovell. In *Nutka 1792*, ed. Mercedes Palau, Freeman Tovell, Pamela Sprätz, and Robin Inglis. Madrid: Ministerio de Asuntos Exteriores de España, Direc-ción General de Relaciones Culturales y Científicas, 1998.

———. "Viaje a la Costa NO de la América Septenrional por don Juan Fran-cisco de la Bodega y Cuadra, del Orden de Santiago, capítan de navío de la Real Armada y comandante del Departamento de San Blas, en las fragatas de su mando, *Santa Gertrudis*, *Aránzazu*, *Princesa* y goleta *Activa*. Año de 1792." In *Juan Francisco de la Bodega y Quadra: El descubrímiento del fín del mundo (1775–1792)*, ed. Salvador Bernabeu Albert. Madrid: Alianza Editorial, 1990.

Cutter, Donald C. "El amigo indio de Bodega: Maquinna, Jefe de Nutka." *Der-roteros de la mar del Sur* 6, 1998.

Inglis, Robin. "Bodega and Vancouver: Protagonists at Nootka, 1792." *Der-roteros de la mar del Sur* 3, 1995.

———. "Otros dos iniciativas: Caamaño en Alaska y Fidalgo en Nuñez Ga-ona." In *Nutka 1792*, ed. Mercedes Palau, Freeman Tovell, Pamela Sprätz, and Robin Inglis. Madrid: Ministerio de Asuntos Exteriores de España, Di-rección General de Relaciones Culturales y Científicas, 1998.

Tovell, Freeman. "The Other Side of the Coin: The Viceroy, Bodega y Quadra, Vancouver and the Nootka Crisis." *BC Studies* 93, Spring 1992.

Jacinto Caamaño

Caamaño, Jacinto. "The Journal of Jacinto Caamaño," ed. Henry R. Wagner and W. A. Newcombe. Part I, *British Columbia Historical Quarterly* 2, no. 3, 1938; Part II, *British Columbia Historical Quarterly* 2, no. 4, 1938.

Tovell, Freeman. "Ending the Search for the Mythical Passage of Admiral Fonte: The 1792 Voyage of Jacinto Caamaño." *BC Studies* 117, Spring, 1998.

S. THE VOYAGES OF GEORGE VANCOUVER AND WILLIAM BROUGHTON

Anderson, Bern. *Surveyor of the Sea: The Life and Voyages of Captain George Vancouver*. Toronto, Ont.: University of Toronto Press, 1960.

Archer, Christon I. "The Voyage of George Vancouver: a Review Article." *BC Studies*, 73, Spring, 1987.

Broughton, William Robert. *A Voyage of Discovery to the North Pacific Ocean*. London: Cadell and Davies, 1804.

David, Andrew. *Vancouver's Artists*. Burnaby, B.C.: Simon Fraser University, Department of History, Vancouver Conference on Exploration and Discovery, 1991.

———. "Vancouver's Survey Methods." In *From Maps to Metaphors: The Pacific World of George Vancouver*, ed. Robin Fisher and Hugh Johnston. Vancouver, B.C.: Douglas & McIntyre, 1993.

Davies, Alun. "Testing a New Technology: Vancouver's Survey and Navigation in Alaskan Waters, 1794." In *Enlightenment and Exploration in the North Pacific, 1741–1805*, ed. Stephen Haycox et al. Seattle: University of Washington Press, 1997.

Fisher, Robin. "Vancouver's Vision of Native Peoples." In *Pacific Empires: Essays in Honour of Glyndwr Williams*, ed. Alan Frost and Jane Samson. Vancouver, B.C.: UBC Press, 1999.

———. *Vancouver's Voyage: Charting the Northwest Coast*. Vancouver, B.C.: Douglas & McIntyre, 1992.

Gillespie, B. Guild. *On Stormy Seas: The Triumphs and Torments of Captain George Vancouver*. Victoria, B.C.: Horsdall & Schubart, 1992.

Gorsline, Jerry, ed. *Rainshadow: Archibald Menzies and the Botanical Exploration of the Olympic Peninsula*. Port Townsend, Wash.: Jefferson County Historical Society, 1992.

Gunther, Erna. "Vancouver and the Indians of Puget Sound." *Pacific Northwest Quarterly* 51, no. 1, 1960.

Lamb, W. Kaye. "Vancouver's Charts of the Northwest Coast." In *Explorations in the History of Canadian Mapping*, ed. Barbara Farrell and Aileen Desbarats. Ottawa: Association of Canadian Map Libraries and Archives, 1988.

Manby, Thomas. *Journal of the Voyages of the H.M.S. Discovery and Chatham*, ed. Glen Adams. Fairfield, Wash.: Ye Galleon Press, 1992.

Meany, Edmond S., ed. *Vancouver's Discovery of Puget Sound: Portraits and Biographies of the Men Honored in the Naming of Geographic Features of Northwest America*. Portland, Ore.: Binfords & Mort, 1957.

Menzies, Archibald. *The Alaska Travel Journal of Archibald Menzies, 1793–1794*. Fairbanks: University of Alaska Press, 1993.

———. *Menzies' Journal of Vancouver's Voyage, April to October 1792*, ed. C. F. Newcombe. Victoria, B.C.: W. H. Cullins, 1923.

Mockford, Jim. "Before Lewis and Clark, Lt. Broughton's River of Names: The Columbia River Exploration of 1792." *Oregon Historical Quarterly* 106, no. 4, 2005.

Naish, John M. "The Health of Mariners: Vancouver's Achievement." In *Enlightenment and Exploration in the North Pacific, 1741–1805*, ed. Stephen Haycox et al. Seattle: University of Washington Press, 1997.

———. *The Interwoven Lives of George Vancouver, Archibald Menzies, Joseph Whidbey and Peter Puget: Exploring the Pacific Northwest Coast*. Lewiston, N.Y.: Edward Mellen Press, 1996.

Puget, Peter. "Peter Puget's Journal of the Exploration of Puget Sound, May 7–June 11, 1792," ed. Bern Anderson. *Pacific Northwest Quarterly* 30, no. 2, 1939.

———. *Vancouver Discovers Vancouver: An Excerpt from the Logs of Second Lieutenant Peter John Puget*, ed. W. K. Lamb. Burnaby, British Columbia: Simon Fraser University, Department of History, Vancouver Conference on Exploration and Discovery, 1991.

Sherriff, John. "John Sherriff on the Columbia, 1792: An Account of William Broughton's Exploration of the Columbia River," ed. Andrew David. *Pacific Northwest Quarterly* 83, no. 2, 1992.

Vancouver, George. *A Discovery Journal: George Vancouver's First Survey Season, 1792*, ed. John E. Roberts. Victoria, B.C.: Trafford, 2005.

———. *A Voyage of Discovery to the North Pacific Ocean and Round the World; in which the Coast of Northwest America has been Carefully Examined and Accurately Surveyed. . . . With a View to Ascertain the Existence of any Navigable Communication between the North Pacific and North Atlantic Ocean; . . . 1790, 1791, 1792, 1793, 1794 and 1795, in the* Discovery *Sloop of War and the Armed Tender* Chatham. 3 vols. and atlas. London: G. C. and J. Robinson, 1798.

———. *The Voyage of George Vancouver*, ed. W. Kaye Lamb with an introduction and appendices. 4 vols. London: Hakluyt Society, 1984.

Whitebrook, Robert B. "From Cape Flattery to Birch Bay: Vancouver's Anchorages on Puget Sound." *Pacific Northwest Quarterly* 44, no. 3, 1953.

Williams, Glyndwr. "George Vancouver, the Admiralty and Exploration in the Late Eighteenth Century." In *Enlightenment and Exploration in the North Pacific, 1741–1805*, ed. Stephen Haycox et al. Seattle: University of Washington Press, 1997.

Wing, Robert C. *Joseph Baker: Lieutenant on the Vancouver Expedition, British Naval Officer for Whom Mt. Baker Was Named.* Seattle, Wash.: Gray Beard, 1992.

T. AMERICAN VOYAGES: EXPLORATION AND THE MARITIME FUR TRADE

Simon Metcalfe

Howay, Frederic William. "Captain Simon Metcalfe and the Brig 'Eleanora.'" *Washington Historical Quarterly* 26, no. 2, 1925.

Richards, Rhys, and Richard A. Pierce. *Captain Simon Metcalfe: Pioneer Fur Trader in the Pacific Northwest, Hawaii and China, 1787–1794.* Kingston, Ont.: Limestone Press, 1991.

Robert Gray and John Kendrick

Hayes, Edmund. "Gray's Adventure Cove [Clayoquot Sound, 1791–1792]." *Oregon Historical Quarterly* 68, no. 2, 1967.

Howay, F. W. "Captain's Gray and Kendrick: the Barrell Letters." *Washington Historical Quarterly* 12, no. 4, 1921.

———. "Letters Relating to the Second Voyage of the Columbia." *Oregon Historical Quarterly* 24, no. 2, 1923.

———, ed. *Voyages of the Columbia to the Northwest Coast, 1787–1790 & 1790–1793.* Boston: Massachusetts Historical Society, 1941. Reprinted by the Oregon Historical Society Press, Portland, 1990.

Howay, F. W., and Albert Matthews. "Some Notes Upon Captain Gray." *Washington Historical Quarterly* 21, no. 1, 1930.

Morison, Samuel Eliot. "The *Columbia*'s Winter Quarters of 1791–1792 Located." *Oregon Historical Quarterly* 39, no. 1, 1938.

Nokes, J. Richard. *Columbia's River: The Voyages of Robert Gray, 1787–1793.* Tacoma: Washington State Historical Society, 1991.

Pipes, Nellie B., ed. "Later Affairs of Kendrick: Barrell Letters." *Oregon Historical Quarterly* 30, no. 2, 1929.

Polich, John Leo. "John Kendrick and the Maritime Fur Trade of the Northwest Coast." M.A. Thesis, University of Southern California, 1964.

Schofield, John. *Hail, Columbia: Robert Gray, John Kendrick and the Pacific Fur Trade.* Portland: Oregon Historical Society, 1993.

Joseph Ingraham

Howay, Frederic W. "The Voyage of the Hope." *Washington Historical Quarterly* 9, no. 1, 1920.

Ingraham, Joseph. *Joseph Ingraham's Journal of the Brigantine Hope on a Voyage to the Northwest Coast of America, 1790–9, illustrated with charts and drawings by the author,* ed. Mark D. Kaplanoff. Barre, Mass.: Imprint Society, 1971.

———. "Nootka Sound in 1789: Joseph Ingraham's Account." *Pacific Northwest Quarterly* 65, no. 4, 1974.

John Boit

Boit, John. *Log of the Union: John Boit's Remarkable Voyage to the Northwest Coast and around the World, 1794–1796,* ed. Edmund Hayes. Portland: Oregon Historical Society Press, 1981.

John Jewitt

Howay, F. W. "An Early Account of the Loss of the Boston, 1803." *Washington Historical Quarterly* 17, no. 4, 1926.

Jewitt, John R. *A Journal kept at Nootka Sound by John R. Jewitt, one of the survivors of the crew of the ship Boston during a captivity among the Indians from March, 1803, to July, 1805.* Reprinted from the original edition, Boston, 1807, with an introduction by Norman L. Dodge. Boston: Charles Goodspeed, 1931.

———. *The Adventures and Sufferings of John R. Jewitt, Captive of Maquinna.* Jewitt's narrative annotated and illustrated by Hilary Stewart. Vancouver, B.C.: Douglas & McIntyre, 1987. Reprinted 1999.

William Sturgis

Sturgis, William. *The Journal of William Sturgis,* ed. S. W. Jackman. Victoria, B.C.: Sono Nis Press, 1978.

———. *A Most Remarkable Enterprise: Lectures on the Northwest Coast Trade and Northwest Coast Indian Life by William Sturgis,* ed. Mary Malloy. Marston Mills, Mass.: Parnassus Imprints, 2000.

U. THE OVERLANDERS

Fur Trade and Westward Expansion: General Works

Barragy, Terence J. "The Trading Age, 1792–1844." *Oregon Historical Quarterly* 76, no. 3, 1975.

Chittenden, Hiram Martin. *The American Fur Trade of the Far West.* Stanford: Academic Reprints, 1954.

Davies, K. G. "From Competition to Union [Hudson's Bay Company and North West Company]." In *Aspects of the Fur Trade: Selected Papers of the*

1965 North American Fur Trade Conference. St. Paul: Minnesota Historical Society, 1967.

Gibson, James R. *The Lifeline of the Oregon Country: The Fraser–Columbia Brigade System, 1811–47.* Vancouver, B.C.: UBC Press, 1997.

Hafen, LeRoy Reuben. *The Mountain Men and the Fur Trade of the Far West: Biographical Sketches of the Participants.* 10 vols. Glendale, Calif.: Arthur H. Clark, 1965–1972.

Karamanski, Theodore J. *Fur Trade and Exploration: Opening of the Far Northwest, 1821–1852.* Norman: University of Oklahoma, 1988.

Lewis, G. Malcolm. "Misinterpretation of Amerindian Information as a Source of Error on Euro-American Maps." *Annals of the Association of American Geographers* 77, no. 4, 1987.

Mackie, Richard Somerset. *Trading Beyond the Mountains: The British Fur Trade on the Pacific, 1793–1843.* Vancouver, B.C.: UBC Press, 1997.

Rich, E. E. *The Fur Trade and the Northwest to 1857.* Toronto: McClelland and Stewart, 1967.

Vaughan, Thomas, and Bill Holm. *Soft Gold: The Fur Trade and Cultural Exchange on the Northwest Coast of America.* Portland: Oregon Historical Society, 1982.

Winnearls, Joan. "Thomas Jefferys's Map of Canada and the Mapping of the Western Part of North America, 1750–1768." In *Images & Icons of the New World: Essays on American Cartography*, ed. Karen Severud Cook. London: The British Library, 1996.

Hudson's Bay Company

Atkin, W. T. "The Snake Country Fur Trade, 1816–1824." *Oregon Historical Quarterly* 35, no. 4, 1934.

Davidson, Donald C. "Relations of the Hudson's Bay Company with the Russian American Company on the Northwest Coast, 1829–1867." *British Columbia Historical Quarterly* 5, no. 1, 1941.

Dean, Jonathon R. "The Hudson's Bay Company and Its Use of Force, 1828–1829." *Oregon Historical Quarterly* 98, no. 3, 1997.

Gibson, J. R. "A Diverse Economy: The Columbia Department of the Hudson's Bay Company, 1821–1846." *Columbia* 5, no. 2, 1991.

Gough, Barry. "The Hudson's Bay Company and the Imperialism of Monopoly: A Review Article." *BC Studies* 18, Summer 1993.

Haines, Francis D. "The Relations of the Hudson's Bay Company with the American Fur Traders in the Pacific Northwest." *Pacific Northwest Quarterly* 40, no. 4, 1949.

Ireland, Willard E. "James Douglas and Russian American Company, 1840." *British Columbia Historical Quarterly* 5, no. 1, 1941.

Murray, Keith A. "The Role of the Hudson's Bay Company in Pacific Northwest History." *Pacific Northwest Quarterly* 52, no. 1, 1961.

Pethick, Derek. *James Douglas: Servant of Two Empires*. Vancouver, B.C.: Mitchell Press, 1969.

Rich, E. E. *The Hudson's Bay Company 1670–1870*. Vol. 2, *1763–1820*. Toronto, Ont.: McClelland and Stewart, 1960.

Ross, Frank E. "The Retreat of the Hudson's Bay Company in the Pacific Northwest." *Canadian Historical Review* 18, no. 3, 1937.

Sage, Walter N. "The Place of Fort Vancouver in the History of the Northwest." *Pacific Northwest Quarterly* 39, no. 2, 1948.

Simpson, [Sir] George. *Fur Trade and Empire, George Simpson's Journal, Remarks, Connected With the Fur Trade in the Course of a Voyage From York Factory to Fort George and Back to York, 1824–25*, ed. Frederick Merk. Cambridge, Mass.: Harvard University Press, 1931.

Swagerty, William R. "The Leviathan of the North: American Perceptions of the Hudson's Bay Company, 1816–1846." *Oregon Historical Quarterly* 104, no. 4, 2003.

North West Company

Campbell, Marjorie Wilkins. *The Northwest Company*. Vancouver, B.C.: Douglas & McIntyre, 1983.

Gough, Barry. "The Northwest Company's 'Adventure to China.'" *Oregon Historical Society Quarterly* 76, no. 4, 1975.

Keith, H. Lloyd. "'Shameful Mismanagement, Wasteful Extravagance, and the Most Unfortunate Dissention': George Simpson's Misconceptions of the North West Company." *Oregon Historical Quarterly* 102, no. 4, 2001.

McLaughlin, Merlyn. "Imperial Aspects of the North-West Company in Western Canada to 1870." Ph.D. thesis, University of Colorado, 1952.

Morton, W. L. "The North West Company: Pedlars Extraordinary." In *Aspects of the Fur Trade: Selected Papers of the 1965 North American Fur Trade Conference*. St. Paul: Minnesota Historical Society, 1967.

O'Neil, Marion. "The Maritime Activities of the North West Company, 1813 to 1821." *Washington Historical Quarterly* 21, no. 3, 1930.

Rumilly, Robert. *La Compagnie du Nord-Ouest: une épopée montréalaise*. 2 vols. Montréal: Fides, 1980.

Samuel Hearne

Hearne, Samuel. *A Journey from Prince of Wales's Fort in Hudson's Bay to the Northern Ocean, 1769, 1770, 1771, 1772*, ed. Richard Glover. Toronto: Macmillan, 1958.

McGoogan, Kenneth. *Ancient Mariner: The Amazing Adventures of Samuel Hearne, the Sailor Who Walked to the Arctic Ocean.* Toronto: Harper-Flamingo Canada, 2003.

Speck, Gordon. *Samuel Hearne and the Northwest Passage.* Caldwell, Idaho: Caxton Printers, 1963.

Peter Pond

Dillon, Richard H. "Peter Pond and the Overland Route to Cook's Inlet." *Pacific Historical Quarterly* 42, no. 4, 1951.

Gough, Barry. "Peter Pond and Athabasca: Fur Trade, Discovery and Empire." *Alberta* 1, no. 2, 1989.

Innis, Harold. "Peter Pond and the Influence of Capt. James Cook on Exploration in the Interior of North America." *Proceedings and Transactions of the Royal Society of Canada*, 3rd series, vol. 22, section 2, 1928.

Ronda, James P. "Peter Pond and the Exploration of the Greater Northwest." In *Encounters with a Distant Land: Exploration and the Greater Northwest*, ed. Carlos A. Schwantes. Moscow: University of Idaho Press, 1994.

Alexander Mackenzie

Gough, Barry. *First Across the Continent: Sir Alexander Mackenzie.* Norman: University of Oklahoma Press, 1997.

———. "Rivers of the West: Alexander Mackenzie's Arctic Adventure." *Columbia* 13, no. 1, 1999.

Hayes, Derek. *First Crossing: Alexander Mackenzie, His Expedition across North America and the Opening of the Continent.* Vancouver, B.C.: Douglas & McIntyre, 2001.

Mackenzie, Alexander. *The Journals and Letters of Sir Alexander Mackenzie*, ed. W. Kaye Lamb. Cambridge: Hakluyt Society, 1970.

———. *Voyages from Montreal on the River St. Laurence through the Continent of North America to the Frozen and Pacific Oceans; in the Years 1789 and 1793. With a Preliminary Account of the Rise, Progress, and Present State of the Fur Trade of That Country.* London: R. Noble for T. Cadell Jun. and W. Davies, Corbett and Morgan, 1801.

Meriwether Lewis and William Clark

Allen, John L. "Thomas Jefferson and the Passage to India: A Pre-Exploratory Image." In *Patterns and Progress: Research in Historical Geography*, ed. Ralph E. Ehrenberg. Washington, D.C.: Howard University Press, 1975.

Ambrose, Stephen E. *Undaunted Courage: Meriwether Lewis, Thomas Jefferson and the Opening of the American West.* New York: Simon and Schuster, 1996.

Ambrose, Stephen E., and Sam Abell. *Lewis and Clark: Voyage of Discovery*. Washington, D.C.: National Geographic Society, 1998.

Brandt, Anthony. *The Journals of Lewis and Clark: Meriwether Lewis and William Clark*. Abridged. Washington, D.C.: National Geographic Society, 2002.

Chinard, E. G. "Thomas Jefferson and the Corps of Discovery." *American West* 12, no. 6, 1975.

Cutright, Paul R. *Lewis and Clark: Pioneering Naturalists*. Urbana: University of Illinois Press, 1969.

Gilman, Carolyn. *Lewis and Clark: Across the Divide*. Washington, D.C.: Smithsonian Institution, 2003.

Karsmizki, Kenneth W. "Cartographic Representations: A Controversy in Mapping Lewis and Clark's Fort Clatsop." *Oregon Historical Quarterly* 105, no. 4, 2004.

Lang, William L. "Describing a New Environment: Lewis and Clark and Enlightenment Science in the Columbia River Basin." *Oregon Historical Quarterly* 105, no. 3, 2004.

———. "Lewis and Clark on the Columbia River: The Power of Landscape in the Exploration Experience." *Pacific Northwest Quarterly* 87, no. 3, 1996.

Lavender, David S. *The Way to the Western Sea: Lewis and Clark across the Continent*. New York: Harper & Row, 1988.

Ronda, James P. *Finding the Way: Explorations with Lewis and Clark*. Albuquerque: University of New Mexico Press, 2001.

———. *Lewis and Clark among the Indians*. Lincoln: University of Nebraska Press, 1984.

———. "Troubled Passages: The Uncertain Journeys of Lewis and Clark." *Oregon Historical Quarterly* 106, no. 4, 2005.

———. *Voyages of Discovery: Essays on the Lewis and Clark Expedition*. Helena: Montana Historical Society, 1998.

Simon Fraser

Fraser, Simon. *The Letters and Journals of Simon Fraser, 1806 –1808*, ed. W. Kaye Lamb. Toronto, Ont.: Macmillan, 1960.

MacKay, Corday. "With Fraser to the Sea." *The Beaver*, December 1944.

John Jacob Astor and Astoria

Bannon, Gary. *The Last Voyage of the* Tonquin*: An Ill-Fated Expedition to the Pacific Northwest*. Waterloo, Ont.: Escart Press, 1992.

Brandon, William. "Wilson Price Hunt." In *The Mountain Men and the Fur Trade of the Far West: Biographical Sketches of the Participants*, ed. LeRoy R. Hafen, vol. 6. Glendale, Calif.: Arthur H. Clark, 1965–1972.

Cox, Ross. *The Columbia River*, ed. Edgar I. Stewart and Jane R. Stewart. Norman: University of Oklahoma Press, 1957.

Franchère, Gabriel. *Journal of a Voyage on the North West Coast of North America during the Years 1811, 1812, 1813, and 1814*, ed. W. Kaye Lamb, vol. 45. Toronto: Champlain Society, 1969.

———. *Voyage à la Côte du Nord-Ouest de l'Amérique et Fondation d'Astoria, 1810–1814*, ed. Georges Aubin. Montréal: Lux Éditeur, 2002.

Giesecke, E. W. "The Search for the *Tonquin*: A Look into the Disappearance of the Pacific Fur Company's Settlement Ship." *Columbia* 14, no. 2, 2000.

Ronda, James P. *Astoria and Empire*. Lincoln: University of Nebraska Press, 1990.

Ross, Alexander. *Adventures of the First Settlers on the Oregon or Columbia River*. London: Smith, Elder & Co., 1849.

Seton, Alfred. *Astorian Adventure: The Journal of Alfred Seton, 1811–1815*, ed. Robert F. Jones. New York: Fordham University Press, 1993.

David Thompson

Beleya, Barbara. "The 'Columbian Enterprise' and A. S. Morton." *BC Studies* 86, Summer 1990.

Jenish, D'Arcy. *Epic Wanderer: David Thompson and the Mapping of the Canadian West*. Lincoln: University of Nebraska, 2004.

Josephy, Alvin M. "David Thompson." In *The Mountain Men and the Fur Trade of the Far West: Biographical Sketches of the Participants*, ed. LeRoy R. Hafen, vol. 3. Glendale, Calif.: Arthur H. Clark, 1965–1972.

Moreau, William. "David Thompson's Claims: Thompson's Three Separate Accounts of His Journey to Astoria Raise More Questions Than They Answer." *Columbia* 15, no. 2, 2001.

Morton, A. S. "The North West Company's Columbia Enterprise and David Thompson." *Canadian Historical Review* 17, no. 3, 1936.

Thompson, David. *Columbia Journals*, ed. Barbara Belyea. Montreal, Québec: McGill-Queens University Press, 1994.

———. *David Thompson's Narrative of His Explorations in Western America, 1784–1812*, ed. J. B. Tyrrell. New York: Greenwood, 1968.

Tyrrell, J. B. "David Thompson and the Columbia River." *Canadian Historical Review* 18, no. 1, 1937.

Peter Skene Ogden

Cline, Gloria Griffin. *Peter Skene Ogden and the Hudson's Bay Company*. Norman: University of Oklahoma Press, 1974.

Maloney, Alice Bay. "Peter Skene Ogden's Trapping Expedition to the Gulf of California, 1829–30." *California Historical Society Quarterly* 19, no. 4, 1940.

Ogden, Peter Skene. *Peter Skene Ogden's Snake Country Journals, 1824–25 and 1825–26*, ed. E. E. Rich. London: Hudson's Bay Records Society, 1950.

———. *Peter Ogden's Snake Country Journals, 1827–28 and 1828–29*, ed. Glyndwr Williams. London: Hudson's Bay Records Society, 1971.

V. BRITISH VOYAGES IN THE 19TH CENTURY

Frederick Beechey

Beechey, Frederick W. *Narrative of a Voyage to the Pacific and Bering's Strait: To co-operate with the Polar Expeditions: performed in* His Majesty's Ship Blossom *under the command of Captain F.W. Beechey, RN, FRS in the Years 1825, 26, 27, 28*. London: Henry Colburn and Richard Bentley, 1831.

Bershed, S. S. "The Drawings and Watercolours by Rear-Admiral Frederick William Beechey, FGS, FRGS (1796–1856) in the Collection of the Arctic Institute of North America, University of Calgary." *Arctic* 33, 1990.

Hooker, William Jackson. *The Botany of Captain Beechey's Voyage: Comprising an Account of the Plants collected by . . . the officers of the Expedition, during the Voyage to the Pacific and Behring's Strait*. London: H. G. Bohn, 1841.

Lincoln, A. "Beechey in Alaska." *Pacific Discovery* 35, no. 1, 1982.

Peard, George. *To the Pacific and Arctic with Beechey: The Journal of Lieutenant George Peard of* HMS Blossom*, 1825–1828*, ed. Barry M. Gough. Cambridge: Hakluyt Society, 1973.

Edward Belcher

Belcher, Edward. *Narrative of a Voyage around the World: Performed in* Her Majesty's Ship Sulphur*, during the years 1836–1842*. London: H. Colburn, 1843.

Belcher, Edward, and Francis Guillemard Simpkinson. HMS Sulphur *on the Northwest and California Coasts, 1837 and 1839: The Accounts of Captain Edward Belcher and Midshipman Francis Guillemard Simpkinson*, ed. Richard A. Pierce and John H. Winslow. Kingston, Ont.: Limestone Press, 1979.

Pierce, Richard A. "Edward Belcher." *Arctic* 35, no. 4, 1982.

Peter Corney

Corney, Peter. *Early Voyages in the North Pacific, 1813–1818*, ed. Glen C. Adams. Fairfield, Wash.: Ye Galleon Press, 1965.

———. *Voyages in the Northern Pacific: Narrative of Several Trading Voyages from 1813 to 1818, between the Northwest Coast of America, the Hawaiian Islands and China with a Description of the Russian Establishments on the Northwest Coast*, ed. W. D. Alexander. Honolulu, Hawaii: Thos. G. Thrum, 1896.

Hydrography in the Region of Vancouver Island

Cook, Andrew S. "The Publication of British Admiralty Charts for British Columbia in the Nineteenth Century." In *Charting Northern Waters: Essays for the Centenary of the Canadian Hydrographic Service*, ed. William Glover. Montreal, Québec.: McGill-Queens University Press, 2004.

Hayes, Derek. "Hydrographic Surveying in British Columbia from 1774–1870." *Resolution* [Maritime Museum of British Columbia] 48, Spring, 2000.

Samson, Jane. "An Empire of Science: The Voyage of HMS *Herald*, 1845–1851." In *Pacific Empires: Essays in Honour of Glyndwr Williams*, ed. Alan Frost and Jane Samson. Vancouver, B.C.: UBC Press, 1999.

Seemann, Berthold. *Narrative of the Voyage of* HMS Herald *during the Years 1845–51: Under the Command of Captain Henry Kellett, being a Circumnavigation of the Globe, and three cruises to the Arctic Regions in search of Sir John Franklin*. London: Reeve and Co., 1853.

The Vancouver Island Pilot, containing Sailing Directions for the Coasts of Vancouver Island, and Part of British Columbia. Compiled from the Surveys made by Captain George Henry Richards, R.N., in H.M. Ships Plumper *and* Hecate, *between the Years 1858 and 1864*. London: Hydrographic Office, Admiralty, 1864.

W. RUSSIAN VOYAGES: EXPLORATION, TRADE, AND SETTLEMENT IN THE 19TH CENTURY

Aleksandr Baranov and the Russian–American Company

Andrews, C. L. *The Story of Sitka*. Seattle: Washington, 1965.

Dauenhauer, Nora Marks, and Richard Dauenhauer. "The Battles of Sitka, 1802 and 1804, from Tlingit, Russian, and Other Points of View." In *Russia in North America: Proceedings of the 2nd International Conference on Russian America, Sitka, Alaska, August, 1987*, ed. Richard Pierce. Kingston, Ont.: Limestone Press, 1990.

Elliott, George Reid. "Empire and Enterprise in the North Pacific, 1785–1825: A Survey and an Interpretation, Emphasizing the Role and Character of Russian Enterprise." Ph.D. thesis, University of Toronto, 1957.

Gibson, James R. "Bostonians and Muscovites on the Northwest Coast, 1788–1841." In *The Western Shore: Oregon Country Essays Honoring the American Revolution*, ed. Thomas Vaughan. Portland: Oregon Historical Society, 1975.

Khlebnikov, Kirill T. *Baranov, Chief Manager of the Russian Colonies in America*, trans. Colin Bearne, ed. Richard A. Pierce. Kingston, Ont.: Limestone Press, 1973.

Lynch, Donald F. "The Historical Geography of New Russia, 1780–1837." Ph.D. thesis, Yale University, 1964.

Mazour, Anatole G. "The Russian–American Company: Private or Government Enterprise." *Pacific Historical Review* 13, no. 2, 1944.

Okun, S. B. *The Russian–American Company*, trans. Carl Ginsburg. Cambridge, Mass.: Harvard University Press, 1951.

Ronda, James P. "Astor and Baranov: Partners in Empire." In *Pacifica* 2, 1990. Republished in *An Alaskan Anthology: Interpreting the Past*, ed. Stephen W. Haycox and Mary Childers Mangusso. Seattle: University of Washington Press, 1996.

Sherwood, Morgan B. "Science in Russian America, 1741–1865." *Pacific Northwest Quarterly* 58, no. 1, 1967.

Tichmenev, P. A. *A History of the Russian American Company*, trans. and ed. Richard A. Pierce and Alton S. Donnelly. Seattle: University of Washington Press, 1978.

———. *A History of the Russian American Company*. Vol. 2, *Documents*. Trans. Dmitri Krenov, ed. Richard A. Pierce and Alton S. Donnelly. Kingston, Ont.: Limestone Press, 1979.

Veniaminov, Innokentii. "The Condition of the Orthodox Church in Russian America," trans. and ed. Robert Nichols and Robert Croskey. *Pacific Northwest Quarterly* 63, no. 2, 1972.

Wheeler, Mary E. "Empires in Conflict and Cooperation: The Bostonians and the Russian–American Company." *Pacific Historical Review* 40, no. 4, 1971.

———. "The Origins of the Russian–American Company." *Jahrbücher für Geschichte Osteuropas*, December 1966.

———. "The Russian–American Company and the Imperial Government: The Early Phase." In *Russia's American Colony*, ed. S. Frederick Starr. Durham, N.C.: Duke University Press, 1987.

Naval Voyages: General

Barratt, Glynn. *Russian Shadows on the British Northwest Coast, 1810–1890*. Vancouver, B.C.: University of British Columbia Press, 1983.

Ivashintsev, N. A. *Russian Voyages of Circumnavigation*, trans. G. R. V. Barratt. Kingston, Ont.: Limestone Press, 1980.

Nozikov, N. *Russian Voyages Round the World*, trans. Ernst Lesser and Mira Lesser, ed. and intro. M. A. Sergeyev. London: Hutchinson, 194-.

Russian Cartography

Longenbaugh, Dee. "Alaska's Own Cartographers." *Terrae Incognitae* 31, 1999.

Sarychev, Gavriil. *Atlas severnoi chasti Vostochnago Okeana, sostavlen v chertezhnoi Gosudarstvennago Admiralteiskago Departamenta s nove'ishikh opisei i kart pod rukovodstvom Vitse Admirala y Gidrografa Sarycheva 1go.* Moskva, 1826.

Teben'kov, Mikhail. *Atlas of the Northwest Coast of America from Bering Strait to Cape Corrientes and the Aleutian Islands . . .* and *Hydrographic Notes accompanying the Atlas of the Northwest Coast of America, the Aleutian Islands and Several Other places in the North Pacific Ocean.* St. Petersburg: 1852. Trans. and ed. R. A. Pierce. Kingston, Ont.: Limestone Press, 1981.

Ivan Kruzenshtern

Kruzenshtern, Ivan. *Voyage round the world, in the years 1803, 1804, 1805 and 1806, by order of His Imperial Majesty Alexander the First, on board the ships* Nadeshda *and* Neva, *under the command of Captain A.J. von Krusenshtern.* London: J. Murray, 1813.

Langsdorff, G. H. von. *Voyage and Travels in Various parts of the World during the Years 1803, 1804, 1805, 1806 and 1807*, part 2. Carlisle, Eng.: George Philips, 1817.

Iurii Lisianskii

Lisiansky, Iurii. *A Voyage round the World, in the Years 1803, 1804, 1805, and 1806 performed by order of His Imperial Majesty Alexander the First, Emperor of Russia in the ship* Neva. London: Booth and Longman, Hurst, Rees, Orme and Brown, 1814.

Otto von Kotzebue

Chamisso, Adelbert. *The Alaska Diary of Adelbert von Chamisso, Naturalist on the Kotzebue Voyage, 1815–1818*, trans. and ed. Robert Fortuine, with assistance of Eva R. Trautmann. Anchorage, Alaska: Cook Inlet Historical Society, 1986.

———. *A Voyage around the World with the Romanzov Exploring Expedition in the Years 1815–1818 in the Brig* Rurik, trans. and ed. Henry Kratz. Honolulu: University of Hawaii Press, 1986.

Choris, Louis. *Voyage pittoresque autour du monde: avec des portraits des sauvages d'Amerique, d'Asie, d'Afrique, et des îles du Grand Océan: des paysages, des vues maritimes, et plusieurs objets d'histoire naturelle*. Paris: F. Didot, 1822.

Kotzebue, Otto von. *A Voyage of Discovery into the South Sea and Behring's Straits for the Purpose of Exploring a North-East Passage: undertaken in the years 1815, 1816, 1817 and 1818 in the ship* Rurick. London: Sir Richard Philips, 1821.

VanStone, James W. "An Early Nineteenth-Century Artist in Alaska: Louis Choris and the First Kotzebue Expedition." *Pacific Northwest Quarterly* 51, no. 4, 1960.

Vasilii Golovnin

Golovnin, V. M. *Around the World on the* Kamchatka, *1817–1819*, trans. and ed. Ella Lury Wiswell. Honolulu: Hawaiian Historical Society and University of Hawaii Press, 1979.

Fedor Litke

Kittlitz, F. H. *Twenty-four views of the vegetation of the coasts and islands of the Pacific; with explanatory descriptions; taken during the exploring voyage of the Russian corvette* Seniavine, *under the command of Capt. Lütke, in the years 1827, 1828, & 1829*, trans. & ed. Berthold Seemann. London: Longman, Green, Longman and Roberts, 1861.

Litke, Frederic. *A Voyage Around the World, 1826–1829*, vol. 1, *To Russian America and Siberia*, trans. Renée Marshall and Joan Moessner, ed. Richard A. Pierce. Kingston, Ont.: Limestone Press, 1987.

Lütke [Litke], F. P. *Voyage autour du monde, exécuté par ordre de Sa Majesté l'empereur Nicolas Ier, sur la corvette* Le Séniavine, *pendant les années 1826, 1827, 1828 & 1829 par Frédéric Lütke, partie historique avec un atlas lithographié d'après les dessins originaux d'Alexandre Postels et du Baron Kittlitz*. 3 vols. and atlas. Paris: Fermin Didot Frères, 1835. Republished by N. Israel, Amsterdam, 1971.

Southeast Alaska

Green, Lewis. *The Boundary Hunters: Surveying the 141st Meridian and the Alaska Panhandle*. Vancouver, B.C.: University of British Columbia Press, 1982.

Grinev, A. V. "The Forgotten Expedition of Dmitrii Tarkhanov on the Copper River." *Alaska History* 12, no. 1, 1997.

Johnson, Stephen Marshall. "Baron Wrangell and the Russian American Company, 1829–1849." Ph.D. thesis, University of Manitoba, 1978.

Khlebnikov, Kirill. "The Condition of Russian America in 1833: The Survey of Kirill Khlebnikov," ed. James R. Gibson. *Pacific Northwest Quarterly* 63, no. 1, 1972.

———. "Russian America in 1821," ed. James R. Gibson. *Oregon Historical Quarterly* 77, no. 2, 1976.

Shelest, J. W. "The *Dryad* Affair: Corporate Welfare and Anglo-Russian Rivalry for the Alaskan Lisière." In *Proceedings for the Borderline Conference*. Whitehorse: Yukon Historical and Museums Society, 1989.

Southwest Alaska, Northwest Alaska, and Interior Exploration

Arndt, Katherine L. "Russian Exploration and Trade in Alaska's Interior." In *Russian America: The Forgotten Frontier*, ed. Barbara Sweetland Smith and Redmond J. Barnett. Tacoma: Washington State Historical Society, 1990.

Glazunov, Andrei. "Russian Exploration in Interior Alaska: An Extract from the Journal of Andrei Glazunov," ed. James W. Vanstone. *Pacific Northwest Quarterly* 50, no. 2, 1959.

Khromchenko, V. S. *V. S. Khromchenko's Coastal Explorations in Southwestern Alaska, 1822*, ed. James W. Vanstone. Anthropology, vol. 64. Chicago: Fieldiana: Field Museum of Natural History, 1973.

Korakovsky, Petr. *Russian Exploration in Southwest Alaska: The Travel Journals of Petr Korakovsky (1818) and Ivan Ya. Vasiliev (1829)*, trans. David A. Kraus, ed. James W. Vanstone. Fairbanks: University of Alaska Press, 1988.

Ray, Dorothy Jean. "Eskimo Place-names in Bering Strait and Vicinity." In *Ethnohistory in the Arctic: The Bering Strait Eskimo*, ed. R. A. Pierce. Kingston, Ont.: Limestone Press, 1983.

———. " The Kheuveren Legend." In *Ethnohistory in the Arctic: The Bering Strait Eskimo*, ed. R. A. Pierce. Kingston, Ont.: Limestone Press, 1983.

———. "The Vasil'ev-Shishmarev Expedition to the Arctic, 1819–1822." In *Ethnohistory in the Arctic: The Bering Strait Eskimo*, ed. R. A. Pierce. Kingston, Ont.: Limestone Press, 1983.

Vasiliev, Ivan Ya. *Russian Exploration in Southwest Alaska: The Travel Journals of Petr Korakovsky (1818) and Ivan Ya. Vasiliev (1829)*, trans. David A. Kraus, ed. James W. Vanstone. Fairbanks: University of Alaska Press, 1988.

Zagoskin, N. P. *Lieutenant Zagoskin's Travels in Russian America, 1842–1844*, trans. Penelope Rainey, ed. Henry N. Michael. Toronto, Ont.: University of Toronto Press, 1967.

Russia and California

Blomkvist, E. E. "A Russian Scientific Expedition to California and Alaska, 1839–1849: The Drawings of I. G. Voznesenskii," trans. Basil Dmytryshyn and E. A. P. Crownhart-Vaughan. *Oregon Historical Quarterly* 73, no. 2, 1972.

Dufour, Clarence John. "The Russian Withdrawal from California." In *Fort Ross: California Outpost of Russian Alaska, 1812–1842*, ed. Richard A. Pierce. Kingston, Ont.: Limestone Press, 1991.

Essig, E. O. "The Russian Settlement at Ross." In *Fort Ross: California Outpost of Russian Alaska, 1812–1842*, ed. Richard A. Pierce. Kingston, Ont.: Limestone Press, 1991.

Mornin, Edward. *Through Alien Eyes: The Visit of the Russian Ship* Rurik *to San Francisco in 1816 and the Men behind the Visit*. North American Studies in 19th-Century German Literature, vol. 32. Bern: Peter Lang, 2002.

Ogden, Adele. "Russian Sea Otter and Seal Hunting on the California Coast." In *Fort Ross: California Outpost of Russian Alaska, 1812–1842*, ed. Richard A. Pierce. Kingston, Ont.: The Limestone Press, 1991.

Pritchard, Diane Spencer. "Joint Tenants of the Frontier: Russian–Hispanic Relationships in Alta California." In *Russian America: The Forgotten Frontier*, ed. Barbara Sweetland Smith and Redmond J. Barnett. Tacoma: Washington State Historical Society, 1990.

Rezanov, Nikolai. *Rezanov Reconnoiters California, 1806*, trans. and ed. Richard A. Pierce. San Francisco: Book Club of San Francisco, 1972.

Shur, Leonid A., and James R. Gibson. "Russian Travel Notes and Journals as Sources for the History of California." *California Historical Society Quarterly* 52, no. 1, 1973.

Temko, Allan. "Russians in California." *American Heritage* 11, no. 3, 1960.

Wrangell, Ferdinand. "Russians in California, 1833: Report of Governor Wrangell," ed. James R. Gibson. *Pacific Northwest Quarterly* 60, no. 4, 1969.

X. THE OREGON TERRITORY TO 1846

General Works

Deutsch, Herman J. "The Evolution of International Boundary in the Inland Empire of the Pacific Northwest." *Pacific Northwest Quarterly* 51, no. 2, 1960.

Gough, Barry. *Fortune's a River: The Collision of Empires in Northwest America*. Madeira Park, B.C.: Harbour Publishing, 2007.

Kushner, Howard I. *Conflict on the Northwest Coast: American–Russian Rivalry in the Pacific Northwest, 1790–1867*. Westport, Conn.: Greenwood, 1975.

Van Alstyne, R. W. "International Rivalries in [the] Pacific Northwest." *Oregon Historical Quarterly* 46, no. 3, 1945.

Walker, James V. "Mapping of the Northwest Boundary of the United States, 1800–1846." *Terrae Incognitae* 31, 1999.

Boundaries 1819 and 1824–1825

Blue, Verne. "The Oregon Question, 1818–1828." *Oregon Historical Quarterly* 23, no. 3, 1922.

Brooks, Philip Coolidge. *Diplomacy and the Borderlands: The Adams–Onís Treaty of 1819.* Berkeley: University of California Press, 1939.

———. "The Pacific Coast's First International Boundary Delineation, 1816–1819." *Pacific Historical Review* 3, no. 1, 1934.

Cloud, Barbara. "Oregon in the 1820s: The Congressional Perspective." *Western Historical Quarterly* 12, no. 2, 1981.

Convention between Great Britain and Russia. [May 16, 1825.] In George Davidson, *The Alaska Boundary.* San Francisco: Alaska Packers Association, 1903.

Convention between the United States of America and His Majesty the Emperor of all the Russias, relative to Navigating, Fishing [and Trading and Establishments on the Northwest Coast of America] *in the Pacific Ocean.* [January 12, 1825.] In George Davidson. *The Alaska Boundary.* San Francisco: Alaska Packers Association, 1903.

Treaty of Amity, Settlement and Limits between The United States of America and His Catholic Majesty. [February 22, 1819.] In *Treaties and Other International Acts of the United States*, vol. 3, ed. Hunter Miller. Washington, D.C.: United States Government Printing Office, 1933.

Camille-Joseph de Roquefeuil

Roquefeuil, Camille de. *Journal d'un voyage autour du monde pendant les années 1816, 1817, 1818 et 1819 par M. Camille de Roquefeuil, lieutenant de vaisseau, commandant du navire* Le Bordelais. 2 vols. Paris: Panthieu, Lésage, Gide fils, 1823.

———. *Voyage around the World, 1816–1819, and Trading for Sea Otter Fur on the Northwest Coast of America*, intro. S. W. A. Gunn. Fairfield, Wash.: Ye Galleon Press, 1981.

———. *A voyage round the world between the years 1816–1819.* London: Sir Richard Philips, 1823.

Rudkin, Charles N. *Camille de Roquefeuil in San Francisco, 1817–1818.* Los Angeles: G. Dawson, 1954.

Eugène Duflot de Mofras

Duflot de Mofras, Eugène. *Duflot de Mofras' Travels on the Pacific Coast*, trans. and ed. Marguerite Eyer Wilbur. Santa Ana, Calif.; Fine Arts Press, 1927.

—————. *Exploration du Territoire de l'Oregon, des Californies et de la mer Vermeille executé pendant les années 1840, 1841 et 1842 par M. Duflot de Mofras*. 2 vols. and atlas. Paris: Arthus Bertrand, 1844.

Charles Wilkes

Goetzmann, William H. "Exploration and Empires for Science." In *New Lands, New Men: America and the Second Great Age of Discovery*. Chapter 7. New York: Viking Penguin, 1986.

Henry, John Frazier. "The Midshipman's Revenge or, The Case of the Missing Islands." [Wilkes and the Survey of the San Juan Islands, 1841.] *Pacific Northwest Quarterly* 73, no. 4, 1982.

Stanton, William. *The United States Great Exploring Expedition of 1838–1842*. Berkeley: University of California Press, 1975.

Viola, Herman J. "The Wilkes Expedition on the Pacific Coast." *Pacific Northwest Quarterly* 80, no. 1, 1989.

Viola, Herman J., and Carolyn Margolis, eds. *Magnificent Voyagers: The U.S. Exploring Expedition, 1838–1842*. Washington, D.C.: Smithsonian Institution, 1985.

Wilkes, Charles. "Diary of Wilkes in the Northwest," ed. Edmond S. Meany. *Washington Historical Quarterly* 16, no. 2, 1925; and 17, no. 1, 1926.

—————. *Narrative of the United States Exploring Expedition during the Years 1838, 1839, 1840, 1841, 1842*. Philadelphia: Lea and Blanchard, 1845.

The Oregon Treaty, 1846, and San Juan Boundary Arbitration, 1872

Anderson, Stuart. "British Threats and the Settlement of the Oregon Boundary Dispute." *Pacific Northwest Quarterly* 66, no. 4, 1975.

Clayton, Daniel W. "Delineating the Oregon Territory." In *Islands of Truth: The Imperial Fashioning of Vancouver Island*. Chapter 12. Vancouver: UBC Press, 2000.

Cramer, Richard S. "British Magazines and the Oregon Question." *Pacific Historical Quarterly* 32, no. 4, 1963.

Galbraith, John S. "France as a Factor in the Oregon Negotiations." *Pacific Northwest Quarterly* 44, no. 2, 1953.

Gough, Barry. "British Naval Intelligence and the Oregon Crisis." In *Pacific Northwest: Essays in Honor of James W. Scott*, ed. Howard J. Critchfield. Bellingham, Wash.: Western Washington University, 1993.

—————. "British Policy in the San Juan Boundary Dispute." *Pacific Northwest Quarterly* 62, no. 2, 1971.

———. "The Royal Navy and the Oregon Crisis, 1844–1846." *BC Studies* 9, Spring 1971.

Graebner, Norman, ed. *Manifest Destiny.* Part 3: "Oregon." Indianapolis: Bobbs-Merrill, 1968.

———. "Politics and the Oregon Compromise." *Pacific Northwest Quarterly* 52, no. 1, 1961.

Hunter, Miller, trans. and ed. *North West Water Boundary: Report of the Experts Summoned by the German Emperor as Arbitrator under Articles 34–42 of the Treaty of Washington of May 8, 1871, Preliminary to His Award dated October 21, 1872.* University of Washington Publications, Social Sciences 13, no. 1. Seattle: University of Washington, 1942.

Jones, Howard, and Donald A. Rakestraw. *Prologue to Manifest Destiny: Anglo-American Relations in the 1840s.* Wilmington, Del.: SR Books, 1997.

Jones, Wilber D., and J. Chal Vinson. "British Preparedness and the Oregon Settlement." *Pacific Historical Review* 22, no. 4, 1953.

Long, John W. "The Origin and Development of the San Juan Island Water Boundary Controversy." *Pacific Historical Quarterly* 43, no. 3, 1952.

McCabe, James O. *The San Juan Water Boundary Question.* Canadian Studies in History and Government, no. 5. Toronto, Ont.: University of Toronto Press, 1964.

McClintock, Thomas C. "British Newspapers and the Oregon Treaty of 1846." *Oregon Historical Quarterly* 104, no. 1, 2003.

Merk, Frederick. "The Oregon Question." In *History of the Westward Movement.* Chapter 35. New York: Alfred A. Knopf, 1978.

———. *The Oregon Question: Essays in Anglo-American Diplomacy and Politics.* Cambridge: Harvard University Press, 1967.

North-West American Water Boundary. Second and Definitive Statement on behalf of the Government of Her Britannic Majesty, submitted to His Majesty the Emperor of Germany. . . . Command Papers/Great Britain. Parliament: Cd. 692. London: Harrison and Sons, 1873.

Opinions and Award of the Commissioners, under the Treaty of July 1, 1863 between Great Britain and the United States, for the Final Settlement of Claims of the Hudson's Bay and Puget Sound Agricultural Companies, pronounced, September 10, 1869. Montreal, P.Q.: John Lovell, 1869.

Papers Relating to the Treaty of Washington. 6 vols. with maps. [Vol. 5, *Berlin Arbitration.*] Washington, D.C.: United States Department of State, 1872–1874.

Pratt, Julius W. "James K. Polk and John Bull." *Canadian Historical Review* 24, no. 4, 1943.

Reply of the United States to the Case of the Government of Her Britannic Majesty, presented to His Majesty the Emperor of Germany as Arbitrator under the Provisions of the Treaty of Washington, June 12, 1872. Washington, D.C.: United States Department of State, 1872.

Scott, Leslie M. "Influence of American Settlement upon the Oregon Boundary Treaty of 1846." *Oregon Historical Quarterly* 29, no. 1, 1928.

Stacey, C. P. "The Hudson's Bay Company and Anglo-American Military Rivalries during the Oregon Dispute." *Canadian Historical Review* 18, no. 3, 1937.

Treaty between Her Majesty and the United States of America for the Settlement of the Oregon Boundary. Signed at Washington, June 15, 1846. . . . Command Papers/Great Britain. Parliament: Cd.106. London: T. R. Harrison, 1846.

About the Author

Robin Inglis was educated at Cambridge University, where he read History. He is a former director of the Vancouver Maritime Museum and the North Vancouver Museum and Archives. A graduate in museology from the University of Toronto, he is also a Fellow of the Canadian Museums Association. A past editor of *Material History Review*, he was the founding editor of the newsletter of the International Congress of Maritime Museums. As curator of major exhibitions on the voyages of Jean François de La Pérouse and Alejandro Malaspina and their visits to the Northwest Coast of America, he became involved in their stories. For over 20 years he has written and lectured on the subject of discovery and exploration on the Northwest Coast. He edited a collection of essays, published in 1991 as *Spain and the North Pacific Coast*, to recognize the bicentennial of the Malaspina Expedition's visit to Pacific North America, and acted as a regional editor for the Hakluyt Society's recent edition of the Malaspina Journal. He is president of the Instituto de Historia del Pacífico Español in Vancouver, where he lives with his wife Beverley, with whom he raised four children.